Mountain Biking
Utah

Gregg Bromka

A FALCON GUIDE®

Falcon® Publishing is continually expanding its list of recreational guidebooks. All books include detailed descriptions, accurate maps, and all information necessary for enjoyable trips. You can order extra copies of this book and get information and prices for other Falcon® books by writing Falcon, P.O. Box 1718, Helena, MT 59624, or by calling toll-free 1-800-582-2665. Also, please ask for a copy of our current catalog. Visit our website at www.FalconOutdoors.com or contact us by e-mail at falcon@falconguide.com.

1 2 3 4 5 6 7 8 9 0 MG 04 03 02 01 00 99

Falcon and FalconGuide are registered trademarks of Falcon® Publishing, Inc.

Library of Congress Cataloging-in-Publication Data

Bromka, Gregg.
    Mountain Biking Utah / by Gregg Bromka
        p.   cm.
    Rev. ed. of: The mountain biker's guide to Utah. c1994
    "A Falcon guide"—T .p. verso
    ISBN 1-56044-654-4. — ISBN 1-56044-824-5 (pbk.)
    1. All terrain cycling—Utah Guidebooks.   2. Utah—Guidebooks.
I. Bromka, Gregg. Mountain biker's guide to Utah. II. Title
GV1045.5.U8B76   1999   98-17495
                                                     CIP

CAUTION

Outdoor recreational activities are by their very nature potentially hazardous. All participants in such activities must assume responsibility for their own actions and safety. The information contained in this guidebook cannot replace sound judgment and good decision-making skills, which help reduce exposure, nor does the scope of this book allow for the disclosure of all the potential hazards and risks involved in such activities.

    Learn as much as possible about the outdoor recreational activities in which you participate, prepare for the unexpected, and be cautious. The reward will be a safer and more enjoyable experience.

 Text pages printed on recycled paper.

Table of Contents

UTAH *RIDE LOCATIONS*

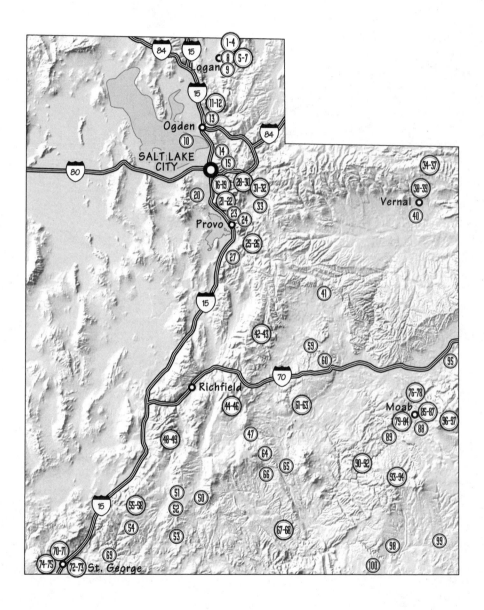

MAP LEGEND

Interstate		Campground	
U.S. Highway		Picnic Area	
State or Other Principal Road		Buildings	
Forest Road		Peak/Elevation	4,507 ft.
Interstate Highway		Bridge/Pass	
Paved Road		Gate	
Gravel Road		Parking Area	
Unimproved Road		Boardwalk/Pier	
Trail (singletrack)		Railroad Track	
Trailhead		Cliffs/Bluff	
Trail Marker		Power Line	
Waterway		Forest Boundary	
Intermittent Waterway		Wall or Enclosure	
Lake/Reservoir		Map Orientation	N
Meadow/Swamp		Scale	0 0.5 1 MILES
Spring			
Elevation	X		
Dam		Tunnel	
Overlook or Point of Interest		Sand	

Dedicated to all those who . . .
"Eat, Sleep, Mountain Bike!"

Acknowledgments

Utah may not be the largest state in the nation, but it packs a helluva lot of mountain-bike rides. If it wasn't for the enthusiastic assistance of many persons, I would still be poring over maps trying to surmise which dotted lines might be Utah's best rides. A tip of the helmet goes to bike-shop owners and employees, fellow writers, and biker buddies who divulged often sacred trail information, knowing that "if you print it they will come." Respectfully, a few of your best kept secrets have been withheld.

I offer sincere gratitude to those employed by the National Forest Service and Bureau of Land Management for the often unappreciated task of providing mountain bikers with continued and near limitless access privileges to federal lands. We applaud your efforts and appreciate the rewards we reap.

High fives to a long list of friends for their companionship on numerous trips (both planned and blind reconnaissance varieties) and for patiently stopping for "just one more photo."

To my mother, Irene, and my family, I thank you all for encouraging me to follow my bliss.

And lest I forget, thank you, Tricia, for immeasurable patience and continued understanding of my two-wheeled obsession.

Introduction

For years Utah has boasted of having the "Greatest Snow on Earth," a motto displayed on its license plates, no less. Perhaps the phrase, ". . . and Mountain Biking, . . ." should be inserted because Utah has proclaimed itself to be the mountain biking capital of the nation. Granted, much of this honor has been generated by one particular town and its most unusual cycling experience, Moab and the Slickrock Bike Trail. Even if Utah did not have Slickrock or the canyon country that surrounds it, this state would still be an outstanding mountain bike destination because its alpine regions, which are extolled as world-class winter playgrounds, define the term "mountain biking." But since good fortune has blessed Utah with the striking diversity of rugged mountains and spacious plateaus contrasted with the surrealistic glow of canyon country, the total package separates this great state from other fat-tire localities. With the help of this guidebook, both locals and visitors from distant abodes may discover, or rediscover, the pleasures of mountain biking in Utah.

It is likely that a guidebook of this nature will increase usage in certain areas and on specific routes; after all, this is a "where-to" book. Consequently, there is a risk of visitors effectively loving a place to death. But visitation to a specific area is normally sparked by curiosity, which in turn fosters awareness and understanding of critical issues that pertain to the area. Conversely, withholding accurate and complete information may feed ignorance or disregard for the same issues.

The routes included in this guidebook were chosen carefully and all were deemed open and appropriate for mountain biking by the land management agencies or entities that oversee them. This guide revisits celebrated destinations while simultaneously directing the mountain biker to emerging venues and previously unknown locations. Most of all, this work strives to provide a broad base for the awareness and appreciation, if not reverence, of mountain biking in Utah while promoting responsible backcountry travel.

SCOPE OF THIS GUIDEBOOK

Initially, the scope of this guidebook was rather simple: Gather together the state's classic mountain bike routes. About 30 or so routes came to mind, including Moab's White Rim, Slickrock, and Porcupine Rim Trails; Brian Head's Dark Hollow Trail and Twisted Forest; Ogden's Skyline Trail; Salt Lake City's Big Water Trail and Wasatch Crest; Deer Valley Resort at Park City; and Fish Lake's Mytoge Mountain, to name a handful. But while these all-time greats were pursued, surrounding routes were uncovered and old favorites were rediscovered. Quickly, the true nature of this project began to

The world's most popular bike trail—The Moab Slickrock Bike Trail.

unfold, or rather, explode. There are far more than a couple dozen great rides throughout Utah; there are literally hundreds from Logan to the Four Corners to St. George, some of which are little known or altogether unknown and are patiently awaiting their moment in the limelight. The outcome in the original edition, *The Mountain Biker's Guide to Utah*, was a compilation of Utah's 80 best mountain bike routes, the cream of the crop. Well, the harvest has become more bounteous, and in this revised and expanded edition, 100 rides are offered. Here's what you'll find.

The Bear River Range of Logan is a nexus for alpine riding. It has an array of dirt roads and singletracks that venture through timbered slopes to lofty summits and waver alongside blue-ribbon streams beneath craggy cliffs. Logan boasts a desirously high trails-to-biker ratio.

Vernal, like Logan, is an untapped reservoir of fat-tire trails and is a fine destination for a weekend trip. Rides adjacent to town take you through terrain that mimics the Moab area, while routes on the nearby Uinta Mountains and in the Flaming Gorge National Recreation area rival those of the Wasatch Range. But you won't have to jockey for a trailhead parking space and solitude is plentiful.

If you want to put the "mountain" back into biking, then you still can't beat the trails of the Wasatch Range. Where else can you ride past 11,000-foot peaks within a stone's throw of a major metropolis, resort towns, and cozy country hamlets? In northern Utah you can have your cake and eat it too.

Are you a singletrack purist? If so, look no farther than Brian Head because its dirt one-laners are the best between the Rockies and the Sierras. Four national parks and monuments nearby guarantee superb scenery while the expansive High Plateaus offer endless opportunities in the pristine backcountry.

Mountain biking is "hot" in St. George nowadays, and it's plenty warm, too! The word is out about outrageous race courses and action-packed desert singletracks. But the real buzz is about a new trail system on Gooseberry Mesa near Zion National Park that combines slickrock *and* bona fide singletrack. Winter may be three months of rotten mountain biking in northern Utah, but in Utah's Dixie, it's prime time.

If you've "been there, done that," with regards to riding in Moab, then it's time to broaden your horizons with spring and fall trips to the San Rafael Swell. Boasting national-park-caliber scenery, but without the national park crowds, the Swell has become the choice of mountain biking desert rats who seek solace in sandstone.

Even if you have ridden them all at Moab, the spring and fall pilgrimage to canyon country will never become passé. Each successive trip captures the anticipation and excitement of your maiden voyage to the promised land. This expanded edition offers two weeks of riding in the slickrock Mecca, and that's just the tip of the iceberg. The truth remains; there is only *one* Moab and it's "da' kine."

Naturally, these 100 rides vary greatly in location, length, difficulty, condition, trail type, and scenic qualities. Overall, there is something for everyone: rides geared for fat-tire neophytes to the most accomplished bikers; family trips to after-work jaunts to week-long vacations; gentle dirt roads; upbeat doubletracks; scintillating singletracks; plus slickrock, of course. A few routes are minutes from metropolitan areas, whereas others venture to the state's (if not the nation's) most remote regions. And finally, nearly every ride offers scenery that is not simply inspiring or even breathtaking but superlative.

So scan the Table of Contents, then page through the chapters. Read up on a region, location, or set of trails. Pick a ride that is well known or one you've never heard of. Saddle up your trusty steed and prepare to embark on some of the finest mountain biking the state, and the nation, has to offer.

REGIONAL SETTING

Topography

Three of the nation's major physiographic provinces converge upon Utah: the Middle Rocky Mountains (Mountainlands), the Colorado Plateau (Canyon Country), and Basin and Range Province. A fourth region is the gradational

Colorado Plateau-Basin and Range Transition Belt (High Plateaus). Consequently, the routes in this guidebook have been grouped according to their physiographic association.

Northern Utah's Mountainlands extend from Logan's Bear River Range and the Idaho border through the Wasatch Range, which serves as a backdrop for a sprawling metropolis centered around the state's capital, Salt Lake City. This region also includes the Uinta Mountains, which stretch from Kamas to Flaming Gorge-Vernal. As can be envisioned from this region's label, rugged peaks coupled with deep mountain valleys prevail. The abruptness of the Wasatch Range offers a spectacular urban setting for the Great Salt Lake valley metropolis, whereas the nearby Uintas are endowed with uncompromised wilderness.

Central Utah's High Plateaus are a band of lofty tablelands arcing through the state's heartland, from where Mountainlands terminates south of Provo to just shy of the state's south-central border with Arizona. This region is alpine in every aspect like northern Utah's mountains, but is characterized by broad, rolling summits offset by long fertile valleys. A necklace of pioneer hamlets envelops the High Plateaus with a quaintness that hallmarks central Utah.

Southern Utah's Canyon Country engulfs a huge wedge of southeastern Utah plus a west-trending panhandle to the state's absolute southwestern corner. This is Utah's famed redrock country, home to a half dozen of the Southwest's acclaimed national parks and monuments, a backdrop for countless western movies, plus, of course, Moab and the world-renowned Slickrock Bike Trail. The Colorado and Green Rivers, plus their associated tributaries, have exposed a hundred shades of the Colorado Plateau's terracotta skin. Floating among the desert seas are three alpine islands: the La Sal, Abajo, and Henry mountains.

Weather

Located midway between the equator and the north pole, centered about 40 degrees latitude, Utah displays four seasons of nearly equal length typical of the Temperate Zone. But because of an elevation gradient exceeding 11,000 feet, temperatures across the state during any one season can be highly variable, which means you can bike in Utah year-round. During winter, when bitter cold grasps Utah's mountains, its lowest deserts may be experiencing near spring-like conditions. That is to say, you can ski champagne powder at Brian Head in the morning and bike in short sleeves at St. George by afternoon. Of course these extremes have new meaning during the height of summer when the mountains are cool and the deserts are sizzling.

Of all the states in the nation, only Nevada receives less precipitation than Utah's 13 inches annually. Such a statistic is apparent when biking through the parched deserts of canyon country. But inasmuch as Utah's mountains act as weather barriers and effectively squeeze moisture from passing storm tracts, Inasmuch, Utah's meteorologists commonly interject "variable" and "unsteady" into their weather forecasts. Week-long drizzles, common of coastal states, are rare, and only occasionally do high-and-dry conditions prevail statewide. Rain and snowstorms typically sweep across the region, dropping moisture in erratic and often copious amounts, then move on to be replaced by clear skies. During summer's monsoon season, cerulean morning skies can be transformed to foreboding thunderheads by afternoon, accompanied by radical drops in temperature. Get caught in just one alpine thunder boomer and a rain jacket will be your constant companion on every outing thereafter.

Flora and fauna

With elevations ranging from a low of 2,500 feet near St. George to a high of 13,528 feet atop Kings Peak in the Uinta Mountains, Utah hosts a wide variety of plant and animal species. Six vegetative life zones are represented in Utah from the Lower Sonoran to Arctic-Alpine.

The Lower Sonoran is restricted to a tract of land in southwestern Utah nourished by the Virgin River. The dry, warm weather of "Utah's Dixie" prompted Mormon pioneers to plant cotton and other crops typical of the nation's southern states. Indigenous plants are more representative of the desert southwest, including cacti, creosote brush, and sporadic occurrences of the Joshua tree. Of the desert's numerous inhabitants, the Gila monster, sidewinder rattlesnake, and desert tortoise maintain small but significant populations.

The most widespread life zone is the Upper Sonoran, which constitutes Utah's high deserts between roughly 4,000 to 7,000 feet. Only the most tenacious plants can thrive in the arid to semi-arid climate, including sage and blackbrush along with the ever-present juniper-pinyon community. Sheltered recesses and washes that receive intermittent moisture support stunted hardwoods such as Gamble oak and bigtooth maple and shade-giving cottonwoods. A variety of rodents scurry about the brush, and deer commonly descend from higher elevations during winter to forage, often in residential neighborhoods located on the mountains' foothills.

More robust trees populate the Transitional Zone, which ranges between 6,000 and 8,000 feet. The mighty ponderosa pine mingles with Douglas fir and other conifers and their wood is prized by the timber industry for their excellent construction properties. With increased elevation and subsequent rainfall of the Canadian Life Zone, the fir-spruce-aspen forests dominate the mountains' slopes and basins up to 10,000 feet. The bristlecone pine, one of the world's oldest living organisms, finds a niche on the crumbly limestone slopes of Utah's southernmost High Plateaus. Wildflowers grow in profusion and bring brilliant color to the verdant hills and valleys. Wildlife is varied and abundant, ranging from the tiny deer mouse to black-tailed rabbit, badger to beaver, mule deer to elk, and bobcat to black bear.

Utah's highest summits announce the Hudsonian to Arctic-Alpine life zones above 10,000 feet. Stoic fir and spruce grow in isolated patches. On ridges and

There's more to Utah than Moab and Slickrock. The state's alpine regions define the word "mountain" biking.

peaks, driving winds mold them to "krumholz" or flag-shaped form. Dwarf plants, matted grasses, and wind-resistant shrubs cling to rocky slopes. Animals must prove their resiliency. Pikas and yellow-bellied marmots hide among the talus, making their presence known with revealing squeaks and chirps.

Utah's first human inhabitants

Although the Mormon trek is chronicled as one of Western America's greatest overland expeditions and largely credited for the opening of Utah, the region's human history began long before the intrusions of European descendants. Excavations by archaeologists have uncovered evidence that Paleo-Indians inhabited Utah at the close of the last ice age at least 12,000 years ago. These peoples were largely nomadic hunters of big game and gatherers of plants and seeds. Centuries later, they developed primitive forms of agriculture that led to a semi-sedentary lifestyle. The ancient Fremont Indians, and their earlier relatives, the Basketmaker culture, occupied central Utah's canyon country from A.D. 500 to 1300. Evidence shows the Fremonts wandered as far north as the Wasatch Front and as far south as Parowan. They stored food in rock granaries, built pit houses, sculpted pottery and clay figurines, and painted and pecked mysterious images on the tarnished canyon walls. Their co-relatives, the Anasazi, occupied the Four Corners area, where they developed advanced forms of agriculture and constructed magnificent multi-story dwellings of stone masonry. For reasons that are still uncertain—drought, warfare, or disease—the Anasazi abandoned their communities suddenly and are believed to have been assimilated into the Pueblo tribes of Arizona and New Mexico. Why the Fremont Indians disappeared remains a mystery. Contemporaneously, Shoshoni-speaking Indians entered northern Utah following herds of game, the Paiutes and Navajos occupied the southern territories, and the Ute Indians expanded their domain from western Colorado to north-central Utah.

The first documented account of Europeans in Utah was that of Spanish friars Francisco Atanasio Domínguez and Silvestre Velez de Escalante in 1776. Their duty was to establish a land route between missions in present-day New Mexico and California. Their circuitous route lead them through the Uinta Basin of north-central Utah, then west across the southern Wasatch Range to where their eyes fell upon "Nuestra Señora de la Merced del Timpanogotzis," which translates to Our Lady of Mercy of the Timpanogotzis Indians—Utah Lake.

With winter rapidly approaching and fearful of uncertainties ahead, the party was compelled to return to New Mexico after reaching southwestern Utah. Domínguez and Escalante endured innumerable hardships while finding a route across the Colorado River's tortuous canyons, and they became the first to report of the desolate badlands that embraced it. Despite their failed attempt to reach California, the path Domínguez and Escalante blazed would become part of the Old Spanish Trail trade route of the early 1800s.

Decades later, in the 1820s, competition among fur companies provoked trappers to turn their attention from the northwest territories to the Intermountain West. Legendary mountain men Jim Bridger, Etienne Provost, and Peter Skene Ogden, all of whom are remembered on maps today, explored and exploited northern Utah's rivers and mountains in search of beaver pelts. It was Bridger who purportedly sipped from the Great Salt Lake and exclaimed he had reached the shore of the Pacific Ocean.

The routes these frontiersmen forged were later used by government-assigned survey parties, including those lead by Captain John C. Fremont. Fremont's first crossing of the Great Salt Lake's hostile deserts caught the eyes of Langsford Hastings, who in 1846, encouraged the Donner-Reed wagon train to steer south from the well-traveled Oregon Trail on his California shortcut across Utah's west desert. But the salt flats' inhospitable conditions claimed the lives of overburdened oxen and caused many wagons to be abandoned. Such time-consuming misfortunes spawned later tragedy when the party was forced to cannibalize its members who had perished when the party became trapped in an autumn Sierra Nevada blizzard.

By this time, the Mormon exodus, lead by Brigham Young, had begun and the group was making preparations for a winter camp on the Great Plains. Despite discouraging reports of the Great Salt Lake valley, Young was set in his plans to seek religious seclusion in a land nobody wanted. On July 24, 1847, the Mormon hand-cart brigade descended from the Wasatch Range to the fringe of the Great Salt Lake valley, and Young, bedridden in his carriage, sat up and proclaimed, "This is the right place, drive on."

Immediately, the pioneers planted crops, built irrigation canals, and plotted their city of Zion to absorb the thousands of Mormons still on the trail and those yet to emigrate. Upon the directive of Brigham Young, the church's devoted members were called upon immediately to colonize and secure the territory by establishing settlements in outlying areas. Reports of iron ore and of land suitable for cotton plantations spawned the settlements of Cedar City and St. George. Although both industries faltered when the newly routed transcontinental railroad brought lower-priced goods to the region, the towns survived. Similarly, Mormon hamlets sprung up throughout Utah. Many must have seemed on the edge of the world, for they were often hundreds of miles from supplies and trade routes. Still, the pioneers survived the numerous hardships brought on by harsh winters, poor crops, and lack of provisions. The encroachment of whites onto Native American lands sparked skirmishes, raids, and prolonged wars. Ironically, it was the Mormons who first procured land from the Paiute Indians to build a fort at Las Vegas.

Despite Young's effort to build an isolated and self-sufficient State of Deseret, he could not stop the inevitable stampede of America's westward expansion because Utah was straight in its path. Hordes of gentiles (those not of the Mormon faith) crossed Utah en route to promising lands in California. Those who stayed in Utah to reap the natural resources of the virgin mountains and deserts forced cultural diversity upon the Mormon's conservative lifestyle. In 1864, silver was discovered in Little Cottonwood Canyon; then a more significant strike was made in 1868 that gave birth to one of the West's best-known mining camps—Park City. The wave of migration turned into a veritable tsunami when in 1869 the Golden Spike was driven near Ogden, and the East and West Coasts were united by the transcontinental railroad. The seclusion Brigham Young and the church's founder, Joseph Smith, sought for their worshipers ultimately turned to inclusion when Utah became the 45th state of the Union in 1896; Utah would now become the "Crossroads of the West."

HOW TO USE THIS GUIDEBOOK

The whole premise behind this and other "where-to" guidebooks is to take a large chunk of guesswork out of where to ride your mountain bike. The dirty work has been done to make your riding experience easier and more enjoyable. But if anything in a ride description doesn't seem to make sense, re-read the following explanation of format. Also, consult the glossary at the end for the definitions of additional terms.

Trail maps: The maps included in this book are clean, easy-to-use navigational tools. Closed trails are not always shown but may be referred to in the ride description. Painstaking effort has been taken to ensure accuracy. While every nook and cranny or bump in the trail may not be depicted, sufficient terrain is shown to keep you on track. The supplemental use of U.S. Geological Survey (USGS) topographic maps is always advised. (See "Maps" below.)

Elevation profiles: These provide a quick look at what's in store by graphically showing altitude and tread change over the ride's length. Out-and-back rides are shown only in one direction. Simply reverse the direction of travel for the return profile. Note the obstacles on such rides since their character may be different on the return.

The rest of the information is listed in an at-a-glance format and is divided into 16 descriptive sections:

Ride number: The numbers are an internal reference and refer to where the ride falls in this guide. Use this number when cross-referencing between rides and to find them on the ride location map in the front of the book. The ride name is the generally accepted name of the trail. Each ride begins with an introduction that provides you with an overview of the route and/or an explanation as to why it is one of Utah's best rides.

General location: Tells where the ride is located in reference to the closest town or other landmark.

Distance: This gives the ride's total length in miles along with the route's configuration: loop, out-and-back, point-to-point, or combination.

Tread: Describes the route's surface and the type of road or trail it follows: gravel road, light-duty dirt road, four-wheel drive road, ATV trail, singletrack, or pack trail.

Aerobic level: This is an estimation of the physical exertion required to complete a ride. The levels are easy, moderate, and strenuous, and are relative only to other rides in this book. They may not be similar to ratings of rides in other locations, states, or publications.

    Easy rides are mostly flat but may include some rolling hills. There may be steep climbs, but they will be short and painless. These rides are best suited for bikers who are new to the sport, ride infrequently, and/or possess only basic off-road handling skills.

    Moderate rides will have climbs; some may be continuous and some may be steep. These rides are geared for cyclists who ride periodically, possess good bike-handling skills, and are usually game for a small adventure.

    Strenuous rides tend to go places that require the use of the granny gear along the way. These are suited for strong bikers who ride on a regular basis, are acclimated to high elevations, and possess advanced handling skills. Endurance, power, and determination are prerequisites.

Remember, these ratings are somewhat subjective and are for the purpose of comparison. Easy rides can still have you gulping for air, and moderate ones can make you walk. Compare your first rides to the levels listed to determine what trails are within your ability. Also, bear in mind that technical sections can add to the aerobic level, making a moderate ride seem strenuous.

An elevation profile accompanies each ride description. Here the ups and downs of the route are graphed on a grid of elevation (in feet above sea level) and miles. Note that these graphs are compressed (squeezed) to fit a small space. The upward angle of the actual slopes you will ride is not the same as that shown on the graph, although at times it seems that way. Some extremely short dips and climbs are too small to show up on the graphs but are mentioned in the description.

Technical difficulty: A measure of the level of bike-handling skill needed or the likelihood that you will have to touch a foot down (a "dab") or dismount to clear obstacles in the tread. Technical difficulty is based on, but not limited to, loose tread, gravel, loose or embedded rocks, sand, ruts, exposed tree roots, fallen tree limbs, or whole trees for that matter, unusually steep ascents or descents, short radius turns, water bars, and water crossings. Levels are 1 to 5.

> **Level 1:** Basic riding skills are needed for riding smooth and obstacle-free routes. Because of the inherent nature of mountain biking in Utah, there are few level-1 rides in this book.
>
> **Level 2:** Mostly smooth tread with minor difficulties. Ruts, gravel, or obstacles may exist but are easily avoided.
>
> **Level 3:** Irregular tread with some rough sections, steeps, obstacles, gravel, sharp turns, slickrock, and other things that make your butt go bumpity bump in the saddle. At this level a mountain bike is being put to its intended use.
>
> **Level 4:** Rough going ahead. The tread is uneven with few smooth sections. The line is limited as it weaves through rocks of varying sizes, sand, eroded sections, downfall, rough slickrock, and ledges. Now we're talking.
>
> **Level 5:** Continuously broken tread or terrain, entrenched or primitive tread, and frequent, sudden, or severe changes in gradient. You are forced to pedal while out of the saddle for long periods of time and to quickly assess a barrage of obstacles. Failure to clear an obstacle or succession of obstacles could have severe physical consequences.

Elevation change: The locations of the route's high and low elevations are given. Elevation gain is the sum of all uphills encountered along the ride, not simply the difference between the highest and lowest elevations. Additional information is provided in the trail's accompanying elevation profile.

Season: This is the best time of year to pedal the route, taking into account trail conditions, riding comfort, and local hunting seasons. Since hunting seasons vary, you should contact the Utah State Department of Natural Resources—Wildlife Resources Division.

Services: Information is provided on where provisions can be found in relation to the trailhead, including food, lodging, campgrounds, gasoline, supplies, bike shop, etc.

Hazards: Special hazards like steep cliffs, great amounts of downfall, or wire fences very close to the trail are noted here. Also any special precautions to be considered before embarking are listed.

Rescue index: Determining how far one is from help on any particular trail can be difficult due to the backcountry nature of most mountain bike rides. The proximity of homes or Forest Service outposts, nearby roads and the frequency of motorists, or the likelihood of encountering others on the trail is noted. Although phone numbers of emergency services are not listed, the general location of a hospital or clinic is provided.

Land status: This category states the land ownership over which a trail crosses. Most rides exist on federal public lands but may also cross state, city, local, or private lands. Note: Every attempt was made to choose trails that were designated as open to bicycles at the time of publication. But because land ownership changes over time, each cyclist must be aware of land status and obey all signs restricting travel. You are ultimately responsible for your actions.

Maps: The maps are 7.5 minute (1:24,000 scale) topographic maps published by the USGS over which the ride traverses. Other maps may be listed when appropriate.

Access: Tells you how to reach the trailhead and where to park your vehicle.

Sources of additional information: Provides sources that can provide additional information on the ride or area. This category is deleted if the only appropriate source is the land management agency listed in "Land status." For a complete list of sources consult Appendix B.

Notes on the trail: This section guides you carefully through any portions of the trail that are particularly difficult. Although the trail descriptions are not "mileage" driven, they are carefully worded so you can easily follow the route and gauge your progress. If a route is straightforward and easy to follow, this category will be brief. Additional information or historical background may also appear here.

This guide doesn't pretend to be omniscient. Ratings and ride accounts are as accurate as possible. However, everyone is different. Individual riders excel in different skills and have different tastes. Use this guide as a starting point.

Though regulations, ownership, and even land itself may change, this guide will help you get home in one piece.

TRAIL ETIQUETTE

Webster defines etiquette as ". . . the forms [and] manners established by convention as acceptable or required for social relations . . ." Etiquette, therefore, applies to tea parties as well as backcountry travel. When it comes to mountain biking, trail etiquette is a subject that cannot be overemphasized because your every action has an impact on the trail, on the environment, and on others.

Only YOU can prevent . . . trail closures.

The following "Rules of the Trail" is reprinted by permission of the International Mountain Bike Association (IMBA), whose mission is to promote environmentally sound and socially responsible mountain biking. Although it may seem lengthy, it boils down to basic common sense: *Ride Aware, Be Prepared, and Share the Trail.*

1. Ride on open trails only. Respect trail and road closures and access restrictions (ask if not sure), avoid possible trespass on private land, and obtain appropriate permits and authorization as may be required. Federal and state wilderness areas are closed to bicycles. Bikes must stay on established roads and designated bike trails in national parks. The way you ride will influence trail management decisions and policies.

2. Leave no trace. Be sensitive to the dirt beneath you and practice low-impact cycling. Even on open (legal) trails, you should not ride under conditions where you will leave evidence of your passing, such as on certain soils shortly after a rain. Recognize different types of soil and trail construction; practice low-impact cycling. This also means staying on existing trails and not creating any new ones. Be sure to pack out at least as much as you pack in.

3. Control your bicycle. Inattention for even a second can cause problems. Obey all bicycle speed regulations and recommendations.

4. Always yield the trail. Make known your approach well in advance. A friendly greeting (or a bell) is considerate and works well; don't startle others. Show your respect when passing by slowing to a walking pace or even stopping. Anticipate other trail users around corners or in blind spots.

5. Never spook animals. All animals are startled by an unannounced approach, a sudden movement, or a loud noise. This can be dangerous for you, others, and the animals. Give animals extra room and time to adjust to you. When passing horses, use special care and follow direction from the horseback rider (ask if uncertain). Running livestock and disturbing wild animals is a serious offense. Leave gates as you found them, or as marked.

6. Plan ahead. Know your equipment, your ability, and the area in which you are riding—and prepare accordingly. Be self-sufficient at all times, keep your equipment in good condition, and carry the necessary supplies for changing weather or other conditions. A well-executed trip is a satisfaction to you and not a burden or offense to others.

Keep trails open by setting a good example of environmentally sound and socially responsible off-road cycling.

Granted, this may seem like a lot to remember when your sole objective is to pedal through the woods or desert. If anything, remember this one point every time you ride: Just because you *can,* doesn't mean you *should!*

TREAD LIGHTLY

"Don't Waste Utah," is the frank but effective slogan of the Utah Department of Transportation's beautification campaign. Whether you are mountain biking, hiking, backpacking, car camping, or picnicking, keep the area you are visiting beautiful and unspoiled for future visitors. It takes little added effort and virtually no extra time to "Leave No Trace."

Backcountry camping

Whenever possible, or if required, camp at developed campgrounds or designated camping sites. Amenities such as water taps, picnic tables, fire pits, tent pads, trash pickup, or outhouses are worth the nominal fee.

When backcountry camping in mountainous terrain, choose a site in a wooded area and, preferably, a site that has been used previously. Camping in meadows damages delicate plant life and is aesthetically unpleasing. Also avoid riparian areas because the community of water-loving plants along streams is precious to wildlife.

In desert terrain, avoid placing tents on top of vegetation, especially cryptobiotic soils, by selecting a site on rock or sand. Avoid dry washes in narrow canyon, because of the danger of flash flooding.

Cooking

Use a gas camp stove whenever possible rather than building a ground fire. If you must have an open fire, use a fire pan and bring your own wood or charcoal. If a fire pit is necessary, use an established site instead of building a new one; otherwise dig through twigs, needles, and sod until cool, moist soil is reached. Make sure there are no tree roots exposed in the bottom of the pit. A rock ring around the pit does little to prevent ashes from spreading, so resist building one. Collect only dead or down wood and think small. Bonfires are dangerous, especially during midsummer when forests are dry. Burn the fire to ashes and douse heavily with water until dead and cold. Finally, cover the cold ashes with the soil that was originally removed from the pit.

National parks prohibit the collection of firewood, even of deadwood that has fallen to the ground. At backcountry camping sites, the use of a fire pan is required and all ashes must be packed out.

National forests may prohibit the use of ground fires during seasons of high fire danger.

Keep a clean campsite

Pack out your trash, recycle it whenever possible, and go the extra distance to clean up after less thoughtful visitors. No one wants to camp where someone has left trash and human waste, and creating a new campsite can stress the environment. Carry plastic bags in your vehicle and pack out all trash if garbage collection is not available.

Washing

Never wash (body, bike, or cooking utensils) in a lake, pond, stream, or desert pothole. The introduction of mud, soap, sunscreen, bike lubricants, and oils can pollute water sources that are critical for animals. Carry wash water away from the source, dispose of dirty water in a small hole, and cover it with dirt. Biodegradable soaps are most effective when rinsed off on land where soil bacteria can degrade it. Screen all camp wash water; then pack out and dispose of food particles appropriately.

Trash

If you made room in your fanny pack or vehicle to bring stuff in with you, then you certainly have the means to *pack it out*. Remember, the little things add up: candy wrappers, fruit peels, nut shells, pop tops, cigarette butts, etc. These items do not decompose readily. Carry a garbage bag in your vehicle for camp waste. On the trail, carry a zipper-top bag for leftovers and to help keep packs mess-free.

Human Waste

Bears do it, cows do it, and soon enough you'll have to do it. Use trailhead facilities whenever possible; otherwise, pick a location several hundred feet away from water sources, trails, campsites, and other uses; then dig a small hole 6 to 12 inches deep in fertile soil, shallower in desert soils. Tissue paper should be packed out. Cover the pit with soil, leaves, and twigs.

In many national parks and some other areas, campers may be required to provide their own washable, reusable toilet system.

SPECIAL ISSUES

Cryptobiotic crusts

"Don't Bust the Crust!" Once known as cryptogams, cryptobiotic crusts are the building blocks of Utah's deserts and effectively *hold the place in place*. This crumbly black soil is made up of fungi, lichen, algae, moss, and bacteria all living together in a symbiotic relationship. Cryptobiotic crusts are important to the desert community because they stabilize the soil, prevent erosion, retain water, and provide important nutrients to plants.

Unfortunately, many activities of man are incompatible with the presence and well-being of cryptobiotic crusts. The fibers that contribute such tensile strength to these crusts are no match for the compressional stress placed upon them by footprints or tire tracks. When trampled, pieces of the crust are loosened and can be carried away by wind or surface water, preventing reattachment, and underlying soil is freed to cover adjacent crusts. Since these organisms are photosynthetic (they need light to live), burial can mean death. When large sandy areas are impacted, previously stable areas can become a series of moving sand dunes in a matter of only a few years. At best a thin veneer (only 2 to 5 millimeters thick) may return in five to seven years; a thick mature crust may take up to 100 years to form!

Learn to recognize cryptobiotic crusts and avoid tramping on them. When your travels take you through the desert, keep your course across rocks or sand. And most of all, *Don't Bust the Crust!*

Archaeological and historical sites

Evidence of early inhabitants abounds throughout Utah, and these sites of antiquity offer enlightenment to any mountain-bike trip. Such forms of prehistoric evidence vary widely from scattered arrowheads and tool fragments to pottery, vessels, and figurines, to rock art panels and cliff dwellings. Historical sites range from old homesteads and town sites to relic fortresses and haunting cemeteries. All of these vestiges are windows to the past and should be preserved for their scientific, cultural, and aesthetic value.

Use caution when visiting a site of antiquity. Avoid touching, scarring, or grasping any remnants or rock art panels. Sites of antiquity located on federal lands are protected by law as provided by the Antiquities Act of 1906. The Archaeological Resources Protection Act of 1979 considerably strengthens the legal base for protecting such archaeological resources with criminal penalties of substantial fines and/or imprisonment. Please preserve these sites for future generations to enjoy.

TRAIL ACCESS POLICIES

United States Forest Service and Bureau of Land Management: The various Forest Service and Bureau of Land Management (BLM) districts in Utah maintain an open policy toward mountain bikes overall. Bicycles are allowed on designated trails and roads unless otherwise posted. Be aware that trails and roads may not be constructed or maintained specifically for bicycles and that you may encounter other trail users, including motor vehicles on some routes. Specific policies and restrictions may vary with the district.

National Parks and Monuments: Bicycles are considered vehicles and are allowed only on roads designated open to vehicles or on paths open specifically to bicycles. Bicyclists must obey all traffic rules of motorized use. All foot and pack trails are closed to bicycles. Bicyclists are required to pay a park entrance fee.

Wilderness Areas and Wilderness Study Areas (WSA): Presently, Utah boasts 15 designated wilderness areas. We all know that mountain biking is not allowed in wilderness areas. It's the law. But what about biking in wilderness study areas (WSAs)?

First, what is a WSA? As was required by Congress, the BLM conducted a survey of its land in Utah during the late 1970s and early 1980s to identify and recommend areas suitable of wilderness characteristics. In 1990, the BLM proposed 83 WSAs, approximately 3.2 million acres, that met minimum wilderness values, including appropriate size, naturalness, outstanding opportunities for solitude or primitive types of recreation, and other special features. WSAs are, therefore, lands that have wilderness characteristics and are to be considered for inclusion in the National Wilderness Preservation System. Only Congress can designate wilderness areas on federal lands. But can you bike in a WSA? Yes and no.

According to the BLM's Interim Management Policy, the use of mechanical transport (including mountain bikes) within WSAs may only be allowed on existing ways and trails designated as "open" to such uses.

The bottom line: Obey all signs restricting travel, stay on roads and trails designated open to mountain bikes, and tread lightly. Should impacts threaten to impair the area's suitability, the BLM may limit or close the affected lands to the types of uses causing the problems. As presented in this guidebook, you will encounter WSAs on routes in the San Rafael Swell and in Moab.

Utah State Parks: Antelope Island State Park is the only state park presented in this guidebook. Mountain bikes are allowed only on designated routes. (See Ride 10: Antelope Island State Park.) Other state parks may have specific policies and restrictions.

Ski Resorts: Ski resorts are either privately owned or operate on national forest lands. All lifts, structures, and buildings are private property. Mountain bikers must be aware that maintenance operations may occur at any time and in any area. Be especially watchful of any activity on slopes above you. Stay on trails designated as open to mountain bikes, obey all signs restricting travel, and do not trespass across lands posted closed to recreational uses or across private lands within the resort.

BEING PREPARED

Mountain biking in Utah ranges from short jaunts to remote backcountry treks. While it is reasonable to adjust your preparedness for each ride, never underestimate your need for water and food, the prospect of rapidly changing weather, and the possibility of having to address a mechanical or health-related emergency. There is more to mountain biking than just mountain biking.

Water and food: Water and food are essential to life, and the lack of either can turn the most blissful ride into an agonizing nightmare. How much you consume may vary with the length and difficulty of the ride, climate and temperature, and your fitness level, nutritional practices, and past experiences. Play it safe and overestimate your consumption of both; the added weight is trivial. Besides, if you have a little extra, you may be a lifesaver for someone who did not plan as carefully as you did. Remember the old cyclists' axiom: Eat before you feel hungry; drink before you feel thirsty. Consume food and water at regular intervals, rather than one large binge midway through the ride.

Bike maintenance and gear: Because of their intended use under rough trail conditions, mountain bikes require regular maintenance. Check and clean your equipment before and after every ride. Repair or replace worn or broken parts immediately. Barring major overhauls, regular maintenance is easy and requires a minimal investment in tools and time. Learn the basic, on-trail repair techniques or ride with someone who has. Don't wait for a mishap on the trail to realize how little you know about your bike.

Tools and repair equipment: Some people ride with just the shirt on their back; others seem to pack a complete hardware store. At the least, carry the "basic tool kit," which can be stuffed easily into a small under-the-saddle pack:

tire levers
patch kit
spare tube
frame-mount pump or compressed-air cartridge
plastic garbage bag (the lightest, most compact, and effective emergency rain slicker on the market)

Now consider these extras:
multipurpose tool
chain tool
crescent wrench, pliers, or vise grips
flat head and/or Phillips screwdrivers
hex and socket wrenches
spoke wrench
duct tape
pocket knife

Still more stuff:
spare brake and derailleur cables
chain lube
sunscreen
lip balm
water purification tablets
toilet paper
zip-locked bags for left-over snacks

A word of advice: If you ride with a group, share the load, but stay close together or regroup often. It does little good for the lead rider to be carrying the pump and patch kit if another rider is a mile behind with a flat. If you ride solo, you may have to carry the whole works.

Emergency gear: Always take into consideration how far your ride is leading you from civilization (or your car) and the prospect of walking home or spending the night on the trail if you have a total mechanical failure at the farthest point.

> waterproof matches or lighter
> compass and map
> flashlight or headlamp
> plastic whistle
> emergency blanket
> first-aid kit

POTENTIAL HAZARDS

Health-related problems can result from lack of preparedness, inadequate physical conditioning, and plain misfortune. The climate of Utah varies between extremes: hot, dry deserts to cool, moist forests, to frigid ridges and peaks. Some rides begin in one climatic extreme and end in another, so you must be aware and plan for current and forecasted weather conditions.

Weather and lightning: During summer, afternoon thunderstorms are common in both desert and mountain environments. They can approach quickly and be violent. Don't be fooled. Morning's cerulean sky can turn to boiling thunderheads accompanied by radical drops in temperatures by midday. If lightning is proximal and strikes are frequent, get off ridges quickly. Seek shelter at lower elevations in valleys, between boulders in rocky slopes, or in heavily forested areas. Avoid shallow caves, open meadows, lone trees, or isolated tree clusters. Separate yourself from your bike. Then sit on a small rock with just your feet and buttocks touching the rock, preferably with insulating material in between you and the rock (foam pad or pack). Clasp your hands around your knees. If you are struck, the lightning may pass around your heart because of the insulation.

Waiting out a storm is a viable option. In many cases, storms pass quickly, and your ride can be resumed. But think ahead by packing along rainwear. At the very least, stuff a plastic garbage bag in your jersey pocket. It is the most effective, compact, and economical rain slicker on the market. However, the best protection against being caught in a thunderstorm is to start your ride early and complete it by mid-afternoon.

Last, in Utah's canyon country in particular, be aware of flash flooding. Dry washes and canyons can turn to torrents when rain cascades off nearby slickrock. The worst cases may result from rain falling over distant highlands that converges on a single stream miles away. Although you may be catching rays at your location, a wall of water may be barreling down on you without your knowing. Don't get stuck in the path.

Hypothermia: The lowering of the body's core temperature is not just a winter-related health threat because air temperature does not have to dip below freezing for exposure to occur. Frigid mountain rains, wind blowing across exposed or wet skin, and lack of food and water can accelerate the onset of hypothermia. Symptoms of mild hypothermia include feeling deep cold or numbness, shivering, poor coordination, slowing of pace, and slurred speech. As hypothermic conditions worsen, a person may develop blueness in the skin, fingers, or lips; severe fatigue; irrationality and disorientation; and decreased shivering followed by stiffening of muscles.

Treat a hypothermic victim by seeking shelter and warmth. Remove wet clothes and replace with dry clothing, or cover the victim with wind-proof materials to prevent additional evaporative heat loss. Encourage the victim to ingest warm fluids (non-alcoholic) and food or to move at a slow and steady pace to raise body temperature.

Heat exhaustion: The opposite of hypothermia is *hyper*thermia (raised body temperature), which is caused by exposure to hot environments and overexertion. Blood vessels in the skin become so dilated to promote internal cooling that blood to the brain and other vital organs is reduced to inadequate levels. Symptoms include nausea, dizziness, mild confusion, headache, mild temperature elevation, and dehydration. In advanced cases, the hyperthermic victim may or may not be sweating, and the skin may be cool to the touch. Cool the victim immediately by seeking shade and shelter. Wet the victim and fan vigorously, and encourage him or her to drink cool fluids (non-alcoholic).

Altitude sickness: Ascending to high elevations without acclimating may produce headaches, fatigue, loss of appetite, drowsiness, and apathy. (It's about the same feeling as a hangover.) Treatment includes rest, adequate consumption of fluids and food, and pain relievers. If you're visiting from low elevations, proceed very slowly at first or allow an extra day to adjust to the new environment.

Bad water: Water does not have to be visually polluted to be bad. Even the clearest mountain streams may be unhealthy to drink because of mine wastes, bacteria and viruses, or a single-celled organism called *Giardia lamblia*. This microorganism causes intestinal distress in the way of severe diarrhea, nausea, cramps, and loss of appetite. In short, it will make your life miserable for weeks if not treated medically. It becomes introduced to surface waters from animal and human waste. To be safe, avoid all surface waters and carry plenty of water with you. There are three effective ways to treat questionable water: boil it for 10 to 15 minutes, purify it through a filtration device, or disinfect it with chemicals (Potable Aqua, Globaline, or iodine).

Hunting season: Big-game hunting season in Utah runs from early September through the end of October, and Utah's mountains, plateaus, and valleys are prime deer and elk habitat. Hunters wear neon orange for a reason. You should do the same if you insist on biking off-road during the autumn hunt. Avoid the opening and closing days of hunting season, stay on main dirt roads, and forfeit remote single-tracks.

Mines: Utah has a deep mining heritage centered about yesteryear's mining activity in desert and alpine terrain alike. Old mining camps, structures, tunnels, and shafts may spark curiosity, but entering one is backcountry roulette. Structures may exist in a state of decay and collapse. Mine openings may contain harmful or lethal gases and low levels of oxygen. Look but do not enter.

NORTHERN UTAH'S MOUNTAINLANDS

Introduction

Two of the nation's prominent and unique mountain ranges converge upon northern Utah: the Wasatch Range and Uinta Mountains. The former plays host to one of the Intermountain West's economic and cultural hubs; the latter is a vast mountain wilderness.

Prominent is the Wasatch Range—a 200-mile-long lineament arcing gently from the state's northern border to its heartland. The Wasatch serves as both westernmost limit of the Middle Rocky Mountains and eastern emergence of the Basin and Range Province. Unique is its geologic complexity that is dominated by the razor-sharp Wasatch Fault Line. On a global scale, the Wasatch Line, which is synonymous with the Wasatch Front, is deemed one of a kind and incomparable to any other of the earth's great fractures. The Front's youth (geologically speaking), tremendous vertical displacements, and consequent lack of well-developed foothills make portions of the Wasatch Front some of the world's steepest rising mountains. Foremost Utah geologist William L. Stokes coined the Wasatch "the Backbone of Utah."

From all points west, the Wasatch Front rises abruptly as a seemingly impervious land barrier above the persistent levelness of the Great Salt Lake valley. Its tallest mountaintops reach 5,000 to 7,000 feet above the valley floor to a maximum elevation of 11,928 feet atop Mount Nebo—monarch of the Wasatch—with two dozen points breaking 11,000 feet. At these elevations, alpine glaciation has been the principal sculptor, shaping lone peaks into horns and ridge lines into serrated arêtes, while scouring out hanging valleys, cirque bowls, and deep U-shaped troughs. Meltwater rivers have notched the mountains' lower canyons into steep-walled conduits, which channel the precious life-giving waters to the valley's fertile farmlands and thirsty inhabitants.

Aesthetically, the Wasatch Range is glorious and beyond compare. Its spectacular silhouette serves as a backdrop for a sprawling metropolis of 1.3 million people (from Logan, through Ogden and Salt Lake City, to Provo), which accounts for three quarters of the state's population. From certain angles, tall mountain jags appear as though they might topple down upon the valley's populus, who gaze up with undying reverence.

But firm and providing is the Wasatch Range. Frontal canyons offer easy and direct access into the heart of this mountain sanctuary where seven designated wilderness areas reside. These outstanding natural areas plus an enormous network of backcountry trails and roads afford a much-desired alpine refuge from the confines of urbanization.

At the western foot of the Wasatch Range lies the smooth saline floor of Pleistocene-age Lake Bonneville, now occupied in part by its offspring, Utah Lake and the Great Salt Lake. On this ancient lake bottom coalesce Utah's urban centers, each laid out according to the systematic grid dictated a century and a half ago by Mormon prophet Brigham Young. Opposing the Central Wasatch are the Oquirrh Mountains, which like the Wasatch, are majestic in

Bob looks over Lake Desolation along the Wasatch Crest Trail.

stature. The dynamic scene of freshwater lake, land-locked saline sea, metropolitan valley, and confining mountains is strictly unique to northern Utah, and when viewed from up high along a mountain-bike route, is utterly breathtaking.

Behind the Wasatch, on its east side, lies a string of fertile parks and valleys. Logan's Cache Valley, nourished by the Bear and Logan rivers, is enveloped by lush farmlands, dairy industries, and cheese factories. During the early nineteenth century, mountain men like Jim Bridger and Jed Smith explored this valley and the Bear River Range in search of beaver and plausible routes through the Intermountain West. Laden with a bounty of skins, trappers often had to "cache" their booty; thus, the region was named.

Ogden, Morgan, and Heber valleys harbor equally fertile agricultural parks but each is also a center for water sports. The Ogden River backs up into amoeba-shaped Pineview Reservoir, East Canyon Reservoir fills a small glen above Morgan Valley, and Heber's Jordanelle and Deer Creek reservoirs are fed by Provo River. On the placid surface of each lake is reflected the Wasatch Range's less-vaunted backside.

Like these valleys, the area once known as Parleys Park lured early settlers from Salt Lake City to pasturelands atop steeply rising Parleys Canyon (through which Interstate 80 now winds). But here in 1868, the rich land produced not only fertile soil but also threads of mineral ore. A silver siren blared in an era of frenzied mining activity that made Park City one of the West's richest mining districts. Mining moguls found their fortunes in Park City, including the Kearns family of Salt Lake City and George Hearst, father of publishing magnate William Randolph Hearst.

Park City was not exempt from the hardships that plagued similar mining boom towns. Fluctuating ore prices, mining disasters, and the 1898 hotel fire that reduced 75 percent of the town to ashen rubble tried the patience of fortune-seeking immigrants and hastened the exodus of those left destitute. By the mid-1900s, Park City had slipped into a deep sleep from which similarly devastated mining towns would never awaken. But the same hills that gave life to Park City a century before would lift its soul again with the modern-day boom of alpine skiing. Today, with its three resorts and refined turn-of-the-century aura, Park City shares its prominence with the likes of Aspen, Vail, and other elite ski towns throughout the Intermountain West.

Equally prominent are the Uinta Mountains (pronounced you-IN-tah), which extend from near Park City 150 miles eastward to Flaming Gorge/Vernal. Utah's tallest peaks reside in the High Uintas Wilderness Area with Kings Peak reaching 13,528 feet. Unique is its physiography, for the Uinta Mountains are the only major east-west trending range in the lower 48 states.

Whereas the Wasatch Range is characterized by a more juvenile assemblage of rough and chaotic glacial terrain, the Uintas expound upon mature glacial topography. During the Pleistocene, the core of the Uintas was blanketed by extensive ice sheets that scoured out broad, flat-bottomed, trough valleys separated by narrow arêtes and gigantic, amphitheater cirques. Thousands of lakes left in the glaciers' wakes and the major drainage patterns that evolved make the Uintas both an invaluable watershed and an angler's paradise.

Since volcanic activity and associated mineral resources are generally absent from the Uintas, these mountains have been a great disappointment to the miner in search of pay dirt. Their bounteous forests, however, have proven attractive to the timber industry, but the range's rugged terrain and hard-to-reach center prevented mass clearing of its woodlands. These combined factors suggest the Uintas have little to offer other than their remoteness and naturalness, two qualities these mountains have in superlative degrees.

In today's age of knobby tires, index shifting, and full suspension, all trails justifiably lead to Moab; however, more than a century ago, pioneer trails converged upon and radiated from the Wasatch Front, which was labeled "Crossroads of the West."

Spanish friars Domínguez and Escalante were perhaps the first Europeans to venture into northern Utah. Their objective was to explore an overland route between Santa Fe, New Mexico, and missions in Monterey, California—a journey that would skirt the Uinta Mountains and lead into Utah Valley, land of an amiable Yuta Indian tribe called the Timpanogotzis. But their 1776 crusade would never come to fruition. With supplies exhausted and hardships frequent, they were forced to return to New Mexico, not along their previous route nor by way of familiar terrain in northern Arizona, but through the tortuously incised canyons and harsh terrain of southern Utah's Canyon Country. A 37-foot tall white cross atop Domínguez Hill at the mouth of Spanish Fork Canyon (Provo) marks their passage.

During the early 1800s, mountain men like Jim Bridger, Jed Smith, Peter Skene Ogden, Etienne Provost, and General Ashley would forge additional routes across northern Utah, and in the process, they would bestow their names upon many sites throughout the Wasatch and Uintas. Their travels were spurred by rich incentives offered by fur-trading companies. Pack trains became common sights, and the annual mountain-man rendezvous on the shore of Bear Lake is reenacted to this day.

While mountain men ventured through northern Utah in search of fur-bearing riches, a group of Easterners persecuted for their religious beliefs sought a "Land of Zion" in the vast West. Guided by divine knowledge, Joseph Smith founded the Church of Jesus Christ of Latter Day Saints as the true church during 1830 in upstate New York and published the first *Book of Mormon*. But local opposition to the new church's beliefs forced Smith and his followers to flee the East to the Midwest where the Mormons established a town in Illinois called Nauvoo—a Hebrew word for "the beautiful location." But the violence and threats continued and culminated with Smith's assassination. Brigham Young, Smith's successor and church prophet, realized that the only peace for the Mormons would be to seek solace in a land "where the Devil cannot dig us out." The exodus to the West would become one of the great treks in American history. Despite glowing reports of California's fruitful lands, Young proclaimed the bleak but visionary Salt Lake Valley as "the right place." Upon this land that nobody else wanted, and even Native Americans seldom inhabited, these determined people would erect their city to God.

These same trails of emigration that led Mormon pioneers to their Promised Land ended their isolation. The short-lived Pony Express would brush by Salt Lake City, a rush for California's gold brought flocks of "gentiles" (those not of the L.D.S. faith) through the Wasatch Front, and a Golden Spike driven into a first-ever transcontinental railroad heralded Ogden as "Junction City."

As you pedal through northern Utah's Mountainlands, think of its back-country paths not simply as a means to perfect a thrill, but envision days long since past when turning wheels were wooden; distances were measured in days, not hours; and trails were replete with life's hardships, not just technical maneuvers.

Logan

RIDE 1 GREEN CANYON

Green Canyon is the locals' favorite because it offers quick and direct access to the heart of the mighty Bear River Range. There is no need to pack up the car for a long haul because you can pedal right from town for a noontime workout or a post-work wind down. If a casual pace is more your speed, then pack along some treats and snuggle up to a shady cottonwood at one of many picnic tables midroute. Terraced limestone slopes 1,500-feet tall support tenacious oak, maple, and pygmy conifers on sunny aspects and pine and fir on shady recesses. Singletrack purists can follow an optional path stemming from the road's end as far as the Mount Naomi Wilderness boundary 1.5 miles away. You might be able to sneak out during the winter because the road is typically snowpacked from cross-country skiers.

General location: 4.5 miles northeast of the center of Logan.

Distance: 8.2 miles out-and-back.

Tread: Light-duty dirt road with gravel, rock, and washboards that is suitable for passenger cars but may be too rough for tag-along child trailers.

Aerobic level: Easy to moderate. The road rises steadily at an average 5 percent grade. Gravel and scattered rocks in the road can make some sections harder than others. When you tire, simply turn around and coast back home.

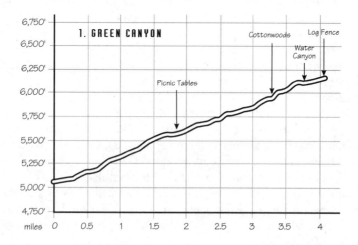

RIDE 1 GREEN CANYON

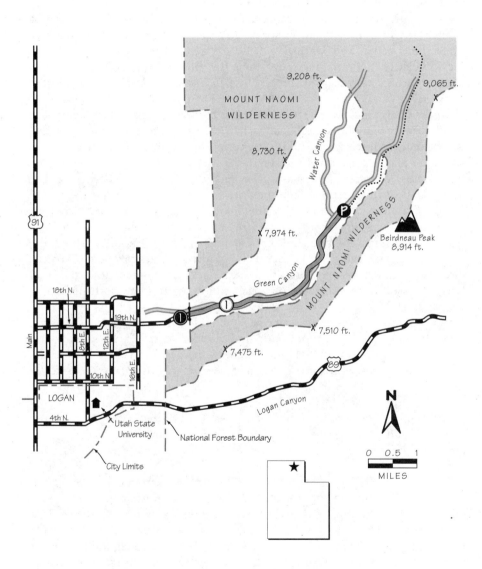

Technical difficulty: Level 2. Gravel, imbedded stones and rocks, and periodic washboards can make handling tricky at times and will keep you out of the saddle for most of the return descent.

Elevation change: The trailhead is at 5,000 feet. The road rises steadily to its end at 6,200 feet for a one-shot, 1,200-foot gain.

Season: April to November. Because the route is relatively low in elevation, it is likely the first to melt out in spring and the last to be dusted in the fall. Midsummer can be very warm.

Services: There is no drinking water along the route, but there are a few picnic tables midroute on which to spread out a picnic lunch. Logan has all visitor services.

Hazards: Gravel and washboards can make cornering tricky when taken with speed. Be alert to motorists, especially where the road narrows to one lane wide.

Rescue index: Motorists and OHVs are common as well as hikers, equestrians, and other bikers. Logan has a hospital.

Land status: Wasatch-Cache National Forest (Logan Ranger District).

Maps: USGS Mt. Elmer and Smithfield, Utah.

Access: From the intersection of Main and 400 North in the center of Logan, travel north on Main (U.S. Highway 91) for 2.6 miles. Turn right on 1800 North/Green Canyon Drive. At 1000 East, a T junction 1.5 miles farther, jog left, then right on 1900 North. Take 1900 North 2.6 miles to where pavement turns to dirt at the national forest boundary. Parking is limited. You can access Green Canyon from elsewhere in Logan simply by heading north until you intersect 1900 North.

Notes on the trail: Directions can't be simpler. Pedal up the road to where it ends after 4.1 miles at a turnaround and wooden fence. This is the parking area for those accessing the Mount Naomi Wilderness.

The road begins with some gravel and washboards that can be physically tiring and mentally tedious. But this is par for the course on a road that attracts motorists and OHVs. About 2 miles up, the gravel and washboards subside but are replaced by imbedded stones that can make the going equally jarring. You'll pass a grove of maples that huddle around a group of picnic tables and keep winding up the canyon. A large stand of cottonwoods signifies the top is near.

When you reach the road's end at the log fence, turn around and coast back down with the wind in your face and the sun on your brow. To add a few extra miles on to your outing, head up the singletrack stemming from the fence. This moderately difficult trail is no steeper than the road but the path is entrenched several inches and may nip at your pedals with each passing stroke. Plus a thick blanket of tall grasses that envelop the path can hide obstacles from your view. As you rise in elevation, trail-side foliage changes to aspen, pine, and fir that thrive in cooler, moister climes. About 1.5 miles up, you'll reach the Mount Naomi Wilderness, and that's the end of the route for bicycles. This isn't just a suggestion; it's the law.

RIDE 2 *JARDINE JUNIPER*

The Old Jardine Juniper is a curious sight. Anchored tenaciously above the craggy cliff-lined walls of Logan Canyon, the stoic cedar clings to life—even after 3,000 years! Grossly twisted limbs stretch from its weather-tortured trunk. Although the tree appears dead and decaying, a small garland sprouting from its crown confirms that the conifer is very much alive.

You'll enjoy diverse scenery on your way up to the juniper. Wood Camp Hollow harbors some of the most active avalanche chutes in northern Utah. There are good views of the Bear River Range, including nearby Mount Naomi Wilderness, and from the trail's end you'll look down at a dizzying angle to the limestone castles that enclose Logan Canyon.

General location: The trail begins 10 miles up Logan Canyon at the Wood Camp/Jardine Juniper turnoff.

Distance: 9 miles out-and-back.

Tread: Doubletrack-turned-singletrack throughout. Portions are smooth-packed dirt; others are gravelly and rutted.

Aerobic level: Moderate to strenuous. Moderate for the first 2 miles, then steep and strenuous thereafter.

Technical difficulty: Level 2 to 4. The lower trail is mostly packed and loose dirt. Midroute, where you climb 1,200 feet through a series of switchbacks, the trail can be loose and rough. The upper section may be furrowed in places from erosion.

Elevation change: The trailhead at Wood Camp Campground sits at 5,360 feet. The trail tops out at 7,200 feet just before reaching Old Jardine. Along

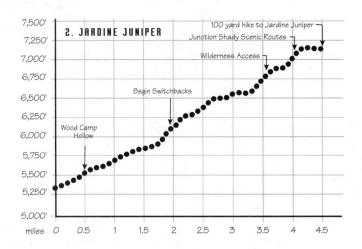

RIDE 2 JARDINE JUNIPER

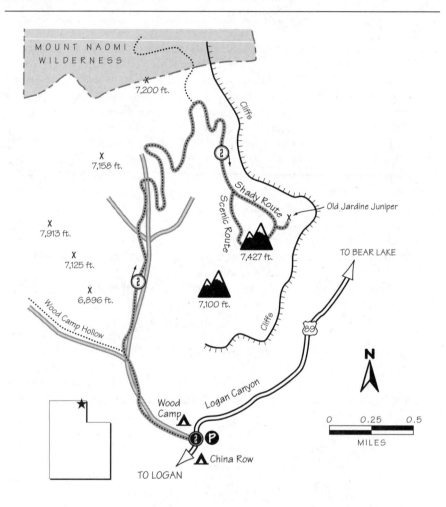

MOUNT NAOMI
WILDERNESS

X
7,200 ft.

Cliffs

X
7,158 ft.

Scenic Route

Shady Route

Old Jardine Juniper

X
7,913 ft.

X
7,125 ft.

7,427 ft.

TO BEAR LAKE

X
6,896 ft.

7,100 ft.

Cliffs

Wood Camp Hollow

89

N

Logan Canyon

Wood
Camp

0   0.25   0.5

MILES

China Row

TO LOGAN

the route's midsection, the trail rises nearly 1,200 feet over 2.5 miles through angular switchbacks. Total elevation gain is 1,800 feet.

Season: May through October. Much of the route crosses south-facing slopes, so it's an oven during midsummer.

Services: No drinking water is available along the route. Wood Camp Campground offers picnic tables, outhouses, and overnight camping, but it does not have water taps. There are many Forest Service campgrounds (fee areas) throughout the canyon. Logan offers all visitor services.

Hazards: Portions of the descent can dump an unsuspecting biker. Watch for loose rock, especially on the steeper switchbacks, and ride cautiously along the narrow, rutted track through the upper meadows. Hiking, instead of biking, the last 100 yards down to the Jardine Juniper is strongly recommended. Hikers use this route to access the nearby Mt. Naomi Wilderness, so be ready and willing to yield the trail.

Rescue index: The trail is popular with hikers and mountain bikers. Logan Canyon is well traveled by motorists. Logan has a hospital.

Land status: Wasatch-Cache National Forest (Logan Ranger District).

Maps: USGS Mt. Elmer, Utah.

Access: From the center of Logan, travel 2 miles east on 400 North/U.S. Highway 89 to Logan Canyon. Park at the turnoff for Wood Camp Campground, about 10 miles up Logan Canyon on the left between mileposts 384 and 385.

Notes on the trail: About 0.5 mile up the wide canyon bottom, Wood Camp Hollow branches left. Note the avalanche-ravaged chutes that have been denuded of trees. Fork right following the sign for Jardine Juniper. Atop the first set of switchbacks, the trail passes a sign for the Mount Naomi Wilderness (bikes are prohibited). Shortly thereafter, the trail ascends a second set of turns and rises to a T junction of trails on a ridge. Both routes circle the knoll and lead to the Old Jardine Juniper: "Shady Route" circles north and ventures through giant aspen groves; "Scenic Route" circles south and crosses open slopes that overlook Logan Canyon and the distant central Wasatch Range. When you round the knoll and come to the trail accessing the juniper, dismount and walk down the final hundred yards to view the old cedar. (It's not a good bike trail.) Return around the knoll on whichever route you did not take on the way out. Then enjoy the long descent back to the trailhead.

RIDE 3 *BEAR HOLLOW TRAIL–TWIN CREEK*

Riding the Bear Hollow Trail to Twin Creek is like racing a Super D downhill course, which is becoming a popular mountain bike race format. The premise behind a Super D ("D" is for descent) is that the finish line is substantially lower than the starting line, but there is some climbing midroute. It rekindles the days of old when cross-country mountain bike racers were disciplined downhillers, too, unlike today's armored breed who ride long-travel tanks and must take a chair lift to get uphill. Get out your old-fashioned, cross-country mountain bike and ride across the Bear River Range on this mostly downhill route.

The route begins at the recreational haven of Tony Grove Lake, an idyllic alpine pond cupped beneath ragged limestone ramparts on the edge of the Mount Naomi Wilderness. You climb briefly above the lake, then begin the

RIDE 3 BEAR HOLLOW–TWIN CREEK

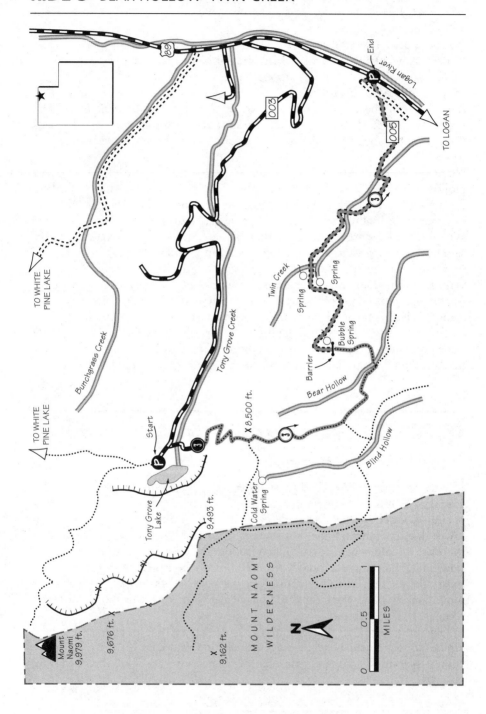

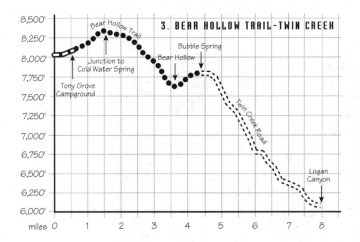

first stage of descending on the little-used Bear Hollow Trail. You'll be thankful your bike is lightweight as you bunny hop logs and ruts and then climb a hill to a broad basin that moose are known to inhabit. The second descent comes on the Twin Creek jeep road, which drops to Logan Canyon. Here gravity is your accelerator and brakes are your friends. If Newton rode a mountain bike, he would love this ride.

General location: Tony Grove Recreation Area (trailhead) is 29 miles east of Logan in Logan Canyon.

Distance: 8 miles point-to-point.

Tread: 1.5 miles of maintained singletrack (uphill), 2.5 miles of primitive singletrack (downhill), 4 miles of steep, sometimes rutted doubletrack (downhill).

Aerobic level: Moderate. The two climbs awaken your legs and lungs but won't make you blow a gasket. Strong forearms are required for constant braking.

Technical difficulty: Level 2 to 4. Bear Hollow Trail is used more by pack horses than foot or bike traffic. Expect narrow, loose, and eroded tread; downed trees and limbs across the trail; and other goodies that make backcountry biking all the more exciting. The Twin Creek doubletrack descends steeply and can be loose and rutted.

Elevation change: Tony Grove Lake (trailhead) is at 8,000 feet. The route tops out above the lake at 8,450 feet. A midroute climb gains 200 feet. The route ends in Logan Canyon at an elevation of 6,100 feet. Total climbing is 650 feet; total descending is 2,520 feet. Good ratio, eh?

Season: June through October. Bear Hollow and Twin Creek may be popular big-game hunting areas during the fall.

Services: Tony Grove has a campground (fee area). The day-use parking area has an outhouse but no water tap. Logan has all visitor services.

Logan Canyon and the Mount Naomi Wilderness are common sights along many Logan-area rides.

Hazards: Hikers and equestrians commonly travel the first 2 miles of the trail to Bear Hollow. Be courteous and yield the trail. Thereafter, your brakes must be in perfect working order for the steep, direct descent on the Twin Creek doubletrack.

Rescue index: Tony Grove is Logan's most popular recreational area. But once you start the descent, solitude will be your constant companion. Bear Hollow Trail and the Twin Creek Road are infrequently traveled. Logan has a hospital.

Land status: Wasatch-Cache National Forest (Logan Ranger District).

Maps: USGS Mount Elmer, Naomi Peak, Temple Mountain, and Tony Grove, Utah.

Access: From the center of Logan, travel 2 miles east on 400 North/U.S. Highway 89 to Logan Canyon. Travel 17.8 miles up Logan Canyon and park at the Twin Creeks Road/Forest Road 005 on the north side of the highway between mileposts 392 and 393. In the shuttle, continue up Logan Canyon for

1.5 miles and turn left for Tony Grove Canyon Recreation Area. (You can park here at the horse trailer lot as well.) Drive 6.7 miles up the paved road to the Tony Grove day-use parking area.

Notes on the trail: Before you get started, please note that bikes are not allowed on the nature trail circling Tony Grove Lake. With that said and done, pedal through the Tony Grove Campground to site 13 and take the trail signed "Cold Water Canyon, Smithfield Canyon, Cottonwood Canyon." As you cross the timbered slopes, ignore a trail forking left and stay straight. (The left fork takes you downhill to the horse parking area.) The trail rises moderately through stands of fir and spruce and around several switchbacks. Too bad the rest of the ride is not on a dreamy trail like this. Just over 1 mile from the campground, the trail tops out and comes to a junction signed for Cold Water Springs (straight), Tony Grove (reverse), and Bear Hollow #600 (left). Your route is left and down Bear Hollow, but if you want to log a couple of extra miles, take the Cold Water Springs Trail to the Mount Naomi Wilderness boundary and back. You'll venture through groves of aspens and then across a sunny alpine basin. (Remember! No bikes allowed in the wilderness!)

The Bear Hollow Trail begins with a steep, rutted descent. After a few hundred yards, the trail bends right and rises gently through crooked aspens underlaid by tall grass and wildflowers. Then you start big-time freewheeling. After 1 mile of coasting, fork left on a flat spot where the Hansen Pond Trail forks right down Blind Hollow. Drop down through the trees to a trail junction in the Bear Hollow meadow. Cut straight across the field, ignoring a trail forking right and descending Bear Hollow. You know you're on course if you start climbing. It's a Super D, remember? (You on your light cross-country rig will make easy work of the half-mile climb; your buddies on their hefty "free ride" bikes will suffer the weight penalty.) Descend past Bubble Spring to a rock barrier, where the trail becomes doubletrack. Curve around the basin on the rolling road while keeping an eye out for moose feeding on the luscious plants nourished by the spring; then begin the Twin Creek descent.

The remainder of the route is a case study of the Laws of Physics. Let's assume for the sake of discussion that we live in an ideal physical world, which means a resistance-free vacuum. All objects regardless of mass (we call it "weight" in the English system) fall toward the earth's surface at the same rate of acceleration—that's gravity acting. A marble and a bowling ball hit the ground at the same time and at the same speed when dropped from the same height. If we know the height of the object, we can determine the speed of impact. Now if that object started at the same height but rolled down a ramp, regardless of length and incline, it would reach the same speed when it contacts the earth as that of a vertical free fall, neglecting rolling resistance of course. "So what," you say?

Let's apply what we've learned. As you begin your descent on the Twin Creek doubletrack, you are 1,600 vertical feet above the trail's end in Logan Canyon. In an ideal world, you would reach a blazing speed of 220 miles per hour at the end of your 4-mile downhill coast. Yikes! And in reality, today's bike manufacturers are attempting to reproduce an ideal world by reducing the resistance in ball bearings, tread design, and aerodynamic clothing. They're trying to kill us!

Flip the coin and you'll find another contingent of bike parts designers who truly love you because they build the stuff that causes friction, and their brakes are your best friends. The bottom line. Use your brakes liberally on this descent.

But if you're a real digit-geek, then stop halfway down and feel your rims. They will be scalding hot; that's your good buddy friction at work. Feel your tires, and they'll be rock hard; that's because friction produces heat, and heat increases pressure in an object of constant volume. Finally, using thermodynamics and strength of materials, you can calculate exactly when your tires are going to blow! Will the new trend be brakes with tiny fans attached to reduce rim heat? No, something better-called disc brakes.

One last physics tidbit. Instead of using your vehicle to gain the height needed for that 220-mile-per-hour descent, pedal up. The Tony Grove Road is a classic road climb, rising 1,800 feet over 6.5 miles (that's a very comfortable 5-percent grade). You'll gaze upon beautifully rugged Logan Canyon and venture through pristine forests. You'll encounter motorists no doubt; some may toot their horn with encouragement.

RIDE 4 *BEAVER CREEK–SINK HOLLOW*

Spanning the Utah/Idaho border, the Sink Hollow loop passes through the rolling backcountry of the Bear River Range. The first half of the loop follows glistening Beaver Creek as it tumbles down a narrow valley filled with willows, sage, and wildflowers. Its course is impeded frequently by shallow ponds that pool up behind beaver dams. On the loop's "back nine" you follow the Great Western Trail as it leaves Idaho and enters Utah on its 3,000-mile course from Canada to Mexico. A spur road leads to the Pat Hollow Memorial where a C-46 transport plane crashed in 1953, killing its civilian crew and 37 military passengers.

General location: 28 miles east of Logan, near the Beaver Mountain Ski Area.
Distance: 12.5-mile loop.
Tread: 6.5 miles of light-duty dirt road followed by 1.5 miles of doubletrack. Sink Hollow Trail begins as an ATV trail, narrows to singletrack, reverts to an ATV trail, and then culminates as doubletrack studded with rocks.
Aerobic level: Moderate. The climb up the Beaver Creek Road is steady but not too tough. There is one short, steep, rough climb up to Gibson Basin; then it's downhill back to the trailhead.

RIDE 4 BEAVER CREEK–SINK HOLLOW

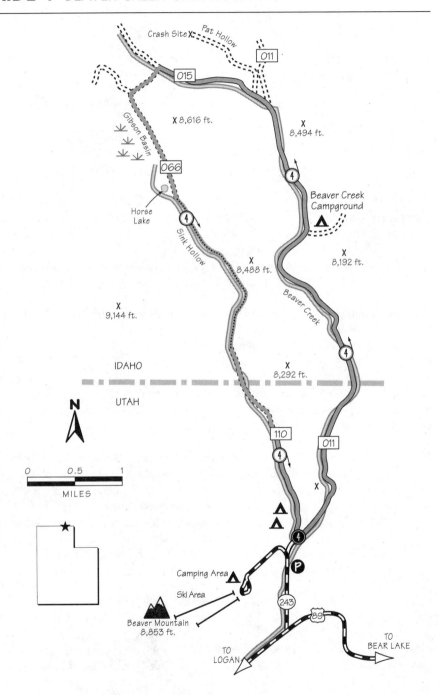

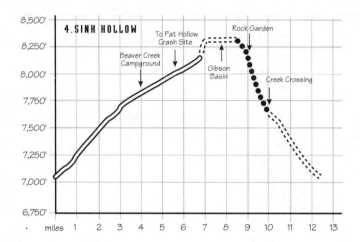

Technical difficulty: Level 2 to 5. Beaver Creek Road poses little challenge other than scattered rocks and a few ruts. The short climb to Gibson Basin is a bugger. Sink Hollow Trail varies from dreamy to pesky. (A brief rock garden, level 5, will force dismounts for all but mystic riders.) The final descent on doubletrack is twisty-turny and pock-marked with boulders that are easily avoided.

Elevation change: The trailhead is the low elevation at 7,070 feet. The route tops out at Gibson Basin at 8,300 feet. Total gain is 1,210 feet.

Season: May through October. This area is popular with big-game hunters in the fall.

Services: There is an outhouse at the trailhead. Beaver Creek Campground, located 4.5 miles into the ride, is a developed Forest Service campground (fee area) with outhouses and water taps. Beaver Mountain Ski Area has a private campground (fee area) with tent sites and RV hookups. Logan offers all visitor services.

Hazards: Motorists and off-highway vehicles may be encountered on the Beaver Creek Road. Sink Hollow Trail has a couple of short, steep descents.

Rescue index: Recreationists and campers are common near the trailhead and at Beaver Creek Campground, especially on weekends and holidays. Emergency assistance may be summoned from Beaver Mountain Ski Area. Motorists are common in Logan Canyon. Logan has medical facilities.

Land status: Wasatch-Cache National Forest (Logan Ranger District).

Maps: USGS Egan Basin and Tony Grove, Utah.

Access: From the center of Logan, travel 2 miles east on 400 North/U.S. Highway 89 to Logan Canyon. Travel 26 miles up Logan Canyon and turn left on Utah State Highway 243 for Beaver Mountain Ski Area. Park 0.6 mile farther at the Sink Hollow/Great Western Trail snowmobile trailhead.

Notes on the trail: From the trailhead, follow the dirt road signed "Entering travel management area." Shortly ahead, the Sink Hollow Road/Forest Road

Serendipitous singletrack highlights the Beaver Creek–Sink Hollow loop.

110 forks left, but stay *right* on the unsigned Beaver Creek Road. (You'll return via Sink Hollow.) Quickly, you leave the sunny meadows and enter thick forests underlaid with riparian growth that engulf Beaver Creek. Cross the Utah/Idaho border, ride out to a broad meadow, and pass Beaver Creek Campground. Thereafter, stay left on the main road next to Beaver Creek. Fork left 2 miles farther on Forest Road 015, heading toward Egan Basin. Climb gently up the narrowing, willow- and wildflower-decked valley, or take the optional 2-mile side trip to the Pat Hollow Crash Site on Forest Road 459. Although the wreckage has long since been removed, a small plaque stands as a memorial to the catastrophe.

One mile from the Beaver Creek Road, fork left on a doubletrack signed for Gibson Basin. Shift to granny gear, take a couple of deep breaths, and power up the steep, boulder-ridden track. At the top of the climb, fork left on a doubletrack that runs southward along the eastern fringe of grassy Gibson Basin. Pass marshy Horse Lake and reenter the woods on a buffed ATV track posted Sink Hollow Trail. Whip through the tightly spaced trees, dodging boulders that are scattered about the path. Slow to a creep and try bunny hopping across a highly technical rock garden. Good luck. Reenter the woods once again, climb a bit, and then descend on a steep, loose singletrack to the shallow ford of Sink Hollow Creek. Here, the path widens to an ATV track, then to a doubletrack, and descends in lively fashion. Swoop through countless turns and wiggle around boulders plopped in the road until you reach the junction with the Beaver Creek Road. The trailhead is a few hundred yards to the right. What fun!

RIDE 5 *OLD EPHRAIM'S GRAVE*

Old Ephraim was neither a famous frontiersman nor a courageous pioneer settler, but a legend just the same. Ephraim was the last grizzly bear to roam Utah, and the largest grizzly ever shot in the continental United States. His penchant for dining on livestock placed him at the top of the locals' "outlaws wanted" list. The 1,100-pound beast was as gigantic as the 11-foot stone monument that marks his 1923 grave site. His massive skull was first sent to the Smithsonian Institute and then transferred to Utah State University in Logan.

This loop crosses the rolling hinterlands of Utah's northern Wasatch Range (locally termed the Bear River Range). Open meadows of alpine grasses and colorful wildflowers carpet groves of aspen and conifer like a patterned blanket. From the route's high points, you'll view Logan Peak to the west, the Mount Naomi Wilderness to the north, and the serrated peaks of the central Wasatch Range to the south.

RIDE 5 OLD EPHRAIM'S GRAVE

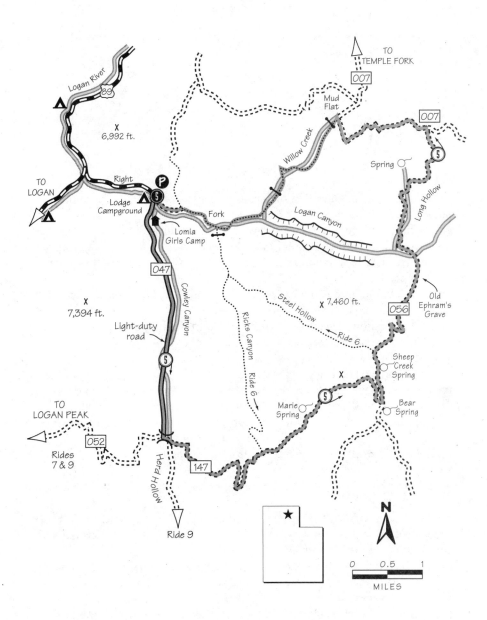

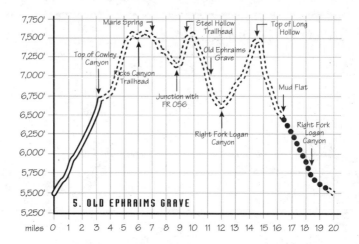

General location: 13 miles east of Logan in Right Fork Logan Canyon.

Distance: 20-mile loop.

Tread: The route begins with 3.5 miles of light-duty dirt road in Cowley Canyon and then follows 12.5 miles of doubletrack past Old Ephraim's Grave to Mud Flat. The loop culminates on the Willow Creek Trail with 4 miles of lively singletrack.

Aerobic level: Moderate to strenuous. The route is a blend of steady climbs and blazing descents.

Technical difficulty: Level 2 to 3. Dirt roads and doubletracks may be littered with imbedded and loose rocks or cut by ruts. Willow Creek Trail is pretty tame but has a few steep sections with loose tread.

Elevation change: The route begins at 5,400 feet. Cowley Canyon rises 1,300 feet over 3.5 miles. The next mile rises at a stiff, 10-percent grade to the upper trailhead for Ricks Canyon Trail. You reach the high point of 7,600 feet near Marie Spring. The descent past Old Ephraim's Grave is a real screamer. It's followed by a near 1,000-foot climb up Long Hollow. The rest is a 2,000-foot drop down Willow Creek and back to the trailhead. Total gain is about 3,300 feet.

Season: May through October. This route may be popular with big-game hunters in the fall.

Services: The Lodge Campground, located near the trailhead, is a Forest Service fee area with water taps and outhouses. Additional campgrounds line Logan Canyon. Logan offers all visitor services.

Hazards: Watch for sections of ruts and loose rocks, especially on the descents. Cattle range in the Willow Creek area, so you may have to dodge "guacamole" in the trail! Who brought the chips?

Rescue index: Cowley Canyon is popular with motorists, especially on weekends. You may encounter ORVs on the loop's more distant sections.

The colossal gravestone
of Old Ephraim.

Willow Creek is popular with hikers and equestrians. Logan Canyon is well traveled by motorists. Logan has a hospital.

Land status: Wasatch-Cache National Forest (Logan Ranger District).

Maps: USGS Boulder Mountain and Temple Peak, Utah.

Access: From the center of Logan, travel 2 miles east on 400 North/U.S. Highway 89 to Logan Canyon. Travel 9 miles up Logan Canyon on US 89, and then turn right for Right Fork, Camp Lomia, and Lodge Campground (between mileposts 383 and 384). Take the gravel road 1 mile and park just past the entrance to Lodge Campground. The loop begins on the Cowley Canyon Road (Forest Road 047).

Notes on the trail: Begin by pedaling up the Cowley Canyon Road (FR 047) next to a trickling stream. The canyon road rises steadily at a moderate grade before breaking out to a clearing and a junction of dirt roads. Take the second left-hand doubletrack (Forest Road 147), which angles southeast and uphill.

(The right fork leads to Logan Peak; the doubletrack straight ahead descends Herd Hollow.) Milk your granny gears while climbing the rough, rutted doubletrack. Descend a bit, and then pass the upper Ricks Canyon Trailhead. Two miles of roller-coaster doubletrack take you past Marie Spring and down to a T junction with Forest Road 056. Fork left/north, climb about 1 mile (passing Sheep Creek Spring and the upper Steel Hollow Trailhead), and then zoom downhill to Old Ephraim's Grave and to Right Fork Logan Canyon. Climb 3 "long" miles up Long Hollow to a saddle that affords a grand view of the terrain you just crossed and of the Bear River Range in the distance. Another bomber downhill takes you to grassy Mud Flat.

Fork left on a faded doubletrack, go through a steel gate, and hop on the Willow Creek Trail. Dart into the aspens and descend alongside the creek. Cross the creek to the west side and wind beneath orange-stained cliffs of conglomerate stone that have dropped pebbles across the trail. Cross the creek a couple times more and come to a gate. Thereafter, the Willow Creek Trail intersects the Right Fork Logan Canyon Trail. You have no choice but to fork right and descend alongside the river because upstream the willow-lined creek disappears into a dark, narrow hallway of limestone.

The next section of trail can be tricky because it first crosses a small talus area and then rolls abruptly through thick trees on the other side of the stream. Pass the junction for Ricks Canyon Trail and return to the Cowley Canyon Road on 0.5 mile of doubletrack.

RIDE 6 *RICKS CANYON–STEEL HOLLOW*

Right Fork Logan Canyon is the nexus of many fat-tire excursions, and the Ricks Canyon-Steel Hollow loop will satiate any singletrack purist; that is, any singletrack purist with legs of steel. Ricks Canyon is no ride through the park because it rises at an average 10 percent grade over its 3.5-mile length. It starts out easy enough and well below the average grade. That means farther on, the grade must exceed 10 percent to meet the average, right? And so it does. Just settle into a comfortable granny gear and let the canyon's lush ecosystem lull you through the toughest spots. It's a bitter pill for novice and intermediate riders, but advanced bikers will find it a tasty treat.

Once you top out of Ricks, the route follows an undulating doubletrack through the Wasatch Range hinterlands to Steel Hollow. Now your legs will have sweet revenge on Ricks as you descend rapidly back to the Right Fork of Logan Canyon. Some ride the loop in reverse, ascending Steel and freewheeling down Ricks. There is little change in difficulty because Steel has some

RIDE 6 RICKS CANYON-STEEL HOLLOW

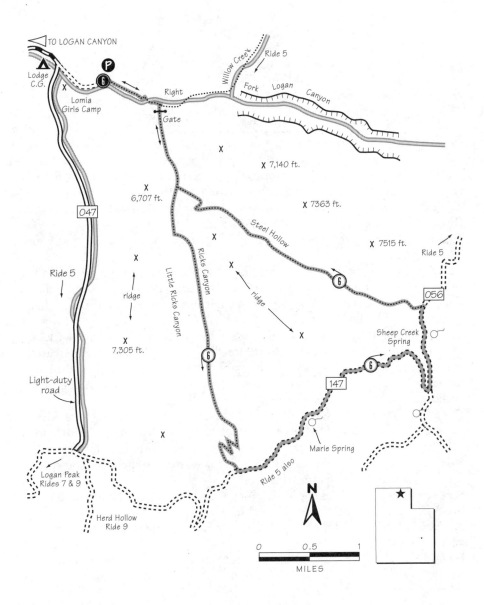

TO LOGAN CANYON

Lodge
C.G.

Lomia
Girls Camp

Right

Gate

Willow Creek

Ride 5

Fork   Logan   Canyon

X

X 7,140 ft.

X
6,707 ft.

X 7363 ft.

Steel Hollow

X

X 7515 ft.

Ride 5

047

Ride 5

X

ridge

X

ridge

056

X
7,305 ft.

Little Ricks Canyon

Ricks Canyon

X

Sheep Creek
Spring

Light-duty
road

147

X

Marie Spring

Logan Peak
Rides 7 & 9

Ride 5 also

Herd Hollow
Ride 9

N

0   0.5   1

MILES

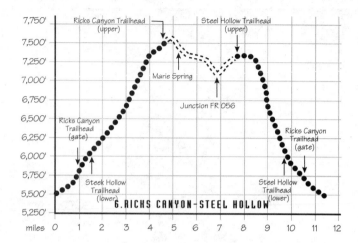

protracted grades as well. Still, if you fancy singletrack, you'll no doubt return to this loop and try it in the opposite direction just for grins.

General location: 14 miles east of Logan in Right Fork Logan Canyon.

Distance: 11.5-mile loop.

Tread: 8 miles of infrequently maintained singletrack and 3.5 miles of doubletrack.

Aerobic level: Strenuous. The climb up Ricks Canyon Trail requires steady effort plus surges of maximum power to clear eroded sections. The doubletrack up top crosses rolling terrain with short, modest climbs and fast descents. Steel Hollow is all downhill.

Technical difficulty: Level 3 to 4. Ricks Canyon Trail has scattered rocks, exposed tree roots, eroded and loose tread. These conditions are increased where the trail is steepest. The doubletrack has trivial rocks and ruts. Many hidden surprises may be awaiting your front wheel while descending Steel Hollow because the trail is narrow and can be overgrown.

Elevation change: The trailhead marks the low point at 5,500 feet. Ricks Canyon Trail gains 1,900 feet. Tack on 500 vertical feet along the rolling doubletrack, which tops out at 7,600 feet. Total gain is about 2,400 feet.

Season: May through October. Midsummer is warm, but there is good shade in Ricks Canyon when you need it most.

Services: There is no drinking water along the route. Lodge Campground near the trailhead is a Forest Service fee area with water taps and outhouses. Numerous Forest Service campgrounds line Logan Canyon. Logan offers all visitor services.

Hazards: Be alert to other trail users on singletracks. Encounters are fewer the farther you go. This area may be popular during hunting season. Foliage draping Steel Hollow Trail may hide obstacles in the tread. Steel Hollow Trail is open to motorcycles.

Right Fork Logan Canyon is the hub of many mountain bike adventures on both singletracks and dirt roads.

Rescue index: Recreationists are common near the trailhead, less so at the route's distant points. Emergency contacts might be made at the Lomia Girls Camp when it is in session. Logan has medical facilities.

Land status: Wasatch-Cache National Forest (Logan Ranger District).

Maps: USGS Boulder Mountain and Temple Peak, Utah.

Access: From the center of Logan, travel 2 miles east on 400 North/U.S. Highway 89 to Logan Canyon. Travel 9 miles up Logan Canyon on US 89 and fork right for Right Fork, Camp Lomia, and Lodge Campground (between mileposts 383 and 384). Take the gravel road 1 mile, fork left (the right fork leads to Lodge Campground and up Cowley Canyon), and continue 0.5 mile to the road's end at the horse corral, passing the girls' camp along the way.

Notes on the trail: The trail begins where the dirt road ends and follows alongside willow-draped Right Fork Logan Canyon River. After 0.5 mile, fork right, cross the creek, and go through a steel gate to head up Ricks Canyon. (The left fork, which stays along the river, leads to Willow Creek Trail—the culmination of Ride 5: Old Ephraim's Grave.) Dodge and hop over rocks as you make your way up the lightly wooded canyon. If you lift your eyes from the trail, you'll find butterflies fluttering through a menagerie of wildflowers.

About 1 mile from the gate, pass the signed junction for Steel Hollow to the left. You'll return on it later. Gradually, isolated stands of aspen commingle until they huddle with profusion, and the trail-side foliage grows to shoulder height. About 1 mile above the junction, you'll settle firmly in your granny gear, and, at times, wish for still lower gears. Inch your way up the canyon, round a few switchbacks that release you from the canyon's clutch, and exit the aspens on to a doubletrack at the trail's summit. Take the track a few hundred yards to the T junction with Forest Road 147.

Fork left and climb the doubletrack; then roll across the hinterlands of the Wasatch Range, spying distance peaks to the south near Ogden and Bountiful. Pass murky Marie Spring and descend to a T junction with Forest Road 056. Turn left and climb the dirt road for less than 1 mile, passing Sheep Creek Spring on the right. Just before the top of the climb, fork left on Steel Hollow Trail.

Cross the sunny field and then enter the shadow-dappled aspens. The going is slow because the trail's tread is often obscured by thick grass and growth; be cautious of concealed obstacles beneath your front wheel. Weave through the forest; then, about 2 miles down, round a rocky point that offers a charming overlook of Logan Canyon in the middle ground and of the Bear River Range on the horizon. A steep, rough shot drops you from the hollow's slope down to the creek's side. Return to the junction with Ricks Canyon; then retrace your tracks to the trailhead.

RIDE 7 *LOGAN PEAK*

Northern Utah's Wasatch Range boasts its fair share of classic fat-tire hill climbs, ones that will burst the blood vessels in your eyes and turn your thighs to hamburger. But the granddaddy is the 5,700-foot grinder to Logan Peak. Only mountain-bike masochists need apply.

You know you've bitten into a whopper when you realize you've passed through three vegetative life zones along the way: the Transitional Life Zone at the trailhead where sage, juniper, pinyon, and scrub hardwoods survive; the Canadian Life Zone midroute where aspens yield to pines and then firs; and the Subalpine Life Zone atop the Logan Peak where conifers become "krumholz" or flag-shaped from incessant winds. Those who make it to the top will be rewarded with unparalleled views of northern Utah's Bear River Range and Wellsville Mountains, both of which reign over fertile Cache Valley.

The climb comes in two discernible sections. The first segment to White Bedground Camp is a moderately difficult but sustained ascent on mostly hard-packed doubletracks. This is a good out-and-back option for intermediate bikers or a simple warm-up for the toughies. The route's second half (reserved for those with mountain-goat chromosomes) is a series of punishing steps up rough four-wheel-drive roads that leave you wishing for one smaller granny gear. Tolerable to tough—just what a hill climb ought to be. Oh yeah, the record is 1 hour, 45 minutes, 30 seconds. Top that!

General location: The trailhead is in Right Fork Logan Canyon located 13 miles east of Logan.

Distance: 28 miles out-and-back.

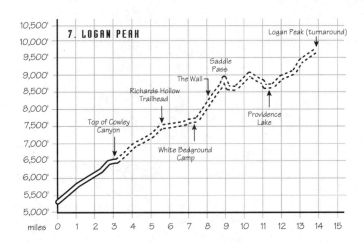

RIDE 7 LOGAN PEAK

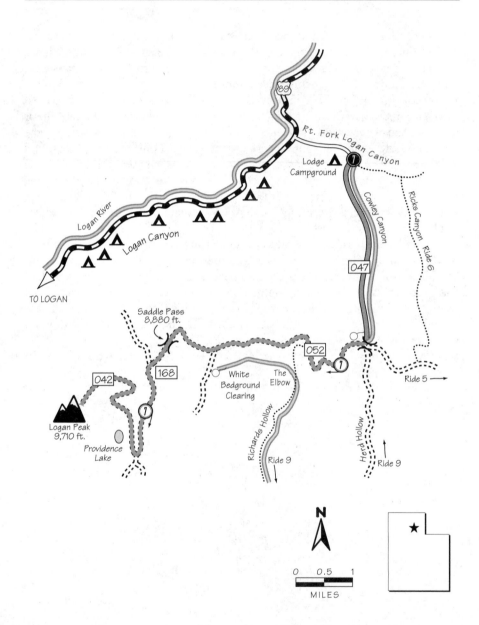

Fields of wildflowers adorn aspen meadows along the climb to Logan Peak.

Tread: 3.5 miles of light-duty dirt road up Cowley Canyon (scattered rocks) followed by 4 miles of mild, four-wheel-drive roads to White Bedground Camp junction, and then 6.5 miles of sometimes severely eroded four-wheel-drive roads to Logan Peak.

Aerobic level: Strenuous. Lungs like bellows and legs like a thoroughbred are prerequisites.

Technical difficulty: Level 2 to 4. There are some embedded stones and ruts on the first half. The second half can be eroded, rocky, and rutted from four-wheel-drive vehicles.

Elevation change: Elevation change is what this ride is all about! The trailhead is at 5,500 feet. The 1,300-foot ascent up Cowley Canyon is a good warm-up. The ensuing climb past Richards Hollow and to White Bedground Camp keeps the blood flowing (2,500 feet so far). The 1,000-foot "head wall" thereafter is downright rude. But what's this, a descent midroute? That means more climbing—a 450-foot teaser followed by the 1,100 coup de grâce up to Logan Peak (elevation 9,710 feet). But add it up and you're still short of the total. Remember that 700-foot descent midroute? Surprise! It's called "muscular meltdown" upon returning. Uh, masseuse, please!

Season: June through October depending on snowmelt and snowfall. Temperature atop Logan Peak can be much cooler than at the trailhead, especially on a breezy day and when you are sopping wet with sweat. Pack a shell or long sleeve. This route may be popular with big-game hunters during the fall.

Services: There is no water along the route. Lodge Campground at the trailhead is a Forest Service fee area with water taps and outhouses. Numerous campgrounds line Logan Canyon. Logan offers all visitor services.

Hazards: Descending the four-wheel-drive roads off Logan Peak requires attentiveness and acute bike-handling skills. Numerous sections are chock-full of loose sediment, gravel, and cobbles, most notably on the steepest grades. The return section from White Bedground Camp to the route's end is an all-out bomber; but watch for occasional vehicles. Be prepared for cool, breezy conditions atop Logan Peak, plus the possibility of afternoon rain.

Rescue index: Logan Peak is no place for a mechanical, physical, or emotional breakdown. Human encounters are less likely the farther you pedal from the trailhead. Cowley Canyon is popular with motorists on weekends. Beyond, you are on your own. Logan has medical facilities.

Land status: Wasatch-Cache National Forest (Logan Ranger District).

Maps: USGS Boulder Mountain, Logan Peak, and Temple Peak, Utah.

Access: From the center of Logan, travel 2 miles east on 400 North/U.S. Highway 89 to Logan Canyon. Travel 9 miles up Logan Canyon on US 89, and then turn right for Right Fork, Camp Lomia, and Lodge Campground (between mileposts 383 and 384). Take the gravel road 1 mile and park just past the entrance to Lodge Campground. The climb begins on the Cowley Canyon Road (Forest Road 047).

Notes on the trail: The Cowley Canyon Road (light-duty dirt with scattered rocks) is a steady 3.5-mile warm-up. At the clearing atop the canyon, fork right/west on Forest Road 052 and continue climbing steadily for 2 miles through a corridor of aspens mixed with conifers. Breathe easier on the 2-mile stretch from the Richards Hollow Trailhead to the junction for White Bedground Camp. This is the turnaround point for an intermediate-level tour.

Now the climbing begins! Continue toward Logan Peak on the protracted, rock-strewn, doubletrack heading west (Forest Road 168). You need brute strength to keep the back wheel turning, and keen handling skills to steer the front wheel on a sane course through the rocks and ruts. After 1.5 miles of soul searching, the road reaches a saddle on a subtle ridge. (Ignore the dirt roads branching north and south.) Glide over the edge and descend to a junction. Stay left/south and climb uphill. Scenery? Who cares about scenery, just keep those pedals turning. If you do lift your nose from the handlebar, you will view the mountain's slopes covered with mixed conifers and mini-meadows filled with picture-worthy wildflowers, all beneath a fortress of banded limestone. The peak you see is a false summit—Logan Peak is behind and out of sight.

Descend to the south again into a back-basin of sorts, ignoring a right-hand spur that dead-ends at a primitive campsite. After 1 mile, fork right and uphill on a doubletrack marked with a carsonite post. At a T junction up ahead, stay right and pass Providence Lake, which dries up midsummer to an ATV velodrome. The doubletrack rises in brutal stair-step fashion for 2 miles to the relay towers atop barren Logan Peak.

From atop Logan Peak, your eyes naturally fall upon Cache Valley, "the garden spot of Utah," states William L. Stokes in *Geology of Utah*. Although the agricultural industry has maintained a stronghold on the fertile valley, and the surrounding communities are bound to their pioneer heritage, Logan has emerged as a renowned industrial and technological center. Utah State University, the Aggies, as they call themselves, has diversified to fields of humanities and scientific research. Several experiments have accompanied recent space shuttle missions.

Cache Valley was not settled until 1859 when Mormons braved cold winters in order to reap the benefit of the prosperous growing season of summer. However, 25 years before the Mormons even arrived in Utah, Anglos scurried about Cache Valley and the Bear River Range. "Sartorial demands of beaver-hatted dandies..." brought mountain men like Jim Bridger and several trapping companies to northern Utah in search of fur-bearing animals in the 1820s and 1830s, according to Ward J. Roylance in *Utah: A Guide to the State*. These explorers-cum-exploiters cached their pelts in underground pits until they could be traded for money, supplies, and drink at the annual fur-trapper rendezvous. One such gathering occurred in Cache Valley; two were held on the shore of nearby Bear Lake.

While you enjoy the view of Cache Valley below and of the mountains that enclose it, eat! Replenish those depleted glycogen stores in your muscles to prepare for the return climb from Providence Lake. Then enjoy the 9.5-mile cruise back to the trailhead.

RIDE 8 *LOGAN RIVER TRAIL*

Every city should have an easily accessible recreation path like the Logan River Trail. Whether a greenbelt corridor or riverside route, such trails increase the quality of life by providing a quick, temporary escape from the confines of urbanism. On the Logan River Trail, you are comforted by the river's rushing sounds, by breezes wafting through thick riparian growth, and by an array of

RIDE 8 LOGAN RIVER TRAIL

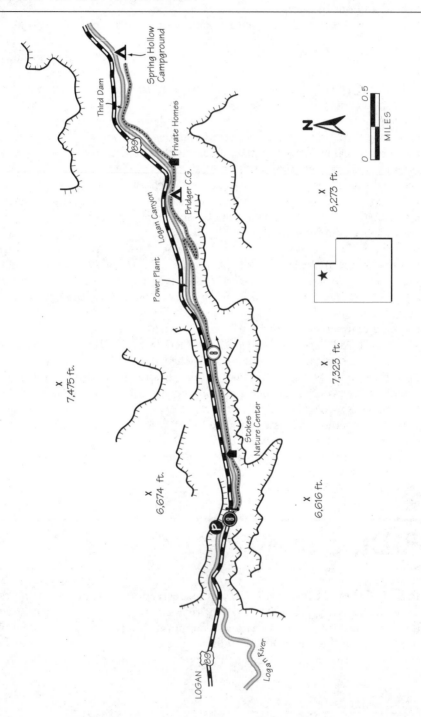

Spring Hollow Campground

Third Dam

Private Homes

Bridger C.G.

Logan Canyon

Power Plant

N

0.5

0 MILES

x 8,273 ft.

x 7,323 ft.

Stokes Nature Center

x 7,475 ft.

x 6,674 ft.

x 6,616 ft.

LOGAN

Logan River

89

89

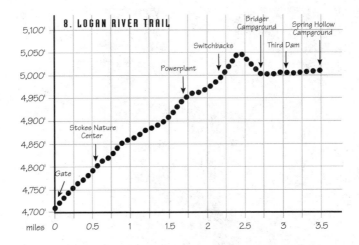

8. LOGAN RIVER TRAIL

animals, waterfowl, and fish that rely upon the river for habitat and sustenance. Logan River Trail can be a quick lunchtime spin, a tension breaker after work, or a family retreat on the weekend.

General location: 2 miles east of Logan near the mouth of Logan Canyon.

Distance: 7.5 miles out-and-back.

Tread: Gravel and native surface multi-recreational path and hand-built singletrack.

Aerobic level: Easy. Much of the trail follows the bank of Logan River. One section, midroute, rises above the river and then again. Although it's a short diversion, it will challenge novice riders and children.

Technical difficulty: Level 1 to 3. The trail along the river's side is a piece of cake. A short uphill singletrack section midroute is a bit more challenging but nothing daunting.

Elevation change: The lower trailhead is at 4,720 feet. The upper trailhead (Spring Hollow Campground) is at 5,020 feet. Adding in a short climb midroute, total elevation gain is merely 400 feet.

Season: March through November. Keep in mind that the trail is on the shady side of the canyon if you're trying to sneak out early or late in the season.

Services: A water tap and outhouse are at Spring Hollow Campground. Logan offers all visitor services.

Hazards: The Logan River Trail is not a racecourse, so leave your heart rate monitor at home. Ride at a prudent, courteous pace and yield to other trail users. Families with children often use the trail. The trail may be busy around the Stokes Nature Center.

Rescue index: The route is very popular with bikers, joggers, pedestrians, and anglers. Campers frequent Red Banks and Spring Hollow Campgrounds. Logan has a hospital.

Land status: Wasatch-Cache National Forest (Logan Ranger District).

A weeping willow alongside the Logan River Trail offers comforting shade.

Maps: USGS Logan, Logan Peak, and Mt. Elmer Utah.

Access: From the center of Logan, travel 2 miles east on 400 North/U.S. Highway 89 to Logan Canyon. The trailhead is 0.7 mile up canyon from where the highway crosses Logan River. Look for a steel gate on the right. Parking at the trailhead is limited to a few vehicles, so park at the pullout on the left/north side of the highway, *before* the trailhead, near the Cache National Forest sign just past milepost 375.

Notes on the trail: From the steel gate, the route follows a dirt and gravel road that is used for maintenance access. It then narrows to a wide single path. The riverside foliage that drapes the trail muffles the steady drone of motor vehicles traveling the highway just a stone's throw away. After about one-half mile, you pass the Stokes Nature Center, which is open by reservation. You then pass the Red Bridge Trailhead and information board. Chalk dust on large boulders tucked in the trees is a telltale sign that technical rock climbers favor the calcareous quartzite cliffs of Logan Canyon. Two miles into your ride, the path narrows to singletrack. It rises steeply above the river to a level where you can view the craggy canyon over the tops of riverside trees. This section is a good test for first-time bikers and children, and it may slow the progress of those with tag-along child trailers. Descend a fun little stretch back to riverside and pass the Gus Lind summer homes area. Pass Third Dam, where anglers and waterfowl congregate, and then arrive at Spring Hollow Campground near site #3.

The trail continues upstream as the Logan Riverside Nature Trail, but bikes are prohibited on the footpath. Make an about face and retrace your tracks to the trailhead while admiring the river from a new and varied perspective.

The river, canyon, and nearby city all share the same name: Logan. But who, or what, was Logan? According to John W. Van Cott in *Utah Place Names*, Logan may have come from one of several sources. One claim is that Logan was the name of an Indian chief who befriended the fur trappers. An entry in the Utah State Historical Society Archives states that a pioneer farmer had an old work ox named Logan, and the town was thus named. The most credible and generally accepted account is that the area was named after Ephraim Logan, a mountain man who trapped with General William H. Ashley and Jedediah Smith. Logan was killed by Indians in 1920 and was buried in the mountains near Logan Canyon.

RIDE 9 *HERD HOLLOW–RICHARDS HOLLOW*

Richards Hollow Trail is the grand-finale descent of the cross-country trek on the Great Western Trail from Logan Canyon to Hyrum. If you tackle that epic tour, be forewarned. The 30 miles of trails and dirt roads preceding Richards is a serious endeavor, one that crosses five topographic quadrangles, demands legs of steel, and requires a monster car shuttle. Here's a long-sought-after, loop alternative. You'll savor the same singletrack descent but with half the distance and one-third less climbing. If you're a singletrack aficionado, you'll find a bit of everything in Richards Hollow: serpentining trail through luscious meadows, multiple water crossings that are a tad too wide to bunny hop, and gnarly technical sections that require adept skills. Richards Hollow will put a grin on your face the shape of a Chiquita banana even during the few times it tries to beat you to a pulp.

General location: 13 miles southeast of Logan in Left Hand Fork Blacksmith Fork Canyon east of Hyrum.

Distance: 15-mile loop.

RIDE 9 HERD HOLLOW-RICHARDS HOLLOW

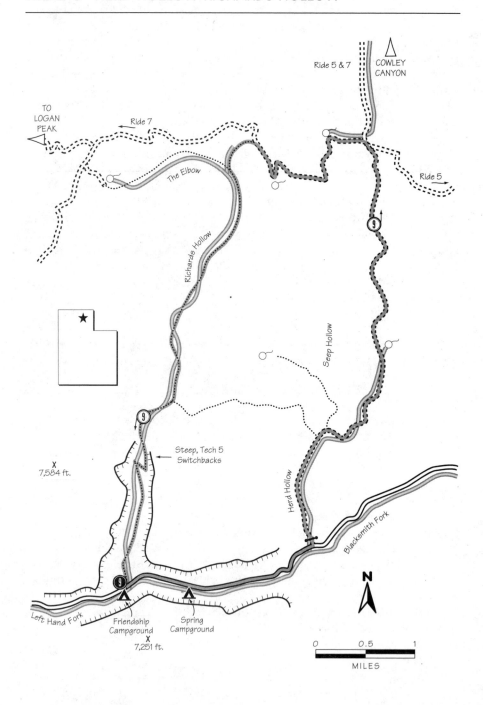

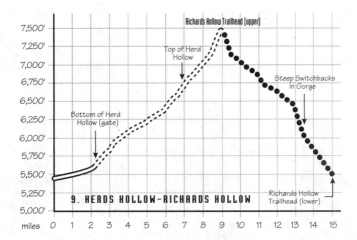

Tread: About 2 miles of light-duty dirt road commence the tour followed by 7 miles of variably rutted doubletrack. The remaining miles follow an infrequently maintained singletrack down Richards Hollow.

Aerobic level: Moderate. The climb up Herd Hollow is steady but not too demanding. The continued ascent to the loop's summit (upper Richards Hollow Trailhead) is moderately difficult and requires sustained effort. Richards Hollow is all downhill, but the increasing technical difficulty usurps energy reserves.

Technical difficulty: Level 2 to 5. The ride up Herd Hollow and then to the route's summit is mostly on hard-packed dirt with token rocks and ruts: level 2. Upper Richards Hollow is a dreamy, twisty pack-trail-cum-singletrack: level 2 to 3. But portions of lower Richards Hollow is marred with steep angular switchbacks, loose rocky tread, outcrop in the tread, and mucky areas, all of which may force prudent dismounts: level 3 to 5. You'll cross the narrow creek in upper Richards Hollow a dozen times. Most are quick splashes that barely wet your toes; others may be gooey bogs depending on horse and livestock traffic.

Elevation change: The trailhead is the low elevation at 5,440 feet. Herd Hollow rises 1,200 feet. The route's summit (7,480 feet) is reached after another 800-foot climb for a total gain of 2,000 feet.

Season: May through October. Cattle are ranged in Richard Hollow seasonally. This is prime big-game hunting ground.

Services: Friendship Campground and Spring Campground in Left Hand Fork Blacksmith Fork Canyon are Forest Service fee areas but do not have water taps. Hyrum offers limited services (food, gasoline, and hardware). Logan offers all visitor services, including bike shops.

Hazards: Left Hand Fork Blacksmith Fork Canyon is popular with ORVs. Richards Hollow Trail, especially the lower half, is frequented by hikers, equestrians, and motorcyclists. Cattle are ranged seasonally in Richards Hollow.

Rescue index: Recreationists and campers are common in Left Hand Fork

Dave and Catherine take wildflower "face shots" descending Richards Hollow.

Blacksmith Fork Canyon, especially on weekends and holidays. Motorists often travel Cowley Canyon, which descends north from the top of Herd Hollow. The prospect of human contact in Richards Hollow increases from doubtful to probable as you descend back to the trailhead.

Land status: Wasatch-Cache National Forest (Logan Ranger District).

Maps: USGS Boulder Mountain and Logan Peak, Utah.

Access: From Logan, travel south on U.S. Highway 89/91 and fork left on Utah State Highway 165 for Providence and Hyrum. Turn left/east in Hyrum on UT 101 for Hardware Ranch and Blacksmith Fork Canyon. Drive 7 miles up Blacksmith Fork Canyon and turn left near milepost 13 for Left Hand Fork Blacksmith Fork Canyon and take the light-duty dirt road 3.7 miles to the Richards Hollow Trailhead opposite Friendship Campground. (The dirt road is sprinkled with small, embedded stones, but it's suitable for passenger cars).

Notes on the trail: Head up Left Hand Fork Blacksmith Fork Canyon and pass Spring Campground after 0.5 mile. Continue up the canyon beneath ragged, terraced cliffs of sullen, charcoal-gray limestone. Fork left 2.2 miles from the trailhead on the unsigned Herd Hollow Road (brown steel gate). One mile up, the road bends right and passes the Seep Hollow trail forking left (a rough, tough shortcut over to Richards Hollow). There's not much to see in Herd Hollow, and the hour-long climb is uneventful, so liven up the ride with a resounding chorus from the *Brady Bunch* or the like. When you reach the top of Herd Hollow (signed four-way junction), fork left for Logan Peak. (The road straight ahead descends Cowley Canyon to Right Fork Logan Canyon; the right fork follows Ride 5 to Old Ephraim's Grave.)

You have to climb 2 miles more to reach the loop's summit. Again scenic vistas are wanting, but the dense roadside aspens underlain with wildflowers are pleasing sights. Where the road tops out, go just past a four-way junction of doubletracks and fork left on the Richards Hollow/Great Western Trail (signed). It begins as an ATV trail then narrows to singletrack as it drops steeply through a patch of conifers. Let the fun begin.

Race down the length of Richards Hollow on the twisted thread of dirt, counting the water crossings as you go. You can blast through most at full speed with little fear of endo-ing. If you ride at a slower pace and let your eyes wander, you'll be captivated by tranquil forests lining the flower- and grass-filled valley.

After the seventh crossing, your rampage will slow as the hollow narrows and the trail becomes progressively more technical. Now you'll have to be quick with your gears, work your brakes, and choose more carefully where to place your front tire. Occasionally, the trail gets mucky or has sloughed along the creek's bank, so expect to dismount periodically. As the limestone cliffs close in, they refrigerate the canyon, and moss grows fat on the trees and rocks. Here, too, the path dives down a nasty set of turns where dismounting is wise. Beyond, the gravelly trail descends directly through oak and maple that tolerate the warmer climate as the canyon opens up. Go through a gate and exit Richards Hollow on the Left Hand Fork Road.

Ogden/Bountiful

RIDE 10 *ANTELOPE ISLAND STATE PARK*

Mountain biking in Utah conjures up images of redrock canyons in the south and of alpine mountains in the north. But would you ever imagine riding on island trails surrounded by aquamarine water? In the Caribbean perhaps, but in Utah? Biking at Antelope Island State Park is a unique experience that will leave an indelible impression that is very different from the rest of the state.

Antelope Island is the largest of the Great Salt Lake's eight islands. Explorers Kit Carson and John C. Fremont named the island in 1845 for the abundant antelope they hunted, and Brigham Young ranged herds of livestock on Antelope Island shortly after the Latter Day Saints arrived in the Salt Lake valley. Although the island's namesake pronghorns disappeared by the 1930s, a population was reintroduced in 1993 and thrives today. The island provides habitat for a variety of land animals, including bighorn sheep, coyotes, bobcats, badgers, jackrabbits, and rodents. But the island is most famous for its bison herd, one of the largest publicly owned herds in the nation. Antelope Island is also a sanctuary for migrating and nesting birds, which are drawn to the lake to gorge on the abundant insects and brine shrimp.

Nearly 30 miles of developed dirt roads and trails take bicyclists, hikers, and equestrians from the lake's white sand beaches to the elevated terraces that are remnant shorelines of ancient Lake Bonneville—the Great Salt Lake's ice-age predecessor. The encompassing views of inland sea, rocky island, and distant

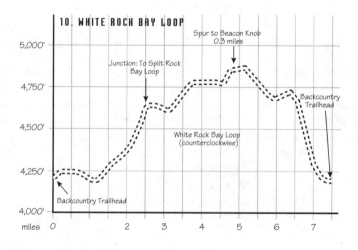

Brad and Aspen look over Split Rock Bay from the Elephant Head Trail.

mountains combined with scents of sea breezes are surreal, and sunsets on Antelope Island are always superlative.

General location: 30 miles northwest of Bountiful.

Distance: Up to 30 miles.

Tread: White Rock Bay Loop and half of Split Rock Bay Loop are double-track; other trails are singletrack.

Aerobic level: Lakeside Trail is easy; White Rock Bay Loop is moderate because of one long, gradual climb; Elephant Head Trail is moderate but

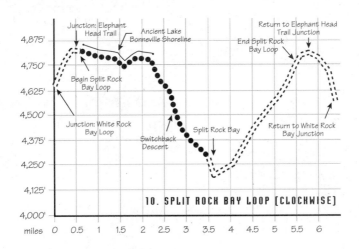

RIDE 10 ANTELOPE ISLAND STATE PARK

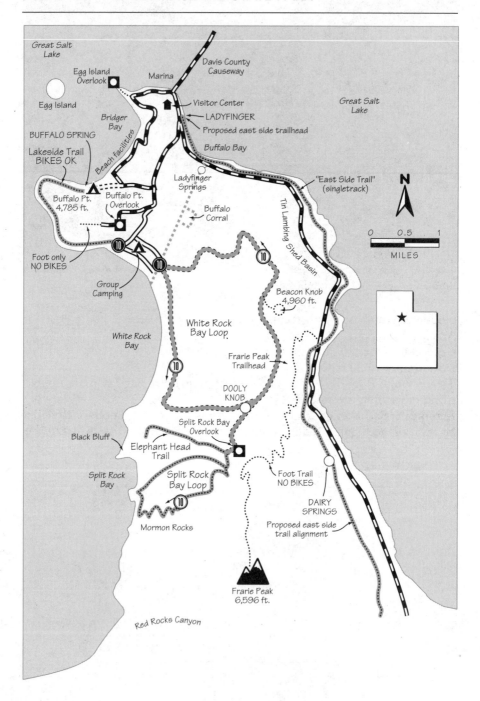

Great Salt Lake

Egg Island Overlook

Marina

Davis County Causeway

Egg Island

Bridger Bay

Visitor Center

LADYFINGER

Proposed east side trailhead

Great Salt Lake

BUFFALO SPRING

Lakeside Trail BIKES OK

Beach facilities

Buffalo Bay

Ladyfinger Springs

Buffalo Corral

"East Side Trail" (singletrack)

N

Buffalo Pt. 4,785 ft.

Buffalo Pt. Overlook

Foot only NO BIKES

Group Camping

0   0.5   1

MILES

Tin Lambing Shed Basin

Beacon Knob 4,960 ft.

White Rock Bay

White Rock Bay Loop

Frarie Peak Trailhead

DOOLY KNOB

Split Rock Bay Overlook

Black Bluff

Elephant Head Trail

Foot Trail NO BIKES

DAIRY SPRINGS

Split Rock Bay

Split Rock Bay Loop

Mormon Rocks

Proposed east side trail alignment

Frarie Peak 6,596 ft.

Red Rocks Canyon

requires a solid climb to reach it; Split Rock Bay Loop is moderate to strenuous; East Side Trail is easy to moderate.

Technical difficulty: Level 2 to 3. Doubletracks and trails are mostly packed and loose sand with some gravel. There are intermittent sections of imbedded boulders and rutted tread.

Elevation change: The backcountry trailhead and Split Rock Bay are the low points at 4,200 feet. The Split Rock Bay Overlook rises to 4,860 feet; Beacon Knob on the White Rock Bay Loop is the high point at 4,960 feet. Gain for the White Rock Bay Loop is about 750 feet. Gain for the Split Rock Bay Loop is about 650 feet. Gain for the Lake Side Trail is trivial. The East Side Trail undulates between 4,200 feet and 4,500 feet.

Season: February through April and September through November are ideal times to visit Antelope Island. You may be able to sneak out during winter when sunny, dry conditions prevail. Summer months can be deathly hot, and insects can eat you alive.

Services: There is no drinking water along the trails. Water is available at the visitor center and at the Bridger Bay beach facilities. The nearby group camping area has an outhouse. The state park has camping and picnic areas, shower facilities, and a visitor center. A concessionaire at Buffalo Point sells snacks and genuine buffalo burgers (not Antelope Island brand, thankfully).

Hazards: Do not approach bison or other wild animals because they are unpredictable and potentially dangerous. Bison can weigh 2,000 pounds and sprint up to 30 mph. It would behoove you to call in advance and inquire about insect populations. After the spring hatch (usually mid to late April), even the most powerful insect repellent is ineffective.

Rescue index: The trails are popular on weekends and holidays, but they are not regularly patrolled. Emergency contact can be made at the visitor center on the north end of the island.

Land status: Utah State Parks.

Maps: USGS Antelope Island North, Antelope Island South, and Buffalo Point, Utah.

Access: From Interstate 15, take Exit 335 for Syracuse and Antelope Island State Park. Travel 7 miles west on Utah State Highway 108 to the park's entrance station and then cross the 7-mile long Davis County Causeway. Upon reaching Antelope Island, turn left on the scenic loop road. The East Side Trail trailhead is at the junction with the East Side Road on the left; otherwise, continue south on the scenic drive. Turn left at the Buffalo Point junction, then right on a gravel road and follow the signs to the backcountry trailhead, located just east of the group camping area. The Lakeside Trail trailhead is at the group camping area.

Sources of additional information: Antelope Island State Park (See Appendix B).

Notes on the trail: Lakeside Trail (4 miles out-and-back, or 6-mile loop): Beginners or families with children will enjoy this easy ride along the shore of the Great Salt Lake. Midroute, you will pass wooden benches from which you can watch the sunset or have a snack. The trail begins at the group camping area on White Rock Bay and travels 3 miles to the Bridger Bay campground. About 2 miles along the trail, you encounter a short boulder-ridden stretch where you must dismount and walk several hundred yards, so turn around here and return to the trailhead. Alternatively, you can ride this as a 6-mile loop by first pedaling up the gravel access road to the Buffalo Point Junction. Follow the paved road north, then fork left for Bridger Bay. Pedal through Bridger Bay campground to pick up the Lakeside Trail. Wrap around Buffalo Point, walking the boulder-ridden stretch, and then coast to the White Rock Bay Trailhead.

White Rock Bay Loop (8-mile loop): Start out from the backcountry trailhead and cross the grassy flats receding from the White Rock Bay shoreline. The doubletrack can be sandy at times and be peppered with rocks. As the trail veers away from the lake's edge, it rises at a deceptively steep grade to a junction. Fork left, plow through short sand traps, and climb to the broad ridge. There's one steep, rough hill before you arrive at Beacon Knob where views are always spectacular. The Wasatch Range reflects off Farmington Bay to the east and the Great Salt Lake catches the setting sun to the west. Round a few sweeping turns and pass two gated roads to the right. Hold on tight for a fast, thrilling descent alongside a wire fence; then cruise back to the trailhead.

Elephant Head Trail (2.6 miles out-and-back): Take the White Rock Bay Trail 2.6 miles to the junction and fork right for the Split Rock Bay Overlook. Climb the steep hill to the overlook and to the junction for Elephant Head Trail. Take the singletrack west for 1.3 miles along the ancient shoreline to its end at a glorious viewpoint high above Split Rock Bay. Most of the trail is easy pedaling because it follows the old wave-cut bench, but sections reach technical levels 3 to 4 because of loose tread, rocks, and short, steep hills. The "Elephant Head" is not discernible from this elevated angle. If you descend to Split Rock Bay and look back at the rocky point, you'll find that the profile of the low, rocky point resembles that of a pachyderm sipping from the lake with its supine trunk.

Split Rock Bay Loop (5-mile loop): This ride follows both doubletrack and hand-built singletrack between Split Rock Bay and the Lake Bonneville bench. The singletrack traces the old shoreline through rugged terrain where rocks dating back 2.7 billion years are exposed as skeletal knobs and cliffs. Part of the Farmington complex, these striped and banded metamorphic rocks record the intense heat and pressure of their formation far beneath the earth's surface. Thereafter, the trail drops through a handful of switchbacks to arcuate beaches before rising back to the loop's trailhead.

The loop begins a few hundred yards beyond the Split Rock Bay Overlook. You can ride in either direction with little change in difficulty. If you ride clockwise, you begin on singletrack along the bench and descend the switchbacks to Split Rock Bay. You'll want to keep your eyes on the trail but should stop often to admire the views. The mile-long return climb follows a sandy doubletrack and can be exasperating. If riding the loop counterclockwise, you'll blaze down the doubletrack to Split Rock Bay first. (Be alert to eroded conditions.) Then you must chug up the switchbacks. The climb can be tedious, but the slow pace will allow you to survey the bizarre scenery without having to track your front wheel.

East Side Trail (24-miles out-and back): The latest addition to Antelope Island is very different from the rest because it follows the island's east shore along the edge of Buffalo and Farmington Bays. The Wasatch Range, which towers above the metropolitan valley across the lake, is your constant companion and reflects off the lake's surface. The route roughly parallels the paved East Side Road, crossing it twice, and ends at the historic Fielding Garr Ranch south of Seagull Point. Built in 1948, the sun-dried adobe ranch was inhabited until 1981 when Antelope Island became a state park. This is a good route to view wildlife on shore, including bison, pronghorn antelope, and bighorn sheep and an array of waterfowl flocking to the lake's mudflat shore.

Backcountry policies:

Trail use is by permit only (free) and is available at the trailhead (self-service).
All users must remain on designated trails.
All users must be out of the backcountry by 8:00 P.M.
Trails are open to non-motorized use only.
Campfires are not allowed on backcountry trails.
Do not disturb plants, wildlife, soil, or minerals.
Hikers and equestrians have the right-of-way.
Pets must be on a leash at all times in the park.
Pack out all trash.
Backcountry trails are closed the last week of October for the annual bison roundup.

Park hours and fees:

The park is open daily from 7 A.M. to 10 P.M. Memorial Day to Labor Day; 7 A.M. to 6 P.M. during winter; and 7 A.M. to shortly after sunset during spring and fall. The visitor center is open 10 A.M. to 5 P.M. year-round. Park entrance fees for 1998 were $7 for motorists and $3 for bikers and in-line skaters who do not drive across the causeway. Camping is $9.

Additional policies apply to the main park. Information is available at the entrance gate and visitor center.

RIDE 11 *SKYLINE TRAIL*

There are big rides, and then there is Olympic-caliber Skyline Trail. This fat-tire enduro is actually the combination of three closely related singletracks: Southern Skyline Trail (Pineview Trailhead), Northern Skyline Trail (North Ogden Pass Trailhead), and Ben Lomond Trail (North Fork Park Trailhead). Each leg defines alpine mountain biking, where long, demanding climbs lead to airy ridges, where mountainsides are blanketed with vibrant wildflowers, and where singletracks are nothing less than riveting.

But wait, there's more. The top-of-the-world views you gain from Lewis and Ben Lomond Peaks are superlative. Where else can your ride through the backcountry for hours and then find yourself hanging over a sprawling metropolis nearly a mile below. Beyond the Ogden/Wasatch Front metro-scene spreads the glistening waters of the Great Salt Lake. In the other direction, reflective Pineview Reservoir fills the fertile North Fork Ogden Valley. And Lewis and Ben Lomond Peaks are two of dozens of Wasatch summits that stuff the cerulean sky like white caps on a rough sea.

The Skyline Olympiad is reserved for off-road experts, endurance junkies, and "mountain-bike-or-die" hammerheads. If 30 miles sounds wimpy, forego the suggested vehicle shuttle and close the loop with an additional 10 miles of pavement. But don't let the route's daunting rating make you start flipping through the pages for a more tame route. Strong intermediate bikers will enjoy out-and-back segments from each of the three trailheads. In doing so, you'll enjoy the same majestic views and outrageous trail conditions but will return to the trailhead satiated, not bonked.

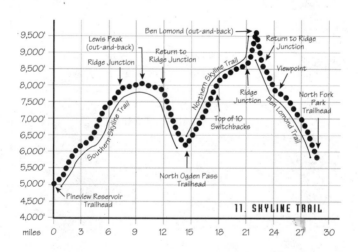

RIDE 11 SKYLINE TRAIL

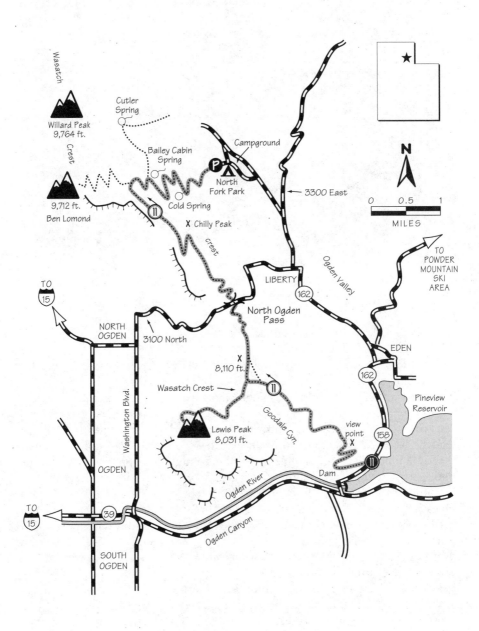

A view of Ben Lomond from near Lewis Peak.

General location: Skyline Trail (Pineview Trailhead) is located 6 miles east of Ogden.

Distance: 28.5 miles point-to-point.

Tread: Singletrack throughout.

Aerobic level: Strenuous is a novel term. Skyline is really a g.a.s.: "gonzo-abusive and sick"

Technical difficulty: Level 2 to 5. The climb from Pineview to Lewis Peak is level 3: some loose tread and rocks. The descent to North Ogden Pass is level 4 to 5: hairpin turns, rocks, ruts, and steep grades. The climb from North Ogden Pass increases rapidly from level 2 to 4: rocks and tight turns, often at the same time. The ridge ramble to Ben Lomond varies from level 2 to 3. The optional ascent to Ben Lomond is level 4 to 5: wicked. And the descent on Ben Lomond Trail is between level 3 to 4: sweet to savage.

Elevation change: Elevation gain comes as three sizeable climbs: the inaugural 3,100-foot ascent over 9 miles from the Pineview Trailhead (elevation 4,900 feet) to Lewis Peak (elevation 8,031 feet); the intermediate 2,500-foot grind over 6 miles from North Ogden Pass (elevation 6,184 feet) to the *base* of Ben Lomond (elevation 8,700 feet); and, legs willing, the optional 1,000-feet ascent to the summit of 9,712-foot Ben Lomond. Total elevation gain is around 6,600 feet. But there is an equal amount of downhill.

Season: Snow may linger on sections of the trail throughout May and perhaps into June, especially on the descent to North Ogden Pass and on the descent to the North Fork Park Trailhead. (Call the Ogden Ranger District for trail conditions.) The sunny, exposed climbs from the Pineview and North Ogden Pass Trailheads may open as early as April and will be scorching by midsummer.

Services: The Pineview Trailhead has an outhouse and water tap. North Ogden Pass Trailhead has an outhouse but no water tap. North Fork Park Trailhead has campsites (fee area), water taps, and outhouses. All visitor services are found in Ogden, North Ogden, and around Pineview Reservoir. Only Ogden has bike shops.

Hazards: This mega-ride will usurp all the energy you can deliver, and then some. Pack along plenty of high-energy food, plenty of water, and extra clothing. Or travel light and leave a cache of food and water midroute at North Ogden Pass. Afternoon storms are common, and there is little or no shelter on the ridges; a rain jacket is always advised. Skyline is a multi-use trail, so expect to encounter other trail users, including equestrians and motorcyclists.

Rescue index: Human contacts along the trail are common, especially on weekends and holidays, but on-trail rescue may be difficult. Medical facilities are located in Ogden.

Land status: Wasatch-Cache National Forest (Ogden Ranger District).

Maps: USGS Huntsville and North Ogden, Utah.

Access: Pineview Trailhead: From Interstate 15, take Exit 347 for 12th South Street, Ogden Canyon, and Recreation Areas. Travel east on Utah State Highway 39 through Ogden and then 5 miles up Ogden Canyon. Turn left on Utah State Highway 158 for Eden, Liberty, and Powder Mountain and cross Pineview Reservoir's dam. The trailhead/parking area is 1 mile farther. (The trail begins about 100 yards to the south and across the road.)

North Ogden Pass Trailhead: From I-15, take Exit 352 for North Ogden, Plain City, and Pleasant View. Drive east on Utah State Highway 134 for 1 mile. Turn right on U.S. Highway 89 followed immediately by a left on UT 235 (2550 North). Turn left/north on Washington Boulevard (400 East). At 2600 North, *ignore* signs for North Ogden Pass; this is a confusing zigzag route through residential streets. Instead, continue north 1 mile to 3100 North and turn right for North Ogden Pass. It's a straight shot into the canyon and then 3 miles up to the pass and trailhead/parking area.

North Fork Park Trailhead: (1) From the Pineview Trailhead, travel north on UT 158 and through Eden. At the junction for Powder Mountain, turn left on Old Highway 162 and travel 3 miles to a T intersection in Liberty. Turn left/west on 4100 North then right/north on 3300 East for North Fork and Avon (four-way stop). Fork left twice following signs for North Fork Park. Turn left a third time for "horse stalls and camping areas" and park near the stone monument. (2) From North Ogden Pass, descend east into Liberty on what becomes 4100 North. At a four-way stop, turn left/north on 3300 East for North Fork and Avon. Then proceed as mentioned above.

Notes on the trail: Southern Skyline Trail rises quickly across warm, sunny slopes and high above rough-cut limestone cliffs encasing Ogden Canyon. Take the short spur to Lookout Point and dream of performing the perfect Nestea plunge into Pineview Reservoir below; then get back to the task at hand.

As you cross the head of Goodale Canyon, you have a stunning view of Mount Ogden's stony crown reigning over Snow Basin Ski Area. Ignore a trail forking right for the Great Western Trail and keep chugging westward up to the main ridge and to a T junction 7 miles from the trailhead. Before you continue your trek, you must bag Lewis Peak first: Fork left on the ridge trail and then fork right about 1 mile out. Climb through groves of aspen while spying Ben Lomond to the north. Scramble up to the summit for the real eye-popper.

Return to the main ridge junction and take the trail northward. Pass a trail, forking sharply right for Pineview Reservoir, and then stay left on a trail that makes a dogleg curve away from, then back to the ridge. Here, you can survey the route's next leg—the switchbacking ascent from North Ogden Pass. Heavy sigh! Now, stop sightseeing and hunker down for the precipitous drop to North Ogden Pass.

North Ogden Pass is the decision-making, halfway point. The next 2.5 miles rise 1,000 feet through a dozen switchbacks that become progressively more difficult. Atop the turns, angle across the back (east side) of the ridge and then cross over to its western face. The overwhelming views and slope-hugging trail battle for your attention. Pass Chilly Peak and chug up to the trail junction in the meadow at the base of Ben Lomond. (Geologically inquisitive types will spot micro-faults transecting the predominant Wasatch Fault. Together, the exposed Paleozoic sedimentary wedge has been tilted, sliced, thrusted, and juxtaposed.)

Decision number two. Just looking at the tortuous path rising to Ben Lomond brings heavy sighs of desperation. This is perhaps the toughest 1 mile of trail in the Wasatch, so consider parking your rig and taking to foot. It starts out reasonably, then turns devilish. But you're entitled to endless bragging rights if you get your bike to the top, whether you ride or drag it there. Spend lots of time atop Ben Lomond because the views are among the finest in the range. The Wasatch Range can be seen stretching nearly 100 miles from near the Idaho border to Salt Lake City. Nevada lies beyond the Great Salt Lake, the Uinta Mountains rise to the east, and the Ogden metro snuggles against the base of the range.

The route's grand finale is the rollicking descent on the Ben Lomond Trail. From the base of Ben Lomond, head due east into the conifers, cross a footbridge, and pass Bailey Cabin Spring. Two dozen switchbacks await. Pass the Cutler Spring Trail forking to the left, but take the spur to the overlook shortly thereafter to gaze across the farmlands of North Ogden Valley. Conifers give way to aspens, then to oak brush, as the trail drops from cool alpine to warm valley. Portions of the trail are as smooth as a baby's butt; others are as rough as a crocodile's spiny back. Keep an eye out for deer and moose that are lured to the marshy meadows near Cold Spring. When you reach the trailhead, pop a cold beverage from your well-stocked cooler and salute your achievement, or chow down your last energy bar as you pound the pavement back to the Pineview Trailhead.

RIDE 12 *WHEELER CREEK TRAIL*

Wedged between ledgy limestone cliffs and lightly forested slopes, Wheeler Creek Trail is a spirited jaunt between Ogden Canyon and Snow Basin Ski Area. A gurgling creek accompanies you along the way while the refrains of songbirds drift from riparian hideaways. And on a warm summer day, nearby Pineview Reservoir offers a cool après-ride plunge. The route is also known as Art Nord Drive. A plaque near the top of the canyon memorializes Arthur George Nord, a Forest Service employee from 1892-1957 for his contributions to the conservation of natural resources.

During 1996, the Ogden Ranger District extended the Wheeler Creek Trail up the old and neglected Maples Trail, which connects upper Wheeler Canyon with the Maples Campground near the base of Snow Basin. The resurrected singletrack curves through grass meadows embraced by moist woods that deer and moose are known to inhabit. Mount Ogden, with its stony frontispiece, is a glorious sight. Although the new trail's grade was kept low and footbridges were installed at strategic water crossings, there are a few sections where

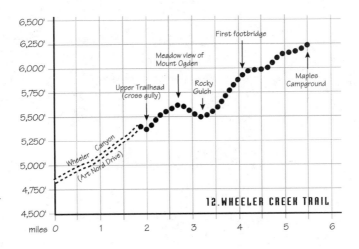

RIDE 12 WHEELER CREEK TRAIL

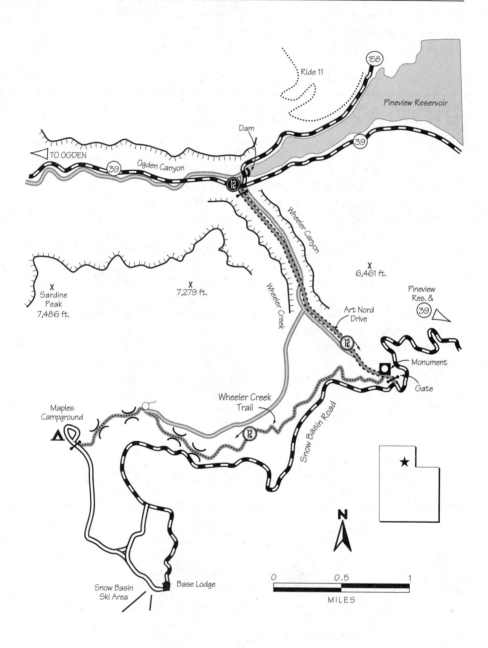

rough conditions prevail. But by and large, Wheeler Creek Trail is perfect for a little pre-season training or to take the edge off a hard day's work.

General location: 5 miles east of Ogden at the head of Ogden Canyon, near the Pineview Reservoir Dam.

Distance: 11 miles out-and-back.

Tread: 2.2 miles of pebbly doubletrack and 3.3 miles of singletrack one way.

Aerobic level: Moderate. Art Nord Drive in Wheeler Canyon is pretty easy, but the Wheeler Creek Trail to Maples Campground requires solid effort.

Technical difficulty: Level 2 to 3. Art Nord Drive in Wheeler Canyon is packed dirt with loose and imbedded stones. Wheeler Creek Trail to the campground can have sections of eroded and rocky tread and a few tight turns.

Elevation change: Art Nord Drive rises 640 feet from the trailhead (4,840 feet) to the Snow Basin Road (5,480 feet). The Wheeler Creek Trail rises another 720 feet to Maples Campground (6,200 feet) for a total gain of 1,060 feet.

Season: Wheeler Canyon may melt out as early as April and remain ridable through November. Midsummer can be very warm.

Services: There are no services at the trailhead. Maples Campground is a Forest Service fee area (outhouse and water tap). There are several cafes and lodges in Ogden Canyon and around Pineview Reservoir. Developed camping is also available on the south shore of Pineview Reservoir. Ogden offers all visitor services, including bike shops.

Hazards: Wheeler Creek Trail is popular with hikers and equestrians, so ride cautiously and courteously.

Rescue index: This route is popular with bikers, hikers, and equestrians, especially on weekends and holidays. Campers are common at Maples Campground. Ogden Canyon is heavily traveled. Telephones can be found at various cafes and lodges around Pineview Reservoir. Ogden has medical facilities.

Land status: Wasatch-Cache National Forest (Ogden Ranger District).

Maps: USGS Huntsville and Snow Basin, Utah.

Access: From Interstate 15, take Exit 347 for 12th Street, Utah State Highway 39, and Ogden Canyon. Travel 5 miles east on UT 39 and up Ogden Canyon, following signs for Recreation Areas. The trailhead is on the right, immediately before the Pineview Reservoir Dam. Park alongside the highway or down the dirt road.

Notes on the trail: Art Nord Drive, now the Wheeler Creek Trail, rises moderately for 2 miles up Wheeler Canyon. The scattered stones in the trail are trivial when climbing but rattle your bones upon descending. As the canyon opens, you pass the rock monument honoring Arthur Nord and come to the Snow Basin Road Trailhead. Fork right, dip through the hollow, and take the singletrack toward Maples Campground.

Struggle up a couple of switchbacks and cross a low divide where you have an unencumbered view of regal Mount Ogden reigning over a court of Wasatch peaks. Upon descending to a gulch, you may have to dismount to negotiate the rough conditions. Farther on, you trade views of rugged summits for interludes with the silent forest. At a Y junction, fork left and cross the creek via a footbridge with steps. (Horses avoid the bridge by taking the right fork.) Rejoin the horse trail, then climb gradually through aspen, oak, and maple to the entrance of Maples Campground. The scent of a smoldering campfire will draw you in. Take a lap around the campground and return to the trailhead by retracing your tracks.

RIDE 13 *BONNEVILLE SHORELINE TRAIL (OGDEN SECTION)*

The Ogden section of the Bonneville Shoreline Trail (BST) offers a variety of riding conditions, scenic attractions, and multiple trailheads for riders of all abilities to enjoy. Families with children can ride a flat, smooth, gravel road to an overlook of Ogden Canyon. Stronger riders can explore sections of the trail that lead to creek-fed canyons creasing the steep foothills beneath Mount Ogden. Gung-ho types can pit their strength and endurance against the whole trail with a 14-mile, out-and-back trip that entails near vertical climbs. Regardless of what part of the BST you target, you'll find stunning views of the Wasatch Range overhead, of the Ogden metropolis below, and of the Great Salt Lake beyond.

General location: Ogden foothills between Ogden Canyon and Beus Canyon.
Distance: 7 miles point-to-point.
Tread: Dirt, sand, and rock singletracks and doubletracks.

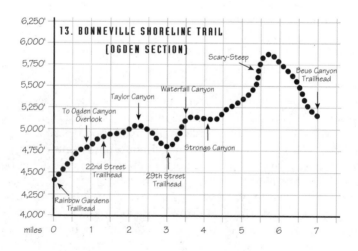

RIDE 13 BONNEVILLE SHORELINE TRAIL (OGDEN SECTION)

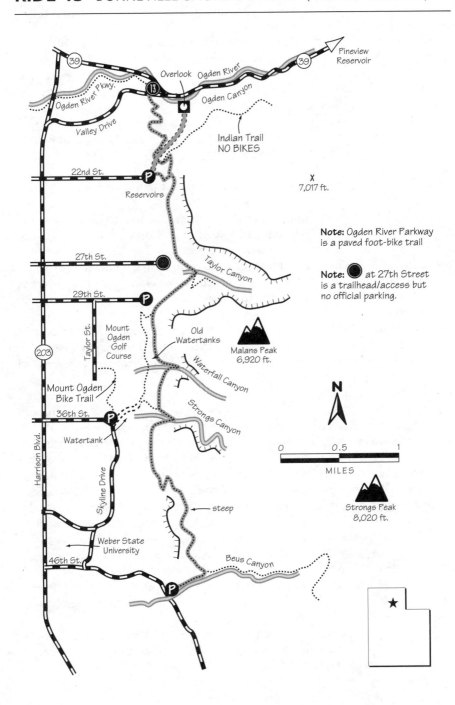

Pineview
Reservoir

39

Overlook   Ogden River

Ogden River Pkwy.

13

Ogden Canyon

39

Valley Drive

Indian Trail
NO BIKES

22nd St.

P

X
7,017 ft.

Reservoirs

Note: Ogden River Parkway
is a paved foot-bike trail

27th St.

Taylor Canyon

Note: ● at 27th Street
is a trailhead/access but
no official parking.

29th St.

P

Taylor St.

Mount
Ogden
Golf
Course

Old
Watertanks

Waterfall Canyon

Malans Peak
6,920 ft.

Mount Ogden
Bike Trail

Strongs Canyon

N

36th St.

P

Harrison Blvd.

Watertank

Skyline Drive

0   0.5   1

MILES

steep

Strongs Peak
8,020 ft.

Weber State
University

46th St.

Beus Canyon

P

★

Aerobic level: Easy to moderate depending on where you start and how much you ride. The entire route, out-and-back, is strenuous because of the abusive climb between Strongs and Beus Canyons. If you eliminate that, the rest is pretty easy. (See "Notes" for options.)

Technical difficulty: Level 2 to 5. Most of the trail is level 2 to 3: sandy and hardpacked dirt punctuated with rocks. The north side of Waterfall Canyon is short, steep, and sandy. The tread between Strongs and Beus Canyons is loose and narrow and the climb is crushing. Beus Canyon is steep, chock-full of boulders, and technical level 5. Ugh!

Elevation change: The Ogden Canyon Trailhead is the low point at 4,400 feet. The trail reaches its highpoint of 5,800 feet between Strongs and Beus Canyons. Between the 22nd Street trailhead and Strongs Canyon, the BST undulates near the 5,100-foot mark.

Season: March through November. Midsummer can be very warm during midday.

Services: There is no drinking water along the trail. Mount Ogden Park and Golf Course near the 29th Street trailhead is your closest water source. You cross several streams, but water should be purified. The Greenery Cafe is at the Rainbow Gardens Trailhead. Ogden offers all visitor services.

Hazards: Rattlesnakes are known to inhabit these warm, dry foothills, but encountering one is rare. Be alert and courteous to other trail users. The trail can be busy.

Rescue index: The BST is popular with hikers, bikers, and equestrians, so on-trail help is usually at hand. You are never more than one-half mile from the city.

Land status: Wasatch-Cache National Forest (Ogden Ranger District) and Ogden City.

Maps: USGS Ogden Utah.

Access: Ogden Canyon Trailhead: From Interstate 15, take Exit 347 for 12th South Street and Recreation Areas. Travel east on Utah State Highway 39/12th South Street to the mouth of Ogden Canyon and turn right on Valley Drive for the Dinosaur Park. Park at the trailhead for the Ogden River Parkway, across the street from Rainbow Gardens. The unsigned trailhead is behind Rainbow Gardens, where the paved lot turns to gravel. Look for a trail heading due south next to a sign stating "slide area, keep out."

Beus Canyon Trailhead: The trailhead/parking area is 1 mile east of Harrison Boulevard on 4600 South Street. (Northbound on I-15, take Exit 326 for South Ogden and travel 13 miles north on U.S. Highway 89, passing I-84 at Weber Canyon. Fork right on UT 203/Harrison Boulevard; 4600 South Street is 2 miles farther. Southbound on I-15, take Exit 343 and take I-84 east for 7 miles to US 89. Take US 89 north for 2 miles, and then fork right on UT 203/Harrison Boulevard.)

Other trailhead/parking areas are at the ends of 22nd Street and 29th Street, and where 36th Street bends and becomes Skyline Drive. All are accessed from Harrison Boulevard/UT 203.

Downtown Ogden is but a stone's throw from the BST.

Sources of additional information: Ogden Trail Network (See Appendix B).
Notes on the trail: The multiple trailheads allow for a variety of options for all ability levels. Novice bikers can start at the 22nd Street trailhead and ride first to the Ogden River Overlook and then to the 29th Street trailhead (about 8 miles round trip). Intermediate bikers can do the same (or start from Ogden Canyon) but keep going to Strongs Canyon, with the option of exploring the peripheral Mount Ogden Bike Trail (10 to 15 miles round trip). Advanced bikers can ride the whole works and test themselves against the protracted climb between Strongs and Beus Canyons (about 14 miles round trip).

Here's the whole ride from Ogden Canyon to Beus Canyon: Climb the twisting trail from Rainbow Gardens across grassy meadows and through oak and maple for 1 mile, passing the peculiar Corkscrew Trail along the way. When you reach the multiple signed junction for the BST (under the power lines), take the gravel road 1 mile (out-and-back) to the Ogden Canyon Overlook.

Back at the power line junction, fork left, struggle up a sandy section, and pass an unsigned four-way junction of trails. (The left fork leads to the Indian Trail where bicycle travel is not allowed; the right fork follows a splinter route of the BST.) Contour along the base of the ledgy foothills on a technical level 2 to 3 trail and wind through Taylor Canyon, passing junctions for 22nd and 27th Street trailheads. About 0.5 mile farther, you come to the signed junction for the 29th Street trailhead. Descend it to take a lap on the Mount Ogden Bike

Path; otherwise, continue straight on the wide, sandy path and climb steeply to Waterfall Canyon. Tiptoe across the creek and continue south on a contour to Strongs Canyon. Upon exiting Strongs Canyon, the BST (singletrack) joins and follows a doubletrack for a few hundred feet then forks left as a gently rising singletrack.

Round two switchbacks and begin the punishing climb over to Beus Canyon. Reward for your effort is a bird's-eye view of the Ogden metropolis, the Great Salt Lake, and the Wasatch Front. Strongs Peak and Mount Ogden bear down with a weighty presence; Ben Lomond is the mammoth chunk of rock to the north. If you descend to the Beus Canyon Trailhead, you'll have to make the nasty climb back over the top again.

When returning to Rainbow Gardens, try this variation. On the north side of Strongs Canyon, fork left on a singletrack that descends along the creek for 0.5 mile. Fork right on the Mount Ogden Bike Trail and roll through a canopy of oak and maple to the Twenty-ninth Street trailhead. Now climb the short path up to the BST and resume your ride northward.

RIDE 14   *MUELLER PARK TRAIL*

The Mueller Park Trail epitomizes the metro-to-mountains convenience of living in the Great Salt Lake Valley at the foot of the Wasatch Range. Within minutes, literally, the nearby suburban jungle is transformed to a tranquil, backcountry ecosystem of lush riparian growth mixed with hardwoods and conifers. The valley's droning clamor is replaced by spirited sounds of nature, and the odor of urbanization succumbs to the wood's deep, earthy bouquet. Through breaks in the forest's cover are good views of the Great Salt Lake and the metropolitan

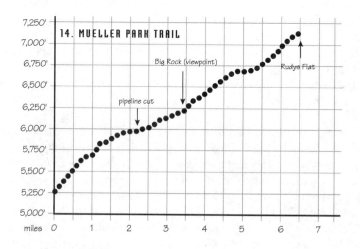

RIDE 14 MUELLER PARK TRAIL

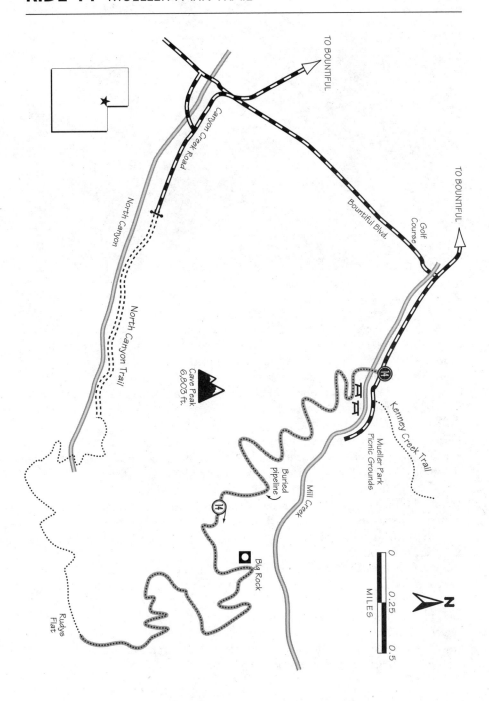

TO BOUNTIFUL

TO BOUNTIFUL

Canyon Creek Road

North Canyon

North Canyon Trail

Bountiful Blvd.

Golf Course

Cave Peak
6,803 ft.

Kenney Creek Trail

Mueller Park
Picnic Grounds

Buried
pipeline

Mill Creek

Big Rock

Rudys
Flat

0   0.25   0.5
MILES

N

Laura enjoys an autumn day on the Mueller Park Trail.

valley. Quick access to the trail, instant submersion in nature, and distant views of the metro you left behind are several reasons why mountain bikers cherish the Mueller Park Trail. Oh, it's one of the best singletracks around, too.

Location: Mueller Park Picnic Ground (trailhead) is located in Mill Creek Canyon in the Bountiful foothills. (Do not confuse this Mill Creek Canyon with the evermore popular canyon of the same name in Salt Lake City.)

Distance: 13 miles out-and-back.

Tread: Dirt and rock singletrack throughout.

Aerobic level: Moderate. Mueller Park Trail is all uphill with many breathers along the way. The first half, to Big Rock, can be knocked off by novice riders. The second half, to Rudy's Flat, is a bit steeper and more technical.

Technical difficulty: Level 2 to 4. The lower trail to Big Rock is level 2 to 3: a few sections of loose tread and rocks. The upper trail from Big Rock to Rudy's Flat is a touch steeper, with longer stretches of rough tread (level 3 to 4) but still plenty of buffed trail, too.

Elevation change: The trailhead is the low point at 5,250 feet. Big Rock, the route's midpoint, is at 6,200 feet. Rudy's Flat is the high point at 7,160 feet for an elevation gain of about 1,910 feet.

Season: Because of its lower elevation, Mueller Park Trail remains snow free longer than most Wasatch routes and may be ridable from late April to November. By the same token, the trail can be very warm during midsummer. Wildflowers reach their peak earlier in the season as well, usually during May.

Services: Picnic tables, water taps, and outhouses are available at Mueller Park Picnic Ground (trailhead). Overnight camping is prohibited. All visitor services are available in Bountiful.

Hazards: Mueller Park Trail is popular with hikers, mountain bikers, equestrians, *and* motorcyclists, so you must be willing to share the trail. Abide by IMBA's "Rules of the Trail" at all times. Always be able to stop—safely and without skidding—within the distance you can see down the trail.

Rescue index: You're rarely alone on the trail, especially on weekends and holidays. Residential areas border the picnic grounds, so emergency contacts are always at hand, but on-trail emergency assistance can be difficult.

Land status: Wasatch-Cache National Forest (Salt Lake Ranger District).

Maps: USGS Fort Douglas, Utah.

Access: From Interstate 15, take Exit 318 for 2600 South and North Salt Lake. Travel east on 2600 South, then continue for 2 miles after 2600 South bends north and becomes Orchard Drive. Turn right/east on 1800 South, and travel 2.5 miles to Mueller Park Picnic Ground. The trail begins at the wooden bridge spanning Mill Creek at the entrance.

Notes on the trail: Cross the footbridge over Mill Creek and round the first of countless switchbacks to come on your climb to Rudy's Flat. Just as quickly, the streamside riparian growth gives way to a mixture of oak, maple, and pine. As the trail weaves into each of numerous side canyons, it penetrates micro forests of cool, shade-giving fir. Cross the remnant swath of the Kearns Pipeline after 2 miles, and make a sharp right turn at the Big Rock overlook 3.4 miles from the trailhead. This is a good turnaround point for novice riders. (For the geologically inquisitive, the marble-white knob is a pegmatite plug—once-molten rock mass of quartz and feldspar that was injected into the surrounding country rock. Its occurrence stems from the nearby Precambrian-age Farmington Complex to the north. These convolute metamorphic rocks are part of the Earth's original foundation and date back approximately 1.5 billion years.)

Now, the route steepens slightly and can be moderately technical at times. Gamble oak grows thick alongside the trail, and it's not until 5 miles up that Douglas fir are commonplace. Round a couple of groovy turns, or is that "grooved" turns, and cross a couple of footbridges. Keep chugging through the forest, whistling while you work, until you reach the small clearing known as Rudy's Flat. The all-freewheeling descent is generous compensation for your effort.

You don't *have* to descend the Mueller Park Trail. You can loop back to the trailhead by continuing past Rudy's Flat and descending North Canyon, which ironically is the next canyon *south* of Mill Creek. North Canyon Trail is steeper, rougher, and shorter than Mueller, but a great ride just the same. A couple of miles down, you leave the singletrack and continue descending on a rough, rutted doubletrack alongside North Canyon Creek. Glide down paved Canyon Creek Road and turn right on Bountiful Boulevard to loop back to Mueller Park. Racers in training like to ride the loop in reverse by ascending the North Canyon Trail—a shorter, more intense climb—and descending Mueller Park Trail. How strong do you feel today?

Salt Lake City/Tooele

RIDE 15 *BONNEVILLE SHORELINE TRAIL (SALT LAKE CITY SECTION)*

The Bonneville Shoreline Trail (BST) is a ride through time. The trail itself takes advantage of the near-level "benches" on the Wasatch Range foothills that mark the remnant shoreline of ancient Lake Bonneville. During the close of the Ice Age, about 10,000 to 100,000 years ago, meltwater from receding continental glaciers filled the lowlands of northern and central Utah such that the Wasatch Range and mountains to the west were colossal islands. Today, these mountains stand in proud relief above a valley that is inhabited by over one million residents. The Great Salt Lake is merely the evaporative offspring of Lake Bonneville.

Fast forward many thousands of years to 1847 when Brigham Young and 144 pioneer travelers entered the Salt Lake Valley, seeking a land where they would be free from religious persecution. According to legend, when the company exited the Wasatch Range through Emigration Canyon, very near the BST's trailhead, Young declared, "This is the right place, drive on," and the Mormons established their land of Zion.

The first section of the BST overlooks a state park named for Brigham Young's poignant proclamation. The second leg traverses the foothills to City Creek Canyon on a section made possible by generous grants from the Steiner

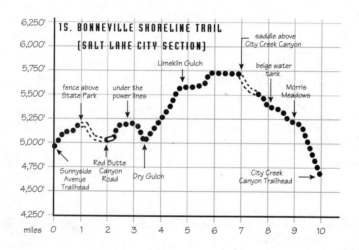

RIDE 15 BONNEVILLE SHORELINE TRAIL (SALT LAKE CITY SECTION)

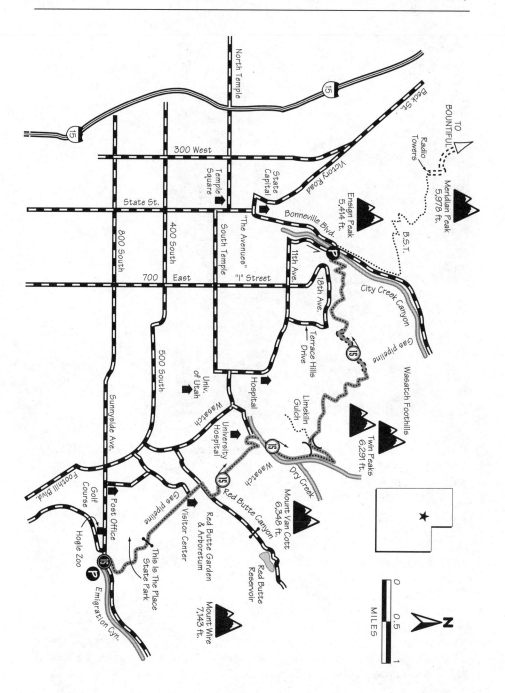

The Bonneville Shoreline Trail offers a quick escape from the confines of urbanism . . . and some stunning views, too.

Foundation and local and state agencies. Additional trail will be constructed to take travelers west and north from City Creek Canyon, past Ensign Peak, and over to Bountiful.

Along the entire route, you'll find staggering views of the Salt Lake Valley, wedged between the Wasatch Range and Oquirrh Mountains. As you ride, think back to an age when water lapped against the mountains, and reflect upon the relief of the weary pioneers as they entered the valley.

General location: Between Emigration Canyon and City Creek Canyon in Salt Lake City's northeastern foothills.

Distance: 10 miles point-to-point.

Tread: Dirt singletrack with short segments of doubletrack.

Aerobic level: Moderate. Although the trail follows the near-level ancient shoreline bench, there are a few short, tough climbs along the way, plus mile-long Dry Gulch. If you ride in reverse, the climb from City Creek Canyon to the Terrace Hills Trailhead is strenuous.

Technical difficulty: Level 2 to 3. Most of the route is packed dirt with few obstacles, but there are a few tricky sections: the gulches behind the University Medical Center, Dry Gulch, and the switchbacks near the City Creek Canyon Trailhead.

Elevation change: The trail reaches 5,800 feet between Dry Gulch and Terrace Hills Drive. The Emigration Canyon Trailhead is at 5,000 feet. The City Creek Canyon Trailhead is at 4,650 feet. Elevation gain is about 1,500 feet.

Season: March through November. Midday during summer can be very warm as temperatures in Salt Lake City can reach 100 degrees F.

Services: There is a water tap at the entrance gate to City Creek Canyon and at the north gate to Red Butte Garden and Arboretum. You are never more than a mile or so from the city's limit.

Hazards: Several sections have gravel and loose rocks that might cause wheels to slide out. Rattlesnakes are known to inhabit these warm foothills, but their occurrence is rare.

Rescue index: The Bonneville Shoreline Trail is very popular because of its inherent concept as an urban perimeter recreational corridor. Residential areas are within 0.5 mile of the trail. You pass very near to the University Medical Center midroute.

Land status: Wasatch National Forest, Salt Lake Ranger District, Salt Lake City Corporation, University of Utah, and private property.

Maps: USGS Fort Douglas and North Salt Lake, Utah.

Access: Emigration Canyon (Sunnyside Avenue) Trailhead: From the intersection of Foothill Drive (1950 East) and Sunnyside Avenue (850 South), take Sunnyside 1 mile east to the mouth of Emigration Canyon. The trailhead/parking area is at the east gate of This is the Place State Park opposite Crestview Drive and Hogle Zoo.

City Creek Canyon Trailhead: From the Emigration Canyon Trailhead, return to the intersection of Foothill Drive and Sunnyside Avenue. Turn right on Foothill Drive and travel north, then west to 1300 East and turn right. Travel four blocks north, turn right on South Temple, and then left on Virginia Street (1345 East) one block farther. Take Virginia uphill, turn left on 11th Avenue, travel west to the T intersection with B Street, and turn right on Bonneville Boulevard (a one-way street). (From any other location, just make your way through the Avenues to 11th Avenue.) The trailhead (limited parking) is at the junction of Bonneville Boulevard and the City Creek Canyon Road. Additional parking is just up the City Creek Canyon Road.

Sources of additional information: Bonneville Shoreline Trail Committee (See Appendix B).

Notes on the trail: You can ride this section of the BST in either direction with little change in difficulty. Many cyclists ride the route as a 20-mile out-and-back trip or start from one of several trailheads midroute. You can make this a loop ride by following residential and city streets. (See "Access.") Many streets have designated bike lanes.

Here's the ride from Emigration Canyon to City Creek Canyon. Squeeze through the gap in the fence and rev up the RPMs because the first little hill is a doozy. As the climb levels, stay left and follow trail signs next to a log fence. When you intersect a doubletrack at the boundary of Old Deseret Village, follow the track uphill to a T junction with a gravel road; fork left. Pass a trail forking right, descend a few hundred feet, fork right on the BST (singletrack) and roll across the grassy, oak-spattered foothills until you reach the fence and an overlook of This is the Place State Park. Coast down the left doubletrack past the entrance to Red Butte Garden and Arboretum, then to paved Red Butte Canyon Road. Take the road to the right along the fence about 100 yards, and fork left on a paved road posted "dead end." Fork right immediately on a doubletrack posted "closed to motor vehicles." Take the track, and then singletrack up to the bench under the power lines. Head north, crossing several gulches. After descending a steep, gravel path, fork right and take the wide gravel road to Dry Gulch. Now it's time to climb.

Lower Dry Gulch rarely lives up to its name, especially during spring when the creek can flood parts of the trail. The upper half, however, is aptly named. You cross the drainage a dozen times then climb steeply to a divide overlooking Limekiln Gulch below and all of Salt Lake City beyond.

Contour across the foothills on a section of hand-built trail for 1 mile to a T junction with an faint doubletrack. Climb the steep track for a few hundred yards, then resume your westward trek on singletrack for 1 mile to a saddle overlooking City Creek Canyon. (A buried gas pipeline crosses here.) Take the doubletrack southward for 0.5 mile, and as you approach the power lines overhead, fork right on a wide trail. If you arrive at Terrace Hills Drive (pavement), you missed the trail junction by about 0.5 mile. Shortly after crossing under the power lines, the route descends steeply toward the city and comes to a four-way junction beside a beige water tank. (Descend left to reach the Terrace Hills Drive trailhead; go straight for a scenic view down the length of the valley.) Fork right, ride the trail around the tank, and then descend to Morris Meadows while ogling City Creek Canyon below. (Morris Reservoir and the 18th Avenue trailhead is 0.5 mile to the left/south.) Go straight across the meadow and descend several steep, sharp turns to the City Creek Canyon Trailhead on Bonneville Boulevard.

Access Policies and Restrictions:

Dogs are not allowed on the first mile of trail from the Emigration Canyon Trailhead to the fence above This is the Place State Park.
Bikes are not allowed on any dirt roads in This is the Place State Park. The park is a fee area.
The main parking area at Red Butte Garden and Arboretum is for garden visitors only. The Arboretum's Nature Trail above the BST is closed to bikes.
Bikes are not allowed in Red Butte Canyon because it is a federal

Research Natural Area (RNA).

Bikes are allowed on the paved City Creek Canyon Road on odd-numbered calendar days, but never on holidays and from Memorial Day to September 31.

RIDE 16 *MILL CREEK PIPELINE TRAIL*

In the early 1990s, the neglected Mill Creek Pipeline Trail was resurrected with the help of the Salt Lake Ranger District, the Utah Mountain Bike Association, and many helping hands. But it wasn't until 1996 when finishing touches made the entire 7-mile trail totally biker friendly. Now, the Pipeline Trail is one of the most popular hiking and biking trails in the Wasatch Range.

The path follows an old water flume that dates back many decades. Consequently, the route descends imperceptibly and is ideal for novice bikers who want a taste of real singletrack without having to scale entire mountains. Since the trail crosses south-facing slopes that grasp every ray of sunshine throughout the day, it melts out in early spring and is ridable long after the peaks are dusted with autumn's snow. To top it off, the Pipeline is especially scenic. When you're not weaving through groves of hardwoods that are nestled in hollows creasing the canyon, you cross sunny slopes that afford grand views of Mill Creek Canyon below and of the mountains that enclose it. If you ride the optional spur to the overlook, you'll gaze across the entire Salt Lake Valley from the State Capitol to Point of the Mountain.

General location: Mill Creek Canyon in the Wasatch Range, 6 miles east of Salt Lake City.

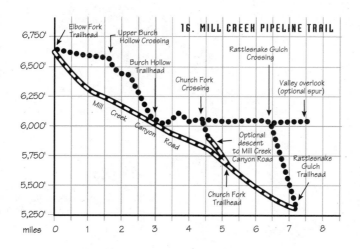

RIDE 16 MILL CREEK PIPELINE TRAIL

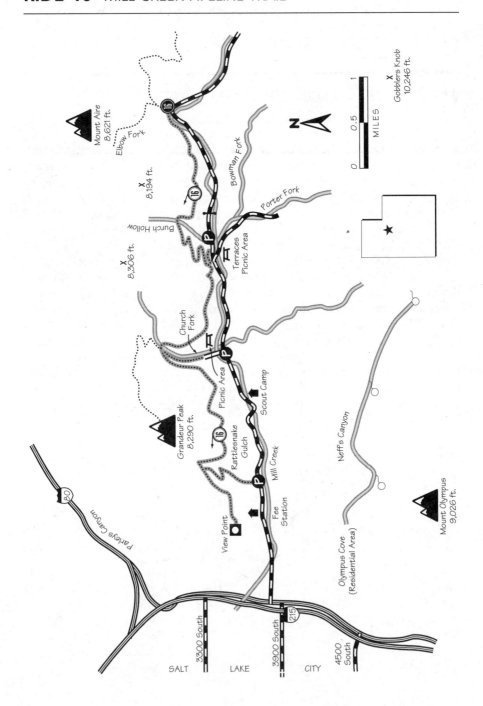

Distance: 7.2 miles point-to-point. Add 2 miles for the out-and-back spur to the overlook. Make this a 12-mile loop by including the paved canyon road.

Tread: Hard-packed singletrack with patches of coarse gravel and talus in the tread.

Aerobic level: Easy. The route is mostly flat with two descents: one fast (Burch Hollow), and one wild (Rattlesnake Gulch).

Technical difficulty: Level 2 to 4. Most of the route is flat and smooth. At times, the tire-wide path winds precariously close to the edge of steep slopes, which may cause concern for acrophobes. Occasionally, coarse gravel eroding from nearby slopes spills onto the trail, and rocks protrude from the tread. The descent to Burch Hollow has hairpin turns. The Rattlesnake Gulch descent is steep and eroded: level 4.

Elevation change: The Elbow Fork Trailhead is at 6,640 feet. The trail contours at 6,600-feet between Elbow Fork and Burch Hollow, and then at 6,000 feet from Burch Hollow to Rattlesnake Gulch. The Rattlesnake Gulch Trailhead is at 5,300 feet for a 1,340-foot elevation loss.

Season: April through November. Midsummer is very warm since the trail crosses south-facing slopes. The upper Mill Creek Canyon Road is closed to motor vehicles at Maple Grove Picnic Area through June (above the Burch Hollow Trailhead). Mill Creek Canyon is busy on weekends and holidays.

Services: There is no drinking water along this route. Church Fork, Terraces, and Maple Grove picnic areas have water taps and outhouses. Overnight camping is prohibited in Mill Creek Canyon. A shopping center and bike shop are near the mouth of Mill Creek Canyon. Salt Lake City offers all visitor services.

Hazards: Occasionally, the trail is narrow, rocky, and winds along the edge of steep slopes. Metal rods, remnant of the old pipeline, poke from the tread periodically and may puncture a tire. The Rattlesnake Gulch descent is steep and technical level 4. Be alert to other trail users and yield the right-of-way.

Rescue index: The trail is popular, especially on weekends and holidays. Mill Creek Canyon is well traveled. Emergency contact can be made at the fee station at the bottom of Mill Creek Canyon, about 0.5 mile down from the Rattlesnake Gulch Trailhead.

Land status: Wasatch-Cache National Forest (Salt Lake Ranger District).

Maps: USGS Mount Aire and Sugarhouse, Utah.

Access: The Mill Creek Canyon Road begins at 3800 South and Wasatch Boulevard in Salt Lake City. (Southbound on Interstate 215, take Exit 3 for 3900 South. Northbound on I-215, take Exit 4 for 3300 South/3900 South.) Take Wasatch Boulevard to 3800 South, and turn right for Mill Creek Canyon. The entrance fee station is 0.5 mile up the canyon. The lower trailhead (Rattlesnake Gulch) is 0.7 mile above the fee station. The upper trailhead (Elbow Fork) is 5 miles farther, just before milepost 6.

Notes on the trail: From the Elbow Fork Trailhead, the trail darts into the brush and crosses a cursed stretch of coarse gravel that has eroded from the

Mount Olympus reigns over the Salt Lake Valley.

crumbling limestone slopes nearby. Thereafter, the trail is a dreamy, hard-packed thread of dirt. Quickly, you find yourself several hundred feet above Mill Creek Canyon as the road below bends out of sight. Gobblers Knob and Mount Raymond are a duo of 10,000-foot peaks rising across the canyon. A hint of the Salt Lake Valley can be seen through the distant V-shaped gap of lower Mill Creek Canyon. These views of peaks above, canyon below, and valley beyond are concealed where the trail penetrates thickets of oak and maple underlain with knee-deep grasses. After rounding a pronounced right-hand curve that affords even better views, the trail begins a 1.5-mile descent to the Burch Hollow Trailhead. This section can be very fast if you don't harness your speed. And if you are not attentive, you might overshoot one of the half-dozen angular turns and find yourself tangled in the trailside brush like a Christmas tree ornament the cat attacked.

Fork left after the descent to reach the Burch Hollow Trailhead 100 yards away; otherwise, continue along the pipeline, weaving through forested hollows and crossing sunny slopes. One mile from Burch Hollow, the trail forks unexpectedly. Slam your gears into granny and power up the right fork; then continue rambling to the Grandeur Peak Trail junction. Fork left to descend to the Church Fork picnic area; otherwise, ride on.

Progressively, the view of Salt Lake City increases as the mouth of Mill Creek Canyon grows wider. When you reach the Rattlesnake Gulch junction, fork left to end the trip on a steep, hair-raising descent; otherwise, stay on the pipeline. This optional 2-mile out-and-back trip receives less traffic than the main trail, and the technical level varies from 3 to 4. If you persevere, you'll behold a sublime view. One thousand feet below, the planar floor of ancient Lake Bonneville is populated with one million plus who are looking your way with undying reverence for the Wasatch Range. Although not the tallest peak in the Wasatch, Mount Olympus, with its stony cockscomb crown, is a mountainous throne of divine proportions guarding Mill Creek Canyon.

RIDE 17 *BIG WATER TRAIL*

Are you new to Salt Lake City, or did you just buy a new rig? If so, then make a beeline for Mill Creek Canyon and ride the Big Water Trail to Dog Lake. Big Water is the locals' favorite twisty, hands down, and chances are it was the first trail ride for most Salt Lakers. What make the Big Water Trail so alluring? It's close to the city and easy to access, it's gentle on first-time singletrack riders, and it's not located in a watershed, so you can take your pet along. But most of all, Big Water Trail is simply *big fun*.

Realize that the Big Water Trail is void of powerful vistas, punishing climbs, and frightening downhills—other Wasatch rides offer plenty of that. Big Water is simply an unintimidating cruise through the forest that ends at a small alpine pond worthy of an afternoon siesta. The intertwined hardwoods and conifers that engulf the trail cast long shadows, and where sunlight filters through, it nourishes a plenitude of wildflowers. Big Water should *not* be a hurried ride, but one on which you can relax and enjoy the nuances of nature. So, whether you're an ambitious beginner or a veteran biker, you'll find Big Water to be a slice of fat-tire heaven.

General location: The Big Water Trail starts at the top of Mill Creek Canyon, 9 miles east of Salt Lake City.

Distance: 6.5 miles out-and-back.

Tread: Dirt singletrack throughout.

Aerobic level: Easy to moderate. Novice riders with a good fitness base should fare well.

RIDE 17 BIG WATER TRAIL

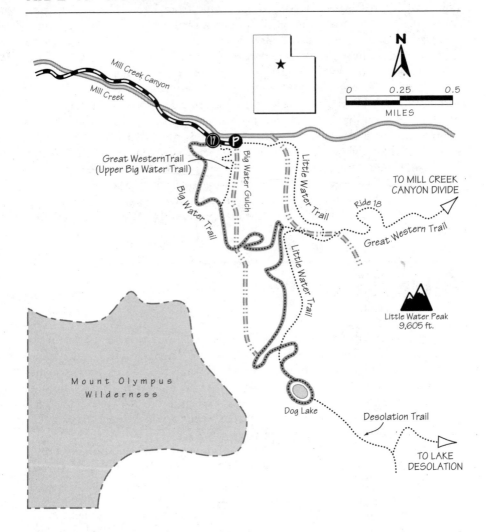

Technical difficulty: Level 2 to 3. Big Water Trail is well maintained. Much of the route is silky-smooth, hard-packed dirt. However, there are numerous switchbacks that require good handling skills to round, and intermittent sections may have loose tread, rocks, and tree roots.

Elevation change: The trailhead is the route's lowest elevation at 7,600 feet. The trail rises 1,200 feet to 8,800 feet at the Desolation Trail junction just above Dog Lake.

Season: Depending upon winter's snow and spring's thaw, the Big Water Trail typically melts out between late May and mid-June and should be ridable

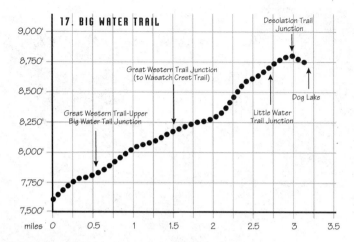

through October. This is a good trail for viewing spring wildflowers and autumn colors. The upper Mill Creek Canyon Road is closed to motor vehicles at Maple Grove Picnic Area through June (milepost 4). Mill Creek Canyon is busy with recreationists and picnickers on weekends and holidays.

Services: An outhouse is at the trailhead but no water tap. Church Fork, Terraces, and Maple Grove picnic areas have water taps and outhouses. Overnight camping is prohibited in Mill Creek Canyon. A shopping center and bike shop are near the mouth of Mill Creek Canyon. Salt Lake City offers all visitor services.

Hazards: The likelihood is high that you will encounter other trail users at any time, including fellow bikers, hikers, and equestrians. Families with children and pets commonly visit the trail. Watch for them since they, especially toddlers, may not be watching for you. Yield the trail, ride in control, and be able to stop safely—without having to skid—at all times. Big Water should be a fun ride, *not* a fast ride. (Rangers do not hesitate to issue citations for excessive speed, recklessness, or biking into the nearby Mount Olympus Wilderness.)

Rescue index: Because of its popularity, you're rarely alone on the Big Water Trail. Forest Service rangers do not patrol the trail on a regular basis. Emergency assistance can be summoned from the fee station at the canyon's entrance.

Land status: Wasatch-Cache National Forest (Salt Lake Ranger District).

Maps: USGS Mount Aire, Utah.

Access: The Mill Creek Canyon Road begins at 3800 South and Wasatch Boulevard in Salt Lake City. (Southbound on Interstate 215, take Exit 3 for 3900 South. Northbound on I-215, take Exit 4 for 3300 South/3900 South.) Take Wasatch Boulevard to 3800 South, and turn right for Mill Creek Canyon. The entrance fee station is 0.5 mile up the canyon. Drive the paved canyon road 9 miles to where it ends. The last 2 miles of road are narrow, so drive cautiously.

Aspen leaves speckle the Big Water Trail.

Notes on the trail: First some fine print. Upper Mill Creek Canyon trails, including the Big Water Trail, are open to mountain bikes on *even*-numbered calendar days only. A fee is collected upon leaving Mill Creek Canyon. For 1998, the fee was $2.25 per vehicle. Pedestrians and bicyclists who do not drive up the Mill Creek Canyon Road do not have to pay the fee upon leaving.

That out of the way, the Big Water Trail begins at the lower of the two parking areas. The first few hundred yards are the steepest, so if you make easy work of that, the rest is a piece of cake.

One half-mile up, the Big Water Trail joins with and follows the Great Western Trail (GWT), which enters from the left. (The GWT begins at the upper parking lot.) Just keep climbing through the rich forest. Cross a footbridge over Big Water Gulch, traverse a sunny slope, and reenter the woods while rounding a couple of tight turns. About 1.5 miles up, the Great Western Trail forks left for upper Mill Creek Canyon and provides access to Ride 18, Wasatch Crest Trail. Stay right on Big Water for Dog Lake and keep chugging up the sun-dappled trail. Stay straight at the four-way junction with the Little Water Trail, round one last turn, and arrive at the Desolation Trail junction and the route's summit. Fork left and descend 100 yards on a gravel path to Dog Lake, where canines have a heyday fetching logs floating in the small alpine pond.

Although the descent may invite unbridled speed, pull back on the reins and resist the urge. Don't jeopardize access privileges for 15 minutes of selfish bliss.

RIDE 18 *WASATCH CREST TRAIL*

The Wasatch Crest Trail is one of northern Utah's premier mountain bike routes. Nearly all singletrack, the Crest Trail traces the spine of the central Wasatch Range, coined by Utah geologist William Lee Stokes as "the Backbone of Utah." Along the initial climb, you venture through sun-kissed forests of aspen, pine, and fir. But when you pedal out the ridge, you are entertained by top-of-the-world views of jagged mountains, glacier-cut canyons, and urban valleys. And when you are not gawking at the topography or prospecting for winter's backcountry ski routes, you'll be riveted to the world-class singletrack trail. Moab's Slickrock Bike Trail might be the state's most popular trail because of its uniqueness, but the Wasatch Crest Trail epitomizes the concept of "mountain" biking.

General location: The Wasatch Crest Trail runs between the tops of Mill Creek and Big Cottonwood Canyons, 9 and 15 miles east of Salt Lake City, respectively.

Distance: 19.5 miles out-and-back.

Tread: Singletrack with a few miles of quasi-doubletrack-turned-singletrack.

Aerobic level: Strenuous. The route rises moderately for the first 4 miles. The following 5 miles are a blend of moderate and steep climbs along the undulating ridge. Remember, those downhills that seemed sweet on the way out will make you sweat on the way back.

Technical difficulty: Level 2 to 4. Up to the Mill Creek Canyon divide, the trail is mostly hard-packed dirt and rarely above level 2. Along the ridge to the turnaround point, the trail varies from level 2 to 4 because of loose and imbedded rocks, stutter bumps, and sections where the narrow path hugs steep

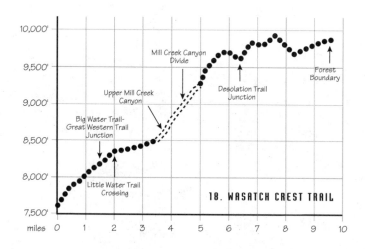

18. WASATCH CREST TRAIL

RIDE 18 WASATCH CREST TRAIL

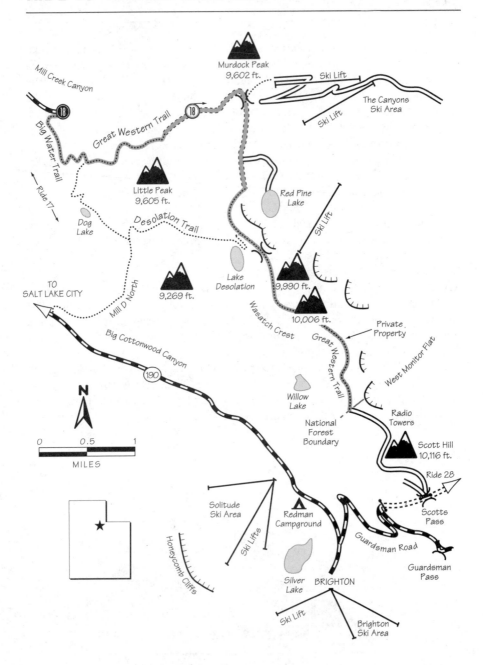

slopes. "The spine" above Lake Desolation is a 100-yard, level 5+ stretch of barren rock; it's a default dismount.

Elevation change: The Big Water Trail trailhead is the route's lowest elevation at 7,600 feet. South of Lake Desolation, the Crest rises to just shy of 10,000 feet. Given the fact that you ride out-and-back along the undulating ridge, total elevation gain is nearly 3,300 feet.

Season: The Wasatch Crest is usually ridable from mid-June to mid-October. The upper Mill Creek Canyon Road is closed to motor vehicles at Maple Grove Picnic Area through June (milepost 4).

Services: An outhouse is at the trailhead but no water tap. Church Fork, Terraces, and Maple Grove picnic areas have water taps and outhouses. Overnight camping is prohibited in Mill Creek Canyon. A shopping center and bike shop are near the mouth of Mill Creek Canyon. Salt Lake City offers all visitor services.

Hazards: Keep an eye on the weather. The mostly treeless ridge offers little shelter from a thunderstorm. The ridge-top singletrack has many demanding sections where loose and imbedded rocks, roots, and exposure to steep side slopes require keen handling skills and your total attention. Commit to walking "the spine" above Lake Desolation before you are forced to dismount involuntarily on the jagged bedrock. Be alert and courteous to other trail users.

Rescue index: The route is popular on weekends and holidays; other times may bring complete solitude. Emergency contacts can be made at the fee station at the entrance to Mill Creek Canyon, but that's 9 miles from the trailhead. From the trail's turnaround point, Brighton and Solitude (Big Cottonwood Canyon) are about 5 miles away via Guardsman Road.

Land status: Wasatch-Cache National Forest (Salt Lake Ranger District).

Maps: USGS Brighton, Mount Aire, and Park West, Utah.

Access: The route begins on the Big Water Trail in upper Mill Creek Canyon. The Mill Creek Canyon Road begins at 3800 South and Wasatch Boulevard in Salt Lake City. (Southbound on Interstate 215, take Exit 3 for 3900 South. Northbound on I-215, take Exit 4 for 3300 South/3900 South.) Take Wasatch Boulevard to 3800 South, and turn right for Mill Creek Canyon. The entrance fee station is 0.5 mile up the canyon. Drive the paved canyon road 9 miles farther to where it ends. The last 2 miles of road are narrow, so drive cautiously.

Notes on the trail: First some fine print. Upper Mill Creek Canyon trails, including the Big Water Trail and Great Western Trail, are open to mountain bikes on *even*-numbered calendar days only. Trail restrictions do not apply to the Wasatch Crest Trail (proper) south of the Mill Creek Canyon divide. Big Cottonwood Canyon is a watershed where pets are not allowed. Therefore, pets are not allowed on the trail south of Lake Desolation. A fee is collected upon leaving Mill Creek Canyon: $2.25 per vehicle in 1998. Pedestrians and

Bob and Julie enjoy an early evening ride on the Wasatch Crest Trail.

bicyclists who do not drive up the Mill Creek Canyon Road do not have to pay the fee upon leaving.

Now let's ride. Start out with easy pedaling up the Big Water Trail from the lower of the two parking lots. Take Big Water 1.5 miles, and then fork left on the Great Western Trail for upper Mill Creek Canyon and the Wasatch Crest. Stay straight at the junction with the Little Water Trail 0.5 miles farther, and keep chugging up through mixed woods and across narrow meadows. Many of the slopes you cross are popular backcountry skiing runs, but bowled-down trees attest to the notorious avalanche danger in these mountains. You'll reach the Mill Creek Canyon divide 4.5 miles from the trailhead. The Canyons Ski Resort, which has gone by "Wolf Mountain" and "Park West" in years past, lies on the other side of the divide.

Now follow the doubletrack to the right/south and uphill. Pass two overlooks of Red Pine Canyon and terrain that was considered prime backcountry skiing until the 1997-1998 expansion of The Canyons Resort. Test your strength and handling skills on a devilish little climb where the doubletrack narrows to singletrack, and then roll along the ridge to the boundary of the Big Cottonwood Watershed. Descend through the aspens to the Desolation Trail junction, fork left for Guardsman Road, and hoof up over "the spine" where the Wasatch's Paleozoic-age skeleton is exposed.

High above Lake Desolation, the Wasatch Crest Trail reaches its full glory. The narrow thread of dirt follows just below the ridge while mimicking its topography. Although the rough-cut profile of the Cottonwood Ridge tugs for your attention, you don't dare take your eyes off the riveting trail. But if you stop from time to time, you'll become immersed by the mountains' beauty and perhaps break into song from *The Sound of Music*.

Singletrack reverts to doubletrack about 3 miles south of Lake Desolation at a sign that signifies you are leaving the Wasatch National Forest. Again, the huge, treeless slopes below the trail reward backcountry skiers with hundreds of steady, uninterrupted turns. This is the recommended turnaround point because the route now crosses private property. (Farther on, the doubletrack passes Scott Hill, descends to Scott's Pass, and eventually drops to Guardsman Road in Big Cottonwood Canyon. Guardsman Road is a popular but unofficial trailhead. Contact the Salt Lake Ranger District for more details.)

Now return to Mill Creek Canyon while enjoying the trail and views from a new perspective. Remember those descents on the way out? Hope you have enough juice left in your legs.

RIDE 19 *ALBION BASIN*

Albion Basin is the heart of the central Wasatch Range. It was here that the Little Cottonwood glacier was born 40 millennia ago. A thick wedge of snow accumulated in these highlands and compressed to ice, which then began creeping down toward the Great Salt Lake Valley. Simultaneously, smaller glaciers descended from the southern ridge to join the main trough. Together, the rivers of ice carved out the U-shaped valley of Little Cottonwood Canyon and a series of hanging valleys that sag beneath a chaotic assemblage of craggy mountaintops. Devil's Castle, Sugarloaf Mountain, Mount Wolverine, and Superior Peak now embrace Albion Basin and the Alta Ski Area. Farther down the canyon, Twin and Dromedary Peaks, the Pfeifferhorn, and Lone Peak are mighty stone sentinels that attest to the slow but powerful forces of erosion by ice and water.

A visit to Albion Basin would not be complete without a trip to Secret Lake. This icy, glacial pool cupped beneath Devil's Castle makes for an ideal lunch spot or midday siesta. The rocky 0.5-mile-long path is closed to bikes, but it is a pleasant hike. Be sure to pack along a camera and plenty of film because the abundance of colorful wildflowers makes a rainbow seem pale.

General location: Albion Basin is located at the top of Little Cottonwood Canyon in the Alta Ski Area, 20 miles southeast of Salt Lake City.

Distance: 6-mile out-and-back.

Tread: 3.5 miles of gravel road with an optional 1.3 miles of doubletrack and 1.2 miles of singletrack.

Aerobic level: Easy to moderate. The climb to the campground is steady but relatively easy. However, "flatlanders" who are visiting the area will feel the constricting effect on their lungs that comes with high elevation.

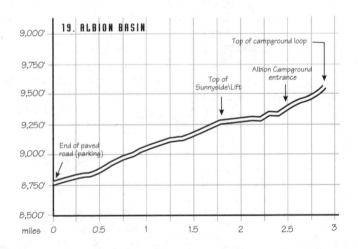

RIDE 19 ALBION BASIN

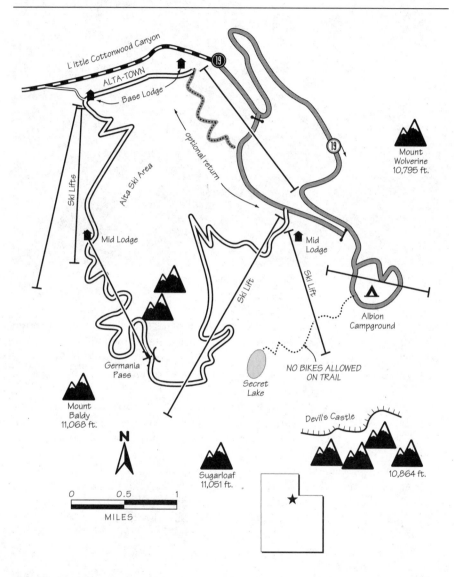

Technical difficulty: Level 1 to 3. The gravel road may develop washboards; the doubletrack section midroute and the culminating singletrack can have loose tread with rocks.

Elevation change: Albion Basin would be one of the easiest routes in the Wasatch Range if not for a trailhead elevation of nearly 9,000 feet. Albion Campground marks the high point at 9,600 feet for a modest 800-foot gain.

Devil's Castle is a chisled backdrop to Albion Basin.

Season: Albion Basin usually melts out by mid-June and is ridable through mid-October, but that is highly dependent on spring snowmelt and autumn snowfall. (Remember, Alta Ski Area typically accumulates 500 inches of snowfall per season, which goes until the end of April.) As always, be prepared for cool and unpredictable alpine weather.

During late summer, Oktoberfest visits the Plaza at Snowbird Resort, 1 mile down Little Cottonwood Canyon. Stop in after your ride to dance a polka, chug Bavarian brew, chow on bratwurst and sauerkraut, and, of course, revel to oom-pah bands.

Services: Water taps and outhouses are at the Albion Basin Campground. A snack stand is located at the route's parking area. Those craving a heartier meal will find an array of continental and international cuisines at restaurants in the town of Alta and at Snowbird Resort 1 mile down the canyon. Lodging is available in Alta and at Snowbird Resort. Mountain bike rentals are available at Snowbird's Activity Center (801) 521-6040. Salt Lake City offers all visitor amenities.

Hazards: The Albion Basin Summer Road is a popular drive for motorists, especially on weekends and holidays. Be alert to hikers on the Albion Meadows Trail. This is alpine terrain, so weather may change from clear in the morning to boiling thunderheads by afternoon.

Rescue index: Albion Basin is a popular mountain retreat from the nearby metropolitan area. Thus, you'll see plenty of motorists, hikers, and other mountain bikers. Telephones are available at lodges near the trailhead. Snowbird Resort has emergency medical facilities.

Land status: Wasatch-Cache National Forest (Salt Lake City Ranger District). Summer homes and all structures in Alta Ski Area are private property, so stay on designated roads and trails.

Maps: USGS Brighton and Dromedary Peak, Utah.

Access: Little Cottonwood Canyon is the southernmost canyon in the Salt Lake section of the Wasatch Range. From Interstate 215 take Exit 6 for 6200 South and Ski Areas. Travel east on 6200 South, and then south on Wasatch Boulevard/Utah State Highway 210 for Alta and Snowbird. Where Wasatch Boulevard forks right for La Caille, stay straight on UT 210 and into Little Cottonwood Canyon. Alta Ski Area is 9 miles up the canyon, 1 mile above Snowbird Resort. Park where pavement ends and the Albion Basin Summer Road begins.

Notes on the trail: Pedal 3 miles up the gravel Albion Summer Road to the Albion Basin Campground. Take a lap around the campground, and return the opposite way. It's that simple.

Naturally, you can return by simply backtracking down the Summer Road, but that is less than eventful. For an optional touch of excitement, return on the Albion Meadows Trail through the lower basin. After exiting the campground, turn left/west on a doubletrack marked by a steel gate and a bike decal. Descend toward the base of the Sugarloaf Lift but not all the way. Fork right/north on a doubletrack that heads down the east side of the valley. Where the doubletrack flattens and before it intersects the Summer Road, fork left on the Albion Meadows Trail. The singletrack winds down toward the Albion Day Lodge just below the parking area. You can explore farther by taking the path down to Goldminer's Daughter Lodge.

The slogan "Alta is for skiers" acclaims a reputation of consistently deep powder and ski terrain that is all-natural with few "cut" runs. But nearly a century and a half ago, miners flocked to Alta, not skiers, to seek their fortune in silver ore. The silver rush began in 1865 with the opening of the Emma Mine, and Alta quickly grew to a population of 5,000 and was served by 26 saloons by 1872. A year later, crashing silver prices and a series of deadly avalanches ended the boom. A second mining surge lasted from 1904 to 1927, but Alta would never regain the mining camps and roaring saloon life of earlier years. Old mine dumps and relics, which can still be seen dotting the hillsides, are silent reminders of the early rollicking history of Little Cottonwood Canyon.

RIDE 20 *COPPER PIT OVERLOOK*

How far will you travel for a small slice of singletrack heaven? If you live in Salt Lake City, you need to drive about 35 miles around the Oquirrh Mountains to Tooele to find a secret little stash that will make you drool. Unfortunately, there's only about 1 mile of one-lane trail, but even at that, it's worth the drive because chances are you'll have it all to yourself.

The heart of the ride is not the singletrack; that's icing on the cake. Your goal is a bird's-eye view of man's largest excavation—Kennecott's Bingham Canyon Mine, dubbed "The Richest Hole on Earth." Beyond the copper pit, your eyes will fall upon 100 miles of the Wasatch Range and on the reverent inhabitants in the valley below. Spin around and you'll view across the eastern margin of the Basin and Range Province, where linear north-south mountain ranges are separated by peneplains like that of Tooele.

The climb to the overlook is steep, the return is raging, and the mile-long singletrack is serendipitous.

General location: 7 miles southeast of Tooele.

Distance: 9.8-mile loop with out-and-back spur.

Tread: 6.8 miles of gravel and rock road that can be rough for passenger cars; 1.8 miles of packed dirt and cobblestone doubletrack; 1.2 miles of primitive singletrack.

Aerobic level: Moderate. The initial 1.5-mile climb to Butterfield Pass averages 12 percent. The remaining climb to the overlook is less severe but steady just the same. Then it's all downhill.

Technical difficulty: Level 2 to 4. The climb to the overlook has gravel, some washboards, and minor pavement bedrock. Doubletracks range from silky

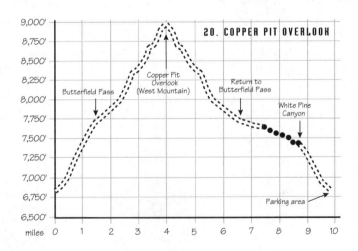

RIDE 20 COPPER PIT OVERLOOK

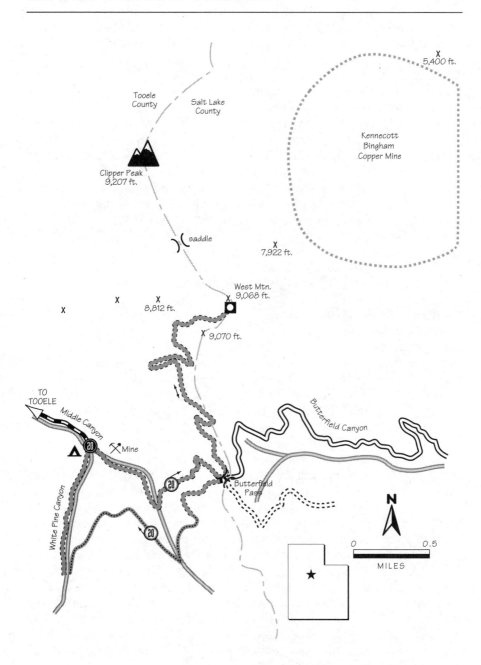

Tooele
County

Salt Lake
County

X
5,400 ft.

Kennecott
Bingham
Copper Mine

Clipper Peak
9,207 ft.

) (saddle

X
7,922 ft.

West Mtn.
X 9,068 ft.

X   X
8,812 ft.

X

X 9,070 ft.

Butterfield Canyon

TO
TOOELE

Middle Canyon

⚒ Mine

20

White Pine Canyon

20

20

Butterfield
Pass

N

0   0.5

★

MILES

smooth to dry cobble streambeds. The wooded singletrack receives little maintenance and is packed dirt.

Elevation change: The trailhead/parking area is at 6,800 feet. The route tops out at the overlook at 9,000 feet for a one-shot gain of 2,200 feet.

Season: May into October. The White Pine Canyon section may be popular with big-game hunters in the fall.

Services: There is no drinking water along this route. The trailhead has a primitive camping area, but no water tap, outhouse, or trash pickup. Tooele offers all visitor services, except a bike shop.

Hazards: You may have to share the road with motorists driving to the overlook. There is one washout on the singletrack that requires dismounting and a short portage downhill. You may encounter hikers and equestrians in White Pine Canyon upon descending to the trailhead.

Rescue index: Passersby are sporadic on the road to the overlook, and campers are few at the trailhead. On the rest of the route, you are on your own.

Land status: Tooele County and private property.

Maps: USGS Bingham Canyon and Lowe Peak, Utah.

Access: From the intersection of Main and Vine in Tooele, travel southeast on Vine for the Oquirrh Overlook. After 7 miles, the narrow paved road turns to dirt and gravel at the White Pine Canyon camping area where you park and embark.

Sources of additional information: *Bicycle Tooele County* (fold out brochure) available from Tooele County Department of Parks and Recreation (See Appendix B).

Notes on the trail: The route through White Pine Canyon crosses private property. It is important that you stay on route and respect the land so that access privileges will continue.

Downshift to granny gear and rev up the RPMs for the no-holds-barred climb from the trailhead. For 1.5 miles the gravel, washboard, and rock road rises at an average 12 percent grade to Butterfield Pass. If you lift your head from the handlebar, your eyes will gravitate to the grass-veneered limestone ledges of White Pine Canyon and to its treeless, glacial-carved peaks piercing the sky. On the return leg, you'll wind through the base of the canyon.

At Butterfield Pass, fork left and continue climbing 2.7 miles, this time at a more tolerable grade, to the mine overlook between West Mountain and Clipper Peak. An entire mountain once stood where the gaping hole now rests. Just how big is the copper pit? It's over 0.5 mile deep and 2.5 miles wide at the top. That means the world's tallest building, the Sears Tower in Chicago, would reach only halfway up, and 40 football fields would fit end-to-end across the top. On a daily basis, 250,000 tons of material are removed—7 days a week, 365 days a year. Each ore shovel can scoop out 40-cubic yards of material in a single bite—that's 70 tons or the equivalent of 35 automobiles. And those haul trucks that seem no bigger than Matchbox cars stand over two stories tall; their tires alone are nearly 10 feet high. It's a modern-day Roman Colosseum.

Descend back to Butterfield Pass and fork right on a doubletrack heading southwest into the trees. In 0.8 mile, the track narrows to a singletrack, and the trailside oak and maple form a wooded tunnel. Sweet. Heed the small sign warning of a washout ahead and dismount!

All good things must come to an end when the path crosses White Pine Canyon creek and connects with a doubletrack that is fraught with river cobbles and makes for sketchy handling (technical level 4 to 5). Farther down, the track is more biker friendly as you return to the trailhead.

Provo

RIDE 21 *RIDGE TRAIL 157*

Like Skyline Trail in Ogden and the Wasatch Crest Trail in Salt Lake City, Ridge Trail 157 captures the essence of mountain biking by following a thrilling singletrack through the heart of a mountain range. You'll need a full repertoire of skills for the varying trail conditions and an extra pair of eyes to lock onto the mountain scenery while pedaling. But if you stop from time to time, you'll be captivated by a skyline shaped by 11,000-foot summits and terrain composed of glacial valleys and river-cut canyons.

American Fork Canyon is a hub for recreational activity. Its reservoirs and streams attract anglers, its solid limestone walls assure technical rock climbers of firm hand holds, and its roadside campsites and picnic areas offer interludes with nature for those less adventurous. But it's American Fork's network of wilderness and non-wilderness trails that have made it a haven for hikers, equestrians, and mountain bikers. Ridge Trail 157 is the backbone of American Fork's non-wilderness trail system. It's a world-class ride in itself. More importantly, it is the framework for an array of peripheral trails that open up countless options for return explorations.

General location: American Fork Canyon, 25 miles northeast of Provo.

Distance: 14 miles point-to-point.

Tread: The route begins with 4 miles of doubletrack and continues with 10 miles of smooth and not-so-smooth singletrack.

Aerobic level: Strenuous. The initial 4-mile climb on doubletrack is moderate to strenuous. Then, Ridge Trail 157 is packed with many tough little climbs.

RIDE 21 RIDGE TRAIL 157

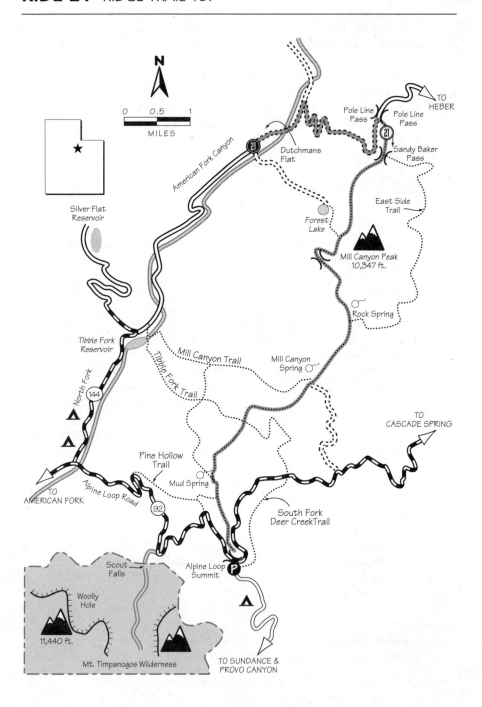

N

0   0.5   1
MILES

American Fork Canyon

Silver Flat
Reservoir

21

Dutchmans
Flat

Pole Line
Pass

Pole Line
Pass

TO
HEBER

21

Sandy Baker
Pass

East Side
Trail

Forest
Lake

Mill Canyon Peak
10,347 ft.

Rock Spring

Tibble Fork
Reservoir

Mill Canyon Trail

Mill Canyon
Spring

Tibble Fork Trail

North Fork

144

TO
CASCADE SPRING

Pine Hollow
Trail

Mud Spring

Alpine Loop Road

92

TO
AMERICAN FORK

South Fork
Deer Creek Trail

Alpine Loop
Summit

P

Scout
Falls

Woolly
Hole

11,440 ft.

Mt. Timpanogos Wilderness

TO SUNDANCE &
PROVO CANYON

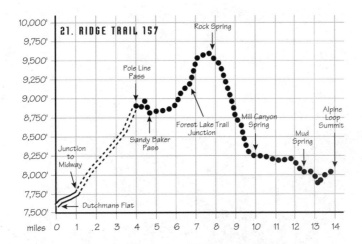

Technical difficulty: Level 3 to 5. The climb to Pole Line Pass on doubletrack can be rocky and rutted in spots. Ridge Trail 157 is packed dirt with the usual assortment of on-trail obstacles. The descent off Mill Canyon Peak to Mill Canyon Spring is notoriously steep and rocky (level 4 to 5).

Elevation change: Dutchmans Flat (trailhead/parking area) is at 7,600 feet. The ride begins with a 1,350-foot climb to Ridge Trail 157 at Pole Line Pass (elevation 8,950 feet). The trail tops out near Rock Spring at 9,600 feet. Although the trail drops to 8,060 feet at the Alpine Scenic Loop Trailhead, you can expect to gain nearly 2,000 feet along the way for total climbing of about 3,300 feet.

Season: June through October, depending on spring thaw and autumn flurries. Hunters converge on American Fork Canyon and its trails in the fall.

Services: A water tap and outhouse are at Tibble Fork Reservoir and at the campgrounds in American Fork Canyon, but there is no drinking water along the trail. Rock Spring and Mill Canyon Spring flow perennially but their potability is uncertain. There is a snack bar at nearby Timpanogos Cave National Monument. Pleasant Grove offers all visitor services, including a bike shop.

Hazards: You may find deadfall on the trail early in the season before Forest Service maintenance crews can sweep the trail. The descent off Mill Canyon Peak to Mill Canyon Spring is steep, direct, rocky, and demands unfaltering skills. The trail is very popular with equestrians, especially over the last several miles between Mill Canyon Spring and the Alpine Scenic Loop Trailhead.

Rescue index: Trail users are more numerous as the ride progresses, especially between Mill Canyon Spring and the Alpine Scenic Loop Trailhead. American Fork Canyon and Tibble Fork Reservoir are popular with campers and anglers. Emergency contacts can be made at Timpanogos Cave National Monument or at the entrance fee station to American Fork Canyon.

The majestic sight of
Mount Timpanogos
stops Scott in his tracks.

Land status: Uinta National Forest (Pleasant Grove Ranger District).
Maps: USGS Aspen Grove, Brighton, Dromedary Peak, and Timpanogos Cave, Utah.
Access: From Interstate 15, take Exit 287 for Alpine and Highland. Travel 8 miles east on Utah State Highway 92 and enter American Fork Canyon (fee station). Stay straight at the North Fork junction (2.5 miles past Timpanogos Cave National Monument) and drive 7 miles to the trailhead/parking area at the summit of the Alpine Scenic Loop.

In the shuttle vehicle, return to the North Fork junction and travel 2 miles up Utah State Highway 144 to Tibble Fork Reservoir. Continue past the lake and up American Fork Canyon on Forest Road 085. The gravel road can be rough but passable for passenger cars due to scattered rocks, washboards, and eroded conditions. Drive 4.5 miles and park at Dutchmans Flat (unsigned). It's before the road crosses the river and marked by numerous backcountry campsites.

Notes on the trail: A recreational use fee is charged for entering American Fork Canyon: $3 per vehicle (three-day pass); $25 per vehicle (one-year pass). Camping fees are additional.

From Dutchman Flat, pedal 1 mile to a junction and fork right on Forest Road 085 for Wasatch State Park and Midway to begin the 3-mile, 1,300-foot, warm-up climb to Pole Line Pass. Sections are steep and rocky and will get your heart pumping. In the clearing at the summit, Ridge Trail 157 heads due south. Round a knoll and descend to Sandy Baker Pass, while enjoying the whopping view of Box Elder Peak due west, the Alpine Ridge to the north, and the Lone Peak Wilderness in between. At the pass, stay right on the upper of two trails and contour around the north and west flank of Mill Canyon Peak.

Let the fun begin! Weave through a mix of aspen and conifers while taking wildflower "face shots" along the way. This is mountain biking at its finest. In the valley below, a swath of bowled-down trees attest to the fury of a winter avalanche. Pass the Forest Lake Trail junction and cross a talus slope of coarse, limestone gravel. Look for wild raspberries growing up slope. Yum! The energy boost may aid in tackling the steep climb ahead.

Atop the climb you'll find a colossal view of the central Wasatch Range. The once-regal Alpine Ridge to the north is now subservient to the Goliath stature of Mount Timpanogos to the south. The main valley gouged out of Timp is the Giant Staircase, which takes hikers and equestrians into the Mount Timpanogos Wilderness and to the Timpanogos glacier. Timp will be your guardian for the rest of the ride.

Contour across the high slopes to Rock Spring, and then hunker down for the wild descent to Mill Canyon Spring, passing a junction for the East Side Trail to the left. The drop is steep and infamous for its rough and rocky conditions. When you reach the clearing at the spring, ignore the dirt road to the left and the Mill Canyon Trail to the right. Stay straight/south on a doubletrack that reverts to singletrack and continues along the ridge.

The remaining route is roller-coaster style, undulating along the ridge beneath the ever-changing face of Mount Timpanogos. Pass the trailheads for South Fork Deer Creek Trail (left) and Tibble Fork Trail (right), curve past Mud Spring, and let gravity pull you past the junction for Pine Hollow Trail (right). You'll have to hoof up one last climb before rambling through the aspens to the trailhead at the summit of the Alpine Scenic Loop. Cheers!

Don't have a car shuttle at hand? Then you have two options. Ride out-and-back along the ridge from the trail's end at the summit of the Alpine Scenic Loop to Mill Canyon Spring (about 10 miles round trip), or knock off Ridge Trail 157 as a 27-mile loop. The former is perfect for intermediate riders, but the latter requires strong legs, indefatigable stamina, and all day. And if you have a penchant for exploring, you can ride for days on the trail network centered about the Alpine Scenic Loop Summit. Without revealing all the goods, check out Pine Hollow and South Fork Deer Creek Trails.

RIDE 22 *SUNDANCE*

In 1969, Robert Redford envisioned a year-round mountain community that would foster the alliance of arts and recreation while preserving the integrity of the land. Out of the old Timphaven ski resort on the North Fork of the Provo River emerged Sundance. At the heart of Sundance is Sundance Village where cottage rooms, picturesque mountain homes, award-winning restaurants, an artisan center, and spacious conference facilities are all tucked amidst pristine forests nestled at the base of 12,000-foot Mount Timpanogos. The unmatched natural scenery and countless activities in every season lend Sundance a truly unique atmosphere. Guests can enjoy nearly every form of recreation from alpine skiing, cross-country ski touring, and snowboarding in the winter, to hiking, horseback riding, mountain biking, and fly fishing during the summer. In addition to the varied recreational opportunities, Sundance offers its guests and community audiences a year-round arts program with weekend film screenings, professional theater, and art studios.

The same terrain that makes skiing and snowboarding at Sundance so incredible also makes for truly outstanding mountain biking. In 1998, Sundance boasted over 20 miles of trails designated for mountain bikes ranging from intermediate to expert, all accessible from Ray's Lift. First-time bikers will enjoy a mellow cruise down Sunnyside Ride, whereas those searching for scintillating singletrack gravitate to Ray's Ride. Ray's With a Twist and Boneyard Loop add more challenging elements reserved for advanced riders. Scott's Pond Loop offers a cross-country tour to a secluded pond.

General location: 10 miles east of Orem.

Distance: Up to 20 miles with more trails slated in the future.

Tread: Singletracks and doubletracks.

Aerobic level: Easy to moderate if you let Ray's Lift do all the work. (See "Notes" for route suggestions.)

Technical difficulty: Level 2 to 5 depending on route chosen. (See "Notes" for route suggestions.)

Elevation change: The base of Ray's Lift is at 6,100 feet. The lift summit is 7,150 feet. Trails are downhill for the most part, but you'll climb a bit on the Scott's Pond-Flathead Loop. If you snub the lift, you'll conquer 1,050 feet of elevation gain.

Season: End of May through mid-October, weather permitting; Monday through Saturday and holidays, 10 A.M. to 6:30 P.M., Sunday 12 noon to 6:30 P.M. Area use fee is $12 for a full-day pass, $10 for a half-day pass (starts at 2:30 P.M. and $6 for a twilight pass (starts at 4:30 P.M.). All passes include unlimited use of Ray's Lift and trail system. A "trails only" pass is $6 for a full day and $3 for a twilight pass.

RIDE 22 SUNDANCE

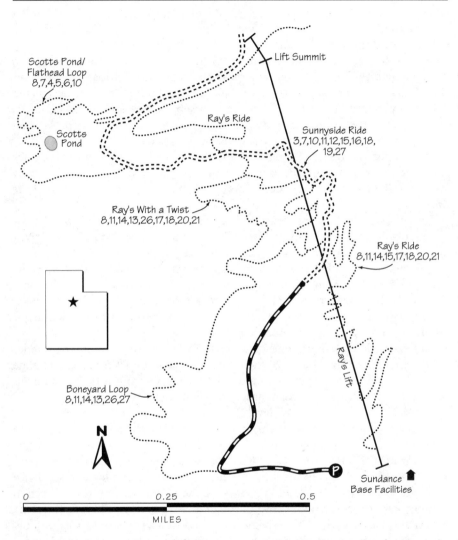

Services: Sundance offers overnight accommodations, gourmet and informal dining, a small general store and deli, and a full-service bike shop with rentals.
Hazards: Although trails are periodically maintained, sections of trails may have loose tread, gravel, rocks, exposed tree roots, ruts, and drop-offs.
Rescue index: Emergency assistance can be summoned from lift attendants at the base and summit of Ray's Lift. Orem and Provo have medical facilities.
Land status: Sundance (private property).

Maps: USGS Aspen Grove and Bridal Veil Falls, Utah.

Access: From Interstate 15, take Exit 275 for 8th North Street (Orem), Sundance, and Provo Canyon Recreation Areas. Travel east on 8th North for 4 miles, and follow U.S. Highway 189 up Provo Canyon for 6.8 miles. Turn left on Utah State Highway 92 for Sundance. The resort is 2.5 miles farther.

Sources of additional information: Sundance (see Appendix B).

Notes on the trail: First some fine print. Helmets are required for all mountain biking activities. Two-way traffic is possible at any time. Ride only on trails and roads that are designated open to bicycles. Separate areas are designated for use by mountain bikers, hikers, and horseback riders to avoid conflicts. Please stay in the appropriate areas as designated by the trail map. An area pass must be purchased even if lift service is not utilized.

Navigating the trails at Sundance is a matter of knowing where to turn since intersections are numbered, but individual sections of trail are typically nameless. Thus, you complete a route by connecting the junctions along the way.

Sunnyside Ride (3 miles, easy, level 2): This easygoing tour is perfect for newcomers who don't want to fret whether they might "stuff" their front wheel. It follows dirt and gravel doubletracks around wide, sweeping turns and across sun-kissed slopes. Ride Ray's Lift past the summit and down to its very end. Ride down the Sunnyside Road (doubletrack); then stay on the main road through intersection 7 and down to intersection 10. Fork left on the Mandan Road (doubletrack), pedal up a gentle hill, and pass trail junction 11. At intersection 12, turn right and descend the road past 15, fork left on a short stretch of singletrack at 16, and wind down to 18. Follow the dirt road under Ray's Lift and across the face of the mountain, pass intersection 19, and glide to the base on the maintenance road, which changes from dirt to pavement. Reload and try Ray's Ride for a little more flair.

Ray's Ride (3.5 miles, easy, level 2 to 3): If you like a ride that's not too tough, not too easy, but just right, you'll love Ray's. It's the main route from the summit to the base and is full of sweet singletrack. But keep an eye in the rearview mirror for armor-clad downhillers who would just as soon put a tire track up your back. From the lift's summit, head toward the black snow fence and take the singletrack around the back side of the lift summit to intersection 8. Stay left on singletrack, drop through the aspens to 11 and cross the Mandan Road. Fork left at 14 (picnic table amidst a thicket of aspens), follow the upcoming doubletrack for a bit, and jump back on the trail from 15 to 17. Cross the dirt road at 18, climb over the aspen and maple knoll, and put on a good show for spectators riding the lift overhead while banking down the main track through 20 and 21 to the base.

Ray's With a Twist (3.25 miles, moderate, level 2 to 5): Up the technical ante on this variation of Ray's Ride with a stretch of level 3 to 5 singletrack, including the infamous rock drop. Descend as you would for Ray's Ride to intersection 14, but fork right to 13 and then to 26. Dip and dive down tight

Steve and Tricia wile away the afternoon at Sundance.

turns and hang your butt way off the back when you come to the drop-off. Shimmy through the woods to connect with 17 and finish off the descent by crossing the road at 21 and following the main singletrack to the base.

Boneyard Loop (4 miles, moderate, level 2 to 5): You can call this ride Ray's With a Double Twist. The route combines Ray's Ride up top with Ray's With a Twist in the middle with a new section of trail that veers away from the main trail system. Boneyard Trail weaves through dense timber to a stunning overlook of North Fork Canyon before looping back to the resort center. You'll swear you've ventured miles into the remote backcountry.

Scott's Pond/Flathead Loop (2.2 miles, moderate, level 2 to 4): Get more bang for your lift-ticket buck on this side trip to Scott's Pond. You'll veer from the main downhill trails by diving through dense groves of maple and then penetrating towering aspens underlaid with ferns that fan your legs as you brush by. You'll perfect your short-radius turning skills while wiggling and giggling through countless curves. At Scott's Pond, take a snack break or cool off with a midday plunge, provided deer or moose haven't claimed first dibs on the grass-rimmed pool. Exit Ray's Lift at the summit and take the singletrack at the end of the black snow fence down to intersection 8, as you would for Ray's Ride. Dive into a canopy of stunted maples on a spaghetti trail, cross the Sunnyside Road at 7, and continue turning, turning, turning. Cross the Long Hollow Road at 4 for more singletrack that enters fern-blanketed aspens. Pass Scott's Pond and climb across meadows, then through timber to intersection 6.

Fork right and continue on challenging singletrack up to 10. Circle back on the Sunnyside Road for another lap, or pursue other routes to the base.

Uphill route (3.5 miles, strenuous, level 1 to 3): "I don't need no stinkin' chair lift," you say? Then pedal Ray's Ride in reverse and uphill. You'll be in granny gear most of the way but that's OK because you'll enjoy the encompassing beauty of Sundance and Mount Timpanogos overhead all the more. And you couldn't ask for a better uphill trail. You'll break a sweat, that's for sure, but the dirt one-laner is a golden thread of dirt. Alternatively, head up Boneyard Loop by starting out on the paved access road. Look for the trail forking left after rounding the big curve. When you reach intersection 26, fork right and cross the mountain over to 17, then up the main trails under Ray's Lift.

If you're a true-blooded cross-country racer, then check out Sundance's informal race series that runs throughout the summer. All these buffed downhill trails make for a dynamite racecourse.

Finally, look for the new back mountain loop of approximately 1.5 miles of singletrack. It will begin at junction 2 and wind down to the base of Arrowhead Lift and promises to be the best yet at Sundance.

RIDE 23 *PROVO RIVER PARKWAY*

The Provo River Parkway is perfect for those who take a simpler approach to mountain biking—lightly spinning the pedals, coasting a bit, stopping for a midafternoon siesta next to a stream—or for those who enjoy a short jaunt with the family.

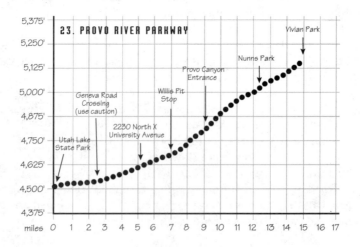

RIDE 23 PROVO RIVER PARKWAY

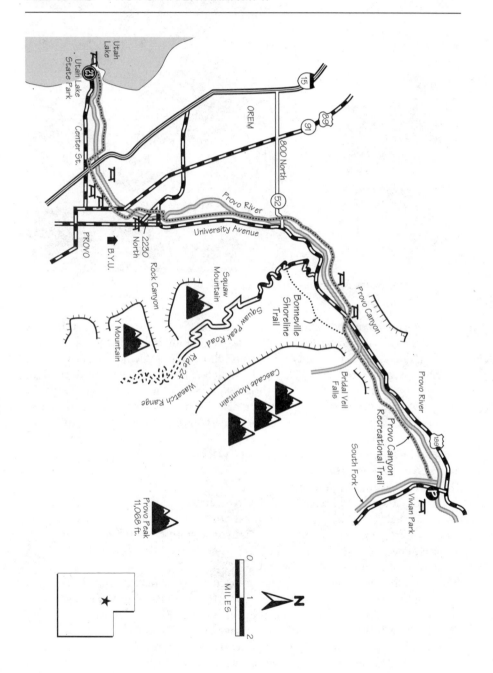

Ever-present Cascade Mountain hovers over the Provo River Parkway.

The Parkway threads through the heart of Provo, connecting Utah Lake State Park and Vivian Park in Provo Canyon. Along the way, the path passes nearly a dozen city and county parks and follows along the banks of the Provo River most of the time. The Wasatch Range is always in view and grows to colossal proportions until it swallows you whole in Provo Canyon. The Parkway attracts not only bikers but also runners, pedestrians, and in-line skaters of all ages. Multiple trailheads allow you to explore a section at a time instead of the entire route.

General location: Provo to Orem, between Utah Lake State Park on Utah Lake and Vivian Park in Provo Canyon.

Distance: 15.5 miles point-to-point.

Tread: Eight-foot-wide paved and dirt recreational path.

Aerobic level: Easy. It's flat as a pancake from Utah Lake State Park to the mouth of Provo Canyon. The Provo Canyon section rises uphill slightly but is a piece of cake just the same.

Technical difficulty: Level 0, zip, none.

Elevation change: Elevation change is hardly worth mentioning. Utah Lake State Park (western trailhead) is at 4,500 feet; the mouth of Provo Canyon is at 4,830 feet; Vivian Park (eastern trailhead) is at 5,200 feet. That's a *whopping* 700-foot climb (less than 1 percent average grade)—just right for tikes.

Season: You can enjoy the Parkway nearly year-round. Midsummer can be very warm. During winter, the path may be covered with snow, which can make for a fun day of ski touring if you are so inclined. City and county parks along the route are open from early April through October.

Services: The Parkway passes through the center of Provo plus ten city and county parks. All parks have water taps and restrooms. Utah Lake State Park has a developed campground (fee area). Provo has all visitor services, including bike shops.

Hazards: Be alert to oncoming recreationists and stay to the right side of the path. Bikes should travel in single file. Watch for gates, entrance labyrinths, or wooden posts that prevent motorized access at trailheads and where the Parkway crosses roadways. Yield to vehicular traffic at crossroads. This is not a time-trials course; travel at prudent speeds and be courteous to other users.

Rescue index: The path is well traveled by recreationists, and it winds through commercial and residential areas where help can be summoned. The initial 1.5 miles from the Utah Lake Trailhead passes through rural lands where residences are more dispersed. Provo has medical facilities.

Land status: Provo City and Utah County Parks and Recreation.

Maps: A trail map is available from Provo City Parks and Recreation.

Access: Utah Lake State Park (western trailhead): From Interstate 15 take Exit 268 for Center Street (Provo) and Utah Lake State Park; then drive 3 miles west on Center Street/Utah State Highway 114. Just before Utah Lake State Park's entrance, turn right/north. The Parkway's trailhead/parking area (unsigned) is immediately ahead on the right.

Vivian Park (eastern trailhead): From I-15, take Exit 275 for Eighth North (Orem) and Provo Canyon. Drive east 3.5 miles on Eighth North/Utah State Highway 52 and enter Provo Canyon via U.S. Highway 189 North. Vivian Park is about 7 miles up Provo Canyon.

Other trailheads:

> **Nunn's Park (mile 12.5):** Take the exit for Nunn's Park 3.3 miles up Provo Canyon on US 189 and park at the trailhead at the bottom of the off ramp. The Bonneville Shoreline Trail branches from the Provo Canyon Recreation Trail a few hundred yards up the path toward Vivian Park.
>
> **Olmsted (mouth of Provo Canyon at mile 9):** Follow the access for Vivian Park, but before entering Provo Canyon on US 189, turn left on 1630 East immediately past the gas station.
>
> **Will's Pit Stop (University Avenue at mile 7):** A small parking area is behind the convenience store at the intersection of University Avenue and 3700 North.
>
> **2230 North (mile 5.5):** There is a small parking area on 2230 North in Provo between University Avenue and 400 West. It's on the west side of the L.D.S. Motion Picture Studio.
>
> **Geneva Road (mile 2.5):** Follow access for the Utah Lake State Park trailhead. But after 0.5 mile on Center Street/UT 114, turn right/north on Geneva Road. The trailhead/parking area is where the road crosses the Provo River.

Sources of additional information: Provo City Parks and Recreation; Utah County Parks (See Appendix B).

Notes on the trail: Here's the route from Utah Lake State Park to Vivian Park—east to west. Mileage markers (noted as MP **x.x**) are posted every half mile beginning at the Utah Lake Trailhead.

The parkway begins as a wide sand-and-gravel path meandering through farm and ranch lands. This section affords striking views of the Wasatch Range from Lone Peak in the north to Mount Nebo in the south. Mount Timpanogos, with its 5-mile-long ridge, is the icon of the Utah Valley. As you click away the miles, the mountains grow majestically until they completely engulf you in Provo Canyon.

At MP **2.5**, the path intersects Geneva Road. The parkway continues across the road and to the south near the entrance to the KOA campground. Just before MP **3**, it passes under I-15; shortly thereafter, the trail dips under railroad tracks. (Watch your head.) Farther along, the parkway begins its namesake tour of several city parks. Paul Reams Wilderness is followed by Riverside Park and Exchange Park (MP **4**). Past the Fire Station trailhead, the trail goes under Columbia Avenue and State Street. Between MP **4.5** and MP **5**, the path crosses a footbridge to the Provo River's northwest bank. Beyond the University Parkway underpass, the trail runs behind apartment complexes and through a maple- and oak-lined park where newlyweds are often photographed.

Past the 2230 North underpass, the Provo River pours over multiple terraces. Cross a footbridge, veer past a power substation, and pedal on the sidewalk along 2230 North; then turn left on University Avenue, again following the wide sidewalk.

After 1.5 miles, cross 3700 North and pass Will's Pit Stop convenience store. (Be alert to motorists entering and exiting side roads and driveways.) The paved path resumes behind the store (MP **7**). Ride parallel to University Avenue for 2 miles to another power substation (MP **9**). Here, the route crosses under UT 52 at the mouth of Provo Canyon and passes the Olmsted Trailhead.

The Provo River Parkway officially ends at Provo Canyon, but the route continues alongside the Provo River as the Provo Canyon Recreation Trail. Near MP **12**, the route passes behind Canyon Glen Park, cuts through Nunn's Park and crosses under US 189. The last (and newly developed) section leads 2.5 miles more to Vivian Park on the South Fork. A few hundred yards up the path from the highway underpass, the Bonneville Shoreline Trail forks right. It starts out steep but then contours the old shoreline bench to Squaw Peak Road. Go on, get a little dirty.

RIDE 24 *SQUAW PEAK ROAD*

Squaw Peak Road reveals some truly exceptional vistas of both the Wasatch Range and Utah Valley. From the outset, the route supplies a grand view of cliff-bound Provo Canyon overshadowed by the Mount Timpanogos Wilderness. From midroute, you'll be mesmerized by Rock Canyon, which fans out from a deeply incised notch lined with convoluted cliffs to pine-covered mountaintops. Only a wedge of Utah Valley can be seen through the gash. Above you, 11,000-foot tall Provo Peak and bulky Cascade Mountain appear to be no more than arm's length away and bear down with a weighty presence. At the route's turnaround at Camel Pass, there are heartthrobbing vistas of the entire route from beginning to end coupled with an aerial perspective of Utah Valley. From here, you can easily trace the razor-sharp Wasatch Fault as it curves around the base of Spanish Fork Peak and Loafer Mountain en route to the Wasatch's monarch, Mount Nebo.

Overall the route is fast-paced and low in technical difficulty. There are a few sizeable climbs that will make you sweat and groan, but you'll find that revenge is sweet on the return leg.

General location: Squaw Peak Road is located high above Provo, between Provo Canyon and Hobble Creek Canyon.

Distance: 27 miles out-and-back.

Tread: 5 miles of gravel road to Rock Canyon Campground, and then 8 miles of rock-studded doubletrack to the turnaround.

Aerobic level: Strenuous. The initial 3-mile climb is steady and moderately difficult—a good warm up. However, the 4-mile climb south of Rock Canyon Campground is a real grinder. Remember, any hills you scream down on the

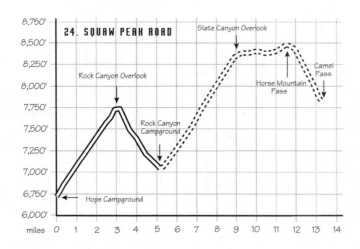

RIDE 24 SQUAW PEAK ROAD

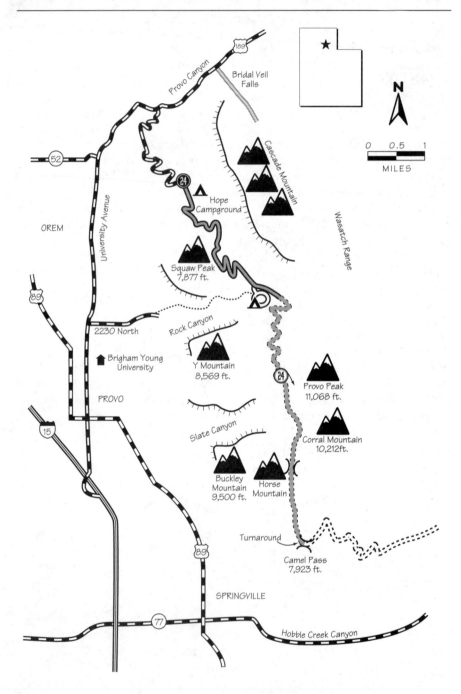

way out might have your legs screaming on the way back, and vice versa.

Technical difficulty: Level 1 to 3. The doubletrack between Rock Canyon Campground and the turnaround can be rutted and peppered with fist-size rocks.

Elevation change: Hope Campground (trailhead) is at 6,700 feet. The road rises to 7,700 feet near the Rock Canyon Overlook, then drops to 7,000 feet at Rock Canyon Campground. The route climbs again to its highest point at 8,400 feet near Horse Mountain before descending to Camel Pass at 7,800 feet. Elevation gain on the way out is 2,400 feet. Add 1,300 feet on the return leg for a total gain of 3,700 feet.

Season: Squaw Peak Road is ridable from May through October, depending on snow thaw and snowfall.

Services: Water taps, an outhouse, and campsites are at Hope and Rock Canyon Campgrounds (Forest Service fee areas open from May through mid-September). This ride is only a few miles from Provo (as the crow flies), with visitor services, including several bike shops.

Hazards: Vehicular traffic between Hope and Rock Canyon Campgrounds can be moderate on weekends and holidays. This route is a local favorite for OHVs and four-wheel-drive vehicles, so ride cautiously and share the road. The doubletrack from Rock Canyon Campground to the Kolob Basin overlook turns to tire-clogging, gear-seizing clay when wet.

Rescue index: This route is popular with cyclists, OHVs, four-wheel-drive vehicles, and weekend sightseers, so help is rarely far away. Campers can be found at both Hope and Rock Canyon Campgrounds. Although the short trail down Rock Canyon to Provo may seem like a shortcut for assistance, it's damn steep and viciously rocky. The return climb is downright brutal.

Land status: Uinta National Forest (Pleasant Grove Ranger District).

Maps: USGS Bridal Veil Falls and Springville, Utah.

Access: From Interstate 15, take Exit 275 for 800 North (Orem) and Provo Canyon. Travel east on 800 North/Utah State Highway 52, then up Provo Canyon on U.S. Highway 189. Turn right on the Squaw Peak Road (Forest Road 027) 1.5 miles up Provo Canyon, and drive 5 miles up the twisting paved road to Hope Campground, where pavement turns to dirt. Park at your discretion near the entrance to the campground or pay the fee to park in the campground.

Notes on the trail: From Hope Campground, pedal 3.5 miles up the all-weather road to the Rock Canyon Overlook. Then zoom downhill 1.5 miles to Rock Canyon Campground, twisting through quaking aspen and oak brush while enjoying both the immensity and proximity of the southern Wasatch Range.

Continue south on the doubletrack labeled Forest Road 027 and up the 4-mile climb to a pass at the Slide Canyon Trailhead. The climb is steady and as difficult as you make it: a good grind for most bikers or a heart-rate-maxing pump for racers in training. When you reach the top, you'll find a view that is

The Provo Peak ridge molds the skyline on the Squaw Peak Road.

very different from other Wasatch scenes. You've risen through a fault-induced valley wedged between the frontal peaks of Squaw Peak and Y Mountain and the predominant Provo Peak ridge.

Over the next 3 miles, the rock-studded jeep road contours beneath Provo Peak and the strong-arm ridge of Corral Mountain. Beyond the Horse Mountain pass, the road descends gradually for nearly 3 miles to a left-hand bend at Camel Pass—the route's recommended turnaround. (From Camel Pass, the doubletrack descends to the Left Fork Hobble Creek Road on a jackhammer descent that leaves you nearly 30 miles from the Hope Campground Trailhead.) The view of the Utah Valley more than 3,000 feet below and of the southern Wasatch Range is truly inspirational. Now make the climb back to the summit, and then get even with the long hill from Rock Canyon Campground by gliding back down with a huge grin on your face. Make the climb from Rock Canyon Campground and coast back to Hope Campground.

RIDE 25   *DIAMOND FORK-STRAWBERRY RIDGE*

Diamond Fork is off the beaten path and easily overlooked, but the word is out that this is the place if you're a singletrack purist. Tucked in the Wasatch hinterlands, Diamond Fork's rolling, forested hills obscure most views of the Wasatch Range. That is, unless you make the climb to Strawberry Ridge, from where the serrated Wasatch can be seen stretching over 60 miles from the Alpine Ridge (Little Cottonwood Canyon) to Mount Nebo. So carry a camera just the same, preferably one that takes panorama-format pictures.

"Go back to that part about being a singletrack purist," you say? This near marathon-length ride is over 60 percent twisty. Do the math and that comes out to about 15 miles of dirt one-laners, including some ATV trails that are arguably parallel singletracks. The four trails this loop ties together are sometimes forgiving, sometime technical, and always big fun. You'll splash through creeks, dodge rocks, duck under trees, and test the performance of your tires' traction and your brake's grip.

But wait, there's more. Pack along a bathing suit because you'll want to soak your weary legs in the natural hot springs in lower Fifth Water Creek near the trail's end. Diamond Fork is as yummy as potato chips—bet you can't ride it just once.

General location: Diamond Fork is about 25 miles southeast of Provo and up Spanish Fork Canyon.

Distance: 24-mile loop. (See "Notes: for an optional shorter loop.)

Tread: 14 miles of singletrack and ATV trails that vary from silky to pebbly to primitive; 9 miles of sometimes rutted doubletrack; and a touch of required pavement. Cattle are herded to and from rangelands along these trails

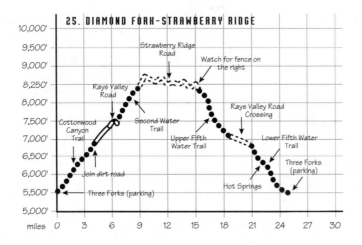

RIDE 25 DIAMOND FORK-STRAWBERRY RIDGE

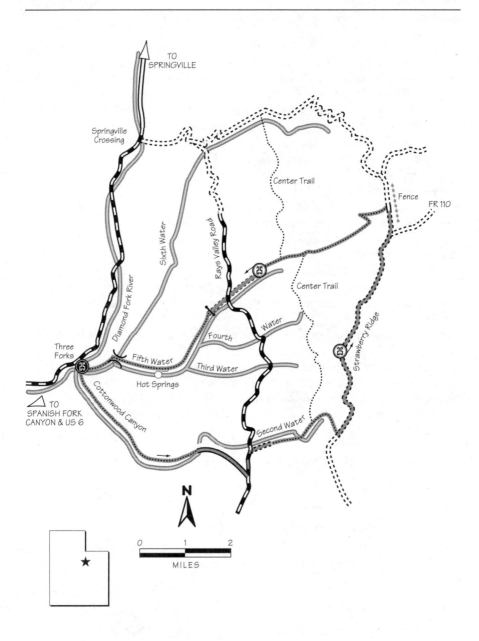

TO
SPRINGVILLE

Springville
Crossing

Center Trail

Fence

FR 110

Sixth Water

Rays Valley Road

Diamond Fork River

Center Trail

Water

Strawberry Ridge

Three
Forks

Fourth

Fifth Water

Third Water

Hot Springs

Cottonwood Canyon

TO
SPANISH FORK
CANYON & US 6

Second Water

N

0   1   2
MILES

seasonally; their impact on the trails can be significant. Contact the Spanish Fork Ranger District to learn where cattle are being ranged and when they are being moved.

Aerobic level: Strenuous. The route begins with nearly two hours of climbing to Strawberry Ridge. One-half dozen short, steep ascents punctuate Strawberry Ridge; each ascent is offset by a blazing downhill. The route culminates with a seemingly endless descent.

Technical difficulty: Level 2 to 4. Cottonwood Canyon and lower Fifth Water Trails are packed dirt with loose stones. Second Water and upper Fifth Water Trails are traveled less frequently, so expect quasi-primitive conditions. The Strawberry Ridge Road is packed dirt with variable rocks and ruts. There are a few level 4 to 5 sections on lower Fifth Trail where the path is rocky and clips the edge of steep slopes.

Elevation change: The trailhead is the lowest elevation at 5,520 feet. Strawberry Ridge undulates between 8,400 and 8,700 feet. Total elevation gain is 3,800 feet.

Season: This route is typically ridable from late May through October. Snowdrifts may linger on Strawberry Ridge. The upper portion of this route, above Rays Valley Road, is prime hunting ground during elk and deer season, which begins in late September and runs through October.

Services: There is no drinking water along this route. Surface waters should be avoided or purified because they may be tainted by cattle and natural hot springs. There are two Forest Service campgrounds (fee areas) 4 miles before the trailhead: Palmyra and Camp Diamond. Fast food restaurants are at the mouth of Spanish Fork Canyon 15 miles from the trailhead. Provo has all visitor services.

Hazards: This ride takes three to four hours for strong riders, more if you take a casual pace, so plan accordingly by packing ample water, food, tools, and clothing. Trail conditions can be highly variable. Avoid the Strawberry Ridge Road when wet; its clay base will clog derailleurs and turn wheels to cement doughnuts. Strawberry Ridge is a dangerous place during a lightning storm because you are often the tallest object. If you miss the unsigned turnoff for upper Fifth Water Trail from the Strawberry Ridge Road, you might add another day to your ride. The route's last 3 miles on lower Fifth Water Trail are very popular with hikers, especially on weekends and holidays, so ride cautiously and courteously.

Rescue index: You'll certainly pass hikers and bikers on the route's last 3 miles in lower Fifth Water. Along the rest of the route, you're on your own. Few motorists travel paved Rays Valley Road, which bisects the loop.

Land status: Uinta National Forest (Spanish Fork Ranger District).

Maps: USGS Rays Valley, Strawberry Reservoir NW, and Strawberry Reservoir SW, Utah.

Access: From Interstate 15, take Exit 261 for U.S. Highway 6 and Price. Travel east on US 6 to Spanish Fork Canyon. Five miles up the canyon, turn left/north

Waterfalls tumble down
lower Fifth Water.

for Diamond Fork, Palmyra, and Diamond campgrounds (between mileposts 183 and 184). The Three Forks parking area is 10 miles up the paved Diamond Fork Road and accommodates up to a dozen vehicles.

Notes on the trail: Cross the narrow footbridge over Diamond Fork, then cross a second footbridge over Sixth Water immediately to the right. Step across Cottonwood Canyon Creek (no footbridge) and you're on your way.

Cottonwood Canyon Trail is moderately strenuous and technical level 2 to 4 with a few more demanding sections thrown in for good measure. You'll cross the creek three times over the 0.5 mile. Each crossing (unbridged) can be deep during spring thaw but ridable later in the year. Pass the signed junction for Jocks Canyon, etc. after 2.8 miles, and then pick a smart line through "derailleur-bender" boulders. No foot dabs allowed! Ahead, the unmistakable odor of sulfur announces the presence of natural hot springs. Cross the creek twice more and then ride through a clearing alongside a wire fence to a doubletrack. Take the pebbly road uphill for 1 mile to paved Rays Valley Road.

Turn left, ride uphill for 0.5 mile, and then turn right at the bottom of the ensuing descent for Second Water Trail, Strawberry Ridge, and Center Trail. The doubletrack immediately turns to singletrack marked for the Great Western Trail. After 1 mile of climbing that takes more effort than seems necessary, cross the creek, push up a steep slope, and bend north to continue up the hollow. Cross the creek three more times while inching up the trail and then dragging your bike up a steep stretch that is chock-full of rocks.

At the signed junction for Center Trail 009 (left), stay right/straight toward Indian Spring and Strawberry Ridge. The singletrack widens to an ATV track and rises gently through charming aspens and conifers. When you reach Strawberry Ridge, take the doubletrack (Forest Road 135) left/north and up the first of five climbs to come. Just grin and bear it, knowing there is a turbo-charged descent beyond each climb.

After 5.5 miles along the ridge, watch for Forest Road 110 branching right/east at the bottom of a high-speed hill. (It's the only prominent doubletrack forking to the right along the ridge.) Continue straight on the ridge road for 0.5 mile. At the base of the next climb and where a wire fence parallels the ridge road on the right, fork sharply *left* onto the unsigned upper Fifth Water Trail, which begins as an ATV track. (A federal geodesic brass cap at the junction assures your location.) Whip through the turns, dodge tree limbs, and bend left to descend off a subtle ridge into the head of Fifth Water.

Follow the ATV track for about 1 mile, cross the creek at a spring, and continue dancing down the canyon on singletrack. Stay straight and down the canyon at the first Center Trail junction (left), cross the creek, and then pass the second Center Trail junction (right). The previous section was fun, but the ensuing track is a rage! Finally, the singletrack crosses the creek once more and joins a doubletrack. (Look for a cheater route to the right that will keep your toes dry.) Take the track through sweeping turns to Rays Valley Road, cross the road, and continue on lower Fifth Water Trail, but be alert to several sections that rate high on the pucker meter.

About 1 mile down, you come to a Y junction. The main trail is the left fork and crosses the creek (unbridged). The right fork is a nasty little cheater route that is the preferred choice during spring runoff when the creek is deep and swift flowing. You rejoin the cheater route 0.5 mile farther after another creek crossing. Pass a double-decker waterfall, then a second waterfall that announces the famed Fifth Water Hot Springs. Soak your bones and culminate the tour on a splendid path along the wooded creek and beneath ruddy cliffs.

You'll no doubt return to the trailhead feeling proud of your accomplishment. After all, that was a big chunk of terrain you just crossed. But you'll be quickly humbled when you reflect upon those who crossed the same terrain two centuries ago—on foot and horseback—without the convenience of trails and roads.

In 1776, Spanish padres Domínguez and Escalante sought a land route between missions in present-day New Mexico and California. Their expedition entered Utah near Vernal and then veered west across the Uinta Basin and toward the southern Wasatch Range. Despite reports from Indian guides about the troublesome terrain ahead, they forged across Strawberry Ridge, toiled through Diamond Fork, and descended rugged Spanish Fork Canyon to find fertile lands and friendly natives in Utah Valley. A 37-foot-tall cross, erected in 1981 atop Domínguez Hill at the mouth of Spanish Fork, commemorates their passage.

Intermediate-level bikers should not write off Diamond Fork because of the long miles and daunting trails. Simply ride the 16-mile inner loop. Take the Cottonwood Canyon Trail as described to Rays Valley Road. Instead of heading up Second Water Trail to Strawberry Ridge, ride Rays Valley Road 5 miles northward—up and down several hills—to the Fifth Water Trail junction. (Look for a stop sign on the left side of the road at the bottom of a screaming descent.) Finish the loop by descending lower Fifth Water Trail past the hot springs. (Be cautious of a few technical level 5 sections.) Ride this loop once and you'll return time and again.

RIDE 26 *MONKS HOLLOW*

As members of the muscle-powered family of recreationists, mountain bikers tend to frown upon energy-consumptive, exhaust-spitting, and otherwise deafening ATVs. But one good thing can be said about our axled brethren: they sure can pack down a good trail. Such is the case with Diamond Fork's Monks Hollow Trail. This designated ATV route is ideal for mountain bikes, and the narrow double-track is built for speed.

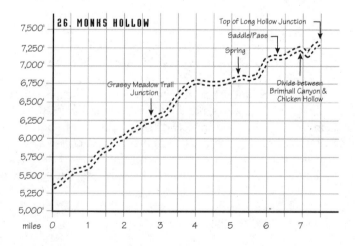

RIDE 26 MONKS HOLLOW

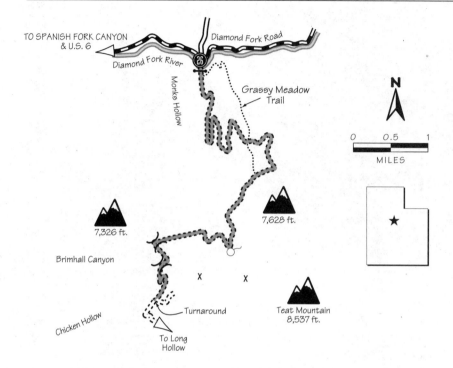

The generally smooth, packed-dirt trail is the main attraction. But there are some good vistas along the way. Early on, the back sides of Provo Peak and Mount Timpanogos line the distant western skyline. Farther up the trail, Spanish Fork Peak and Loafer Mountain vie for your attention. At the trail's summit, the tri-peaked arête of Mount Nebo cracks the southern horizon.

General location: Monks Hollow is in Diamond Fork, about 25 miles southeast of Provo.

Distance: 15 miles out-and-back, rather, up-and-back-down.

Tread: ATV trail: a narrow doubletrack to pessimists or dual singletracks for optimists.

Aerobic level: Moderate. It's all uphill at a steady grade, so the climb is what you make of it. The last mile is the steepest.

Technical difficulty: Level 2 to 3. Packed dirt with sections of sand, gravel, and rocks, but nothing too intimidating for even novice riders.

Elevation change: The trailhead is at 5,340 feet. The route rises steadily to 7,280 feet at the ridge separating Chicken Hollow and Long Hollow. Total climbing is just shy of 2,000 feet.

A distant view of Mount Nebo—monarch of the Wasatch—from atop Monks Hollow.

Season: April through October. This is an intermediate elevation ride, so it melts out relatively early in spring and may stay open after the first snow hits the nearby peaks.

Services: There is no drinking water along this route. There are two Forest Service campgrounds (fee areas) in Diamond Fork a few miles before the trailhead: Palmyra and Camp Diamond. There are fast food restaurants near the mouth of Spanish Fork Canyon on Utah State Highway 6. Provo has all visitor services.

Hazards: The faster you ride the more cautious you should be of changing trail conditions. Watch for other trail users, particularly ATVs. If returning to the trailhead via the optional, high-speed, grassy meadow route, anticipate an *unannounced,* sharp left-hand turn at the clearing's north end followed by a cobble-stuffed drop to the trailhead.

Rescue index: The farther you pedal from the trailhead the less likely you are to encounter others. ATV traffic is common on weekends and holidays. Motorists are numerous in Diamond Fork. Emergency contacts might be made from campground hosts at Palmyra and Camp Diamond Campgrounds.

Land status: Uinta National Forest (Spanish Fork Ranger District).

Maps: USGS Billies Mountain and Rays Valley, Utah.

Access: From Interstate 15, take Exit 261 for U.S. Highway 6 and Price. Travel east on US 6 and into Spanish Fork Canyon. Five miles up the canyon, turn left/north for Diamond Fork, Palmyra, and Diamond campgrounds (between mileposts 183 and 184). The trailhead (Forest Road 072) is 7.5 miles up the paved Diamond Fork Road. Look for a one-lane bridge over the river, a green steel gate, and a wooden barn in a clearing. It's just past a particularly scenic, Moab-esque redrock canyon.

Notes on the trail: From the trailhead next to the barn, pedal due south for 0.5 mile, fork left, and go through a gate signed "Monks Hollow Trail 126." Dip through the gully and crank up the opposing bank. Curve to the right and you are on your way up the ATV trail.

After the fourth switchback, the path crosses the top of a grassy meadow sloping downhill to the left. Watch for an unsigned ATV trail crossing the main route at right angles. (This is the optional grassy meadow return route to the trailhead. It's a Mach II, adrenaline-laden blast across the clearing. If you do take this route back to the trailhead, pull back on the reins at the meadow's north end because the trail turns sharply left at a cliff's edge. It then drops quickly on a rough, rock-strewn road to the trailhead.)

Keep chugging uphill and pass by a spring enclosed by a wooden fence. One mile farther, the trail crosses a saddle on a ridge overlooking Brimhall Canyon. One-half mile beyond, the trail crosses a second ridge that supplies distant but impressive views of Mount Nebo on the southern skyline. Drop through the whoop-te-doos and power up one more hill to a sloping ridge dividing Chicken Hollow from Long Hollow. This is the route's high point and suggested turnaround, although a trail forks left and climbs another 0.5 mile to a dead end. The return descent is a real screamer that offers opportunities to perfect your "YEE-HAs," unlike Billie Crystal who never really got the hang of it in the movie *City Slickers*.

RIDE 27 *BLACKHAWK TRAIL*

The Blackhawk Trail is for meat eaters—real carnivores who like their T-bones cooked rare. It's bloody good! Those who prefer well-done, pre-fab burgers disguised with special sauce had best look elsewhere. Blackhawk is way off the beaten path, but those who make the effort to find it and follow it will score big.

You'll need strong legs and keen handling skills for the many hills and ever-changing trail conditions. A good sense of direction will help because more than half of the route is not shown on the USGS quadrangles. This loop is more a collection of pack trails than government-issue, multi-recreational paths. Equestrians have known about Blackhawk for years and have effectively kept it a secret. Now mountain bikers are on to them.

RIDE 27 BLACKHAWK TRAIL

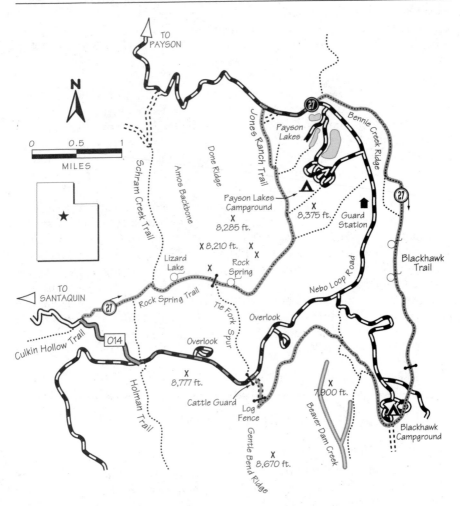

If you demand quality scenery to complement your outing, then Blackhawk serves up some beauties. You'll see angles of the southern Wasatch Range and distant Wasatch Plateau of which few others can boast. Mount Nebo, the monarch of the Wasatch at 11,928 feet, makes a brief but commanding appearance at midroute. When you ride, you'll learn quickly that Blackhawk is a stepping stone to a week's worth of trails that rarely feel a knobby's tread, but you'll have to be the tenacious, tolerant breed to chase down these elusive paths.

General location: Payson Canyon, 26 miles south of Provo.

Distance: 17.5-mile loop.

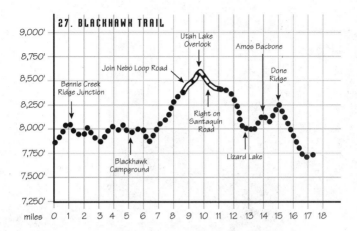

Tread: 14.5 miles of singletrack, 2 miles of pavement, 1 mile of gravel road.

Aerobic level: Strenuous. There are many incremental climbs of varying length and difficulty along the way.

Technical difficulty: Level 2 to 4. Trails are used more by horses than by bikers so expect variably eroded conditions.

Elevation change: The trailhead is at 7,700 feet. The highest point of 8,400 feet is reached along the Nebo Loop Road midroute. You'll tackle a dozen or so climbs, but each is no more than a few hundred vertical feet. Total gain is about 2,200 feet.

Season: June through October. Beware of hunters during the fall.

Services: Drinking water is available at Blackhawk and Payson Lakes Campgrounds (Forest Service fee areas). Payson offers most visitor services and a small bike shop.

Hazards: The trail's clay-based tread turns to gooey slop when wet and will stop you dead in your tracks. Allow one to two days of solid sunshine to dry the trail after a rain. This area may be popular during elk and deer hunting season in the fall. Be alert to and yield the trail to equestrians. After all, they were using these trails long before mountain bikes came on to the scene.

Rescue index: The trails are variably traveled by bikers, hikers, and equestrians. Campers regularly visit Blackhawk and Payson Lakes Campgrounds. Provo has medical facilities.

Land status: Uinta National Forest (Spanish Fork Ranger District).

Maps: USGS Birdseye and Payson Lakes, Utah.

Access: From Interstate 15, take Exit 254 for Payson and Utah State Highway 115 and follow the signs for Mount Nebo Scenic Loop. In Payson, turn left on 100 North/Utah State Highway 198, then right on 600 East (may be signed for Nebo Scenic Loop) and drive up Payson Canyon. The roadside trailhead/parking area is about 13 miles from town, near milepost 10, and is signed for Loafer Mountain Trail. If you reach Payson Lakes, you just missed the trailhead.

Brad leads the way along the Blackhawk Trail.

Notes on the trail: Go through the log fence and fork right on Blackhawk Trail 084 after a few hundred feet (Loafer Mountain Trail forks left). Climb gradually for 1.5 miles across meadows and through woods to an unsigned Y junction on the subtle Bennie Creek Ridge. Fork left/east, descend a steep gravelly shot, and then follow the trail southward, crossing meadows and mucky springs. Continue past a junction where a trail (signed for Blackhawk Trail) joins from the right/uphill. Here, the trail you just traveled is tagged for Loafer Mountain, contrary to signs near the trailhead. Regardless, you are on the straight and narrow now.

Blast down across a meadow, tiptoe through the spring, and climb into the musky woods. Ignore a faint path forking left atop the hill amidst groves of oak and maple, and continue contouring across nondescript terrain to a steel gate. Shortly thereafter, you'll connect with a doubletrack that intersects the paved access road to Blackhawk Campground (outhouse to left). Making your way through the cloverleaf campground is the most confusing part of the ride. Cross the road and continue on singletrack. Cross a second road and fork right in the middle of the large grassy field, angling toward a distant outhouse. Cross the campground road a third time and continue on the Blackhawk Trail. Climb, then descend to a four-way junction of trails. Stay straight to continue, or fork right and drop to a picnic site for a midroute snack and to collect your bearings. Whew!

Now the trail roughly contours high above the Beaver Dam Creek basin. Less than 1 mile ahead, you come to an unsigned Y junction; fork right and uphill. (The left fork descends quickly to Beaver Dam Creek.) About 1 mile farther, on a small ridge, you reach a multiple-signed junction. Stay straight for Blackhawk Trail 084 or fork right (uphill) to bail out to the Nebo Scenic Loop Road. The next mile receives less use than previous sections and can be technical level 3 to 4 at times. When you reach a log fence, fork right and pedal up a doubletrack to the paved road. Chow down some food and gulp a bottle of water because the half dozen climbs on the loop's "back nine" will sap your energy reserves.

Climb left up the Nebo Loop Road and pass a scenic pullout providing a view of Mount Nebo to the south and of Utah Lake to the north. Read the interpretive plaque about the region's human history. At the bottom of the ensuing descent, fork right on the Santaquin Canyon Road (Forest Road 014). Now, listen up!

Glide down the gravel road for 1 mile, not an inch farther, and fork right on the *unobtrusively* signed Rock Spring Trail 010. It's opposite the signed Culkin Hollow Trail. Descend like a bat out of hell, passing Holman Trail to the right and Schram Trail to the left. Pass Lizard Lake (more a marshy pond than a lake) and make the tough climb to a fence atop Amos Backbone. You're not done climbing until you reach the top of Done Ridge.

Now, for some well-earned descending on Jones Ranch Trail, stay left at three junctions where trails fork right to Payson Lakes. The trail forks immediately after the third junction and just beyond a fence. Stay left on what seems to be the less-traveled trail that rises over a small hump. Descend another 0.5 mile to the Nebo Loop Road; the trailhead is 0.5 mile uphill to the right. Now go find a steakhouse and order up a Fred Flintstone-size slab of "dead red." If you're a vegetarian, a Garden Burger will prove equally satisfying.

Park City/Kamas

RIDE 28 *PARK CITY MOUNTAIN RESORT*

Answering the plea for more public access to private lands surrounding town, Park City Mountain Resort has graciously opened its doors, rather its mountain, to the community of non-motorized recreationists. To the resort, mountain biker's are indebted and grateful. A newly designated network of dirt roads, doubletracks, and singletracks caters to bikers of intermediate ability and above. Unlike Deer Valley Resort across town, where you can "get a lift" and coast downhill all day, Park City Mountain Resort recaptures the original precept of cross-country mountain biking.

Although nearly 30 miles of routes are available on the resort, this abbreviated tour features many of the newly constructed singletrack trails. Your goal is Shadow Lake, a glacial pond that reflects some of the resort's steepest runs in Jupiter Bowl. But this route is more than simply logging miles on one- and two-lane dirt. It is a window to the bygone days when the clamber of picks and shovels shattered the still mountain air, and miners searched feverishly for pay dirt.

You'll pass a half dozen defunct mine sites along the way, many of which brought fortune to prospectors and mining magnates alike. Some brought only ruin. The story of Solon Spiro, after which one trail was named, is perhaps the most heart-breaking of all. The nephew of a pioneer merchant, Solon labored

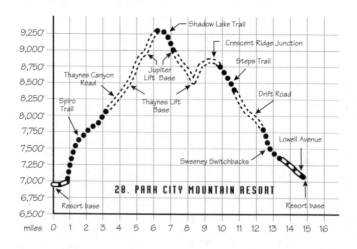

RIDE 28 PARK CITY MOUNTAIN RESORT

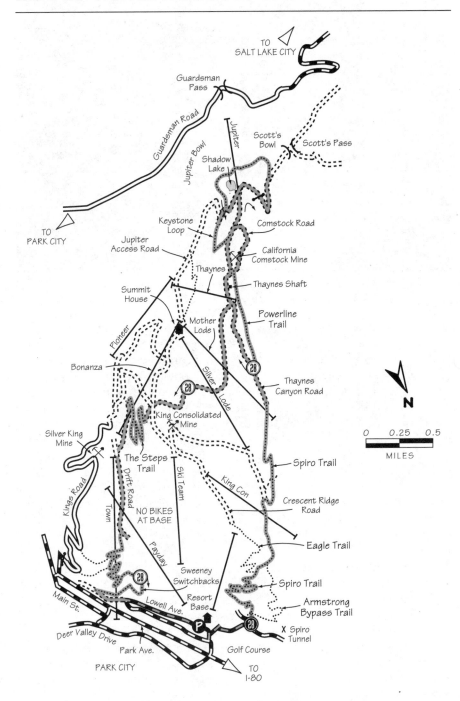

TO
SALT LAKE CITY

Guardsman
Pass

Guardsman Road

Jupiter Bowl

Jupiter

Scott's
Bowl

Scott's Pass

Shadow
Lake

Keystone
Loop

Comstock Road

Jupiter
Access Road

California
Comstock Mine

Thaynes

Thaynes Shaft

TO
PARK CITY

Summit
House

Pioneer

Mother
Lode

Powerline
Trail

Bonanza

Silver Lode

28

28

Thaynes
Canyon Road

King Consolidated
Mine

Silver King
Mine

The Steps
Trail

Drift Road

Ski Team

King Con

Spiro Trail

Crescent Ridge
Road

Kings Road

Town

NO BIKES
AT BASE

Payday

Eagle Trail

Sweeney
Switchbacks

Spiro Trail

28

Armstrong
Bypass Trail

Main St.

Lowell Ave.

Resort
Base

P

28

X Spiro
Tunnel

Deer Valley Drive

Park Ave.

Park City

Golf Course

TO
I-80

N

0   0.25   0.5

MILES

Rick and Jeff take a lap around Shadow Lake in Jupiter Bowl.

away in his uncle's store, saving his meager wages and buying stock in other mines. By the early 1900s, he amassed respectable wealth, bought claims bordering the golöath Silver King Mine, and incorporated his own company— Silver King Consolidated. But his workings produced little ore and the shaft was constantly flooded with icy waters. Pumping the water out was too expensive, so Spiro drove a tunnel nearly 3 miles long, and so straight you could see daylight from its end, to drain the water. He continued burrowing his mine until it was 5 miles into the mountain. But with little ore to show for his effort and with funds depleted, Spiro succumbed to defeat and sold his claim to his competitor, the Silver King, at a bargain price. Adding the greatest insult to injury, the Silver King tunneled just 40 feet farther in Spiro's old mine and struck a giant body of ore, one that Solon predicted was there all along.

General location: Park City Mountain Resort in Park City.

Distance: 14.5-mile loop, but there are over 30 miles of available routes on the resort.

Tread: 1.2 miles of pavement, 7.3 miles of doubletrack, 6 miles of singletrack.

Aerobic level: Moderate to strenuous. The first half is a long, moderate climb to and around Shadow Lake. After a short, steep grind midroute, the rest is downhill. Many peripheral routes can make your ride easier or tougher.

Technical difficulty: Level 2 to 4. The majority of the route is level 2 to 3, but Sweeney Switchbacks is level 4 because of rock outcropping in the tread.

Elevation change: The resort's parking lot at 6,900 feet. The Shadow Lake Trail rises to 9,300 feet. A midroute climb to Crescent Ridge brings the total gain to 2,600 feet.

Season: June through October, depending on snow thaw and snowfall.

Services: There is no drinking water along the route. Park City Mountain Resort Center offers dining and lodging. Park City offers all visitor services.

Hazards: Ride at prudent speeds, and be courteous to other trail users. Always yield to hikers, equestrians, and motor vehicles. The Steps Trail has sharp turns, and Sweeney Switchbacks has sharp, rocky turns. Be alert to maintenance operations and heavy machinery at any time and at any place on the resort. Do not enter any mines or mining structures because they may be in a state of decay and collapse. Mines may contain low levels of oxygen. All mining areas are private property.

Rescue index: These trails are frequently traveled but are not patrolled. Emergency assistance may be summoned from the resort center.

Land status: Park City Mountain Resort (private property).

Maps: USGS Brighton, Heber, Park City East, and Park City West, Utah. (Most trails are not shown; in fact, half of Park City is not shown on these grossly outdated maps.)

Access: From the intersection of Park Avenue and Deer Valley Drive, travel east to Park City Mountain Resort. Turn left on Lowell Avenue and park at the resort center. Parking is prohibited at the Crescent Road trailhead (tow zone).

Sources of additional information: Park City Mountain Resort (See Appendix B).

Notes on the trail: First some fine print. Park City may limit access or close any trails or roads to public use at any time. Obey all signs restricting travel and ride on open trails and roads only. Trail maps are available at the Crescent Road, Sweeney Switchbacks (Lowell-Empire Avenues), and King Road Trailheads, or by contacting the resort.

From the resort center, return down Lowell Avenue, turn left on Silver King, right on Three Kings Drive, then left on Crescent Road, all edging the golf course. The signed trailhead is at the upcoming left bend where a dirt road forks right. Fork left on the wide singletrack, and you're on your way to the top. After a few hundred yards, you come to a four-way junction of trails: Armstrong Bypass Trail forks right, a bailout to Crescent Road is left, Spiro Trail (your route) is straight. Gear down and inch up the mile-long climb through thick aspens and around a dozen turns. A lone aspen that was spared the trail builder's saw marks the junction with Eagle Trail. Stay straight (right) on Spiro and after 0.1 mile stay straight again (left) at the junction with upper Armstrong Bypass. (If you're a masochist for steeps, then Eagle Trail is your ticket to the top; others will blow a gasket.)

Spiro Trail rises gently to moderately through profuse timber and crosses sunny ski runs. Cross under King Con Lift, then descend to a right-hand curve across Broadway ski run where Claim Jumper Trail forks left. Stay on Spiro, cross a doubletrack (closed to bikes), keep climbing, and then fork left on the

Thaynes Canyon jeep road. (Lower Thaynes Canyon is closed to bikes.) The doubletrack rises steadily for almost 1 mile to the base of Thaynes Lift. If you're a singletrack purist, fork right 0.3 miles up the road on Thaynes Canyon Power Line Trail to reach the lift. It's a true backcountry one-laner that rarely feels the imprint of knobbies.

Just past Thaynes Lift and the massive tailing pile of the Thaynes Shaft, fork right to continue climbing on the Comstock Mine Road past the classic turn-of-the-century wooden mill. Fork left at a T junction and take the doubletrack 0.1 mile to the Thaynes Canyon jeep road. Jupiter Lift and Shadow Lake are 0.5 mile uphill.

Take a lap around Shadow Lake (counterclockwise) by first climbing the loose, rocky doubletrack. About 0.5 mile past the steel gate, fork left on a faint doubletrack that curves across Scott's Bowl and then narrows to singletrack around Shadow Lake. When you intersect a good doubletrack (the Jupiter Access Road), fork right, then immediately left, on Keystone Loops and return to the base of Thaynes Lift.

If your legs say it's "Miller Time," then retrace your tracks down Spiro to the resort center and belly up to the bar. Otherwise, fork right and climb the doubletrack to Crescent Ridge. It's steep initially, but then it levels for big-chain-ring cruising under Motherload and Silverload Lifts to Crescent Ridge (four-way junction of dirt roads). Here, your choices are many: fork right to climb to the Summit House for another lap to Shadow Lake, go straight and bomb down King Road to upper Main Street, or fork left and descend the Crescent Ridge Road then Eagle Trail to the trailhead.

But why ride doubletracks when there is more singletrack? Take the faded doubletrack to the *right* of the Crescent Ridge Road and head north from the resort signs for Silver Queen, etc. After 0.2 mile, fork right on The Steps Trail and descend 1 mile to the old gondola angle house. Pass the resort signs next to Town Lift and take the Drift Road downhill for 1 mile at the speed of sound. Fork right on a doubletrack signed for Payday and Town Runs (the lower Drift Road/Blanche ski run is closed to bikes); then fork left on a short singletrack that loops around to rejoin the Payday Road. Cross straight over and into the conifers (uphill from a resort sign for Creole and Quittin' Time) to culminate on the dizzying Sweeney Switchbacks Trail.

Conditions get pretty technical (level 4) on this famed dirt twisty, so watch your front wheel. To navigate the many intersections, remember this: *Always* fork in the direction that takes you back under the Town Lift overhead. When you join with a dirt road overlooking town, fork left, cross under Town Lift (again), and exit to Lowell Avenue. Coast to the resort center for après-bike festivities.

RIDE 29 *TOUR DE SUDS*

The Tour de Suds mountain-bike race is a long-standing Park City tradition dating back to 1983, when mountain bikes had fewer gears than fingers and toes and were nearly double the weight of today's high-tech breeds. The Tour began as an impromptu year-end event when local road racers would hop on their ATBs or cyclo-cross bikes and spend the day competing on dirt trails rather than on paved roads. Today, the fall classic is still the grand finale to a prosperous summer of fat-tire racing and adventures in the surrounding Wasatch Range. Although the present-day tour draws up to hundreds of entrants, both devoted racers and admitted non-competitive types, it has maintained its lighthearted, tongue-in-cheek appeal and is every bit a social event as it is a timed race. And it still culminates with a festive picnic with plenty of suds.

The Tour de Suds overflows with Park City history, starting with a blend of nineteenth- and twentieth-century architectural themes that make up Historic Main Street. Main is one of only a few business districts in the nation to be named to the National Register of Historic Places. In Daly Canyon (called Empire Canyon in the olden days), the route penetrates the haunting silence of yesteryear's silver boom, which literally put Park City, Utah, on the map in 1868. Farther on, the route passes the modernized Ontario Mine where, today, visitors can descend a mine shaft 1,500 feet and explore the old tunnels. On the route's top half, you cross the ski slopes of Deer Valley Resort, which has contributed to Park City's current boom.

General location: The Tour de Suds begins at the top of Main Street in Park City.

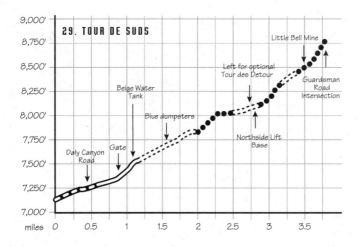

RIDE 29 TOUR DE SUDS

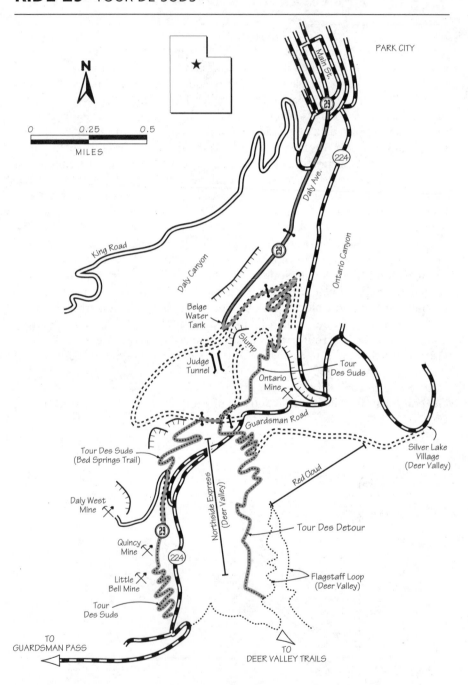

N

0   0.25   0.5

MILES

PARK CITY

Main St.

29

224

Daly Ave.

King Road

Daly Canyon

29

Ontario Canyon

Beige
Water
Tank

Slump

Judge
Tunnel

Ontario
Mine

Tour
Des Suds

Guardsman Road

Tour Des Suds
(Bed Springs Trail)

Northside Express
(Deer Valley)

Red Cloud

Silver Lake
Village
(Deer Valley)

Daly West
Mine

Quincy
Mine

29

224

Tour Des Detour

Little
Bell Mine

Tour
Des Suds

Flagstaff Loop
(Deer Valley)

TO
GUARDSMAN PASS

TO
DEER VALLEY TRAILS

Distance: About 4 miles one-way uphill. Distance changes slightly every time the trail is rerouted.

Tread: 1 mile of pavement, a bit of doubletrack, and the rest is twisting singletrack.

Aerobic level: Strenuous. The Tour de Suds is all uphill, but according to the laws of physics, what goes up must come down. The return ride is always exciting by either backtracking or descending any one of the trails at Deer Valley Resort.

Technical difficulty: Level 2 to 4. Portions of singletrack can have loose and imbedded stones, ruts, exposed roots, and hairpin turns.

Elevation change: The top of Main Street is at 7,100 feet. You'll climb to 8,800 feet on Guardsman Road for an elevation gain of 1,700 feet.

Season: Snow lingers on upper sections of the trail into May or June. The trail is usually ridable through October.

Services: There is no drinking water along the route. All visitor services are available in Park City.

Hazards: Do not enter any mines or mining structures because they may be in a state of decay and collapse. Mines may contain low levels of oxygen. All mining areas are private property. Be aware of and stay clear of construction activity on Deer Valley Resort.

Rescue index: This route is a local's favorite, so you'll likely encounter other trail users. Motorists commonly travel Guardsman Road. Emergency contacts can be made with lift operators and patrols in Deer Valley Resort. Park City has medical facilities.

Land status: The route crosses private property owned by Deer Valley Resort and United Park City Mines. Although it is often difficult to stay on course, be aware that not all trails in this area are open to public use or to mountain bikes. Obey all signs restricting travel.

Maps: USGS Brighton, Heber, Park City East, and Park City West, Utah. None of the trail is shown.

Access: The public parking lot at the top of Main Street and next to the Wasatch Brew Pub makes for a good staging area. It's strategically located for après-ride festivities, too.

Sources of additional information: Deer Valley Resort; Mountain Trails Foundation (See Appendix B).

Notes on the trail: The Tour de Suds Trail has been rerouted in the past and will no doubt be rerouted in the future to accommodate Deer Valley Resort expansion. Deer Valley is committed to relocating and resigning the trail as is necessary. Every year brings a surprise. The lower half has been status quo for some time; the upper half gets booted around because it is impinged upon by new ski runs and lifts.

The Tour de Suds is nearly impossible to describe, difficult to navigate your first time, but always loads of fun to ride. Watch for green trail buttons and orange trail disks marking the route. If you get off track, don't worry, be

Mountain bike first;
drink "suds" later.

happy. There are miles of trails crisscrossing the area; exploring them and devising your own route is half the fun.

From the parking lot next to the Wasatch Brew Pub, pedal up Main Street then continue up Daly Avenue. In less than 1 mile, pavement turns to dirt and broken asphalt. Go around the gate (the landowner graciously allows access for hikers and bikers), then counterclockwise around the big beige water tank. Pass a dirt road forking right (it leads to the Judge Tunnel and Lower Daly Canyon) and continue climbing on the doubletrack.

Turn *sharply* right at the blue dumpster and steel posts and follow the doubletrack on the right/west side of the small ridge. Ignore the singletrack running up the ridge and under the power lines, unless you like crushing climbs. The track narrows briefly to singletrack where it passes through a heap of rustic, and rusted, mine equipment. Bend sharply left and then right to an overlook of Ontario Canyon and paved Guardsman Road. Pedal up the doubletrack on the left/east side of the small ridge. Ignore the first right but take the second right just after passing under the power lines. Fork sharply left and follow the green trail button up a steep, twisting singletrack through dense aspens. When the trail levels, stay right and connect with a doubletrack. Take the track up to a T junction with a good dirt road near the base of Northside Express Lift. Whew! Don't give up hope.

The old classic route went to the right and then up the "Bed Springs" Trail, a serpentining singletrack to Guardsman Road. But in 1998 that section was closed for resort construction. The alternate route follows the new "Tour des De Tour." (Orange trail disks should mark the way.)

Ready? At the T junction, take the twisty singletrack to the left, cross paved Guardsman Road, and continue on singletrack. This section is steep, forever turning, and laced with tree roots. When you intersect a doubletrack, your choices are two. Bail out and descend to Silver Lake Village Deer Valley's mountain bike center) or keep climbing. If you choose the later, climb the road for about 0.25 mile and fork left on the continued Tour des De Tour. Climb for nearly 2 miles up sometimes steep, sometimes cruising, singletrack until you intersect Flagstaff Loop (Trail 8) at a dirt road. More choices. Return the way you came, or take Flagstaff over to Deer Valley's main trail system and descend any number of trails to Silver Lake Lodge. (See Ride 30 Deer Valley Resort.)

RIDE 30 *DEER VALLEY RESORT*

Deer Valley has long been recognized as one of the nation's most sophisticated ski areas. Set in an atmosphere of rustic mountain elegance, the resort is renowned for its manicured ski runs, uncompromised hospitality, and gourmet, slope-side dining.

Deer Valley has emerged as an acclaimed mountain-bike destination also, blending a network of trails into its refined alpine surroundings. The resort's singletrack riding is beyond compare, just like its ski runs, but Deer Valley is also a hub for exploring peripheral routes stemming to Park City and the nearby Wasatch Range.

Deer Valley caters to first-time through advanced mountain bikers, offering meandering trails and exacting descents. The resort boasts over 45 miles of trails accessible from Sterling Lift with more than 10 miles of additional trails on the lower mountain from Snow Park Lodge (chair lift access). Mountain bike sales, rentals, and repairs are available at Silver Lake Village. Instructional clinics and tours can be arranged by reservation. All together, Deer Valley offers the ultimate mountain-biking package for visitors and locals alike.

General location: Deer Valley is located in Park City.

RIDE 30 UPPER DEER VALLEY RESORT

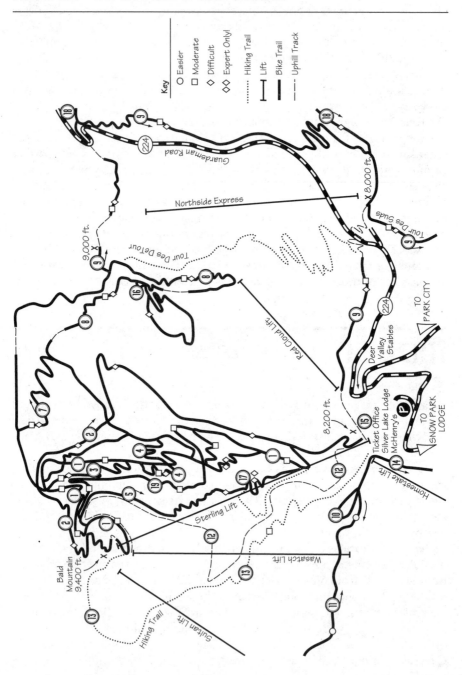

RIDE 30 LOWER DEER VALLEY RESORT

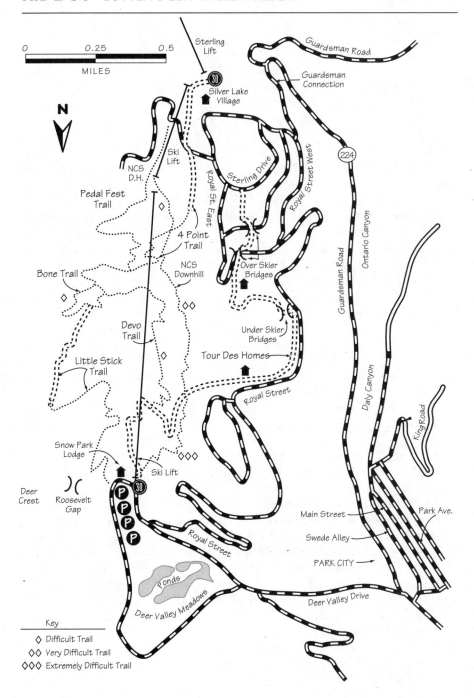

0   0.25   0.5
MILES

N

Sterling
Lift

Guardsman Road

Guardsman
Connection

30

Silver Lake
Village

Ski
Lift

NCS
D.H.

Royal St. East

Sterling Drive

Royal Street West

224

Guardsman Road

Ontario Canyon

Pedal Fest
Trail

4 Point
Trail

NCS
Downhill

Over Skier
Bridges

Bone Trail

Devo
Trail

Under Skier
Bridges

Tour Des Homes

Daly Canyon

King Road

Little Stick
Trail

Royal Street

Snow Park
Lodge

Ski Lift

Deer
Crest

Roosevelt
Gap

P
30
P
P
P

Royal Street

Main Street

Park Ave.

Swede Alley

PARK CITY

Ponds

Deer Valley Meadows

Deer Valley Drive

Key

◇ Difficult Trail
◇◇ Very Difficult Trail
◇◇◇ Extremely Difficult Trail

Distance: More than 45 miles of trails accessible from Sterling Lift at Silver Lake Village. More than 10 miles of trails on the lower mountain between Silver Lake Village and Snow Park Lodge.

Tread: Singletrack with a bit of doubletrack connectors.

Aerobic level: Easy to moderate. How tough can it be riding downhill all day?

Technical difficulty: Level 2 to 5. Only McHenry's Loop and Sultan Road are level 2. Other trails range from silky to savage.

Elevation change: The base of Sterling Lift (Silver Lake Village) is at 8,200 feet. The lift's summit atop Bald Mountain is at 9,400 feet. Elevation change is 1,200 feet. Squeeze in seven chair rides and you'll tally nearly 10,000 feet of vertical.

Season: Chair lift service operates Wednesday through Sunday, 10 A.M. to 5:30 P.M., from mid-June through September, conditions permitting, and on weekends only after Labor Day. Ride passes for 1998 were $15 all-day, $8 single ride, and $5 single ride for seniors and children. Before and after the resort's official season, the trail system is available for use, but your own two legs must provide the needed lift.

Services: Lodging, dining, bike service, and rentals are available at Silver Lake Village. All visitor services are available in Park City.

Hazards: Although the trail system is regularly maintained, heavy use can cause eroded conditions. Know your skill level and choose your trail accordingly. Trails may have any combination of packed and loose sediment, exposed rocks and roots, steep descents, sharp turns, and trees very nearby. The most thrilling and challenging trails often combine all these elements at once.

Rescue index: The trail system is not regularly patrolled. Assistance can be summoned from lift operators at the base and summit of Sterling Lift. Don't send up a distress flare if you get a flat tire. Park City has a hospital.

Land status: Deer Valley is a privately owned and operated resort. Routes leaving the resort's designated trail system enter adjacent private lands where public recreational use may not be permitted.

Maps: Pick up a Deer Valley Resort biking and hiking map at Silver Lake Village.

Access: From Interstate 80, take Exit 145 for Park City. Travel south on Utah State Highway 224 and into Park City via Park Avenue. At a stoplight, turn left on Deer Valley Drive. After 1 mile, bear left, following signs for Deer Valley Ski Resort to access Snow Park Lodge and the mountain's lower trails. (A sharp, right turn leads to the bottom of Park City's Main Street.) To reach Silver Lake Village, bear right on Marsac Avenue, and then travel up Ontario Canyon on Guardsman Road/UT 224. Just past the Ontario Mine and where Guardsman Road bends sharply right at the horse stables, turn left on Guardsman Connection Road. Shortly uphill, turn right on Royal Street East to reach Silver Lake Village. Underground parking is available, but clearance is too low for most bike-topped cars!

Who says getting to the top is tough?

Sources of additional information: Deer Valley Resort; Mountain Trails Foundation (See Appendix B).

Notes on the trail: In 1998, Deer Valley claimed to have 18 trails on the upper mountain and 6 trails on the lower mountain. Here are some highlights:

Naildriver Downhill #1 (2.9 miles, level 2 to 3): This is Deer Valley's least difficult downhill route. At the top, you'll enjoy a grand vista of the Wasatch Range to the west, of the Uinta Mountains to the east, and of Jordanelle Reservoir in the valley below. Watch for a few sharp turns, loose tread, and washboards. From the top of Sterling Lift, go right/west and descend the switchbacks off the back of Bald Mountain to the meadow junction. Follow brown posts for Trail 1 and coast all the way to the lift's base at Silver Lake Village. Hop on the lift and start exploring other routes.

Homeward Bound #2 (3 miles, level 2 to 4): Those who "feel the need for speed" will gravitate to Homeward Bound for its tight turns up top, sweeping curves midroute, and fast straightaways near the bottom. For the full downhill effect, head up to the reflector shields atop Bald Mountain from the lift's summit. Ricochet off the backside of Bald Mountain, race through the meadow, and curve back into the trees. Then let gravity pull you downhill at breakneck speeds to the base of Sterling Lift.

Super G Trees #3 and G.S. Trees #4 (1.3 miles combined, technical level 3 to 4): These trails are the fat-tire equivalent to ski racing, only the gates are densely packed, unyielding aspen trees. The turns just keep on coming which means you must shift quickly and finesse your brakes. Your riding skill will improve tenfold after just one run. Descend off Bald Mountain on Naildriver #1, but when you reach the meadow junction, fork right and slightly uphill to enter the aspen "gates." Yield to other bikers where the path crosses Naildriver several times.

Aspen Slalom #5 and Freestyle #17 (2 miles, level 3 to 5): Like a double shot of espresso, these trails will have you wide-eyed and "amp'd." Tight turns through aspens lead to even tighter, steeper turns. Much of the route follows under the Sterling Lift, so you can wow others who are critiquing from above. Exit the summit of Sterling Lift as you would for Naildriver but do not descend off the back to the meadow junction. Instead fork right on a doubletrack, and descend Sunset Ski Run. One-half mile down and under the lift, fork left on Aspen Slalom #5. Freestyle #17 forks left from Aspen Slalom farther down.

Flagstaff Loop #8 (4 miles, level 2 to 3): Milk your single-ride lift pass by touring the resort's western slopes on a rolling cross-country loop through meadows, aspens, and conifers with a big view of the resort below. You'll actually give your legs a workout and maybe even break a sweat. Descend off Bald Mountain on either Naildriver or Homeward Bound to the meadow junction. Fork left and take a doubletrack westward along the resort's perimeter. Descend, then climb toward Flagstaff Peak but not all the way to the top. Fork right on a meadow-bound singletrack and race into the aspens. Be quick with the shifters or you'll stall midstroke on a pair of sharp, steep turns. Pass the turnoff for (upper) Tour de Suds, cross a dirt road, and race to the summit of Red Cloud Lift, then back. Retrace your outbound tracks to Naildriver #1 at the meadow junction, or take a curving course to Deer Camp and Homeward Bound.

Twist and Shout #6 (0.5 mile, level 4 to 5): a.k.a., "twitch and pitch," this is a quick but thrilling, white-knuckle drop through steep, angular turns, and past sideswiping trees. Needless to say, the double-black-diamond rating is for fearless types who have perfected short radius turns and "hang-your-butt-off-the-back" descending. Twist and Shout forks right off Naildriver 1.7 miles from the top of Sterling Lift, then rejoins Naildriver at the old mine after which the trail was named.

McHenry's Loop #10 (0.7 mile, level 1 to 2): This is the perfect trail to test your skills and check out your bike. It's ideal for children before they head up the lift. From the base of Sterling Lift, take the dirt road to the left past the base of Homestake Lift and enter the trees. Take a lap through the muffled woods, and return to Sterling Lift geared up for bigger adventures.

Uphill Route #12 (1.9 miles, 1,200-foot gain at about 10 percent grade, level 2): In the *real* world of mountain biking, there is no such thing as a free lunch—you have to earn your downhills. Snub the Sterling Lift and put the hammer down. You'll enjoy good views of Jordenelle Reservoir and the western Uinta Mountains if you dare lift your nose from the handlebar. From the base of Sterling Lift, take the doubletrack uphill and under the lift. (Do not ride up Naildriver #1.) A few hundred feet up, fork left and take the gravel road all the way to the top. Join the pro-circuit if you beat your buddies who are lounging on the lift.

Four Point Trail #14 (1 to 2 miles, level 3 to 5): This trail connects Silver Lake Village with Snow Park Lodge on the lower mountain and accesses a variety of trails. You'll leave the lift-served area, so be prepared to ride back up on Tour de Homes. Most trails are unsigned, so be willing to accept the consequences of whatever turn you take. All trails have highly technical sections, but Little Stick has a straightaway where you can approach highway speeds. From the base of Sterling Lift, pedal uphill beneath Homestake Lift and alongside the condominiums. Cross a paved road and climb a gravelly doubletrack. Where the track crosses a ski run, go straight, and dart into the fir trees on a singletrack. You'll wind through groves of fir and cross more ski runs. Regardless of the route you choose, you'll end up at Snow Park Lodge below.

Tour de Homes (1.5 miles, level 2): This is the main uphill route from Snow Park Lodge to Silver Lake Village and is popular with racers in training. In fact, it is the cornerstone of the NORBA National Championship Series racecourse. The route follows doubletracks and singletracks and gains about 800 feet. From Snow Park Lodge, pedal up the gravel access road on the right side of Clipper Lift. Round a right-hand turn, climb 0.25 mile, and bend sharply left at an overlook of Park City. At a junction of trails a few hundred yards ahead, fork right, and follow alongside condos whose property lines are posted "no trespassing." A flat stretch precedes a section where you overlook Ontario Canyon. Pass under a skier's bridge, and then bend sharply right. The route narrows to singletrack and runs behind slope-side condos. You'll cross over two skier's bridges, each requiring a short blast of power, and then intersect paved Sterling Drive. Take the road left or right to Silver Lake Village.

Twistin' and shoutin' at Deer Valley.

Deer Valley has played host to numerous mountain biking competitions, including the annual Park City Pedalfest, NORBA National Championship Series, and the Deer Valley Rally (Utah State Championship Race). But there is more to do at Deer Valley than mountain bike. The resort boasts a full calendar of summer activities, including performances by the Utah Symphony, Repertory Dance Theater, and folk and bluegrass bands. Plus there are many shops and restaurants at Silver Lake Village. At Deer Valley Stables you can hop in the saddle of a real steed and ride horseback on a variety of trails.

RIDE 31 *BEAVER CREEK TRAIL*

Punishing climbs, white-knuckle descents, and the pursuit of high-caliber singletrack (arguably the purest form of mountain biking) lure many to the world of fat-tire cycling. But for those who are just starting out, or for families with children, something a bit more mellow might be in order. Like a radio station that plays easy-listening tunes rather than head-banging rock, the Beaver Creek Trail is perfect for those seeking the softer side of mountain biking. You won't have to worry about dicing it up with a pack of wanna-be NORBA champs; they're too busy charting their heart rate on marathon rides

RIDE 31 BEAVER CREEK TRAIL

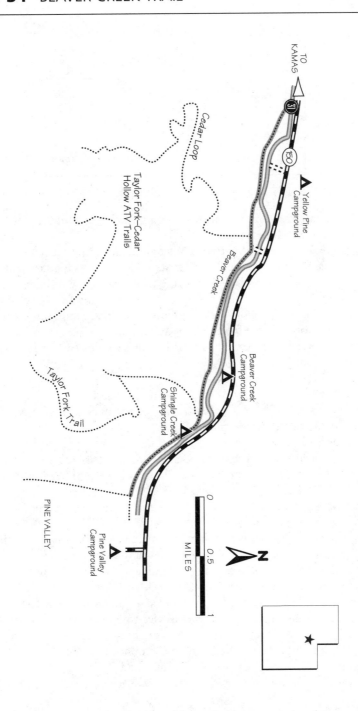

TO KAMAS

150

Yellow Pine Campground

Cedar Loop

Taylor Fork–Cedar Hollow ATV Trails

Beaver Creek

Beaver Creek Campground

Shingle Creek Campground

Taylor Fork Trail

PINE VALLEY

Pine Valley Campground

0

0.5

1

MILES

N

★

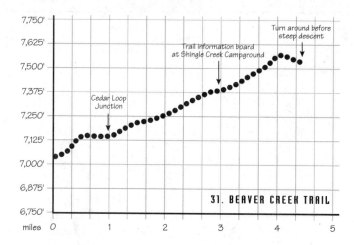

across entire mountain ranges. Instead, you'll likely encounter other first-time bikers with their children, too.

Beaver Creek is neither dirt road nor singletrack but rather a "mega-track." It is part of the Taylor Fork ATV trail system. Sure, ATVs tend to be noisy and obtrusive, but they can pack down a fine trail for mountain bikes. The route parallels a gently meandering creek pooled occasionally by beaver dams. On one side lies the creek's willow- and grass-filled floodplain, and on the other side, forested slopes of the lower Uinta Mountains.

General location: Beaver Creek Trail is located 6 miles east of Kamas on the Mirror Lake Highway.

Distance: 9.5 miles out-and-back.

Tread: ATV trail. Think of it as an ultra-wide singletrack.

Aerobic level: Easy. There's a rude little hill at the outset; thereafter, it's about as flat as a true off-road ride can be.

Technical difficulty: Level 2. Mostly packed dirt but there are ruts here and there plus sections of small rocks that may make your saddle spank your butt lightly.

Elevation change: The route is virtually flat. The trailhead is the lowest elevation at 7,020 feet. The trail rises to 7,600 feet at the trail's turnaround for a *whopping* elevation gain of 600 feet. You'll feel fresh at day's end, not bonked.

Season: Beaver Creek Trail is ridable from mid-May through October. The trail and adjacent campgrounds may be very active on weekends and holidays.

Services: There is no water tap at the trailhead, but you'll find water taps, outhouses, and picnic tables at Shingle Creek and Beaver Creek campgrounds. Most visitor services are found in Kamas (6 miles west of the trailhead); otherwise, Park City is the closest full-service town (15 miles west of Kamas).

Hazards: This route is pretty tame. A few short, rocky patches may prove challenging for children and first-time mountain bikers. Beaver Creek Trail is part of the Taylor Fork ATV area, so watch for OHVs.

A beaver pond reflects forested slopes of the Uinta Mountains.

Rescue index: The campgrounds passed along the trail are very popular on weekends and holidays, and the Mirror Lake Highway/Utah State Highway 150 is well traveled. The nearest telephone is at the Beaver Creek Inn, located 3 miles west of the trailhead. Kamas has a medical clinic; Park City (15 miles west of Kamas) has a hospital.

Land status: Wasatch-Cache National Forest (Kamas Ranger District).

Maps: USGS Hoyt Peak and Woodland, Utah. Also, Wasatch-Cache National Forest: Taylor Fork-Cedar Hollow ATV Trail System (available through the Kamas Ranger District).

Access: From the intersection of Main and Center Streets in Kamas, travel east on the Mirror Lake Highway/Utah State Highway 150 to milepost 6 at the Wasatch-Cache National Forest boundary. The trailhead is on the right/south side of the highway.

Notes on the trail: The Kamas Ranger District has initiated a recreational use fee for the Mirror Lake Highway/UT 150. Fees per vehicle for 1998 were $3 per day and $6 per week if you park and recreate anywhere along the Mirror Lake Highway.

From the trailhead, cross the wooden footbridge over Beaver Creek and follow the trail left/east alongside the lush floodplain. Tackle the short, modest hill and then breathe a sign of relief knowing that the tough part is over.

One-half mile down the trail, a dirt road enters from the left; stay straight. One-half mile farther, pass a trail to the right signed for Cedar Loop; it's a good climb for hammerheads. Shortly ahead, a second dirt road enters from the left, marked by a steel gate. Again, stay straight on what is now a dirt road and pass a corral where the route reverts to an ATV trail. A short, rocky stretch, a.k.a. a rock garden, will test your handling skills.

Pass Beaver Creek Campground and a trail information board 3 miles from the trailhead. It directs ATV users toward Cedar Loop—rough and rocky (uphill) or Beaver Creek—not so tough (straight). Hmm, let's go straight. Go through Shingle Creek Campground and stay on a westward bearing where the trail joins and branches from campground roads; then pass a reflective pool created by the trail's namesake rodents.

Descend a bit and enter a small clearing marked by a ponderosa pine with a split trunk on the north side of the trail. This is the recommended turnaround point because the trail ahead descends steeply to Pine Valley Campground and ends anyway. Return in the opposite direction, using caution while descending the steep hill near the trailhead.

For a shorter version, embark from Shingle Creek or Beaver Creek Campgrounds at midroute.

RIDE 32 *SOAPSTONE BASIN*

Soapstone Basin is a fast-paced, backcountry tour looping around a broad valley pocketed with groves of fir and aspen. Miniature wildflowers speckle the sunny, alpine meadows like paint spattered from an artist's brush. By and large, you won't find staggering views of mountain peaks along the main loop, although the Uinta Mountains do reveal themselves shyly from time to time. If you venture off course to the Bluffs overlook, however, you'll find a view that will make acrophobes tremble. Here, the Duchesne River has carved a gorge over 2,000 feet deep. The river's headwaters trickle from snowfields that cloak the Uinta Mountains—home to Utah's tallest peak, King's Peak, rising to 13,528 feet.

General location: Soapstone Basin is located about 15 miles east of Kamas and 4 miles south of the Mirror Lake Highway.

Distance: 16.5-mile loop, including a 2.5-mile spur.

Tread: Packed- and soft-dirt doubletracks with variable imbedded rocks and ruts.

Aerobic level: Moderate. The initial hill is the toughest, and it's not that bad. The rest of your time will be spent cruising on mostly fast-paced doubletracks around the rolling alpine basin. The optional spur up to the Bluffs involves a short-steep climb.

RIDE 32 SOAPSTONE BASIN

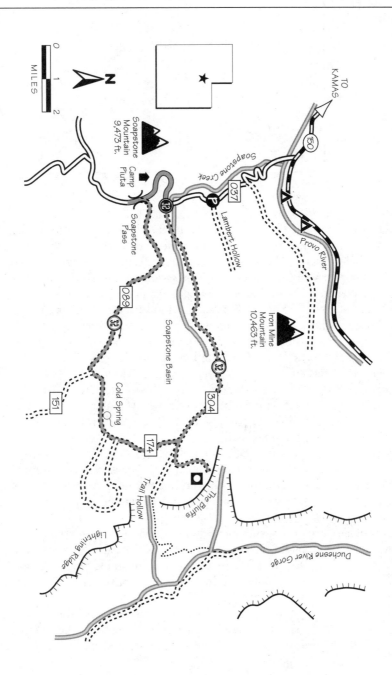

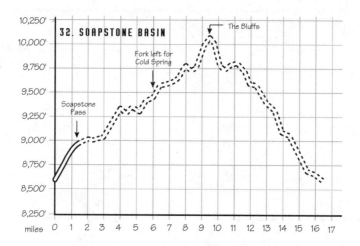

Technical difficulty: Level 2 to 3. Most of the doubletracks are packed dirt with some imbedded rocks, but the tread can turn to soft dirt during prolonged dry spells. The loop's second half follows a lumpy and bumpy doubletrack that will force you out of the saddle to absorb the shock.

Elevation change: The trailhead/parking area near Lambert Hollow is the route's lowest elevation at 8,570 feet. The loop begins with a sustained, 1.5-mile, 480-foot climb to Soapstone Pass (elevation 9,080 feet). The route rolls gently across the basin, rising to 9,800 feet at its eastern tip. It then drops slowly back to the trailhead. Total climbing for the loop is about 1,320 feet. If you venture to the Bluffs overlook, you'll face a 0.5-mile-long, 360-foot climb.

Season: The Soapstone Basin road is usually snow free from late May/early June through October. This route is extremely popular with outdoorsmen during elk and deer hunting season (end of September through October). Sheep range in the basin seasonally.

Services: There is no drinking water along this route. The Mirror Lake Highway/Utah State Highway 150 is lined with Forest Service Campgrounds (fee areas). Kamas offers most visitor services but no bike shop. Backcountry camping is available near the trailhead and along the route, unless posted otherwise.

Hazards: There are no unusual hazards along the loop. Be alert to OHVs and four-wheel-drive vehicles. If you take the spur to the Bluffs overlook, use caution near cliffs; the blocky limestone may be unstable and break away. Be prepared for changing alpine weather. The open basin can be a dangerous place during a lightning storm.

Rescue index: You may encounter OHVs and vehicles along the route. Campers and motorists are numerous along the Mirror Lake Highway/UT 150. Kamas (17 miles away) has a medical clinic, and Park City (nearly 30 miles away) has a hospital.

A vertigo-inducing view of the Duchesne River gorge from the Bluffs.

Land status: Wasatch-Cache National Forest (Kamas Ranger District).

Maps: USGS Iron Mine Mountain and Soapstone Basin, Utah.

Access: From the center of Kamas, travel 14.5 miles east on the Mirror Lake Highway/UT 150 and then turn right on the Soapstone Basin Road (Forest Road 037). The gravel road can be rough for passenger cars. Drive uphill 2 miles, turn right at the Iron Mine Lake junction toward Camp Piuta and Wolf Creek Road, and continue on Forest Road 037. Park 1 mile farther at a backcountry campsite near Lambert Hollow, or continue for another mile to where the loop officially begins.

Notes on the trail: The Kamas Ranger District collects a recreational use fee of $3 per vehicle per day or $6 per vehicle per week for any travelers who park and recreate along and adjacent to the Mirror Lake Highway.

The loop begins where Forest Road 304 intersects Forest Road 037. Head up FR 037 (right) toward Wolf Creek and Piuta; you'll return on FR 304 from Cold Spring. After 1.5 miles of steady climbing (stop grumbling), you reach Soapstone Pass. Fork left for Cold Spring on Forest Road 089 (a designated ATV route) and enter, then exit, a darkened grove of trees. At a T junction about 4.5 miles from Soapstone Pass, fork left on Forest Road 174 for Cold Spring and Iron Mine Creek. Wheel across breezy meadows endowed with a plethora of wildflowers.

Pass Cold Spring, then stay left at two junctions where doubletracks fork right toward Lightning Ridge. On the east side of the basin, you come to the junction for Trail Hollow Trail. Fork left to continue the loop on FR 304; fork right for Trail Hollow Trail to take the optional, but highly recommended, 1.5-mile out-and-back spur to the Bluffs overlook. If you choose the latter (and you should), then descend the doubletrack a few hundred yards and fork left. Climb a short, tough hill and wander to the Bluffs overlook. You'll know when to stop!

Unlike the mediocre vistas along the main loop, the view from the Bluffs takes your breath away like an Arctic plunge. You toe the edge of the 2,000-foot-deep Duchesne River gorge and gaze at 12,000-foot-tall Uinta Mountain peaks. The combined negative and positive relief exceeds a vertical mile.

Although you might never guess, the Uinta Mountains are a physiographic oddity because they are the only major mountain range in the nation that run west-east. The Uinta's crest is the axis of a major anticline that bowed and lifted miles of the Earth's crust from great depths. Uplift and subsequent erosion, most recently by glaciers, have exposed the fold's quartzite core in the range's tallest peaks. These metamorphic rocks date back over 1.5 billion years to the Precambrian Era.

Return to the loop junction and continue northwest on FR 304. Climb a bit, and then enjoy the gradual 5-mile-long descent back to the trailhead. Some sections along the way can be jarring because of rocks in the road, and your toes may get soaked when crossing Soapstone Creek, but memories of views enjoyed earlier will smooth the ride.

RIDE 33 *LITTLE SOUTH FORK OF PROVO RIVER TRAIL*

Little South Fork of Provo River Trail is another of those way-out-there singletracks that mountain bikers have recently gone gaga over. The 8.5-mile downhill trail is well worth the hour-and-a-half drive from the Wasatch Front. But the thrill does not come easy. The near 3,000-foot climb to the upper trailhead consumes a couple of hours of solid effort. But when you reach the summit, you'll poach some good views of the distant Uinta Mountains, which shape the skyline like humpbacked whales breaching the ocean. Then you'll embark on an 8-mile descent on a singletrack that you'll wish was right in your backyard. You won't find Little South Fork splashed on posters or mentioned in flashy magazines. Let's keep it that way.

General location: 25 miles southeast of Park City; 25 miles northeast of Heber.

Distance: A gung-ho, 22-mile loop or a wimpy, 10-mile point-to-point (see "Notes").

Tread: 5 miles of pavement, 3 miles of gravel road, 6 miles of doubletrack, and 8 miles of singletrack.

Aerobic level: Strenuous. It's all uphill to the upper trailhead, then all downhill to the finish except for one short, rude hill near the end.

Technical difficulty: Level 1 to 3. Gravel roads can have washboards; doubletracks can have ruts and rocks; and singletracks can have variable rocks, loose tread, and deadfall. The upper trail has several small, shallow creek fords. The lower trail has one significant creek ford (see "Hazards").

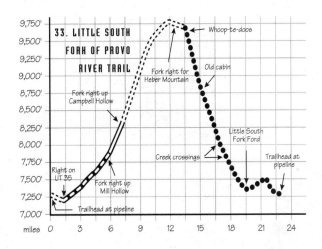

RIDE 33 LITTLE SOUTH FORK OF PROVO RIVER TRAIL

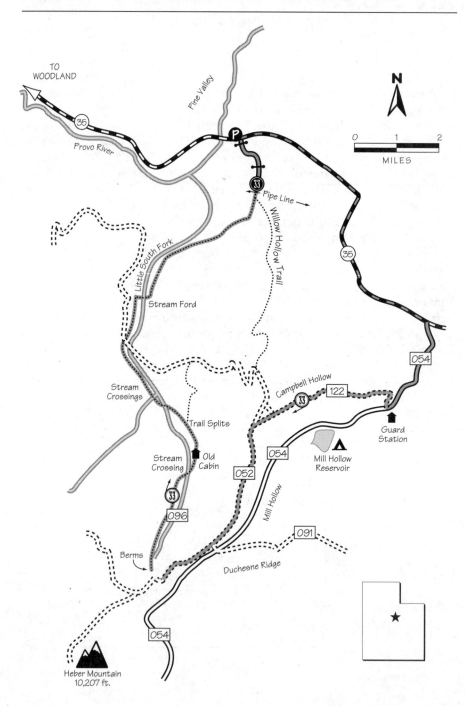

TO
WOODLAND

Pine Valley

N

35

Provo River

Pipe Line →

Willow Hollow Trail

33

35

Little South Fork

Stream Ford

054

Stream
Crossings

Campbell Hollow

122

33

Trail Splits

054

Guard
Station

Stream
Crossing

Old
Cabin

052

Mill Hollow
Reservoir

33

096

Mill Hollow

091

Berms

Duchesne Ridge

054

Heber Mountain
10,207 ft.

0   1   2
MILES

★

Heading down Little South Fork.

Elevation change: The trailhead is at 7,320 feet, but the lowest point of 7,200 feet is on Utah State Highway 35. The route tops out at 9,800 feet at the head of Mill Hollow. Add in the contemptuous climb near the end for a total elevation gain of about 2,800 feet.

Season: Upper Little South Fork Trail is well shaded and may not melt out until mid-June. It is typically ridable throughout October, but it's not the wisest choice during elk and deer hunting season.

Services: There is no drinking water along this route. Surface waters should be purified. Nearby Mill Hollow Campground is a Forest Service fee area. Woodland, a few miles from the trailhead, offers no visitor services. Francis has a small convenience store, Kamas has most services, Park City and Heber have it all, including bike shops.

Hazards: Upper Little South Fork Trail is a primitive path and not maintained. Lower Little South Fork is maintained on an irregular basis. Deadfall may be encountered on any section of singletrack. The trail is unsigned throughout, so route-finding skills are required. There are several creek fords on the upper trail. None pose a significant problem. But one ford on the lower half can be knee deep and swift flowing during spring thaw. Later in the year, you should be able to hop across on exposed rocks. Finally, signs posted at Mill Hollow Campground warn of "Bear Frequenting Area."

Rescue index: You'll find few trail users on Little South Fork Trail. Motorists travel Utah State Highway 35. Campers and anglers enjoy Mill Hollow

Campground, especially on weekends and holidays. Heber and Park City, each about 25 miles away, have medical facilities.

Land status: Uinta National Forest (Heber Ranger District).

Maps: USGS Heber Mountain, Soapstone Basin, Wolf Creek Summit, and Woodland, Utah.

Access: From Park City, travel east on Utah State Highway 248 to Kamas, and turn right/south on UT 35/32. Turn left in Francis after 2 miles (flashing stoplight) on Village Way/UT 35 for Woodland. About 9.5 miles from Francis, turn right on a gravel road signed for Willow Hollow Trail and Little South Fork just after crossing the Provo River. Take the dirt road uphill 0.8 miles to the trailhead/parking area adjacent to a gas pipeline corridor. Leave all gates as you find them. Passenger cars should use caution over the last 0.3 mile because the road can be rough. Alternatively, park alongside the highway at the turnoff.

From Heber, travel 4 miles north on U.S. Highway 40/189. Turn right on US 189 for Kamas and wrap around Jordenelle Reservoir. Go through Francis (flashing stoplight) and proceed as mentioned above.

Notes on the trail: From the trailhead/parking area, descend back to UT 35 and pedal the highway right/east for 5 miles. Take Forest Road 054 (gravel road) up Mill Hollow for 1.5 miles. Immediately after passing the Mill Hollow Guard Station, fork right on Forest Road 122 for Campbell Hollow and Overflow Camping. This doubletrack is steeper and rockier than the Mill Hollow Road but has less traffic, dust, and washboards. As Campbell Hollow levels, stay left at two junctions with doubletracks and cruise along the gentle ridge on Forest Road 052. Fork right at a multiple-signed junction on Forest Road 096 toward Heber Mountain and Camp Hollow.

Just short of 1 mile from the previous junction and at the bottom of a descent, look for a wooden post and "Road Closed" sign. This is the inconspicuous Little South Fork Trailhead. There are a dozen earthen berms awaiting, some worthy of air time. After number 12, the route appears to veer left and uphill, but fork right and downhill on a singletrack (look for "dotted i" tree blazes). Beyond, the route is readily apparent.

Blaze across a meadow, drop down a sketchy hill, and dart into the damp woods. Cross upper Little South Fork creek (just a trickle here), enter the opposing meadow, and pass the remains of an old cabin. Here the trail, marked by a solitary wooden post, continues *due north* and crosses a side drainage. (Do not take the tempting path rising up the hollow to the right/east.) The trail veers away from the Little South Fork drainage while crossing meadows cut by small rivulets.

About 1 mile from the old cabin, the trail forks. Stay *left,* as Robert Frost would, on the path that appears less traveled. (The junction is just after a rocky stretch. Also look for a tree etched with the words "Willow Hollow" and "L S X." If you miss this turn and come to a T junction with a doubletrack, take it down a steep hill and ford Little South Fork creek.) The upbeat and utterly serendipitous descent continues as you enter cool, moist evergreens. Cross two creeks, enter a narrow sagebrush valley, and come to a doubletrack at the ever-widening Little South Fork creek.

Listen up! Do not cross the creek here. Instead, pedal down the doubletrack for about 100 yards on the west side of the creek, while noting tree blazes in the aspens, and then fork right on an unsigned singletrack. One mile down the trail you must ford the creek, which now flows with confidence. Resume jammin' down the trail but get ready for a rude climb. Grin and bear it; don't let it ruin your day. Finish off the ride with a bonzai drop off the hill, and then casually cruise along the fence back to the trailhead.

Knock down the aerobic level one big notch by shuttling to the top of Mill Hollow and riding 8 miles downhill to the trailhead. When driving up Mill Hollow (gravel road), pass the turnoff for Campbell Hollow as mentioned above, continue past Mill Hollow Reservoir to Duchesne Ridge, and come to the junction with Forest Road 091. Park and embark. Ride FR 052 west about 0.25 mile, and then fork right and climb a doubletrack to the multiple signed junction mentioned above at the top of Campbell Hollow. Fork left on Forest Road 096 toward Heber Mountain, and proceed as above. Just keep in mind that you're not entitled to any bragging rights if you don't ride the loop and pedal to the top.

Vernal/Flaming Gorge

RIDE 34 ELK PARK

The grandeur of the 100-mile-long Uinta Mountains is unfurled in its midsection where Kings Peak, Utah's tallest at 13,528 feet, and attendant summits boldly display the erosional effects of glaciation. Massive cirques have been stamped from the range's hardened quartzite core as cleanly as a giant's heel depresses damp sand. Mile-long ridges embrace the rock amphitheaters and direct countless streams from these highlands to the basins below. So grand are the High Uintas that they harbor the state's largest wilderness area.

Here on the eastern slope, however, the Uintas are more subtle in form and less brash in topography. Treeless summits still rise to majestic heights of over 12,000 feet, but glaciers had a gentler touch as evidenced by shallow bowls, rounded peaks, and oblique mountainsides wrapped in a thick shawl of

RIDE 34 ELK PARK

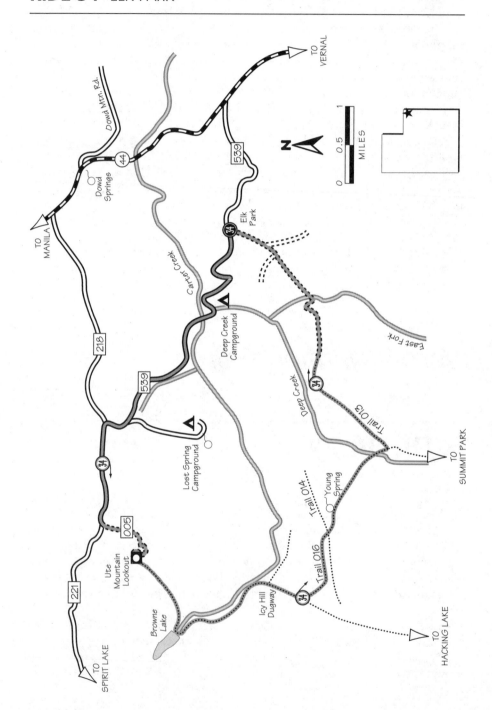

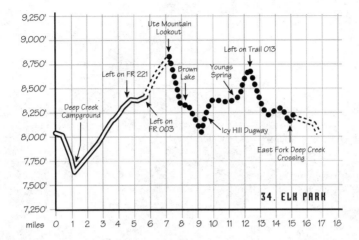

timber. Since the eastern slope is outside the wilderness, its trails beckon mountain bikes.

The Elk Park loop takes you across the Uinta's eastern slope. From the Ute Mountain Lookout, the first of Utah's fire detection towers built in 1935 and on the National Register of Historic Places, you can survey the land and study its topography. Then, you'll follow trails along crystalline streams and across breezy meadows cuddled by dense timber.

General location: Elk Park is in the eastern Uinta Mountains, 50 miles north of Vernal and 15 miles south of Manila.

Distance: 17-mile loop.

Tread: The loop begins on well-traveled doubletracks to the Ute Mountain Lookout. Thereafter, the route follows a short stretch of singletrack followed by ATV trails all the way around.

Aerobic level: Strenuous. The 2.5-mile climb from Deep Creek Campground is moderate and steady; the shorter ascent to the Ute Mountain Lookout takes solid effort. You'll have to hoof up Icy Hill Dugway and then produce maximum effort for 1 mile up to Deep Creek. Last, the short portage out of East Fork Creek stings like a sucker punch.

Technical difficulty: Level 1 to 5. Dirt roads and doubletracks are of little consequence—some gravel and washboards. The real action takes place on the singletracks and ATV trails. The descent from Ute Mountain Lookout to Brownie Lake has rough stretches that rate 3 to 5, so watch your front wheel. Icy Hill Dugway is level 5, but it is too steep to ride anyhow, so give it up. The mile-long, cobbly climb to Deep Creek is level 3 to 4 and ridable with maximum effort. Succumb to walking the wall out of East Fork Creek. The rest is sandy, grassy, rocky, lumpy, bumpy level 2 to 4.

Elevation change: The trailhead in Elk Park is at 8,020 feet where the route quickly drops to Deep Creek Campground at 7,644 feet. The route's highpoint

Dean finds Elk Park to his liking.

is Ute Mountain Lookout at 8,834 feet. After descending along Carter Creek, there is 700 feet of climbing to Deep Creek—the route's second high point of 8,700 feet. Total climbing is about 2,200 feet. (Add 50 feet more of gain if you climb the steps to the lookout's viewing deck.)

Season: This section of the Uintas should melt out by late May and be ridable through much of October. Portions of the route may be wet and muddy during spring. Insect repellent is recommended. Afternoon clouds may produce chilling rains and lightning. As its name implies, this backcountry route may not be the wisest choice during autumn's hunting season.

Services: There is no drinking water along the route. Deep Creek Campground and Ute Mountain Lookout have outhouses but no water taps. There are Forest Service campgrounds (fee areas) near the Red Canyon Visitor Center, 10 miles away. Red Canyon Lodge (same location) has a restaurant, small general store, telephone, cabins, and mountain bike rentals. Manila has a few cafes and motels, a small grocery store, and gasoline. Vernal has all visitor services.

Hazards: Portions of the loop are remote, so travel well equipped. Motorists commonly travel the dirt roads at the loop's beginning.

Rescue index: The loop's backside is remote and seldom traveled. Campers frequent Deep Creek Campground. The Ute Mountain Lookout is staffed most daylight hours, May through September, and has radio communication. Medical facilities are in Vernal 50 miles away.

Land status: Ashley National Forest (Flaming Gorge Ranger District).

Maps: USGS Elk Park, Jessen Butte, and Leidy Peak, Utah.

Access: From Vernal, travel 36 miles north on U.S. Highway 191/Utah State Highway 44 to where US 191 forks right for Flaming Gorge Dam. Continue left on UT 44 for 11.5 miles, and fork left on Forest Road 539 for Deep Creek and Elk Park. (The light-duty dirt road may be unsuitable for passenger cars when wet). The trailhead is 2 miles ahead at a sign for Elk Park Trails #013, #014, and Old Carter Trail. From Manila, the Deep Creek turnoff is 16 miles south on UT 44.

Notes on the trail: Begin by pedaling west on the FR 539 and descending feverishly to Deep Creek Campground at Carter Creek. Find a comfortable gear for the 2.7-mile, moderate climb out of the canyon. There are numerous cliff-side viewpoints worthy of a brief stop and a few photographs. Turn left/west on Forest Road 221 (gravel road) for Spirit Lake, Browne Lake, and Sheep Creek Lake and take it 1.5 miles; then fork left on Forest Road 5 for Ute Mountain.

The climb to the Ute Mountain Lookout requires low gears and steady effort. Be sure to climb the tower itself if it's open, and take in the circumambient view from its deck. Now hop on the Ute Mountain Trail #005 and descend toward Browne Lake. You'll race down smooth sections and nearly come to a halt while bunny hopping others.

The Ute Mountain Lookout tower.

If the trail is not flooded where it enters a grassy meadow, cross the field and rise up to the fence at Browne Lake; otherwise, take a detour route to the right. Ride south alongside the fence for 200 feet or so, and then fork left to cut across the lower edge of the meadow on singletrack. Watch for trail markers because the path can be indistinct. The path becomes quite obvious, and a helluva good time, as it follows Carter Creek.

About 1 mile down Carter Creek, cross two tributaries, then come to a junction where Lost Spring Trail #007 forks left/east. Stay straight for Youngs Spring Park and hoof up the mucky, boulder-ridden Icy Hill Dugway. (No doubt this hill turns to solid ice in winter.) Shortly thereafter, fork left/east for Youngs Spring. (If you miss this turn and continue straight toward Hacking Lake, you'll face an unbearably steep climb and waver far off course.)

Test your skills and strength against a short technical hill, and then enter a "park" signed for Old Carter Trail #016. (By now you'll agree this route is no spin through the park. The park you enter is "a level, open area surrounded by mountains or forest" according to Webster.) Head east across the meadow following carsonite posts for #016. (Note: Trail #014 also crosses this meadow diagonally from *southwest to northeast*. Don't get confused; where the two trails intersect, stay to the right on the mountain side of the meadow.) Pass Youngs Spring on the meadow's eastern perimeter. It's less a seep, and more a river, emanating from the ground. Now back in the forest, gear up for a mile-long climb where you'll have to cant-and-ratchet, surge at full power, and finesse your wheels over and around loose cobbles.

Keep a close watch for the less-than-obvious junction to the left for South Elk Park Trail #013 and Elk Park 4 miles. It's your route back to the trailhead. (The Carter Trail continues straight toward Summit Park, up a punishing trail that averages nearly 15 percent grade.)

Now, for a little payback, race through the woods down the grassy path, at times kicking up crunchy pine needles and other times splitting rocks. Dive to East Fork of Deep Creek, and then haul your rig up the opposing wall to join with a doubletrack. In a clearing, fork right, then left (marked with a post reading "trails"), and wind back to the trailhead.

While in the area, plan a few hours to drive (or half a day to bike) through Sheep Creek Canyon, located north of Elk Park. Sheep Creek is an outdoor geologic classroom where 80- to 600-million-year-old rocks are a window to the past when lakes, marshes, deserts, and tropical seas covered the land. Many formations, originally horizontal when formed, have been tilted to near vertical by the Uinta Fault, which traces the north slope of the Uinta Mountains for nearly 100 miles. Movement along the fault uplifted the nation's only major east-west trending mountain range.

The Sheep Creek route is marked with roadside signs describing the various rock layers and their environments of deposition. Obtain the "Wheels of Time" tour guide from the Flaming Gorge Ranger District in Manila, the Vernal Ranger District in Vernal, or the Dinosaurland Welcome Center in Vernal.

RIDE 35 *DOWD MOUNTAIN*

For decades, anglers have gloated over the trophy-size fish pulled from Flaming Gorge Reservoir, and boaters have been awe-struck by its cliff-bound shoreline. Landlubbers, like hikers and horseback riders, have relished the nearby High Uinta Wilderness for its solitude and pristine terrain. Now mountain bikers are reaping similar rewards around the Flaming Gorge area through the proactive efforts of the Ashley National Forest.

Tucked away on the east flank of the Uinta Mountains are a handful of designated mountain bike routes worth centering your next vacation around, and Dowd Mountain is a fine introduction to the region and its trails. This undaunting loop winds through stands of dispersed ponderosa and lodgepole pine trees that shield wildflower-speckled alpine meadows from the glaring sun. The Uintas rise to lofty heights above timberline in one direction, while Wyoming's parched prairies sprawl to the earth's curvature in the other. In between, a huge wedge of colorful, sedimentary rocks spanning 200 million years in age has been tossed about by conspicuous faults. And the canyons that resulted from these tectonic episodes have since been inundated by the aquamarine waters of Flaming Gorge Reservoir. From the route's goal, the Dowd Mountain overlook, all of these dazzling elements are yours for the viewing.

The combination of easy-to-follow and easy-to-ride doubletracks and singletracks makes Dowd Mountain perfect for novice and intermediate riders. But aggressive riders should tag along, too, and test themselves against the optional Hideout Canyon Trail, which links the canyon's rim with the reservoir's shore 1,700 feet below. The test is the climb out.

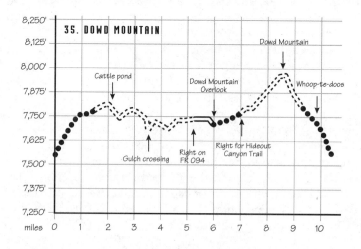

RIDE 35 DOWD MOUNTAIN

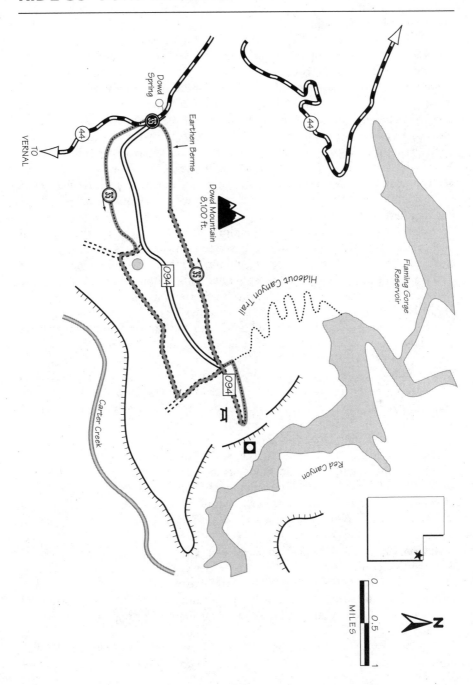

General location: Dowd Mountain is 50 miles north of Vernal (10 miles north of the Red Canyon Visitor Center) and 14 miles south of Manila.

Distance: 10.5-mile loop. Add on another 10 miles out-and-back for the arduous Hideout Canyon Trail.

Tread: A few miles of singletrack; the rest is doubletrack.

Aerobic level: Easy to moderate. The optional Hideout Canyon Trail is for those with excess testosterone.

Technical difficulty: Level 2 to 3. Dirt trails and doubletracks may have some ruts and rocks. The handful of earthen berms crossing the trail near the end can be interesting and technical level 3 to 4, but they are easily skirted.

Elevation change: The parking area is the route's lowest elevation at 7,520 feet. The loop reaches its highest elevation of 8,000 feet on the side of Dowd Mountain. Total elevation gain is about 850 feet.

Season: May through October. Days during midsummer are pleasantly warm while nights are cool. Rainstorms accompanied by lightning are common during afternoons.

Services: There is no drinking water along this route. The overlook has an outhouse and picnic tables. Manila has a few cafes, motels, a small grocery store, and gasoline. Lodging, dining, minor supplies, and bike rentals are at Red Canyon Lodge. There are Forest Service campgrounds (fee areas) near the Red Canyon Visitor Center 10 miles south. Vernal has all visitor services.

Hazards: The earthen berms (whoop-te-doos) near the trail's end can be hazardous if you take to the air and land with the rubber side up and helmet side down. Use caution along cliff edges because the blocky rock may be unstable and break away.

Rescue index: Motorists occasionally drive the gravel road to the overlook. They are common on Utah State Highway 44. Emergency contacts can be made in Manila, at Red Canyon Lodge, and at Red Canyon Visitor Center. Vernal has medical facilities, but it's 50 miles away.

Land status: Flaming Gorge National Recreation Area.

Maps: USGS Elk Park, Flaming Gorge, and Manila, Utah.

Access: From Vernal, travel 36 miles north on U.S. Highway 191/UT 44 to where US 191 forks right for Flaming Gorge Dam. Continue left on UT 44 for 14 miles to the signed turnoff for Dowd Mountain. Park near the cattle guard. (From Manila, travel 14 miles south on UT 44 to the Dowd Mountain turnoff.)

Notes on the trail: A recreation use fee is charged within Flaming Gorge National Recreation Area. In 1998, the fee per vehicle was $2 for one day, $5 for 16 days, and $20 year-long. The pass is available at the Vernal Ranger District office in Vernal, the Flaming Gorge Ranger District office in Manila, Red Canyon Visitor Center, and at most businesses throughout the Vernal/Flaming Gorge area.

There are two ways to ride to the Dowd Mountain overlook: ride 9 miles out-and-back on the gravel road, or ride the 11-mile loop on doubletracks and

The Hideout Trail drops from Dowd Mountain to the shoreline of Flaming Gorge Reservoir.

singletracks. The out-and-back option via Forest Road 094 is straightforward. Here's directions for the loop version.

Pick an easy gear and start out on the singletrack that branches right/south on the other side of the cattle guard. You'll climb gently to moderately for nearly 2 miles, and then intersect Forest Road 613. Fork right, and take the doubletrack south. About 0.5 mile past a mucky cattle pond on the left, fork left on a little-used doubletrack while following blue diamond trail markers. Zigzag through dispersed lodgepole and ponderosa pines underlain by fragrant sage and grasses. Dip through a gulch, pass a wire fence enclosure, and turn left at a T junction with a good doubletrack. After 1 mile of gentle climbing, you intersect FR 094; turn right and take it 0.6 mile to the overlook.

Spend lots of time here ogling the contrast between mountain summits, tilted strata, and blue-green water. The driving force behind the tectonics was the Uinta Fault, which runs over 100 miles along the northern base of the range. While it was responsible for the mountain's uplift, it also deformed the adjoining rocks.

Near the outhouse, hop on the singletrack signed for Dowd Mountain and Hideout Trail. It wraps around the rounded ridge and passes a rock monument. When you intersect a doubletrack, turn left, and pedal uphill to a gate. (Or pursue the Hideout Canyon Trail by taking the doubletrack right and off the rim.) Just past the gate (and immediately before re-joining FR 094), turn right/west on the doubletrack-turned-singletrack tagged Forest Road 613. Pedal 1.5 miles up the gently sloping flank of Dowd Mountain and culminate the loop on a full-throttle descent back to the parking area. The approaching earthen berms start out as mere bumps but grow to the size of a buried VW Beetle with sharp fronts and off-camber backs. Slip and slide down the gully, and return to the parking area.

OK, so all you hammerheads may be thinking: "Big deal. Where is the leg burn, maximum heart rate, anaerobic threshold?" Tack on an additional 1,700 feet of vertical by pursuing the 10-mile, down-and-back-up Hideout Canyon Trail. This old jeep road is bittersweet—sweet in that it takes you to the lake's edge where a plunge is utterly refreshing, bitter in that you'll be sweating buckets on the ride back up. Sorry, but there is no drinking water at the bottom either.

RIDE 36 *CANYON RIM TRAIL-SWETT RANCH*

"At a distance . . . a brilliant red gorge is seen, the red being surrounded by broad bands of mottled buff and gray at the summit of cliffs, and curving down to the water's edge on the nearer slopes of the mountain. This is where the river enters the mountain range . . . the first canyon we are to explore, or rather, an introductory canyon to a series made by the river . . . We have named it Flaming Gorge," wrote Major John Wesley Powell in 1869. This was the initial leg of Powell's historic expedition down the Green and Colorado Rivers, culminating with the first-ever recorded journey through the mighty Grand Canyon.

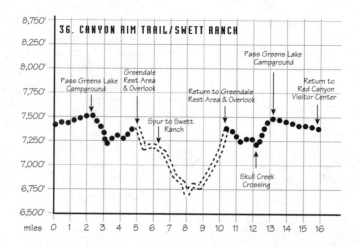

RIDE 36 CANYON RIM TRAIL-SWETT RANCH

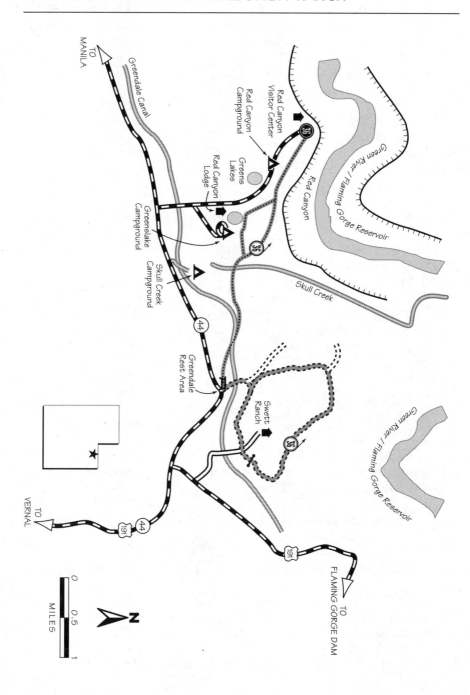

With a depth of 1,700 feet and a width of 4,000 feet, Red Canyon is an inspiring sight. Its maroon- and rust-colored sandstone cliffs, peppered with pine forests, cascade down to the sinuous aquamarine pool of Flaming Gorge Reservoir. Above rise the rugged slopes of the Uinta Mountains; beyond lie the endless prairie deserts of southern Wyoming. This contrast in scenery is the West's trademark.

In addition to overlooks of Red Canyon, this route ventures to a turn-of-the-century homestead at Swett Ranch. Oscar Swett and his family worked the ranch (claimed in 1909) in pleasant isolation until it was sold in 1968. A graveyard of antiquated horse-drawn plows, a small sawmill, and several log-hewn cabins testify to Swett's penchant for pioneer living with minimal technological influence. Today, the Forest Service-maintained ranch is listed on both the Utah and National Registers of Historic Sites.

General location: Red Canyon Visitor Center is located 40 miles north of Vernal or 31 miles south of Manila.

Distance: 16-miles out-and-back with loop. (See "Notes" for shorter, easier versions.)

Tread: Rock-studded and dirt singletracks from the visitor center to the Greendale Overlook. Light-duty dirt roads and doubletracks on the Swett Ranch loop.

Aerobic level: Easy to strenuous depending on options. Out-and-back from the visitor center to Greens Lake Campground is easy. The Rim Trail's upper look is moderate. Out-and-back from the visitor center to the Greendale Overlook is moderate. The whole shebang around the Swett Ranch loop and back is moderate to strenuous.

Technical difficulty: Level 2 to 4. The Rim Trail from the visitor center to Greens Lake Campground is mostly smooth with a few rocky patches. However, the trail from Greens Lake to the Greendale Overlook is loaded with quartzite "pavers." Full-suspension rigs will float over the rocks; a hard rail will harden your tail for sure. The Swett Ranch loop follows good dirt roads and lumpy, bermed doubletracks.

Elevation change: Red Canyon Visitor Center is at 7,400 feet. The singletrack descends to 7,200 near Skull Creek, then rises up to 7,420 feet at the Greendale Overlook. Swett Ranch Loop descends to 6,750 feet, so the climb back to the Greendale Overlook is nearly 700 feet. Total climbing for the entire route is about 1,140 feet.

Season: May through October. Summer days are warm, but evenings can be cool. Insect repellent is recommended. You're pretty safe from hunters on this ride.

Services: The Red Canyon Visitor Center has vending machines, a water fountain, restrooms, and a pay telephone. The trail passes three Forest Service campgrounds (fee areas) plus the Red Canyon Lodge. Red Canyon Lodge offers overnight accommodations in two-person rustic cabins and multi-family log homes. The lodge has a restaurant, small general store, and mountain-bike

Pooled behind the Flaming Gorge dam, the Green River floods Red Canyon.

rentals. There are no services at Swett Ranch. Gasoline is available at nearby Flaming Gorge Lodge. Vernal has all visitor services, including bike shops.

Hazards: Pedestrians are common on the Rim Trail between the visitor center and Greens Lake. The trail can be rocky and eroded in spots, so watch your front tire. The pebbly descent from the Greendale Overlook to begin the Swett Ranch loop can be very fast.

Rescue index: Emergency contacts can be made at the visitor center and at Red Canyon Lodge. A volunteer Forest Service ranger is stationed at Swett Ranch. Vernal has a hospital.

Land status: Flaming Gorge National Recreation Area.

Maps: USGS Dutch John, East Park Reservoir, Flaming Gorge, and Mount Lena, Utah.

Access: From Vernal, travel north on U.S. Highway 191/Utah State Highway 44 and ascend the eastern Uinta Mountains. Stay left on UT 44 where US 191 forks right for the Flaming Gorge Dam. Continue on UT 44 for 3.5 miles (passing the Greendale Overlook after 1.3 miles), and turn right for Red Canyon Recreation Area (Visitor Center, Red Canyon Lodge, and Greens Lake). The Red Canyon Visitor Center is 3 miles to the north. (Red Canyon Lodge, which you pass along the way, is a fine trailhead as well and is exempt from the recreational use fee.)

Notes on the trail: A recreation use fee is charged within Flaming Gorge National Recreation Area. In 1998, the fee per vehicle was $2 for one day, $5 for 16 days, and $20 year-long. The pass is available at the Vernal Ranger District office in Vernal, the Flaming Gorge Ranger District office in Manila, the Red Canyon Visitor Center, and at most businesses throughout the Vernal/ Flaming Gorge area.

Before you begin, walk the paved footpaths from the visitor center to the overlooks of Flaming Gorge and brush up on the human, geologic, and natural history of the area. Then, from the parking area, follow the dirt and gravel Canyon Rim Trail southeastward. Stay left at the many junctions that lead to Red Canyon Campground; just follow posts that are marked for Rim Trail or that are tacked with blue diamond trail markers. The several rock-fortified overlooks of the gorge are worth stopping at.

The trail forks about 1 mile from the visitor center. Stay right/south, heading away from the canyon's rim for Red Canyon Lodge on a singletrack that widens to an old doubletrack. You'll return on the left fork (Rim Trail) later on. About 0.5 mile farther, fork left on a singletrack, go through a wooden swinging gate, and circle around the shore of reflective East Greens Lake. (If you miss this turn, you'll end up at the cabin area of Red Canyon Lodge.)

At the entrance to Greens Lake Campground, fork left to continue to the Greendale Overlook and Swett Ranch loop. (Novice riders can turn around here, or continue with the option of circling back to the visitor center on the technical level 2 to 3 Rim Trail up ahead.)

Descend 0.3 mile on the rock-studded trail (technical level 3) through dispersed lodgepole and ponderosa pines to the junction where the Rim Trail forks left. There are enough blue diamond trail markers here to open a jewelry store! Stay straight for Greendale, or circle back to the visitor center via the 2.5-mile-long Rim Trail. Cross the Skull Creek gulch, and climb gradually for 2 miles on the sometimes smooth, sometimes rocky trail to the Greendale Overlook, crossing the Greendale Canal along the way.

If your legs are feeling fresh, then continue on the Swett Ranch loop; if you're pooped, you'd better head back while you still can. (If you dread returning on the trail, then circle back on the highway. It's much easier.)

Go to the east end of the parking area, and fork left on Forest Road 157 to begin the 6-mile Swett Ranch loop. Rage down the pebbly half-mile-long hill, and then fork right at a four-way junction. (You'll finish the loop on the middle fork; ignore the left fork, signed "dead end.") After 1 mile, fork left to visit the historic ranch 0.5 mile away; otherwise, continue a few hundred feet on the main road and then fork left following a post with a blue trail diamond. Go around a steel gate and stay left at an upcoming junction while cruising downhill. The road narrows to an unimproved doubletrack then to pseudo-singletrack and crosses two creeks engulfed by aspens. Roll across the open sage hills and fork left at a T junction of doubletracks. (The right fork may be signed "dead end.") Climb 1 mile to the four-way junction you encountered when descending, then take FR 157 back up to the Greendale Overlook.

If your legs are still feeling fresh, take the singletrack back to the visitor center. If you're woozy, take the gently rolling highway.

RIDE 37 *LITTLE HOLE NATIONAL RECREATION TRAIL*

Right when you're about to stow away the bike and wax the skis, head to Flaming Gorge to squeeze in one last alpine ride on the Little Hole National Recreation Trail along the Green River. "Why wait," you say? Because the trail is closed to bicycles from April to September to allow uncontested river side access for the large numbers of anglers. Your patience will be duly rewarded when you ride this fun-loving trail along the banks of this blue-ribbon hatchery. Pack along a pole and hook your quota of trout, or try to snatch one bare-handed as schools team up in the calm, bank-side eddies just a few feet from the path.

The route begins at the base of a colossal slab of concrete called Flaming Gorge Dam. As you sneak away from the monstrosity of water retention, it's just you, the Green River, and 1,000-foot-deep Red Canyon. John Wesley Powell floated these gentle rapids in 1869 as he embarked on his legendary expedition to the Grand Canyon. You'll shadow rafters who are content with replicating only a fraction of the journey.

Want to know more about Flaming Gorge? Here are the "dam" facts. Construction of Flaming Gorge Dam began in 1958 and was completed in 1964 at a cost of 65 million dollars. It is one of four units on the Colorado River Storage Project that produces electricity for the Intermountain West. Rising 502 feet above bedrock, with a base thickness of 131 feet and a top thickness of 27 feet, the dam impounds water of the Green River to form Flaming Gorge Reservoir, which extends 91 miles to the north and into

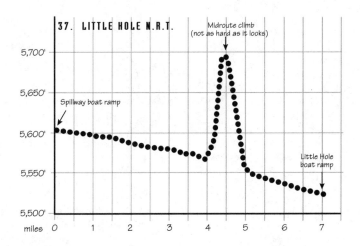

RIDE 37 LITTLE HOLE NATIONAL RECREATION TRAIL

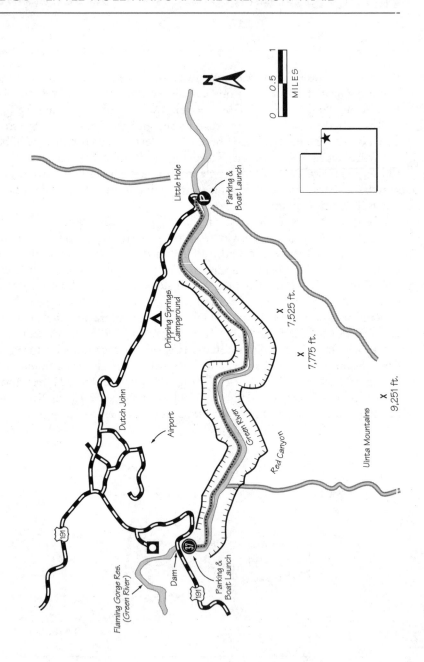

Wyoming. The roadway across the dam's crest is 0.25 mile long. Nearly one million cubic yards of concrete were used to build the dam, and its three turbine-powered generators can produce a maximum of 150 megawatts. That's a lot of light bulbs! Guided tours offered at the visitor center take you deep within the dam to view the power plants.

General location: 42 miles north of Vernal at the Flaming Gorge Dam.

Distance: 7 miles point-to-point.

Tread: Dirt and rock singletrack.

Aerobic level: Moderate. The path follows the banks of the Green River, but there are numerous "bumps" that require surges of power plus a more lengthy climb midroute. The technical aspect of the trail consumes more energy than the ups and downs.

Technical difficulty: Level 2 to 4. The Little Hole Trail is not maintained for bike traffic, so you expect the three Rs: rocks, roots, and (e)roded tread. Occasionally, the narrow, rock-studded trail is wedged between cliffs brushing your left shoulder and the river's banks below your right foot. Good balance is required to stay on the straight-and-narrow. Several sections cross "gabions" where the tread is a caged-in row of rocks. Portions of the trail can be overgrown and conceal the tread.

Elevation change: The spillway trailhead is at 5,620 feet. The trail descends to 5,530 feet at Little Hole. A midroute climb gains about 150 feet. But you'll face numerous bumps along the way that keep you from coasting.

Season: The Little Hole Trail is closed to mountain bikes from April 1 to Labor Day. Autumn (after Labor Day and through October) is the best time of year, although you might be able to sneak out during early spring (mid-March) because of the trail's relatively low elevation.

Services: There is no water tap at the spillway trailhead. However, there is a water tap at Little Hole, but it may be turned off during the times of the year when bikes are allowed on the trail. There are several Forest Service campgrounds (fee areas) nearby. Overnight accommodations and dining are available at Flaming Gorge Lodge west of the dam.

Hazards: Rocks and tree roots in the tread can make riding conditions tricky. Sometimes these conditions present themselves when the path is wedged between a rock wall on the left and the river's embankment on the right. A fall to the river, although not more than a few feet, could smart. The trail is often elevated a few feet where it crosses gabions—long rows of rocks enclosed by wire netting. These sections are bumpy, and there is little room for dismounting. Be alert to back-casting anglers.

Rescue index: This trail is very popular with anglers, and boaters commonly run the river. Emergency assistance can be summoned from the Flaming Gorge Dam Visitor Center. Vernal has a hospital.

Land status: Flaming Gorge National Recreation Area.

Maps: USGS Dutch John and Goslin Mountain, Utah.

Are we having fun yet, Tina?

Access: From Vernal, travel 36 north on U.S. Highway 191/Utah State Highway 44 and ascend the eastern Uinta Mountains. Turn right on US 191 for Flaming Gorge Dam and Dutch John. Cross the dam after 6.4 miles; then 0.4 mile farther, turn right at milepost 282 for "River Access." The trail begins at the boat ramp next to the outhouses.

Notes on the trail: A recreational use fee is charged within the Flaming Gorge National Recreation Area. A pass can be purchased from the Forest Service district offices, visitor centers, or most businesses in the region, and it must be displayed on your vehicle.

Right from the start, the quirky Little Hole Trail tests your bike-handling skills as you negotiate scattered boulders, roots, and dips in the tread. This is the fare for the day: smooth dirt tread interrupted with things that make you go bump. Early on, the canyon's terraced maroon-sandstone walls close in on the trail and attempt to push you overboard into the river. Watch your head as you brush by, and focus on where your wheel should be—not where it shouldn't be. The slower you ride, the harder it is to stay upright. Periodically, the trail crosses gabions, where the tread has been fortified by rocks caged by wire netting to prevent trail erosion during high water flow. The elevated 4-foot-wide rock-and-wire path bucks you around, and you need good balance to roll over the rough surface.

A few miles downstream, the path crosses a wooden boardwalk alongside overhanging cliffs. Between miles 4 and 5, the path rises uphill sharply to a vantage point 150 feet above the river. One mile farther, you reach an outhouse near a crescent-shaped sand beach on a river bend. Continue alongside the river for 1.5 miles to reach Little Hole, where Red Canyon has widened to grassy fields on opposing banks.

To avoid the car shuttle, you have two options: Ride out-and-back or pedal paved roads for a 17-mile loop. If you choose the former, novice riders will find a 4-mile out-and-back trip from the Little Hole Trailhead to their liking. Starting from the spillway trailhead is more scenic but technically more difficult.

For the loop version, circle back to the dam on the paved Little Hole Road. You'll face two long-winded climbs along the way, each about 1 mile long, and gain nearly 1,000 feet total. When you reach an unsigned T junction just past Dutch John, fork left on US 191 to return to the dam. Most of the route crosses rolling hills populated with fir and pine. The last 0.5 mile, however, is an eyeful where the roadway curves high above the dammed reservoir, and then descends furiously to the spillway.

RIDE 38 *RED CLOUD LOOP*

Nowadays, everyone knows Vernal is the heart of Dinosaurland. But beyond "Dino," which adorns nearly every cafe, motel, and gift shop, Vernal is a hub from which radiates a variety of summertime activities. In addition to Dinosaur National Monument and white-water rafting on the Green River, mountain biking is gaining a slow but steady stronghold. Vernal may not have world-class singletrack—the trails crossing the Uinta's high country are best suited for boots or horses—but a network of backcountry roads transport fat-tire enthusiasts through a scenic montage that is decidedly northeastern Utah.

Vernal sits in a high desert basin rimmed by sunbaked; redrock terrain similar to that of southern Utah's canyon country. Yet, nourishing this otherwise parched land are crystalline ribbons of life-giving water cascading down from the Uinta Mountain's snowcapped peaks. Ashley Creek, a prominent waterway descending from the mountains and through town, was named for General William H. Ashley who crossed the area in search of fur in 1825. Reports of perennial streams cascading down from 10,000-foot peaks inspired pioneers to settle the valley in the 1870s. In recent times, the oil and gas industry has brought boom-and-bust cycles to the region.

You'll learn about the region's geology while accessing the trailhead on U.S. Highway 191, otherwise known as the "Drive through the Ages." Interpretive signs at pullouts explain the 600 million years of tilted layer-cake geology, the associated mineral resources, and life forms that once thrived in the ancient environment.

The Red Cloud Loop takes you across the slopes of the Uinta Mountains through pine forests and across alpine meadows. Then you'll descend off the

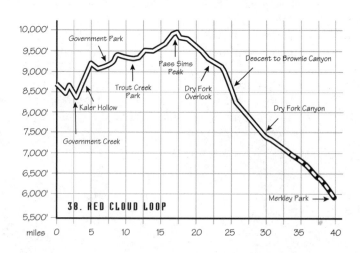

RIDE 38 RED CLOUD LOOP

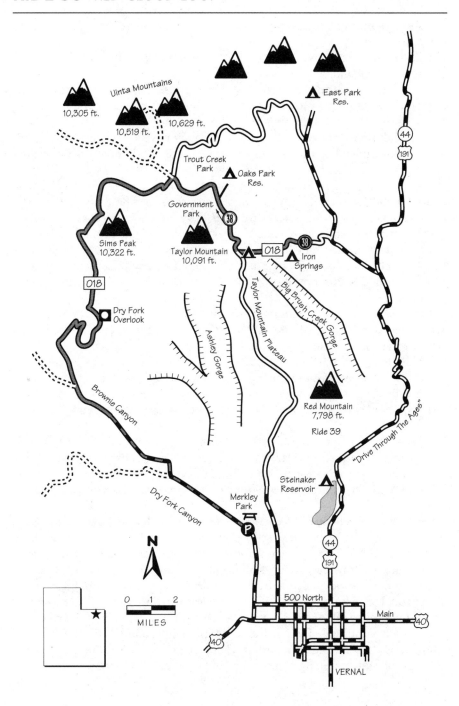

mountain and enter sandstone canyons that enclose fertile valleys.

General location: The Red Cloud Loop is 23 miles north of Vernal on the southern flank of the eastern Uinta Mountains.

Distance: 40 miles point-to-point, or pack up the panniers for a 70-mile, two-day loop.

Tread: Gravel roads and rock-studded doubletracks with a few miles of pavement at the end.

Aerobic level: Moderate to strenuous. There are several tough climbs as you cross the mountain on the tour's first half, but then it's all downhill back to Vernal. Still, 40 miles is nothing to scoff at.

Technical difficulty: Level 2 to 3. Dirt roads may have gravel and washboards mixed with imbedded stones. On descents, these conditions can rattle your bones and make bike handling unnerving.

Elevation change: Iron Springs (trailhead) is at 8,700 feet. The route barely clears 10,000 feet near Sims Peak, and then drops to 5,860 feet in Dry Fork Canyon. The 3,400-foot descent through Brownie and Dry Fork canyons is both exhilarating and highly scenic. Total elevation gain is around 2,500 feet.

Season: Much of the Red Cloud Loop is strictly alpine. Highest portions may not melt out until June and may be snowbound by early October. Changing alpine weather is common during summer months. Insect repellent is highly recommended.

Services: Water taps and outhouses are at Iron Springs Campground (Forest Service fee area). There are no other services along this route. Vernal has all visitor services, including bike shops.

Hazards: Since the route is a Utah Scenic Backway, motorists may be common, especially on weekends and holidays. Be prepared to share the road, and use extreme caution when rounding blind corners. There are many brisk, if not furious, descents on gravel and washboard dirt roads that may make handling difficult.

Rescue index: Campers frequent Iron Springs Campground. Motorists commonly travel the route on weekends and holidays. Vernal has medical facilities.

Land status: Ashley National Forest (Vernal Ranger District).

Maps: USGS Dry Fork, Dyer Mountain, Steinaker Reservoir, and Taylor Mountain, Utah.

Access: Leave a vehicle at "Remember the Maine (Merkley) Park," where an American flag has been painted high on a sandstone cliff. From Vernal, head north on 500 West and west on 500 North. Turn right at the "Red Cloud Loop" sign and proceed about 4 miles into the mouth of Dry Fork Canyon. Look for the flag on the cliff. In the shuttle vehicle, drive 20 miles north of Vernal on U.S. Highway 191. Turn left/west on Forest Road 018 for Red Cloud Loop, then left again 3.3 miles farther on the gravel road for Red Cloud Loop and Iron Springs. Park at Iron Springs Campground 1 mile farther.

Notes on the trail: From Iron Springs Campground, head west on FR 018 and descend through sweeping turns to upper Brush Creek Canyon. Shift to your

TYRANNOSAURUS
RĖX
WELCOMES YOU
TO
VERNAL UTAH
SOMEPLACE SPECIAL

This area is maintained

Vernal is a modern day
Jurassic Park.

granny gear, and chug 1.5 miles up the 10-percent grade in Kaler Hollow on the other side. Pass the road to Taylor Mountain forking to the left, and top out at Twin Parks where a pair of sunny meadows are separated by groves of aspens. Enjoy the easy pedaling alongside Government Creek and across Government Park.

Pass the turnoff for Oaks Park Reservoir, staying left/west on FR 018, and cut across the expansive alpine meadows of Trout Creek Park. Fork left in Trout Creek Park for Hacking Lake and Vernal via Dry Fork Canyon, continuing on FR 018 (the right fork loops around to East Park Reservoir).

Ahead, the road enters thick stands of lodgepole pine that hide countless lakes and ponds. Shadows cast by these pine lances stripe the road with an alpine bar code. A few miles of gradual climbing around the flank of Sims Peak is followed by big-chain-ring cruising. Take a break at the Dry Fork

Overlook to survey the remainder of the route. Marsh Peak hovers above the widening canyon that descends from pine to redrock.

Now let the fun begin! The downhill action is subtle at first but intensifies as the road bends north and angles downward. Watch out for a handful of gravelly, washboard switchbacks that drop you to upper Brownie Canyon. Stay left and downhill through Dry Fork Canyon. The air warms progressively as pine succumbs to juniper, pinyon, and sage, which inhabit the high desert. You'll swear you have been transported through space and time to southern Utah's canyon country, except for the weighty presence of the imposing Uintas. Dirt turns to pavement as the sandstone walls widen and lush farmlands fill the valley. File into a pace line and hammer down the paved road, or kick back and enjoy the incredibly diverse scene of mountain and high desert.

RIDE 39 *RED MOUNTAIN*

Who says you have to travel to Moab to ride burly trails over denuded sandstone? Red Mountain offers a taste of southern Utah's canyon country but is miles away in northern Utah's mountainlands. This ride is a real mouthful, and depending on your fat-tire palate, you'll either chomp at Red Mountain like a prehistoric carnivore or spit it out in disgust.

Red Mountain is Vernal's version of the infamous Moab Rim jeep trail—it's straight up and unyielding. Although Red is double the elevation (gulp!), it's many times longer. That means the grade is tolerable (whew!). But unlike the Moab Rim, where tire traction is impeccable, the route up Red has been busted into ledges stacked atop one another and all dusted heavily with sand

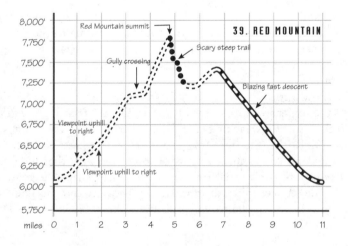

RIDE 39 RED MOUNTAIN

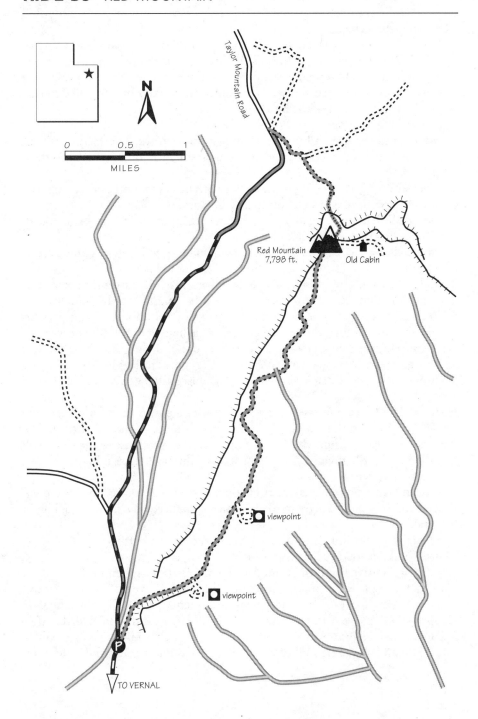

N

0   0.5   1
MILES

Taylor Mountain Road

Red Mountain
7,798 ft.

Old Cabin

viewpoint

viewpoint

P

TO VERNAL

and loose rock. Brute power, finesse, and unfaltering balance are needed for the many calculated moves and precision gruntwork. Start this route with 100 points and deduct one for each dab. He or she with the most points atop Red Mountain is the champ.

As the elevation increases, so do the views of the Uinta Basin below and of the Uinta Mountains above. Steinaker Reservoir interrupts the lower desert lands with its shimmering, ultramarine surface, while treeless peaks rise sluggishly above timbered slopes. Each holds additional promising bike routes.

General location: 9 miles north of Vernal.

Distance: 11-mile loop.

Tread: 6 miles of sand and broken slickrock doubletrack/ATV trail, 1 mile of gravel road, 3.8 miles of pavement, and a smidgen of humorously steep singletrack.

Aerobic level: Strenuous (an understatement). The climb is all granny gear and downright brutal, plus it's technical as hell. Gotta love it!

Technical difficulty: Level 4 to 5 plus. Red Mountain is one big, eroded, crumbling slickrock staircase.

Elevation change: The trailhead is the low point at 6,040 feet. The route crests Red Mountain at 7,790 feet for a direct 1,750-foot climb.

Season: March through June and September through November. You can attempt this route during summer but it will be deathly hot by midday. The singletrack descent off Red Mountain's north slope is on a shaded aspect, so wet conditions can linger when the south face is high and dry. Recent weather can adversely affect portions of the route: too dry and it's a sand box, too wet and it's gumbo mud, somewhere in between and it's "just right."

Services: There is no drinking water along this route. Vernal has all visitor services.

Hazards: The entire route is a hazard for some or a playground for others. The singletrack drop off the mountain is steep, deeply eroded, and is better walked than ridden. Use caution when descending the roadway back to the trailhead; you'll reach near-highway speeds. Portions of the trail, especially down low, are impassable when wet.

Rescue index: The route is infrequently traveled, so you're on your own. Rescue becomes increasingly more difficult the higher you climb. Vernal has a hospital.

Land status: Bureau of Land Management (Vernal Field Office).

Maps: USGS Steinaker Reservoir, Utah.

Sources of additional information: Altitude Cycles (See Appendix B).

Finding the trail: From the intersection of Main and Vernal Avenue, travel west on Main for 0.6 mile and then turn right on 500 West/Utah State Highway 121. Drive north 0.5 mile then bend left/west on 500 North. After 2.5 miles, turn right/north on 2500 West. Travel 5.7 miles, passing Ashley substation and a logging mill after 3.2 miles, to a doubletrack and pullout on the right. Park and embark. (It's just before the roadway dips through Spring Creek—a usually dry wash surrounded by low sandstone ledges.)

Notes on the trail: The route is laced with peripheral tracks laid down by ATVs and motorcycles, so navigation can be difficult. But these motor heads share a common goal to reach the top. The consensus of tracks is usually the main route.

From the parking area, take the sandy doubletrack northward, roughly parallel to the paved roadway, and then veer right in less than 0.5 mile up a draw creasing the mountain's flank. About 1 mile from the trailhead, the route dips not more than 20 vertical feet and then forks. Stay left and down the small draw; then get back to climbing. (The right fork rises to an overlook of distant Steinaker Reservoir.) About 0.7 mile farther, the route forks again, so stay left again. (The right fork rises steeply toward the sandstone cliffs to a second overlook of the faraway reservoir.)

Battle the slickrock and come to yet a third fork in the trail. Pick your poison; they rejoin a few hundred feet ahead. If you're feeling like a superhero at this point, then the upcoming stretch is a heavy dose of kryptonite; it will squash you like a mere mortal. Haul your rig over the sandstone knuckles and then bounce through a section where the rock has eroded to an audience of ghoulish eyes.

Now 3.3 miles up, the trail bends eastward and flattens. Time to use that neglected middle chain ring, but not for long. Step down a pair of 2-foot ledges and then bend around a juniper-inhabited rock gulch. About 1 mile farther, the trail changes complexion as it levels slightly and winds through open stands of pines underlain with more sand than rock. Without much warning, bam, you're on top and looking northward at the sloping Uinta Mountains that have been dissected by Brush Creek Gorge to the right and Ashley Gorge to the left.

The doubletrack bends right, but don't take it unless you want to visit the old cabin .2 mile away. Instead look for a faint singletrack on the right side of the mountain's ledgy summit. That's your route down. Succumb to walking; you'll save the trail and your skin. Drop to the red clay slopes below, then stumble down another frightful descent. Cross the sage flats on a doubletrack and veer left to the Taylor Mountain Road/Forest Road 044. Now you can rest easy. Take the gravel road south for 1 mile and culminate the loop on a wind-howling-through-the-helmet descent on pavement back to the trailhead. "Piece of cake," you say? Take another lap!

If you're spending more time in the basin, check in with Altitude Cycles for additional Vernal-area rides.

RIDE 40 *HORSESHOE BEND*

If you chum around the mountain-biking circle in Vernal, you'll learn that the Horseshoe Bend loop goes by several names; regardless, it's a locals' favorite. The loop takes you across the broken high desert west of town that announces the onset of the expansive Uinta Basin. En route to the trailhead, you'll swear you've been lead astray because McCoy Flat is a veritable wasteland offering few signs of life and little promise of a decent ride. But as you scurry off the treeless mesa on a roaring descent, you catch sight of a line of cottonwoods in the distance that can mean only one thing—water. Progressively, the Green River grows nearer; then you follow along the banks of northeastern Utah's lifeblood.

Miles away upstream on a stretch called the Gates of Ladore, the Green boils with foaming rapids. Far downstream, the Green again tumbles through Desolation Canyon. But here, the river is rippleless and meanders on a circuitous course across broad tablelands, not through deep, confining canyons. A side spur takes you to the Notch where the river has doubled back on itself after making an 8-mile-long gooseneck around Horseshoe Bend. Towing memories of the Green River and of the fertile streamside pastures it nourishes, you surmount the terraced mesa to return to the trailhead. Indeed, McCoy Flat is desolate; indeed, there *is* decent riding out here.

General location: 12 miles west of Vernal.

Distance: 13-mile loop, including two spurs.

Tread: Dirt, sand, pebble, and rock doubletracks.

Aerobic level: Moderate. The climb back to the trailhead from the Green River is the toughest part and it's not altogether that tough. It rises gently to moderately with one steep shot up a short dugway cut into the terraced mesa.

Technical difficulty: Level 2 to 4. Doubletracks are packed dirt mixed with loose sand, pebbles, rocks, and variable ruts—typical of high desert terrain.

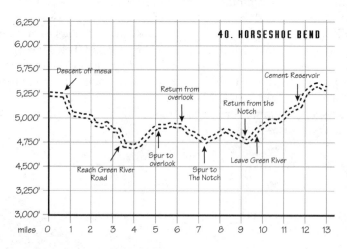

RIDE 40 HORSESHOE BEND

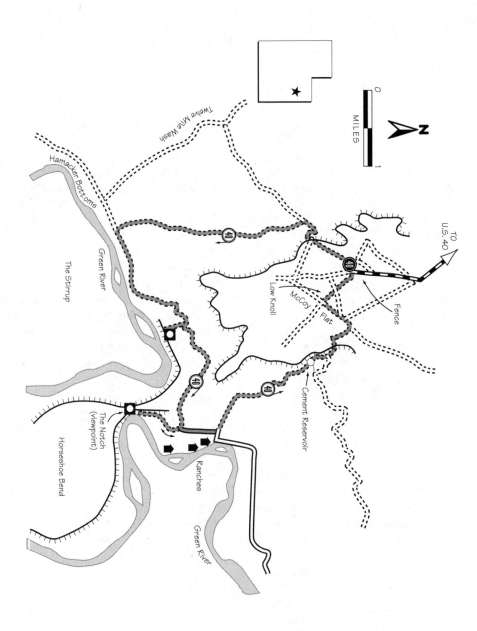

Elevation change: The trailhead is the highest point at 5,280 feet. The route drops to 4,700 feet alongside the Green River. Most climbing occurs over the last few miles when returning to the trailhead. Total gain is 900 feet.

Season: March through June and September through November. The warmth of spring can bring an increase in bugs near the river. Midday during summer can be unbearably warm. Fall is perfect.

Services: There is no drinking water along this route. Vernal has all visitor services.

Hazards: If you venture off route, you could be out for hours and wind up miles from where you want to be. Use caution while descending the doubletracks to the river. Eroded conditions can pitch an inattentive biker. Carry insect repellent just in case. Portions of the route can be impassable to bikes when wet, especially along the Green River Road.

Rescue index: You'll be the only traveler on the descending and ascending doubletracks. The river road might receive an occasional motorist. Emergency assistance might be summoned from the ranches along the river, east of the Notch. Vernal has a hospital.

Land status: Bureau of Land Management (Vernal Field Office).

Maps: USGS Vernal SE, Utah.

Sources of additional information: Altitude Cycles (See Appendix B).

Access: From the intersection of Main and Vernal Avenue in Vernal, travel west on Main/U.S. Highway 40. Crest Asphalt Ridge after 5 miles. Turn left 1.5 miles down from the summit on a secondary paved road marked solely with a stop sign between mileposts 139 and 140. Take the asphalt road 5.1 miles to its end next to a wire enclosure at McCoy Flat, marked "Seismologic Observatory" on the topography map. (In 1998 a flash flood washed out the McCoy Flat Road 4 miles from US 40. You'll have to park at the washout and pedal the last mile to the trailhead until the road is rebuilt.)

Notes on the trail: Three doubletracks branch southward from the trailhead at the road's end; take the right-hand track over a broad 20-foot-tall hump, then out the mesa top for 0.6 mile. Descend the pebbly dugway off the mesa to the sage plain; then fork left/south on a doubletrack 0.2 miles after the descent. (If you miss this turn, fear not. You'll continue descending southwest for 2.2 miles to the junction with the graded Twelve-Mile Wash Road. Turn left and ride 2 miles to the Green River Road. Turn left again and after 0.5 mile, you'll be back on track.)

Make a beeline due south for 2.5 miles beneath the mesa's rim over which you just dropped and descend off successive terraces stepping down to the river. The pace is fast and furious and the periodically eroded conditions make for an exciting ride, so keep your eye on your front tire. Intersect the river road and fork left.

The road crosses the river's floodplain for 1 mile then veers left to rise steeply to a pass. Where the hill flattens after 1 mile, take the 0.5-mile spur right/south to a rim-edge view of the placid Green as it exits Horseshoe Bend. Return, climb a bit more, and then rage down the ledgy canyon of Collier Hole. At a T junction, fork right and climb the 0.9-mile spur to the Notch.

Bob looks over the Green River from the Notch.

In the near geologic future, the quiet Green will gnaw away at the Notch and eventually dissect it as the waterway seeks the shortest route to its confluence with the Colorado River half a state away. Horseshoe Bend will then become a silty oxbow, and the central highland will be a rincon. To the east, the Green's broad banks support farmers' crops and pastures; to the west, the river attempts to undercut a 200-foot rampart called the Wall.

Return from the Notch and head north on the much-improved river road for 0.4 mile. Where the road bends 90 degrees to the right along a fence, fork left on an unsigned doubletrack that angles northwest toward the banded mesa. Climb gradually for 2 miles, then bend through a gulch marked by a broken structure that is presumably a remnant of Cement Reservoir (so called on the topography map). Pass a doubletrack forking right, head to the mesa's base, and then struggle up the rough-cut dugway to the table top.

A web of old roads makes the return to the trailhead tough to navigate. From the top of the dugway, stay left at a junction, make a U-turn across a shallow, dry gulch, and head southwestward. Ignore a track forking right; then at a four-way junction of sandy doubletracks 0.5 mile farther, take the right fork. Skirt a low knoll on your left, and stay on the straight-and-narrow to return to the trailhead.

Be sure to quiz the folks at Altitude Cycles about other Vernal-area rides, including the newly configured and long-sought-after Grail Trail on nearby Asphalt Ridge.

CENTRAL UTAH'S
HIGH PLATEAUS

Introduction

Central Utah is distinguished by its High Plateaus—a series of lofty, alpine tablelands arcing from the state's heartland to its southwestern reaches. There are eight elevated tracts that comprise the High Plateaus, beginning in the north with the Wasatch Plateau (not to be confused with northern Utah's backbone, the Wasatch Range) and extending southward through the Fish Lake, Awapa, Aquarius, Table Cliff, Sevier, Paunsagunt, and Markagunt Plateaus.

Three of the nation's major physiographic provinces converge upon the High Plateaus: the Colorado Plateau (Utah's Canyon Country) from the south and east; the Middle Rocky Mountains (Northern Utah's Mountainlands) from the north; and the Basin and Range Province from the west. Consequently, the High Plateaus have a combination of attributes characteristic to each of these neighboring regions.

The High Plateaus' southern and eastern margins are largely the products of land stripped away by the erosively insatiable Colorado River and its attendant tributaries. This denudation of the Colorado Plateau, coupled with the High Plateaus' gradual uplift, has created a band of prominent cliffs and terraced slopes that drop from the plateaus' tabletops. Pedal out to the great promontories of Powell Point (Table Cliff Plateau), Pink Cliffs (Paunsagunt Plateau), or Strawberry Point (Markagunt Plateau), and you'll gaze across a descending series of colorful terraces that look like massive steps, otherwise known as the Grand Staircase of the Colorado Plateau. Ultimately, this sequence of sedimentary rock units, or stratigraphic section, drops layer after layer across the Utah/Arizona border to the depths of the Grand Canyon. In the process, more than 100 miles and 500 million years of geologic time are crossed.

The faults and folds that border the High Plateaus' western slopes have dual significance. First, they announce the beginning of the Basin and Range Province, which encompasses western Utah and all of Nevada. Second, they are extensions of northern Utah's great Wasatch Fault, which lifted up the rugged Wasatch Range. Wallace Stegner explains in *Beyond the Hundredth Meridian,* "To the traveler from the east or west . . . the Plateau Province presents difficulties. It is easy to skirt the region, hard to cross it, for from Bear Lake at its northern border to the Vermilion Cliffs along the south, Utah has a spine like a Stegosaurus."

Other recreationists and visitors have long since uncovered the countless treasures harbored in the High Plateaus: anglers and hunters seek trophy catches in vitreous lakes and endless forests; boaters skim the surface of Joes Valley Reservoir in the Wasatch Plateau; four-wheelers rally to the Tushars and surrounding mountains during the annual Piute ATV Jamboree; skiers fly down snow-covered slopes at Elk Meadows and Brian Head resorts; hikers venture into the ghostly chasms of the Box Death Hollow Wilderness Area or are absorbed by the fantasy lands of Bryce Canyon National Park and Cedar Breaks National Monument; historians study the cultural significance of Utah's earliest inhabitants at Fremont Indian and Anasazi State Parks; and motorists tour scenic byways that are rated among the nation's best drives. Now mountain bikers are able to discover the abundant riches that await in these alpine hideaways.

Along the plateaus' crests, you will feel suspended between earth and sky.

You'll be awed by views of bounteous forests, shimmering lakes, and glistening creeks that nourish flower-speckled meadows. And best of all, you'll enjoy a delightfully cool escape from stifling redrock deserts that bake under a relentless midsummer sun.

CAPTAIN CLARENCE E. DUTTON

Accounts of travelers who ventured through the Colorado Plateau during the late eighteenth and early nineteenth centuries abound. Franciscan padres Domínguez and Escalante in 1776 laid the foundation for what would become the Old Spanish Trail; the 1830s trapper Denis Julien incised his name in canyon walls; John C. Fremont led numerous route-finding expeditions in the mid-1800s; railroad crews surveyed corridors for a potential transcontinental route; and dutiful Mormon pioneers proliferated the Church's presence across the territory.

Despite these efforts, the Colorado Plateau and subsequently half of Utah, remained enshrouded with fables of the unknown. As a master atlas of the western states and territories was being compiled during the mid-1800s, the Four Corners Area was largely left blank or splashed with the word "unexplored." It was Major John Wesley Powell's famed 1869 exploration of the Green and Colorado Rivers (which ultimately became the first documented voyage through the Grand Canyon) and subsequent second journey in 1871 that are credited for the opening of the Colorado Plateau. His expeditions provided the impetus for a number of government-funded surveys to this remote section of the West.

However, Powell had many interests that steered him away from the surveys he created, including Native American ethnology. Of all the topographers, geographers, anthropologists, and geologists that comprised Powell's crews, none would provide the lasting visionary impact that geologist Captain Clarence E. Dutton did.

Assigned by Powell to map and decipher the geology of Utah's High Plateaus and adjacent Plateau Province (Colorado Plateau), Dutton did so with a literary flair that veered far from the exceedingly terse prose that was considered standard presentation of geologic discoveries and discussions. Perhaps this was because Dutton was more than a student of science, but was also an "omnibiblical" tourist and lover of nature. His superfluous and aesthetic geologic accounts are recited and revered more than a century later, not only by the scientific community but also by inquisitive Plateau travelers.

Wallace Stegner, in his biography of Powell, et al., *Beyond the Hundredth Meridian,* claimed that "Dutton loved a grand view, a sweeping panorama. What [others] loved to paint—the big, spectacular, colorful view—Dutton loved to describe. [And] . . . like a painter . . . his drift was constantly away from the meticulous and toward the suggestive."

Whether you are making your first or fifth mountain bike trip to Utah's High Plateaus or Canyon Country, keep an open mind when you're traveling through this bizarre land, as Dutton did when he described the Grand Canyon:

Bryce Canyon National Park is " . . . one mighty ruined colonade . . . now chained up in a spell of enchantment," C.E. Dutton described more than a century ago.

The lover of nature, whose perceptions have been trained in the Alps, in Italy, Germany, or New England, in the Appalachians or Cordilleras, in Scotland or Colorado, would enter into this strange region with a shock, and dwell there for a time with a sense of oppression, and perhaps horror. Whatsoever things he had learned to regard as beautiful and noble he would seldom or never see. . . . Whatsoever might be bold and striking would at first seem only grotesque. The colors would be the very ones he had learned to shun as tawdry and bizarre. The tones and shades . . . in which his fancy had always taken special delight, would be the ones which are conspicuously absent. But time would bring a change. . . . outlines which at first seemed harsh and trivial have grace and meaning; forms which seemed grotesque are full of dignity; . . . colors which had been esteemed unrefined, immodest, and glaring, are as expressive, tender, changeful, and capacious of effects as any other. [The Colorado Plateau is] a great invention in modern ideas of scenery . . . whose full appreciation [is] a special culture. . . . if planted upon the plains of Central Europe, would have influenced modern art.

As Stegner notes, these are strange and poetic words for a geologist. It is through Powell's adventures that we feel the power of the Colorado River and its significance in sculpting the Colorado Plateau. But it is with Dutton's eye that we are able to look beyond what is superficial and become utterly spellbound by the bizarre shapes and colors of this unique geologic showcase.

Northern Plateaus

RIDE 41 *NINE MILE CANYON*

Nine Mile Canyon is considerably longer than its name implies. The creek runs over 40 miles, beginning northeast of Price and emptying into the Green River at the head of Desolation Canyon. On its way, the creek penetrates the arid and austere Book Cliffs, one of the largest de facto wilderness areas in the continental United States. The canyon received its name from one of John Wesley Powell's topographers named Bishop who did a nine-mile triangulation drawing of the area in 1869.

There are many places that are the scenic equal of Nine Mile Canyon, with its banded, red stone cliffs peppered with sage and pygmy evergreens, but few rival its archaeological riches. This is where the Fremont Indians, relatives of the Anasazi, were first identified and described. With more than 10,000 estimated sites, the canyon contains the largest concentration of Indian rock art in North America. Most are petroglyphs—a form of rock art created by chipping off the oxidized outer surface to expose the lighter rock underneath. Displays are of both individual figures and complex panels. Often you'll have to look closely to find them because they are hidden from direct line of sight or faded from age. The Fremonts constructed rock-walled granaries for food storage as well. Many are still intact but are often tucked high into the canyon's walls. You'll have a field day if you pack along binoculars.

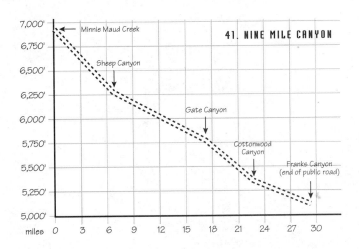

RIDE 41 NINE MILE CANYON

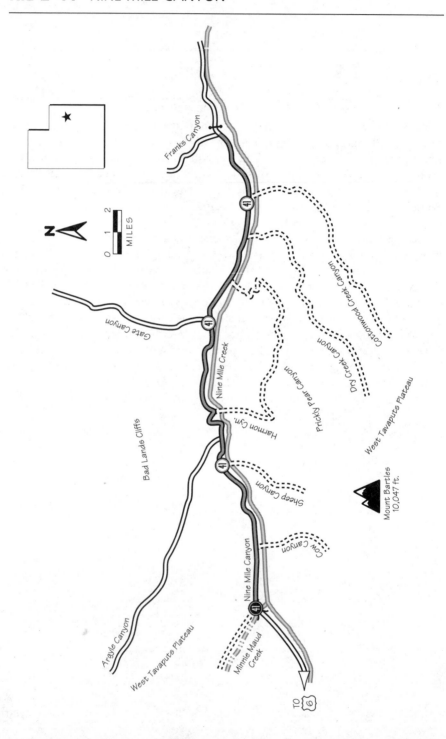

Nine Mile Canyon has a fruitful recent history as well. Long before Utah State Highway 6 connected Interstates 15 and 70, Nine Mile was the main route of travel and commerce between the Uinta Basin and Price in the late 1880s. Old homesteads echo the romantic era of the West's evolution. The canyon has supported extensive livestock ranching to this very day, and the old Nutter Ranch, which dates back to the 1890s, is one of Utah's longest-continuing operations. And although the surrounding Book and Roan cliffs give not a hint of mineral wealth from a distance, these sedimentary ramparts are important sources of carbon dioxide and bituminous coal.

General location: Nine Mile Canyon is located about 25 miles east of Price off U.S. Highway 6.

Distance: 58 miles out-and-back (between Minnie Maud Creek and the road's end at private property), but shorter routes are possible.

Tread: Light-duty, dirt road suitable for passenger cars when dry but may stymie even four-wheel-drive vehicles when wet.

Aerobic level: Easy to strenuous depending on your chosen trailhead and turnaround. The entire 58-mile round trip is nothing to scoff at despite Nine Mile's nearly imperceptible grade. See "Notes" for options.

Technical difficulty: Level 1. The road is mostly packed dirt but may develop soft silt during dry periods and ruts from passing motorists after it rains.

Elevation change: The elevation of Nine Mile Canyon is 6,950 feet at Minnie Maud Creek; 6,250 feet at Sheep Canyon; 5,780 feet at Gate Canyon; 5,300 feet at Cottonwood Canyon; and 5,100 where the road ends at private

One of hundreds of mysterious messages left by the ancient Fremont Indians.

property. On average, the Nine Mile Canyon Road descends at a nearly imperceptible 1 percent grade.

Season: Nine Mile Canyon is at its best whenever it is dry. However, the area can be stifling hot during midsummer. Spring is a good choice to view budding cacti. Autumn is appealing when cottonwood trees turn golden.

Services: Services, what services? Water can be filtered from Nine Mile Creek, but Wellington is the last outpost for drinking water and, more importantly, beer, ice, and junk food. There are a few motels and restaurants in Wellington. Price has all visitor services including a bike shop. Beyond that, it's Sticksville. Backcountry camping is allowed up the passable side canyons. Avoid camping at ruins, rock art panels, or on private property.

Hazards: The area can be hot in the summer, so bring an adequate water supply. Traveling the Nine Mile Canyon Road is not recommended when it's wet because the clayey road can turn to potter's slip instantly. The remote network of optional side routes, which are dead dry and utterly deserted, can be confusing. But don't be daunted; many routes are worth exploring. Be sure to take a map, compass, repair kit, knowledge, food, and more water than you think on these adventures . . . or you'll end up buzzard meat.

Rescue index: Anyone who finds his/her way into Nine Mile Canyon will realize how remote this area is. Emergency help might be available at the various ranches in the canyon, but medical attention (Price) is at least an hour's drive away. Price has a hospital.

Land status: Bureau of Land Management (Price Field Office). Private lands fill much of Nine Mile Canyon and border the road. The main road and most side canyon roads are on public land. Obey all signs restricting travel.

Maps: USGS Cowboy Bench, Currant Canyon, Minnie Maud Creek West, Pine Canyon, Pinnacle Canyon, and Wood Canyon, Utah; USGS 1:100,000 metric series: Price, Utah.

Access: From Price, drive 8 miles southeast on US 6 through Wellington, and turn left for Nine Mile Canyon on Soldier Creek Road between mileposts 249 and 250. The 21-mile drive to the bridge over Minnie Maud Creek begins as paved and then turns to dirt road. This is where mileage to selected sites begins in the informative pamphlet *Nine Mile Canyon: A Guide*. Continue 8 miles to Sheep Canyon, 16 miles to Gate Canyon, or 23 miles to Cottonwood Canyon for abbreviated tours.

Sources of additional information:

Castle Country Travel Council; Price, Utah 84501
435-637-2788

Nine Mile Canyon: A Guide, by Castle Country Travel Council (See Appendix A).

Notes on the trail: Here are some highlights excerpted from *Nine Mile Canyon: A Guide* if you set out from Minnie Maude Creek for the entire 58-mile round-trip tour.

Mile 1.5: On the left is an old homestead that dates back to a time when the saddle you rode on was strapped to a horse not bolted to aluminum tubes with knobby tires.

Mile 4.8: The first major petroglyph panels are to the left on a rocky point. How many different figures and designs can you identify? There are more images on the ledge above.

Mile 8: Sheep Canyon Excavation: To view a rock structure built by the Fremont Indians look to your left at a large sagebrush hill. Locate a flat-topped rock and follow the slope several hundred yards below and to the left to find a round rock structure. Five pit houses are on a low ridge to the right.

Mile 9: Pass the ghost town of Harper. Argyle Canyon enters from the left.

Mile 10.4: The road rounds a curve next to a balanced rock that resembles the cartoon character Porky Pig. An excellent art panel is just beyond.

Mile 13.2: Stop alongside a line of poplar trees and sight halfway up the hillside to a smooth black rock face for a snake design. With binoculars you will find may more interesting images.

Mile 16.7: Pass Gate Canyon, which makes a good trailhead for easy and moderate level rides. Look up the slope at a 45-degree angle to view a granary. Although the front has decayed away, the walls and ceiling are still intact. A fully intact granary can be found one mile farther after crossing a cattle guard.

Mile 19.2: The rocks near the side of the road are an ancient structure. Observe the stone work up close, but do not disturb the site.

Mile 21.7: Dry Canyon enters from the right and is guarded by the Mummy rock formation. On the north side of Nine Mile Canyon, excavators unearthed several mummies in Rassmussuen's Cave that also has pictographs (rock art paintings).

Mile 22.7: The road up Cottonwood Canyon forks right. Pedal about 1.5 miles up to view a classic Fremont hunting scene.

Mile 25: You pass a panel above a ledge that depicts a turkey, scorpion, bird, and humanoids.

Mile 27.4: Fork left up a doubletrack and go around the outcrop of rock on the right side of the road. Where the cliff face becomes a smooth half circle, look half way up to find a well-preserved granary perched on a small ledge. It is a wonder how the Fremonts accessed this site.

Mile 29: You reach a gate that ends public access and announces private property. There is much more to see, but you must obtain permission from the landowner to continue. Turn around and admire Nine Mile Canyon and its wonderful history from a new perspective.

RIDE 42 *SKYLINE DRIVE*

What the White Rim Trail is to Utah's canyon country, Skyline Drive is to Utah's plateau country—a multi-day, epic bike tour along a famed Utah scenic backway. Whereas the White Rim penetrates the Colorado Plateau's layer-cake strata of sun-baked sandstones, Skyline Drive traces the 10,500-foot crest of central Utah's Wasatch Plateau, dancing among clouds and scraping the belly of the heavens.

Along Skyline, you will not face chiseled peaks and improbable mountain passes, which characterize northern Utah's formidable Wasatch Range. The summit of the Wasatch Plateau is an open, rolling expanse of virgin tundra meadows pocketed with stands of fir. Graceful, horseshoe-shaped amphitheaters embrace broad, ice-carved valleys and bow to solitary limestone crowns. During the 1880s, Captain Clarence E. Dutton, John Wesley Powell's protégé, surveyed Utah's high plateaus and described the Wasatch: "On the plateaus stand buttes, lone mountains. The buttes are mountain cameos, horizontal strata with escarped sides—they are mountains of circumdenudation."

Anglo explorers who first ventured through central Utah in the early 1800s mapped the Wasatch Plateau as merely an extension of Wasatch Range to the north. But geologists have long since separated the association. On the contrary, the Wasatch Plateau is a transitional feature that shares characteristics of the Colorado Plateau to the east (layered strata) and of the Basin and Range to the west (parallel fault zones).

To Mormon pioneers, the Wasatch Plateau was both lifeblood and formidable obstacle. Streams that cascaded west from its crest nourished the farmlands and quenched the Mormon hamlets of Sanpete Valley, which was settled in

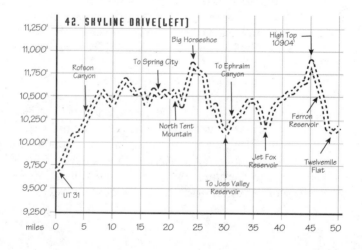

1849. Today, these half-dozen towns, strung like pearls on a necklace, cling tightly to their pioneer heritage and display some of the finest periodic architecture and cultural elements in the state. No town is sizably larger than the next, and each town has vital institutions, even though the valley has been effectively bypassed by Interstate 15.

As Sanpete Valley grew, so did the pressures on vital water sources. In 1877, one week before his death, Brigham Young called upon the people of Sanpete Valley to cross the Wasatch Plateau and establish settlements in Castle Valley. A smattering of homesteads were soon concentrated to a string of towns that would mark the last effort of Young's indomitable drive to colonize the Intermountain West. Third- and fourth-generation residents still farm and ranch today, but the key industry is coal mining and energy production provided by the Wasatch Plateau.

General location: Skyline Drive and the Wasatch Plateau are located in the center of Utah, neatly packaged between U.S. Highway 6 to the north (Spanish Fork Canyon) and Interstate 70 to the south.

Distance: 80 miles point-to-point.

Tread: Light-duty dirt roads and doubletracks throughout. Although many sections are suitable for passenger cars, your support vehicle should have high clearance and preferably four-wheel-drive for the rougher parts.

Aerobic level: Beyond strenuous if self-supported; intermediate to advanced depending on how much biking and driving you do on a vehicle-supported trip.

Technical difficulty: Level 2 to 3. Most of the time you'll cruise on packed dirt or pebbly doubletracks. Some sections are rutted; a few are peppered with imbedded rocks that make the riding teeth chatter but are not unbearable.

Elevation change: Skyline Drive begins at 9,700 feet (at the junction with Utah State Highway 31) and undulates to 10,987 feet at High Top (midroute). The

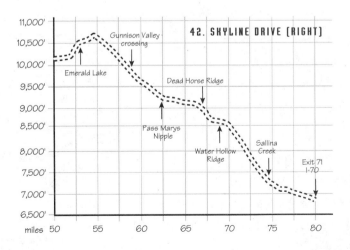

RIDE 42 SKYLINE DRIVE (NORTH SECTION)

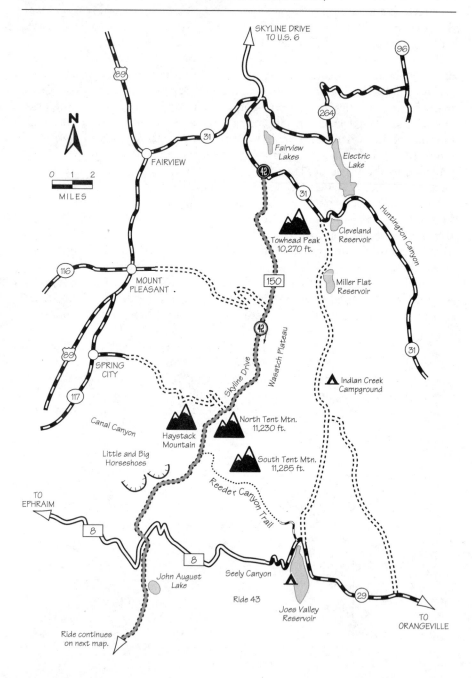

RIDE 42 SKYLINE DRIVE (SOUTH SECTION)

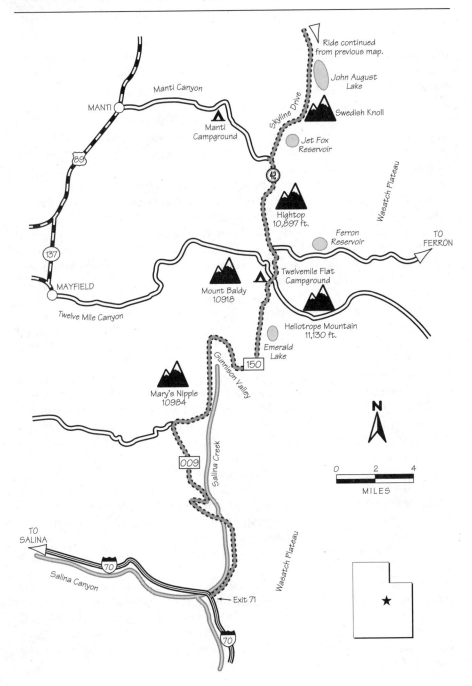

Ride continued from previous map.

John August Lake

Swedish Knoll

Skyline Drive

Manti Canyon

MANTI

Manti Campground

Jet Fox Reservoir

89

42

Hightop 10,897 ft.

Wasatch Plateau

137

Ferron Reservoir

TO FERRON

MAYFIELD

Mount Baldy 10918

Twelvemile Flat Campground

Twelve Mile Canyon

Heliotrope Mountain 11,130 ft.

Emerald Lake

150

Mary's Nipple 10984

Gunnison Valley

009

Salina Creek

N

0   2   4
MILES

TO SALINA

70

Salina Canyon

Wasatch Plateau

Exit 71

70

★

route peaks again at 10,780 feet above Blue Lake before beginning its famed 20-mile descent to I-70 at 6,660 feet. Although net elevation change along the plateau's rolling crest is about 1,000 feet, total climbing approaches 5,000 feet. Total descending is nearly double.

Season: Skyline Drive has a relatively short biking season, from late June-early July through late September. Evenings will be crisp, perhaps near freezing; midday temperatures may reach 70 to 80 degrees. Because of the high elevation, a rainstorm during summer may bring high winds, radical drops in temperature, and possibly hail. Carry rain gear.

As the warmth of midsummer intensifies so does a pallet of brilliant wildflowers. Aster, lupine, bluebell, alpine paintbrush, penstemon, wild rose, geraniums, mule ear, and skyrockets populate open meadows, painting the plateau with a rainbow of vibrant colors.

Services: There are no services along this route. There is a Forest Service campground (fee area) 2 miles north of the trailhead at Fairview Lakes. Campgrounds are midroute at Ferron Reservoir and Twelvemile Flat (each nearly 50 miles into the ride). Water is restricted to a few springs, small reservoirs, and irrigation ditches; all should be purified because of sheepherding. Rustic cabins and limited provisions are available at Ferron Reservoir's Skyhaven Lodge, but inquire first.

The towns of Sanpete Valley (west) and Castle Valley (east) offer basic visitor services, including lodging, food, and gasoline; but there are no bike shops. More extensive services and bike shops are in Price, Provo, and Richfield. All are several hours away by vehicle. A hospital is located in Mount Pleasant (Sanpete Valley).

Hazards: Skyline Drive itself poses no significant hazards for mountain bike travel; however, chassis-deep mud holes after recent rains and lingering snowdrifts (notorious near the Horseshoes and High Top) may hinder support vehicles. Although bikes may be portaged around these obstacles, vehicles may have to descend off the plateau along variably maintained dirt roads and then ascend the plateau via the next canyon.

Route conditions vary from hard-packed dirt and gravel when dry, to greasy, potter's clay when wet. A high-clearance vehicle equipped with four-wheel-drive is recommended for support and should be stocked with emergency equipment, including a full-size spare tire, shovel, tow rope, high-lift jack, and perhaps a few sturdy wooden planks.

Prepare for temperate days and cold nights; bring sunscreen and carry adequate water supplies.

Rescue index: Motorists, recreationists, and campers are common near the route's beginning on UT 31, in Manti Canyon, at Joes Valley Reservoir, and at Ferron Reservoir. Along the route's midsection, however, you'll see few travelers other than occasional ranchers. Towns located in Sanpete Valley (west) are often 20 miles and several bike hours from Skyline Drive; those located in Castle Valley (east) are much farther.

Emerald Lake on the
Wasatch Plateau.

Emergency assistance might be summoned at the cafe/boat dock at Joes Valley Reservoir or nearby Olsen Ranger Field Station and perhaps at Skyhaven Lodge (Ferron Reservoir). Mount Pleasant (Sanpete Valley) has a hospital; Manti, Ephraim, Salina (all in Sanpete Valley), and Castle Dale (Castle Valley) have medical clinics.

Land status: Manti–La Sal National Forest (Ferron, Price, and Sanpete Ranger Districts) and Fish Lake National Forest (Richfield Ranger District).

Maps: USGS Danish Knoll, Fairview Lakes, Ferron Reservoir, Heliotrope Mountain, Huntington Reservoir, South Tent Mountain, Spring City, Water Hollow Ridge, and Woods Lake, Utah. 1:100,000 scale topographic series: Manti, Nephi, and Salina, Utah.

Access: Skyline Drive/Forest Road 150 begins where UT 31 crosses the Wasatch Plateau, about 15 miles east of Fairview (Sanpete Valley) or 35 miles northwest of Huntington (Castle Valley). You can also reach Skyline Drive via

Utah State Highway 96 and Utah State Highway 264 from Scofield (south of US 6 at Soldier Summit). The route ends at I-70 (Exit 71) 35 miles east of Salina. Park at your discretion.

Sources of additional information: Skyhaven Lodge (See Appendix A).

Notes on the trail: Skyline Drive begins with a modest climb around Towhead Peak, followed by a generous descent across the head of Rolfson Canyon spiced with a few ruts, mud holes, and scattered rocks. These conditions are the general fare for the next 75 miles as you rise and descend the gigantic roller coaster.

Early on, road conditions are good and the ride progresses rapidly. Here, the Wasatch Plateau's crest is quite narrow with sharp, craggy canyons plunging west, countered by broad, shallow bowls opening to the east. As the route progresses, the plateau widens, canyons lengthen, and scarped buttes cap the summit.

After 8 miles, Forest Road 37 branches right and descends to Mount Pleasant. Two miles ahead and under the power lines, the clay-based road can get real messy when wet, and even four-wheel-drive can be futile.

Around mile 18, Forest Road 036 cuts off and drops to Spring City. Beyond is the domed assemblage of North Tent and South Tent Peaks, two of the plateau's tallest at 11,230 feet and 11,285 feet, respectively. The road winds around their western flanks pinned between precipitous limestone cliffs and steep head walls of Canal Canyon.

The two ice-carved scallops of Big and Little Horseshoe soon come into view. Along with Mary's Nipple to the south, the Horseshoes are the Wasatch Plateau's most pronounced landforms, easily visible from Sanpete Valley. There is a long, grinding climb to the crest of the Horseshoes followed by one of Skyline's great descents—a 4-mile all-out bomber. As the downhill flattens, UT 29/Forest Road 8 crosses Skyline. It descends left/east to Joes Valley Reservoir and right/west to Ephraim.

You are 30 miles in with 50 to go. Pass Snow Lake and Jet Fox Reservoir and climb gradually to High Top, elevation 10,897 feet and signed "Highest Point on Skyline Drive." Break out the cameras to record the event.

As you descend off High Top, you need to make a route choice regarding overnight accommodations: Ferron Reservoir or Twelvemile Flat. To reach Ferron, you must descend 900 feet off Skyline, then regain the route later. Twelvemile Flat is straight ahead on Skyline. But if you are linked up with a rustic cabin at Ferron Reservoir, the return climb may be worth a bed and roof overhead.

Huge meadows mark Twelvemile Flat. Pass through the log fence and bear right to continue on Skyline beneath the barren flanks of Mount Baldy. The valley to the east is the headwater catch basin of Muddy Creek. Muddy eventually cuts deeply into the San Rafael Swell 50 miles away, disappearing into the darkened sandstone narrows of the Chutes (an adventuresome hike).

Tackle the last formidable climb past Emerald Lake, and then breathe a sigh of relief, for you have beaten Skyline. Except for a couple of uphill teasers, the remaining 20 miles is mostly a cruise. The beacon of the Wasatch Plateau, Mary's Nipple (Musinia Peak), guides you across grass-covered Gunnison Valley and down Salina Creek to I-70. (On the south flank of Mary's Nipple, Skyline continues as Forest Road 009; the Great Western Trail branches right.) Say farewell to the tundra, fir, and aspen of the plateau's crest and welcome the oak, sage, and cacti of the Sonoran high desert.

RIDE 43 *PETE'S HOLE*

You won't find many mountain bikers in this part of the state for two reasons: it is remote and generally unknown. Ask someone where Joes Valley Reservoir is, or the Wasatch Plateau for that matter, and they will likely stare quizzically and shrug their shoulders. Perhaps that is good. Many people don't know that the Wasatch Plateau, located bull's-eye in the center of the state, hosts an untapped wealth of recreational opportunities. Most people don't realize that this section of the Wasatch Plateau is blessed with a gorgeous reservoir overshadowed by 10,000-foot plateaus. Even more people are not aware of the many outstanding mountain bike adventures waiting to be discovered. Pete's Hole loop incorporates all of these Wasatch Plateau elements plus a good chunk of fine singletrack.

Although mountain bikers have only recently discovered the Wasatch Plateau, the region was inhabited by archaic peoples nearly a millennium ago. The nomadic Fremont Indians have long been known to wander about the

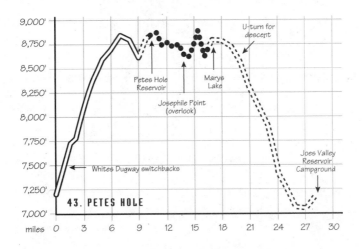

RIDE 43 PETE'S HOLE

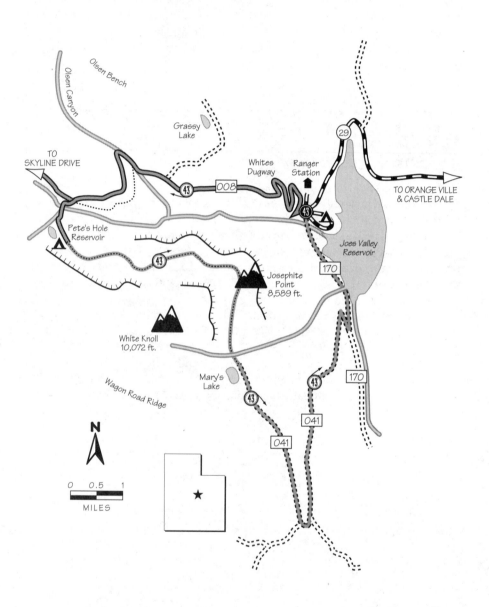

Olsen Canyon

Olsen Bench

Grassy Lake

TO SKYLINE DRIVE

Whites Dugway

Ranger Station

29

TO ORANGE VILLE & CASTLE DALE

43   008   43

Pete's Hole Reservoir

43

Joes Valley Reservoir

170

Josephite Point 8,589 ft.

White Knoll 10,072 ft.

170

Mary's Lake

43

43

170

Wagon Road Ridge

041

041

N

0   0.5   1
MILES

★

desert canyons of central Utah, as is documented in prolific rock art panels. But items excavated from an alcove at Joes Valley Reservoir, including basketry and corn cobs, suggest that the Fremonts ventured to the mountains and may have adopted a more sedentary lifestyle by practicing basic agriculture techniques. In 1990, an 11,000-year-old mammoth was uncovered in Huntington Canyon along with spear tips. These finds give clear insight as to the extent of prehistoric fauna and to early man's existence in Utah.

General location: Pete's Hole is located near Joes Valley Reservoir in the heart of the Wasatch Plateau, located 40 miles south and west of Price.

Distance: 28-mile loop.

Tread: 8 miles of light-duty dirt road, 13.5 miles of doubletrack, and 6.5 miles of pseudo-primitive singletrack.

Aerobic level: Strenuous. The route begins with a hefty climb on a dirt road and follows singletrack punctuated with incremental climbs. Intermediate cyclists can ride out-and-back to Pete's Hole, and legs willing, continue around the loop.

Technical difficulty: Level 2 to 4. Dirt roads and doubletracks are fast paced and have scattered rocks and ruts. The singletrack from Pete's Hole to Mary's Lake may vary from a primitive pack trail to a buffed ATV track.

Elevation change: The trailhead/parking area at Joes Valley Reservoir is at 7,000 feet. The route commences with a 1,400-foot climb up Whites Dugway. The route's high point of 9,000 feet is near Josephite Point. A raucous 1,700-foot descent concludes the route. Total elevation gain is 3,000 feet.

Season: This section of the Wasatch Plateau should melt out by mid-June and be ridable through mid-October. The area is very popular during autumn's hunting season.

Services: Limited services (food, camping supplies, and sometimes gasoline) are available at the boat-ramp cafe near the trailhead and across the reservoir at a second cafe. Meat and potatoes are generally the cuisine. A Forest Service campground (fee area) is at the trailhead. There is no drinking water along the route. (A primitive campground and picnic area is at Pete's Hole, but there is no water tap.) Most visitor services are available in Castle Dale and Orangeville 15 miles from the reservoir. Price has the closest bike shops.

Hazards: Portions of the singletrack exist in near-primitive condition. You may encounter some motorists on the initial climb up Whites Dugway. Whites Dugway is notoriously muddy and ill-advised to travel when wet.

Rescue index: Joes Valley Reservoir is popular with boaters, campers, and anglers. Recreationists regularly visit Pete's Hole Reservoir. Dirt roads are irregularly traveled, and the singletrack section receives few users. A telephone is at the reservoir's boat dock (if the cafe is open) and at the cafe across the lake. Assistance may be summoned from the Forest Service Field Station near the campground, but it may be manned irregularly. Castle Dale has a medical clinic; Price has a hospital.

Land status: Manti–La Sal National Forest (Ferron Ranger District).

Maps: USGS Danish Knoll, Ferron Canyon, Joes Valley Reservoir, Utah.

Access: From Price, travel 26 miles south on Utah State Highway 10. Turn west on Utah State Highway 29 for Orangeville, and follow the signs for Joes Valley Reservoir. Travel 15 miles up "twisting" Straight Canyon, and circle the reservoir to the campground and boat ramp. Day-use parking is available.

From Interstate 70, take Exit 89 and travel about 40 miles north on UT 10. Connect with Utah State Highway 57, which leads to UT 29 in Orangeville. Follow the signs for Joes Valley Reservoir as mentioned above.

Notes on the trail: From the day-use parking area or campground, pedal west on UT 29/Forest Road 008, which is hard-packed dirt when dry and gumbo stew when wet. The route commences with a 5-mile warm-up climb up Whites Dugway. Switchbacks quickly take you high above the reservoir and to overlooks of Seeley Creek—a deep V-notched canyon marred by avalanches. Josephite Point is the prominent butte across the canyon. In an hour or so, you'll be there, looking back here.

Juniper and pinyon flirt with ponderosa, all of which gradually succumb to aspen and mixed fir. Pass the junction for Grassy Lake to the right after 5.5 miles. About 1.4 miles farther, the road bends sharply left as it wraps through Olsen Canyon. Thereafter you can fork left on a spirited 2-mile-long ATV trail (tagged for the Great Western Trail) or continue on the main road for the same distance. If you choose the later, turn left for Thistle Flat and Beaver Dams, and then arrive at Pete's Hole Reservoir for a lunch stop. (The ATV trail also leads to Pete's Hole.)

On the reservoir's southeast side, take the trail signed for Josephite Point Trail. Let the fun begin! This semi-primitive path crosses breezy meadows lying beneath layered cliffs and passes small reservoirs and beaver-dammed ponds. You'll dip through gullies filled with small creeks and dart into dense, fragrant forests. When the trail bends south at Josephite Point, hike out the slope to find a glorious overlook of Joes Valley Reservoir.

You don't need an advanced degree in geology to notice the conspicuous shape of the valley in which the reservoir resides. A valley like this one, long and narrow with steep, tall sides, is a sure indicator of faulting. In this case, the valley is a "graben," or a block-dropped valley wedged between parallel faults.

The singletrack continues southward through more fields and timber with one long, gut-busting climb. At Mary's Lake, the route proceeds south as a doubletrack for 4 miles to a T junction. Turn left and downhill, then left again, now heading north. A long, paint-shaker downhill quickly drops you back to the valley floor. Turn left once more, and pedal 2 easy miles back to the boat ramp, where a cool plunge in the reservoir awaits.

RIDE 44 *U M PASS*

The U M Pass loop ventures up one meadow-filled valley and then down another. In between, however, you cross U M Pass and descend an old doubletrack-turned-singletrack loaded with air-worthy earthen berms, a.k.a. whoop-te-doos. Your bike will buck like a bronco, trying to toss you from its saddle. But hold on tight and wait for the horn to blow before you bail.

In addition to the exciting descent, the U M Pass tour overflows with scenic charm. Both the Sevenmile Creek and U M Creek Valleys, on either side of the pass, are wide plains, threaded by a meandering creek. The Sevenmile Cirques along with Mounts Terrill and Marvine neatly package the Sevenmile Creek Valley with glacial accents. The U M Plateau and Windstorm Peak flank U M Valley with subtler forms. Along the loop's last leg, Johnson Valley Reservoir reflects its aspen-rimmed shore and the elevated plateau tops.

According to John W. Van Cott in *Utah Place Names,* U M Pass gets its name from the United Moroni Order, a group of Mormon stockmen who ranged livestock in the area during pioneer days. U M was their brand, and Moroni was a prophet in the Book of Mormon.

Others had trod these valleys, not herding livestock, but packing stolen treasures. Legend has it that after Butch Cassidy robbed the Union Pacific Flyer in Wilcox, Wyoming, he dashed off on his favorite escape route through northeastern Utah. To elude the posse, he dove into the San Rafael Swell, then crossed the Fish Lake region en route to a hideout in the Henry Mountains. Somewhere between the U M and Sevenmile Creek Valleys, the loot hit the trail and presumably still lies buried today.

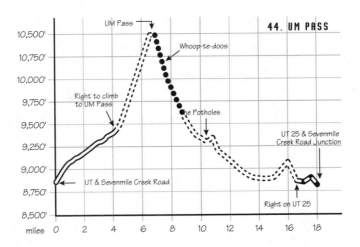

RIDE 44 U M PASS

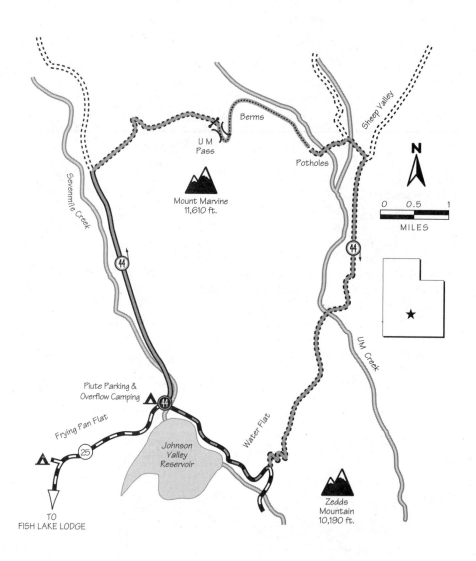

General location: The U M Pass loop is 5 miles north of Fish Lake, which is between Richfield and Torrey in central Utah.

Distance: 19-mile loop.

Tread: 13 miles of variably rutted and washboard doubletrack, 3 miles of doubletrack-turned-singletrack, and 3 miles of pavement.

Aerobic level: Moderate. The Sevenmile Creek Road rises gently, but the climb to U M Pass requires solid effort. The cruise down U M Valley is, well, a cruise, except for a short, protracted hill on the south end. Utah State Highway 25 undulates back to the trailhead.

Technical difficulty: Level 2 to 4. Doubletracks are pretty tame with some gravel, washboards, and ruts. The drop off U M Pass over the whoop-te-doos can be exciting and approach level 4 briefly. You must accept the consequences if you dare let your tires leave contact with Mother Earth. The bumps have claimed the collarbones of unsuspecting bikers in the past.

Elevation change: The trailhead is at 8,850 feet. U M Pass rises to 10,500 feet. U M Valley drops to 8,900 feet. There are two small climbs upon returning to the trailhead via UT 25. Total elevation gain is 2,000 feet.

Season: Snow can linger through May and return by mid-October. Midsummer days are temperate; nights are crisp. Wildflowers are showy during July and August, and fall colors are among the best in the state. The area is very popular with hunters in the fall.

Services: There is no drinking water along the route. The parking area has an outhouse but no water tap. Bowery Haven and Lakeside Resorts have cafes, cabins for rent, general supplies, gasoline, and public pay showers. Fish Lake Lodge has overnight accommodations and a full-service restaurant. There are several Forest Service campgrounds (fee areas) along the lake. Richfield has the closest bike shop.

Hazards: The whoop-te-doo descent from U M Pass warrants caution. Look before you leap! You may encounter motorists along the paved highway and OHVs on dirt roads.

Rescue index: Motorists are common along the highway on the loop's last leg. Anglers commonly work the banks of Sevenmile Creek. U M Pass and the U M Creek Valley receive few visitors.

Telephones are at Bowery Haven, Fish Lake Lodge, and Lakeside Resort. A Forest Service ranger station is across the road from Fish Lake Lodge. Richfield has a hospital.

Land status: Fish Lake National Forest (Loa Ranger District).

Maps: USGS Fish Lake, Forsyth Reservoir, Hilgard Mountain, and Mount Terrill, Utah.

Access: The Piute Parking Area, 8 miles north of Fish Lake Lodge, makes a good trailhead.

From Interstate 70 (east of Richfield), take Exit 48 for Sigurd and travel south on UT 24 toward Capitol Reef National Park. After 33 miles, turn left/east on UT 25, travel 8 miles to Fish Lake Lodge, and then drive 8 miles farther to the trailhead.

From I-70 (west of Green River), take Exit 89 or Exit 85, and then travel 30 miles south on UT 72. Two miles south of the National Forest boundary and Forsyth Reservoir, turn right/west on UT 25 and travel about 16 miles to the trailhead.

From the south (Capitol Reef National Park and Torrey), travel west and then north on UT 24. About 13 miles north of Loa, turn right on UT 25. Fish Lake Lodge is 8 miles ahead; the trailhead is 8 miles farther.

Notes on the trail: Pedal north from the parking area and turn left on Forest Road 640 for Sevenmile Creek and Gooseberry. Your heart gets a jump start as the road rises quickly. It becomes an idle ramble shortly thereafter where it breaks out across the valley's broad, hummocky meadows. After 4 miles, fork right/east on Forest Road 042. This doubletrack may be unsigned but is marked by a wooden information board. Begin the 2.7-mile, 1,000-foot climb to U M Pass.

Groves of aspen quiver in the cool midday breezes. Across the valley, the crest of the Fish Lake Hightop has been stamped with a succession of glacial imprints called Sevenmile Cirques. Mount Marvine, with its craggy cockscomb ridge, creates the southern gate to U M Pass, whereas the subtle stature of Mount Terrill guards the north.

At U M Pass, the road bends south and ends at a log-and-wire fence. Enjoy the view east of sky, mountain, and valley. Hilgard Mountain, an inclined plateau across the valley, is the prominent landform.   .

Now lower your seat and securely fasten your brain bucket. At first, the trail drops quickly, and the berms are steep and abrupt. Check your weight distribution and hang your butt off the back if needed. Feather the brakes—not too much pressure on the front. As the trail flattens, the bumps lessen in severity and allow for a little air to gather between the ground and your tires. But keep things in perspective; you are not trying to jump the Caesar's Palace fountain like Evel Knievel.

Keep an eye on the trail as it wavers through the potholes; it can be faint and confusing. Splash through U M Creek and then a larger water trap at Black Flat. Keep pedaling eastward over an aspen-covered knoll. Turn right on Forest Road 015 and ramble down the length of U M Valley. After cresting and then banking down a rough hill at the valley's southern end, turn right on UT 25 to wind around Johnson Valley Reservoir and return to the parking area.

RIDE 45 *MYTOGE MOUNTAIN*

Mytoge Mountain is a Fish Lake classic and is the featured tour of the Fish Lake in the Fall Mountain Bike Festival held annually in September. The laid-back but well-catered event attracts hundreds of fat-tire enthusiasts to the aquamarine waters of Utah's mountain jewel. Three days of guided tours lead through pristine forests, across stream-cut meadows, and to lofty viewpoints of shimmering lakes with sweeping panoramas of the surrounding plateaus.

Be sure to pack a rod and reel when visiting Fish Lake because trophy-size Mackinaw and rainbow trout lurk in the lake's frigid, spring-fed waters. When Kit Carson visited Fish Lake in 1847, he wrote in his diary that ". . . fish were so plentiful that you could walk on the back of their fins to cross the creek and catch hundreds with your bare hands within minutes." Perhaps fish are not as abundant today, but anglers feverishly cast their lines in hopes of landing that elusive 36-pound lunker, which stands as an all-time record catch.

Upon hearing Carson's glowing reports, Mormon pioneers and ranchers sought the prosperity of the Fish Lake Valley. But their arrival intruded upon the traditional hunting and fishing grounds of the Ute Indians. In the decades to come, many people were killed in battles between white settlers and Native Americans over this land. In 1873, the Mormons sent a delegation to Fish Lake to sign a peace treaty with the Utes; the treaty held firm and was never broken.

The traditional Mytoge Mountain loop received a face-lift in 1998 when the Loa Ranger District applied the finishing touches to the Lakeshore Trail. Instead of riding on paved roads and doubletracks, you can now make the loop on nearly all singletrack. There are steep climbs along the way and one

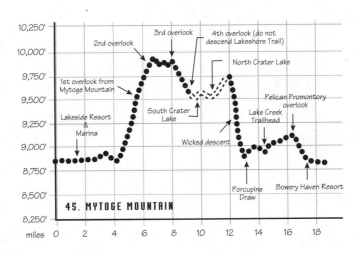

RIDE 45 MYTOGE MOUNTAIN

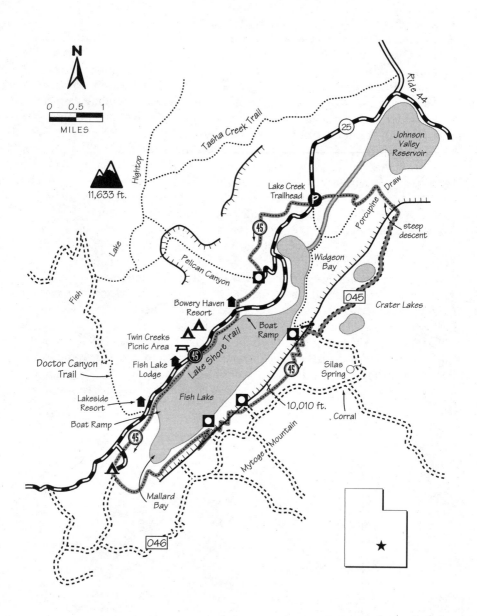

N

0   0.5   1
MILES

Ride 44

Johnson
Valley
Reservoir

Tasha Creek Trail

25

Hightop

11,633 ft.

Lake Creek
Trailhead

P

Porcupine Draw

steep
descent

45

Widgeon
Bay

Lake

Pelican Canyon

045

Crater Lakes

Bowery Haven
Resort

Boat
Ramp

Fish

Twin Creeks
Picnic Area

Lake Shore Trail

Doctor Canyon
Trail

Fish Lake
Lodge

45

Silas
Spring

45

Lakeside
Resort

Fish Lake

10,010 ft.

Corral

Boat Ramp

45

Mytoge Mountain

Mallard
Bay

046

★

hair-raising descent where even elite riders may balk. Those with lesser skills and endurance should not be deterred. Walk the toughest stretches and enjoy the stunning scenery.

General location: Fish Lake is between Richfield and Torrey in central Utah. Mytoge Mountain forms the eastern wall that encloses the lake.

Distance: 19-mile loop.

Tread: 15.5 miles of singletrack, and 3.5 miles of doubletrack.

Aerobic level: Strenuous. The 0.5-mile 500-foot climb to Mytoge is painfully steep and even elite bikers may have to walk some sections. Along the crest and in Porcupine Draw, you'll face several short pulses that pump up your heart and legs. The last climb is a moderate ascent from the Lake Creek Trailhead up to Pelican Promontory.

Technical difficulty: Level 1 to 5. The Lakeshore Trail is dirt, sand, and gravel for the first 4 miles (level 1 to 2). The climb to Mytoge is steep, rough, and has several angular switchbacks (level 3 to 4). There are some rough sections along the crest (level 2 to 4). The wicked descent off Mytoge to Porcupine Draw pushes the technical scale to level 5 and beyond because of the steep grade, menacing rocks, and eroded conditions. The culminating Lakeshore Trail is level 2 to 3.

Elevation change: The trailhead on the lake's shore is at 8,860 feet. The route climbs to 10,000 feet just past the second overlook atop Mytoge Mountain. Total vertical is about 2,000 feet.

Season: Snow lingers into May or June and may return by mid-October. Midsummer days are temperate; nights are crisp. Although terribly inviting for a post-ride plunge, Fish Lake is numbing cold. The backcountry around Fish Lake is popular hunting grounds in the fall.

Services: There is no drinking water once you venture beyond the campgrounds and lodges on the lake's west side. Fish Lake Lodge has a full-service restaurant and snack shop plus overnight accommodations in rustic cabins or deluxe lodges. Lakeside and Bowery Haven Resorts each have a cafe, small general store, gasoline, pay showers, and lodging. There are several Forest Service campgrounds (fee areas) along the lake. Richfield has the closest bike shop.

Hazards: The infamous descent off Mytoge to Porcupine Draw is one of the loop's highlights, but it can be treacherous for all but highly skilled bikers. Save your skin and the trail by walking the scariest spots.

Rescue index: Telephones are at Bowery Haven, Fish Lake Lodge, and Lakeside Resort. Human contact is almost nonexistent once you're into the heart of the ride. A Forest Service ranger station is located across the road from Fish Lake Lodge. Richfield has a hospital.

Land status: Fish Lake National Forest (Loa Ranger District).

Maps: USGS Fish Lake, Utah.

Access: Park and embark from the Twin Creeks Picnic Area just north of Fish Lake Lodge. From Interstate 70 (east of Richfield), take Exit 48 for Sigurd and

Fish Lake—the jewel of Utah's High Plateaus.

travel south on Utah State Highway 24 toward Capitol Reef National Park. After 33 miles, turn left/east on Utah State Highway 25. Fish Lake Lodge is 8 miles ahead.

From I-70 (west of Green River), take Exit 89 or Exit 85, and then travel about 30 miles south on UT 72. Two miles south of the National Forest boundary and Forsyth Reservoir, turn right/west on UT 25 and travel 25 miles to the Twin Creek Picnic Area just north of Fish Lake Lodge.

From the south (Capitol Reef National Park and Torrey), travel west and then north on UT 24. About 13 miles north of Loa, turn right on UT 25. Fish Lake Lodge is 8 miles ahead.

Notes on the trail: From the Twin Creek Picnic Area, take the Lakeshore Trail south and behind Fish Lake Lodge. The lodge is one of the great rustic resorts of the West. Stout hand-hewn logs support a trestle roof over a grand ballroom and a noble dining room.

Take the gravel and dirt path past the rustic cabins and along the lake's edge through willows and hardwoods. Pass the Lakeside Resort marina, cross the paved entrance road to Doctor Creek Campground, and pass the RV dump station. Wind through towering aspens on the fine-gravel path.

Where the trail intersects a doubletrack, fork left and take the track about 100 feet to a broken log fence; fork left again on the continued path (may not be signed) and skirt the corral. Climb briefly into the aspens, and then follow the lake's edge past several doubletracks and back into the trees.

The past 4 miles of trail has been a piece of cake. Well, you are about to burp up that cake. The trail rises for 1 mile up the face of Mytoge Mountain, gently at first, then at agonizing grades over the last 0.5 mile. Technical difficulty increases proportional to the trail's steepness, and several turns are humorously sharp. Just grin and bear it.

Oftentimes, perseverance is a virtue in this sport, and if you persevere you will be rewarded with the first of several stunning viewpoints to come. Soak up the sight of Mallard Bay on the lake's south end and of the Hightop Plateau across the way. Shake out your legs, and take the trail uphill. Crank full-steam ahead on the steeps and spin idly on the breathers.

Just over 1 mile farther, you reach the second viewpoint directly across from Fish Lake Lodge and the 11,300-foot crest of the Hightop Plateau. If fall colors are at their peak, you'll spot the "Aspen Heart" above the lodge on the plateau's forested flank. According to Indian legend, this grove of blood-red aspens marks the site where a Paiute princess died of a broken heart when her lover, a warrior brave, did not return from battle. After her death, the brave did return badly wounded to claim his princess. But when he learned of her death, he too climbed the hillside and died beside her grave. The brilliant leaves of the Aspen Heart symbolize their love and devotion for each other.

Roll across the top of Mytoge for 1 mile to the third overlook. Cross a wire fence with iron steps that prevents livestock from crossing (may be gated in the future) and bank down the slope for a half-mile to a fourth overlook and the junction with Forest Road 045 (doubletrack). Here, you are across from Pelican Point and Pelican Canyon. A glacier once occupied the canyon and scoured out its conspicuous U shape. As the ice tongue slowly plowed down the canyon, the debris that was pushed ahead of it nearly pinched off Widgeon Bay from the rest of the lake.

Now it's time to leave the Lakeshore Trail, temporarily. (At this point, the trail *does* descend to the lake's shore, but if you take it, you'll stumble and tumble down a menacing path and then hack through a tangle of brush and trees along the shore. In the future, this section will be reconstructed and may be biker friendly.) There's a better way. Take the doubletrack (FR 045) northerly and around the west side of South Crater Lake 0.25 mile ahead. Deer often venture from the forest's cover to forage on the marshy grasses that surround the depression. Curve around the *east/right* side of North Crater Lake, cross a fence, and climb back into the aspens on the doubletrack-turned-singletrack. Watch for trail markers. After the path exits the trees to a clearing, head to the wire fence and trail marker. Now, drop your seat *way down*, secure your helmet, and plunge headlong off Mytoge's rim down the horrific but exciting trail and to the clearing in Porcupine Draw.

Fork left and follow trail markers up the draw on a faint trail that wavers through the sage and rocks. Before entering the trees, fork right for Lake Creek. Struggle over a small ridge, descend, and cross to Lake Creek (you'll have to hopscotch on rocks), and arrive at a parking area. Here, you have two choices: Pound the pavement back to the trailhead or cross the road and continue on the Lakeshore Trail.

If you choose the latter, follow the doubletrack for about 0.5 mile to a wire fence and corral. Take the trail up the right side of the fence along the interface between an aspen grove and a large meadow. Cross footbridges over Jorgenson Creek, and then contour slopes above Widgeon Bay for almost 2 miles to Pelican Promontory. Here, the Lakeshore Trail descends a gravel doubletrack due south to Bowery Haven Resort. Cross the highway to the marina and pick up the trail for a 1.3-mile cool down.

RIDE 46 *LAKESHORE NATIONAL RECREATION TRAIL*

Completed in 1998, the Lakeshore National Recreation Trail offers pedestrians and casual-paced bicyclists interludes with central Utah's aquatic jewel—Fish Lake—and the forested slopes that cradle it. The route is nearly 9 miles long from Mallard Bay on the southern tip of Fish Lake to the Lake Creek Trailhead on the northern end. But you don't have to knock off the whole route at once. Embark from one of several trailheads midroute and ride in either direction. Then make an about-face and enjoy the trail from a different perspective.

Interpretive signs along the trail tell about the area's prehistoric, human, and geologic history. Take the kids and make a day of it by casting a line from shore or having lunch at a lakeside lodge. If you are a member of the Polar

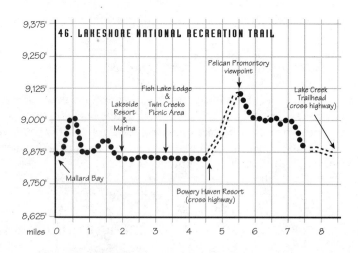

RIDE 46 LAKESHORE NATIONAL RECREATION TRAIL

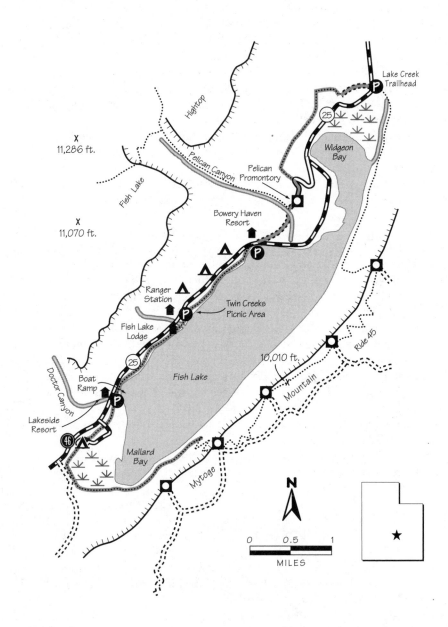

Bear Club, then you can brave the lake's frigid waters with a midroute plunge.

Last, the Lakeshore Trail is not a racecourse, so leave your heart rate monitor behind. Head up to Mytoge Mountain or circle around U M Pass if you are craving a solid workout.

Location: Fish Lake is between Richfield and Torrey in central Utah.

Distance: 8.5 miles from Mallard Bay to the Lake Creek Trailhead.

Tread: Dirt, sand, and gravel multi-recreational trail.

Aerobic level: Easy. If you stay along the lake's shore, the trail is as easy as pie and is perfect for first-time bikers, children, and perhaps tag-along child trailers. The section from Bowery Haven Resort to Lake Creek Trailhead has a short, steep climb over Pelican Promontory.

Technical difficulty: Level 1 to 3. Again, the trail alongside the lake is a breeze. The climb to Pelican Promontory from Bowery haven is steep with some gravel and rocks.

Elevation change: The lake's shore is at 8,850 feet. Pelican Promontory rises to 9,070 feet for a 220-foot gain. Double that if you ride out and back to the Lake Creek Trailhead.

Season: May through October. You're safe from big-game hunters on this trail.

Services: Fish Lake Lodge has a full-service restaurant and snack shop, plus overnight accommodations in rustic cabins or deluxe lodges. Lakeside and Bowery Haven Resorts each have a cafe, general store, gasoline, pay showers, and lodging. There are several Forest Service campgrounds (fee areas) along the lake. Richfield has the closest bike shop.

Hazards: None to speak of. Be alert and courteous to other trail users and perhaps back-casting anglers. Use caution crossing the highway near Bowery Haven Resort.

Rescue index: Telephones are at Bowery Haven, Fish Lake Lodge, and Lakeside Resort. A Forest Service ranger station is located across the road from Fish Lake Lodge. Richfield has a hospital.

Land status: Fish Lake National Forest (Loa Ranger District).

Maps: USGS Fish Lake, Utah.

Access: Begin at one of the following trailheads: Doctor Creek Campground, Twin Creek Picnic Area, Bowery Haven Marina (fishermen's parking area), or the Lake Creek Trailhead.

From Interstate 70 (east of Richfield), take Exit 48 for Sigurd and travel south on Utah State Highway 24 toward Capitol Reef National Park. After 33 miles, turn left/east on UT 25. Fish Lake is 8 miles ahead.

From I-70 (west of Green River), take Exit 89 or Exit 85 and then travel about 30 miles south on Utah State Highway 72. Two miles south of the National Forest boundary and Forsyth Reservoir, turn right/west on UT 25 and travel 25 miles to Fish Lake Lodge.

From the south (Capitol Reef National Park and Torrey), travel west and then north on UT 24. About 13 miles north of Loa, turn right on UT 25. Fish Lake is 8 miles ahead.

Emerging from the aspens near Pelican Promontory on the Lakeshore N.R.T.

Notes on the trail: For the full effect, start at Doctor Creek Campground and take the trail north past the Lakeside Resort marina. (Or begin with a 3-mile out-and-back trip around Mallard Bay. Turn around when the trail starts scaling Mytoge Mountain.) Read the plaque describing the local geology about how faulting formed the valley, and learn about a truce that was declared between warring Ute Indians and white settlers. You'll learn more about the Black Hawk Wars at Pelican Promontory.

Wander along the edge of the lake, which flickers through white-bark aspens. Pass the rustic cabins and then Fish Lake Lodge. On the return leg, enjoy a treat on its back porch and reflect on the vision of Charles Skougaard, who in the early 1900s urged his pony over the mountain and declared to his companions, "Someday, boys, people are coming a long way to fish and rest here." Looking back over the rough trail, the others just shook their heads in doubt. Yet in 1911 Skougaard brought his dreams to Fish Lake and built a small lakeshore tent resort that harbored 12 boats. Steadily, nature seekers stout enough to make the rough trip from the nearby Sevier Valley marveled at its spectacular setting, and this prompted Skougaard to build the noble Fish Lake Lodge. With its hand-hewn timber and open-air trestles, Fish Lake is one of the grand log lodges of the West that rivals those of many national parks.

At Twin Creek Picnic Area you can read a plaque about Kit Carson's visit to the lake in 1847 and the plenitude of fish he caught. Take the wide, dirt-and-gravel path past several spurs for Mackinaw and Bowery Creek Camp-grounds. Stop to read the interpretive sign that rekindles the adventures of Native Americans and Anglos who traveled across the plateaus and valleys long before bicycles came on the scene.

Exit the trail at the Bowery Haven marina, and pick it up again across the highway just north of the resort. Here, the trail follows a doubletrack of native surface (dirt, pebbles, and rocks) and climbs quickly to Pelican Promontory where a glorious view of lake, valley, and plateaus awaits. Take the dirt road to a right-hand bend, and then fork left on the continued trail, which now has the character of a true singletrack. Contour the slopes high above Widgeon Bay and cross footbridges over Jorgenson Creek. Descend to a wire fence and corral and take the doubletrack to the Lake Creek Trailhead across the highway. Round out your history class by envisioning a time when mammoths and prehistoric bison roamed the land 12,000 years ago and were hunted by Paleo-Indians.

If you're not looking forward to surmounting Promontory Point again, then simply ride the highway to Bowery Haven, and hop back on the Lakeshore Trail. Be alert to motorists and lumbering RVs.

RIDE 47 *VELVET RIDGE*

If your travels take you to Capitol Reef National Park, spend half a day outside the park and just west of Torrey exploring Velvet Ridge. This is a quick, fun ride that clips the edge of the Torrey Breaks where a beautiful complex of canyons, cliffs, ledges, buttes, and mesas wrap the shoulder of Thousand Lake Mountain.

The route takes you along the fertile Fremont River and through the Red Gate where the Fremont has carved a valley passageway between Thousand Lake Mountain to the north and Boulder Mountain (Aquarius Plateau) to the south. Thousand Lake Mountain's high flanks are trimmed with alpine timber. Lower on the mountain, glowing sedimentary strata, typical of southern Utah's canyon country, step down as a series of cliffs and alcoves to the river valley. A wavering row of chocolate-brown, Grecian columns of stone called the Fluted Wall contain the river; atop the wall are hummocky, calico-striped mounds of Chinle clay and bentonite called the Velvet Ridge. The combination of verdant forests, terra-cotta strata, and fanciful forms make the Velvet Ridge loop surreal.

General location: The Velvet Ridge loop is located immediately west of Torrey on the north side of the Fremont River Valley.

Distance: 14-mile loop.

Tread: 5.5 miles of pavement with the rest of the trail sandy doubletrack.

Aerobic level: Easy to moderate. The road work is easy. The initial climb to Velvet Ridge is tough but short. The remainder of the ride is marked by rolling hills, drift sand, and a generous descent.

Technical difficulty: Level 2 to 3. Doubletracks can have some ruts, drift sand, and scattered rocks; none is of significant consequence.

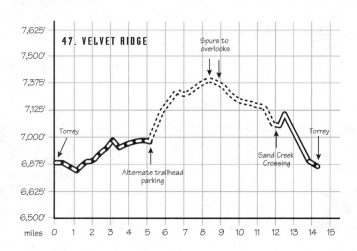

RIDE 47 VELVET RIDGE

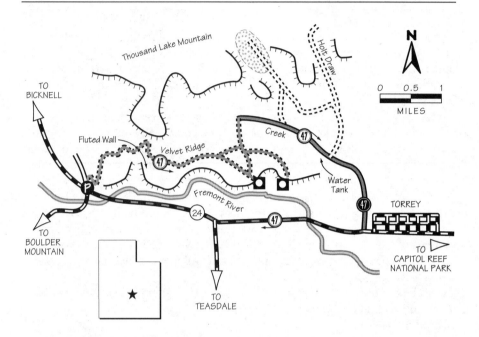

Elevation change: The route's trailhead (Torrey) is the low point at 6,850 feet. The trail rises to just shy of 7,400 atop the Fluted Wall. Adding in a few undulations, total climbing is about 700 feet.

Season: Because of its mid-elevation and good southern exposure, Velvet Ridge could be ridable from March through much of November. But *do not* attempt this route when wet. The bentonite clays of Velvet Ridge turn even the knobbiest tires to smooth, concrete doughnuts and shoes to cement slippers. The Catch-22 is that after prolonged dry spells, the clay breaks down to powdery silt—but at least you can pedal through the silt.

Services: There is no drinking water along the route. Torrey offers all visitor services. Wild Hare Expeditions in Torrey offers bike rentals, repairs, and shuttle service (435-425-3999). Additional visitor services are in nearby Bicknell and Loa.

Hazards: Doubletracks wander everywhere on Velvet Ridge, but the main route is marked with signs and carsonite posts. Again, avoid this route after recent rains. Use caution when seeking the ideal viewpoint from the cliff's rim.

Rescue index: There's a good chance you'll experience complete solitude on Velvet Ridge. You're never more than 4 miles from the highway. Bicknell has a medical clinic.

Land status: Fish Lake National Forest (Loa Ranger District).

Maps: USGS Bicknell and Torrey, Utah.

Access: Start this ride from anywhere in Torrey; otherwise, travel west out of Torrey 0.5 mile and turn right/north on Sand Creek Road. Park about 1 mile up the gravel road at the Great Western Trail information board.

Notes on the trail: From Torrey, pedal west on Utah State Highway 24 and pass Sand Creek Road to the right after 0.5 mile. You'll return via Sand Creek later. (If you parked up Sand Creek Road, then hop on board at this point.) Pedal the highway up the Fremont River Valley for 5 miles to a trailhead kiosk where the road bends north toward Bicknell. You'll pass a two-story gristmill set back among the trees that operated from 1890 to 1940 and is a national historic landmark. From the kiosk, take the doubletrack veering right and up a rough and tough hill. (The left/lower road leads to an electrical substation.) This short grinder is a good workout for advanced cyclists and a make-or-break initiation for novice cyclists.

The going is much easier once you're on top of the bench. Here, you'll pass the Velvet Ridge. Its rounded humps striped in gray, maroon, and light green are part of the Chinle Formation which was formed along the shore of a fluctuating, shallow seashore about 200 million years ago. Keep an eye out for pebbles of silica and petrified wood. About 3 miles out the ridge, follow a wooden post directing you to the right, and then veer right again at a second post tagged for Scenic Point (right), Sand Creek (left), and Highway 24 (reverse). Take this right fork for 0.5 mile to a cliff-edge view of the Fremont River Valley.

The Fremont River was named for Captain John C. Fremont who lead several expeditions through Utah between 1840 and 1853. His colorful accounts and detailed maps had a major influence on the Mormon's quest to colonize Utah. The Fremont Indians, who occupied central Utah from 700 A.D. to 1300 A.D., also share the explorer's name. But it was archaeologist Noel Morss who named the culture in the late 1920s. By studying the extensive artifacts left behind in the Fremont Valley by the now-vanished tribe, Morss determined that the Fremonts were a separate and distinct culture from the more widespread and populated Anasazi group of the Four Corners area.

Return from the overlook to the previous junction and head north for Sand Creek. A few hundred yards ahead, you can fork right and ride 1 mile to an equally stunning overlook of the valley, plateaus, and national park; otherwise, stay on a northerly course toward Thousand Lake Mountain. Surf the sand, dip through a gully, and fork right/east at a junction tagged for Velvet Ridge. One-half mile farther, stay right at two junctions with doubletracks. (Actually, these roads form the corners of a large triangle-shaped junction with the upper Sand Creek Road.) Coast downhill, plow through the sand, and cross Sand Creek. Fork right at the Holt Draw Road junction, cross Sand Creek a second time, power up a short ramp, and pass a water tank. Round the western tip of the Fluted Wall, and cruise back to town on Sand Creek Road/Great Western Trail.

Barry passes the historic gristmill outside of Torrey on the Velvet Ridge loop.

Torrey, the Fremont River Valley, and the Capitol Reef area were some of the last regions in Utah to be discovered and settled. It wasn't until the 1870s, more than 25 years after the Mormons arrived in Utah, that settlers took hold of the fertile valley and found the weather and soil ideal for fruit trees. Small orchards still bear luscious fruit near the entrance to Capitol Reef National Park at the old town site of Fruita. Like most small towns throughout Utah, Torrey has gone by many previous names, including Central, Poverty Flat, and Bonita. Its current name honors Colonel Torrey who fought in the Spanish American War.

RIDE 48 *SKYLINE NATIONAL RECREATION TRAIL*

The Tushar Mountains east of Beaver are one of Utah's alpine hideaways— seldom visited and largely unknown. Ardent skiers may be familiar with the quaint resort of Elk Meadows, and big-game hunters might know of a good camp spot or two, but the Tushars have successfully eluded the fevered quest of mountain bikers.

The majority of the Tushars' backcountry trails can shred even the most hard-core mountain biker since the paths are more suited for hooves and boots

RIDE 48 SKYLINE NATIONAL RECREATION TRAIL

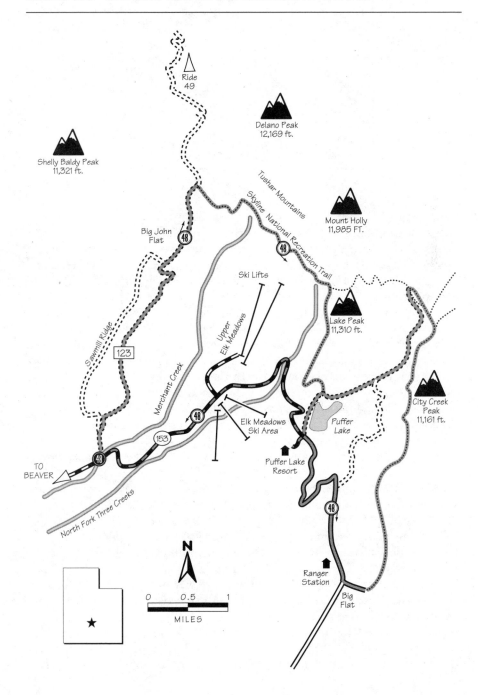

Ride 49

Delano Peak
12,169 ft.

Shelly Baldy Peak
11,321 ft.

Tushar Mountains

Skyline National Recreation Trail

Mount Holly
11,985 FT.

Big John
Flat

48

48

Ski Lifts

Lake Peak
11,310 ft.

Upper
Elk Meadows

Sawmill Ridge

123

Merchant Creek

48

Elk Meadows
Ski Area

Puffer
Lake

City Creek
Peak
11,161 ft.

153

Puffer Lake
Resort

TO
BEAVER

48

North Fork Three Creeks

48

N

Ranger
Station

Big
Flat

0   0.5   1

MILES

★

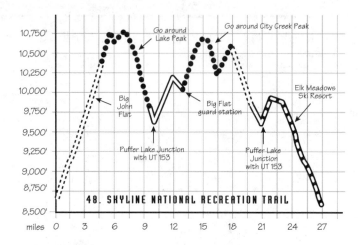

than fat-tires. Skyline National Recreation Trail, on the other hand, is a serendipitous find. Keep in mind that this is no place for flatlanders or first timers; Skyline is a tough ride. Its semi-primitive tread demands advanced handling skills, its long climbs require solid quads, and its high elevation strangles the lungs of those not acclimated. Start the day with a huge bowl of Wheaties topped with PowerBars.

Skyline National Recreation Trail (Skyline NRT) crosses terrain that is alpine in every aspect; where groves of subalpine fir and quaking aspen flirt with tundra meadows and treeless peaks; where sparkling creeks tumble down from winter's snowfields to merge with blue-ribbon hatcheries; and where distant views extend across southwestern Utah into Nevada's Basin and Range Province. Along the way you'll pass Puffer Lake and Elk Meadows Ski Area, which provide additional summertime activities.

General location: 20 miles east of Beaver in the Tushar Mountains.

Distance: 27-mile figure-eight loop.

Tread: 12 miles of dirt roads and doubletracks, 10 miles of singletrack, 5 miles of pavement.

Aerobic level: Strenuous. Mountain bikes were not on the scene when Skyline was designated as a National Recreation Trail, so expect sections that are not altogether biker friendly. Several sections require short episodes of portaging uphill. Trail signs are minimal, so route-finding skills are required.

Technical difficulty: Level 3 to 5. The initial climb on doubletrack is mostly packed dirt (level 2). Although designated as a National Recreation Trail, Skyline is semi-primitive in spots and not regularly maintained, which means rocks, loose tread, and eroded conditions can exist (level 3 to 5). Some sections, however, are as smooth as silk.

Elevation change: The starting point in Beaver Canyon is the lowest elevation at 8,620 feet. The ride begins with an inaugural 5.5-mile, 2,200-foot climb. The Delano Peak section of singletrack traverses at about 10,800 feet. A midroute descent to Puffer Lake drops to 9,660 feet. The second loop tops out at 10,720 feet aside City Creek Peak. Total elevation gain is nearly 4,400 feet. Yikes!

Season: High elevations mean snow may linger well into late June and return by early October. Expect mild daytime temperatures (70s) and cold nights (40s) during summer. Since the Tushars are the first major landmass encountered by eastbound weather systems crossing Utah's western desert, clear morning skies can produce thunderstorms by afternoon. This route crosses prime big-game hunting grounds and should be avoided in the fall.

Services: A water tap is at the Big Flat Ranger Station, located along Utah State Highway 153 a few miles south of Puffer Lake. Food and beverages *may* be available midroute at Puffer Lake Resort, but in years past, offerings were scant. (There is a pool table, though.)

Puffer Lake Resort has rustic cabins and a campground (private) at Puffer Lake. Forest Service campgrounds (fee areas) are in Beaver Canyon. Overnight lodging (but no dining) is available at Elk Meadows Ski Area. Elk Meadows' upper lodge may be open for lunches. Beaver offers all visitor services, but no bike shop.

Hazards: Much of Skyline NRT requires attentive biking else you might twitch and pitch or be lead far off course by a wrong turn. Be alert and courteous to horseback riders; mountain bikes are still alien in these parts. Route-finding (and -following) skills are required.

Daydreaming in the Tushar Mountains.

Part of the route follows UT 153, which is paved between the trailhead and Puffer Lake. Be aware of vehicular traffic and changing road conditions, especially on the fast, descent back to the trailhead.

Rescue index: Motorists are common along UT 153. Campers, fishermen, and recreationists visit Puffer Lake, Big John Flat, and Big Flat. Emergency contacts can be made at Elk Meadows and Puffer Lake Resort. Beaver has a medical clinic.

Land status: Fish Lake National Forest (Beaver Ranger District).

Maps: USGS Delano Peak and Shelly Baldy Peak, Utah.

Access: From Interstate 15, take either Exit 109 or Exit 112; both are for Beaver. In the center of town, travel east on UT 153 for Elk Meadows. Drive 16.5 miles up Beaver Canyon and park near the junction with Forest Road 123, signed for Big John Flat. Park at your discretion. Alternatively, park midroute at Puffer Lake 5 miles farther up UT 153.

Notes on the trail: After a sustained, 3.5-mile, 1,300-foot warm-up climb, a sign welcomes you to Big John Flat—elevation 9,954 feet. Pedal around the basin, staying right when the road splits and following Piute ATV trail markers. A short, punishing climb brings you to the signed trailhead for Delano Trail, Puffer Lake, and Skyline NRT 225.

The old doubletrack rises steeply to a small ridge (tree blazes mark the route) and then turns eastward to cross the head of Merchant Creek basin. You would never guess from its subtle shape that Delano Peak is the monarch of the Tushars, capping 12,169 feet, and is the sixth tallest peak in Utah. Travel across Delano's treeless flanks on the technical level 3 to 5 trail. Push up and over a small ridge of talus cobbles, and then traverse the flank of Mount Holly. Lake Peak comes into full view after you cross a small nose extending from the south face of Mount Holly. Ahead, you come to a trail junction signed Big Flat (straight), Big John Flat (reverse), and Puffer Lake Trail 175 (sharp right). Turn right on the Puffer Lake Trail and start descending, but not too far! (Ignore any trails that drop into the North Fork of Three Forks basin.) Take the trail eastward across the head of the basin directly toward Lake Peak; aim for the conifers mid-slope. (If you descend to a pioneer cabin deep within the basin, you have gone too far downhill.)

The well-defined Lake Peak segment of the trail enters a darkened tunnel of conifers on a mat of crunchy pine needles. Serendipity! Descend steep switchbacks through aspens to the shore of Puffer Lake and take the doubletrack south to UT 153.

If you have had enough adventure for the day, simply ride the paved highway 5 miles back to your vehicle. Otherwise, head up UT 153 (gravel road). Pass the Big Flat Ranger Station after 3 miles, and then fork left to continue on Skyline NRT. Pedal around the northern edge of Big Flat to a wooden staging ramp for horses. Skyline NRT is signed Big John Flat 8.3 miles (left/north). This section is moderately technical and semi-primitive. Watch for tree blazes and other trail indicators.

After 2 miles, the path crosses a knob of bedrock. This is a fine rest stop that boasts powerful views of the Tushars' regal high peaks, of valleys a mile below, of central Utah's High Plateaus, and of Nevada on the western skyline. The singletrack wraps around City Creek Peak and then descends through angular switchbacks to a saddle that appears to have been cleared of its timber. The trail can be elusive here. Head due north across the saddle, and push up a heinous pitch back into the forest. You'll pass a trail sign reading "Bears Hole, Cottonwood."

There are two trail junctions over the next half mile; stay left and along the subtle ridge. As the trail crosses over to the ridge's west side, it splits again (that's the third junction). Stay right and descend gradually past a sign for Big John and to a meadow at the base of Mount Holly.

Skyline Trail (proper) continues west and up to a saddle between Lake Peak and Mount Holly. This section is difficult to follow, full of dismounts, and provokes endless cursing, so descend left/south on Forest Road 642. Control your speed; the ride is fast! After 1 mile, intersect Cullen Creek Road (Forest Road 129) and stay right for Puffer Lake. Upon connecting with UT 153 again, turn right on the paved road, chug up one last hill (make it burn!), and then take delight in a full-blown, screaming descent past Elk Meadows on the highway. (Stay attentive to vehicular traffic and variable road conditions). The S turns announce the approaching turnoff for Big John Flat and your vehicle.

RIDE 49 *KIMBERLY ROAD*

Not many people know of the Tushar Mountains. Perhaps that is understandable; perhaps that is good. The Tushars' presence is peripheral, if not subliminal, as you cruise past the wayside town of Beaver on Interstate 15. From afar the Tushars rise sluggishly through subtle contours to seemingly submissive heights. A snowcapped peak or two hovers above timberline, and a shadow-filled canyon creases a slope; but all are too distant and ill-defined to spark real curiosity. But if you dare exit the freeway and wander into Tushars' heartland, you will find that your preconceptions pleasantly erred. The Tushars are the state's third highest range (behind the Uintas and La Sals) and are home to Utah's sixth tallest peak, Delano Peak, at 12,169 feet. Herds of elk populate the pristine woods and commonly leave their protective cover to forage the mountain's meadows.

The Tushars are rich in history. Mormon pioneers established a settlement at the mouth of Beaver Canyon in 1856 and raised sheep amidst seclusion and tranquility. The calm was shattered in 1860 when silver and gold were discovered in the San Francisco Mountains to the west and then again when precious ore was uncovered on the Tushars' north slope in the 1880s.

RIDE 49 KIMBERLY ROAD

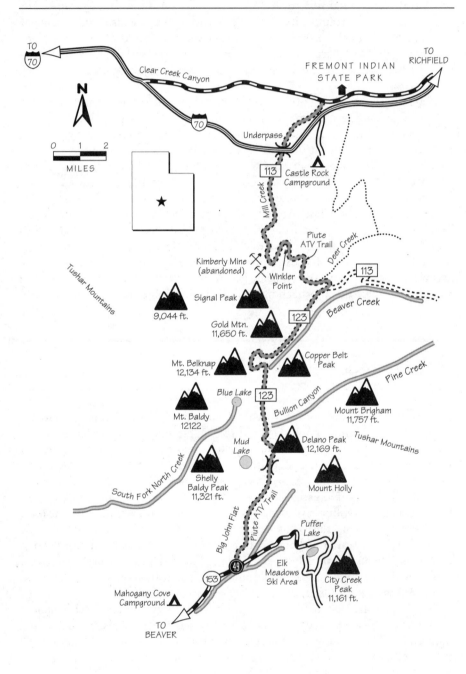

The Kimberly Road takes you over the Tushars, across meadows that invite deer, and within arm's reach of its tallest peaks. You'll find the air to be mighty thin up here because this route reaches an elevation higher than every other route in this book—11,500 feet. Then you descend for what seems an eternity and pass the defunct mining center after which the route is named. You can round out your tour with a visit to Fremont Indian State Park and study artifacts of this ancient tribe and hike to mystical rock panels. The entire route is part of the Piute ATV trail.

General location: The Tushar Mountains form the predominant massif east of Beaver. The Kimberly Road connects Beaver Canyon/Utah State Highway 153 with Interstate 70 near Fremont Indian State Park.

Distance: 32 miles point-to-point.

Tread: Packed dirt and rock doubletracks throughout are suitable for high clearance and/or four-wheel-drive vehicles.

Aerobic level: Strenuous. High elevations and the hefty elevation gain require strong legs and acclimated lungs.

Technical difficulty: Level 2 to 4. Doubletracks are packed dirt with variable rocks and ruts. The descent through Mill Creek Canyon (past Kimberly) is steep and pebbly, which demands continual braking and a firm grip on the bars.

Elevation change: The tour's starting point in Beaver Canyon is at 8,620 feet. The road tops out at 11,500 feet about 8 miles into the ride. The descent to Deer Creek drops to 8,740 feet, where you must climb again to 10,000 feet at Winkler Point. The route culminates with a 12-mile, break-neck descent down Mill Creek Canyon to Fremont Indian State Park at 5,800 feet. Total elevation gain is 4,140 feet; total elevation loss is 7,000 feet.

Season: Because of the high elevations, this route has a short biking season from early July through September. Since elevation changes are extreme, so might be the weather. Pack extra clothes and rainwear just to be safe because precipitation at the summit can be bone chilling.

Services: There is no drinking water along this route. Beaver offers all visitor services, but it does not have a bike shop. Fremont Indian State Park has a campground (fee area), located a few miles from the visitor center. There are Forest Service campgrounds (fee areas) in Beaver Canyon.

Hazards: Because of the high elevations, weather can be erratic. Be aware of current weather patterns and pack appropriate clothing. The road descending Mill Creek Canyon past the Kimberly mine site is steep and gravelly; bike cautiously.

Rescue index: Steel gates close the highest portions of the route until the snow has melted. Although these gates do not impede bike travel, they will stymie vehicle support or rescues. Motorists are frequent in Beaver Canyon. Campers are common at Big John Flat, especially on weekends and holidays. Between

Mount Belknap blocks the horizon.

Big John Flat and Fremont Indian State Park you're on your own. A pay phone is at Fremont Indian State Park. Beaver has a medical clinic.

Land status: Fish Lake National Forest (Beaver Ranger District).

Maps: USGS Marysvale Canyon, Mount Belknap, Mount Brigham, Shelly Baldy Peak, and Trail Mountain, Utah.

Access: Leave a vehicle at or near Fremont Indian State Park, located 20 miles west of Richfield on I-70 (take Exit 23 or Exit 17) and 17 miles east of the

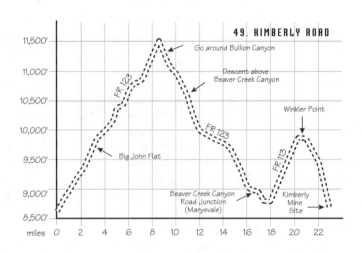

I-70/I-15 interchange (Exit 132 off I-15). Be aware that the parking lot's gate is locked when the visitor center closes (usually about 5 P.M.). Otherwise, leave a vehicle near the park's campground on the south side of I-70 about a mile up the gravel road.

In the shuttle vehicle, drive 17 miles west on I-70 to the interchange with I-15. Travel south on I-15 and take Exit 112 for Beaver. Drive to the center of town, and turn left/east on Utah State Highway 153 for Elk Meadows and Beaver Canyon. Drive 16.5 miles up UT 153 and park near the junction with Forest Road 123, signed for Big John Flat. Or drive up to Big John Flat and knock off the 3-mile, 1,300-foot warm-up climb.

Sources of additional information: Fremont Indian State Park (See Appendix A).
Notes on the trail: After a 3-mile, 1,300-foot warm-up climb, a sign welcomes you to Big John Flat—elevation 9,954 feet. While skirting this glorious meadow, you will be introduced to the Tushars' high peaks. From afar, Shelly Baldy's smoothly contoured slopes seem to welcome explorations by foot, but its savage talus of angular volcanic scree is a hiker's lament. Delano Peak to the east, on the other hand, is cloaked with a carpet of tundra grasses. Hiking to its 12,169-foot summit is surprisingly easy for the sixth tallest peak in Utah.

Quickly, the doubletrack rises with little regard for those lacking aerobic stamina. Stay right where the road splits on the east side of the basin, and pass the trailhead for Skyline National Recreational Trail. A protracted grade announces Mud Lake (a generous name) and the commencement of the final switchbacks rising to the basin's divide.

At the divide you are greeted by a dynamic mountain scene; stream-fed basins drop in all directions, and naked, conical peaks swarm the ultramarine sky. The Paiute called the range T'shar, meaning "white" in reference to the light-colored peaks. The Tushars are quite different geologically from the rest of the central High Plateaus, which are dominated by uplifted and eroded sedimentary strata capped with basaltic lavas.

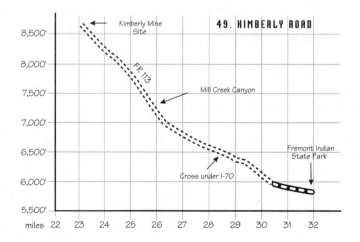

The Tushars are the remains of a collapsed caldera—a massive volcanic vent—whose fiery, molten deposits of lava, ash, and pyroclastic flows covered a broad area. Some events were violent, like the eruption of Mount St. Helens; others produced thick, slow-flowing rivers of magma. Volcanic rocks tend to be quite drab in color, but because of weathering and oxidation of primarily iron minerals, many of the Tushars' high peaks are streaked with yellow, orange/brown, light green, and pale violet.

From the divide, you reap the first payoff in the way of an 8-mile roaring descent around the flanks of Mount Belknap and Gold Mountain while remaining high above luxuriant Big Meadow. Just stay on the main road signed "Piute ATV Trail 01."

Upon reaching the Beaver Creek Road junction, fork left for Piute ATV, Kimberly, and I-70, and enter the alpine jungle that engulfs Deer Creek. Hopefully your legs are still fresh for the 2 miles of 12-percent grade up to Winkler Point. Take a break at Winkler Point (named in honor of Ernest Winkler, who had an illustrious career with the Forest Service from 1923 to 1936). Savor this last great viewpoint of the San Pitch Mountains and Wasatch Plateau to the north and the flanks of the Tushars elsewhere, for in a moment's time, you'll be concentrating squarely on the road before your front wheel.

The descent through Upper and Lower Kimberly is brisk, and you'll be braking the whole way. Stop periodically to let your rims cool and to search for dilapidated cabins, mine structures, and vacant foundations lining the road and hiding in the forest. You may even catch a glimpse of the sad skeleton of the Annie Laurie Mill. Between 1899 to 1908, the town site rang with activity as thousands of miners extracted gold from the wily, volcanic-country rock. But like most boomtowns, prosperity faded as the pay dirt ran thin.

Cross Mill Creek and continue the rampage. Note the peculiar, conical rock formations lining the slopes above the drainage—seems like the area was carpet-bombed with a bunch of duds. Pass under I-70 and follow the frontage road back toward Fremont Indian State Park.

Southern Plateaus

RIDE 50 *POWELL POINT*

The salient of Powell Point is as distinct as the nineteenth-century geologist and western explorer after whom it was named. Its stately presence and ocean-liner profile can be seen from great distances throughout the region. But the point is more than another of the many lofty vantages that terminate the wavering edge of southern Utah's High Plateaus. It is a titanic viewpoint from where the Great Architect oversees his handiwork in the Grand Staircase-Escalante National Monument. Geologist Clarence E. Dutton, John Wesley Powell's protégé, wrote of the terminus in his 1880 report *Geology of the High Plateaus of Utah* as ". . . the aspect of a vast Acropolis crowned with a Parthenon. Such glorious tints, such keen contrast of light and shade, such profusion of sculptured forms, can never be forgotten by him who has once beheld it. This is one of the grand panoramas of the Plateau Country . . ."

A short and long version of this ride caters to novice-intermediate bikers and advanced bikers. Regardless of the route taken, all will cross the forested crest of the Table Cliff Plateau on a rolling doubletrack and then take a spirited singletrack to the point. There you'll find a stunning view that has captured the souls of travelers for a century and a half.

General location: Powell Point is located 25 miles northeast of Bryce Canyon National Park in south-central Utah.

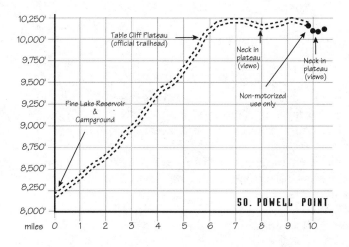

RIDE 50 POWELL POINT

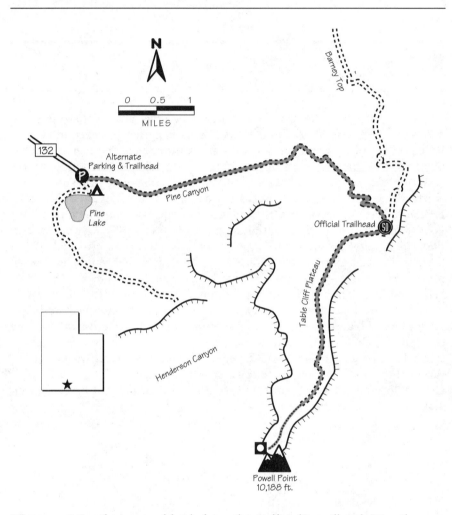

Distance: 9.2 miles out-and-back from the "official" trailhead; 21 miles out-and-back from the alternate trailhead at Pine Lake. (See "Notes.")

Tread: About 6 miles of light-duty dirt road from Pine Lake to Table Cliff Plateau (rough for passenger cars). Thereafter, 4 miles of dirt doubletrack (high clearance recommended) along the plateau and 0.6 mile of singletrack.

Aerobic level: Easy to moderate. The route rolls gently atop the plateau, but there is one short, steep hill along the singletrack. The high elevation can enfeeble flatlanders.

Technical difficulty: Level 2 to 3. The doubletrack is packed dirt with token rocks and ruts. The singletrack can have some eroded conditions.

Elevation change: The trailhead atop the Table Cliff Plateau is at 10,120 feet. The route rolls gently to a high point at midroute of 10,260 feet. Total climbing is merely 500 feet. If you start from Pine Lake at 8,200 feet (the long version), you'll begin with a 6-mile, 2,000-foot climb to reach the trailhead on the plateau. (See "Notes.")

Season: Because the Table Cliff Plateau receives considerable snow during winter and is at high elevation, the route may not melt out until late May to mid-June. It should be ridable throughout October. The point is usually breezy, so pack a light jacket.

Services: There is no drinking water along this route. Pine Lake has a Forest Service campground (fee area). Lodging, dining, gasoline, and curios shopping are at Bryce Junction (intersection of Utah State Highways 12 and 22). Mountain bikes can be rented from Ruby's Inn, located at the entrance to Bryce Canyon National Park.

Hazards: Use caution when scouting the viewpoints at Powell Point; the friable limestone may crumble and break away. Any fall could prove fatal. Be prepared for changing alpine weather.

Rescue index: Campers, anglers, and other recreationists frequently visit Pine Lake and its campground. The Powell Point Trail is not heavily traveled. Emergency contacts can be made from businesses at Bryce Junction (junction of UT 12 and UT 22). Panguitch has a hospital.

Land status: Dixie National Forest (Escalante Ranger District).

Maps: USGS Griffin Point, Pine Lake, Sweetwater Creek, and Upper Valley, Utah.

Access: From Bryce Junction (UT 12 and UT 22, 2 miles north of Bryce Canyon National Park), travel 11 miles north on UT 22 for Antimony and Pine Lake. Turn right on Forest Road 132 (gravel road) for Pine Lake and Table Cliff Plateau and drive 5.5 miles to Pine Lake. Those opting for the long version should park and embark here; those banking on the short version should continue driving 6 miles up Pine Canyon on FR 132 to where it bends conspicuously left atop the plateau. A high clearance vehicle is recommended.

Notes on the trail: Let's start at Pine Lake for those choosing the long version. Head out from the reservoir and ride 6 miles up Pine Canyon on FR 132 to the crest of the Table Cliff Plateau. Directions are that simple. But the climb can be more difficult. At times the road can be coated with coarse limestone gravel that is transported during sudden rains from the sparsely vegetated slopes across the road. No bother. As the climb progresses, the road steepens and may be rocky and rutted. You have fleeting glimpses of the Table Cliff Plateau's salmon-hued cliffs as ponderosa pines meld with spruce and fir higher up. After rounding several switchbacks you come to the plateau's crest where the road bends conspicuously left/north. Here you have a sweeping view off the plateau's east rim; the doubletrack to Powell Point forks right/south. Those opting for the short version will park and embark here.

The Wasatch Formation fortifies Powell Point.

But before heading out to Powell Point, take in the staggering view eastward from the plateau's edge and across southern Utah. The Table Cliff Plateau blends with the Aquarius Plateau to the north. Their sheer slopes descend to Upper Valley, which directs numerous streams toward the Escalante River. Although the Escalante is hidden from sight, the down-cutting handiwork of its attendant tributaries can be seen in the incised, naked sandstones of the Box-Death Hollow Wilderness. When Dutton viewed the wilderness from atop the Aquarius Plateau, he was obviously stunned by its destitute nature.

> The view . . . is dismal and suggestive of the terrible. It is a maze of cliffs and terraces lined off with stratifications, of crumbling buttes, red and white domes, rock platforms gashed with profound canyons, burning plains barren even of sage—all glowing with bright color and flooded with blazing sunlight. Everything visible tells of ruin and decay. It is the extreme of desolation, the blankest solitude, a superlative desert.

The ruler-true lineament off to the right is the Straight Cliffs of the Grand Staircase-Escalante National Monument's Kaiparowits Plateau province. The Henry Mountains define the horizon.

The playful doubletrack crosses the broad, flat-topped mountain through a corridor of fir and aspen. Periodically, the crest pinches to a narrow backbone that affords more astounding views across the vast emptiness below. After nearly 4 miles, the doubletrack ends and singletrack begins (motorized use is prohibited). As you round the first curve, you'll sneak a peek of colossal views yet to come. Cross a neck in the plateau and ramble to Powell Point. You'll know when to stop!

You are standing on the top rung of a sequence of mammoth, stratigraphic terraces that step down layer after layer across the Utah-Arizona border to the brink of the Grand Canyon. Collectively they are called the Grand Staircase. Here at Powell Point, like at Bryce Canyon National Park and Cedar Breaks National Monument (the latter nearly 60 miles west) the Wasatch Formation erodes to a pastel frieze, called the Pink Cliffs, that breaks from the forested plateaus.

When you are visually satiated, retrace your tracks to the trailhead and bomb down to Pine Lake if that's your destination. Fond memories of grand views and that killer little singletrack will steer you home.

RIDE 51 *CASTO CANYON*

Bryce Canyon National Park is not a canyon at all but coalescing amphitheaters of salmon-colored cliffs that break sharply from the rim of the forested Paunsagunt Plateau. The Paiute Indians called it "Unka-timpe-wa-wince-pock-itch," which translates to "red rocks standing like men in a bowl."

If only mountain bikes were allowed on Bryce Canyon's trails, what a dream ride it would be. But attempt that sort of stunt and you'll be counting bricks lining your cell inside the town poky. There is an alternative: Casto Canyon. Casto is a miniature version of the nearby national park and it beckons fat tires. Casto boasts much of the phantasmagoria of Bryce Canyon, and all can be seen from a playful trail.

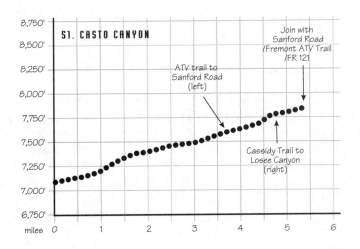

RIDE 51 CASTO CANYON

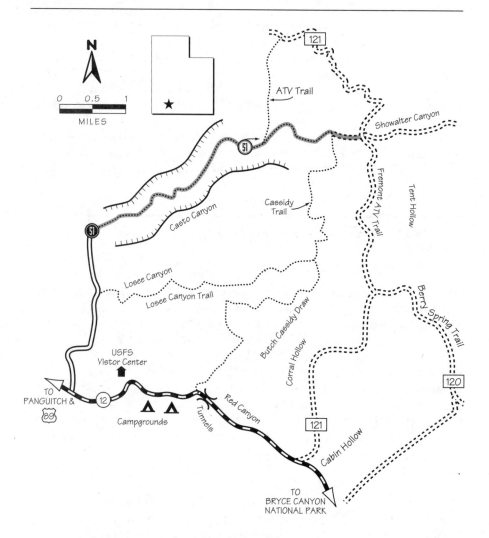

Like in Bryce Canyon National Park, your imagination will run wild in Casto Canyon. The flesh-tone rocks have eroded to delicate forms that mimic obelisks, steeples, and temples; sentinels armed with spears; castle walls and darkened windows manned by hooded monks and robed priests.

Butch Cassidy and the Wild Bunch used these labyrinthine canyons to elude the law after a heist. Purportedly, one of his rock hideouts was built into Casto Canyon's deep crevasses. Nearby Cassidy Trail and Butch Cassidy Draw bear the outlaw's name.

The standard approach to Casto Canyon is to ride out-and-back. But you can venture out of Casto and chase trails that lead to higher ground and neighboring canyons or to Red Canyon on backcountry roads and trails.

General location: 12 miles southeast of Panguitch.

Distance: 10.8 miles out-and-back.

Tread: 3.6 miles of ATV trail and 1.8 miles of primitive singletrack.

Aerobic level: Easy to moderate. The trail rises gently but crosses the wash many times. Each crossing requires good handling skills and a bit of "oomph" to plow through sand, bound over rocks, and hop back onto the bank.

Technical difficulty: Level 2 to 4. Where the trail follows on the creek's bank, it's easy. But when it crosses the (usually) dry wash, the sand and rocks can make steering tricky and traction poor. Walking a bit means you have more time to ogle the sights.

Elevation change: The trailhead/parking area is at 7,080 feet. The top of Casto Canyon rises to 7,880 feet, for a gain of 800 feet. If you loop south up Tent Hollow to Red Canyon (optional), you'll gain another 500 feet.

Season: Despite all the redrock, Casto Canyon and the Paunsagunt Plateau are hardly desert, but low alpine terrain. Daytime temperatures are temperate (70s and 80s) and nights are cool (40s). This route is ridable from April through October.

Services: There is no drinking water along the trail. The trailhead/parking area has an outhouse. The Red Canyon Visitor Center has a water tap, restroom, and vending machine. Red Canyon Campground is a Forest Service fee area. Camping at the trailhead is prohibited. Lodging, cafes, and gift shops are along Utah State Highway 12. Mountain bike rentals are available at Ruby's Inn near the entrance to Bryce Canyon National Park. Panguitch has all visitor services, including a full-service bike shop.

Hazards: Use caution when crossing the wash; sand and rocks can nab your front tire. Use caution if looping to UT 12 and descending Red Canyon. Red Canyon's overwhelming scenery may distract your attention and that of motorists, too.

Rescue index: Casto is popular with ATVs, equestrians, and fellow bikers, but the route is by no means heavily traveled. You'll likely find solitude. Motorists are numerous on UT 12 in Red Canyon. Emergency assistance may be summoned from the Dixie National Forest's Red Canyon Visitor Center, about 1 mile up Red Canyon. Panguitch has a hospital.

Land status: Dixie National Forest (Powell Ranger District).

Maps: USGS Casto Canyon and Wilson Peak, Utah.

Access: From the junction of U.S. Highway 89 and UT 12 (7 miles south of Panguitch), travel east on UT 12 toward Bryce Canyon National Park. Turn left at milepost 2 for Casto and Losee Canyons and take the gravel road 3 miles to Casto Canyon, passing Losee Canyon after 2 miles.

Tricia mingles with the hoodoos in Casto Canyon.

From the east, pass the turnoff for Bryce Canyon National Park (junction of UT 12 and UT 63) and continue west on UT 12, then down Red Canyon. One-half mile after exiting Red Canyon, turn right/north at milepost 2 for Casto and Losee Canyons and proceed as above.

Notes on the trail: From the parking area, pedal the ATV trail into the fiery mouth of Casto Canyon. There is no wanting of scenic reward, for you are instantly engulfed by national-park-caliber sights. Periodically, the trail crosses the (usually) dry creek bed. The soft sand and scattered rocks may stymie your progress unless you charge ahead at full steam. During prolonged dry spells, a clean path gets beaten down through the wash. However, if rains cause the creek to flow, the trail may be partially erased. Fussy little trail.

About 3.5 miles up the trail, the canyon's walls begin to subside, and you reach a trail junction. The ATV trail forks left up a side canyon and is signed for Sanford Road and Barney Cove. You can explore up there and loop clockwise via Forest Road 121/Fremont ATV Trail to reenter Casto Canyon farther up. But for this out-and-back version, fork right and stay on an easterly bearing up the rest of Casto. Novice riders may opt to turn around.

Now the trail is less an ATV path and more a cattle trail. Continue up the widening canyon for another 1.8 miles, passing Cassidy Trail and Casto Spring along the way. When you intersect the Sanford Road/FR 121, turn around and enjoy Casto Canyon's beauty and the trail's playfulness from the varied perspective.

Strong riders have two options from upper Casto Canyon: follow the Cassidy Trail south to neighboring Losee Canyon or take FR 121 to Red Canyon. If you pursue either, you will loop back to Casto on the access road.

The former, Cassidy Trail, is a temperamental path that is used infrequently by equestrians and less by bikers. Although it is highly scenic, it is technically challenging and difficult to follow. If you're good at sniffing out a trail, you can ride 4 miles on Cassidy, descend 3 miles through Losee, and loop back to Casto for a 13-mile loop.

The latter follows doubletracks southward to UT 12 in Red Canyon. Take the Sanford Road/FR 121 right/south and grind up the steep 1.5-mile-long hill in Tent Hollow. After reaching the top and descending another mile to a prominent junction, fork right on FR 121 for Cabin Hollow and UT 12. (Forest Road 120 forks left for the Fremont ATV Trail). Descend 4 miles to UT 12, coast 3 miles through Red Canyon, and take the access road 3 miles back to Casto for a 20-mile loop. Like passing motorists, you'll be rubbernecking the whole way down Red Canyon.

RIDE 52 *SUNSET CLIFFS*

It would be a grave injustice if you did not visit Bryce Canyon National Park while you're in this area, for it is truly a remarkable sight to behold. But after scrounging for a parking space, sightseeing from fenced-in viewpoints, and hiking with the masses, you can find solitude by mountain biking in the adjacent Dixie National Forest.

This loop takes you from the fertile East Fork Sevier River Valley to Bryce Canyon's alter ego—the Sunset Cliffs—on the west rim of the Paunsagunt Plateau. Here, too, water and wind have exposed the flesh of the Pink Cliffs and created a blazing frieze on the rim of the forested plateau. But you'll be sharing the sights with sparrows overhead, laying claim to your own viewing deck, and yielding the trail to foraging deer.

The miniature Bryce Canyon-esque formations passed on the way up to the cliffs will spark your curiosity. At the rim, you'll be socked with an eyeful of blinding color and fanciful shapes that become indelible memories as you race back to the trailhead. As their name suggests, the cliffs are set aglow when the sun wanes in the western sky. So pack along a flashlight or ride like mad with what little daylight remains if you plan to hold your ground until the burning orb drops below the horizon. Bring a fishing pole, too, because trout are always biting at Tropic Reservoir.

General location: 27 miles southeast of Panguitch and 15 miles west of Bryce Canyon National Park Tropic Reservoir (2 miles as the crow flies).

Distance: 17.5-mile loop.

Tread: Hard-packed dirt and pebbly doubletracks and light-duty dirt roads.

Aerobic level: Moderate. The ride up Badger Creek starts out gentle for a few miles and then rises in stair-step manner where moderate pulses are offset by recovery zones. The road can be rocky at the switchbacks near the top. The descent is blazing fast and forever curving.

Technical difficulty: Level 1 to 3. Doubletracks are generally packed dirt but can have scattered pebbles and rocks, especially on the steeper switchbacks.

Elevation change: Tropic Reservoir is at 7,835 feet. The loop rises to 9,250 feet atop the Sunset Cliffs. Total elevation gain is about 1,400 feet.

Season: The route is ridable from late April through October. Despite the redrock rimming the Paunsagunt Plateau, the terrain is decidedly alpine. Daytime temperatures during summer are moderate (70s to 80s) and nights are cool (40s). This area is popular with big-game hunters in the fall.

Services: Kings Creek Campground is a Forest Service fee area with water taps and outhouses. The Tropic Water Stop is a spring-fed fountain near the end of the loop. Lodging, dining, and curios shopping are along Utah State Highway 12. Panguitch has all visitor services, including a full-service bike shop.

RIDE 52   SUNSET CLIFFS

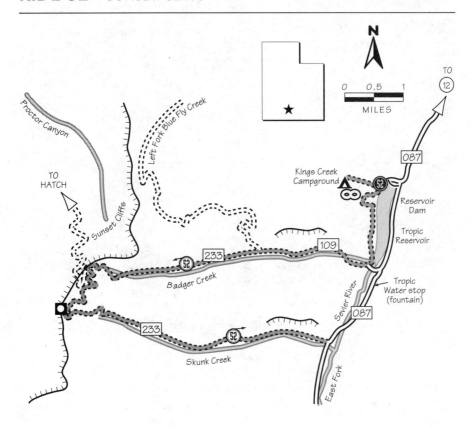

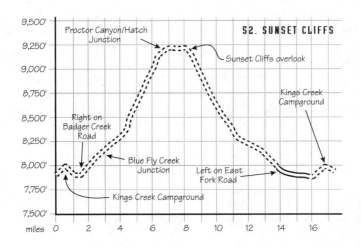

What did you expect to find at Sunset Cliffs?

Mountain bikes can be rented at Ruby's Inn near the entrance to Bryce Canyon National Park.

Hazards: Use caution if hiking along the rim of Sunset Cliffs; the friable limestone may crumble and break away. The descent is raging-fast, so know your limits and watch your front wheel. Be alert to changes in the road's tread and to the possibility of oncoming OHVs and motorists, especially around blind curves. Be aware of changing alpine weather; doubletracks may become impassable when wet.

Rescue index: Campers, anglers, and other recreationists commonly visit Tropic Reservoir. However, few travel this backcountry route. Panguitch has a hospital.

Land status: Dixie National Forest (Powell Ranger District).

Maps: USGS Tropic Reservoir, Utah.

Access: From the junction of U.S. Highway 89 and UT 12 (7 miles south of Panguitch), travel east on UT 12 toward Bryce Canyon National Park for 11 miles. Between mileposts 10 and 11, turn right/south on Forest Road 087 for Kings Creek Campground and Tropic Reservoir. Drive 7 miles on the gravel road to Tropic Reservoir, cross the dam, and park at the boat ramp.

Notes on the trail: From the reservoir's boat ramp/day-use parking area, pedal south past the entrance to Kings Creek Campground, and then roll along the west lake road for about 1 mile. Fork right on Forest Road 109 for Badger Creek and Proctor Canyon. After 0.5 mile, fork right and cross the luxuriant, grass-filled valley to its north side. Hoodoo rock formations, similar to those at Bryce Canyon but less brash, peek through the open stands of ponderosa pines on the slopes above. Keep an eye out for deer and elk at dawn and dusk.

When you reach a junction 2 miles up the Badger Creek Valley, stay straight/left on Forest Road 233 for Skunk Creek and Proctor Canyon. (FR 109 forks right to Blue Fly Creek.) Now the road rises in stair-step fashion as the grassy valley narrows and pines succumb to aspen and fir. Each moderately difficult riser is offset with a gentle recovery zone. Round two pair of steep, loose switchbacks and arrive at a junction. Fork left/south on FR 233 for Skunk Creek and East Fork. (The right fork descends Proctor Canyon to Hatch.) The climb is essentially over as the doubletrack contours around knolls that conceal Sunset Cliffs. After about 1 mile, the road brushes the cliff's edge.

Park your bike and take a hike, literally, northward up the small knoll. There you will have the whole Sunset Cliffs to yourself. Beneath the cliffs, Proctor Canyon collects whatever rainfall and spring water trickles off the scarp and feeds it to the Sevier River in the distant valley. Beyond the Sevier, the Markagunt Plateau shapes the western skyline. Those with a penchant for land forms will recognize the asymmetrical profile of Brian Head Peak over 30 miles away. Did you find the small natural arch below the rim?

Now race down Skunk Creek, banking around the sweeping turns at mach speed like a skier on a giant slalom course. Feather your brakes lightly while leaning into the turns. Feel the tire's knobs grip. Then shift your weight for the next curve. As the forest opens and the valley widens, let gravity take over, but let one eye roam the hillsides for more hoodoos and for deer and elk.

Upon intersecting the East Fork Road (FR 087), fork left and take it 1.5 miles to the Tropic Water Stop (spring-fed fountain). Fork left on FR 109 and circle back to the boat ramp on the west lake road.

RIDE 53 *PINK CLIFFS*

From Brian Head to Powell Point, a distance of nearly 60 miles by line of sight, the Pink Cliffs decorate the wavering rims of the Markagunt, Paunsagunt, and Table Cliff Plateaus with a stony entablature of striking color and fantastic form. The Cliffs' propensity for what geologists call "differential weathering" culminates at Cedar Breaks National Monument and Bryce Canyon National Park where colossal amphitheaters are stuffed with ornate erosional features that defy the imagination.

But you don't have to visit the national parks to mingle with the hoodoos. Here at the absolute terminus of the Paunsagunt Plateau, you can toe the edge of the Pink Cliffs and stand spellbound by the intricacies of erosion. Also,

RIDE 53 PINK CLIFFS

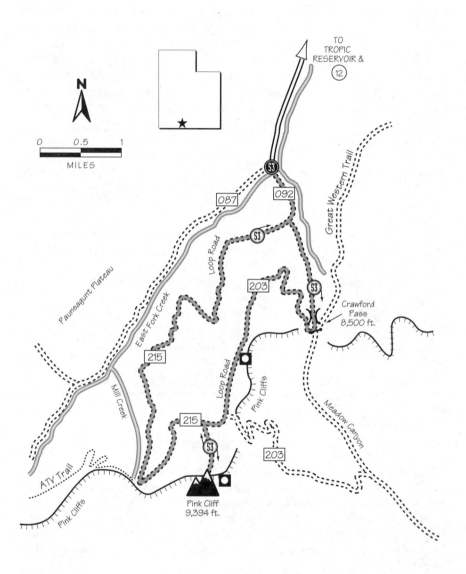

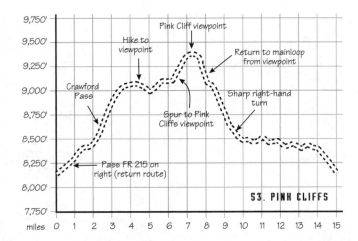

you'll stare out over a vast region of mammoth terraces incised by rivers and bound by scarps called the Grand Staircase. In the fall of 1996, by presidential proclamation, Bill Clinton created the namesake national monument and forever preserved this unique landscape.

When you're not gawking across the land, you'll be pedaling through the Paunsagunt Plateau's rich forests and stream-fed valleys. The Paiute Indians made their home among the "place of the beavers" over a century ago, hunting its woodlands and fishing its streams. When they spied the Pink Cliffs, they applied simple but evocative names. They called Bryce Canyon "Unka-timpe-wa-wince-pock-itch" or "red rocks standing like men in a bowl"; Cedar Breaks was "Un-cap-i-cun-ump" or "circle of red or painted cliffs." You, too, will follow the footsteps of the Paiutes and stare with awe at bands of tribesmen that have been cast in stone.

General location: 35 miles southeast of Panguitch at the southern tip of the Paunsagunt Plateau in south-central Utah.

Distance: 15-mile loop.

Tread: Dirt, sand, and rock-peppered doubletracks.

Aerobic level: Moderate. There are no crushing climbs on this route, but several heart-pumpers just the same.

Technical difficulty: Level 2 to 3. Doubletracks are mostly packed dirt with minor ruts. The loop's "back nine" is locally spattered with imbedded pebbles and has a few sandy stretches that can grab your front wheel. Mostly, the loop is cruisey.

Elevation change: The trailhead is the lowest elevation at 8,100 feet. The route rises to 9,394 at the Pink Cliffs themselves. Total elevation gain is about 1,600 feet.

Season: Despite the tour's redrock undertones, the Paunsagunt Plateau resides in the Canadian Life Zone where midsummer daytime temperatures are temperate (70s and 80s) and nights are cool (40s). Expect changing alpine weather; afternoon thunderstorms are common. The entire area is very popular with big-game hunters during the fall.

Storm clouds gather over the Pink Cliffs.

Services: There is no drinking water along the trail. The Podunk Guard Station does not have public drinking water and is not always manned. Kings Creek Campground at Tropic Reservoir is a Forest Service fee area. Lodging, dining, and curios shopping are available along Utah State Highway 12. Panguitch has all visitor services and the closest full-service bike shop. Mountain bike rentals are available at Ruby's Inn near the entrance to Bryce Canyon National Park.

Hazards: Use caution when walking along the cliffs' rims; the limestone may crumble and break away. Don't mess around during hunting season (late September through October); wear fluorescent orange, or ride somewhere else, because this is prime elk habitat. Be aware of changing alpine weather; doubletracks may become impassable when wet.

Rescue index: This route is remote. At the farthest point, you are 8 miles from your vehicle, 18 miles from UT 12, and 35 miles from medical attention. Panguitch has a hospital.

Land status: Dixie National Forest (Powell Ranger District).

Maps: USGS Podunk Creek, Utah.

Access: From the junction of U.S. Highway 89 and UT 12 (7 miles south of Panguitch), travel east on UT 12 toward Bryce Canyon National Park for 11 miles. Between mileposts 10 and 11, turn right/south on Forest Road 087 for Kings Creek Campground and Tropic Reservoir. Drive 18 miles on the gravel road to a Y junction for Crawford Pass and Meadow Canyon (left) and Robinson Canyon (right), passing Tropic Reservoir after 7 miles and the

Podunk Guard Station after 16.5 miles. Park alongside the road at your discretion.

Notes on the trail: From the junction, pedal up the left fork toward Crawford Creek and Meadow Canyon. After 0.7 miles, Forest Road 215 joins sharply from the right. (This is the loop's return route.) Stay straight, and climb gently for 1.5 miles more to Crawford Pass, marked by a cattle guard. Turn right/south on Forest Road 203 signed for Loop Road and Pink Cliffs and keep chugging up the moderate grade to a subtle divide.

As the road bends south and descends, it winds to within a few feet of the Pink Cliffs, which are drenched in white, orange, and pink. Hike up the knoll to the north to view a scalloped bowl stuffed with hoodoos that rival those of Bryce Canyon National Park.

At the upcoming Y junction, stay right on FR 215. (FR 203 forks left and descends to Meadow Canyon. The views are mediocre from down there, and you won't enjoy the return climb!) About 0.5 mile farther, fork left from FR 215 and climb a numberless doubletrack signed for Pink Cliffs. The pedaling is the toughest yet (still moderate), and the track is laced with ruts and peppered with small rocks. In the clearing at the top, fork left again, and follow an ATV trail for a few hundred yards to the plateau's absolute terminus.

John Wesley Powell enjoyed this view over a century ago. He established a triangulation station here from which he surveyed distant points and landmarks. Until recent years, his weathered, three-sided marker made of interlocked logs remained and echoed his pioneering days.

Look south and east from the rim and over the Grand Staircase-Escalante National Monument. The plateau's crimson cliffs descend to a forested terrace that stretches southward until terminated by another eroded scarp—the White Cliffs. In turn, the White Cliffs yield to the Vermillion Cliffs, then to the Chocolate Cliffs. Thereafter, the stratigraphic sequence crosses the Utah-Arizona border and culminates on the north rim of the Grand Canyon. Uplift and faulting have since dissected the region and the Colorado River, along with its attendant tributaries, has carved deep scars into its skin.

Return to the previous junction with FR 215, turn left, zoom downhill, and round a sharp, right-hand turn. Now the road heads northward and enters timbered slopes above Mill Creek that elk are known to inhabit. Rousing a bedded herd electrifies the still air with stampeding hooves and thrashing antlers. Who startles whom more? The doubletrack roughly contours the hillsides for 5 miles, rising and falling gently. Portions are baby-butt smooth; others are lumpy and bumpy. Upon intersecting the Crawford Pass Road, fork left, and coast less than 1 mile back to your vehicle.

RIDE 54 *VIRGIN RIVER RIM TRAIL*

The Virgin River Rim Trail (VRRT) is one of the newest trails in the Dixie National Forest and has instantly become a new-found classic. The trail follows the edge of the Markagunt Plateau, which is rimmed by the always-captivating Pink Cliffs. These salmon-hued limestones are the foundation of nearby Cedar Breaks National Monument and Bryce Canyon National Park and exude a propensity to erode to ornate shapes. Springs seeping from the lip of the Markagunt nourish the trail's namesake Virgin River, which has cut the famous Narrows of Zion National Park far downstream. From many points along the VRRT, you'll gaze from the rim of the Pink Cliffs across forested platforms to the shadow-clad canyons and sandstoned temples of Zion. Geologist Clarence E. Dutton described the sublime spectacle in his 1880 report, *Geology of the High Plateaus of Utah.*

> We stand upon the great cliff of Tertiary beds [Pink Cliffs] which meanders to the eastward till lost in the distance, sculptured into strange and even startling forms, and lit up with colors so rich and glowing that they awaken enthusiasm in the most apathetic.

The scenery along the VRRT is inspirational, but the trail riding is superlative. The route is predominately singletrack, blending sections that were either hand-built or machine-cut. The route winds through fragrant pine and fir forests mixed with aspens, cuts across wildflower-blanketed alpine meadows, and passes the shore of ultramarine Navajo Lake.

The entire 33-mile, point-to-point route is reserved for advanced cyclists who are acclimated to high altitudes. But intermediate and novice riders alike will revel in the VRRT by starting from numerous trailheads at midroute and exploring part of the epic course.

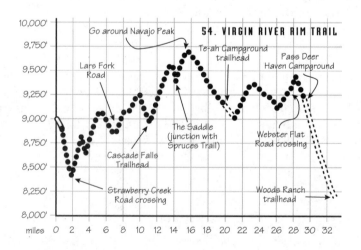

RIDE 54 VIRGIN RIVER RIM TRAIL

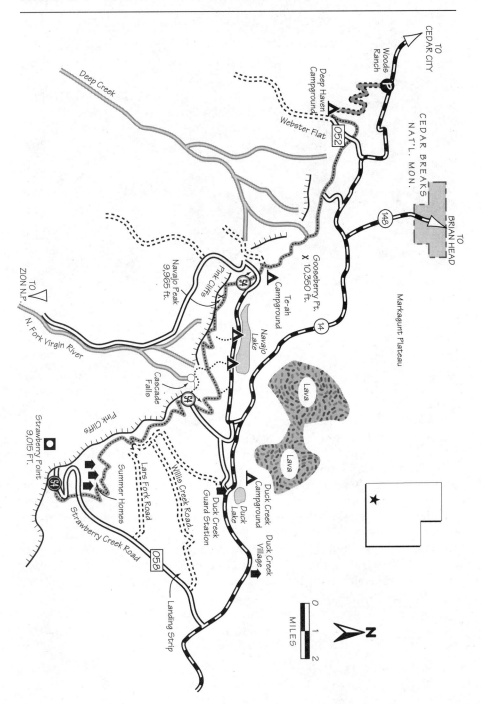

TO CEDAR CITY

Woods Ranch

Deep Creek

Deep Haven Campground

Webster Flat

052

CEDAR BREAKS NAT'L. MON.

148

TO BRIAN HEAD

Gooseberry Pt. × 10,350 ft.

Navajo Peak 9,965 ft.

Pink Cliffs

TO ZION N.P.

N. Fork Virgin River

Te-ah Campground

Navajo Lake

14

Markagunt Plateau

Lava

Lava

Cascade Falls

Pink Cliffs

Strawberry Point 9,015 FT.

Summer Homes

Lars Fork Road

Willis Creek Road

Duck Creek Guard Station

Duck Lake

Duck

Duck Creek Campground

Duck Creek Village

Strawberry Creek Road

058

Landing Strip

0 1 2 MILES

N

Jim gazes across the Grand Staircase to Zion National Park from Strawberry Point.

General location: 28 miles east of Cedar City and centered about Navajo Lake.

Distance: 33 miles point-to-point.

Tread: Nearly all singletrack with just a touch of requisite doubletrack midroute. The 3-mile descent to the Woods Ranch Trailhead is on a pebbly doubletrack.

Aerobic level: Strenuous. Although the trail is claimed never to exceed the fed's maximum 8-percent-grade guideline, an 8-percent grade on a dirt trail is nothing to scoff at. And there are many 8-percent-grade climbs along the way that effectively turn ambitious legs to Silly Putty.

Technical difficulty: Level 2 to 3. The VRRT offers the whole gamut of singletrack elements in a fun and enticing way: dizzying turns, angular switchbacks, loose and rocky tread, short and extended climbs, and lots of silky smooth, pine-needle-encrusted trail.

Elevation change: The VRRT has a mean elevation of about 9,000 feet, but the trail undulates constantly. The highest elevation is 9,800 feet near Navajo Peak above Navajo Lake; the lowest is Woods Ranch at 8,200 feet. Total elevation gain is nearly 4,100 feet.

Season: The trail should be ridable late May through October, although snow may linger near Navajo Lake well into June. Midsummer daytime temperatures are mild (70s and 80s) and nights are cool (40s).

Services: A water tap is at Te-ah Campground on the west end of Navajo Lake. Navajo Lake Lodge, 1 mile east of Te-ah, has a bare-bones general store. Additional Forest Service campgrounds (fee areas) are at Navajo Lake. Limited services are available at Duck Creek Village, 5 miles east of Navajo Lake. Brian Head and Cedar City offer all visitor services, including bike shops.

Hazards: The VRRT is a huge ride; plan on being in the saddle for six to ten hours depending on the amount of sightseeing. The route winds near the edge of sheer cliffs several times, so use caution when scouting viewpoints because the eroded surface may crumble and break away. The trail is generally free of significant hazards, but some switchbacks can be tricky. Be alert and courteous to other trail users. Some sections of the trail can impede your progress when wet.

Rescue index: By and large, the VRRT provides overwhelming solitude. Hikers frequent the Cascade Falls National Recreation Trail. Emergency assistance can be summoned from the numerous summer homes near Strawberry Point and from campgrounds at Navajo Lake. The Duck Creek Visitor Center has a pay phone. Cedar City and Brian Head have medical facilities.

Land status: Dixie National Forest (Cedar Ranger District).

Maps: USGS Navajo Lake, Straight Canyon, Strawberry Point, and Webster Flat, Utah.

Access: This route requires a vehicle shuttle. Drop a vehicle at Woods Ranch, which is located 11.5 miles east of Cedar City on Utah State Highway 14 (between mileposts 11 and 12). Then drive 21 miles east on UT 14 to Strawberry Road/Forest Road 058 (between mileposts 32 and 33). Take Strawberry Road (gravel road) 9 miles south to Strawberry Point. Navajo Lake is between the endpoints near milepost 18 on UT 14.

Notes on the trail: The standard approach to the VRRT is to ride from Strawberry Point to Woods Ranch, east to west, although you can create countless options of varying difficulty from the many trailheads midroute.

Before you saddle up and head out from Strawberry Point, take a few minutes to visit the point itself and gaze pensively from the top rung of the Grand Staircase to Zion National Park. This is truly one of the great power spots on Utah's High Plateaus. Now pedal down the main road 0.5 mile and fork right on the signed VRRT. Swoop down the raveled ribbon of dirt, and cross the Strawberry Road. Zero your altimeter watch because now you officially begin climbing.

A series of switchbacks takes you up to a doubletrack. Follow it left and uphill less than 0.3 mile, fork left on the continued trail, and dive down more turns. Cross a lightly flowing creek, and climb the track coiled like a serpent. Keep climbing on alternating sections of trail and doubletrack (watch for trail signs) until you reach the Pink Cliffs again. Big view!

Ahead, the trail clips the top of the Lars Fork Jeep Road, and you must inch up switchbacks alongside the road. Once on top, the route mellows and veers away from the plateau's edge to penetrate a mix of hardwoods and evergreens. A few miles farther, the path rejoins the rim and passes a timbered point that extends from the plateau. Bank around several turns connected by long straightaways and arrive at the trailhead/parking area for the Cascade Falls National Recreation Trail. If you hike the 0.5-mile foot path (bikes are not allowed), you'll visit the small cave that serves as both "drain pipe" of Navajo Lake and headwaters to the North Fork Virgin River. Gulp some carbo and wolf a few energy bars; 11 miles down, 22 to go.

From the Cascade Falls parking area, the trail rises at a despicable 8-percent government-issue grade, through a half-dozen turns for about 1 mile. Breathe easy during a respite, climb again, and pass the junction for the Dike Trail. Zig then zag down to The Saddle and pass the junction for Spruces Trail. Shift down once gain to climb through stands of old-growth aspens. Pass the junction for Navajo Trail and round the north side of Navajo Point. Give your weary legs a deserved rest on the 2-mile, rampaging descent to Te-ah Campground, passing Lodge Trail along the way, 20 miles down, 13 to go.

Go to the bend signed for North Fork and take the doubletrack to the right/ north. Descend the track 0.25 mile and fork right on the continued VRRT. Over the next 8 miles, you'll work your gears constantly as the trail winds through countless hollows that crease the slopes descending from Gooseberry Point. Each individual climb is trivial by itself, but when they gang up on you, the cumulative effect can shred already tired legs. From here on, you'll have to rely on fond memories of the Pink Cliffs and of the vistas across the Grand Staircase, because throngs of aspen and fir block any potential views.

Intersect a doubletrack, follow it uphill, and fork left on the VRRT toward Stucki Spring. When you intersect the Webster Flat Road, take either the VRRT over the knoll and past Lundell Spring, or circle around on the level road. Near the entrance to Deer Haven Campground, fork right/north on a doubletrack and cross the wire fence.

Check your brakes, because the VRRT culminates with a 1,000-foot drop to Woods Ranch. Sections of the doubletrack are pebbly, rough, and slow; others are smooth and blazing fast. And watch out for those berms crossing the road. There is no point in ruining a perfectly good ride at this point just because you want to catch some air. When you reach Woods Ranch, grab a cold beverage from your well-stocked cooler and salute Utah's latest and greatest fat-tire tour.

RIDE 55   *RIGHT FORK OF BUNKER CREEK*

Like Dark Hollow-Second Left Hand Canyon, Right Fork of Bunker Creek showcases the downhill trail riding and mind-numbing vistas that have become synonymous with Brian Head. But instead of dropping to Parowan on the west side of the mountain, like on Dark Hollow, you'll head east off the backside to Panguitch Lake. Powerful overlooks from tundra meadows inaugurate the route, a sassy, singletrack descent adds spice, and a turbo-charged freewheeler is the coup de grâce. And like Dark Hollow, the stats of Right Fork Bunker Creek are totally biker friendly: 80 percent downhill and 100 percent thrill.

General location: 4 miles east of Brian Head, between Brian Head Peak and Panguitch Lake.

Distance: 11.5 miles point-to-point.

Tread: 7 miles of singletrack, 4.5 miles of doubletrack.

Aerobic level: Easy to moderate. Yet another of those mega-descent rides. There are a few rolling hills on Sidney Peaks Ridge and a short riser on the doubletrack below Right Fork. Don't forget, the trailhead elevation is at an oxygen-deprived 11,000 feet.

Technical difficulty: Level 2 to 4. You'll hop over and steer around a few boulders on the ridge trail. Right Fork is mostly tame but can be eroded locally. There is one rock garden on upper Right Fork that rates level 4, but after a quick dismount, you're back in the saddle. The whoop-te-doos on the lower doubletrack are what you make them.

Elevation change: The trailhead on the Brian Head Peak Road is at 11,000 feet. The ridge trail undulates gently and tops out a tad higher. Then, down you go to 8,400 feet. Total climbing is less than 400 feet.

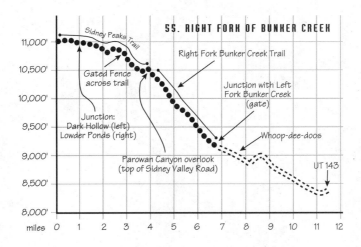

RIDE 55 RIGHT FORK OF BUNKER CREEK

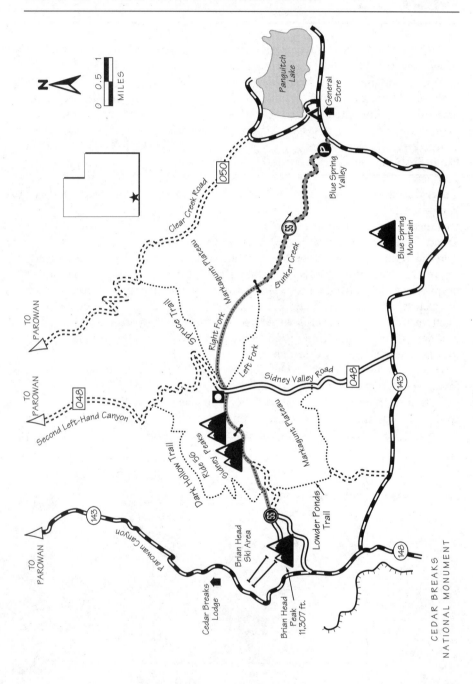

Approaching warp speed
on lower Right Fork
Bunker Creek.

Season: Snowdrifts may linger at Brain Head well into June. Flurries can dust
the area by October. Midsummer days at Brian Head are moderate (70s to
80s) and nights are crisp (40s). Apply sunscreen liberally. Carry a rain jacket
because afternoon storms can be chilling.

Services: There is no drinking water along this route. An outhouse is at the
trailhead. Panguitch Lake General Store near the route's end has limited
groceries and gasoline. Lodging, dining, groceries, gasoline, and bike shops are
at Brian Head. Lodging is at Panguitch Lake. Public campgrounds (fee areas)
are at Panguitch Lake, Cedar Breaks National Monument, and down Parowan
Canyon in First Left Hand Canyon. All bike shops in Brian Head offer shuttle
services.

Hazards: If you daydream on Right Fork Bunker Creek, you might twitch and
pitch, so watch for the usual singletrack accouterments.

Rescue index: The route draws a fair amount of use on weekends; other times, solitude prevails. Motorists commonly travel Utah State Highway 143 between Panguitch Lake and Brian Head. Emergency assistance can be summoned from the Panguitch Lake General Store. Brian Head has a medical clinic; Panguitch has a hospital.

Land status: Dixie National Forest (Cedar City Ranger District).

Maps: USGS Brian Head and Panguitch Lake, Utah.

Access: Shuttle a vehicle to the trail's end by first driving 4 miles south of Brian Head on UT 143 to the intersection with UT 148 (Cedar Breaks National Monument). Turn left and continue on UT 143 for 12.5 miles to Blue Spring Valley/Forest Road 081. Or, continue down the highway another mile to the Panguitch Lake General Store. (Ask permission to park; a fee may be required.) Return to Brian Head (Mammoth Summit), and take the Brian Head Peak Road 1.8 miles up to the Sidney Peaks Trail parking area, just before the U-bend.

Notes on the trail: From the parking area on the Brian Head Peak Road, take the Sidney Peaks Trail out the tundra ridge through islands of fir and spruce. Pass the Dark Hollow/Lowder Ponds Trail junction after 1 mile, and continue north on the ridge trail. Cross a broad, treeless saddle, and climb gently around Sidney Peaks. Funny how high altitude seems to cut your fitness level in half. Enter and exit the trees, and descend to a right-hand bend at a photoworthy overlook of Parowan Canyon. Dart into the trees again and bound over their roots on a steep little descent; then arrive at the main viewing deck of Parowan Canyon.

First and Second Left Hand Canyons crease the forested valley below. Noah's Ark and the Grand Castle interrupt the pervasive greenery with bright strawberry hues that seem more indicative of canyon country than alpine terrain. Autumn is glorious, for the colors in the canyon below are as varied as a box of Crayolas.

Take the doubletrack across the clearing to the signed Right Fork Bunker Creek Trailhead. Cross straight over Sidney Valley Road/Forest Road 048, and start your singletrack descent on Trail 040. (Right and Left Fork Bunker Creek share a common trailhead. If you mistakenly take Left Fork, don't worry; you'll be just as happy you did.) The path drops quickly into the timbered drainage, and you'll have to think quick whether or not to "ride the rocks." After crossing the creek, the trail is more playful as it banks through the commingling fir and aspen woods. You'll be wearing a mile-wide grin.

Three miles of blissful singletrack are gone in a flash as the trail joins with a doubletrack beyond a steel gate. (Left Fork of Bunker Creek joins from the right.) But that's not to say the fun is over. On the contrary, the excitement is yet to begin. Kick in the afterburners and race down the track, letting a prudent amount of air filter between your treads and the earth as you launch off successive berms. About 1 mile down from the gate, the road forks. Stay *left* and round the bend, then climb gently into the aspens. Shift to high gear again and scream downhill through sweeping curves to Blue Spring Valley. Cross the creek on a bridge, and pump up to the highway to complete the tour. With a cold beverage from Panguitch Lake General Store in one hand and a mustard-smeared wiener from the Doggie Delight in the other, celebrate your freewheeling adventure.

RIDE 56 *DARK HOLLOW–SECOND LEFT HAND CANYON*

Dubbed the "Vertical Mile," Dark Hollow-Second Left Hand Canyon is a downhiller's delight. If you have just one day in Brian Head, this is the only choice. The route begins atop Brian Head Peak at 11,307 feet (quite possibly Utah's highest mountain-biking trailhead) and ends in Parowan Canyon after a near 5,000-foot descent. Needless to say, gravity is your accelerator and brakes are your friends. But it's not the quantity of downhilling that makes this route a Utah classic; it's the quality. The 7 miles of one-lane twisty that lead off the tour are among the finest anywhere. The doubletrack thereafter is

Mike surveys Cedar Breaks National Monument from atop Brian Head Peak before embarking on the Dark Hollow Trail.

RIDE 56 DARK HOLLOW–SECOND LEFT HAND CANYON

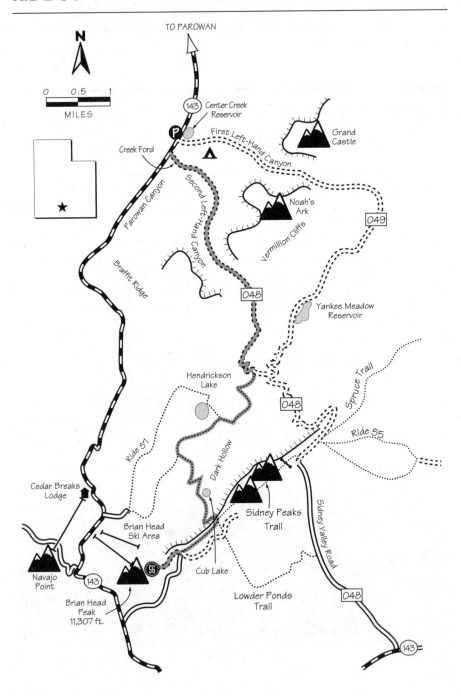

N

0   0.5   1
MILES

TO PAROWAN

143 Center Creek Reservoir

First Left-Hand Canyon

Grand Castle

Creek Ford

Second Left-Hand Canyon

Parowan Canyon

Noah's Ark

Vermillion Cliffs

049

Braffit Ridge

048

Yankee Meadow Reservoir

Hendrickson Lake

048

Spruce Trail

Ride 51

Ride 55

Dark Hollow

Cedar Breaks Lodge

Sidney Peaks Trail

Brian Head Ski Area

Sidney Valley Road

Navajo Point

56

143

Cub Lake

048

Brian Head Peak 11,307 ft.

Lowder Ponds Trail

143

Tom leads Katie, Mary, and Scott down the Dark Hollow Trail.

an all-out bomber that ends with a soak-you-to-the-bones creek ford if you attack at full throttle.

Those who descend at a more casual pace will be spellbound by the ever-changing scenery. From the summit you gaze out across all of southwestern Utah and into adjoining states. But your eyes naturally gravitate to the multi-hued scarps of Cedar Breaks National Monument below Brian Head Peak. Measuring 3.5 miles wide and 2,000 feet deep, the amphitheater is a pastel intaglio of crenulated ridges adorned with spires and intricate shapes—all sculpted from the forested plateau. It's a Bryce Canyon National Park in the making.

As you roll off the tundra peak, you enter dense timber that effectively conceals all views of the surrounding land. But when you connect with the Second Left Hand Canyon Road, you will be immersed in the salmon-colored hoodoos that you viewed from afar earlier.

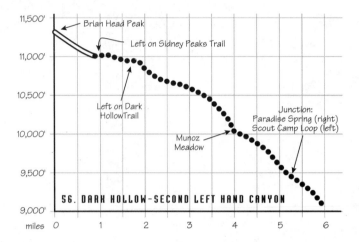

Brian Head Peak

Left on Sidney Peaks Trail

Left on Dark Hollow Trail

Munoz Meadow

Junction:
Paradise Spring (right)
Scout Camp Loop (left)

56. DARK HOLLOW-SECOND LEFT HAND CANYON

General location: This route begins 4 miles east of Brian Head atop Brian Head Peak and ends in Parowan Canyon.

Distance: 12 miles point-to-point.

Tread: The route begins with 0.8 mile of gravel road, followed by 6 miles of singletrack midroute, and ends with 5 miles of doubletrack plus a touch of pavement.

Aerobic level: Easy (see "Technical difficulty"). There are two short climbs way down on the singletrack that rudely awaken your legs and lungs. All this downhill means you need strong forearms for constant breaking and good handling skills for the varying trail conditions. You'll be out of the saddle with your legs acting like shocks much of the way.

Technical difficulty: Level 2 to 3. The short, rough drop off the ridge can be scary for first-time bikers; walking it is a wise choice. Thereafter, the Dark Hollow Trail turns constantly and descends rapidly. Singletrack conditions range from smooth, pine-needle-coated tread to loose dirt mixed with gravel, ruts, and rocks. The Second Left Hand Canyon Road is blazing fast, but it can also be rutted and coated with pebbles that slide under your wheels like ball bearings. The Center Creek ford at the route's end can be ankle- to calf-deep depending on spring runoff and afternoon storms.

Elevation change: This route is all about descending—nearly 5,000 vertical feet. Elevation gain is trivial. The two short climbs below Paradise Spring amount to a couple hundred feet, max. Brian Head Peak is the high point at 11,307 feet; Parowan Canyon is at 6,600 feet. Although you're freewheeling most of the time, you'll be sucking wind just the same because of the high elevation.

Season: Brian Head is a ski resort town, and snowdrifts can linger well into June. Flurries can dust the peak by late September. Midsummer days at Brian Head are moderate (70s to 80s) and nights are crisp (40s). Apply sunscreen liberally. Carry a rain jacket because afternoon storms can be chilling.

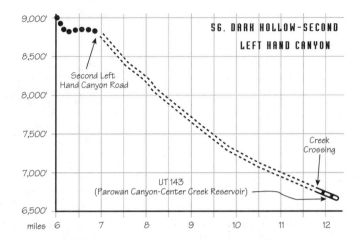

Services: There is no drinking water along this route. There is an outhouse at the Sidney Peaks Trailhead on the Brian Head Peak Road. Brian Head offers all visitor services but on a limited scale. Developed campgrounds (fee areas) are in Parowan Canyon (First Left Hand Canyon) and at Cedar Breaks National Monument. In 1998, Brian Head had five bike shops and about 100 permanent residents, making it the most biker friendly town in the world! All bike shops offer shuttle services.

Hazards: Brakes should be in perfect working order. Deadfall may cross the trail at any place. Be alert to logging activity near the trail. Watch for (infrequent) vehicles on the Second Left Hand Canyon Road and for sections where the road is eroded.

Rescue index: The route is popular on weekends and holidays; you may have it to yourself during midweek. Emergency assistance can be summoned from Brian Head or Parowan. Brian Head has a medical clinic.

Land status: Dixie National Forest (Cedar City Ranger District).

Maps: USGS Brian Head and Parowan, Utah.

Access: This route requires a vehicle shuttle. Leave one vehicle alongside Utah State Highway 143 at Center Creek Reservoir near First Left Hand Canyon, located 3.7 miles up from Parowan or 9 miles down from The Mall at Brian Head. Return to Brian Head and drive 2.5 miles up UT 143 to the Brian Head Peak Road. Take the gravel road 1.8 miles to the Sidney Peaks Trailhead or, preferably, 0.8 mile farther to Brian Head Peak for the full effect.

Notes on the trail: After you're visually satiated atop Brian Head Peak, coast down the gravel road to the bend and fork left on the Sidney Peaks Trail. Be sure to follow the singletrack and not the doubletrack. One mile out the ridge, you come to a four-way trail junction. Fork left on Dark Hollow Trail, and take the plunge off the ridge. The path is notoriously rocky and the turns are sharp, but it's over with quickly. Thereafter, the trail mellows as it passes Cub

Lake. Once back in the trees, the path descends quickly again but this time more playfully.

Cross Muñoz Meadow, passing the junction for Steam Engine Meadow to the left, and descend the twisting trail through stands of aspen and fir to a log fence. Ahead, the trail can be steep and technical level 3 to 4 in spots, so pick a good line and anticipate boulder booby traps lurking around curves. At the junction for Scout Camp Loop-Hendrickson Lake, fork right for Paradise Spring Trail and descend more stellar singletrack through profuse aspens. You'll have to climb two short hills before joining the Second Left Hand Canyon Road, small dues for such outrageous descending, then it's back on the brakes.

Descend the Second Left Hand Canyon Road (doubletrack) alongside the moss-encrusted creek and around sweeping turns. Soon, you are totally immersed in the redrock fantasyland that was viewed from afar atop Brian Head Peak. Only Dr. Seuss could conjure up such peculiar shapes.

Complete the freewheel tour with a saturating splash through Center Creek. Accept your fate by taking the plunge at full throttle, or be prudent and scout the miniature rapids first. Although rarely more than pedal-deep, rocks lurk in the channel and await your front tire. When you intersect UT 143 in Parowan Canyon, coast a few hundred yards downhill to your vehicle at Center Creek Reservoir next to First Left Hand Canyon.

RIDE 57 *SCOUT CAMP LOOP*

During the early 1990s, Brian Head emerged as one of southern Utah's premier mountain-biking venues, second only to Moab, naturally. The two towns are worlds apart, both in distance and surroundings. Ride the canyon country of Moab in spring and fall, but during summer, head to Brian Head for the best alpine trails between the Rockies and the Sierras.

Scout Camp Loop should top your list of must-do rides. It features the energetic singletracks for which Brian Head has gained fame; plus it's a loop ride. No vehicle shuttle is needed, and you'll actually get a workout instead of cruising downhill all day as on neighboring trails. In fact, it was Scout Camp Loop that convinced this author, as well as an ever-growing number of singletrack purists, that Brian Head must become an annual pilgrimage, as is Moab.

Granted, Scout Camp lacks the eye-popping scenic views that hallmark other Brian Head rides. That's OK. You trade sweeping vistas for unadulterated alpine singletrack that pumps your veins full of adrenaline. Scout Camp Loop has been the chosen course of the Brian Header mountain-bike race for years, and for good reason—it's outrageous.

RIDE 57 SCOUT CAMP LOOP

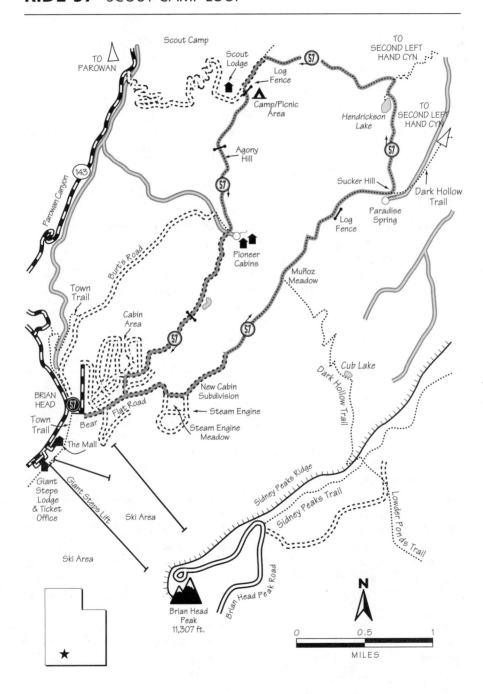

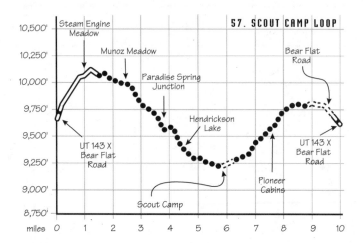

General location: Scout Camp Loop begins in the town of Brian Head.

Distance: 10-mile loop.

Tread: 4 miles of doubletrack, 6 miles of wooded singletrack.

Aerobic level: Moderate. The loop begins with a good warm-up climb on Bear Flat Road; then the singletrack undulates and descends 5 miles to the scout camp. After hoofing up "agony hill," you climb intermittently back to Bear Flat Road.

Technical difficulty: Level 2 to 4. Singletrack varies from smooth and silky to pebbly and rocky, but with no significant threats. "Agony hill," however, is a fly in the ointment—a short, sinister climb chock full of cobbles just beyond the scout camp. It's level 4 to 5, so unless you possess Zen-like abilities, take a hike.

Elevation change: This loop begins in town at an elevation of 9,656 feet. Bear Flat Road rises to 10,100 feet at Steam Engine Meadow; then the route undulates but descends to 9,200 at the scout camp. The route concludes with intermittent hills up to 9,800 feet. Total climbing is about 1,200 feet.

Season: Brian Head is a ski-resort town, so snowdrifts can linger well into June. Flurries can dust the area by late September. Midsummer days at Brian Head are moderate (70s to 80s) and nights are crisp (40s). Apply sunscreen liberally. Carry a rain jacket because afternoon storms can be chilling.

Services: There is no drinking water along this route. Brian Head offers all visitor services but on a limited scale. Developed campgrounds (fee areas) are in Parowan Canyon (First Left Hand Canyon) and at Cedar Breaks National Monument. In 1998, Brian Head had five bike shops per 100 permanent residents; you do the math!

Hazards: You can expect the usual assortment of singletrack goodies, including exposed roots, loose rocks and gravel, deadfall, and firmly embedded boulders. None of these should deter any rider; in fact, they add to the route's overall excitement. Be aware of other trail users, and be courteous when riding through the Thunder Ridge Scout Camp. Use caution when riding through the new cabin development adjacent to Steam Engine Meadow and stay clear of construction activity.

Rescue index: Emergency contacts can be made in Brian Head. Assistance might be sought at the scout camp when it's in session. Brian Head has a medical clinic.

Land status: Dixie National Forest (Cedar City Ranger District) and private property. Stay on the designated route and obey all signs restricting travel.

Maps: USGS Brian Head, Utah.

Access: Start from anywhere in Brian Head by first pedaling up Bear Flat Road, just north of The Mall at Brian Head.

Notes on the trail: The route begins with a rude little hill up Bear Flat Road (gravel road). The climb would prove trivial at lower elevations, but here at Brian Head (10,000 feet), it can suck the life out of you. About 1 mile up, the road bends right and levels. Fork left and enter Steam Engine Meadow, and ride toward the old turbine's rusted hull. Decades ago and long before the skiing industry took hold, timber sustained the local economy. But the recent spruce beetle infestation has jeopardized the health of the forest.

Head north of the boiler along the edge of the conifers and enter a new cabin development that popped up in 1998. The trail was obliterated then, but trail markers showed the way through the construction zone for about 0.5 mile to the continued singletrack. Although this section may get booted

Riders pass reflective Hendrickson Lake.

around in the future, the town, resort, forest service, and landowners are dedicated to preserving access to the loop; time will tell.

Let the fun begin! Zoom across fields linked by stands of fir and aspen and skirt the west edge of expansive Muñoz Meadow. (The Dark Hollow Trail joins from the right and follows your route.) Bank down the wooded trail to where it nips a log fence, and then hopscotch over the boulders. Descend 0.5 mile on the sometimes cushy, other times wild, trail to the Paradise Spring junction. Fork left for Scout Camp and Hendrickson Lake, slam your gears into granny, and pump up the short "sucker" hill.

Now on the loop's back nine, you'll dance the singletrack boogie and shake your bootie through profuse aspens and fir trees. Travolta's got nothing over this. Pass the spur left leading down to Hendrickson Lake and zig right on the main trail. A few hundred feet farther, zag left at a junction where a trail forks right and drops precipitously to Second Left Hand Canyon. Keep gyrating along the trail until you exit the woods to a meadow on the north end of the scout camp property. Take the doubletrack along the edge of the meadow for 0.5 mile, fork left at a log fence signed for Brian Head, and curve through the camp/picnic area amidst the aspens. (If you reach the camp's lodge, you missed the turn.)

Doubletrack reverts to singletrack, and then you come face to face with "agony hill" at a steel gate. Float like a ballerina but jab like a heavyweight while rocks chomp at your tires. Thereafter, climb gently through the forest to a junction on the edge of a meadow. Ignore the right fork for Burts Road and Town Trail and cross the meadow to reenter the timber on a doubletrack. A pair of pioneer cabins at the top of the meadow is worth visiting. Take the track through the woods past secretive ponds and across meadows, until you enter a cabin subdivision. Turn left at each intersection and stay on the main road until you reach Bear Flat Road. Descend to town or take another lap. Expert racers during the Brian Header take three!

RIDE 58 *TWISTED FOREST*

The name Twisted Forest evokes childhood fairy tales of a foreboding woodland where country folk spend eternity under villainous spells. This Twisted Forest, on the contrary, is open, sunny, brightly colored, and welcomes curious travelers. Twisted it is, however, for these hillsides harbor large communities of bristlecone pines, one of the earth's oldest living organisms. These tenacious conifers have been known to live for more than 2,000 years. With tangled roots that sprawl across the crumbly limestone, contorted limbs curled into spirals, and sprouts of pine garlands at the tips of

RIDE 58 TWISTED FOREST

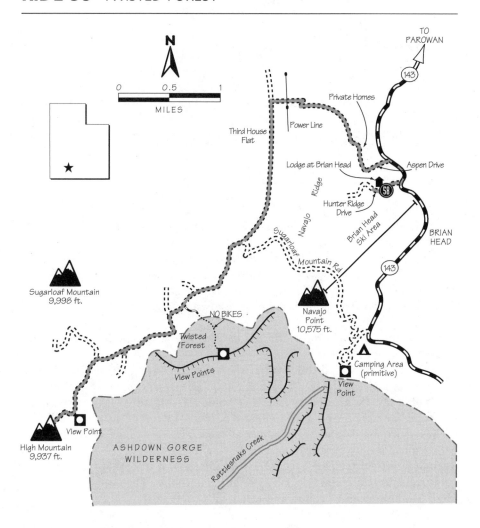

branches, they appear feeble and arthritic. But they are sturdy and stoic. Hug one!

This route takes you to the forest's trailhead where you then must hike among the age-old pines. Bikes are not allowed in the Twisted Forest because it is in the Ashdown Gorge Wilderness. If you make the effort, you'll stand rimrocked on the edge of the wilderness and stare eye-level at the grand amphitheater of Cedar Breaks National Monument. You'll understand how the monument received its name by the way the Pink Cliffs break abruptly

from the plateau's forested edge. The Paiute Indians called Cedar Breaks "Un-cap-i-cum-ump" or "circle of red or painted cliffs."

Save this ride for early evening when the waning sun sets the fleshy stone aglow. Time permitting, ride a couple miles farther to the top of High Mountain for more stunning views of the Markagunt Plateau.

General location: The route begins in the town of Brian Head.

Distance: 12.5 miles out-and-back.

Tread: 5 miles of light-duty dirt roads. The spur to High Mountain is on mostly tame doubletrack.

Aerobic level: Moderate but within the reach of strong-novice riders. The route starts and ends with a nasty, 0.3-mile, 15-percent pitch (to use a rock-climbing term). Novice riders will walk no doubt, and advanced riders will be searching for their easiest gear. Grin and bear it. The rest of the route rolls idly or has short, moderately tough hills at most. The mile-long climb to High Mountain is steady but, oh, so scenic.

Technical difficulty: Level 1 to 3. Most of the route is smooth dirt. There may be gravel and scattered rocks on some turns and hills. The doubletrack up to High Mountain can be rutted and laced with roots in spots.

Elevation change: Brian Head (town) is at 9,700 feet roughly. Third House Flat is the lowest point at 9,500 feet. The Twisted Forest Trailhead is at 9,800 feet, and High Mountain rises to 9,937 feet, for a total gain of 1,700 feet.

Season: The route should be free of snow by mid-June and ridable to mid-October. Midsummer daytime temperatures are temperate (70s to 80s) and nights are crisp (40s). Sheep commonly graze near High Mountain during summer.

Services: There is no drinking water along this route. Brian Head offers all visitor services, but on a limited scale, and has no shortage of bike shops.

Mary and Katie wander up to High Mountain for a whopping view of Brian Head Peak and Cedar Breaks.

Developed campgrounds (fee areas) are in Parowan Canyon (First Left Hand Canyon) and at Cedar Breaks National Monument.

Hazards: Use caution when hiking through the Twisted Forest, especially along cliffs, because the limestone substrate may crumble and break away. Be alert to motorists traveling these roads.

Rescue index: The Twisted Forest is infrequently visited. Emergency assistance can be obtained at Brian Head. Brian Head has a medical clinic.

Land status: Dixie National Forest (Cedar City Ranger District).

Maps: USGS Brian Head and Flanigan Arch, Utah.

Access: Head out from Brian Head Cross Country in the Lodge at Brian Head (up Hunter Ridge Drive) or from anywhere in town.

Notes on the trail: From Brian Head Cross Country in the Lodge at Brian Head, coast down Utah State Highway 143 toward Parowan for 0.2 mile and fork left on Aspen Drive. Bend right, and after the pavement ends, climb a crushing hill through the cabin subdivision to Columbine Circle on Navajo Ridge. Stay on the main dirt road, cross the forested ridge, and descend the other side cautiously. It's way steep. Bummer, you'll have to face this monster on the way back. Let gravity pull you across Third House Flat to the junction with Dry Lakes Road. Fork left and take the dirt road into the aspens.

After 1 mile, you reach the junction with the Sugarloaf Mountain Road, which joins from the left and uphill. Here, the main road bends right and follows the Sugarloaf Mountain Road. Descend a bit and round a curve over Brown Creek. One-half mile farther and on the edge of a clearing, fork left to access the Twisted Forest Trailhead. Read the interpretive plaques, stash or lock your rig, and take to foot. (Bikes are not allowed in the Twisted Forest because it's within the Ashdown Gorge Wilderness.) When the footpath peters out, you must "free hike." Set your bearings for east by southeast and cross several small ridges inhabited by legions of bristlecone pines. About 0.5 mile out (you'll know when to stop), you tiptoe the edge of the Pink Cliffs and stare into the gullet of Cedar Breaks National Monument. The Breaks are framed by Navajo Ridge and Brian Head Peak to the north and Blowhard Mountain (FAA radar globes) to the south. Cedar Breaks feeds Ashdown Gorge, which in turn funnels to Coal Creek Canyon outside of Cedar City.

Do not be content with this view, as striking as it is. Return to the Sugarloaf Mountain Road and take it left. Pass the trailhead for the High Mountain Trail, ride 0.5 mile farther to where the main road bends right, and then fork left on the High Mountain Jeep Road. (The junction should be signed; otherwise, look for a snowmobile decal tacked to a tree.) Climb through the aspens and enter a meadow. Fork left to reach another viewpoint or take the doubletrack to the bald summit of High Mountain for the full effect. Burn through some film if you have it. If not, gaze pensively until the scene is etched permanently on your mind.

SOUTHERN UTAH'S
CANYON COUNTRY

Introduction

Utah's Canyon Country lies within the northwest sector of the greater Colorado Plateau and is defined by classic redrock terrain. It is easy for the mountain biker to succumb to the obvious when venturing into Canyon Country by making a beeline to Moab—mountain bike Mecca, and arguably, center of the universe. There is good reason for such haste since the area has been widely acclaimed, offers endless services, and is a veritable utopia for fat tires. By all means, experience the hyperactivity of Moab, but do not overlook Canyon Country's multitudinous offerings of open space and endless adventures.

Southern Utah is home to numerous world-renowned national parks, including Arches, Canyonlands, Capitol Reef, and Zion, plus Natural Bridges and Grand Staircase-Escalante National Monuments, Monument Valley Navajo Tribal Park, and Glen Canyon National Recreation Area. All have something to offer the mountain biker, either in the way of scenic roads that venture through these parks' interiors, or backcountry routes located just beyond their boundaries.

Some national parks are becoming less revered as sanctuaries of solitude, though. For those seeking intimate relations between self, bike, and nature, Canyon Country is well suited. One of the region's less celebrated treasures is the San Rafael Swell. This kidney-shaped uplift located just west of Green River is national-park caliber indeed. San Rafael Swell is neatly bisected by Interstate 70, so you might assume it to be easy prey for concessionaires and the RV crowds they attract. On the contrary, despite easy (but often elusive) access, the Swell has remained remote, rugged, and a desert biker's haven. With a little perseverance (and the assistance of this guidebook), you will experience redrock pageantry thought only to exist in the Moab area.

The same can be said for the remainder of Canyon Country's outback. If your penchant is gazing at the Milky Way's twinkling swath, swigging coffee sweetened with sand, and awakening to a sunrise intensified by the burnt-umber walls it rebounds off, Canyon Country will quickly draw you deeper into its embrace.

Despite the all-encompassing nature of this region's redrocks, there are three alpine retreats worth seeking for midsummer refuge: the La Sal, Abajo, and Henry Mountains. Each beckons the desert biker with the promise of cool breezes and fragrant forests.

Finally, if winter-long powder skiing has become mundane, cartop down to St. George where off-season biking is always pleasant. You can even squeeze in a round of golf.

There are many opportunities to study ancient Indian cultures in southeastern Utah, particularly the Anasazi and Fremont Indians who inhabited central and southeastern Utah, roughly between 500 A.D. and 1300 A.D.. The Anasazi, who occupied the Four Corners Area, first lived in underground pit houses during what is called the Basketmaker period. As the culture developed into the Pueblo period, life became centered around small villages. The Anasazi mastered stone masonry and built multilevel dwellings in protective cliffs and

Canyon Country—an ensemble of desert, mountains, and sky.

alcoves, some the size of castles. As a more sedentary life evolved, the Anasazi became skilled artisans, began to cultivate and store crops, and produced ornamented pottery. The kiva, an underground chamber believed to be a ceremonial room, is a symbol of Anasazi culture.

The Fremont Indians roamed widely throughout central Utah, inhabiting both desert and mountainous areas. Less is known about the Fremont Indians since they were considered nomadic hunters and gatherers rather than a sedentary tribe. They lived in small villages and occupied pit houses, like the early Anasazi, but moved their villages seasonally or to seek more productive grounds. The Fremont Indians were also craftsmen who produced primitive baskets and clay figurines. In addition, the Fremont adorned the desert's walls with mystical rock art. Mysteriously, though, both the Anasazi and Fremont cultures disappeared around 1300 A.D., arguably the result of climatic changes and subsequent unfavorable living conditions, or of the hostile encroachment of neighboring tribes.

Mesa Verde National Park hosts the famous and spectacular displays of Anasazi masonry, but the scattered ruins at Hovenweep National Monument are especially haunting. Edge of the Cedars (Blanding), Anasazi (Boulder), and Fremont Indian (Richfield) State Parks offer modern museums and displays with interpretive trails. Newspaper Rock State Park on route to Canyonlands National Park's Needles District is a veritable tabloid of prehistoric and modern headlines etched into stone.

As informative and spectacular as these parks are, there is immeasurable enchantment in spying prehistoric vestiges during a backcountry bike ride. A small granary perched precariously in a cliff alcove, a broken arrowhead or pottery shard, or a curious arrangement of rough-cut rocks that outline a dwelling are all windows into a clouded past.

Rock art is particularly captivating and has been subject to considerable interpretive efforts at scientific, cultural, and aesthetic levels. Whimsical images depict the cultures' routine activities and relay messages with religious and spiritual undertones. A single bighorn sheep or spiral on a tilted boulder is every bit as compelling as panels composed of shamanistic humanoids and elaborate hunting scenes.

Please remember that prehistoric ruins, remains, and rock art displays are delicate, irreplaceable, and protected by federal law (see "Special Issues" on page 16). Even the best-intentioned visitor can cause irreparable damage with a gentle touch. Take with you only your emotional and visual impact while allowing future visitors to experience the same.

SLICKROCK

Slickrock is not simply the evocative tag given to the world's most popularized mountain-bike trail, nor is it a riding surface that is restricted to that specific locale or any particular rock formation. Rather, "It's more like the whole country is slickrock, even where it's crumbling away," Edward Abbey explained in his book *Slickrock*.

Slickrock gained its name from early settlers whose metal-shod horses found the smooth, barren sandstone slick to cross. But in the realm of mountain biking, it is exactly the opposite; this naturally abrasive surface is about as "slick" as sandpaper and soft as concrete. Arguably, this unique riding medium allows a mountain bike its fullest expression but at the same time is absolutely unforgiving. Slickrock may intimidate the first-time or tentative biker because it can hold the bike at angles that seem to defy gravity. But if you accept and then master its apparent distemper, you might profess—as Moabite Todd Campbell, who wrote the book on the stuff—that the two-wheeled experience is "the most fun you can have with your clothes on."

To gain an appreciation for slickrock—its rough-to-the-touch surface and its boundless extent—it helps to have a basic understanding of the geologic processes that formed and exposed these rocks for us to enjoy. Geologic history can confound many people because it involves events that took place over millions of years.

In a nutshell, the geologic complexity of the Colorado Plateau (inclusive of Canyon Country) is based on huge volumes of sediments derived from various sources and deposited under various environmental conditions, followed by

Slickrock bizarrerie.

tectonic-related uplift and subsequent down-cutting by erosional forces. Sounds a bit complicated, doesn't it? Still, like chapters of a book lying flat on your desk, the sequence of these layers (stratigraphic sections) can be read even by the untrained eye. Of course, keep in mind that pages and whole chapters are often missing due to lapses in deposition or long periods of erosion, and that the entire book has been bent, broken, cut up, and deeply grooved in some places. But it is this chapter-by-chapter progression that gives Canyon Country its trademark "layer-cake" appearance.

The geologic history of the Colorado Plateau (including Utah's Canyon Country) dates back about 550 million years when a primordial sea encroached upon the Four Corners Area, covering the continent's Precambrian crystalline core with mud and limestone. These ancient strata and the schist they buried are visible only in the absolute bottom of the Grand Canyon.

From the Cambrian Period to the Tertiary Period (a span of 500 million years), the environment of the relatively low-lying Colorado Plateau varied from shallow seas with shoreline tidal flats, to thin freshwater lakes fed by rivers, to basins of blowing and drifting sand dunes. The products of these environmental episodes are the terra cotta rocks that can be seen throughout southwestern Utah. Throughout this great time span, plate tectonics (the movement of the Earth's crust) would uplift and fold areas of Canyon Country. But it would not be until the very last page in this book of geologic history, the late Tertiary Period, that erosively voracious rivers, like the

Colorado, would carve the landscape into the deep canyons and curious shapes we see today.

Of all the sedimentary rock layers deposited across the Colorado Plateau, perhaps the most extensive and easily recognized is the Glen Canyon Group. (A "group" is a stratigraphic sequence of two or more rock units, or formations, that are closely related in composition and origin of deposition.) The Glen Canyon Group consists of three layers of sandstone formations: Wingate, Kayenta, and Navajo—oldest (bottom) to youngest (top), respectively. Specifically, the sequence spans the interface of the Triassic and Jurassic periods roughly 210 million years ago. As a whole, the Glen Canyon Group represents an environmental episode when vast deserts and dune fields swept across the Colorado Plateau. William L. Stokes notes in *Geology of Utah* that some geologists half-jokingly refer to these strata as the "Great Sand Pile."

Glen Canyon, the type area after which the group was named, is mostly submerged beneath Lake Powell, but you can see rocks of the Glen Canyon Group from Zion through Capitol Reef and Canyonlands National Parks to Moab. The Glen Canyon Group is largely responsible for the colossal vertical walls, overhanging alcoves, fins, towers, and domes that are the hallmark of Canyon Country.

The reddish orange Wingate Sandstone forms sheer walls, mesa peninsulas, or island spires. This homogeneous sandstone has a desert-dune origin. The Kayenta, which lies atop the Wingate, typically forms steep, broken terraces and varies in color from red to purple to brown layered with gray. A mixture of sandstone and shale, the Kayenta originated in delta areas of slow-flowing rivers. Finally, the Navajo Sandstone (atop the Kayenta) produces sheer cliffs and massive towers capped with hummocky domes, fins, and rounded humps. The trademark of the Navajo is its near-white color and gigantic, sweeping crossbeds, indicative of desert sand dunes.

Where is the Glen Canyon Group best displayed? Good exposures include: the San Rafael Reef; Moab Rim, and the Portal of the Colorado River (Moab); Amasa Back, Poison Spider Mesa, and the Slickrock Bike Trail (the latter rolls over the Navajo Sandstone entirely); the looming walls above the White Rim Trail and beneath Panorama Point off Canyonlands National Park; the Waterpocket Fold of Capitol Reef National Park; the canyons of the Escalante River; and, of course, Checkerboard Mesa, and the majestic towers of Zion National Park.

This colorful sequence is just the beginning of a rewarding process of paging through the varied chapters that comprise Canyon Country's geologic history. Expand your geologic awareness both up and down strata by comparing the different rock structures of Arches National Park with those of the Canyonlands' Needles District, and in turn, with those of Monument Valley. Once you get the hang of it, "slickrock" will take on a whole new meaning.

Central Canyon Country

RIDE 59 *BUCKHORN WASH— THE WEDGE OVERLOOK*

The San Rafael Swell is graced with redrock architecture that hallmarks southern Utah's famed national parks. But unlike those national parking lots to which Edward Abbey has referred, the San Rafael Swell sees far fewer visitors, thus enabling it to retain its primitive beauty.

Interstate 70 bisects the Swell, making access utterly convenient. Still, the region is visited by few, although crossed by many. Is it the lack of enticing off-ramps from the freeway? "Ranch Exit" is hardly inviting. Or are motorists freaked by road signs near Green River and Salina cautioning of "no water or services for the next 100 miles"? The grip tightens on the wheel and the temperature gauge is carefully eyed. Perhaps a whisper from Captain John W. Gunnison, who lead a government survey party through this torrid desert in the mid-1800s, wafts on gentle breezes but threatens like a billowing thunderhead: "an absolutely sterile country . . . not even a wolf could make a living."

Whatever the reason, let the passersby pass on by and be content with a fleeting glimpse in their mirror or with the token, two-dimensional keepsake snapped from the scenic overlook.

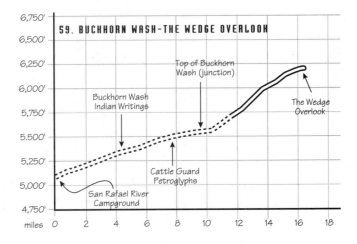

RIDE 59 BUCKHORN WASH—THE WEDGE OVERLOOK

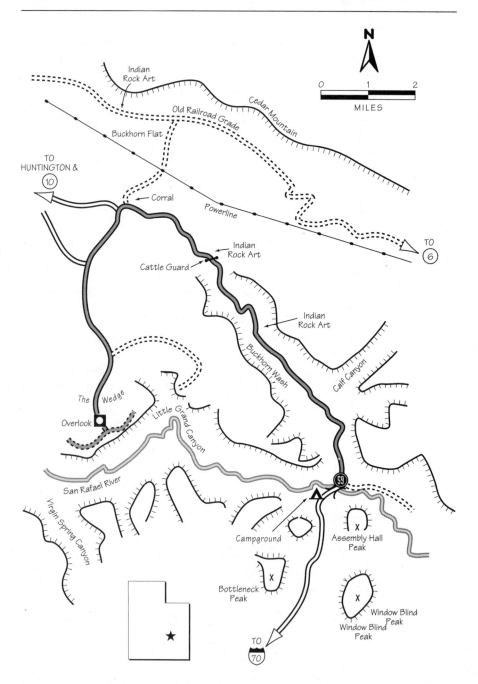

N

0   1   2
MILES

Indian Rock Art

Old Railroad Grade

Cedar Mountain

Buckhorn Flat

TO HUNTINGTON & 10

Corral

Powerline

TO 6

Indian Rock Art

Cattle Guard

Indian Rock Art

Buckhorn Wash

Calf Canyon

The Wedge

Overlook

Little Grand Canyon

San Rafael River

Virgin Spring Canyon

59

Campground

Assembly Hall Peak

Bottleneck Peak

Window Blind Peak

Window Blind Peak

TO 70

The fat-tire desert rat on the other hand, who cares not that skin turns to leather under the searing sun or that hair becomes a bristly mop when caked with dust, will enter the Swell and not resurface for days until this desert sanctuary has filled the soul. For those somewhere in between, who are intrigued by the San Rafael Swell's austere offerings but are not of the nomadic breed, the Buckhorn Wash-Wedge Overlook tour is a fine introduction.

This route begins at the San Rafael River campground and follows a comforting dirt road past marvelous buttes, then up a sandstone hallway that could be easily paved and tagged Buckhorn Wash Scenic Drive. Designated turnouts fenced off by federal land managers direct the curious to rock art panels left by ancient civilizations. Then at the Wedge Overlook, you'll tip toe the edge of Utah's Little Grand Canyon and squint into this mammoth chasm to where your tour began hours ago. You pay good money for stuff like this elsewhere. In the San Rafael Swell it's yours free for the taking in return for your respect of the land.

General location: Buckhorn Wash-Wedge Overlook is in the northern San Rafael Swell, 50 miles northwest of Green River and 45 miles southeast of Price.

Distance: 33 miles out-and-back. This tour is actually the combination of two adjoining routes: Buckhorn Wash, 20 miles out-and-back and the Wedge Overlook, 13 miles out-and-back.

Tread: Light-duty sand and dirt roads, with variable washboards that are suitable for passenger cars when dry.

Aerobic level: Moderate. Each route by itself is easy.

Technical difficulty: Level 1 to 2. There are sand and washboards on the Buckhorn Wash Road, gravel and scattered rocks on the Wedge Overlook Road.

Elevation change: The San Rafael River campground at the mouth of Buckhorn Wash is the route's lowest elevation at 5,100 feet. The top of Buckhorn Wash is 5,600 feet, a mere 500-foot gain. Extending the ride to the Wedge Overlook entails an additional 700-foot gain to a maximum elevation of 6,300 feet.

Season: Spring (March into May) and fall (September into mid-November) are the best times to visit the San Rafael Swell. Midsummer brings searing heat and insects can be intolerable. Rain may make dirt roads impassable. Blooming desert flowers peak in late April/early May. Fall is surprisingly striking when golden hues of cottonwoods, willows, and tamarisks complement the fiery tones of the surrounding sandstones.

Services: There is no drinking water along this route or at the trailhead's campground. Carry extra in your vehicle. The San Rafael River campground (fee area) has tables and outhouses only. Backcountry camping is allowed throughout the Swell, unless posted otherwise. Huntington and Castle Dale (both west of the Swell in Castle Valley) offer most visitor services. The closest bike shop is in Price.

Hazards: Dirt roads are suitable for passenger cars when dry but can be slippery when wet. This is a bona fide desert; carry plenty of water both on your bike and in your vehicle. All surface waters should be purified. Apply sunscreen liberally.

Buckhorn Wash is the main thoroughfare through the northern San Rafael Swell, so expect to encounter motorists; stay to the right side of the road and use caution when rounding blind corners. OHVs visit the area, especially on weekends and holidays.

Rescue index: Buckhorn Wash is popular with motorists and other recreationists, but you are a minimum of 30 miles from emergency contacts (Castle Dale and Huntington) and about 50 miles from a hospital (Price).

Land status: Bureau of Land Management (Price Field Office).

Maps: USGS Bob Hill Knob, Bottleneck Peak, Buckhorn Reservoir, and Sids Mountain, Utah.

Access: From Green River, travel about 30 miles west on I-70 and take Exit 129 for Ranch Exit. Take the light-duty dirt road north for 21 miles to the bridge over the San Rafael River. (The road is suitable for passenger cars but can be rough locally.) The campground is a good trailhead.

From Price, head south on Utah State Highway 10, pass through Huntington, and then continue 7.5 miles toward Castle Dale. Look for an old wooden corral next to a dirt road (between mileposts 40 and 39) marked with a Bureau of Land Management sign reading "Buckhorn Wash, Wedge Overlook." Follow the light-duty dirt road 13 miles to the Wedge Overlook Road. Stay left and travel 2 miles farther to the top of the Buckhorn Wash Road. Drive down Buckhorn Wash to the San Rafael River. Or, if you don't want to see Buckhorn twice, start from the top of the wash by descending first.

Notes on the trail: Before you head out, remember that the San Rafael Swell is a fragile ecosystem. Stay to roads and designated trails open to mountain bikes; never ride cross-country.

From the San Rafael River bridge, pedal up the main dirt road into the redrock gash of Buckhorn Wash, leaving behind the trio of guardian buttes, Bottleneck, Window Blind, and Assembly Hall. Immediately, precipitous walls lock the canyon in an open embrace. Sandstone domes top the cliffs and above the domes are more cliffs. Buttes rest atop buttes; dark alcoves hide in high ledges, and rock ceilings arch overhead. After 2 miles, Calf Canyon enters from the right. Although tempting, this doubletrack is just one big sandbox. Two miles farther, you pass the Buckhorn Indian Writings. Although these 1,000-year-old vestiges of the Fremont Indian culture are faded and abhorrently vandalized, the assemblage of winged, anthropomorphous humanoids, coiled serpents, and other indecipherable pictographs (paintings on rock) demand long, pensive study and many photographs.

At the cattle guard (7.5 miles up canyon), stash your bike and walk the path toward the northern cliffs. There you'll find another fine rock art panel of petroglyphs, this time of box-shaped deer, bighorn sheep, stick figures, rows of

Early morning fog enshrouds Bottleneck Peak.

dots, and linked humanoids. Two miles past the cattle guard, the canyon walls subside and the wash rises up to meet the broad desert prairies. At the road junction, fork left/west toward Huntington, Castle Dale, and UT 10. As the road bends right, fork left again on an unsigned dirt road that rises over shallow hills. After 1.5 miles of gentle climbing, turn left on the gravel Wedge Overlook Road.

A distant peppering of junipers will be your only companion as you pedal across a bleak and painfully desolate landscape no more productive than the moon. If you persevere, however, you will be duly rewarded when, without much warning at all, the earth opens up to a yawning chasm of incomprehensible size. This is the Wedge Overlook. Beneath you drops the San Rafael River gorge, "Utah's Little Grand Canyon." Earlier in the day when you were beside the river's bridge, the San Rafael was a fair stream; rimrocked at the Wedge Overlook, the river appears to be no more than a twisted green thread. Assimilate the sublime view and return down Buckhorn, packing fond memories.

RIDE 60 *BLACK DRAGON CANYON*

The San Rafael (pronounced san ra-fel´) Swell is neither a mountain nor a plateau, but a colossal geologic blister on the earth's skin. The most stunning sight is the San Rafael's eastern perimeter, marked by a formidable sawtooth ridge of protracted strata that juts abruptly from the surrounding desert plains. The "Reef," as it is called, is not a cliff or a straight crest, ". . . but a row of cusps like a battery of shark's teeth on a large scale," described

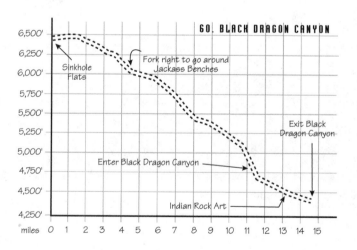

RIDE 60 BLACK DRAGON CANYON

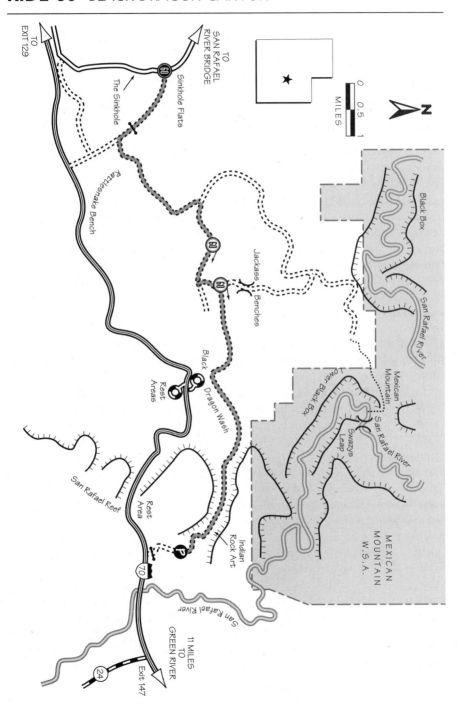

geologist C. E. Dutton in the 1880s. Seemingly impenetrable from afar, the Reef is actually breached by sinuous canyons, or "narrows." Some of these slots constrict to less than shoulder width and block all but a mere sliver of sky above.

Black Dragon Canyon is a trip through one of the Reef's sandstone hallways. The route begins up high in the Swell's Sinbad Country where low rising mesas mingle with high desert prairies. But the route draws you toward the Reef's menacing cusps until you are swallowed whole by Black Dragon Canyon. Although this passageway does not pinch to claustrophobic widths, it is bound by overhanging alcoves and vertical walls nearly 1,000 feet tall. Fremont Indian rock art adorns the canyon, including the elusive "black dragon" pictograph. In a cave along the way, you'll see handprints and drawings that resemble necklaces, plus what appears to be a primitive form of accounting, a Fremont-age abacus of sorts.

And if you made easy work of the mostly downhill trip, then you can bust a cog on the massive slickrock ramp upon exiting Black Dragon Canyon. There are no painted dashes to follow like Moab's variety; it's all freestyle. If you make it to the top, you'll peer into the chasm you just rode through. Hope you're not acrophobic!

General location: The San Rafael Swell is located in central Utah about 15 miles west of Green River. Black Dragon Canyon is just north of Interstate 70 on the edge of the Reef.

Distance: 14.5 miles point-to-point.

Tread: Packed dirt and sandy doubletracks with intermittent rocky sections.

Aerobic level: Easy to moderate. The ride is mostly downhill. The hills you do climb are tame.

Technical difficulty: Level 2 to 3. The upper portion of the route (Jackass Benches) follows packed dirt and sand doubletracks with sporadic loose stones, patches of pavement bedrock, and a few ruts. The doubletrack through Black Dragon Canyon is mostly soft sand, but your tires float, making the plowing easy.

Elevation change: The trailhead is the route's highest elevation at 6,500 feet. The route is virtually downhill all the way to the mouth of Black Dragon Canyon at 4,360 feet, for an elevation loss of just over 2,100 feet.

Season: Spring (March into May) and fall (September into November) are the best times to visit the San Rafael Swell. Midsummer is *very* warm and insects can be bothersome. Rain may make dirt roads impassable. Blooming desert flowers peak by late April.

Services: There is no drinking water along this route or any services. Backcountry camping is allowed throughout the Swell unless posted otherwise. Camping is not allowed along the lower 2 miles of Black Dragon Canyon. Remember, if you pack it in, pack it out. Green River, located 15 miles from the trail's end, offers all visitor services, but Price has the closest bike shop.

Deep inside Black
Dragon Canyon.

Hazards: Since this is a desert environment, carry plenty of water both on your bike and in your vehicle. You'll be craning your neck once you enter Black Dragon Canyon, so pay attention to where your front wheel is heading. If you're exploring the slickrock at the canyon's mouth, you are strictly on your own. Know your limits; the rock is utterly unforgiving. Use extreme caution near cliff edges.

Rescue index: The San Rafael Swell is getting more and more popular with recreationists. But you aren't likely to encounter others along the route until you're well into Black Dragon Canyon. There you'll likely visit with sightseers, especially on weekends. Green River, located 15 miles east of the route's end, has a medical clinic.

Land status: Bureau of Land Management (Price Field Office).

Maps: USGS Drowned Hole Draw and Spotted Wolf Canyon, Utah.

Access: From Green River, travel west on I-70 and pass Exit 147 for Utah State Highway 24 and Hanksville. One-half mile past the San Rafael River, look for a dirt road leaving the edge of the freeway between mileposts 145 and 144. (There is no exit ramp.) Pass through the wire gate (close it behind you) and drive the light-duty dirt road about 1 mile to the mouth of Black Dragon Canyon. Leave a vehicle here. If the road is impassable, park at your discretion near the highway or at the rest area 1 mile west on the freeway at the edge of the Reef.

In your shuttle vehicle, drive west on I-70 through Spotted Wolf Canyon and take Exit 129 for Ranch Exit. Double back to the east on the frontage road (gravel road) and then travel north for 6 miles to a doubletrack for Sinkhole Flats and Jackass Benches. Park and embark.

Notes on the trail: Pedal eastward on the doubletrack for 1.1 miles and cross a cattle guard at a wire fence. One-half mile farther, fork left at a Y junction on a good dirt road. Ride like the wind for 2.6 miles to an unsigned but prominent Y junction. The low, honey-blonde platform of Jackass Benches rises immediately to the north. Fork right and open up the throttle while skirting the bench. Continue around a 90-degree bend, ignoring a faint doubletrack forking to the right, and come to the signed turnoff for Black Dragon Wash 0.5 mile farther. (If you continue on the main road, you'll climb through a notch between the mesa tops.) Descend along the base of the benches for 4.5 miles and enter the Reef. Protracted walls of the Glen Canyon Group jut from the canyon as titanic ramparts.

The Glen Canyon Group is the classic southern Utah assemblage of cliff-forming sandstones. It is defined by the red-brown, perfectly cleaved Wingate Formation at the base, which represents ancient sand dunes. Laying on top of the Wingate is the thinner Kayenta Formation characterized by terraced orange-brown sandstones formed by a fluctuated river delta-tidal flat. Capping the sequence are the white-tan "beehive" domes of the Navajo Sandstone—the stuff the Slickrock Bike Trail is made of—which also represents drifting dunes fields.

Once fully engulfed by Black Dragon Canyon, you'll want to slow the pace a bit and let your eyes wander from your front tire to overhead. You can't miss the pictographs nowadays because they are bound by log fences installed by the BLM to preserve the site's integrity. Look but do not touch. A single finger dab, repeated by thousands of visitors, can cause irreversible damage. Equally fascinating as the Black Dragon itself is the nearby "Counter Cave."

You breach the Reef 0.5 mile past the rock art panels. When you do, look for a track immediately to the left and leading to a ramp of sandstone. That's the entry to the slickrock playground should you choose to awaken you heart, legs, and lungs.

RIDE 61 REDS CANYON

The San Rafael Swell's remarkable scenic diversity and mining nostalgia are amplified on the Reds Canyon loop. Inasmuch as this is one of the most remote corners in the Swell, solitude abounds and rings with deafening silence. If you feel the need to escape the confines of urbanism, Reds Canyon fits the bill.

The route commences with many miles of cruising across Sinbad Country's grass-carpeted, high desert plains from where you can view distant mountains and plateaus. Thereafter you drop into the heart of the western San Rafael Swell and follow an 800-foot deep canyon guarded by twin towers of stone and drenched with desert varnish—nature's bar coding. Prospectors poked and prodded the sedimentary rocks in search of radioactive ore many decades ago. Today, their efforts exist as ghostly reminders of boom days long since past. The route culminates with a steep but not-too-painful climb out of the canyon back to the flats above.

General location: 50 miles southwest of Green River.

Distance: 31.5-mile loop.

Tread: Dirt and sand doubletracks throughout that may be suitable for passenger cars when dry but are rough locally.

Aerobic level: Strenuous. The first half is a breeze, with easy pedaling followed by a fast descent. The second half follows a doubletrack in a dry wash where pedaling is still pretty good. A stiff climb out of the canyon culminates the loop.

Technical difficulty: Level 1 to 3. Most of the route is easygoing, but portions may be rutted or have sand and scattered rocks.

Elevation change: The route tops out at 6,960 feet near the trailhead and drops to 5,120 feet at Tomsich Butte. Gain is about 2,000 feet.

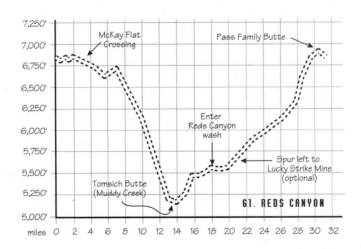

RIDE 61 REDS CANYON

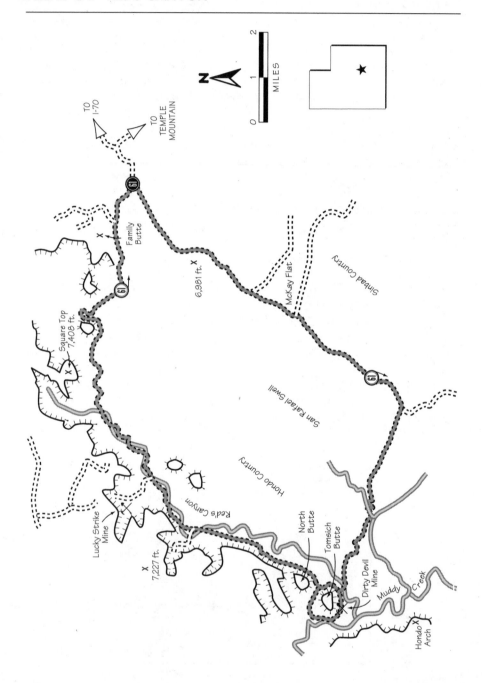

Season: Spring (mid-March into June) and fall (September into November). Bugs can be annoying around water sources by June.

Services: There are no services or sources of reliable water along this route. Muddy Creek is generally too silty to filter. Springs may seep from rocks that are tainted with radioactive minerals.

Hazards: Preparedness is paramount because the route is remote. Carry plenty of water because you'll consume most over the loop's second half. Avoid venturing into mine tunnels and structures because they may be unstable and collapse. Low oxygen levels may exist in tunnels, and undetectable and potentially harmful radon daughters may be present. Wild horses and burros are known to inhabit the area. Do not disturb them and keep your distance.

Rescue index: The entire route is accessible by vehicle, but organized rescue will take a half-day to arrive. Your closest emergency contact would be at Goblin Valley State Park, located about 8 miles south of Temple Mountain.

Land status: Bureau of Land Management (Price Field Office).

Maps: USGS Copper Globe, Horse Valley, San Rafael Knob, and Tomsich Butte, Utah.

Access: Two light-duty dirt roads access Reds Canyon, one via Interstate 70 and the other via Utah State Highway 24 and Temple Mountain.

Via I-70, drive 29 miles west of Green River and take Exit 129 for Ranch Exit. Cross under the freeway, drive west, then south for 10.3 miles on the light-duty dirt road (suitable for passenger cars when dry), and fork right for Reds Canyon and Tan Seep. (If you miss this turn, you'll have another opportunity after 3 miles.) Four miles farther, fork right again for Reds Canyon and Tan Seep. Within 1 mile, you'll come to a junction signed for McKay Flat (left) and Reds Canyon (right). Park near the junction.

Via Temple Mountain, travel 11 miles west of Green River on I-70 and take Exit 147 for UT 24 and Hanksville. Travel 25 miles to milepost 137 and turn right for Goblin Valley State Park and Temple Mountain. Pass the turnoff for Goblin Valley, staying straight, and cut through the San Rafael Reef (pavement turns to a light-duty dirt road). Drive the sand, rock, and washboard road west for 9 miles, and then fork left for Reds Canyon and Tan Seep. Fork left again for Reds Canyon after 4 miles. and then come to the junction for McKay Flat (left) and Reds Canyon (right) 1 mile thereafter. Park near the junction.

Notes on the trail: Strike out southward and click away the miles across the grass, sage, and juniper flats. First impressions are less than impressive, but perseverance is a virtue. The landscape unfolds slowly at first, then more dramatically. A long, impending cliff hovers to the west, and soon you'll ride along its base. On the horizon rise the mighty Henry Mountains—volcano wanna-bes like the La Sals near Moab—and the flat-topped plateau of Boulder Mountain.

After 8.5 miles, fork right for Reds Canyon and descend gradually at first, then more rapidly. Watch out for ruts, rocks, and hairpin turns, because the magnificently sculpted desert draws your attention away from your front

Overlooking Reds Canyon and the western San Rafael Swell.

wheel. The road forks at the base of Tomsich Butte. The main road goes right, but fork left for a 1.5-mile loop around the butte. Dozens of mine portals, tailings aprons, and rusted mine equipment scar the Chinle and Moenkopi formations, which forms a varicolored skirt beneath the block of Wingate Sandstone. The Dirty Devil Mine saw its heyday here in the mid-1940s as the nation entered the atomic age; now it lies in eerie silence. Beyond the tamarisks and willows flows Muddy Creek. Miles downstream, it cuts through the narrow confines of the Chutes. Trace the cliffs south and you'll spot Hondo Arch—an inverted triangular span that resembles the small loop at the end of a cowboy's lariat.

Stay right near a lone cottonwood and take the doubletrack around the butte. When you reach a dry gully, take the track up the gully and to the pass between Tomsich and North buttes. Head north and dip into the dry wash of Reds Canyon. Vehicles usually pack the sand and gravel to a firm base, so your tires should float over without bogging down. Overhead, the cliffs you viewed earlier from afar bear down heavily and will accompany you for the next 10 miles.

About 6 miles from Tomsich Butte, the sandstone palisades open to a massive alcove that harbors the long-since-abandoned Lucky Strike Mine. Take the spur to explore a bit; otherwise, keep wavering up Reds Canyon, passing Sulphur Canyon and Square Top along the way. A right-hand switchback announces the moderately strenuous, 1.5-mile climb out of the canyon. Wind down with 2 miles of easy pedaling past Family Butte and San Rafael Knob to the north. Knowing that the closest convenience store is hours away, you stocked your cooler, didn't you?

RIDE 62 *IRON DIVIDE TRAIL SYSTEM*

If you chum around in the right circles, you'll hear secretive talk about the Iron Divide Trail System in the southern San Rafael Swell. Some disguise it as the cutesy "Rainbow Trails," others water it down as the dull-sounding "Twin Knolls," and many refer to it as the menacing "Five Miles of Hell." Whatever the title, Iron Divide beckons mountain bikes to its network of doubletracks, ATV trails, and desert singletrack. Desert singletrack? Granted these two words seem worlds apart, but here in the Swell it works and it's damn good.

The Iron Divide Trail System was created by the Price motocross crowd in the late 1970s. Later, the routes were accepted and signed by the Bureau of Land Management for OHV use. Now mountain bikers are onto the news and are exalting the virtues of their piston-powered brethren. Funny, didn't this happen in Moab a while back with some trail called Slickrock? Don't be misled; Iron Divide and the San Rafael Swell will never be destined the same fate as Moab, because this region is categorically no man's land. But that's the allure. Although dead dry and utterly deserted, the San Rafael Swell charms those who make the effort with its sun-charred redrock and sinuous canyons.

Despite its remoteness, the color-coded Iron Divide Trail System caters to all ability levels. The Blue Trail is tranquil and non-threatening. It's like dipping

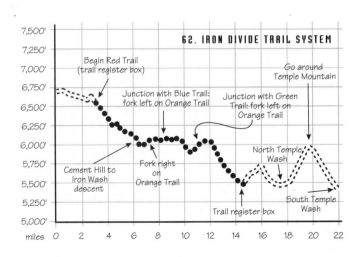

RIDE 62 IRON DIVIDE TRAIL SYSTEM

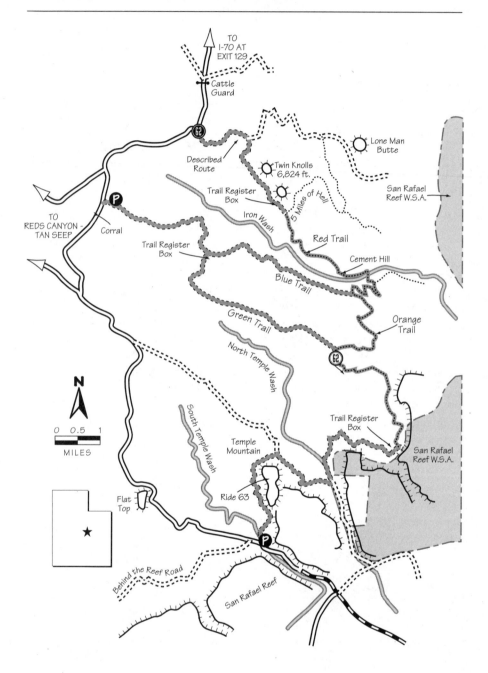

TO
I-70 AT
EXIT 129

Cattle
Guard

62

Described
Route

Lone Man
Butte

Twin Knolls
6,824 ft.

Trail Register
Box

5 Miles of Hell

San Rafael
Reef W.S.A.

Iron Wash

TO
REDS CANYON –
TAN SEEP

Corral

Red Trail

Trail Register
Box

Cement Hill

Blue Trail

Orange
Trail

Green Trail

North Temple Wash

62

Trail Register
Box

N

0   0.5   1

MILES

South Temple Wash

San Rafael
Reef W.S.A.

Temple
Mountain

Flat
Top

Ride 63

Behind the Reef Road

San Rafael Reef

your toe in a lake to test the water without plunging in headlong. Green means go, and don't look back. Set your gears in cruise mode and wander the desert floor like a nomad—but with a mission. You'll rave about the miles you crossed, the twisting trails, and the scenery that made your eyes bug out. Orange is for the flood of color radiating from the sun-baked rock and for the warming comfort of the distant San Rafael Reef that grows to colossal proportions. Orange is a warm color, and this trail will make you sweat. You'll be fully engaged in the trail system and shun the preconceived notion that singletracks are found in mountains and forests. But Red means blood, and the buzzards will feast on the flesh you leave behind if you balk at the technical stunts or let testosterone pollute your brain. Red is also for hell—Five Miles of Hell.

General location: Southern San Rafael Swell behind Temple Mountain, about 45 miles southeast of Green River.

Distance: 22 miles point-to-point. (See options in "Notes on the trail.")

Tread: Sand and rock doubletracks; smooth, rough, and hellish ATV trails and desert singletracks.

Aerobic level: Strenuous. More so than requisite brute strength and indefatigable stamina, you'll need collective trail-finding skills for the Red Trail (Five Miles of Hell). See "Notes" for options.

Technical difficulty: Level 2 to 5+. The easy parts are easy and the hard parts are off the scale. Red Trail has broken slickrock, ledge drops, and boulder-ridden staircases, all of which require a full repertoire of handling skills (level 5+). Although "Cement Hill" sounds like a comical prop from the *Beverly Hillbillies,* it's vicious and demands careful scrutiny. Orange Trail has lesser amounts of stunts coupled with sandy ATV trails (level 3 to 5). Blue and Green Trails are sand and rock doubletracks (level 2 to 4). (See "Notes.")

Elevation change: The Twin Knolls Trailhead is the highest elevation at 6,720 feet. The route drops to 5,400 feet at North Temple Wash. You hit two 500-foot climbs near the end: a 1.5-mile grind after exiting the Orange Trail and the 0.5-mile spanker around Temple Mountain. Total climbing is about 2,000 feet.

Season: Spring (March through May) and fall (September through November) are the best times to visit the San Rafael Swell. Midsummer can be unbearably warm. Rain may make dirt roads impassable to both bikes and vehicles.

Services: Nada, nadie, ninguno. In English that means nothing! If you don't have it on your bike or in your car, you're S.O.L. Green River, which has all visitor services except a bike shop, is an hour's drive from either trailhead. Backcountry camping is allowed throughout the San Rafael Swell unless posted otherwise. Goblin Valley State Park (fee area), located 7 miles south of Temple Mountain via a gravel road, has developed camping and showers. But you must pay the entrance fee even if you wish only to use the rest rooms or stock up on water.

Hazards: Survival will be your greatest concern, especially if you have a mechanical or mental breakdown, get off track, or run out of water. One invariably leads to the others. Make a sound assessment of your ability and that of others in your group; remember the old adage about the weak link in the chain. Take a ton of water and sensible food. (Saltine crackers are not sensible.) Pack a hardware store of tools and a spare inner tube, and make sure your patch kit glue is not dry. Watch for oncoming motorcycles, especially in wash gullies where the sound of their sputtering motors is muffled.

Rescue index: Any chance of timely organized rescue is farfetched. It's an hour's drive to Green River from either trailhead. If you are stranded midroute, it's a day's walk just to reach one of the trailheads. Passersby are unlikely. Green River has a medical clinic. The closest hospital is in Price, several hours away. There is a park ranger (and radio communication) at Goblin Valley State Park, located about 10 miles south of the Temple Mountain Trailhead.

Land status: Bureau of Land Management (Price Field Office).

Maps: USGS Horse Valley, San Rafael Knob, Temple Mountain, and Twin Knolls, Utah. (Much of the trail system is not shown.)

Access: Temple Mountain Trailhead: From Green River drive 11 miles west on Interstate 70 and take Exit 147 for Utah State Highway 24 and Hanksville. Travel 25 miles south on UT 24. At milepost 137 turn right for Goblin Valley and Temple Mountain, and drive 5 miles on the paved road to the Goblin Valley turnoff. Continue straight/west on the South Temple Wash Road and enter the San Rafael Reef, where pavement turns to dirt. Where the road breaches the Reef, pull off to the right and park a vehicle in the dirt clearing on the south side of Temple Mountain.

Twin Knolls Trailhead from Temple Mountain: In the shuttle vehicle, travel west, then north on the South Temple Wash Road for 9 miles to a Y junction for Reds Canyon (left), but fork right for I-70. Pass a corral on the left 1.8 miles farther. About 0.2 miles from the corral, a doubletrack forks right, signed "Motorcycle Trailhead." Use this for the Blue and Green Trails option. To reach the Twin Knolls Trailhead (Red Trail), continue for 0.7 miles to a second junction signed for Reds Canyon and Tan Seep (left). Stay right/straight and continue 2.4 miles from the junction to a faint doubletrack forking right. There may be a sign for motorcycle trailhead set back from the main road.

Twin Knolls Trailhead from I-70: Drive 29 miles west of Green River on I-70, and take Exit 129 for Ranch Exit. Cross under the freeway and drive west, then south for 7 miles on the dirt road. The trailhead is 0.9 mile south of a four-way junction with doubletracks marked by a cattle guard and a sign cautioning of a winding road and 15 mph.

Note: All dirt access roads are graded occasionally and are suitable for passenger cars when dry (rough in some spots). These dirt roads may be *impassable* when wet!

Notes on the trail: First some fine print. Although the BLM has signs and registration boxes at some trailheads, the BLM does not maintain the trail system, nor did it paint the trails. The trails were painted on an individual or group basis by trail users. The trail exists in its natural state and does not receive any maintenance, and the paint-on-rock trail indicators can wear off or fade away. Oftentimes, the only indication of the trail (Red Trail especially) is the track left by the last visitor. The BLM will not tolerate resource damage to lands adjacent to the trail and will close the trail system to all mechanized uses should environmental impacts compromise current management objectives. *Stay on route,* as difficult as that may be at times!

Now, here's the lowdown on the 22-mile, aerobically strenuous, technical level 5+ ride from Twin Knolls to Temple Mountain, including the infamous Five Miles of Hell.

From the Twin Knolls Trailhead, sneak away from your link to civilization and don't look back. Round the south flank of the flat-topped knoll and pedal roughly eastward across the broken, nondescript terrain peppered with pygmy evergreens. Lone Man Butte topped with a solitary sandstone digit is a lighthouse to desert rats like yourself. In the eastern haze, the La Sal Mountains hover above Moab and snicker at the droves of gearheads who "hurry up and wait" on the Slickrock Bike Trail.

After 1.5 miles, fork right at a Y junction, staying on the main doubletrack signed "BLM Motorcycle Trailhead." You're heading southeast now. About 1.5 miles farther, you round Twin Knolls—a pair of honey-blonde buttes topped with rusted caps—and come to a metal trail registration box. Let the desert know you are ready to take it on. The doubletrack narrows to a sandy ATV trail which becomes progressively more rocky as you are eased into Five Miles of Hell.

Over the next 3 miles you are on your own to find and follow the route. Fortunately, the scenery doesn't warrant your undivided attention, so keep your eyes glued to the trail. You'll need to instantly assess the barrage of obstacles awaiting your front tire and to scout for vestiges of trail markers: red painted dashes or arrows on rocks, small piles of rocks (called cairns), and tire tracks from others who ventured before you.

A rust-stained slash in the middle ground grows closer and deeper, and after a short respite from the pounding, you dive down the jumbled slickrock ramp of Cement Hill to bone-dry Iron Wash. If bike and body are unscathed at this point, you can breathe a sign of relief—you passed the test. There are more wild sections ahead, but they are far less threatening. ("Why is Five Miles of Hell only 3 miles long?" you say. That's because we skipped several miles of doom, despair, and agony to the north, which make this last section seem like a spin through the park. Three miles is plenty.)

Slog down the wash through ankle-deep sand for 0.5 miles, not an inch farther, and look to the right for the exit trail (may be marked with small cairns). Buzzards circling overhead eagerly await those who miss this turn.

Enough said!

Struggle out of the wash, blast over more technical stunts, pass a sign for Cement Hill, and intersect the Orange Trail. Fork right! (The left fork, which leads toward the San Rafael Reef Wilderness Study Area, is seldom traveled and is not recommended for bicycles.)

Now for that killer desert singletrack—the motorheads have carved up a nice little twisty out here in cowboy country, and you'll have a chance to shift up to your neglected higher gears. Bank through the turns, charge up a slope of broken rock, and intersect the Blue Trail. A sign rates the previous Orange Trail as ". . . not recommended for inexperienced riders." (Now you tell me!) Fork left on the continued Orange Trail to head over to Temple Mountain; fork right to bail out to the main road 7 miles away via the Blue Trail.

The technical punches keep on coming, but these jabs land more gently than the numbing blows soaked up earlier on the Red Trail. Round the mesa on your right, descend and climb through the alcove, and then descend a sketchy little ridge that drops to a dry wash. Cross over. Cross a second wash, but when you reach a third wash, fork right and pedal up the sand-filled gulch for 0.4 miles; then fork left up a dry tributary. (Look for orange paint on a rock and follow the consensus of tire tracks.) After 0.5 mile of intermittent slickrock, you break from the gully and reach the junction with the Green Trail, marked by a low-honey-blonde mesa to the south and a pair of 40-foot-tall blocky mounds to the right. Fork left for BLM–Iron Divide Trail on the continued Orange Trail. (The right fork is tagged BLM–North Temple Trail. It's 8 miles of long and drawn-out, sandy doubletrack.)

Take the ATV trail southeast and gear down for "the Wall." (Don't bother; even the Hall of Famers can't clear it.) Cross a broad, elevated ledge of purple, ripple-marked Moenkopi sandstone and let gravity pull you down the twisting luge track toward the ever-growing San Rafael Reef. Drop into a wide, dry wash like a semi plowing down a runaway truck ramp, and surf down the sandy gully in high gear for 2 miles to a junction signed for the Iron Divide Motorcycle Trail and Temple Mountain. Sign out at the registration box. Follow the latter, but first chug some fluids and chow down some treats, because now you climb.

Desert singletrack is no more, but excitement still waits. The road turns upward quickly, and you exhaust your gear selection. After about 1 mile of steady climbing, the road bends across the top of a ridge and banks down the other side. Before you rip down the sweeping turns, twirl around and scoop up the circumambient view of this beautifully deserted desert crowned by Temple Mountain. The Henry Mountains define the distant south.

Drop to another dry wash and pedal down it idly for 0.5 mile to a T junction with North Temple Wash. Fork right on a wide, purple-sand doubletrack to round the backside of Temple, passing satellite doubletracks, a mine camp, and vintage cars circa 1940. (If you're pooped, head down North Temple Wash then along the Reef to the South Temple Wash Road. (See Ride 63, Temple Mountain.) This option is a few miles longer but is virtually flat and gentle on weary legs.)

One-half mile past the mine camp, the road forks. Stay *left*, as Robert Frost would, on the steeper, rougher, rutted, and seemingly less-traveled road and climb for 0.4 mile. Yeah, it hurts! (The right fork, smooth and gentle, tempts you to a labyrinth of canyons in Sinbad Country.) When you are beneath a "thumb" of rock peeling away from the northwest corner Temple Mountain, fork right and drop off a 20-foot ramp. Fork left/south for the denouement.

With whatever energy you can muster, charge down the maroon-sand doubletrack that rolls and descends off the shoulder of Temple like a giant-slalom course. If you have faith in your knobs, put your bike on edge and carve. But be leery of sucker ruts that invariably angle across the road. Your car and the cold, bubbly contents in your cooler draws you in at breakneck speeds. Twist the cap or pop the top. Moab isn't the only place with da' kine trails!

Now for the options: Green Trail-Orange Trail to Temple Mountain (16.5 miles point-to-point, moderate, technical level 2 to 4).

Here's the easier of two cheater routes if Five Miles of Hell sounds too much like a blood-and-guts slasher movie. Arrange a shuttle from Temple Mountain to the motorcycle trailhead located between the two junctions for Tan Seeps and Reds Canyon (see "Access"). Pedal down the doubletrack for 3.2 miles to a trail registration box at a junction. Twin Knolls can be seen periodically off to the northeast. Sign in and fork right on the Green Trail, and follow the little-used, sand-and-rock doubletrack south, then east. (The route may not be signed, but look for spots of lichen-green paint on rocks in and alongside the track.) Roll across the bleak and forsaken terrain for 4.3 miles to a signed junction, spying Temple Mountain between gaps in the low mesas along the way. Fork right for BLM–Iron Divide Trail via the Orange Trail and pick up the main description above at mile 11.1.

Blue Trail-Orange Trail to Temple Mountain (20.7 miles point-to-point, strenuous, technical level 2 to 5): Here's the tougher of the cheater routes that allow you to snub Five Miles of Hell. Oh, you'll get a good taste of what you're missing, but at least it's palatable. Arrange a shuttle from Temple Mountain to the motorcycle trailhead located between the two junctions for Tan Seeps and Reds Canyon (see "Access"). Pedal down the doubletrack for 3.2 miles to a trail registration box at a junction. Twin Knolls sneer at you from the distance; just jeer right back. Fork left on the Blue Trail (doubletrack), and follow the north flank of the low, wavering mesa through shade-giving juniper and pinyon. Ride about 3.5 miles to a not-so-obvious junction with the Orange Trail, where the doubletrack has narrowed to singletrack. Now, you'll follow the main description above from mile 8.3 by taking the technical level 4 to 5 Orange Trail to the right and around the east end of the mesa.

Blue Trail (14 miles out-and-back, easy to moderate, technical level 2 to 3): Here's one for the kids to try. Start out at the motorcycle trailhead located between the two junctions for Tan Seeps and Reds Canyon (see "Access"). Pedal down the doubletrack for 3.2 miles to a trail registration box at a junction, or drive to this point for a shorter ride. Fork left, and take the Blue Trail (doubletrack) around the north side of the low mesa. Wind in and out of the hollows creasing the tabletop and dodge the juniper and pinyon boughs overhanging the track. There are a few rough and rutted sections, but for the most part, the road rises and drops gently. About 3.5 miles from the trail box, you'll intersect the Orange Trail, where the route narrows to singletrack and becomes instantly more technical. If you're feeling gutsy, head north on the Orange Trail a ways and see how you fare; then turn around.

Red Trail-Blue Trail: (18.5-mile loop, strenuous, technical level 2 to 5+): Pit your testosterone against Five Miles of Hell, but bail out when you intersect the Blue Trail. You'll loop right back to your car after 7 miles of rolling doubletrack and 3.1 miles of smooth dirt road. This is the perfect loop if no shuttle is available. Naturally, you can add on a few more miles of rock-hopping by staying on the Orange Trail and then looping back on the Green Trail. The extra miles of challenging desert singletrack outweigh the lengthy and utterly monotonous legwork along the Green Trail.

The Big Bubba, or Big Betty, Loop: (36-mile loop, aerobically strenuous, technical level 2 to 5+). "We Don't Need No Stinkin' Shuttle!" If that's your philosophy, then this is your ride, and it comes complete with unabashed bragging rights. Start out at Temple Mountain and knock off the 14-mile shuttle to the Twin Knolls Trailhead. (See "Access.") You begin with a 4-mile, 800-foot warm-up climb from Temple to Flat Top, then roll through Sinbad Country, gaining another 800 feet along the way. The road is wide, mostly smooth, and fast-paced. When you reach the Twin Knolls Trailhead, your legs should be feeling pumped but absolutely fresh or you're buzzard meat later on. Epic ride!

RIDE 63 *TEMPLE MOUNTAIN*

Temple Mountain is a hub of recreational activity, from mountain biking to narrows hiking to exploring mining history. The tower-capped butte received its name for its resemblance to the many Mormon temples throughout Utah. From afar, it stands out as the beacon of the southern San Rafael Swell.

In the past, the Temple drew a strong following of worshipers—but not a religious-minded congregation. The atomic age of the 1940s and 1950s heralded a flurry of activity to the Colorado Plateau and desert southwest. Temple Mountain was the focus of much attention when prospectors and

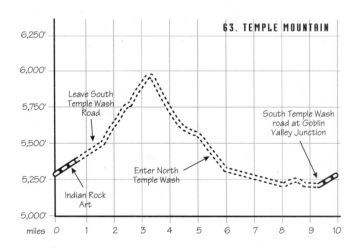

RIDE 63 TEMPLE MOUNTAIN

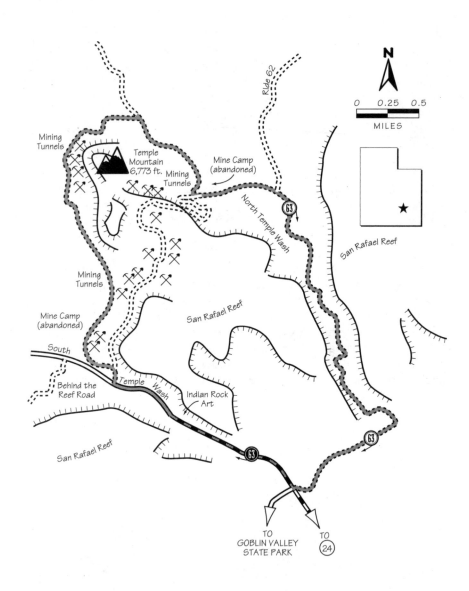

mining magnates alike scurried about Utah's Canyon Country in search of uranium and other radioactive minerals. The butte's maroon, gray, and chalk-white banded slopes were honeycombed with tunnels and shafts while a sizeable mining community prospered. Many found quick fortunes while others found financial ruin. Although its life span was short, Temple Mountain's boom days are reflected in the abandoned mining camps and defunct mine workings that litter the district.

General location: Temple Mountain is in the southern San Rafael Swell, about 40 miles southwest of Green River.

Distance: 10-mile loop.

Tread: Variably sandy and rocky doubletracks.

Aerobic level: Moderate. The climb around the west side of Temple Mountain is moderate and the route's toughest part. The rest is downhill or nearly flat. Sand traps in North Temple Wash require a little oomph to plow through.

Technical difficulty: Level 2 to 3. Doubletracks can be sandy, and the descent on the north side of Temple Mountain is littered with small rocks—nothing too scary.

Elevation change: The route's trailhead/parking area is at 5,320 feet. The lowest point is 5,210 feet upon exiting North Temple Wash. The loop rises to 6,200 feet on the northwest flank of Temple Mountain, for total climbing of 1,000 feet.

Season: Spring (March into May) and fall (September into November) are the best times to visit the San Rafael Swell. Midsummer can be unbearably warm. Rain may make dirt roads impassable to both bikes and vehicles. Easter weekend brings hordes of recreationists to nearby Goblin Valley State Park with many spilling over to the Temple Mountain area.

Services: There is no drinking water or services along the route or in the immediate area. Backcountry camping is allowed throughout the San Rafael Swell, unless posted otherwise. Goblin Valley State Park (fee area), located 7 miles south of Temple Mountain via a gravel road, has developed camping and showers. But you must pay the entrance fee even if you only wish to use the restrooms or stock up on water.

Hazards: Since this is a desert environment, carry plenty of water both on your bike and in your vehicle. Avoid venturing into mine tunnels and structures because they may be unstable and collapse. Low oxygen levels may exist in tunnels, and undetectable and potentially harmful radon daughters may be present.

Rescue index: You are likely to encounter others near the trailhead, but less so as the route winds around Temple Mountain. There is a park ranger (and radio communication) at Goblin Valley State Park, located about 7 miles south of the parking area/trailhead. Green River, located about 40 miles northeast of Temple Mountain, has a medical clinic.

Land status: Bureau of Land Management (Price Field Office).

Maps: USGS Temple Mountain, Utah.

An abandoned mining camp haunts Temple Mountain.

Access: From Green River, travel 11 miles west on Interstate 70 and take Exit 147 for Utah State Highway 24 and Hanksville. Travel 25 miles south on UT 24. At milepost 137, turn right for Goblin Valley State Park and Temple Mountain, and drive 5 miles on the paved road to the Goblin Valley turnoff. Continue straight/west on the South Temple Wash Road for less than 0.5 mile and park in the large pullout on the left just before entering the canyon piercing the San Rafael Reef. From Hanksville, travel about 20 miles north on UT 24 to milepost 137. Turn left/west and proceed as described above. (If you don't want to hang out in RV-City, just drive through the Reef and park on the other side.)

Notes on the trail: From the parking area/trailhead, pedal west on the South Temple Wash Road as it slices through the inclined San Rafael Reef. The canyon's walls reveal classic exposures of the Triassic-Jurassic Glen Canyon Group. This prominent trio of sandstones is visible throughout much of Utah's Canyon Country, and forms many of the colorful features that typify the Southwest. The Navajo Sandstone, recognized by its off-white color, sweeping crossbeds, and hummocky surface, comprises the outer/western face of the Reef. The Navajo's conspicuous structure and uniform sand composition indicate it was once an ancient sand dune field that consumed much of southern Utah about 200 million years ago. Beneath the Navajo, the Kayenta Formation forms alternating orange and brown ledges. These layers of dirty sand suggest a near-shore depositional environment, perhaps a widespread

river delta that formed nearly 220 million years ago. The base of the
is supported by the reddish-orange Wingate Sandstone, which forms th.
ramparts on the backside of the Reef. Like the Navajo Sandstone, the Wi.
is also believed to represent drifting sand dunes dating back 240 million yea.
Since these once-flat-lying layers have been upended here at the Reef, you can
casually cross 40 million years of the earth's evolution without the aid of rock-
climbing gear.

About 0.5 mile inside the Reef, fork right to a backcountry campsite
beneath a cliff face. You'll find pictographs of anthropomorphs (humanoids)
and box-shaped animals drawn by the ancient Fremont Indians, who inhabited central Utah between 700 A.D. and 1300 A.D. Immediately thereafter,
pavement turns to dirt, and the road breaches the Reef. Beyond is Sinbad
Country, a barren and bleak wasteland of varicolored terraces etched in low
relief. Temple Mountain now comes into clear view, wrapped in a lithified
shawl of purple and white.

Turn right/north on a doubletrack that passes a few abandoned mine huts.
The road angles around the western flank of Temple Mountain, rising gently
at first and then more steeply as it passes dozens of deserted mine tunnels and
structures. Ignore all tracks forking from the main road, unless you choose to
explore.

The road ends on the northwest side of the mountain. Back up a few feet,
fork right/east on another doubletrack, and push up a 20-foot ramp. Now
descend the steep, rough track around the mountain's north side—steady as
she goes. Stay on the main doubletrack and curve past a junked car and then
more mining camps. Sinbad Country recedes as the sandy road drops to North
Temple Wash, yet another incision in the Reef. Fork right and enter the cut,
following the wide, sandy road that has been plowed for vehicle use. Your
imagination will run wild when you're greeted by hollow eyes, ghoulish
shapes, and melting figures that have eroded from the seemingly solid
sandstone.

As you approach the end of the canyon, ignore the track to the right rising
up a sandy hill. Instead, exit the Reef completely, and then fork right on a
much mellower track. Take this dirt road back along the face of the Reef and
to the South Temple Wash Road to complete the loop.

While you're in the area, schedule an extra day to romp on foot among
battalions of gremlin soldiers wearing mushrooms for helmets and other
oddly-shaped hoodoos in the bizarre fantasy land of Goblin Valley State Park.
Also, you can hike the many narrows (slot canyons) that slice the Reef south of
Temple Mountain, including Chute, Crack, Little Wild Horse, and Bells
Canyons. Since these canyons are within the Crack Canyon Wilderness Study
Area, mountain bikes are not allowed.

RIDE 64 *TANTALUS FLATS*

Capitol Reef National Park's Waterpocket Fold is the decided focus of the Tantalus Flats tour with its uplifted and inclined sandstones played in colors of white, gold, and reddish orange; profound canyons that elude sunshine; and rotundas of lithified dunes. Of course you can waltz through similar terrain elsewhere in southern Utah's canyon country. But no other route combines such desert splendor with an alpine approach.

The tour begins on the shoulder of Boulder Mountain, where cool breezes waft through aspen, fir, and pine; where icy creeks tumble down boulder-ridden, moss-encrusted channels; and where glaciation has stamped a series of arcuate recesses and promontories from the plateau's rim.

From a break in the timber, your eyes fall upon juniper and pinyon chaparrals that surround grass meadows far below. Pulsating through heat vapors rising from the distant desert floor awaits Capitol Reef, marked by the Waterpocket Fold's unwavering lineation of naked sandstone knobs. And the Henry Mountains, which tower above the Reef, add additional alpine components. You embark from the alpine while viewing the desert; by midday, you'll be engulfed by the desert and look back at Boulder.

General location: East flank of Boulder Mountain to Capitol Reef National Park in south-central Utah, about 15 miles south of Torrey.

Distance: 24 miles point-to-point.

Tread: The route starts with 3 miles of pavement on Utah State Highway 12, followed by 3.5 miles of packed dirt doubletrack to near Lower Bowns Reservoir. Thereafter the route follows doubletracks that vary from packed dirt, to rock-studded, to sand.

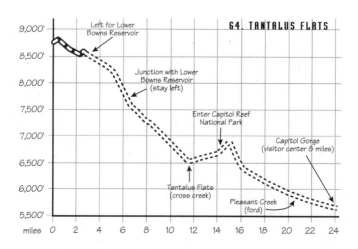

RIDE 64 TANTALUS FLATS

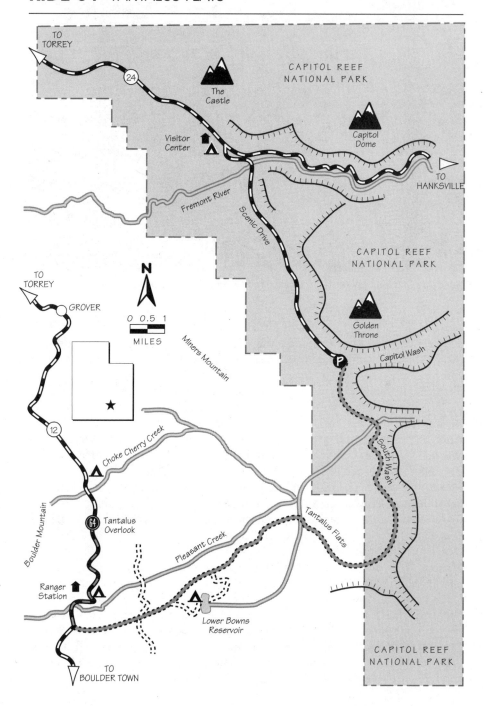

Rounding out the day on the scenic drive in Capitol Reef National Park.

Aerobic level: Moderate. You'll hit some sand midroute that will slow your progress. If you opt to culminate the ride with the 8-mile-long scenic drive to the visitor center, the route is rated strenuous because there are several steady climbs along the way. The full-on loop is 55 miles and rated expert—epic.

Technical difficulty: Level 2 to 3. The doubletrack descent to Tantalus Flats is periodically studded with small rocks that make for bumpy conditions. Beyond Tantalus you'll plow through sand traps. The climb to, and the descent from, the park boundary can have loose cobbles and low rock ledges. South Wash is firm sand and gravel that lets your knobbies float. The ford of Pleasant Creek is usually ridable but can be hub-deep during high flow.

Elevation change: The trailhead/parking area is the route's highest elevation at 8,750 feet. The lowest elevation is 5,650 feet at the trail's end where the scenic drive meets Capitol Gorge. Although this is largely a downhill ride, there are a few climbs along the way that total to about 700 feet. Total descending is closer to 3,800 feet. Nice ratio!

Season: This route has a fairly long season beginning in early spring (March) and extending through fall (late October). Temperatures can fluctuate dramatically from cool on Boulder to sweltering in Capitol Reef National Park.

Services: There is no drinking water along this route once you pass the campgrounds along UT 12. Lower Bowns Reservoir has a Forest Service campground but no water tap. Tantalus Creek and Pleasant Creek flow perennially but must be purified. There are several Forest Service campgrounds (fee areas) along UT 12 on Boulder Mountain. Capitol Reef National Park has a campground (fee area). Torrey offers most visitor services, including lodging, dining, limited groceries, gasoline, and minor vehicle services. Wild Hare Expeditions in Torrey offers bike rentals, repairs, and shuttle service (435-425-3999).

Hazards: Be alert to motorists on UT 12. You must ford both Tantalus Creek and Pleasant Creek. Both are usually ridable (hub-deep) but may deepen and flow swiftly during heavy spring runoff or flash floods. Check with rangers at the visitor center.

Rescue index: Motorists are common on UT 12 and along the Scenic Drive in Capitol Reef National Park. Anglers and campers visit Lower Bowns Reservoir. But the route's midsection (Tantalus Flats through South Wash) is remote, and you'll see few, if any, travelers. Emergency assistance can be summoned from the park's visitor center. Bicknell has a medical clinic.

Land status: Dixie National Forest (Teasdale Ranger District) and Capitol Reef National Park.

Maps: USGS Bear Canyon, Fruita, Golden Throne, Grover, and Lower Bowns Reservoir, Utah.

Access: Drop one vehicle at the end of the Scenic Drive in Capitol Reef National Park, located 8 miles south of the visitor center (park entrance fee is required). In the shuttle vehicle, travel 10 miles west of the park on Utah State Highway 24 to Torrey. Turn left/south on UT 12 and travel 14 miles up the flank of Boulder Mountain to the Tantalus Overlook, located between mileposts 110 and 109. Park and embark.

Sources of additional information: *Tour of the Waterpocket Fold,* by Ward J. Roylance (available at the Capitol Reef National Park Visitor Center, see Appendix B).

Notes on the trail: As you saddle up, reflect upon those who ventured this way over a century ago, like geologist Clarence E. Dutton. He described the scenic Pandemonium in his 1880 report, *The Geology of the High Plateaus of Utah*:

> Perhaps the most striking part of the picture is the middle ground, where the great Water Pocket fold turns up the truncated beds of the [Triassic] and [Jurassic] . . . great gashes cut across the fold or perpendicular to the face of the outcrop [carving] the stratum into colossal crags and domes.
>
> Directly east of us, beyond the domes of the flexure, rise the Henry Mountains. Among innumerable flat crest-lines, terminating in walls, they rise up grandly into peaks of Alpine form and grace like a modern cathedral among catacombs—the gothic order of architecture contrasting with the elephantine.

From the Tantalus Overlook, pedal 2.5 miles south on UT 12 to the Wildcat Ranger Station and then another 0.5 mile to the signed turnoff for Lower Bowns Reservoir. Glide down Forest Road 181 on packed dirt and gravel for 3.5 miles; then fork left on Forest Road 168 for Tantalus 5. (The right fork leads to the reservoir after another mile.) Rapidly the ecosystem has changed from the Canadian Life Zone (aspen and fir) to the Upper Sonoran (juniper and pinyon), and you'll be shedding layers of clothing.

A mile farther, veer left for Jorgensen Flat. This stretch descends gradually and the tread constantly changes from hard-packed, to sandy, to rocky. Pleasant Creek canyon flashes through the junipers and pinyons lining the left side of the road. Its gape widens and deepens quickly between terra cotta walls. If you take a side trip down the rough spur to Pleasant Creek, you can soak in bathtub-size potholes carved into the sandstone-lined streambed.

The main route descends to Tantalus Creek, where similar sun-drenched walls of stone enclose micro-parks of tall grasses. Splash through the creek and continue eastward across the flats on the gently rising but deep sand doubletrack. Unless you ride right after a rain, there is a good chance you'll be slogging through this part. The climbing becomes more aggressive—sand gives way to loose rocks—as the route crosses the park boundary and rises up to a low pass.

Take a break, grab a snack, and absorb the contrasting environment. The forested flank of Boulder Mountain has long since receded, and grass meadows bound by glowing sandstone mesas lie behind. Ahead the Waterpocket Fold stretches far north; it will be your companion for the remaining 10 miles. The Henry Mountain's 12,000-foot summits reveal themselves shyly as they peek through canyons that are notched into the colossal stone barrier.

Now here's today's geology lesson. As its name suggests, the Waterpocket Fold is a flexure in the Earth's crust. Folds are not unusual, except that this spine of barren rock stretches for nearly 100 miles but is only a few miles wide. Geologists call it a monocline because only the eastern face, which is hidden from sight behind a wall of rock, dips steeply into the ground. The western face gives rise to the multitude of sheer cliffs topped with white beehive domes composed of the famed Navajo Sandstone. Tanks (erosional depressions) that form in the Navajo hold "pockets" of water after a rain and give life to many of the desert's creatures. The Fold has created a seemingly impenetrable land barrier, or reef, to use a nautical term. Pioneers who ventured into this region noted that many of the rock domes capping the reef resembled the rotunda on the U.S. Capitol building. Capitol Dome is the prime example and adds to the park's name.

The descent from the pass can be technical level 3 because of loose cobbles and ledgy pavement rock in the tread. Drop to South Wash and snake down the dry wash bottom. Even without the outstanding desert scenery, this luge-style run would be worth the trip.

When you reach Pleasant Creek, which is ridable most of the time, you can either hit it full-bore and unreconnoitered or cross it cautiously after a little scouting. Either way, you'll get wet. Three more miles of dirt road bring you to the scenic drive at Capitol Gorge and the tour's end, unless you have opted to pound the pavement for 8 miles to the visitor center.

RIDE 65 *MOUNT ELLEN*

The Henry Mountains were the last major range to be named in the lower 48 states, mainly because the rugged area surrounding the mountains discouraged early settlers and explorers. It wasn't until 1882 that polygamist Ebenezer Hanks sought the isolation of the area and founded the settlement of Hanksville. At the same time, bandits following the famed Outlaw Trail used the remote canyons east of Hanksville to elude posses. These mountain islands floating on the Colorado Plateau were named after Professor Joseph Henry of the Smithsonian Institute. He was an active supporter of the John Wesley Powell expeditions, which explored the Colorado River and surrounding areas in 1869 and for years to follow.

The Henrys are home to the only free-roaming herd of American bison in the continental U.S. In 1941, 18 head of the once-threatened species were transplanted from Yellowstone National Park to the Henry Mountains area. Today over 200 buffalo roam the western lower benches in the winter and higher elevations during summer. Seeing them up-close is a rare but treasured moment.

Like the La Sal and Abajo Mountains, the Henrys are would-be volcanoes whose magma never reached the surface. Semi-molten rock from deep beneath the earth's crust pushed upward but was thwarted by a massive pile of sedimentary rock. Unable to breach the surface, the magma domed the overlying rock layers and spread laterally between them, forming laccolithic intrusions. As they stand today, the Henry Mountains represent the core of the magma chamber after the capping rocks have been eroded away. Evidence of these once-overlying layers is revealed in the arched sedimentary units lapping

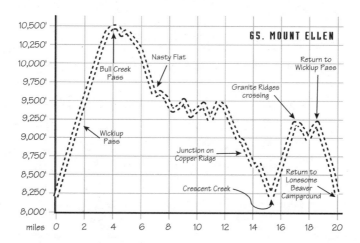

RIDE 65 MOUNT ELLEN

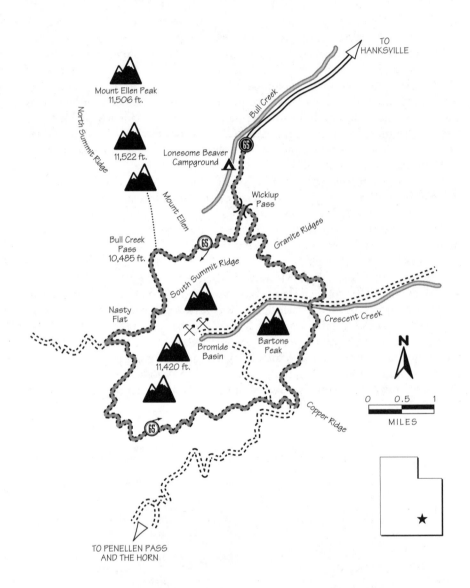

against the mountains' flanks.

General location: The Mount Ellen loop encircles the northernmost massif of the Henry Mountains and is located 21 miles south of Hanksville.

Distance: 20-mile loop.

Tread: Dirt doubletracks.

Aerobic level: Strenuous. Two punishing climbs hallmark this loop. The first is twofold: a 1.6-mile, 12-percent grunt right from the starting gate to Wickiup Pass followed by a 2.5-mile, 9-percent incline to Bull Creek Pass. The second, upon returning to Wickiup Pass, is a gentler 3.3-mile grind at an average 6-percent grade, but like the Energizer rabbit, it keeps going and going . . .

Technical difficulty: Level 2 to 3. Doubletracks are passable to high clearance vehicles and are generally hard-packed dirt with variable ruts and rocks. You may encounter some eroded conditions periodically. Descents can be wicked fast.

Elevation change: Lonesome Beaver Campground (trailhead) shares the route's lowest elevation with Crescent Creek at 8,200 feet. Bull Creek Pass, which separates North and South Summit Ridge of Mount Ellen, caps the loop at 10,485 feet. Total elevation gain is about 4,400 feet.

Season: Although the Henry Mountains melt out by May or June, notorious snowdrifts may block Wickiup and Bull Creek Passes throughout June and possibly into July depending on spring thaw. The route should be ridable through September and into October. Midday temperatures are warm and nights are pleasantly cool. Afternoon thunderstorms are common and can be severe.

Services: There is no drinking water along this route. Lonesome Beaver Campground is a Forest Service fee area with water taps. Creek water should be purified, or better yet, avoided, because creeks may drain old mine sites. Hanksville offers limited services, including lodging, food, and gasoline. There are no bike shops within a day's drive.

Hazards: This route is remote, so ride well equipped with repair tools, ample water and food, and appropriate clothing. Obtain a current weather forecast before embarking. When weather turns foul at these elevations, it can be merciless. There is little shelter, and what shelter there is may be an easy target for lightning.

Rescue index: Campers rarely visit Lonesome Beaver Campground or back-country sites. Motorists are few and far between. It is 20 slow miles on dirt roads from Lonesome Beaver Campground to Hanksville, and then 60 miles to Green River and medical attention.

Land status: Bureau of Land Management (Hanksville Field Office).

Maps: USGS Mount Ellen, Utah.

Access: From the intersection of 100 North and 100 East in Hanksville (next to the post office), drive south for "Sawmill Basin, Lonesome Beaver 21" (as in miles). The graded road is hard-packed dirt and sand and provides good cruising for 12 miles to a signed junction near a ranch. As you continue

On reconnaissance in the Henry Mountains.

straight/south toward Lonesome Beaver, the road becomes progressively rougher. Clearance is not a problem, but the abundance of imbedded gravel and stones test both your patience and your car's suspension. Passenger cars may be stymied 8 miles ahead at a double creek crossing. A primitive campground is 1 mile beyond the creeks. Lonesome Beaver is 0.5 mile farther, but coarse gravel and angular cobbles may make the primitive campground a more inviting parking area. High clearance vehicles should not have problems. **Notes on the trail:** From Lonesome Beaver Campground, the route begins with an unforgiving, 1,000-foot, 1.6-mile climb to multi-signed Wickiup Pass. Catch your breath but don't dally or lactic acid will lock up your thighs. Grind away at the mountain toward Bull Creek Pass, which is 2.5 miles and another 1,200 feet away. The route rises through mixed forests to open tundra meadows. To hell with lactic acid buildup, on second thought, and take a well-deserved break at the pass.

For a rewarding deviation, hike the path northward from Bull Creek Pass along Mount Ellen's North Summit Ridge. From the treeless ridge you'll find a top-of-the-world view of the confounding landscapes that compose south-central Utah. The faceted badlands of the Blue Hills and Factory Butte lie north of the Henrys and are backed by the domed San Rafael Swell with its cusped reef; the Waterpocket Fold of Capitol Reef National Park interrupts the western valley with a 100-mile, inclined barrier of stone; the Aquarius,

Thousand Lake, and Fish Lake plateaus give levelness to the western skyline; the burning wastelands of Canyonlands' Maze District is nature's jigsaw puzzle to the east; and sibling mountain islands of the Abajos and La Sals rise above the desert's heat vapors.

Undulate around the mountain's west flank and then scream downhill to the pleasing meadow and charming aspen groves at Nasty Flat. At the junction signed for McMillon Spring and Utah State Highway 24, turn sharply left/ eastward and round the southwestern tip of South Summit Ridge.

Here you can see how Mount Ellen is separated from its spouse, Mount Pennell, by the spacious void of Pennellen Pass. The Horn, a muscular but topographically insignificant hump cuddled in the pass, is the igneous offspring produced by these parental massifs and is an attraction for rock climbers.

The road continues eastward around South Summit Ridge, winding into lightly forested drainages that crease the mountain's massive flank, then back out across sloping knolls that extend from the main crest. A number of ramps that keep the thighs well pumped and lungs fully expanded are offset by equal amounts of freewheeling.

About 12 miles into the ride, you come to a junction where a doubletrack forks left and crosses upper Copper Basin en route to Bromide Basin above. Ignore it and stay right and descend switchbacks to a second junction at Copper Ridge. Now fork left/north and cross lower Copper Basin and then Copper Creek on the mountain's east side.

A huge view of desert and hopelessly deserted wilderness extends eastward ad infinitum from the base of the Henrys. The Dirty Devil, Green, and Colorado rivers, backed by intermittently voracious tributaries, have indiscriminately consumed this bleak and unproductive terrain. The parts that are more resistant to erosion have created an impossible-to-reconnoiter sandstone labyrinth. That's exactly what desperadoes Butch Cassidy, the Wild Bunch, and the Robber's Roost gang banked on. From 1875 to 1905, the maze of canyons provided reliable water and excellent protection from surprise. According to Ward J. Roylance in *Utah: A Guide to the State,* not a single lawman entered the Roost to capture the outlaws.

Descend to and cross Crescent Creek and then hunker down for the climb back to Wickiup Pass. It starts out easy enough, but then it turns ugly. There's a short respite when you cross Granite Ridge, then you bust a gut up to Wickiup Pass. No flowery superlatives can smooth over the requisite chore. Forget the scenery and stop conversing. Concentrate on "power breathing" and pedaling in smooth circles to take advantage of every muscle. Remember, if you're pedaling, you're not walking! And if you still feel fresh upon reaching the pass, place bets on who can make it the farthest up the angular doubletrack rising due south. Ugh! Finish the loop with the palm-bruising, but vengeful, descent to Lonesome Beaver.

RIDE 66 *WOLVERINE ROAD*

The Wolverine Road takes you into the colorful past of prehistoric southern Utah. The route leads to the Wolverine Petrified Wood Natural Area within the Grand Staircase-Escalante National Monument. More than 200 million years ago, these trees were buried under a protective layer of soil. While buried, the wood dissolved and was replaced by a silica material. Through erosion, these hardwoods have been liberated from the shaley tombs.

Much of this ride's allure is the journey to it via the Boulder-Bullfrog Road, otherwise known as the Burr Trail. The approach begins high on the cool alpine slopes of flat-topped Boulder Mountain, then dives into a quickly changing realm of slickrock beehive domes and checkerboard mesas. The road pursues the sun-drenched crease of Long Canyon, a postcard-perfect corridor encased by luminous Wingate sandstone palisades, to the brink of the Circle Cliffs. The Cliffs, which stand in bold relief, ring a terminally forsaken, but decidedly pristine, desert basin. Many feared this segment of the Wild West was destined to vanish forever when the Burr Trail was paved in the late 1980s. But in 1996, the designation of the Grand Staircase-Escalante National Monument preserved this rough-and-tumble land from future intrusions by the civilized world.

General location: The Wolverine Road is 18 miles east of Boulder along the Boulder-Bullfrog Road.

Distance: 36-mile loop.

Tread: 26 miles of dirt, sand, and rock roads; 10 miles of pavement.

Aerobic level: Strenuous. The first 9 miles descend gently, followed by 17 miles of more ups than downs. The paved Burr Trail rolls along without any menacing climbs.

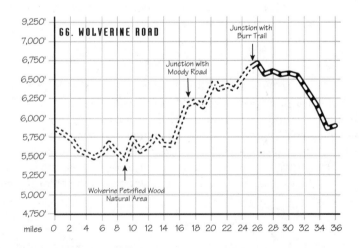

RIDE 66 WOLVERINE ROAD

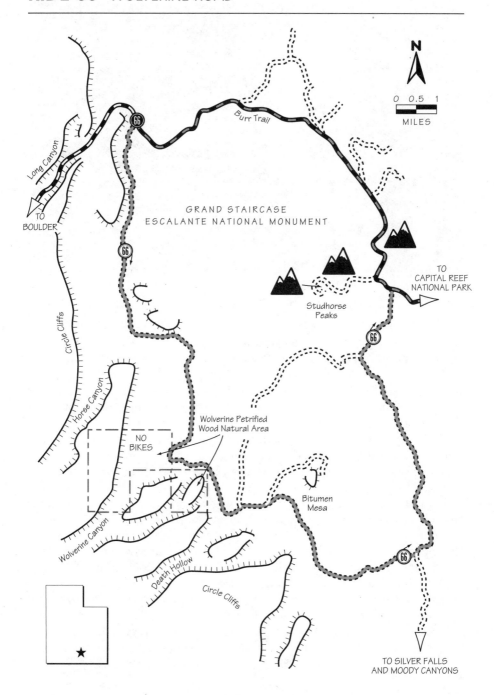

N

0   0.5   1
MILES

Long Canyon

66

Burr Trail

TO
BOULDER

GRAND STAIRCASE
ESCALANTE NATIONAL MONUMENT

66

Circle Cliffs

Studhorse
Peaks

TO
CAPITAL REEF
NATIONAL PARK

66

Horse Canyon

Wolverine Petrified
Wood Natural Area

NO
BIKES

Bitumen
Mesa

Wolverine Canyon

Death Hollow

Circle Cliffs

66

★

TO SILVER FALLS
AND MOODY CANYONS

The Burr Trail slips into Long Canyon.

Technical difficulty: Level 1 to 3. Dirt roads periodically receive the blade of a plow but may be rough for passenger cars.

Elevation change: The Wolverine Road's western junction on the Burr Trail (trailhead) is at 5,880 feet. The road descends gently to 5,400 feet at the Wolverine Petrified Wood Natural Area. Thereafter, the route oscillates up to 6,800 feet at the Wolverine Road's eastern junction with the Burr Trail. Total elevation gain is about 2,800 feet.

Season: This route is best enjoyed during spring (April through June) and fall (September through October). Midsummer is very warm and insects are annoying. Rain may swell otherwise dry creeks making them impassable to vehicles.

Services: There is no drinking water along this route. Deer Creek Campground, 6 miles east of Boulder and 12 miles west of the trailhead, is a Bureau of Land Management fee area but does not have a water tap. Boulder offers bare-bones visitor amenities: a few cafes, about the same number of motels, very limited groceries, and gasoline—usually. Beyond Boulder, it is 40 miles north to Torrey and 30 miles south to Escalante.

Hazards: Lack of preparedness is the greatest potential hazard. This route is remote, dry, and desolate, so carry plenty of water, food, and repair tools. Rain may turn portions of hard-packed road into viscous, clayey mud. Downpours may swell otherwise dry creeks and make them impassable to vehicles.

Rescue index: With the paving of Burr Trail, tourist traffic has increased between Boulder and points east (Capitol Reef and Lake Powell's Bullfrog Marina). Even so, you won't see a steady stream of motorists. Solitude is the norm along the Wolverine Road, except for a visitor or two at the Petrified Wood Natural Area. Emergency contacts can be made from Boulder, but Escalante (30 miles away) has the closest medical clinic.

Land status: Grand Staircase-Escalante National Monument.

Maps: USGS Bitter Creek Divide, Bitumen Mesa, Lamp Stand, and Wagon Box Mesa, Utah.

Access: From Boulder and Utah State Highway 12, travel east on the Boulder–Bullfrog Scenic Backway (the Burr Trail). Drop to "The Gulch" (an outstanding natural area), then wind up scenic Long Canyon. Descend from the top of Long Canyon 1.7 miles to the junction with the Wolverine Road. You'll find a sign for Boulder 19 and Burr Trail 17. Park at your discretion.

Notes on the trail: From the western junction of the Wolverine Road and Burr Trail, pedal south on the dirt road. The hard-packed sand and clay track descends gently, so the pace is brisk. After 4 miles, the road dips through a (usually) dry creek bed coated with thick sand and gravel. A mile farther, hop through another gulch marked with a BLM sign for Horse Canyon. Float through intermittent sand, gravel, and gulches for 4 more miles to a signed junction that reads "Wolverine Petrified Wood Area." There is a small parking area up ahead to the right. Lock, tether, or stash your bike and take to foot.

Inside the fence, there is a trail (of sorts) that leads through sage and cactus, over knolls, into dry washes, and across sandy wastes. Hoof out about a mile staying generally in or close to the somewhat prominent creek bed. Your destination is the band of spreading slopes that flare out like calico skirts below the rust-orange cliffs to the west. These smoothly weathered humps of gray, tan, maroon, and chocolate-brown clays host the silicified timber.

Small pieces of petrified wood are scattered everywhere. You'll find cracked but aligned segments of partial limbs and whole logs. Stumps and severed trunks form perfect stools, ottomans, and end tables; other pieces are simply rough-cut wheels from Fred Flintstone's Stone-Age car. *Note: collecting petrified wood is prohibited.* Besides, a fist-sized specimen will quickly defeat the purpose of your several-hundred-dollars' worth of titanium add-ons. And, of course, a feather-light bike takes precedence over whimsical paperweights.

Back to the trailhead/parking area, head east on the main road to continue the loop. Three miles ahead, pass a wooden corral and stay straight where a spur branches left/north. Big-chain-ring cruising precedes several miles of gradual but sustained climbing to the Moody Road, where you turn left at a sign for the Burr Trail. The right fork is signed "Silver Falls and Moody Canyons." You'll reach the paved Burr Trail after 8 endless miles of soul searching across a pictureless land of dust and scrub.

The Burr Trail was one of Utah's great backcountry roadways that lead through this stark but pristine desert landscape. In the 1980s the Burr became a battleground between environmentalists, land managers, and county com- missioners. The heated debate centered on whether the Burr Trail should remain a four-wheel-drive dirt road or be upgraded to boat-towing RV standards. After hearings, appeals, and quick court actions, the Burr met its demise and was "improved," but only after a few incidences of attempted sabotage no doubt inspired by Edward Abbey's novel, *The Monkey Wrench Gang.*

Even a staunch environmentalist will welcome pavement, for the past laborious miles can leave you feeling "bonked." The remaining 10 miles is easy cruising, and the complex scenery of desert growth, redrock palisades, and distant forested plateaus is overwhelming.

While in the area, be sure to stop at Anasazi State Park in Boulder to learn of the habitation and cultural significance of the "Ancient Ones." You'll find exhibits, murals, and a wealth of literature inside the small museum. Outside, a short, self-guided walking tour takes you through a partially excavated village.

RIDE 67 *FIFTYMILE BENCH*

As you drive out the Hole-in-the-Rock Road through the Grand Staircase- Escalante National Monument, two topographic contrasts are readily appar- ent. To the east, the Escalante Desert is a despairing wasteland of desert scrub and cacti, drift sand, and sun-baked slickrock. Discernible positive relief only periodically interrupts the general levelness. If you attempt traveling toward the center of this tableland, however, your progress will be impeded by hundred- or thousand-foot drops from an unforeseen canyon's edge.

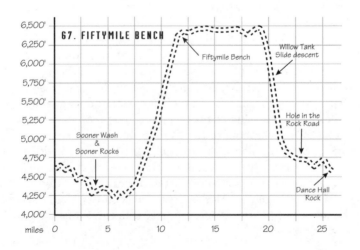

RIDE 67 FIFTYMILE BENCH

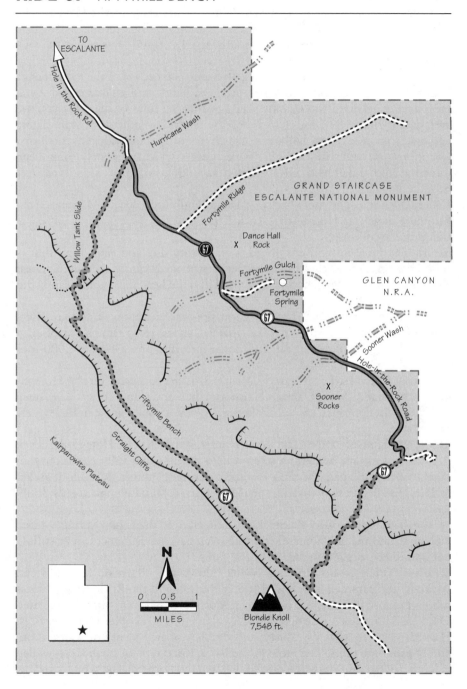

TO
ESCALANTE

Hole in the Rock Rd.

Hurricane Wash

Fortymile Ridge

GRAND STAIRCASE
ESCALANTE NATIONAL MONUMENT

Dance Hall
67 X Rock

Fortymile Gulch

Fortymile
Spring

GLEN CANYON
N.R.A.

67

Willow Tank Slide

Sooner Wash

Hole-in-the-Rock Road

X
Sooner
Rocks

Fiftymile Bench

Straight Cliffs

Kaiparowits Plateau

67

67

N

0   0.5   1

MILES

Blondie Knoll
7,548 ft.

★

To the west, the Escalante Desert is bound by a line of two superimposed cliffs extending as far as the eye can see. The upper tier is a ruler-straight escarpment, hence named the Straight Cliffs of the Kaiparowits Plateau. The lower platform, Fiftymile Bench, is a succession of cusps jutting out from a common bench. Fifty miles to the south, the Escalante Desert and the two terraces converge.

From atop Fiftymile Bench, you'll gain a true perspective of the monument's Escalante Canyons Province. The lower badlands are characterized by a profusion of inverted topography. The meandering lines of darkness you see are shadow-filled canyons, etched into the desert's weather-torn skin. These narrow slots feed deep hallways, which in turn join widened corridors. Corridors fuse with the Escalante River gorge, which ultimately joins Glen Canyon. But the depths of Glen Canyon have long since been smoothed over by Lake Powell.

General location: The route begins at Dance Hall Rock, located 42 miles from Escalante down the Hole-in-the- Rock Road.

Distance: 26-mile loop.

Tread: The Hole-in-the-Rock Road is light-duty dirt and sand road that is suitable for passenger cars when dry, but washboards can be tedious. The rest of the route up to, along, and down from Fiftymile Bench, is on dirt, sand, and rock doubletracks.

Aerobic level: Strenuous. This is a good pre-season training ride that offers miles of flat ground to dial in your cadence, short, steep climbs out of deep gullies that boost your heart rate like doing intervals, and a 4-mile, 2,000-foot grinder thrown in for good measure.

Technical difficulty: Level 2 to 5. Washboards are incessant on the Hole-in-the-Rock Road. Doubletracks up top can be sandy and rocky. The steep descend from the bench can be choked with loose cobbles and can be severely eroded.

Elevation change: Dance Hall Rock is at 4,600 feet. The Hole-in-the-Rock Road dips through numerous steep-walled gulches that tally elevation gain quickly. But you'll gain the most elevation during the direct, 2,000-foot ascent to Fiftymile Bench that tops out at 6,500 feet. Total climbing exceeds 3,200 feet.

Season: This region of southern Utah is best enjoyed during the spring (March into June) and the fall (September into November). Midsummer can be stifling hot and insects are a nuisance.

Services: There is no drinking water along the route or any services. Backcountry camping is allowed along the Hole-in-the-Rock Road, unless otherwise posted. Escalante has an outdoor store that may offer bike-related supplies, but it's not a true bike shop. Escalante offers all other visitor services.

Hazards: This route is dry, dusty, and desolate. Carry plenty of water, food, and appropriate tools. The Hole-in-the-Rock Road dips through steep-walled gulches, so use caution when descending around corners. The white-knuckle, free-falling descent off Fiftymile Bench requires steadfast bike handling. Afternoon cloudbursts may produce flash floods that can make the usually dry creek beds along the Hole-in-the-Rock Road impassable. High-clearance and four-wheel-drive vehicles have an obvious advantage.

Rescue index: The farther you venture from Escalante on the Hole-in-the-Rock Road, the less likely you are to encounter others. You may run across OHVs on Fiftymile Bench. Escalante has medical facilities but is located more than 40 miles away via the washboarded Hole-in-the-Rock Road.

Land status: Grand Staircase-Escalante National Monument.

Maps: USGS Big Hollow Wash, Blackburn Canyon, and Sooner Bench, Utah.

Access: The Hole-in-the-Rock Road branches south from Utah State Highway 12 about 5 miles east of Escalante (near milepost 65). Dance Hall Rock is 37 miles down the regularly maintained, but sand-and-washboard road. The first 5 to 10 miles are smooth and suitable for near highway speeds. Beyond, the road can be the most devilish washboard imaginable. Whether you travel at 5 mph or 50 mph, your teeth will chatter and bolts will rattle.

Notes on the trail: This route begins at Dance Hall Rock, a solitary hump of sandstone that doubled as an outdoor amphitheater during the 1879 Mormon pioneer trek to Hole-in-the-Rock.

From the Rock, follow the Hole-in-the-Rock Road 3.6 miles south to Sooner Wash and Sooner Rocks, and then pedal another 2.8 miles to the signed Fiftymile Bench Road. Turn right/west to begin the 2,000-foot ascent. The road begins as soft but graded sand and gravel. Gradually, the road angles upward. With elevation, the road's quality deteriorates for vehicles but actually improves for mountain bikes because the soft sand turns to packed dirt and rock.

This is a great hill climb—unyielding, but not relentless, demanding, but not agonizing. It does require well-conditioned legs and bellows for lungs. You'll reach a false summit 0.5 mile beyond a steel gate. The true summit awaits another 1.5 miles ahead and is marked by a T junction.

Turn right/north at the T junction on a doubletrack that passes through juniper, pinyon, and mixed pine, plus a few aspens sheltered in recessed canyons. During springtime, purple lupine bloom with profusion on the Bench. The Straight Cliffs rise another 1,000 feet immediately overhead. For the next 7 miles, the bench road maintains a near level keel but is punctuated with short climbs that require surges of power.

Pass a wooden corral and a small pasture. A few miles beyond, the road begins to descend. A mile downhill you'll reach a junction at the head of Willow Tank Slide Canyon. This is a good time to lower your seat, cinch down the helmet, and secure all belongings; the plunge off Fiftymile Bench is wicked. Your forearms will burn, your back will ache, and your brakes will smoke.

Once you're off Fiftymile Bench, you'll pedal down a doubletrack of soft sand for 2 miles to the Hole-in-the-Rock Road. One mile of washboard takes you back to Dance Hall Rock.

RIDE 68 *HOLE-IN-THE-ROCK*

To extend its boundaries and promote its principles, leaders of the Mormon Church organized a mission to settle the wild lands of the Four Corners Area. During October of 1879, 236 men, women, and children received their call and left Escalante with 1,000 head of cattle and 80 wagons packed with supplies on a historic migration across Utah's southeastern desert. The chosen route would require an unfathomable descent from the rim of the Colorado River Gorge down through the precipitous passageway called the Hole-in-the-Rock.

Crossing the inhospitable Escalante Desert was the travelers' first challenge. Midway to the Hole-in-the-Rock, the pioneers found temporary solace at the natural sandstone amphitheater of Dance Hall Rock. Here, music, song, and merriment erased the hardships they had endured and kept anxious thoughts of the Hole momentarily at bay.

Before the migrants could descend to and then cross the Colorado River, the passageway through the Hole had to be forged. Courageous blasting crews were lowered in rope-tethered barrels to drill holes in the rock for powder charges; rock was chiseled to open the notch to wagon width; and a platform road of log, brush, rock, and gravel was tacked along a ledge to prevent wagon wheels from slipping over and pulling rig and team into a perilous plunge.

The travelers, along with wagons and livestock, made their way 1,000 feet down the rock-wall slot to the Colorado River, where a hand-hewn ferry awaited to carry them across. Their midwinter trek then continued across equally godforsaken lands where additional hardships were faced and conquered. After what was expected to be a six-week journey turned into a six-month expedition, the weary migrants settled in what is known today as Bluff. Surprisingly, not a soul, wagon, or animal was lost.

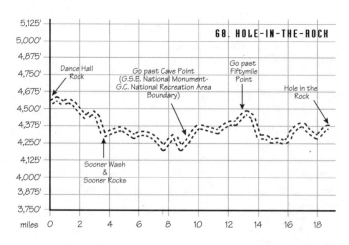

RIDE 68 HOLE-IN-THE-ROCK

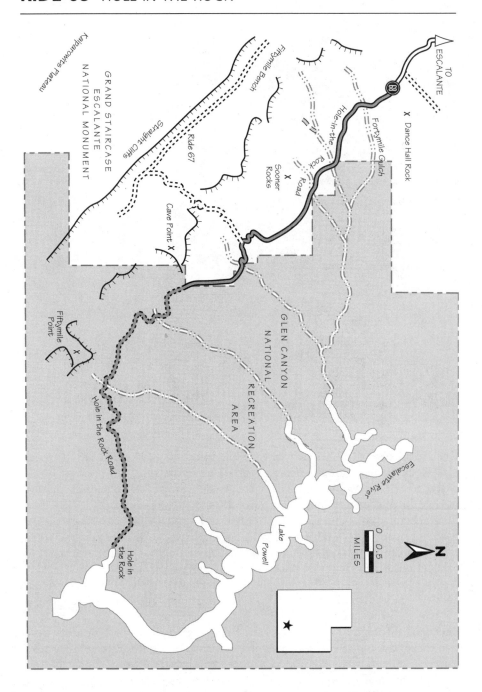

An aerial view of
Lake Powell above
Hole-in-the-Rock.

General location: This segment of the Hole-in-the-Rock Road begins at Dance Hall Rock, located about 42 miles southeast of Escalante.

Distance: 37 miles out-and-back. The route can be shortened by driving farther down the Hole-in-the-Rock Road.

Tread: Light-duty sand and gravel road for 13 miles that may be rough for passenger cars but suitable for high-clearance vehicles. Thereafter the route follows a doubletrack that combines sand and slickrock that is restricted to vehicles with high clearance and four-wheel-drive.

Aerobic level: Strenuous, but intermediate bikers will fare well if they drive out about 10 miles from Dance Hall Rock before embarking. No single climb is a monster, but the constantly undulating route takes its toll.

Technical difficulty: Level 1 to 4. The first 13 miles follow a light-duty sand and rock road, but the washboards and numerous dry gulches the road crosses can be rough. Beyond Fiftymile Point, the road degrades to a sandy double-track punctuated with pavement sandstone that rates technical level 4.

Elevation change: The elevation of Dance Hall Rock is 4,600 feet. The Hole-in-the-Rock Road ends above Lake Powell at 4,400 feet. Don't let the net elevation change mislead you. Granted, there are no whopping climbs along this route, but it undulates constantly in and out of sometimes steep washes and gulches. Incremental climbs are usually less than 100 feet, but there are dozens of them. Total elevation gain, out-and-back, approaches a respectable 2,800 feet.

Season: This region of southern Utah is best enjoyed during the spring (March into June) and the fall (September into November). Midsummer can be stifling hot, and insects can be a nuisance.

Services: There is no drinking water along this route and springs may not be reliable. Water can be purified out of Lake Powell but it lies at the bottom of a 700-foot scramble down through the Hole. Escalante offers all visitor services. The town has an outdoor store that may offer bike-related supplies, but it's not a true bike shop.

Hazards: This route is dry, dusty, and desolate. Carry plenty of water, food, and appropriate tools. Use caution where the road descends into and rises out of numerous gulches; turns can be blind and the road base can be gravelly. Use extreme caution when exploring the cliff-bound gash of the Hole-in-the-Rock. A fall could be fatal. Afternoon cloudbursts may produce flash floods that can make sections of the Hole-in-the-Rock Road impassable to passenger cars. High-clearance and four-wheel-drive vehicles have an obvious advantage.

Rescue index: The farther you venture from Escalante on the Hole-in-the-Rock Road, the less likely you are to encounter others. Motorists with four-wheel-drive occasionally venture all the way out to the Hole-in-the-Rock itself, but don't rely on them. Escalante has medical facilities but is located 40 miles away from the trailhead via slow-going washboard roads.

Land status: Grand Staircase-Escalante National Monument and Glen Canyon National Recreation Area. (*Note:* Bicycling off designated roads is prohibited in the Glen Canyon National Recreation Area; that is, no slickrock exploring!)

Maps: USGS Davis Gulch and Sooner Bench, Utah.

Access: The Hole-in-the-Rock Road branches south from Utah State Highway 12 about 5 miles east of Escalante (near milepost 65). Dance Hall Rock is located 37 miles down the regularly maintained sand and dirt road. The first 5 to 10 miles are smooth and suitable for passenger cars at near-highway speeds. Beyond, the road can have devilish washboards that become tedious whether traveled slow or fast. You can shorten this ride by driving 13 miles farther to Fiftymile Point, but high clearance is recommended.

Notes on the trail: From Dance Hall Rock, pedal southeast on the Hole-in-the-Rock Road. Fiftymile Bench is a succession of salient cusps protruding from the unwavering Straight Cliffs above. Opposing the cliffs, an endless expanse of burnt slickrock extends to the east. Portions of the road are smooth; others are washboarded. You dip into, and struggle out of, numerous dry washes that cross the road. After 4 miles, pass the floating sandstone domes of Sooner Rocks.

Near Cave Point, the road leaves the national monument and enters Glen Canyon National Recreation Area. At Fiftymile Point (mile 13) the road turns to doubletrack and requires four-wheel-drive as it drops off a shallow bench and bends eastward. There are a few technical level 4 rock ledges that are tougher for vehicles than for mountain bikes. The symmetrical hump of Navajo Mountain, which marks the Utah/Arizona border, comes into full view. Six miles of doubletrack and broken bedrock lead to the road's end and a visitor registration box at the top of the Hole-in-the-Rock itself.

If you scramble down the Hole, you can take a cool swim in Lake Powell. On your way down, notice the drill holes, chiseled steps, and deep scars scratched by wagon wheels. Or hike up the neighboring sandstone exposures and enjoy inspiring overlooks of Glen Canyon and Lake Powell. With your new and enlightened perspective of this bleak but priceless land, return to Dance Hall Rock. As you cross the miles on your highly efficient wheeled machine, reflect upon those who made this trip over a century ago, and the hardships they endured. Regardless of your religious beliefs, you'll agree that the Mormon pioneers were a faithful, indefatigable bunch.

RIDE 69 *GOOSEBERRY MESA*

Biking off-road within Zion National Park is strictly forbidden, but that's OK. Stroll through this divine gallery of rock towers, weeping alcoves, and sunshine-eluding canyons; then leave the tourists behind and pedal your mountain bike on Gooseberry Mesa. In years past, riding on Gooseberry Mesa was simply a matter of following the dusty doubletrack to a rimrocked

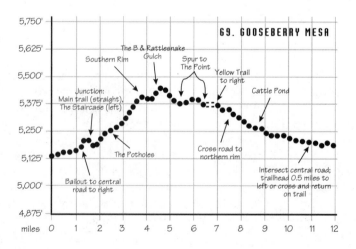

RIDE 69 GOOSEBERRY MESA

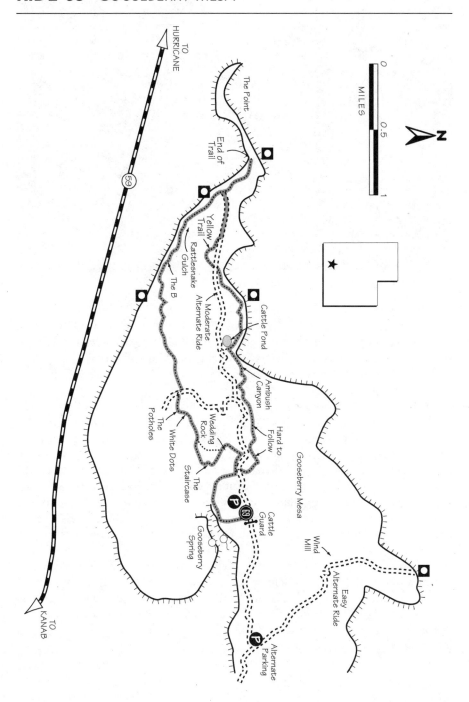

The scenic side of Gooseberry Mesa.

viewpoint and back again—highly scenic but somewhat uneventful. Now the locals in Utah's Dixie are spreading the word about an elusive trail system on Gooseberry that comes complete with slickrock. "Eh, slickrock—been there done that," you say? How about slickrock mixed with singletrack? Can't find that in Moab, so let's talk.

It's true. Tucked neatly away on the end of this pointy mesa you'll find a 12-mile track laid out amidst the sage, manzanita, juniper, and ponderosa. Granted, these slickrock sections are not the free-flowing, catch-a-wave expanses that hallmark the original formula in Moab. But Gooseberry's recipe is every bit as delectable and demands adept skills to clean the hundreds of audacious stunts. While you're not busting a cog on the rock, you're twisting a number on soft, loamy, one-laners coated with crunchy pine needles—not the runaway bike ramps-cum-sand traps of the Moab variety. This is the real stuff that will satisfy any singletrack purist. On Gooseberry, you get your cake and can eat it too.

Oh, you want scenic views, too? Well, Gooseberry serves up some real beauties that will seduce the lens of any shutterbug. From selected points on the trail, you toe the edge of southern Utah's Grand Staircase and gaze upon its successive rungs, each named for the distinctive colors of the rocks exposed. Mark this trail for late afternoon when the sun starts its westward arc and intensifies the hue of each step and fills crevasses with slivers of darkness.

Location: Gooseberry Mesa is about 15 miles southwest of Springdale, 21 miles east of Hurricane, and 38 miles east of St. George.

Distance: 12-mile pseudo-loop.

Tread: Intermittent slickrock and dirt-sand singletrack.

Aerobic level: Strenuous. (See "Notes" for options that are rated easy to moderate.) Although there are no long-winded climbs, the countless protracted ramps require sudden blasts of maximum power. You'll rarely shift out of granny gear when crossing slickrock, but on the singletrack segments you can charge full steam ahead.

Technical difficulty: Level 3 to 5+. Gooseberry Mesa is every bit as tough as the real deal in Moab (Slickrock Bike Trail) and requires a full repertoire of riding skills. If you're not on top of your game, you walk. It's that simple.

Elevation change: The trailhead is roughly 5,160 feet. The trail tops out at 5,450 feet midroute. It's nearly impossible to tally the elevation gain because the innumerable climbs are usually less than the standard 40-foot contour interval or are less than can be recorded by an altimeter watch. Let your legs be the gauge at route's end.

Season: At an average elevation of 5,200 feet, Gooseberry Mesa is pleasantly cooler than the surrounding desert of Utah's Dixie. Thus, the season extends from March through June and September through November. Midsummer is hot, unless you start at daybreak.

Services: There is no drinking water along this route. All visitor services, including bike shops, can be found in Springdale and in St. George. Hurricane offers most visitor services but has no bike shop.

Hazards: The trail itself is inherently hazardous; that's why it's so much fun. Know your ability, your limits, and the performance of your bike; if in doubt, err toward conservatism. Use caution when walking along the edge of cliffs. Rock could break away and take you with it. The slickrock/singletrack can be very difficult to follow and requires good route-finding skills. The access road may be impassable to even four-wheel-drive vehicles when wet.

Rescue index: There are few visitors out on Gooseberry Mesa, although the trail is becoming increasingly popular. Springdale has a medical clinic; St. George has a hospital.

Land status: Bureau of Land Management (St. George Field Office).

Maps: USGS Little Creek Mountain, Smithsonian Butte, Springdale West, and Virgin, Utah.

Access: Southbound on Interstate 15 (from Cedar City), take Exit 27 and travel south on Utah State Highway 17 to La Verkin. Then take Utah State Highway 9 east toward Springdale and Zion National Park. In Rockville (a few miles before Springdale), turn right/south on Bridge Street and follow the Smithsonian Butte National Backcountry Highway (light-duty dirt road) for 6.5 miles toward Utah State Highway 59. (One steep hill can be rough on passenger cars.) Where the road flattens, turn right on the Gooseberry Mesa road and cross the cattle guard.

Northbound on I-15 (from St. George), take Exit 16 for Harrisburg Junction and travel south 1 mile to State Street/UT 9. Turn left and travel 6.5 miles on UT 9 to Hurricane. Turn right on Main Street/UT 59 for Grand Canyon and Kanab; then turn left on 100 South to continue on UT 59. Take UT 59 for 14 miles, and then turn left/north on the Smithsonian Butte National Backcountry Highway between mileposts 8 and 9 (marked by a stop sign). Take the light-duty dirt road 3 miles to the Gooseberry Mesa Road and cross the cattle guard.

The Gooseberry Mesa Road is a light-duty dirt road that is suitable for passenger cars when dry but should be avoided when wet. Drive 3.6 miles out the Gooseberry Mesa Road, ignoring doubletracks forking left and right, and come to a prominent Y junction that may be marked by a rock cairn (just past the second cattle guard). Fork left on the doubletrack and take it 1.1 miles. Park on the west side of the cattle guard/fence. (This doubletrack may be too rough for passenger cars; if so, park near the Y junction. High clearance vehicles should fare well.)

Notes on the trail: At the time of publication, the Gooseberry Mesa Trail was difficult to follow and even harder to describe. Trail markers consisted of sometimes sporadic and faded dots painted on the slickrock and a consensus of tire tracks on the singletrack. The Bureau of Land Management may adopt and develop this trail in the future.

From the parking area at the cattle guard, head south on the singletrack through the sage, then into juniper, pinyon, and ponderosa pines. Weave along the tire-wide dirt path and hop over bands of sandstone while scanning the ground for green dots painted on the rock. After 1 mile, the trail bends northward and rises up a ledgy, slickrock ramp to an ill-defined junction. If you feel you're in over your head, then bail out to the right and take the central road (doubletrack) either back to the trailhead or to the mesa's point. If you're foaming at the mouth for more technical treats, then fork left. About 0.5 mile farther, the trail bends left around a prominent, overhanging point called Wedding Rock, where Glen (the proprietor of Red Rock Bicycles in St. George) and wife Kaylene were wed.

The trail forks in the conifers ahead. Stay straight for the easier shortcut, or fork left to face the Staircase. Where the two trails rejoin, head westward and across a section of slickrock potholes that is marked with white dots. Intersect a doubletrack and take the track to the right/north a few hundred yards. Then fork left near a large rock on the right to continue on the green-dot trail, or bail out by following the doubletrack north to the mesa's central road. One mile farther, the trail reaches and follows the southern rim of Gooseberry Mesa.

Take a gander from the 500-foot rim of the banded rocks flaring out from it and of Little Creek Mesa rising across the highway-striped valley. Follow the rim trail to an improbable maneuver that goes by a variety of cursed names

Glen rounds "Wedding Rock."

(most commonly The B—— rhymes with "itch"); then practice your short radius turns and track stands while reconnoitering Rattlesnake Gulch.

After a fast stretch of rimmed-side singletrack about 5 miles from the trailhead, the path curves northward and clips the edge of a colossal amphitheater of calico-striped slopes. When you intersect the mesa's central road, make a mental note of your surroundings because it tends to look different when you return from Gooseberry Point. To reach the point, take the jeep road left a few hundred yards, then fork left on an elusive trail that leads 0.5 mile to the rim-edge viewing deck.

You are looking over a huge chunk of the Grand Staircase. Gooseberry Mesa sits atop one of the lower rungs called the Chocolate or Banded Cliffs. Smithsonian Butte and Eagle Crags to the east constitute the Vermillion Cliffs. The massive flesh-toned walls of Zion National Park occupy the White Cliffs. And the top step, the Pink Cliffs, is on the timbered horizon below Brian Head

Peak. That's Smith Mesa across the Virgin River Valley where the government conducted numerous tests of rocket-powered vehicles and ejection seats. And the Pine Valley Mountains host Utah's southernmost alpine wilderness area.

Return to the junction with the central road and follow it east for 0.5 mile, and then fork right on the utterly unobtrusive yellow trail. (Look for yellow paint on a tree limb and a rock cairn.) After just over 0.5 mile, rejoin the main road, take it to the right for 50 feet, and then fork left on the continued green-dot trail. Now you'll wind along the edge of the mesa's north rim and ride more singletrack than slickrock. Pass a cattle water catchment pond (may be dry) 1.3 miles from the central road and wander eastward away from the rim. (You can bail out to the central road at the pond also.) Ahead you twist up a narrow sandstone hallway the author calls Ambush Canyon and cross nondescript terrain.

If you've made it this far, then you are a master navigator. Now comes the real test of your route-finding skills because the green dots tend to be few and far between. One mile past the cattle pond, you come to a T junction of sorts. The old route forks right (green dots) and intersects the central road. Fork left if you're still hell-bent on pedaling every inch of singletrack. After 1 mile more, you'll intersect the central road. Take the doubletrack left and back to the parking area. Or fork right/west and take the road 50 feet, then fork left on a singletrack to retrace your outgoing tracks back to the trailhead. Whew!

Novice and intermediate bikers can avoid the navigational nightmare of the slickrock/singletrack by just riding the mesa's central road to Gooseberry Point for a 6-mile, out-and-back trip. The central road undulates gently but can be rough and rocky or soft and sandy. Alternatively, if you parked at the Y junction, follow the right fork for an easy 4-mile, out-and-back trip to the mesa's north rim. This route is nearly flat and easy cruising.

Oh yeah. If you come across two middle-aged, somewhat portly bikers that are the mirror image of each other, except for different colored Cannondale V bikes, tip your helmet to Mike and Morgan of Hurricane. The new Gooseberry Mesa Trail was their brainchild. Nicely done, guys.

RIDE 70 *SILVER REEF*

The Silver Reef tour travels along a broad bench of juniper, pinyon, and ponderosa pine that separates the Pine Valley Mountains from deep, redrock canyons. The route affords scenic vistas of sandstone temples and majestic peaks of distant Zion National Park, including the Guardian Angels and Towers of the Virgin. Stop occasionally, especially at the route's higher points, to catch over-the-shoulder glimpses of this famed gallery of sculpted rock.

RIDE 70 SILVER REEF

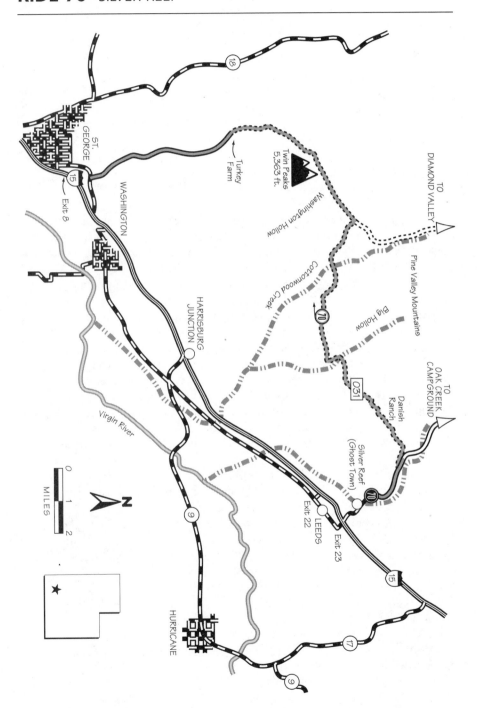

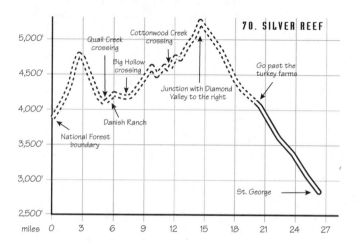

Overhead, rugged slopes of the Pine Valley Mountains Wilderness Area contrast with checkerboard swirls etched into sandstone canyons below. Toward the route's end, looming red cliffs above Warner Valley and the cultivated fields east of Washington are in view. The final descent to St. George is highlighted by miles of rock-hopping, from juniper and pinyon communities, to sagebrush country, to steaming desert prairies.

General location: The Silver Reef tour begins 15 miles northeast of St. George and traverses the southern flank of the Pine Valley Mountains.

Distance: 26 miles point-to-point.

Tread: The route begins on a light-duty dirt road rising up from Silver Reef. The midsection traverses a pebbly packed-dirt doubletrack. The ride culminates on a light-duty dirt road with gravel and rock.

Aerobic level: Strenuous. The route starts with its toughest climb. Along the traverse of the Pine Mountains, the route undulates and has only a few arduous sections. The route culminates with miles and miles of freewheeling to St. George.

Technical difficulty: Level 2 to 3. Doubletracks are packed dirt with variable amounts of sand, rocks, and ruts. The descent at the end is on a pebbly dirt road that keeps you out of the saddle.

Elevation change: From Silver Reef, elevation 3,900 feet, the ride begins with a strenuous 1,000-foot climb. Afterward, the road crosses several ridges that separate various drainages and caps 5,300 feet prior to the final descent. You'll finish the route with a long descent to St. George at an elevation of 2,800 feet. Total elevation gain is about 2,500 feet.

Season: The St. George area (coined "Utah's Dixie") is noted for superb off-season mountain biking. Spring, fall, and most of winter are quite pleasant, but midsummer can be terribly hot with daytime temperatures near or above 100 degrees in St. George and a few degrees less midroute. Start this route at daybreak during summer.

Services: There is no drinking water or services along this route. This area can be very warm, so carry ample water. St. George offers all visitor services, including bike shops. Camping (fee areas) is available nearby at Quail Creek Reservoir (Bureau of Land Management), located 12 miles northeast of St. George, and at Oak Creek (Forest Service), located 8 miles north of Silver Reef.

Hazards: If you're riding during midsummer, daytime temperatures can approach 100 degrees. Carry extra water and apply sunscreen liberally. Start your ride at dawn to avoid the hottest part of the day. Normally dry creek beds may flow during spring runoff and after heavy rains. Wet weather may turn sections of the doubletrack midroute into viscous clay—the type that eats derailleurs and clogs wheels.

Rescue index: Expect complete solitude on weekdays. On weekends or holidays, you may have to share the road with a few passing vehicles or with ranchers. St. George has medical facilities.

Land status: Dixie National Forest (Pine Valley Ranger District) and Bureau of Land Management (Dixie Resource Area).

Maps: USGS Harrisburg Junction, Pintura, Signal Peak, and Washington, Utah.

Access: This route requires a vehicle shuttle, although experienced long-distance cyclists could make the ride a loop. Park at your discretion in St. George. Hop on Interstate 15 at Exit 8 (St. George Boulevard) and drive 14 miles north to Exit 22/Leeds. (Those riding a loop should take Red Cliff Drive/Frontage Road.) Drive through town about a mile, and turn left/north toward Silver Reef and Oak Creek Campground. Travel to the end of the pavement at the Dixie National Forest boundary. Park and embark.

Sources of additional information: Bicycles Unlimited (See Appendix B).

Notes on the trail: Before you begin, take some time to visit the old Wells Fargo and Pony Express Station in Silver Reef. Silver Reef was a raucous mining town that produced millions of dollars in silver from the surrounding sandstone during the 1870s and 1880s. This unusual association of precious metal ore in sandstone is the only known occurrence in the United States. Once supporting a population of 1,500, the community of Silver Reef was a stark contrast to the sedate Mormon communities around it. The old mail transfer station is now home to Jerry Anderson's Art Gallery, where you can view paintings and sculptures based on southwestern themes.

From the national forest boundary, pedal up the graded dirt road past red cliffs and along rugged Leeds Creek. After 1.6 miles, turn west on Forest Service Road 031 signed "Danish Ranch, St. George." Continue ascending through juniper and pinyon. Look back periodically to catch retreating views of the majestic towers of Zion National Park. A generous descent takes you to a rugged canyon marking the headwaters of Quail Creek. Climb gradually out the other side and roll across ledgy slopes peppered with juniper and pinyon. Pass through the apple orchard and pastures of Danish Ranch (private property) and then cross another creek. A wooden Forest Service sign announces the Big Hollow Trail; judging from the tread it is popular with OHVs and motorcycles. Just around the corner, the Big Hollow Creek dives into a labyrinthine sandstone canyon. The canyon's walls are etched with swirling and checkerboard-style crossbeds. The distance holds more views of Zion's Guardian Angels and Towers of the Virgin.

Fourteen miles into the ride, you cross a ridge marking the route's high point. Say goodbye to the sights eastward and get ready to freewheel. Stay left at a junction of doubletracks; the right fork leads north to Diamond Valley. The route now bends south and begins an endless descent on Forest Road 033. As the descent progresses, the doubletrack widens to a gravel and rock road. Pass the turkey farm on the left; then glide 6 miles more into town.

RIDE 71 *CHURCH ROCKS*

If you crave slickrock, then you'll get a quick fix on Church Rocks. Once you start the loop section, the route is nearly all rock, whether open expanses or broken ledges. And it's a known fact that riding any type of slickrock is better than riding no slickrock.

You won't really find solitude on Church Rocks because the entire route is within earshot of Interstate 15. Sure, the paved four-laner is intrusive, but the highway actually lends to the ride's intrigue. Early on, you pedal under the freeway, not via a lofty bridged underpass, but through a football-field-long drainpipe. When you enter the tunnel you might think, "This is dumb," but halfway through it gets damn spooky when your front tire disappears from

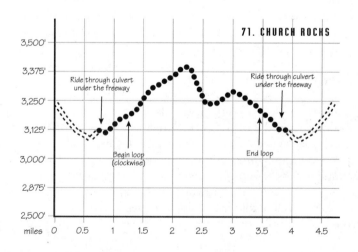

RIDE 71 CHURCH ROCKS

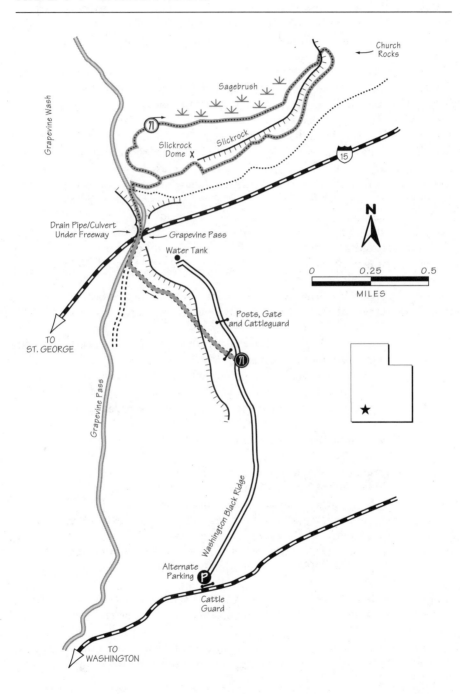

sight. You'll pray that the roof doesn't cave in or that all of St. George doesn't flush the toilet at once.

Once you're out on the loop, you can turn your back on the streaming traffic and be charmed by the terraced sandstones backdropped by the Pine Valley Mountains and by the ever-present temples of Zion National Park on the eastern skyline.

This route enters the Red Cliffs Desert Reserve, which serves as protected habitat of the threatened desert tortoise. Spying one of the slow-moving lumps is rare, but you should be on the lookout just the same.

Location: 7 miles northeast of St. George.

Distance: 4.7 miles out-and-back with loop.

Tread: Sand and rock doubletrack for 0.5 mile, a short section of sandy singletrack, and then nearly 3 miles of broken slickrock.

Aerobic level: Moderate. A few short, steep climbs on slickrock at the loop's beginning are tough. The rest descends or rolls gently. You need to climb a steep 0.5-mile doubletrack to return to the trailhead.

Technical difficulty: Level 3 to 4. Sandy sections can also have loose rocks. Slickrock sections are always a test of your bike-handling skills.

Elevation change: The loop wanders between 3,200 feet and 3,400 feet with an elevation gain of about 400 feet.

Season: Year-round. During midsummer (mid-June to September) you should ride at the crack of dawn because daytime temperatures may exceed 100 degrees.

Services: There is no drinking water along this route. St. George offers all visitor services, including bike shops.

Hazards: As with any route that crosses slickrock, you must be alert as to where your front tire is heading and of steep drop-offs nearby. Heavy rains or spring runoff may swell Grapevine Pass Wash and make pedaling through the long culvert dangerous or impossible.

Rescue index: Although I-15 is a stone's throw away, you're pretty much on your own. St. George has a hospital.

Land status: Bureau of Land Management (St. George Field Office).

Maps: USGS Harrisburg Junction, Utah.

Access: From St. George, take St. George Boulevard east to Red Cliff Drive (Exit 8 off I-15). Turn left and travel 3 miles on Red Cliff Drive to Washington. Continue east on Telegraph Street for 2.5 miles; then turn left on a gravel road marked by a cattle guard at the top of the hill on Washington Black Ridge. (Watch for oncoming traffic rising over the blind hill.) Take the gravel road 1 mile north to a Y junction and park on the ridge.

Sources of additional information: Red Rock Bicycle Co. (See Appendix B).

Notes on the trail: This route enters the Red Cliffs Desert Reserve, so it is imperative that you stay on route.

From the parking area atop Washington Black Ridge, take the left fork past the steel gate, and descend the rutted, rocky doubletrack to Grapevine Pass

A Joshua tree frames Church Rocks.

Wash. Follow the sandy track toward the freeway, and immediately before reaching the base of the embankment, fork left in the willows on a singletrack that drops to the massive, 8-foot-tall culvert running under the freeway. That's your route!

Regardless of the fun you have later on, riding through this tunnel of darkness under the freeway is totally bizarre. What seems to be a mile away, but not more than a hundred yards, is a pinhole of light that draws you through. Halfway in, or halfway out if you're an optimist, what little daylight that filters into the tunnel from its endpoints has all but dissipated and you are biking by Braille. Instinctively, you'll howl like a dog at the moon. Gradually, the end of the tunnel approaches and you exit to the blinding light of day.

Turn on your homing device, because the next 0.5 mile is tricky to follow. Take the sand and rock trail north from the drainpipe for 0.25 mile and cross Grapevine Pass Wash (usually dry). About 20 feet thereafter the trail splits; fork left and ride parallel to the Wash, which is to the left/west. As you approach the sandstone ledges, bend right and pedal up the slickrock ramp. (Look for rock art in this area.) After a few hundred feet, bend left/north and follow tire tracks across the rock and sand; then veer left again (west) toward Grapevine Pass Wash and inch over ledgy redrock. Your goal is to pedal around and up the backside of the prominent 50-foot-tall sandstone dome to your right. Watch for small cairns, tire tracks, and painted dots and dashes that can easily be mistaken for lichens growing on the rock. (Or is that follow the lichens that look like the painted dots and dashes?)

Once on the backside of the slickrock ridge, veer east, then south, and climb the dome. Here you can look over the edge at your previous route and at the loop's return trail below and to the left. Now the route is easier to follow. Head east (toward Zion) on a trail that hugs the interface between brushy soil to the left and barren rock to the right. Gradually the pesky but entertaining trail descends off the rock ridge. When you see Church Rocks floating in the sand and sage far ahead (they look more like a matching set of terra cotta teapots), the trail bends right and doubles back to the west below the ridge you just rode atop.

Cross the sand, sage, and rock slabs on the low sloping terrace. As Grapevine Pass Wash nears, you'll notice a trail running parallel to yours but in the dry wash below to your left. Ignore it; stay on the straight and narrow following the rows of purposefully placed pebbles lining your route. Bend 90 degrees to the right/north to cross to an adjacent ledge, then veer left to return to the initial slickrock ramp to close the loop. Retrace your tracks down the wash and reenter the spooky drainpipe.

The Mojave tortoise, commonly called the desert tortoise and scientifically *Gopherus agassizzi,* is one of many tenacious reptiles that has survived the earth's evolution since the age of dinosaurs. Three distinct types of the same species inhabit part of the shared California-Arizona-Nevada desert, including extreme southwest Utah. Like all chelonians, or turtles, they are cold-blooded and cannot regulate their body temperature. Thus, they keep from boiling or freezing by seeking shelter under rock ledges and brush or by burrowing beneath the sand where temperatures are more constant.

An adult tortoise can grow to 15 inches in shell length and weigh 20 to 25 pounds. They reach sexual maturity in 15 to 20 years and at least one individual tortoise lived 150 years. That makes it the longest-lived of any vertebrate, including man.

Tortoise populations have been victimized to a large extent by livestock grazing, and in certain areas, tortoise densities have declined at alarming rates. Immediately north of St. George, livestock grazing is less a problem. Here, the desert tortoise finds its home amidst prime undeveloped real estate. The Red Cliffs Desert Reserve was established in 1996 to help protect the desert tortoise and other unique and threatened wildlife and to provide open space for the people of Washington County. The desert tortoise has effectively survived 100 million years of adverse conditions and wants little more than to be left alone so that it may continue its deliberate existence.

RIDE 72 *WARNER VALLEY*

This easy ride is located just east of St. George. It is excellent for a family outing since you can vary its length by altering where you park and embark.

The Warner Valley tour is loaded with history—human, prehistoric, and geologic. In an era 200 million years ago, when great sand dunes blanketed other parts of southern Utah, dinosaurs stomped through what was then a local floodplain. Evidence of these beasts is found at the route's end in a series of footprints stamped into a layer of Moenave siltstone. These three-toed impressions left by bipedal coelurasaurids and plateosaurids are considered some of the finest examples of creatures of their age in North America.

In more recent times, the Spanish Franciscan padres Domínguez and Escalante passed through southwestern Utah in 1776 seeking a land route between missions in New Mexico and California. A century later, during the mid-1880s, Warner Valley was dubbed the Honeymoon Trail. Caravans of Mormon settlers (from towns as far away as Phoenix), including soon-to-be newlyweds, traveled to St. George, where the only Mormon temple in the territory existed at the time.

While Latter Day Saint immigrants colonized the region, they were persistently attacked by bands of marauding Indians. Such attacks increased during the Black Hawk Wars of 1865 to 1869. Consequently, pioneers constructed Fort Pearce as a defensive stronghold. You'll find the old stone fortress a short distance off the main route.

Location: 8 miles east of St. George.

Distance: 18 miles out-and-back.

Tread: Soft and packed-sand doubletracks

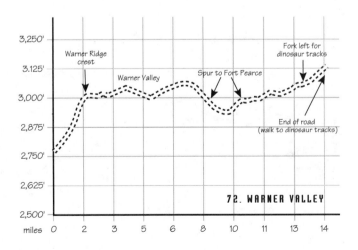

RIDE 72 WARNER VALLEY

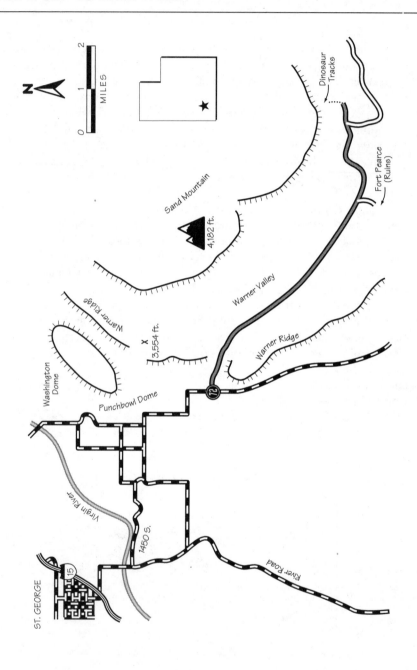

Three-toed dinosaur
tracks.

Aerobic level: Easy to moderate. Except for the 200-foot climb from the outset, the route is flat to gently rolling.

Technical difficulty: Level 1 to 2. You may encounter a few sand traps after prolonged dry spells.

Elevation change: The route begins at an elevation of 2,770 feet and rises to 3,100 feet—once just before the Fort Pearce turnoff and again at the foot trail for the dinosaur tracks. Except for the modest climb up through Warner Ridge to Warner Valley, the rest of the route is quite level. Total elevation gain is about 450 feet.

Season: September through May is the best time of year to pedal through Warner Valley. The route is dusty and hot during the summer. Winter can be pleasant when dry conditions persist. Don't take this road if it's wet; its clay base can turn to thick mud.

Services: There is no drinking water along this route or any services. St. George offers all visitor services, including bike shops.

Hazards: The route can be very warm, so always carry adequate water. This route receives some vehicular traffic, so yield the right of way to motorists.

Rescue index: Emergency contacts will have to be made in St. George or from scattered residences along the route's access drive. St. George has medical facilities.

Land status: Bureau of Land Management (Dixie Field Office).

Maps: USGS St. George, The Divide, and Washington Dome, Utah.

Access: From St. George, drive east on 700 South and turn right/south on River Road toward Bloomington Hills. Just past the Virgin River Bridge, turn left/east on 1450 South toward Washington Fields. After 2 miles, follow the sharp right-hand bend. Immediately thereafter, fork left/east, following signs for Warner Valley and Fort Pearce. Drive east for 1.5 miles, and then turn right/south. About 1.5 miles farther, turn left on a road that becomes dirt and gravel heading east and uphill through a cut in Warner Ridge. Park at your discretion near this junction, up atop the hill, or out along the road, depending on how energetic you feel.

Sources of additional information: Bicycles Unlimited (see Appendix B).

Notes on the trail: From the parking area, where the Warner Valley Road turns to gravel, begin your tour with a modest climb through a notch in Warner Ridge and then out across Warner Valley. Pedal southeast through this sage and brush valley beneath the looming red cliffs of Sand Mountain. About 5.2 miles into the ride, turn right and pedal 0.5 mile to historic Fort Pearce.

Upon returning from Fort Pearce, continue on the Warner Valley Road eastward for 2 miles, and then fork left on a dead-end road. A short 200-yard hike leads to the dinosaur tracks and a sign describing them. Return through Warner Valley by retracing your tracks while admiring Sand Mountain at your side and the Pine Valley Mountains in the distance.

RIDE 73 *RED ROCK RAMPAGE*

Renowned as a retirement community boasting a multitude of golf courses and discount, factory-outlet shops, St. George is quickly becoming a hotspot for mountain biking. It's not because this southwest corner of Utah is noted for its balmy summers and temperate winters, thus called Dixie, but largely due to glowing reports from mountain-bike racers who have bragged about the outrageous Red Rock Rampage. In fact, the response has been so positive that St. George has played host to the World Senior Games and American Mountain Bike Challenge (AMBC) Finals.

The Rampage, sponsored by Red Rocks Bicycle Company, has changed venues over the years but has now settled in the castaway Price City Hills just

RIDE 73 RED ROCK RAMPAGE

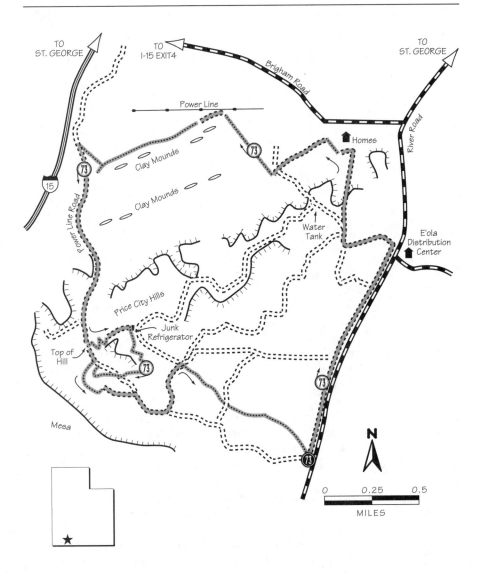

south of town. They say you shouldn't judge a book by its cover. Keep that in mind when you pull up to the trailhead, for the area is scenically deprived except for a distant glimpse of the Pine Valley Mountains. But racing is the game—fast doubletracks and wild desert singletracks. Scout out the course's many junctions and collect your bearings on your first lap; then nudge the starting line with your buddies and charge at race pace on ensuing loops.

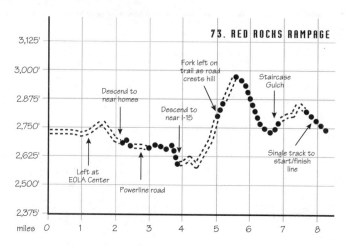

When you're through, you'll no doubt mark your calendar and start training for the springtime event.

Location: 5 miles southeast of St. George.

Distance: 8.5-mile loop.

Tread: 5.2 miles of sand and rock doubletrack and 3.3 miles of desert singletrack.

Aerobic level: Moderate. There is one strenuous climb on the route's backside. The rest is rolling hills and moderate climbs.

Technical difficulty: Level 2 to 5. ATV trails and doubletracks have scattered rocks and ruts. Singletrack sections have more of the same with berms and bumps mixed in. The backside singletrack has a steep, rough descent followed by a climb up a rock-paved dry wash.

Elevation change: The trailhead is at 2,734 feet. The loop tops out at 2,980 feet on the backside singletrack. Total elevation gain is about 800 feet.

Season: Early fall through late spring. Midday during summer can be unbearably hot, so set out at the break of day.

Services: There is no drinking water or services along this route. St. George has all visitor services.

Hazards: Carry plenty of water. Keep your eye on the trail and watch where you place your front wheel. If you twitch, you could pitch. Be alert to four-wheel-drive vehicles and OHVs.

Rescue index: The route is growing in popularity as a result of many successful races, but you won't find hordes of bikers out here. Motorcyclists and OHVs may use these trails. Mostly you'll be on your own. St. George has medical facilities.

Land status: Utah State Land and Bureau of Land Management (Dixie Field Office).

Maps: USGS St. George, Utah.

Access: From St. George, travel east on 700 South. Turn right on River Road, cross the Virgin River, and travel 2.8 miles to the junction with Brigham Road. (Southbound on Interstate 15, take Exit 8 for St. George Boulevard and take River Road south from the intersection with Red Cliff Drive at the factory malls. Northbound on I-15, take Exit 6 for Bluff Street and turn right/east on Brigham Road.) Continue south on River Road for 0.7 mile to the E'ola Distribution Center, then 1.3 miles farther to a dirt clearing on the right side of the road. The doubletrack paralleling River Road is the first leg of the loop.

Sources of additional information: Red Rock Bicycle Company (See Appendix B).

Notes on the trail: From the dirt clearing/starting line, head north on the doubletrack paralleling River Road for 1.2 miles. Opposite the E'ola Distribution Center, the road bends left and rises up a rough doubletrack to a multiple junction beneath a hill capped with a water tank. You'll be overlooking St. George. Fork right/north and descend the rutted doubletrack under the power lines toward the private homes.

Near the edge of private property, the route bends left and narrows to singletrack. Stay near the homes and come to a four-way junction, where an eroded doubletrack descends steeply from the water tank. Stay straight, dip through the gully, and follow the trail angling northwest toward town over clay mounds and multiple jumps. Intersect and follow the power line doubletrack to the left. Count three poles, and then fork left on more singletrack that rolls over the badlands terrain. No time for coasting or you'll

The Pine Valley Mountains interrupt the pervasive deserts surrounding St. George.

relinquish your lead. Bear right at a faint junction, and descend a steep shot to a doubletrack very near I-15. (If you find yourself atop a knoll and facing a scary vertical drop, you missed the turn by 100 feet.)

Fork left/south and climb the power line road around the Price City Hills' backside. About 1 mile from I-15, stay left at a Y junction at the base of an orange- and tan-banded bluff on your right and pump up a near-vertical pitch. Atop the climb, fork left on a singletrack, and grind up through multiple turns and continue on a doubletrack up the ridge but not to the top. (You're about 5 miles into the loop.) Fork right on a singletrack (may be marked by an old refrigerator) that traverses the hillside southeast and overlooks a valley beneath a mesa with a ruler-straight rim. Hold on for a twisty, technical level 4 descent to the valley.

Now here's the tricky part, as if the preceding section was easily navigated. Cross three doubletracks. The trail loops right and intersects the power line road. Take the road left a couple hundred feet, as if backtracking, and fork left on a singletrack that leads up a dry gully that is a veritable staircase of rock. The mesa looms over your right shoulder. Connect with and follow the main doubletrack to where it flattens. (Note the miscellaneous wreckage to the right.) Take the first doubletrack left, pedal up a hill, and descend 0.1 mile to a Y junction. Search for an elusive singletrack peeling off to the right. The trail makes a beeline back to the trailhead/starting line, crossing one doubletrack along the way. Kick in the afterburners, but watch the path; it will do its best to buck you from the saddle. Now for a second lap!

RIDE 74 *GREEN VALLEY*

Every city should have a ride like this. It's close to town, (so close you can pedal right from town), it's a killer little workout, and it's a helluva good time. Ride Green Valley to get your fat-tire fix during lunch hour or to wind down after work. Or head out anytime you want to rekindle the days of old when you raced through neighborhood sand lots on your purple Sting-Ray decked out with monkey bars up front and a sissy bar in back.

Green Valley is one big BMX course filled with thrills and potential spills. The names of four white-knuckle sections say it all: Three Fingers of Death, Acid Drops, Clavicle Hill, and Roller Coaster. If you miscalculate or push your limits beyond the envelope's edge, you can easily ruin the rest of your bike season. On the other hand, if you are successful in proving your handling prowess, or just your lack of fear, you will be ennobled to a mountain-bike guru. But fear not, these are not mandatory stunts; each has a cheater route to the side.

RIDE 74 GREEN VALLEY

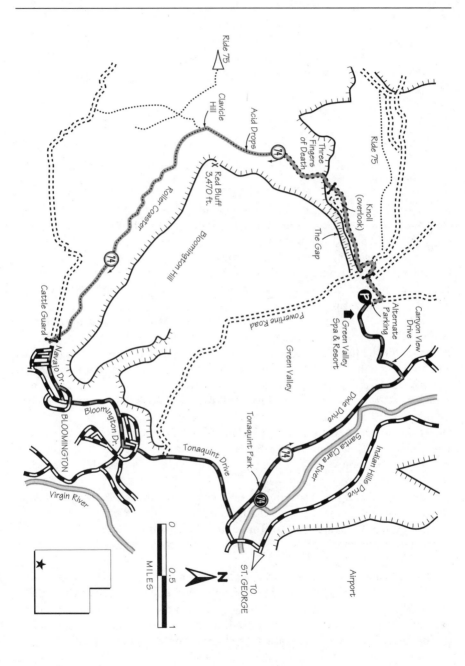

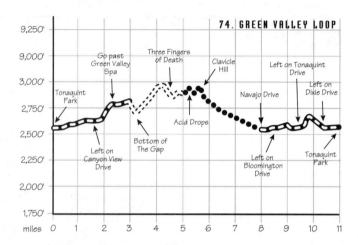

The route is not solely about cashing in on your nine lives. There are charming views of Zion National Park, Pine Valley Mountains, and Snow Canyon State Park from the route's highpoint.

Location: Immediately west of St. George.

Distance: 11-mile loop.

Tread: 5.3 miles of paved roads, 2.3 miles of rock and sand doubletracks, and 3.3 miles of dirt ATV trail and singletracks.

Aerobic level: Moderate. The climb up The Gap will have you huffing and puffing, but the rest undulates over micro-hills and countless whoop-te-doos.

Technical difficulty: Level 3 to 5+. The doubletrack up The Gap is dirt and broken pavement rock. The last 2 miles roll over low whoop-te-doos that can be technical level 2 to 4 depending on how abrupt the bumps are and how fast you ride. Warning: Three sections of roll-over-drop-offs midroute are *highly* technical. (The *italics* are for a reason.) Look before you leap!

Elevation change: Navajo Drive in Bloomington is the low point at 2,560 feet. The climb up The Gap rises at a near 10-percent grade for 0.5 mile to a maximum elevation of 3,010 feet. The rest is rolling or downhill. Elevation gain is about 700 feet.

Season: Year-round but midsummer, unless you get out at the crack of dawn, because daytime temperatures typically cap the century mark.

Services: There's a water tap at Tonaquint Park (trailhead) but no drinking water along the route. St. George offers all visitor services, including bike shops.

Hazards: As mentioned above, there are three notoriously technical sections where the trail drops steeply and out of sight. A prudent biker will scout these sections first. The rolling whoop-te-doos later on can easily pitch an inattentive biker. The route can be deathly hot during summer. Avoid this route when wet because the powdery clay turns to slop and hardens like cement.

Rescue index: The route receives regular use, so others may be encountered. You are never more than about 2 miles from residential areas. St. George has a hospital.

Land status: Bureau of Land Management (Dixie Field Office), Utah State lands, and private property.

Maps: USGS St. George and White Hills, Utah.

Access: Make your way through St. George to the intersection of Bluff Street and Main (Exit 6 off Interstate 15). Cross Bluff and proceed on Hilton Drive for 1 mile, veer left on Tonaquint Drive, and pass through Southgate Golf Course. Turn right on Dixie Drive 0.3 mile past the golf course and drive 0.4 mile to Tonaquint Park.

Sources of additional information: Red Rock Bicycle Co. (See Appendix B).

Notes on the trail: From Tonaquint Park, pedal along Dixie Drive 1.6 miles, turn left on Canyon View Drive, pump up the hill past Green Valley Spa and Resort, and take a quick break where the pavement ends atop a low knoll.

Look west into the small valley that rests at the base of a deep gash in the earth called The Gap. Your route follows the right/north side of The Gap up a doubletrack that starts with a Superman S turn and then parallels the canyon's rim. So descend to the fence in the valley and start climbing. (Ride 75, Stucki Spring, forks right from the left-hand bend in the road as you begin your climb.) Ignore tracks spurring left; these are access points to The Gap's craggy handholds used by technical rock climbers.

The rough doubletrack splits about halfway up (less than 0.5 mile); both forks meet on the northwest side of the treeless knoll ahead. The right route is less technical and less steep; the left route is not. But stay left because it affords views you won't want to miss. Zion National Park molds the eastern skyline with its sandstone temples and towers. The Pine Valley Mountains to the northeast interrupt Dixie's pervasive deserts with an alpine anomaly. Due north, Snow Canyon State Park is a multi-tiered rampart of deep orange and snow-white sandstones. Beneath your tires, The Gap's shadowy depths open to a broad calico-striped basin that seems devoid of life. Most importantly, you can see your route ahead where it drops abruptly from the bluff to the desert's clutch.

Descend northward off the knoll on the technical level 4 to 5 track, join with the lower road, and follow it west to a fence. Ease over the top and descend Three Fingers of Death—a trio of rib-like mounds of clay that plunge to the dry wash feeding The Gap. Pucker-factor increases from left to right, so "choose wisely, grasshopper" and hang your butt *way* off the back.

Head up the sandy wash (right) for less than 0.5 mile and exit the wash to the left on a rolling ATV trail. As you round Red Bluff, you rise to the brink of Acid Drops—a hallucinating series of cascading rollovers that resemble the successive rapids of the Colorado River in Cataract Canyon. Like on the Colorado, where a turbulent hole lies leeward and out of sight of each white-capped wave, the ill will that awaits your front tire remains a mystery until

Glen takes the plunge off Clavicle Hill.

you roll over each Drop to the point of no return. Butt off the back, chest to the saddle, death grip on the bars, and you should emerge unscathed. Feeling uneasy about taking the plunge? Then follow the cheater route to the left.

A few rollers later, the trail disappears over Clavicle Hill. No explanation is needed, other than it rates high on the "Oh sh*t!" meter. Even intrepid white-water rafters scout the most menacing rapids. You should do the same here or else stuff your wheel in the sucker hole that hides from view beneath the lip. This is also a good place to survey the remainder of the route. You'll want to follow the rolling singletrack left/southeast along the interface of Bloomington Hill's red terraced slopes and the white clay mounds that sprawl from its base. *Do not* venture south or west, or you'll enter a maze of trails that would baffle a GPS receiver.

With bones and bike intact, hopefully, kick in the afterburners and launch yourself down the Roller Coaster. This section is 2 miles of BMX-style whoop-te-doos and banked turns that just keep coming; you'll be as giddy as a kid in a candy shop. Although the area is a braided web of trails, the main route is readily evident because it receives the most traffic. It's important that you stay on track and do not wander about, because the route crosses habitat of the endangered Bear Poppy. This is the only area in the world where the desert flower blooms annually during the spring. Step over the wire fence and exit to paved Navajo Drive in the ritzy Bloomington subdivision.

The dirt riding is through; it's time to pound the pavement and recap the tricks you mastered and the ones you choked on. At the intersection of Navajo and Geronimo, stop at Petroglyph Park to view an impressive display of Indian rock art on a huge, cleaved boulder. Turn left/north on Bloomington Drive West (becomes Bloomington Drive North), left on Tonaquint Drive, and return to Dixie Drive. Tonaquint Park is 0.4 mile left on Dixie.

Note: The route may be altered or closed in the future at the end of Canyon View Drive because of proposed residential developments. Contact Red Rock Bicycles for updates and obey all signs restricting travel.

RIDE 75 *STUCKI SPRING*

The Stucki Spring Trail is yet another reason why St. George has become an alluring mountain-bike destination, especially when you thought it was safe to stow your bike away for the winter. On the contrary, keep it well lubed and take a break from skiing Utah's frothy powder with a weekend jaunt to balmy Dixie.

Stucki Spring is a bona fide mountain-bike rodeo, and you'll have to hold on tight to make it until the bell. Hallmarking this route is mile upon mile of rolling desert singletrack punctuated with endless berms and whoop-te-doos that toss you around like a bucking bronco. There is a fair amount of climbing involved before you're let loose from the gate, which makes the roller-coaster-style trail that much more worthwhile.

The loop ventures through the White Hills west of St. George where a network of trails has been a haven for motorcyclists long before mountain

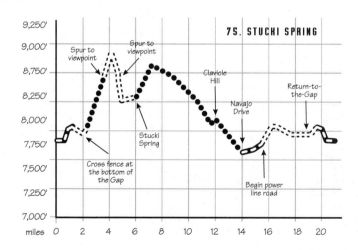

RIDE 75 *STUCKI SPRING*

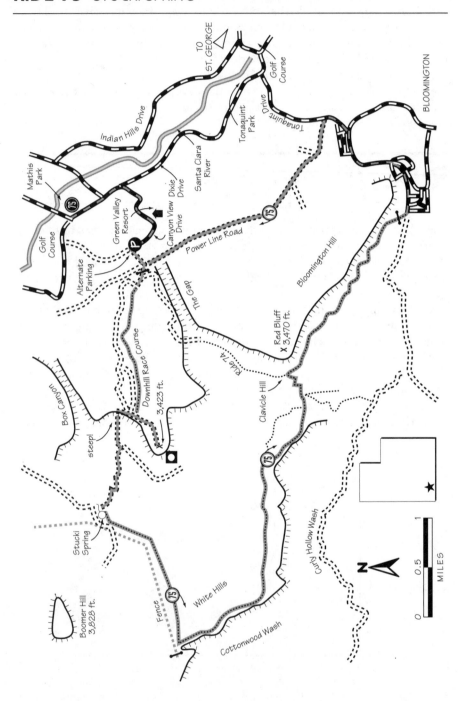

bikes came on to the scene. The gently sloping, clayey mesas are painfully bleak and despairingly unproductive in and of themselves, but from high points you'll find impressive views of distant sandstone features in national and state parks separated by an anomalous hunk of alpine wilderness.

You'll need a good sense of direction because there are a number of crucial unsigned turns along the way. But do not let this deter you. If you pay attention to the trail and to the surroundings, you'll stay on track and round out the day with a beaming grin.

General location: 4 miles west of St. George.

Distance: 21.5-mile loop.

Tread: 4.6 miles of pavement, 6.9 miles of dirt and rock doubletrack, and 10 miles of sand and silt singletrack-cum-ATV trails.

Aerobic level: Strenuous. There is one notable climb: the ascent of the Red Rock Rampage downhill racecourse early in the loop. A second, less apparent climb is from Stucki Spring to the rim of the White Hills. The gradual grade and loose tread of the latter can tire legs in a subliminal kind of way. The undulating singletrack descends overall but allows for little rest time. The culminating power line road is rolling and requires lasting stamina.

Technical difficulty: Level 2 to 5. The downhill racecourse singletrack crosses ledgy sandstone (level 4). The descent off the mesa rim is frighteningly steep (level 4 to 5). The remaining route is packed with small, playful whoop-te-doos that can dump an inattentive biker (level 3 to 4). The power line road has scattered rocks (level 2 to 3).

Elevation change: Mathis Park (trailhead) is at 2,660 feet. The route tops out beyond Stucki Springs at 3,320 feet and bottoms at Navajo Drive at 2,560 feet. Total climbing is about 1,800 feet.

Season: Early fall through late spring. During midsummer, you'll have to ride at daybreak before the sun bakes St. George to a crisp with daytime temperatures exceeding 100 degrees.

Services: There is no drinking water or any services along this route, but the trailhead is only a few miles from town where all services are available, including bike shops.

Hazards: Look before you leap off the mesa rim after climbing the downhill singletrack racecourse. The descent seems near vertical, and ruts await your front tire. The barrage of dips and dives on the trail's remainder is a hoot but requires constant attention. Carry plenty of water because this route can suck your body dry.

Rescue index: After the climb up the downhill racecourse, it's you, the desert, and the creatures that eke out a living in this parched land. You may encounter a motorcyclist but do not plan on it. You might make emergency contacts from residences near the trailhead. St. George has medical facilities.

Land status: Bureau of Land Management (Dixie Field Office), Utah State, and private property.

Maps: USGS St. George and White Hills, Utah.

Endless whoop-te-doos will keep you whooping it up on the Stucki Spring Trail.

Access: Make your way through St. George to the intersection of Bluff Street and Main (Exit 6 off Interstate 15). Cross Bluff and proceed on Hilton Drive for 1 mile, veer left on Tonaquint Drive, and pass through Southgate Golf Course. Turn right on Dixie Drive 0.3 mile past the golf course and drive 2.9 miles farther to Mathis Park opposite Sunbrook Golf Course.

Alternatively, to knock off a few miles of pavement, park at the end of Canyon View Drive where pavement turns to dirt (see "Notes"). This is an unofficial trailhead that may be altered by future residential developments.

Sources of additional information: Red Rock Bicycle Co. (See Appendix B).

Notes on the trail: From Mathis Park, return down Dixie Drive for 0.8 mile, fork right on Canyon View Drive, and climb past Green Valley Spa and Resort to where the pavement ends atop a knoll adjacent to red-tile-roofed homes.

It would behoove you to survey the upcoming route from atop the knoll. Most apparent is The Gap, a deep gash in the earth's crust. The doubletrack rising up The Gap's north rim is the Green Valley Loop. The Stucki Spring route stems from the sweeping left-hand turn at the bottom of The Gap road *across* the fence in the valley. *Do not* take the prominent doubletrack heading northward alongside the fence. Also, you'll see a pair of distant doubletracks rising up the sloping mesa north of The Gap. You'll ride a singletrack parallel to and just left/south of these doubletracks in a moment's time. Now ride what you viewed; descend to the valley, cross the wash and fence, and fork right on the doubletrack branching from the left-hand bend. After 200 feet, fork left on a faint, unsigned singletrack that crosses sandstone outcrop (Red Rock Rampage downhill racecourse). The path is readily apparent after a few pedal strokes. (If you continue on the doubletrack and find yourself in a dry wash, you missed the trail.)

The singletrack's loose tread and ledgy bedrock can be technical level 3 to 5, but it is good, clean, technical fun. Imagine racing downhill at warp speed. Whoa! You'll face a steep pitch after 0.5 mile and then bend very close to a doubletrack. After 1.7 miles from the bottom, the path joins with the doubletrack you just passed. Take the track uphill 0.3 mile to the overlook atop the inclined mesa. Enjoy the circumambient view of Utah's Dixie from the Arizona border in the south to Zion National Park's stoic temples in the east, and to Snow Canyon State Park's two-tiered palisades in the north. The Pine Valley Mountains appear as an alpine mirage rising above the desert's pervasiveness.

Again, survey your route. Trace the mesa's rim northward about 0.5 mile. The doubletrack that drops precipitously from the rim to the valley is your route. About 0.2 mile after the descent, the track splits at a Y junction. Take the right fork for Stucki Springs. Eventually, you'll ride the low rim in the western middle ground all the way around to the base of Bloomington Hill to the south. Now ride what you mapped out mentally. Be forewarned; the descent off the rim is a near free fall, so ride your brakes until they smoke.

The rolling doubletrack leads 1.2 miles across the sage valley to Stucki Spring, marked by a wire fence, metal water tank, and a T junction. Fork left/west about 100 feet *before* the fence and T junction, on a vague singletrack on the south side of the tamarisk-lined wash enclosing Stucki Spring. The path parallels the wash, fence, and dirt road—all on your right—and is obvious after a few tentative pedal strokes. The soft, silty track makes a beeline west for 1.8 miles, rising steadily up the sloping mesa, except for one brash drop mid-route.

Atop a short, steep hill on the edge of a small canyon that opens to Cottonwood Wash, the path meets the same wire fence that it paralleled at Stucki Spring. Fork left/south on the continued motorcycle trail along the rim of the canyon. *Do not* continue west through the gated fence and around the canyon or you're buzzard meat.

IEEE-ha! It's rodeo time. Take the undulating trail south along the White Hill's banded rim over countless "mega-ripples," catching air if you dare. After about 1.5 miles, the path bends eastward toward The Gap with Zion in the background. The small patch of greenery (Bloomington subdivision) on the south edge of Bloomington Hill is your destination. You'll wander to and from the rim's edge for another 1.5 miles to where the track bends right/south and forks. Take the right-hand track, which again wanders along the mesa's now-subtle edge. (The left fork descends a dry wash that is less than eventful.) One mile farther, both routes merge and are followed by a four-way junction of trails near the base of Bloomington Hill.

Fork left, and pump up the white terraced clay mounds to the top of Clavicle Hill. (If you miss this turn, you'll end up on the Curly Hollow Road, a light-duty dirt road. Take it left to Navajo Drive.) Survey once more. Your route is the well-worn path heading southeast, hugging the interface of Bloomington Hill's red terraced flank and white clay mounds at its base. The next 2 miles have more dips, dives, and bumps than Mr. Toad's Wild Ride at Disneyland. Hang on and "keep your arms and legs inside the ride at all times." Step over the wire fence closing the area to motorized use to protect the rare Bear Poppy, and exit to Navajo Drive in Bloomington.

Pass Petroglyph Park, turn left on Bloomington Drive West, then left again on Tonaquint. When you crest the hill, fork left on the power line access road (doubletrack) that returns you to The Gap 2.7 miles away. Stay left at a junction in 0.7 mile, then right at a second junction 0.3 mile farther, always following under the power lines. After going through a gated wire fence (close the gate), the road veers away from the lines overhead. Pass through a second wire gate and return to the valley at the base of The Gap to close the loop. Chug up the knoll to Canyon View Drive or follow a doubletrack northward atop the knoll to Sunbrook Golf Course and back to Mathis Park.

Moab/Canyonlands

RIDE 76 BARTLETT WASH

There is a generally accepted, but scientifically unproven, theorem that states, "The more time spent mountain biking in Moab, the farther from town your explorations will lead." Ride the big-name trails near town first, by all means, then pursue lesser-known and infrequently visited areas to round out your Moab portfolio. Bartlett Wash supports a second corollary: "Not all slickrock is created equally."

Bartlett Wash lies on the northern fringe of Canyon Country, beyond which the colorful sandstones dissipate to bleak and hopelessly unproductive sagebrush plains and shallow, charcoal-colored washes. The slickrock along this route is a member (or subdivision) of the Entrada Sandstone, which on the whole forms the wonderful creations that give Arches National Park its name. Here, the gray, tan, and salmon-hued Entrada delights the eye with both soft color and smooth form. Compared to the Slickrock Bike Trail, which rolls

RIDE 76 *BARTLETT WASH*

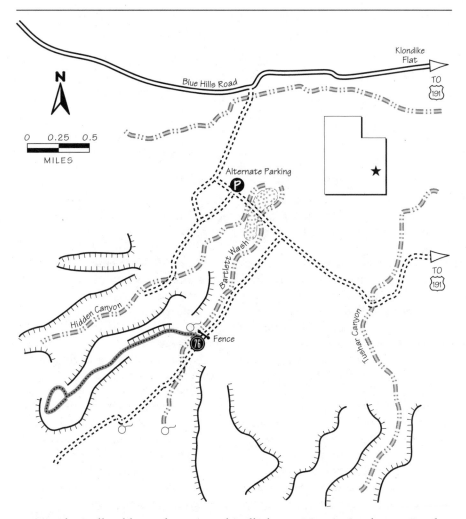

over geologically older and stratigraphically lower Navajo Sandstone, Bartlett Wash might be likened to riding on fine sandpaper rather than coarse sandpaper. Still, Bartlett's abbreviated, but wavelike, expanse of barren sandstone provides hours of mountain bike gymnastics.

General location: 18 miles north of Moab.

Distance: 4 miles out-and-back.

Tread: Slickrock with one short sandbox.

Aerobic level: Moderate. You can spend hours out here exploring every nook and cranny and pitting your fat-tire savvy against the rock. Your legs will tell you when it's time to go home.

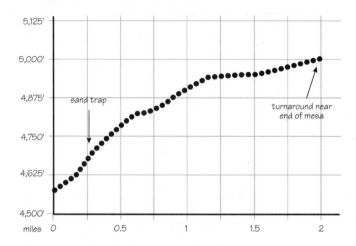

Technical difficulty: Level 3 to 5. Technical difficulty is directly proportional to the extent you defy gravity and experiment with traction.

Elevation change: The trail begins at 4,620 feet and rises to 5,000 feet at the turnaround point. Simple subtraction yields a gain of 380 feet, but because of the route's freestyle nature, you can expect to gain a few hundred feet extra.

Season: Spring (March into June) and fall (September into November). Midsummer will be hot and bugs may be annoying, especially near water sources. You can sneak out during winter when dry conditions prevail, but be cautious of lingering snow and ice on shaded aspects.

Services: There is no drinking water along this route. All visitor services are in Moab. A gas station/convenience store is located at Crescent Junction, 15 miles north of Bartlett Wash at the junction of U.S. Highway 191 and Interstate 70.

Hazards: Bartlett Wash's main attraction, slickrock, doubles as the route's greatest peril. The sandstone's smooth surface and swirling, plate-like crossbeds can provide excellent traction—or lack of traction—depending on how it's exposed. Be prudent when pursuing "Zen and the Art of Fat-Tire Friction."

Rescue index: Although located just a few miles from heavily traveled US 191, Bartlett Wash is seldom visited and considered remote. A telephone is at Crescent Junction, 14.5 miles north at the junction of US 191 and I-70. Moab has a hospital.

Land status: Bureau of Land Management (Moab Field Office).

Maps: USGS Jug Rock, Utah.

Access: From the intersection of Main and Center in Moab, drive 17.2 miles north on US 191 and turn left on Blue Hills Road (near milepost 143). (Blue Hills Road is located 14.5 miles south of I-70.) Turn left/south after 2.2 miles along this light-duty dirt and sand road (impassable when wet). At the second junction 0.8 mile farther, stay left/straight (right fork leads to Hidden Canyon) and come to a deep, sandy section. Scout the sand to determine if your vehicle can cross it. If not, park and embark. If you cross, go up the small hill, fork right, and drop to Bartlett Wash. The trail begins about 1 mile south at a fence marked by an old cottonwood and small, grassy meadow.

Notes on the trail: At the fence that crosses Bartlett Wash, go right toward the old cottonwood and cross the micro-meadow. In the brush you'll find a slickrock ramp that provides access to the sandstone playground. Pedal southward on the ledge and within 0.5 mile trudge through a long sand trap, and then hop back on the salmon-hued slickrock. Continue southwestward beneath the mesa on your right, which is capped with sandstone bonnets and lithified elephant toes.

You are on your own to construct a feasible route; there are no paint-on-rock dashes to provide direction. Improvisation leads to hours of bicycle frivolity. There are numerous arcuate bowls to surf in, solution pockets to dodge, and protracted slopes to test muscle against balance against the coefficient of friction. Just remember to keep your wheels on rock and away from pothole garden.

About 1.5 miles out, the lens of slickrock wraps around the mesa's abutment, and Hidden Canyon cuts in from the west. You can construct a loop ride by portaging off the rock to Hidden Canyon and slogging through sand, but why bother? There is too much fun to be had here. The route ends 0.5 mile farther, where broken cliffs plunge to the valley floor. Turn around and retrace your tracks or follow your bliss—diving, dodging, and feeling free on two wheels.

Exploring the nooks and crannies of Bartlett Wash.

RIDE 77 *KLONDIKE BLUFFS*

Klondike Bluffs can be considered *the* introduction to mountain biking in Moab for two reasons. First, Klondike is a varietal blend of the riding mediums you will encounter around the region, grading from clay, to sand, to washboard, to rock-studded doubletracks and smooth, to broken slickrock. Second, Klondike is the first trail to greet you when making the final approach to Moab from Interstate 70. If Klondike raises your brow, then you will be primed for happy times ahead. Conversely, if Klondike is not your cup of tea, then plan on spending more time on a bar stool than on your bike.

Klondike Bluffs is a primer of Canyon Country scenery, too. The route initially crosses bleak clay mounds that support little life. Scenery was of little concern to waves of mining prospectors who prodded the land for mineral resources decades ago. At midroute, however, you climb an inclined slickrock ramp and pass imprints of three-toed dinosaurs that tramped across mud flats and river bottoms about 170 million years ago. At route's end, you can hike across the trail's namesake bluffs, which erode to bonnets and elephant toes atop fractured fins and alcoves. Features of Arches National Park can be seen in the distance, backed by the stoic La Sal Mountains, and scenery is superlative.

General location: 16.5 miles north of Moab and 15 miles south of I-70.

Distance: 15.2 miles out-and-back.

Tread: 2.9 miles of sandy, pebbly, sometimes washboarded, light-duty dirt road; 4.7 miles of sand and rock doubletrack, including slickrock.

Aerobic level: Moderate from the highway trailhead, a bit easier from the alternate trailhead 2.9 miles in. The route is mostly uphill on the way in, but

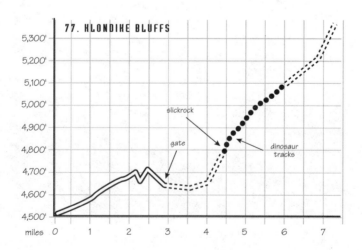

RIDE 77 KLONDIKE BLUFFS

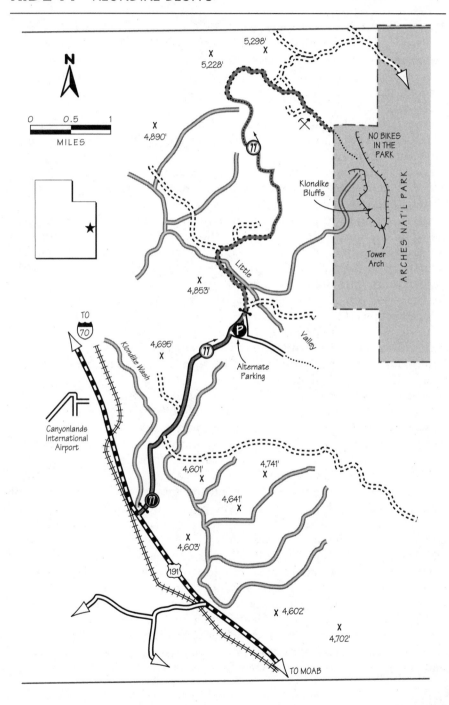

N

0   0.5   1
MILES

X
5,228'

5,298'
X

X
4,890'

77

NO BIKES
IN THE
PARK

Klondike
Bluffs

ARCHES NAT'L PARK

Tower
Arch

X
4,853'

Little

TO
70

P

Valley

Klondike Wash

4,695'
X

77

Alternate
Parking

Canyonlands
International
Airport

4,601'
X

4,741'
X

4,641'
X

77

X
4,603'

191

X 4,602'

X
4,702'

TO MOAB

reserve some juice for a few "bumps" on the way out. Budget extra time, energy, water, and food if you choose to hike out to Klondike Bluffs beyond the route's turnaround.

Technical difficulty: Level 1 to 3. Sand and washboards are followed by sand and rock doubletracks, then slickrock, and more bumpy doubletracks.

Elevation change: The trailhead is the lowest elevation at 4,520 feet. The route rises progressively to 5,360 feet at the turnaround at the boundary of Arches National Park. You'll climb a bit on the way out for a total gain of about 1,250 feet.

Season: Spring (March into June) and fall (September into November). Midsummer will be hot. You can sneak out during parts of the winter when dry conditions prevail.

Services: There is no drinking water along this route. All visitor services are in Moab. A gas station/convenience store is at Crescent Junction, 15 miles north of the trailhead at I-70.

Hazards: Always watch your front wheel and nearby terrain changes when riding slickrock exposures. Use caution if hiking from the trail's end out across Klondike Bluffs (proper) in Arches National Park; the informal route requires scrambling over slickrock and skirting edges of cliffs. The first 3 miles should be avoided by bike and vehicle when wet.

Rescue index: Although located on the outskirts of Moab, the route is popular, especially on weekends. U.S. Highway 191 is heavily traveled. A telephone is at Crescent Junction, located 15 miles north at I-70 and at the Canyonlands Airport across the highway. Moab has a hospital.

Land status: State of Utah and Arches National Park (turnaround point).

Maps: USGS Klondike Bluffs, Utah.

Access: From the intersection of Main and Center in Moab, travel 16.5 miles north on US 191. From Crescent Junction on I-70 (Exit 180), travel 15.1 miles south on US 191. The dirt parking area is on the east side of the highway next to a gated wire fence (keep closed) between mileposts 142 and 143. (Look for a small sign for Klondike Bluffs across the fence.) Novice riders might opt to drive the first 2.6 miles to the alternate parking area.

Notes on the trail: The turnaround point for this ride is at the boundary of Arches National Park. Beyond, bikes and pets are not permitted, but the 0.5-mile hike out Klondike Bluffs is worth pursuing. Wear shoes that are comfortable for walking. If you are hesitant about leaving your bike unattended while you hike, bring a cable lock and secure your rig to a tree.

From the roadside parking area, the ride to Klondike Bluffs begins with a gentle warm-up across the badlands. About 1 mile out, fork left to continue on the graded road, passing a doubletrack forking right. Ignore doubletracks forking left thereafter until you descend to a large junction in a broad valley 2.6 miles out. Stay left for the alternate parking area (large clearing) and then come to a fence. Angle northward on the sandy doubletrack up Little Valley and past calico-striped hills on your left. Cross the sandy wash; then at a T junction immediately thereafter, fork right following trail markers. Klondike Bluffs peek through a notch on the skyline. Pass a doubletrack forking left to an old mine and enter a wash lined with sandstone ledges. A small alcove on the right resembles Fred Flintstone's front porch.

Now 4 miles into the ride, you hit a slickrock ramp. There is plenty of room for play, but you'll find that the rock's fractures confine the navigable route to the far left where the sandstone laps against the ledgy bluff. Just follow the three-toed "animal-oid" footprints painted on the rock. (They look more like duck tracks than dino tracks.) Near the top of the ramp, you pass imprints in the stone of the real prehistoric beasts. (Typically, the prints are encircled by rows of rocks to prevent passersby from treading on them.)

Round a ledgy point marked with a huge rock cairn that serves as your beacon on the return leg, descend a bit, then veer right onto the slickrock ribs. Follow the route markers carefully. If you are inattentive, you'll end up on the wrong rock rib and have to cross fragile garden areas to get on track, and that's *bad form*.

As you approach a short dugway rising up a line of low cliffs, fork right and circle south toward Klondike Bluffs, ignoring spurs leading to old mine sites. One mile more takes you to the trail's turnaround at the signed boundary of Arches National Park.

Take a hike, literally, because bikes are not allowed beyond this point. Walk out the path, then across rock as far as you desire or until you are rimrocked. The view of Klondike Bluffs at your feet, expansive Salt Lake Valley beyond, and Arches in the distance makes choking down an energy bar and swilling warm carbo juice a five-star dining experience. Return to the trailhead by retracing your tracks. Watch closely for trail markers at junctions and when crossing slickrock.

RIDE 78 *COURTHOUSE WASH*

The Courthouse Wash tour loops through Arches National Park, which harbors all the redrock wonderment captured in postcards, movies, and especially one popular Saturday morning cartoon. Although you won't likely encounter frolicking roadrunners and conniving coyotes, it is easy to envision their comical antics in this desert world that is not overly exaggerated in the Looney Tunes.

You begin by pedaling up the remains of old highway 191, predecessor to today's thoroughfare, and follow the Moab Fault out of Spanish Valley. The fracture has lifted the earth's crust west of the highway hundreds of feet higher than that beneath you on the east side. As you make your way north, you'll be

RIDE 78 COURTHOUSE WASH

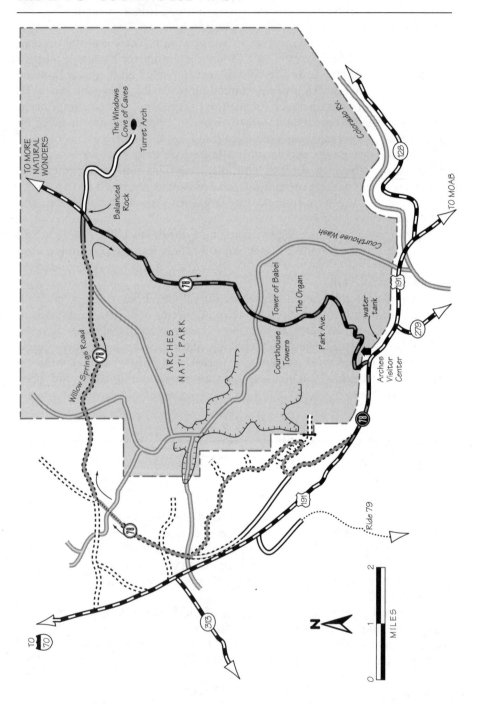

entertained by the Arches' distant features backdropped by the ever-present La Sal Mountains. Midroute, you'll follow the Willow Springs Road into the park and arrive at one of nature's most curious sights: Balanced Rock. The remaining 9 miles follows the park's scenic drive past features that no doubt inspired The Roadrunner cartoon and ends with a wind-howling-through-the-helmet descent to the visitor center.

Granted, there is a good chunk of pavement on this loop, but viewing Arches National Park from the seat of a bicycle creates an intimacy with nature that cannot be duplicated from behind a bug-splattered windshield.

General location: 5.5 miles north of Moab.

Distance: 26-mile loop. (See "Notes" for a point-to-point option.)

Tread: 16 miles of pebbly and sandy doubletrack, 10 miles of pavement.

Aerobic level: Moderate to strenuous. (See "Notes" for an easier option.) The first 3 miles rise gently up the old highway; then it rolls and descends along a pipeline corridor. The middle section rises moderately to Arches National Park Scenic Drive. The remainder is mostly downhill and ends with a steep glide to the visitor center.

Technical difficulty: Level 2 to 3. The old highway is broken pavement and dirt followed by a pebbly doubletrack. A short singletrack stint is level 3 to 4. There is a level 5 drop-off on the pipeline road that is a walker by default. The rest of the doubletrack is level 1 to 3. The scenic drive is level 0 unless you rub elbows with traffic.

Elevation change: Arches National Park Visitor Center is the low point at 4,100 feet. The route tops out at 5,040 feet near Balanced Rock in the park. Total elevation gain is about 1,900 feet.

Season: Spring (March into May) and fall (September into November) are the most enjoyable times to bike around the Moab area. June through August can be very warm, and insects may be a nuisance. Carry plenty of water regardless of the season.

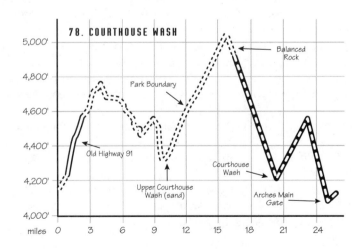

A side trip to the Windows Section in Arches National Park.

Services: Drinking water and a restroom are available at the park's visitor center. Arches National Park has a campground (fee area). Moab offers all visitor services.

Hazards: You'll exercise your route-finding skills between miles 3 and 8 because many tracks branch from the main route. Use caution when pedaling the scenic drive through Arches National Park: stay to the far right, pedal in single file, and be watchful of rubbernecking motorists. The final descent to the visitor center is fast and rounds tight curves; watch for oncoming traffic. The 0.6-mile section along U.S. Highway 191 from Arches to the trailhead has little or no shoulder; be alert to traffic approaching from the stern.

Rescue index: The first 10 miles are within a short distance of heavily traveled US 191. The 6-mile-long Willow Springs Road is infrequently traveled. Motorists are common in the park, and emergency assistance can be summoned from the visitor center. Park patrols are infrequent. Moab has a hospital.

Land status: Arches National Park and Bureau of Land Management (Moab Field Office).

Maps: USGS Gold Bar Canyon, Merrimac Butte, Moab, and The Windows Section, Utah.

Access: From the center of Moab, travel 5.2 miles north on US 191, pass the entrance to Arches National Park, and park 0.6 mile farther at the large pullout on the right side of the highway.

Notes on the trail: Bicyclists are required to pay a $5 fee (as of 1998) when exiting Arches National Park. Carry some cash. Within Arches National Park, mountain bikes are allowed only on roads that are designated as open to vehicular traffic. Bikes are not allowed on any foot trails nor on any roads closed to vehicles.

From the pullout, start up the old highway at a gentle to moderate grade. Broken pavement mixed with dirt and gravel is the fare. After the road levels 2.6 miles up, fork right and leave the old roadway on a doubletrack, and plug in your homing device, because tracks branch every which way. The main doubletrack curves east, then southeast toward the distant La Sal Mountains, and splits 0.5 mile from the old highway. Fork left, then fork left again. (If you stayed right at the split and continued toward the mountains, you would come to a gated fence marking the park boundary; back up.)

Now you should be heading northward on a doubletrack that follows the interface between low, red soil knolls on your left and cream-colored, barren rock on your right. Make a mental image of this roadside contrast because it is the key to navigation.

Over the next 2 miles, ignore two roads forking right and crossing the slickrock. (If you do choose to explore, be mindful of the park boundary.) Remember, the route heads northward along the soil/slickrock interface. Pass a rather obvious, anvil-shaped rock on the left. Beyond, the route peters out across intermittent slickrock. Again stay near the soil/slickrock interface. Be sure to ride cleanly by keeping tires solely on rock and not on cryptobiotic soils. Leaving no trace of your passage is good form.

The route narrows to singletrack (technical level 3 to 4) as it rounds the boxed-in head of Sevenmile Canyon. Cross a wire fence and continue on the doubletrack (pipeline corridor) that gradually angles northeast away from nearby US 191. Stay straight at a four-way junction of doubletracks 0.5 mile farther, continuing on the pipeline road. Plunge over, rather, walk down, a ledgy drop and into the wide, sandy bottom of upper Courthouse Wash. Just beyond the opposing embankment, fork right/east on the sandy Willow Springs Road (The junction is marked by a corrugated metal shack on the right).

Pedal 6 miles due east on the Willow Springs Road to the paved scenic drive, crossing the park boundary after 1.6 miles and passing the spur left/north for Tower Arch after 4.9 miles. The road gains nearly 700 feet, and at times the sand and rock can be exasperating, but your effort will be duly rewarded when your eyes fall upon Balanced Rock and other erosional oddities in Arches National Park. Seems the coyote was unsuccessful in prying loose this hunk of rock. Turn right/south and take the scenic drive to the visitor center 9 miles away, but consider tacking on 5.5 miles (out-and-back) to the Windows Section (left); it's the "holiest" place on Earth.

Hopefully a head wind won't spoil the long, gradual downhill on pavement to Courthouse Wash. From there, the road rises gently past a wealth of peculiar features, including Three Gossips, The Organ, and Tower of Babel. Just past the South Park Avenue Trailhead, the road winds steeply down to the visitor center.

Final note: To bypass the exasperating reconnoiter from the trailhead to the Willow Springs Road, cartop 5.3 miles to the parking area at the intersection of US 191 and Utah State Highway 313. Then pedal north on US 191 1.8 miles to the unsigned Willow Springs Road between mileposts 138 and 139. It's marked by a vertical orange pipe and a tubular steel/wire gate. When you reach the corrugated metal shack at the pipeline junction, stay straight/east to venture into the park.

RIDE 79 *GEMINI BRIDGES*

Gemini Bridges is one of those routes that everyone loves to ride time and again, especially if they're not hell-bent on pitting testosterone against slickrock or stamina against marathon rides. It's perfect for fledgling bikers because the route is largely downhill. However, it's hardly a cruise through the park because the sometimes rough conditions work your arms and the mile-long climb out of Little Canyon is a little devil. But the sweeping panorama of Monitor and Merrimac buttes to the north, Gold Bar Rim to the east, and the La Sal Mountains and Behind the Rocks to the southeast outweigh any hardships endured.

What makes this route unique is that it places you on top of the namesake arches rather than making you crane your neck skyward from underneath. In fact, it's easy to pass right by the bridges unknowingly. The fun comes when

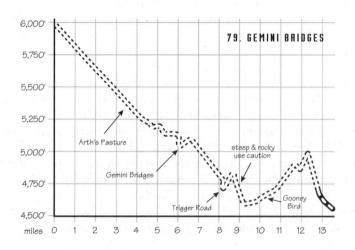

RIDE 79 GEMINI BRIDGES

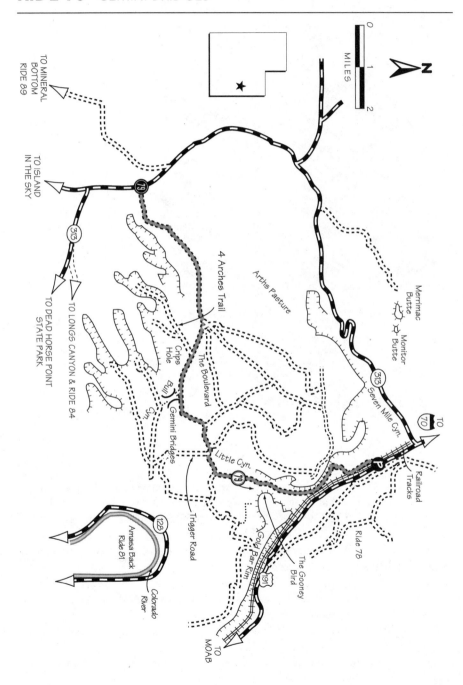

TO MINERAL BOTTOM RIDE 89

TO ISLAND IN THE SKY

313

TO DEAD HORSE POINT STATE PARK

TO LONGS CANYON & RIDE 84

4 Arches Trail

Arths Pasture

Merrimac Butte

Monitor Butte

Crips Hole

Bull Cyn.

The Boulevard

Gemini Bridges

Little Cyn.

313

Seven Mile Cyn.

TO 70

79

Railroad Tracks

Ride 78

79

Trigger Road

128

Amasa Back Ride 81

Colorado River

Gold Bar Rim

The Gooney Bird

191

TO MOAB

MILES
0
1
2

N

A lone rider approaches
the Gooney Bird.

you step out onto their flat tops and peer into the acoustically resounding alcove below. Acrophobics might want to stay on the mainland. Later, the route wanders up the hanging valley of Little Canyon and to the rim of orange-brown cliffs that overlook Moab Canyon and Arches National Park.

General location: The lower trailhead is 10 miles north of Moab; the upper trail is 24.5 miles north and west of Moab.

Distance: 13.7 miles point-to-point.

Tread: Rock-studded and sand doubletracks.

Aerobic level: Easy to moderate. The route is all downhill except the 1-mile climb out of Little Canyon. The paint-shaker conditions early on keep you out of the saddle and work your arms.

Technical difficulty: Level 2 to 4. The ride's first half is lumpy and bumpy from pebbles and broken pavement rock. The spur to the bridges has slickrock ledges. A steep, loose descent midroute is technical level 4, but it's short. You may have to trudge through sand in Little Canyon.

Elevation change: The upper trailhead is at 6,000 feet. The lower trailhead is at 4,575 feet. The 300-foot climb out of Little Canyon awakens your legs and lungs.

Season: Spring (March into June) and fall (September into November). Summer is usually too hot for an enjoyable or safe ride, unless you set out at daybreak.

Services: There are no services or water along this route. Moab offers all visitor services. Bike shops and taxi companies offer shuttle services.

Hazards: If you venture from the main route, you can explore (or be lost) for days. Use extreme caution atop Gemini Bridges and leave your bike on the mainland; a fall can be fatal.

Rescue index: This is a popular route and is frequently traveled during the spring and the fall. Moab has medical facilities.

Land status: Bureau of Land Management (Moab Field Office).

Maps: USGS Gold Bar Canyon, The Knoll, and Merrimac Butte, Utah.

Access: From the intersection of Main and Center in Moab, travel 10 miles north on U.S. Highway 191 to a dirt pullout on the left next to the railroad tracks and marked with a BLM travel information board. Drop one vehicle here; then continue on US 191 for 1.2 miles and turn left on Utah State Highway 313 for Canyonlands National Park and Dead Horse Point State Park. Drive 13.2 miles to a dirt road on the left tagged for Gemini Bridges between mileposts 10 and 9 (about 1.5 miles before the intersection of UT 313 and the Island in the Sky Road).

Notes on the trail: Head east through juniper and pinyon woodlands, and let gravity slowly pull you down the bumpy doubletrack. Ever-widening gaps in the earth's crust to the right remind you that this is indeed Canyon Country. Descend a bit faster and after 4 miles come to a junction of roads leading left/ north across Arths Pasture, but stay straight/east following the trail markers. Pass the spur right leading to Four Arches Trail and Crips Hole 0.7 mile farther; then 1 mile more fork right to access Gemini Bridges. In years past, a myriad of possible routes led to the twin spans and virtually trashed the place. Today the spur is marked with painted stripes on the ledgy rock. Stay on route to minimize your impact.

You could practically roll right across the flat-topped connectors without knowing it, except that the earth drops 200 feet into the boxed-in canyon. Bask on the rock like a lizard, then send your voice bouncing off the canyon's walls below.

Return to the main road (again following the stripes) and continue your descent eastward for nearly 2 miles to a prominent junction. Fork left to continue; fork right for the 8-mile, out-and-back trip to Bull Canyon to view Gemini Bridges from below. (Stay right at all junctions if choosing the latter, and be prepared for sand.) Descend a steep technical 4 to 5 hill laden with sand, loose rock, and ledges; then fork left at the junction when you reach the bottom. Take this main doubletrack north up Little Canyon and past the

Gooney Bird formation on the right. About 1 mile past the sandstoned cuckoo, the canyon widens and the road starts rising, gradually at first, then at a rather rude incline. Just when you think you've made it to the top, the road curves and rises up one last pitch. The descent on the sand, rock, and rutted doubletrack is as fast and fearful as you dare make it. But if you work the brakes, you can enjoy the stunning view from the cliff's edge of the valley below and of Arches in the distance. (Be alert to uphill bikers who have opted to ride out-and-back.) Finally, follow the power lines to the lower trailhead. If you need to return to town on your bike, you are advised to cross the highway, go through the fence, and follow old Highway 191. (See Ride 78 Courthouse Wash.)

No shuttle? No problem. Park and embark from the lower trailhead and ride 15.5 miles out-and-back to Gemini Bridges. This option is moderately difficult because it's mostly uphill to the bridges. Plus you'll face that little bruiser of a hill on the way back. Total elevation gain is nearly 1,300 feet.

RIDE 80 *POISON SPIDER MESA*

Few Moab-area rides are as visually rewarding and physically demanding as Poison Spider Mesa. The route affords astonishing vistas of Behind the Rocks, where an entourage of sandstone fins march in echelon toward the idyllically emplaced La Sal Mountains. From the rimmed-side viewing deck at Little Arch, the route's goal, you toe the edge of the Portal where the nourishing Colorado River leaves Moab and slips between confining 600-foot-tall cliffs. In the distance, Arches National Park displays a wonderment of nature's architectural talent.

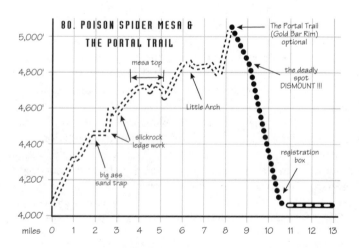

RIDE 80 POISON SPIDER MESA

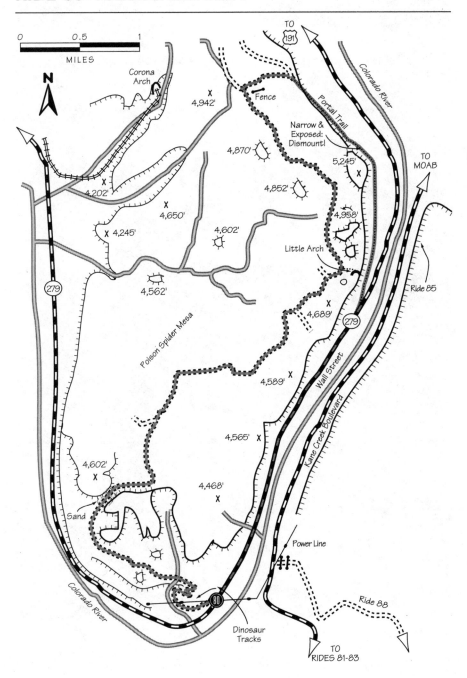

0   0.5   1
MILES

N

Corona
Arch

X
4,942'

Fence

TO
191

Colorado River

Portal Trail

Narrow &
Exposed:
Dismount!

5,245'
X

TO
MOAB

4,870'

4,852'

4,958'

4,602'

Little Arch

X 4,245'

4,650'
X

279

X
4,202'

4,562'

Poison Spider Mesa

X
4,689'

279

Ride 85

X
4,589'

Wall Street

Kane Creek Boulevard

4,565' X

4,602'
X

4,468'
X

Sand

Power Line

Ride 88

Colorado River

80

Dinosaur
Tracks

TO
RIDES 81-83

Julie and Tricia find a route across Poison Spider Mesa.

Poison Spider is renowned for its technical sections that will challenge the most resolute trail rider. A half dozen rock staircases require brute strength and unfaltering skills to master. Near the turnaround, you can "rock out" to your heart's delight on a ramp of naked Navajo Sandstone that will satisfy any slickrock purist. Although the route follows paint-on-rock markers, a short lapse of attentiveness may prompt an anxious voyage across nondescript lands rimmed by unscalable cliffs.

Poison Spider Mesa is described here as a 12-mile, out-and-back route geared for strong intermediate riders. But *expert* riders can pursue a 12.7-mile loop by descending the infamous Portal Trail—a precarious path scratched into a 600-foot cliff. "Expert" refers to one who possesses both exacting skills *and* unclouded objectivity about when to dismount and portage. As the multitude of mountain bikers attempt to wear the Colorado Plateau down to sea level, the Portal Trail has become humorously difficult over the years. But there is nothing humorous about the fact that three bikers have fallen to their deaths from the Portal Trail. A sobering note indeed, but one that stresses the potential gravity of the trail.

General location: 10 miles west of Moab.

Distance: 12 miles out-and-back. (See "Notes" for the 12.7-mile loop via the Portal Trail.)

Tread: Sandy doubletrack with smooth and rough-cut slickrock.

Aerobic level: Moderately strenuous. Sand is exasperating, rock ledges are technical as hell, and the slickrock wave at the turnaround is a steep creep.

Technical difficulty: Level 3 to 5+. You'll trudge through deep sand, portage over improbable rock steps, yank innumerable wheelies over ledges, and defy friction on inclined slickrock. Ya gotta love it!

Elevation change: The trailhead/parking area is the route's lowest elevation of 4,000 feet. The route rises to 4,800 feet at Little Arch. Total gain is around 1,000 feet.

Season: Spring (March into June) and fall (September into November). You can sneak out during winter months when Moab is high and dry, but riding the Portal Trail is ill-advised because snow and wet conditions may linger on the well-shaded trail. Midsummer is oppressively hot.

Services: There are no services or water sources along this route. The parking area has an outhouse. Camping along the Colorado River is restricted to Bureau of Land Management designated camping areas (fee areas), but none have drinking water. Moab offers all visitor services.

Hazards: Poison Spider can be a handful for even adept bikers. Know your ability and limits when attempting technically difficult sections. Use caution when hiking along cliff edges. The Portal Trail is a hazard in its entirety; involuntary dismounts have proven fatal three times.

Rescue index: This route is popular, but organized rescue is exceedingly difficult and time consuming. The Potash Road is regularly traveled by motorists and visited by campers, rock climbers, and sightseers. Moab has a hospital.

Land status: Bureau of Land Management (Moab Field Office).

Maps: USGS Gold Bar Canyon and Moab, Utah.

Access: From the intersection of Center and Main in Moab, travel 4.1 miles north on U.S. Highway 191 and turn left on Utah State Highway 279 for Potash. The trailhead is 6 miles down the road. Park at the newly developed trailhead up the gravel road on the right.

Notes on the trail: Take a minute to view the dinosaur tracks near the trailhead and conjure up a prehistoric time when land lizards were king and the hardened trail was a quiescent river delta. The route begins with a nice little warm-up on the sand and rock doubletrack. Pass a spur forking left toward the power lines overhead and round the first switchback. After the fourth turn, the road rises up a heinous hill clogged with fist-size cobbles. Go ahead, blow a gasket. Atop the hill, the view of Behind the Rocks is photo worthy, but save the film for later. Find a feasible route through a cleft in the bedrock and then cruise across a sage plain bound by hummocky Navajo Sandstone domes on the right.

At 2 miles, the doubletrack curves north and enters a narrow canyon filled with one big-ass sand trap that stalls the knobbiest tires and saps the strongest legs. Beyond, you face the first of several rock staircases to come. If you teeter, back up and try again. Arrows and jeep icons painted on the rock steer you to the starboard thereafter (that's *right* for the nautically impaired).

The route splits after the third hurdle. The left fork, marked with white diamonds, is less unridable than the sandpit to the right. Both join after 0.1 mile. Power up a fourth ledge and come to a junction marked by a brown carsonite post on an elevated plain. Head due north, crossing directly over shallow slickrock humps that resemble sandstone whales breaching the desert's floor for a gasp of parched air. (On the return leg, do not follow the doubletrack westward from the post; head due south.)

Speed across the black-brush plain on the sand and pebble doubletrack. Where the track drops abruptly, it forks. Again the left route (marked with post and jeep icons) is more ridable than the right fork; both rejoin in 0.1 mile. Unfolding before you is a jumbled expanse of slickrock that you must cross, so watch carefully for those jeep icons—they don't lie. Veer right as recommended by a painted arrow and the word "bike" and then come to a T junction marked with a post; fork right and grind up the huge bubble of rock, angling northeastward. Dip through a sandy lane amidst junipers and chug up another slickrock ramp. Park your rig, hike down to Little Arch, and peer over the edge at the life-giving Colorado River. Intrepid bikers can be seen descending the Portal Trail directly beneath you and ascending the Moab Rim Trail across the river. Retrace your tracks for the return leg, exploring the earth's hardened skin if you care to.

All you "experts" jonesing for the Portal Trail should head northwestward from Little Arch, again closely following the jeep icons. First you cross blisters of slickrock then descend to and follow a sandy doubletrack. The route bends north, then northwest, and passes a wire fence that warns jeepers of a 10-foot drop-off. Immediately thereafter (0.1 mile), you come to a junction of doubletracks marked with posts; fork right and climb 0.5 mile up the sandy, ledgy doubletrack to Gold Bar Rim. (The left fork heads due west between two rock ridges. If you're slogging more than riding, you're off course.)

Take in the God-sent view of the Moab Valley, Behind the Rocks, Slickrock Bike Trail, and the blessed La Sals; assess your willingness to continue; then ease down the Portal Trail. Don't be fooled by the trail's initially buffed conditions because the rest is wicked:

> wicked (wik′id) adj. 1. exceeding the limits of what is normal or tolerable. 2. giving trouble or anxiety. 3. marked by a high level of ability or skill. 4. involving the possibility of injury, pain, or loss. 5. having, showing, or indicative of intense, often vicious, ill will, *a wicked descent.*

Acrophobics will shudder over the next mile where the tire-wide path is pinned between a wall on the right and emptiness on the left. Heed the advice of three signs emplaced by the Moab Bike Patrol that warn of technical conditions ahead. About a mile down the trail, you reach the skinny part where the cliff below cuts into the trail and reduces your margin of error to nil. No heroes, *dismount,* please! Just beyond you can peer over the edge from a rock slab signed "Portal Overlook, end of maintained trail."

The remaining mile of trail is a steady stream of gnashing rocks and jackhammer stunts that redline the technical meter, but the cliffs are set back to a comforting distance. Exclaim your thoughts to the world at the trail register box. One rider wrote, "I don't think we're in Kansas anymore Toto." A second wrote, "A 9 on the sphincter scale." Two miles of road and riverside pedaling lead past Wall Street, a popular rock-climbing area, back to the trailhead. The shoulder is narrow, so stay to the "right of the white."

RIDE 81 *AMASA BACK*

Amasa Back is a thumb-shaped mesa bound on three sides by a gooseneck bend in the Colorado River. Over millions of years, the Colorado River shaped this landlocked peninsula. Within a short span of geologic time to come, the river will undoubtedly bisect the Back as the waterway forever seeks the shortest route to the Pacific Ocean. Amasa will then exist as a rincon encircled by a silted-in moat of the Colorado's abandoned meander.

Amasa Back is a relatively short ride that packs a wallop, but in the most endearing way. On the initial climb, you'll reach deep into your bag of two-wheel stunts to pull off a variety of maneuvers needed to clear the many technical tricks along the way. On the return descent, you'll have to be equally crafty to undo the feats you attempted earlier.

RIDE 81 AMASA BACK

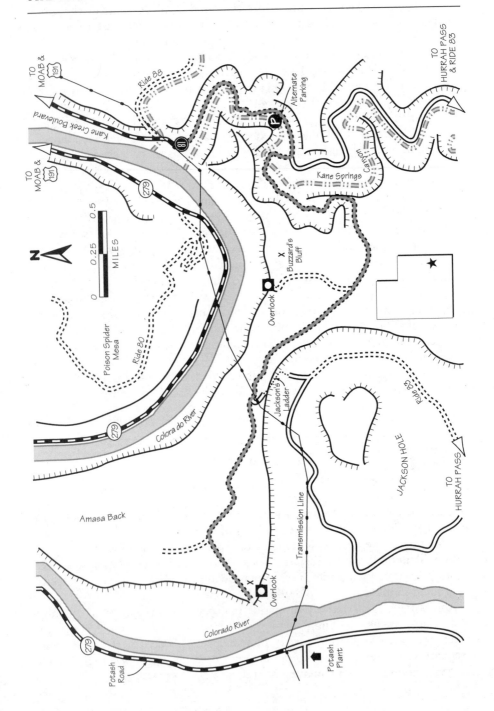

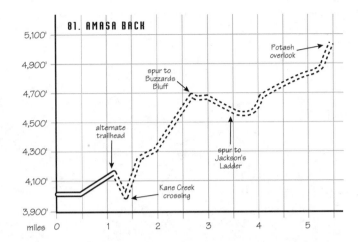

Along with the gain in elevation come superlative views of the land embracing Moab. The Colorado River slips through the Portal's dueling walls and the fractured fins of Behind the Rocks march toward the distant La Sal Mountains like a parade of sandstone pachyderms. While you're sweating buckets on the way up, you might scoff at bikers who have opted for the tamer route below on the Kane Springs Canyon Road to Hurrah Pass. But at midroute you'll be dumbfounded when you learn those same bikers dared to continue past Hurrah only to hoof up the 500-foot-tall rock ladder from Jackson Hole. Whoa!

General location: 5.5 miles southwest of Moab on Kane Creek Boulevard.

Distance: 11 miles out-and-back, less if you don't venture out to Amasa's western viewpoint.

Tread: 1.2 miles of light-duty dirt, gravel, and washboard road; 3 miles of identifiable doubletrack; 1.4 miles of create-as-you-go broken slickrock.

Aerobic level: Moderate to strenuous. The climb to Amasa is steep and technical and no place for spinning at high cadence. It's all power pedaling. A short respite atop is followed by more rock-hopping.

Technical difficulty: Level 3 to 5. Going up and down is equally as tricky with pavement slickrock, broken slickrock, and ledgy slickrock. There is more of the same as you pursue Amasa's western elbow.

Elevation change: The parking area on Kane Creek Boulevard is at 4,000 feet. The main climb rims out at 4,700 feet. A slight descent is followed by another climb to 5,100 feet at the viewpoint/turnaround. Total elevation gain is about 1,300 feet.

Season: Spring (March into June) and fall (September into November). Midsummer can be stifling, and insects can be annoying, especially near water. The route can be ridden during winter when it is dry.

Services: There are no services or drinking water along this route, and all surface waters should be purified. Camping along Colorado Riverway is

A side route leads to a compelling view of the Colorado River corridor.

restricted to Bureau of Land Management designated camping areas (fee areas) along Kane Creek Boulevard. All camping areas have outhouses but no drinking water. Moab has all visitor services.

Hazards: The technical conditions of the trail, both up and down, warrant keen attention. Be aware of loose rocks and overhanging ledges when near cliff edges. If pedaling from town, be alert to motorists on Kane Creek Boulevard.

Rescue index: Amasa Back is remote and difficult to reach by organized rescue. Motorists frequently travel Kane Creek Boulevard but less so on the dirt section. Moab has a hospital.

Land status: Bureau of Land Management (Moab Field Office).

Maps: USGS Gold Bar Canyon and Moab, Utah.

Access: From the intersection of Main and Center in Moab, travel south on Main 0.7 mile and turn right on Kane Creek Boulevard. Bend left 0.7 mile farther at the "dangerous intersection" sign where 500 West joins from the right. Continue 4 miles on Kane Creek Boulevard to where pavement turns to dirt and park at the pullout on the right near the BLM information board. To pedal from town, take 100 North to 100 West, turn left, then immediately right on Williams Way. At the T intersection, turn left/south on 500 West, then right on Kane Creek Boulevard at the "dangerous intersection" sign and proceed as above.

Notes on the trail: Take the light-duty dirt road into Kane Springs Canyon. At 1.2 miles, turn right on the old prospector's road and dive over ledgy bedrock (technical level 5). Plow through the sand, cross Kane Springs Creek, and start climbing. The doubletrack rises quickly above the canyon floor and is marked by rock cairns where it periodically crosses barren rock.

Two miles from the Kane Springs Canyon Road, the route reaches a summit and crosses over to Amasa Back's western side. At the Y junction, take the spur right for the optional (but highly recommended) 2 miles out-and-back trip to a compelling viewpoint of the Colorado River, the Portal, Poison Spider Mesa, Behind the Rocks, and more.

Back on the main route, continue north out Amasa Back along the edge of the 500-foot-deep rincon called Jackson Hole. Drop over a rock staircase, hop over the pipeline, and pass under the power lines. Take the optional left fork 0.2 mile to the top of Jackson's Ladder just to muse at any bikers hoofing up from the depths of Jackson Hole. (See Ride 83 Jackson Hole.)

Beyond the spur to Jackson's Ladder there are about 2 miles of pursuable trail; however, the track dissipates to broken slickrock marked periodically with cairns. How far you go out on the Amasa peninsula depends on your perseverance. Remember, keep your wheels on rock and avoid delicate soils. The western elbow of the rim affords overwhelming vistas of Jackson Hole, Colorado River, Island in the Sky District, Behind the Rocks, and the ever-present La Sal Mountains.

RIDE 82 *HURRAH PASS*

All this talk about Slickrock: precision grunt work, interval straining; friction, stiction, and traction; butt off the back, nose to the bars; pitch and twitch, potato chip, crotch split; rock rash; prodigious, profound, and improbable maneuvers; protracted acclivities, free-falling declivities; sandstone surfing. You can get winded just thinking about it.

If you long for a straightforward, scenically captivating ride, head out to Hurrah Pass. Here you'll have opportunities for viewing petroglyph panels, quenching your thirst at a fern-encrusted spring, plus a whole lot of canyon country viewing. From the pass, you'll sight across a huge chunk of incised terrain carved out by the Colorado River and preserved in Canyonlands National Park. Since technical difficulty is generally low, you can spend more time sightseeing than worrying whether you might stuff your front wheel.

Despite the generous amounts of graded roads, 20 miles is nothing to scoff at. Strong novice riders will fare well if they pace themselves and keep well-watered and fed. The return leg can seem endless if you reach Hurrah Pass with your fuel gauge reading near empty.

RIDE 82 HURRAH PASS

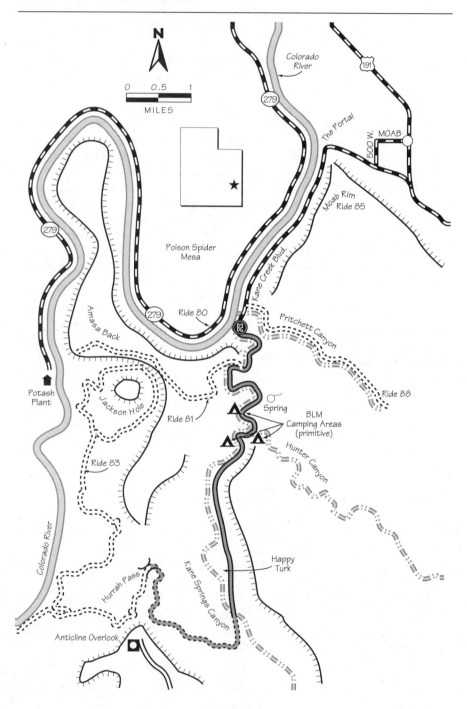

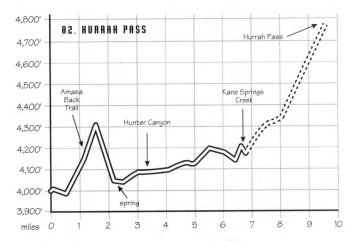

General location: 5.5 miles southwest of Moab on Kane Creek Boulevard.

Distance: 19.5 miles out-and-back, 29 miles if starting in town.

Tread: 7 miles of light-duty sand and rock road, 2.2 miles of sand and rock doubletrack. Two creek crossings will wet your toes.

Aerobic level: Moderate. The toughest parts are the 1.5-mile, 400-foot climb to Hurrah Pass itself and then the 0.6-mile, 250-foot climb on the way back from the roadside spring. The route can be made easier by driving out to the Hunter Canyon Trailhead or made harder by biking from town.

Technical difficulty: Level 1 to 3. The Kane Spring Canyon Road is sand, gravel, rock, and light washboards: easy stuff. The road deteriorates to sand and rock slabs in the tread on the last 1.5 miles to the pass (technical level 3).

Elevation change: The route's trailhead/parking area is at 3,980 feet. Hurrah Pass rises to 4,780 feet. Total elevation gain is about 1,600 feet.

Season: Spring (March into June) and fall (September into November). Midsummer is hot and insects can be bothersome, especially near water sources. Parts of winter can be enjoyable when the route is dry and weather cooperates.

Services: There is no drinking water along this route. A perennial spring (untreated water) is located 2.2 miles from the trailhead. Camping along the Colorado Riverway is restricted to Bureau of Land Management designated camping areas (fee areas). All camping areas have outhouses but no drinking water. Moab has all visitor services.

Hazards: Although Hurrah Pass is rated as one of Moab's easiest rides, you should carry ample water and food; the return leg can be tiresome for novice riders. Traction may be poor at sharp turns and on steeper grades because of erosion from vehicles. Be alert to motorists, ride in single file, and stay to the right. The return descent from Hurrah Pass requires attention to navigate intermittent sand and bedrock in the road. You must cross Hunter Creek (usually shallow) and Kane Springs Creek (could be shallow, could be hub-deep depending on runoff).

Wingate Sandstone palisades dwarf a lone rider.

Rescue index: This is a popular route, so you are likely to encounter other bikers. Vehicular traffic is more likely near the trailhead and less likely farther out. Moab has a hospital.

Land status: Bureau of Land Management (Moab Field Office).

Maps: USGS Moab and Trough Springs Canyon, Utah.

Access: From the intersection of Main and Center in Moab, travel south on Main 0.7 mile and turn right on Kane Creek Boulevard. Bend left 0.7 mile farther at the "dangerous intersection" sign where 500 West joins from the right. Continue 4 miles on Kane Creek Boulevard to where pavement turns to dirt and park at the pullout on the right near the BLM information board. To pedal from town, take 100 North to 100 West, turn left then immediately right on Williams Way. At the T intersection, turn left/south on 500 West, then right on Kane Creek Boulevard at the "dangerous intersection" sign and proceed as above.

Notes on the trail: From the parking area, leave the Colorado River behind and pedal out the dirt and gravel Kane Spring Canyon Road beneath sandstone palisades of the prolific Glen Canyon Group. Kane Springs Creek below nourishes shade-giving cottonwoods that interrupt the pervasive desert hues with mellow emerald tones. Pass the Amasa Back Trail after 1.2 miles; then drop down the steep, switchbacking road and pass a moss-encrusted spring on the left. The next mile follows a sandstone hallway walled in by 400-foot cliffs that glow warmly in the midday sun. Pass the Hunter Canyon Trailhead and camping area (alternate parking) 3.1 miles from the parking area and cross Hunter Creek. Beyond, Kane Springs Canyon widens to a broad valley ringed by colorfully banded sediments and vertical walls of stone that were poked and probed by prospectors decades ago.

A gentle, but noticeable, incline is capped by Happy Turk Rock on the right and a teed-up golf ball on the left. Gather prudent speed to carry you through the Kane Springs Creek crossing up ahead (may be shallow, may be hub-deep); then bend right/west for Hurrah Pass where a sandy doubletrack forks left and heads up the remaining length of the valley. The road steepens and deteriorates with patchy pavement bedrock as it fails to hold a straight course up to Hurrah Pass. Each passing turn brings a more compelling view of the rock-rimmed valley you just crossed.

West of Hurrah Pass, the Colorado River meanders out of sight through Canyonlands National Park's Island in the Sky District and toward its mating with the Green River. The resultant layer-cake strata hallmarks the White Rim Trail. Even a geologic layman can trace the arched sediments bowed by the Canyonlands' Anticline. Closer at hand, the strikingly blue evaporation ponds of the Potash Plant remind you of humankind's penchant for utilizing nature's resources.

When you are visually satiated, make an about-face and retrace your tracks while enjoying a varied perspective of Kane Springs Canyon. Take a shower under the spring to freshen up before making the climb back to the trailhead.

RIDE 83 *JACKSON HOLE*

The Jackson Hole loop is a g.a.s.—*gonzo, abusive, and sick*—and comes with chest-pounding bragging rights. Whoever first biked this improbable connector between Hurrah Pass and Amasa Back is a few fries short of a Happy Meal, and whoever selected it as the long-standing course of the Tour of Canyonlands Mountain Bike Race is downright twisted. Hallmarking this otherwise highly scenic ride is the infamous Jackson's Ladder, a 0.25-mile-long, near-vertical portage—uphill mind you—carved into the side of a 400-foot cliff. You can't ride up, that's for sure, and with your bike dangling from your shoulder the scramble is dubious. Halfway up, you'll shake your head in wonderment. John Jackson, on the other hand, forged the route and used it purposefully during the pioneer era to run horses to and from town and pastures on the Colorado River.

The ride to and from the hike-a-bike is pure Moab. From the outset you click away the miles on the smooth-sailing Kane Springs Canyon Road to Hurrah Pass. Beyond the pass the route degrades to a rock- and sand-infested doubletrack, descends wildly, and winds through some of the most remote country bordering Moab. Then comes the portage. Ugh! The loop culminates with the thrilling descent off Amasa Back that is packed with countless ledgy slickrock stunts. Straggling back to the trailhead, you'll concur that Jackson Hole is a g.a.s., but totally cool. Oh yeah, pro racers complete the loop in about 1 hour, 35 minutes.

Location: 5.5 miles southwest of Moab.

Distance: 23-mile loop.

Tread: 8 miles of light-duty dirt road; 13 miles of sand and rock doubletrack; 2 miles of broken slickrock doubletrack; and a 0.25-mile, 400-foot portage. Three creek crossings will soak your toes.

Aerobic level: Strenuous, and that's just the on-bike part. The bike-on-back portage up Jackson's Ladder is silly by most standards and redlines the difficulty meter.

Technical difficulty: Level 1 to 4+ for the on-bike portion. The descent from Hurrah Pass pushes level 4 if taken with speed, and the descent from Amasa Back pushes level 5 even at a creep. Jackson's Ladder is the mother of all portages and is categorically unridable.

Elevation change: The route's trailhead/parking area is at 3,980 feet. Hurrah Pass rises to 4,780 feet. After the portage, the trail tops out again at 4,700 feet on Amasa Back. Total gain is about 2,500 feet.

Season: Spring (March into June) and fall (September into November). If inadvertently ridden during the annual spring race, you'll have to wait your turn as hundreds of bikers march single file up the portage like ants at a picnic.

RIDE 83 JACKSON HOLE

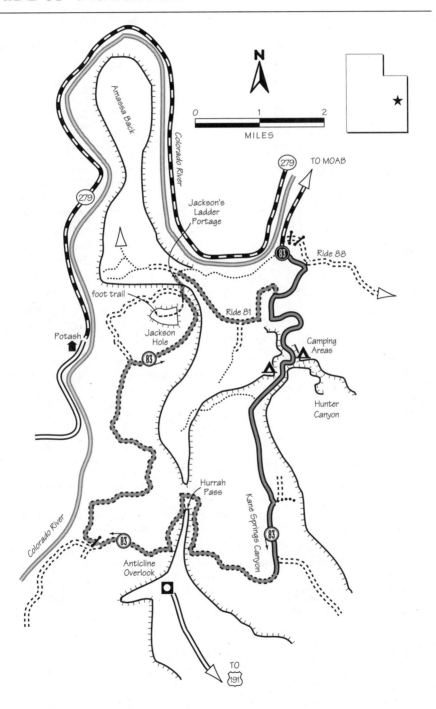

N

0   1   2
MILES

TO MOAB

279

Amassa Back

Colorado River

Jackson's
Ladder
Portage

83

Ride 88

foot trail

Ride 81

Potash

Jackson
Hole

83

Camping
Areas

Hunter
Canyon

Hurrah
Pass

Kane Springs Canyon

Colorado River

83

83

Anticline
Overlook

TO
191

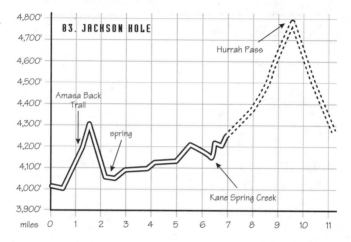

Services: There is no drinking water along this route. A perennial spring (untreated water) is located 2.2 miles from the trailhead. Camping along the Colorado Riverway is restricted to Bureau of Land Management designated camping areas (fee areas). All camping areas have outhouses but no drinking water. Moab has all visitor services.

Hazards: If you haven't guessed by now, Jackson's Ladder in not for the tentative or fainthearted. It is a three-point scramble; that is, two feet and one free hand up a steep pack trail that is loaded with loose and ledgy rocks. The descents from both Hurrah Pass and Amasa Back warrant caution. Watch for motorists on the Kane Springs Canyon Road. Pack along your smarts, lots of water, food, and a well-equipped tool kit. Sections to and through Jackson Hole turn to goo when wet.

Rescue index: Hurrah Pass is a popular destination for bikers and occasional motorists. Amasa Back is a popular bike route, also. But the loop's backside through Jackson Hole is remote. Rescue would be difficult and time consuming.

Land status: Bureau of Land Management (Moab Field Office).

Maps: USGS Gold Bar Canyon, Moab, Shafer Basin, and Trough Springs Canyon, Utah.

Access: From the intersection of Main and Center in Moab, travel south on Main 0.7 mile and turn right on Kane Creek Boulevard. Bend left 0.7 mile farther at the "dangerous intersection" sign where 500 West joins from the right. Continue 4 miles on Kane Creek Boulevard to where pavement turns to dirt and park at the pullout on the right near the BLM information board. To pedal from town, take 100 North to 100 West, turn left, then immediately right on Williams Way. At the T intersection, turn left/south on 500 West, then right on Kane Creek Boulevard at the "dangerous intersection" sign and proceed as above.

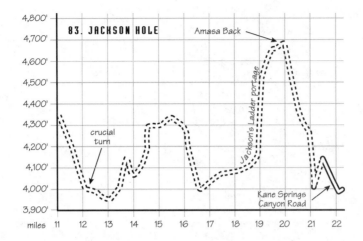

Notes on the trail: From the parking area, leave the Colorado River behind and pedal into the sandstone corridor of Kane Springs Canyon. Pass the Amasa Back Trail after 1.2 miles, and then drop down a steep hill and around a pair of rough switchbacks. Pass a moss-encrusted spring on the left, and then cross Hunter Creek. Break from the canyon's firm embrace past the Hunter Canyon trailhead/camping area and enter the ever-widening valley. Tip your helmet to Happy Turk Rock after a gradual climb and cross Kane Springs Creek (may be shallow, may be hub-deep). Bend right/west where a sandy doubletrack forks left up the remaining length of the valley. The road steepens and deteriorates with patchy pavement bedrock in the tread as it wavers up to Hurrah Pass, where you must decide whether to press on or bail out by backtracking.

Take in the view from the pass and then bomb down the other side on the rock-studded and slickrock-paved doubletrack (technical level 4). After a jackhammer straightaway, the road dips into a gully and begins a short, gentle rise. *Thou shalt not ride uphill!* Instead, fork right into a dry wash enclosed by low sandstone ledges. Look for cairns and an old wire fence marking the turnoff. (If you reach the Colorado River, you missed it by a long shot.) Slog through the sand for a few hundred yards, hop back in the saddle, and then slog some more.

With the maroon ledges at your side, the track swings right 0.5 mile from the turnoff and rises up a ramp of pebbly gray limestone. Hurrah Pass has swung around and is now square in your sights on the skyline. Descend a bit and toil up another grueling hill to a platform at the base of the wavering purplish cliffs overhead. The road bends west, then north, and takes you down a speedy mile-long descent with rocks lashing at your tires. During the springtime race, this descent is littered with both ejected biker goods and with bikers frantically repairing snake-bit tubes. The Potash Plant is at 11 o'clock and across the river.

Just "grin and bear it."

As the descent mellows, the track enters a wash lined with low sandstone ledges. Look for an *unobtrusive* doubletrack forking sharp right. Take the sandy track counterclockwise around Jackson Hole for nearly 2 miles. Once upon a time, the Colorado River flowed around the mesa centered in Jackson Hole. But this sand-filled meandering loop, called a rincon, has long since been abandoned. If and when the Colorado bisects Amasa Back, Jackson Hole will once again flow.

Now pinned between the butte on the left and Amasa Back on the right, fork right toward a pair of lone junipers that mark the gateway to the portage. Fashion a sling from a spare tube and start hoofing. As Igor would say in the movie *Young Frankenstein,* "It could be worse, it could be raining!"

In 20 minutes' time, the deed is done and you're back in the saddle. Follow the power line right to a T junction and fork right. Struggle up a couple of cursed hills along the edge of Jackson Hole, curve around the top of Amasa Back, and take a face-shot of the La Sal Mountains looming above Behind the Rocks. With legs weary and vision bleary from the portage, carefully descend the ledgy prospector's road off Amasa Back to Kane Springs Creek. Slog through the sand one last time and struggle up to the Kane Springs Canyon Road, surrendering to the waterless cascade of rock near the junction. Fork left, and relish 1 mile of easy pedaling to the parking area.

RIDE 84 *JUGHANDLE LOOP*

If you can't arrange a trip on the White Rim, then the Jughandle Loop is the next best alternative. Like the White Rim, Jughandle is a continual scenic highlight. The loop commences along the Colorado River and then rises up to the Island in the Sky District of Canyonlands National Park. Along the way, the route crosses nearly 100 million years of geologic boundaries that represent an ancient time when shallow seas, shoreline flats, river deltas, and drifting dunes buried southeastern Utah under a massive wedge of mud and sand. The sediments' flat-laying nature has been preserved largely intact, but headward erosion and down-cutting rivers have peeled back the earth's skin to reveal Canyonlands' famed layer-cake strata.

Hallmarking the loop is the Shafer Trail's infamous switchbacks—a raveled jeep road scratched into the face of a sheer cliff. Whether you blow a gasket by charging up at race pace or take your time in order to soak up the unfolding scenery, the accomplishment entitles you to interminable chest beating. And according to the laws of physics, "what goes up must come down." Long Canyon is one long, downhill thrill. You'll need to watch your front wheel as you round switchbacks and drop through "Pucker Pass," but if you lift your eyes they will fall upon the parading fins of Behind the Rocks backed by the ever-present La Sal Mountains.

General location: 5 miles west of Moab as the crow flies, 18 miles by vehicle.
Distance: 36.5-mile loop.
Tread: 10.5 miles of pavement, 26 miles of variably sandy, rocky, and washboarded doubletrack.
Aerobic level: Strenuous. This would be a solid ride even if it was all paved, but it's not. Innumerable rollers along the Potash and Shafer Trails keep you

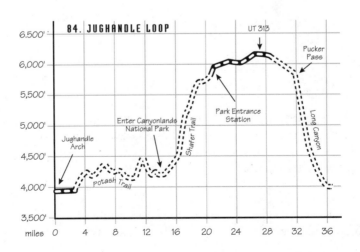

RIDE 84 JUGHANDLE LOOP

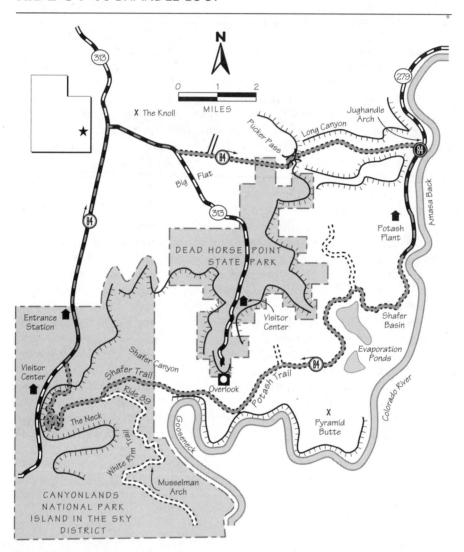

huffing up to the intersection with the White Rim Trail. Thereafter, the legendary Shafer Trail switchbacks are a 2-mile, eye-popping grind. The paved Island in the Sky Road is a breeze unless the breeze is blowing in your face. While descending Long Canyon, your legs are needed only as shock absorbers for the many miles of freewheeling.

Technical difficulty: Level 2 to 4. The Potash Trail follows a resistant limestone bench that typically erodes to hardened knuckles and coarse gravel; the Shafer Trail switchbacks are generally in good shape but can be gouged from erosion and four-wheel-drive traffic. Conditions are most rough in upper Long Canyon and through Pucker Pass (level 3 to 4).

Elevation change: The trailhead is the lowest elevation at 3,960 feet. The route tops out at 6,190 feet at the intersection of Utah State Highway 313 and the Island in the Sky Road. Total gain is about 3,200 feet. One third comes on the 1.9-mile grind up the Shafer Trail switchbacks. Long Canyon is a long descent where you lose nearly all the elevation you gained in one swoop.

Season: Spring (mid-March into June) and fall (September through October). The route reaches high country by local standards where the desert can be fanned by cooler breezes.

Services: There are no services along the route other than an outhouse at the intersection of the Shafer Trail and the White Rim Road. The Island in the Sky Visitor Center, located 1 mile from the top of the Shafer Trail, sells bottled water—usually. Backcountry camping along the Colorado Riverway is restricted to Bureau of Land Management designated camping areas (fee areas). Moab has all visitor services, including bike shops.

Hazards: Considering the ride's length and the warm high desert it crosses, do not skimp on your water and food rations. Allow all day to complete the ride, especially if sightseeing is a priority. Obtain a current forecast because large portions of the route may be impassable when wet.

Rescue index: Emergency assistance on this ride depends on your timing and where you are when you need help. The Potash Trail outside of Canyonlands National Park is not frequently traveled by motorists. Within the park and during high season, passersby may be encountered, especially along the paved Island in the Sky Road. Still, you might find complete solitude at any time. Park patrols are irregular on the Shafer Trail. Emergency contacts can be made from the Island in the Sky Visitor Center, 1 mile from where the Shafer Trail tops out.

Land status: Bureau of Land Management (Moab Field Office) and Canyonlands National Park (Island in the Sky District).

Maps: USGS Gold Bar Canyon, Musselman Arch, Shafer Basin, and The Knoll, Utah.

Access: From the center of Moab, travel 4.1 miles north on U.S. Highway 191, and then turn left on Utah State Highway 279/Potash Road. Drive south alongside the Colorado River 13.7 miles and park at the bottom of Long Canyon, just past Jughandle Arch.

Notes on the trail: First some fine print. Bicycles must stay *on* the Potash and Shafer Trails. You may be cited if your bike ventures from the road's edge. Bicyclists must pay the $5 park fee when exiting Canyonlands National Park on the Island in the Sky Road.

Beginning at Jughandle Arch, follow UT 279 south along the Colorado River. At the entrance to the Potash Plant, stay straight on the highway and along the sandbar riverbank of Jackson Bottom. To your left, the Colorado River once snuggled against Amasa Back as it meandered around Jackson

A rider drops through Pucker Pass.

Hole. In due time, geologically speaking, the Colorado will likely bisect the neck of Amasa and once again find a route through the rincon.

About 3 miles out, pavement turns to dirt (now called the Potash Trail), passes the boat launch, and begins climbing away from the river. Roll down, then up, then down again and come to a four-way junction marked by a stop sign. Stay straight on the public road and climb a stiff hill next to brick-red rocks of the Cutler Formation and pass Fred Flintstone's golf ball atop the hill. Follow the fence-lined road around the potash evaporation ponds in Shafer Basin. Leave the Potash property by crossing a wire fence 8.5 miles out and curve past Pyramid Butte on the left and a monolithic tower on the right.

Colossal amphitheaters have been stamped from the rim like glacially sculpted bowls. But tongues of ice had no hand in shaping these lands. Rather, the wavering cliffs and terraced strata at their bases are the result of headward erosion as first described by geologist Clarence E. Dutton in his 1880 publication, *Report on the Geology of the High Plateaus of Utah*: ". . . the brunt of erosion throughout the Plateau Country [Colorado Plateau] is directed against the edges of the strata and not against the surfaces . . . Thus the battering of time is here directed against the scarps and falls lightly but on the terrepleins." This relentless "pushing back" of the earth's skin gives Canyonlands its striking layer-cake characteristics.

A thin layer of resistant limestone interfingered within the Cutler Formation's iron-rich mudstone. This limestone forms a bench for the road and is also the culprit for the incessant teeth-chattering conditions. After a tough and rough 1-mile climb, the road finds a narrow passage between a towering butte overhead and a 400-foot sheer wall below that steers the Colorado River. Around the bend, the road is nearly pinched off by cliffs underneath and overhead and affords a dizzying view into the river gorge. Search the northern rim for the overlook at Dead Horse Point State Park. Two miles later, the road clips the edge of the Colorado River corridor again where the waterway loops around the highly photogenic Gooseneck mesa. Veer away from the Colorado, climb in and out of the South Fork of Shafer Canyon several long-winded times, and enter the Canyonlands on what is now called the Shafer Trail. You'll find an outhouse at the intersection with the White Rim Trail; use it if you need to lighten your load before tackling the climb ahead.

The Shafer Trail makes a beeline toward the base of the sandstone fortress, and you might wonder if you took a wrong turn on a dead-end street. But as you near the wall and exhaust your gears, the task of the Shafer Trail switchbacks becomes all too apparent: 1,000 feet, 1.5 miles, 12-percent grade. Grin and bear it. After the last turn, the road levels and you'll have many opportunities to gaze with bewilderment across the land you just crossed and of the feat you just accomplished.

Upon connecting with pavement, race north across the mesa for 6 miles (paying the fee at the park's gate) and fork right on UT 313 toward Dead

Horse Point State Park. After 1.7 miles, veer left on a graded dirt road (marked with a stop sign) where UT 313 bends right. Pull back on the reins as the earth opens up to Long Canyon, ricochet around the rough curves, and squeeze tightly down Pucker Pass (on the brakes that is). Four-wheelers can chew up the tread, so steady as she goes. Farther down, the road passes under a bus-size rock slab that fell from the canyon's rim in 1997. (Where are the cautionary highway signs warning of falling rock?) Ride the jackhammer down through two more sets of turns and then enjoy the mellow cruise back to the trailhead within the firm embrace of Long Canyon.

RIDE 85 *MOAB RIM*

The Moab Rim is the mother of all hill climbs. Sure, there are other ascents that are longer and gain ungodly amounts of elevation, but few are as merciless. You start out in granny gear and never leave it. The jeep road rises 900 feet in about 0.8 mile—an average 21-percent grade. But the law of averages can be misleading. The lower third is somewhat tolerable and, no doubt, less than the average grade, which means the upper third seems near vertical. And all along the way, the fractured, ledgy Kayenta slickrock is technical as hell. Don't go blaming lack of traction for your shortcomings either, because your rear tire sticks to the rock like glue.

So why bother? Other than pounding your chest like a gorilla when you reach the top, which you are certainly entitled to, you'll find the Moab Rim to be highly scenic. If you dare raise your nose from the handlebar, you'll look down upon the Colorado River as it slips through the sandstone confines of

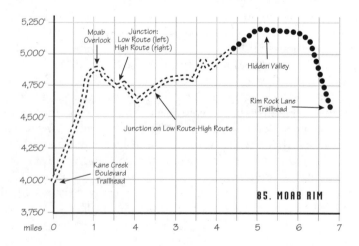

RIDE 85 MOAB RIM

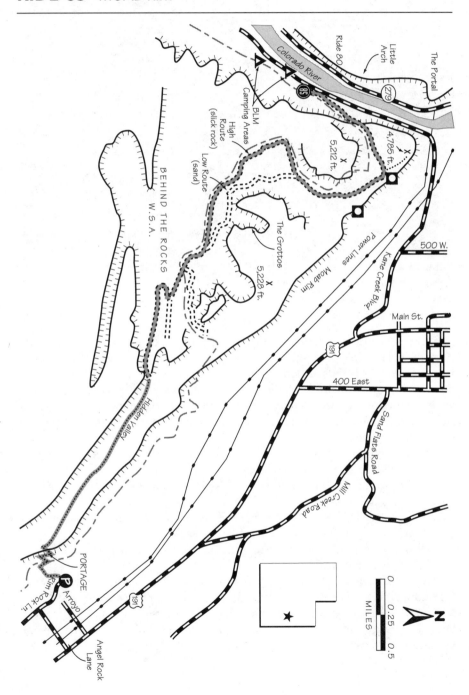

Moab/Canyonlands

Colorado River

Ride 80

Little Arch

The Portal

279

85

BLM

Camping Areas

High Route (slick rock)

Low Route (sand)

5,212 ft.

4,785 ft.

BEHIND THE ROCKS W.S.A.

The Grottos

5,228 ft.

Power Lines

Moab Rim

Kane Creek Blvd.

500 W.

Main St.

191

400 East

Sand Flats Road

Mill Creek Road

Hidden Valley

PORTAGE

Rim Rock Ln.

Arroyo

Angel Rock Lane

191

0   0.25   0.5

MILES

N

Scenery abounds on the Moab Rim Trail—if you dare raise your nose from the handlebar.

the Portal. On the rim across the river, bikers peer down at you from Little Arch on Poison Spider Mesa. When you top out, you gaze upon Moab Valley wedged within a wondrous land of naked, sunburned rock. If you continue on the optional route to Hidden Valley, you'll have opportunities to view rock art, ancient Indian ruins, and shadow-filled grottos. But the culminating descent is a silly portage on a boulder-ridden pack trail that plummets to the valley more steeply than the ride up.

Oh yeah, bikers raced up the Moab Rim in years past during the annual Canyonlands Fat Tire Festival. The record time was 12 minutes!

General location: 3.3 miles southwest of Moab on Kane Creek Boulevard.

Distance: 1.6 miles out-and-back with an optional 12-mile loop.

Tread: Fractured slickrock to the rim; sandy doubletracks; dirt, sand, and rock singletrack; and pavement on the optional loop.

Aerobic level: Strenuous has a warm, fuzzy sound to it. It may very well be the toughest mile in the world.

Technical difficulty: Level 5. Ledgy, fractured slickrock the whole way.

Elevation change: The trailhead is at 3,980 feet. The route rims out at 4,880 feet for a 900-foot gain. The optional loop adds another 600 feet.

Season: Spring (mid-March into June) and fall (September into November). Good southern exposure means you can often ride during winter.

Services: There is no drinking water along this route. Camping along the Colorado Riverway is restricted to Bureau of Land Management designated camping areas (fee areas). All have outhouses but none have water taps. Moab has all visitor services.

Hazards: The technical nature of the trail is inherently hazardous. Those with weak hearts and elementary skills had best look elsewhere. The return descent requires unfaltering skills and perfectly tuned brakes. The optional loop via Hidden Valley Trail ends with a 400-foot portage down a steep, boulder-ridden pack trail.

Rescue index: Since this route does not cater to the masses, you will not encounter hordes of bikers. Hikers, on the other hand, are more common and you might share the ascent with the token jeeper. You are, at most, 0.8 mile from frequently traveled Kane Creek Boulevard. The loop option crosses seldom traveled remote areas. Moab has a hospital.

Land status: Private property and Bureau of Land Management (Moab Field Office). Portions of this route enter the Behind the Rocks Wilderness Study Area (see "Notes").

Maps: USGS Moab, Utah.

Access: From the center of Moab, drive south on Main/U.S. Highway 191 for 0.7 mile and turn right on Kane Creek Boulevard. Bend left 0.7 mile farther at the "dangerous intersection" sign where 500 West joins from the right. Continue 1.8 miles to the signed trailhead on the left. Parking is limited. Consider biking to the trailhead to warm up your legs before the climb. For a shortcut, take 100 North to 100 West, turn left, then immediately right on Williams Way. At the T intersection, turn left/south on 500 West, then right on Kane Creek Boulevard at the "dangerous intersection" sign. The trailhead is 1.8 miles down the road.

Notes on the trail: First some fine print. The optional Hidden Valley Trail enters the Behind the Rocks Wilderness Study Area (WSA). Bicycle traffic is currently permitted on existing trails in the WSA, although it is not encouraged. Be aware that bicycle access may change in the future if: (1) the U.S. Congress upgrades the WSA to a Wilderness Area, then all mechanized travel will be prohibited; and (2) the BLM determines that bicycles are causing excessive environmental impacts and are compromising current management objectives. Stay on the existing trail and do not let your course waver!

Now for the ride: Directions are pretty simple—up. You'll get a good feel for the ride in the first few feet where you must bunny hop, cant-and-ratchet, and power over ledges and around boulders. When you reach the rim, press your eyeballs back into their sockets, and soak up the view of the valley below and of the surrounding land. Then make an about-face and seek vengeance on the rim road.

To pursue the optional loop, continue on the doubletrack as it curves southward and passes a spur left to a second viewpoint. About 0.6 mile farther and where a large alcove opens to the far right, you come to an unobtrusive junction (may be marked with a lonely cairn). The recommended route is to the right, which stays high and crosses sand and rock. Pay attention to trail markers (remnant cairns, tire tracks, blood stains), especially when crossing slickrock. (The left fork descends a bit, follows a sandy wash, and passes the Grottos.) In 1.5 miles (a little less if you take the lower route) the two tracks merge.

Head eastward, drop to a wash, and stay straight at a junction. The doubletrack now makes a beeline up a steep, pebbly hill that ends near an Indian ruin. About halfway up, fork right (look for a post tagged "trail"), descend through an S curve, and pedal uphill and eastward across rock and sand. The track ends at a rock ledge where singletrack takes over. Coast through grassy Hidden Valley on a fine section of trail for 1 mile. (It is imperative that you stay on the trail and do not blaze parallel tracks through the valley. Such contemptuous behavior is scorned upon by land managers and will quickly bring the demise of bike access.) All good things must come to an end. Sling your bike over your shoulder and hoof down the sketchy path to the valley below. Close the loop by riding the highway back to town or Kane Creek Boulevard around to the trailhead.

RIDE 86 *SLICKROCK BIKE TRAIL*

For most people, the Slickrock Bike Trail needs no introduction. It's the ride that made Moab the self-proclaimed center of the mountain-bike universe and may very well be the world's most popular and visited trail. Its uniqueness stems from its peculiar riding medium—solid rock—more precisely Navajo Sandstone. The

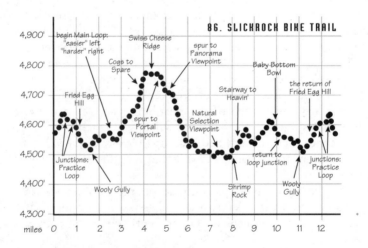

RIDE 86 SLICKROCK BIKE TRAIL

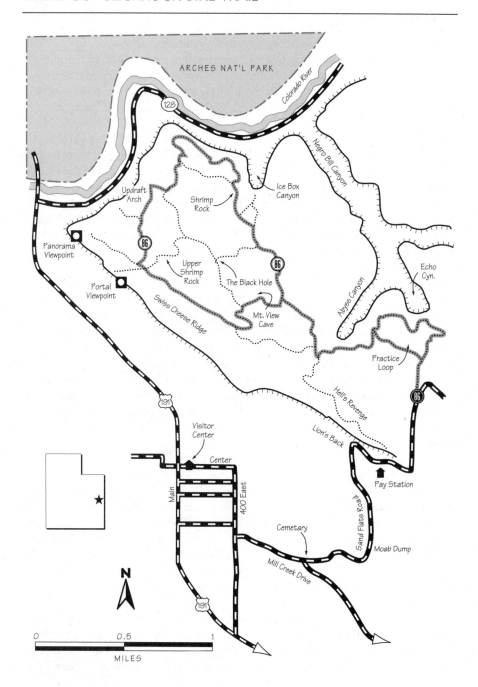

ARCHES NAT'L PARK

Colorado River

128

Negro Bill Canyon

Ice Box Canyon

Updraft Arch

Shrimp Rock

Panorama Viewpoint

86

Echo Cyn.

Upper Shrimp Rock

The Black Hole

86

Abyss Canyon

Portal Viewpoint

Swiss Cheese Ridge

Mt. View Cave

Practice Loop

Hell's Revenge

86

Lion's Back

Visitor Center

Center

Main

400 East

Pay Station

Cemetary

Sand Flats Road

191

Moab Dump

Mill Creek Drive

191

N

0   0.5   1

MILES

opportunity, and often necessity, to find seemingly impossible paths around or over the rock's eroded features coupled with its steep frictional surfaces is a tribute to its legendary difficulty. Slickrock has played proving ground for bike and component manufacturers worldwide.

But don't be overly daunted if this is your first outing or if you're a novice rider. A cautionary approach, common sense, and a willingness to dismount and walk will get you through the technically and physically demanding sections. Then you can feel out the less threatening aspects. It's easy to be intimidated by others who display Zen-like abilities. Whether you're walking or riding, you're a "rocker" just the same.

The tendency to focus on where to place your front tire and to stay glued to the paint-on-rock dashes often overshadows Slickrock's immediate and surrounding beauty. Wandering eyes will discover intricate shapes in the lithified dunes that constitute the trail. Pockets of sand support tenacious shrubs, cacti, and cryptobiotic soils—the building blocks of this semi-arid desert. Apparently lifeless potholes hold a microcosm of organisms that await the next rainfall. When ridden at different times of the day, the Navajo Sandstone has chameleon characteristics, changing in color from creamy white, to radiant gold, to salmon or lavender.

The entire trail crosses an elevated platform of sandstone bound by cliffs on two sides cut by the Colorado River and its tributaries. There are many opportunities to peer into shadow-filled canyons or gaze at features of Arches National Park across the Colorado. The La Sal Mountains on the eastern skyline, with treeless 12,000-foot summits that collect snow from fall through spring, provide a surreal backdrop to any Slickrock photograph.

And did you know that Slickrock was not originally a mountain bike trail? Off-road motorcyclists established the trail in 1969. Years thereafter, mountain bikers simply adopted and dominated the trail. If you pass the occasional pistoned brethren, tip your helmet in gratitude.

Location: 3.7 miles east of Moab.

Distance: The main trail is 9 miles according to the BLM Moab Slickrock Bike Trail Map, 12.5 miles according to the mileage markers painted on the rock, and in between, by the author's gauge. Regardless, allow two to four hours to ride the entire trail, no lie. There are over 4 miles of additional connecting and spur trails painted with dots instead of dashes, plus you can free ride to your heart's (and legs') content. Just avoid cryptobiotic soils and delicate potholes by staying strictly on rock. The Practice Loop by itself is just over 2 miles long from the trailhead.

Tread: Except for short sand traps, the entire route crosses barren, solid sandstone.

Aerobic level: Strenuous. Slickrock is perhaps the toughest 12 miles you'll ever ride and is the equivalent of riding 100 intervals up short, steep pitches at maximum power in your lowest gears. The alternative is simply dismounting and walking. The whole ride is a full-body workout and a true test of your bike-

The author spends a
"day at the office."

handling prowess. Rest zones are many but short in duration. Slickrock will
whoop the butt of anyone who underestimates it.

Riding the main loop clockwise is claimed to be easier than counterclockwise
because you'll knock off a big chunk of elevation up a hill dubbed "Cogs to
Spare" to Swiss Cheese Ridge. Either way, you'll face every challenge Slickrock
has to offer.

The Practice Loop is no easier than the main loop; it's just shorter and allows
novice and intermediate bikers the comfort of bailing out within a reasonable
distance of the trailhead. Out-and-back trips on the main trail are as enjoyable as
the whole shebang. Just make sure you turn around before you're bone dry or
bonked.

Technical difficulty: Level 5. The trail crosses barren sandstone throughout,
interrupted periodically with patches of sand. You'll climb and descend perplex-
ingly steep hills, skirt ledges and drop-offs, and creep over rippled crossbeds
cemented in the lithified dunes. Don't feel compelled to keep your tires glued to

the dashes; cheater routes around improbable stunts are often a few feet away.

Elevation change: The low point is 4,500 feet on the north side of the loop (about mile 7.5); the high is 4,800 feet on Swiss Cheese Ridge (about mile 4). The trailhead is midway at 4,650 feet. Because of the trail's undulating nature, elevation gain is close to 2,000 feet.

Season: Spring (March into June) and fall (September into November) are best. Midsummer is deathly hot unless you head out at the crack of dawn because midday temperatures typically exceed 100 degrees. Winter can be enjoyable when the trail is dry. Be aware of changing weather. Afternoon can bring intense thunderstorms, and when wet, Slickrock lives up to its name.

Services: There is no drinking water along the trail. The trailhead parking area has an outhouse. Camping in the Sand Flats Recreation Area is permitted only at designated sites (fee areas). There are outhouses but no water taps. All services are available in Moab.

Hazards: The entire trail can be hazardous for the unskilled, inattentive, or overly zealous biker. Expert sections are marked with yellow dots inside white dashes ("fried eggs"), and hazards are marked with "comb" symbols—stay clear. Portions of the trail cross steep side slopes, traverse narrow ledges, and venture close to cliffs varying in height from tens to hundreds of feet.

Slickrock is somewhat of a misnomer because if you fall, you won't slide like on an ice rink; rather, any spill will produce USDA Grade A road rash, and that's on the mild end of the injury spectrum. Be alert to where your front wheel is heading and to where your body might tumble if you must dismount.

Carry plenty of water and food, perhaps the equivalent for a ride three times this length. Physical exertion, warm weather, lack of shade, and the reflective sandstone can overheat, dehydrate, and deplete your body quickly.

Make sure your bike, especially your brakes, are well tuned. First-time and novice bikers should not ride alone.

Rescue index: It's rare to find solitude on Slickrock nowadays. The route is marked at 0.5-mile increments, which aid in search and rescue and to gauge your progress. Rescue by four-wheel-drive emergency vehicle is difficult, time-consuming, and expensive. Helicopter airlift is used for serious injuries at remote locations, but your landing destination will be the hospital in Grand Junction, Colorado. Moab has a hospital with emergency facilities (719 West 400 North).

Land status: Bureau of Land Management (Moab Field Office).

Maps: USGS Moab, Utah, BLM Moab Slickrock Bike Trail Map (free with access fee).

Access: From the intersection of Main and Center Streets, travel east to 400 East and turn right. Turn left after 0.4 mile on Mill Creek Drive; then 0.5 mile farther, stay straight on Sand Flats Road (near the cemetery) where Mill Creek bends right/south. Pass "America's most scenic dump," pay the fee at the Sand Flats Recreation Area entrance station, and park at the trailhead lot.

If you're biking from town to the trail, the distance is 3.7 miles with a 700-foot gain.

Sources of additional information: The Community Sand Flats Team, Slick-rock Bike Trail Map by Latitude 40° (an aerial photo of Slickrock with the dozens of humorous but accurately named stunts, many of which are referred to below. See Appendix B).

Notes on the trail: Now first the fine print. A recreation use fee is required for the Sand Flats Recreation Area and is collected at the entrance station about 0.7 mile before the trailhead. Fees during 1998 were $5 per vehicle or $2 per bicyclist if pedaling to the trail. Camping fees were $6 per night (two persons) and $2 for each additional person.

These notes are based on mile markers painted on the trail (mm ##). Your exact mileage may differ.

Your first order of business is an introductory hill dubbed Hurry Up & Wait. During high season, bikers congregate in force sizing up others and being sized up by others. Thereafter, fork right for the Practice Loop or left for the main trail. (If you choose the former, the trail jogs east for a postcard perfect view of the La Sals rising over Porcupine Rim. Around the bend, you can opt to fork right, descend a bit, and peer into the depths of Echo Canyon; heed the cautionary markers as to where to dismount. Blast through two sand traps and rejoin the main trail 0.8 miles from the trailhead.)

Onward for the real McCoy: A huge descending ramp called Fried Egg Hill sets the frictional tone for the day by placing undying faith in your brakes. Invincible types launch from the lip on a death-defying plunge into the half pipe below while others hover like bloodthirsty vultures. Round a ledgy area (keep that left pedal up), pass Abyss Viewpoint (mm 1.5), and drop down a tricky staircase section to a sandy gulch called Wooly Gully.

A series of humorously steep ramps quickly separate the pack into "riders with moxie" and "mere bipeds" (mm 2.0). Weave through Snake Alley, or take the cheater route to the side, and then come to the junction for the main loop (mm2.5). If you're sporting a grin the size of a Chiquita banana, then press on, because more thrills and views await. If you're bedraggled, then perhaps your cooler is calling. One-half mile to the left (we're heading clockwise), the trail passes appropriately named Mt. View Cave and a connecting trail leading past The Black Hole. Slog through the sand and cast your eyes upon the dreaded climb up Cogs to Spare (mm 3.5). Deft bikers make it look way too easy. Rev up the rpms to carry you gracefully over the steps at the bottom—don't just bash into them full throttle, or you'll be on your head—then blow a gasket by creeping up the rest at a painfully slow pace. Alas, Swiss Cheese Ridge (mm 4.0 to 4.5) allows you to shift up to that neglected middle chain ring, briefly albeit. The spur left to the Portal Viewpoint releases you from your intense technical focus with a sublime visual perspective of why you made the journey here in the first place. Those on Poison Spider Mesa or the Moab Rim are no doubt gazing your way with the same devotion.

Back on route and after a quick drop, a spur heads left to Panorama Viewpoint where you can toe the edge of the Colorado River corridor from dizzying heights. Plow through the sand, hop on the rock, and relish the fact you are descending Interval Straining. Pass a spur left to a viewpoint near Updraft Arch (mm5.5), and wander across Slickrock's back nine to the Darwinist-sounding Natural Selection Viewpoint (mm7.0 to 7.5). Chug through the sand once more (hey what did you expect of sandstone) and arrive at socially gravitating Shrimp Rock.

Now, this clockwise version was claimed to be easier than counterclockwise, but not easy, for the upcoming sections will burst your anaerobic threshold and make you long for the frosties in your cooler (mm8.0 to 9.5). Your effort is rewarded with a few roller coaster laps around the half pipe at Baby Bottom Bowl (mm9.5 to 10.0). Return to the loop junction and descend those blasted ramps with a vengeful grin—and a death grip on the brakes!

Ahead looms Fried Egg Hill, a.k.a. Fried "Legs" Hill. Roll up your dragging tongue and try to look fresh as you pass the vultures' perch. Pass the Practice Loop junction and you're virtually home free. Those packing excess testosterone can tackle the silly incline on the right before returning to Hurry Up & Wait Hill. And watch out for that last dip before the gate—no point cracking your melon with 50 feet to go.

RIDE 87 *PORCUPINE RIM*

This route takes you to Moab's high country, by local standards, and to an overlook of redrock monoliths poking up from Castle Valley. For millennia the formations Castle Rock and Priest and Nuns have preached a silent sermon to a congregation of canyons, mesas, and mountain peaks. You, too, will be enlightened by their desert oration from Porcupine Rim's 1,000-foot altar.

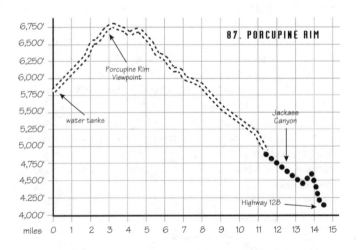

RIDE 87 PORCUPINE RIM

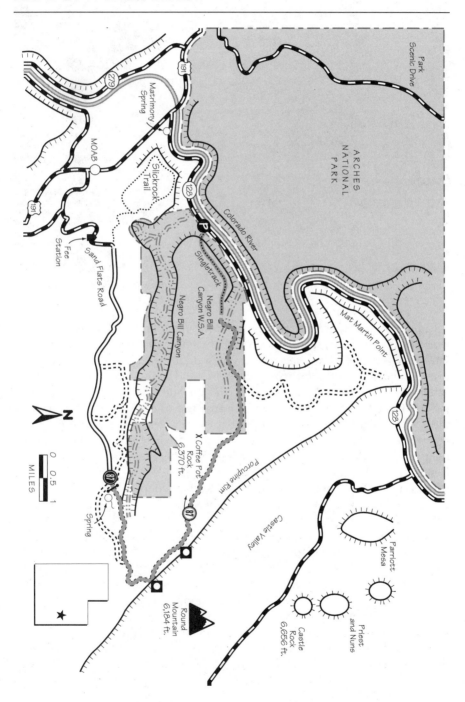

279

191

Matrimony Spring

MOAB

128

191

Slickrock Trail

Fee Station

Sand Flats Road

ARCHES NATIONAL PARK

Park Scenic Drive

Colorado River

P

Singletrack

Negro Bill Canyon W.S.A.

Negro Bill Canyon

Mat Martin Point

128

N

MILES 0 0.5 1

87

X Coffee Pot Rock 6,370 ft.

Porcupine Rim

87

Spring

★

Castle Valley

Round Mountain 6,184 ft.

Parriott Mesa

Priest and Nuns

Castle Rock 6,656 ft.

Riders become afflicted with the dreaded disease *Porcupinus invertium*.

Riding conditions are bittersweet, and your upper body will receive a bigger workout than your legs. The climb to Porcupine is a constant battle against sandstone ledges outcropping in the sandy doubletrack, and you'll yank on your handlebars to lift your front wheel time and again. The rim road is more agitating than a paint-shaker and leaves you blurry eyed. And the famous Jackass Canyon singletrack descent is a true test of one's handling savvy and capacity for high places; it's blissful for some or a despairing walk for others. But when you factor in where you've been and where you're going and the sights enjoyed along the way, Porcupine Rim truly is a world-class ride.

General location: 10 miles east of Moab.

Distance: 14.8 miles point-to-point or a 30.5-mile loop.

Tread: 11.7 miles of sand, pebble, and broken slickrock doubletracks; 3.1 miles of dirt and ledgy singletrack.

Aerobic level: Moderate to strenuous. Almost all of the climbing is tackled within 3.5 miles of the starting gate. Although the rest is generally downhill, the rough conditions and occasional risers can easily drain your fuel tank to the point you'll be running near empty when you embark on the highly technical singletrack descent. If ridden as a loop, Porcupine is strenuous and requires *all day* to complete.

Technical difficulty: Level 3 to 5. The doubletrack ascent to the rim is over broken slickrock steps (level 4). The rim road is sand, loose rock, and slickrock "chatter strips" (level 3 to 4). The Jackass Canyon singletrack descent is narrow, chock-full of rocks and ledge drops, has a few short portage sections, and is exposed to steep slopes and cliffs (level 4 to 5). What a ride!

Elevation change: The route begins on the Sand Flats Road at 5,840 feet. You top out on Porcupine Rim at 6,800 feet and drop to 4,000 feet at the Colorado River. Total gain is about 1,200 feet.

Season: Spring (April to mid-June) and fall (September through October). Because of the route's higher elevation, it has a later opening date in the spring and earlier closing date in the fall. When the La Sal Mountains get belted with autumn's snow, Porcupine Rim will likely get dusted, too. Wet conditions may linger on the singletrack descent because of its north-facing exposure. Give the trail time to dry after wet weather to prevent erosion.

Services: No drinking water or services are available on this route. The trailhead and trail end have outhouses. Camping along the Colorado River-way is restricted to Bureau of Land Management designated camping areas (fee areas). Bike shops and taxi companies offer shuttle services.

Hazards: Although the Jackass Canyon singletrack is one of the route's highlights, it is highly technical and can be dangerous to the inattentive and unskilled biker. Common sense goes a long way. Navigating the route has always been tricky over the years, but now the way is well marked with carsonite posts and cairns. Don't be fooled by the modest elevation gain; this is a long ride that requires stamina, and consequently, a generous supply of water and food.

Ron and Bob pass a rim-edge view of Castle Rock and Priest and Nuns.

Rescue index: Porcupine Rim Trail is well attended by bikers. The Sand Flats Road from Moab to the trailhead is fairly well traveled, and Utah State Highway 128 along the Colorado River is busy. Porcupine Rim Trail itself is remote, and organized rescue can be difficult and time consuming.

Land status: Bureau of Land Management (Moab Field Office). The Jackass Canyon singletrack enters the Negro Bill Wilderness Study area. Time and the U.S. Congress will determine the trail's fate.

Maps: USGS Big Bend, Moab, and Rill Creek, Utah.

Access: To arrange your shuttle, first drive 2.5 miles north from Moab. Turn right on UT 128 and travel 3.1 miles along the Colorado River to the Negro Bill Canyon Trailhead. Return to town, turn left on Center, right on 400 East, and left on Mill Creek Drive at Dave's Corner Market. Fork left in 0.5 mile (actually you stay straight) on Sand Flats Road where Mill Creek bends right/south. Pass the Moab Dump, and pay the fee at the Sands Flat Recreation Area entrance station ($5 per vehicle or $2 per biker in 1998). Pass the Slickrock Bike Trail and drive 6.4 miles farther to the trailhead/parking area. (Sand Flats Road past Slickrock is sand, rock, and washboard and is suitable for passenger cars but can be rough locally.)

Notes on the trail: Take the doubletrack at the northeast corner of the parking area, descend a bit, and then start climbing along the upper reaches of Negro Bill Canyon. You'll pull innumerable wheelies as you thrust your bike over repetitive sandstone ledges. After 1.9 miles, stay straight/left where a double-track forks right, and keep testing your might against the rock-jumbled road. Where the track bends left/north you are greeted with a welcome, but brief, respite and a widespread view westward across Negro Bill Canyon to the Moab Rim. Inch up one more hill to reach the rim-edge viewing deck that is typically cluttered with bikes and bodies. Join the pack and share the view.

Porcupine Rim is a ruler-sharp escarpment rising 1,000 feet above the wide gape of Castle Valley. A linear mesa to the northeast interrupts the levelness. It is capped with a fractured fin of Wingate Sandstone—Castle Rock and Priest and Nuns—that has served as backdrop for many commercials and movies. Somewhere on the mesas pinned between the valleys and the hulking flank of the La Sal Mountains, Kokopelli's Trail makes its way toward Moab from Loma, Colorado.

Back on board, continue northward along the rim, while futilely seeking a smooth line in the rock-rippled road. About 1 mile along, the road clips the rim at what has been dubbed "High Anxiety Viewpoint." This is your last chance to toe the rim and gasp at the view, so get out the camera and record the moment. Gradually the road veers away from the rim as it begins descending; then it turns more westward, passes Coffee Pot Rock in the distance, and skirts the port side of a widening valley. If gravity had its way, you would be freewheeling at near highway speeds, but you'll succumb to a slower pace for fear that the incessant sandstone chatter strips will shake loose your dentures or burst your spleen. Numerous spur roads fork left and right, so follow posts and cairns marking the main route. (In 1996, two bikers veered off course and perished while attempting to scramble down canyons and exit the desert.)

About 2 miles from Porcupine Rim, you enter the speed zone where the track smooths briefly. At last, you can shift up and sit down. An S turn swings your bow directly in the path of the distant La Sals, then turns you to stern to avoid the titanic collision. Hold a straight and steady course across a slickrock area 10.5 miles from the trailhead. Thereafter, stay left at a junction and say hello to the La Sals once more. Dip through the head of Jackass Canyon and climb up to a major junction that is obtrusively signed "Dead End." Get the hint? Go right for the righteous singletrack.

Initially, the smooth sand trail reels you in at high speed, but it changes quickly to a slow-paced trail course along a ledge high above Jackass Canyon and the Colorado River. Loosen the tension on your clipless pedals and watch where you put your front wheel; a tumble will be nasty if not fatal. Besides, a prudent dismount will allow your eyes to wander from the trail to the glorious sight of the Colorado far below and of Arches National Park beyond. Bend, or rather portage, through a side canyon and welcome gentler conditions down to the highway.

RIDE 88 *PRITCHETT CANYON*

You get a little bit of everything on the Pritchett Canyon tour, including a generous amount of descending. Located 13 miles south of Moab, this route circles around the Behind the Rocks Wilderness Study Area and then descends a rock-walled canyon to the Colorado River. Early on, you'll cross grass pastures and pass seductive Prostitute Butte and showy Picture Frame Arch. Spur roads lead you to overlooks of Kane Springs Canyon and distant Hurrah Pass before a rollicking descent takes you to the WSA boundary bordering Pritchett Canyon. A short hike leads to spacious seating at the Pritchett Arch bistro where you can enjoy a midroute snack among deep canyons and sandstone domes that bubble up all over. The route culminates with a wide-eyed descent through a notch in upper Pritchett Canyon called White Knuckle Hill, followed by miles of an old Euro-style cobblestone track through lower Pritchett to the Colorado River corridor.

General location: 13 miles south of Moab.

Distance: 20 miles point-to-point.

Tread: The route begins with 11 miles of sand and gravel roads that are best suited for high-clearance vehicles. Thereafter, the road degrades to sand, rock, cobble, and bedrock doubletracks that can stymie even the most resolute four-wheel-driver.

RIDE 88 PRITCHETT CANYON

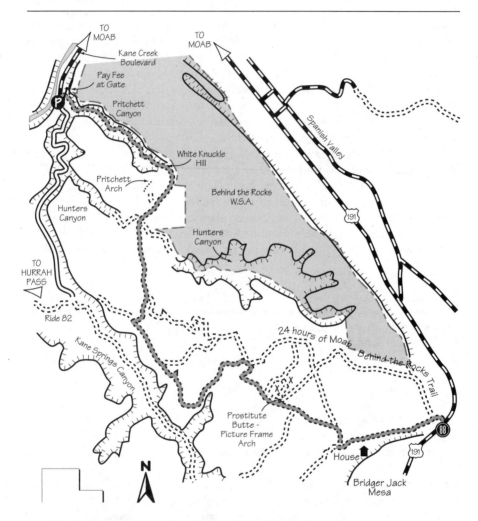

Aerobic level: Moderate. The first half is a blend of gentle to moderate rolling hills. Pritchett Canyon, the second half, is virtually all downhill. It's a far cry from a joy ride, however, and you'll rarely ride while seated because of the rough and sometimes highly technical conditions.

Technical difficulty: Level 2 to 5. Except for "catch-a-wave" slickrock, you'll encounter just about every other desert riding medium from sand and gravel, to ledgy bedrock, to dry cobble creek bed. White Knuckle Hill, the entry gate to Pritchett Canyon, lives up to its name. But it is manageable to walk the toughest spots.

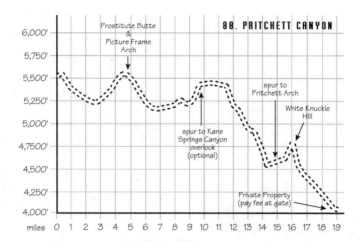

Elevation change: The trailhead is at 5,510 feet. For 11.5 miles the route undulates within a couple hundred feet of 5,300 feet. The remaining miles descend to 4,000 feet upon exiting Pritchett Canyon. Total gain is a modest 1,040 feet.

Season: Spring (mid-March into June) and fall (September into November). Midsummer is hot. One weekend in early October brings a carnival atmosphere to the route's early miles with the 24 Hours of Moab endurance mountain-bike race.

Services: There is no drinking water or services along this route. Camping along the Colorado Riverway is restricted to Bureau of Land Management designated camping areas (fee areas but no water taps). Backcountry camping is allowed near the trailhead. There is a private camping area at the mouth of Pritchett Canyon (fee area) with water and pay showers available. Moab offers all visitor services.

Hazards: A midroute descent on a rough, ledgy doubletrack rates technical level 4. A few miles thereafter you descend White Knuckle Hill, which is infamous for technical level 5 conditions including waist-high ledge drops. As always, carry plenty of water.

Rescue index: You may pass other bikers and four-wheel-drive vehicles along the route, or you may experience complete solitude. The first 11 miles are accessible by high-clearance vehicles, but vehicle rescue is difficult if not impossible in Pritchett Canyon. Emergency contacts might be made from the Hole in the Rock Gift Shop 3 miles past the trailhead turnoff on U.S. Highway 191.

Land status: Bureau of Land Management (Moab Field Office) and private property upon exiting Pritchett Canyon (fee required).

Maps: USGS Kane Springs, Moab, and Trough Springs Canyon, Utah.

Access: To arrange a shuttle, first drop a vehicle at the bottom of Pritchett Canyon. From the intersection of Main and Center in Moab, travel south on

Bob and Ron drop off White Knuckle Hill to enter Pritchett Canyon.

Main 0.7 mile and turn right on Kane Creek Boulevard. Bend left 0.7 mile farther at the "dangerous intersection" sign where 500 West joins from the right. Continue 4 miles on Kane Creek Boulevard to the pullout on the left with a BLM information board for Pritchett Canyon. Return to the intersection of Kane Creek Boulevard and US 191 and travel south on US 191 for 12.4 miles. As the road tops a hill just past milepost 113, turn right on a dirt road signed for Behind the Rocks and Pritchett Canyon and park near the junction. **Notes on the trail:** You must pay a $1 fee (in 1998) for the privilege of crossing private property upon exiting Pritchett Canyon to Kane Springs Boulevard.

Strike out northward on the sand and bedrock road for 0.5 mile and then bend left/west to descend gradually across a widening grass pasture between Bridger Jack Mesa and Behind the Rocks. (The right fork at 0.5 mile follows the Behind the Rocks Trail and the 24 Hours of Moab racecourse.) Stay on the main road as it bends gradually right and rises uphill gently toward curvaceous Prostitute Butte in the distance. Ignore several sandy doubletracks along the way.

Pass Prostitute Butte 5 miles out and continue westward following a sign for Pritchett Canyon, or digress and take the highly scenic 2-mile loop around the butte and visit Picture Frame Arch. Descend the sand and rock road to a junction in a dry wash. Stay left on the flats; do not fork right/north and climb around the towering butte next to the road. After 2 miles of easy pedaling, the road bends right/north around a point and then rises up a steep, pebbly dugway beneath broken cliffs. At the top, you can take an obscure and optional 1-mile out-and-back spur left to an overlook of Kane Springs Canyon. Then cruise northward across the plateau for 2 miles and fork right to descend for nearly 3 miles to a junction of doubletracks in the dry wash of Hunters Canyon. This descent rates technical level 3 to 5 as it crosses rock ledges, slickrock, and cobbles. (In the wash, the right fork signed for Behind the Rocks loops back toward the trailhead, but it's a long, laborious ride.)

Cross Hunters Canyon wash and proceed slightly uphill. After 0.5 mile, you come to the signed 0.5-mile-long spur road that accesses the 0.5-mile-long hike to Pritchett Arch. Have lunch at the rock span and preview the route's remaining miles.

After 1 mile of sandy doubletrack, you must climb a short, difficult pitch called Yellow Hill to the brink of White Knuckle Hill. Spectators hover like vultures during the annual Red Rock Jeep Safari on Easter weekend while four-wheelers defy mechanical capabilities by creeping over improbable ledges.

As the canyon widens upon descending, stay right, round more switchbacks, leap off more ledges, and drop into the sand and cobble creek bed of Pritchett Canyon. A 3-mile bump-and-grind takes you down the dry stream to the gate marking private property. Buck up and tip your helmet graciously.

RIDE 89 *WHITE RIM TRAIL*

The White Rim Trail is the granddaddy of multi-day mountain bike tours in the Colorado Plateau, for in few other places is the sense of open space as lucid and overwhelming. Scenic beauty is everywhere along the White Rim and is largely the product of erosion by water. Water laid down the thick sedimentary framework 200 to 300 million years ago and in most recent geologic time has attempted to strip that framework bare. The Colorado and Green Rivers are the master sculptors of Canyonlands' Island in the Sky District by roughing out its V-shaped terraced highland. But rain and groundwater are the artisans by shaping blocks of stone with both intricate detail and brash form.

The route is made possible by the erosionally resistant White Rim sandstone, a frosting layer in the otherwise ruddy geologic wedding cake of the Island in the Sky District. The White Rim's bench-forming nature, located mid-level in the district's 2,000-foot stratigraphic profile, allows the cyclist to penetrate a land of gross positive and negative relief. Above the Rim, headward erosion makes easy work of denuding the sedimentary stack until it reaches the strong-arm Wingate Sandstone, which resists attack with 400-foot-tall bulwarks of rusty stone. Below, a landscape of sheer and overhanging cliffs

RIDE 89 WHITE RIM TRAIL

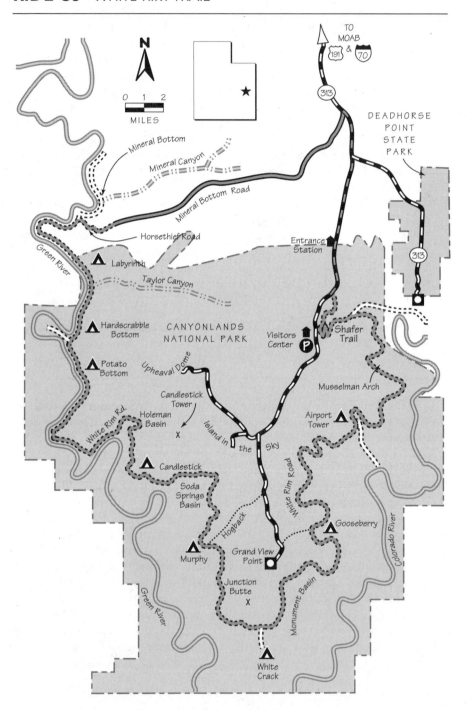

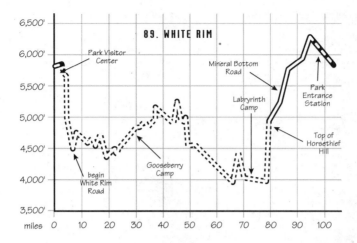

capped by the White Rim appears to have been stamped by a giant's cookie cutter.

To fully appreciate the White Rim Trail means embarking on a three- to four-day trip with stays in designated camping areas along the way. Some elite bikers are quick to boast of knocking off the White Rim in a single day, but they are missing the point. A White Rim trip is more than pounding out an off-road century; you can do that anywhere. You'll want the extra time to bond with the desert, to feel its pulse, and revere its wonderment.

General location: The White Rim Road is located in the Island in the Sky District of Canyonlands National Park, 33 miles west of Moab.

Distance: 100.5-mile loop.

Tread: 10.2 miles of pavement; 12.9 miles of light-duty dirt road; and 77.4 miles of four-wheel-drive roads. Some sections may be harder and slower for a support vehicle than for a bike.

Aerobic level: Moderate as a three- to four-day vehicle-supported trip with shared driving duties; moderate to strenuous as a multi-day vehicle-supported trip but where you pedal the whole way; strenuous to extreme as a multi-day, self-supported trip. A single-day trip is an incomprehensible feat for the average biker and one that shatters the difficulty scale.

Three significant climbs will be encountered: Murphy Hogback and Hardscrabble Hill on the White Rim Trail (proper) and the formidable Shafer Trail or Horsethief Trail switchbacks at either end. Depending on your direction of travel, you'll descend one and ascend the other; both are despairingly steep.

Technical difficulty: Level 3 to 4. The White Rim Trail varies between packed and loose sediment that is often rock-studded and rutted or has pavement bedrock. Murphy Hogback and Hardscrabble Hill are technical level 4 because of steep grades and eroded conditions. Both the Shafer Trail and Horsethief Trail can have loose, eroded tread, but it is their steepness that makes them legendary.

The ever-present Wingate
Sandstone forms fortress
walls above the White
Rim Trail.

Elevation change: The route's highest elevation of 6,000 feet is along the paved Island in the Sky Road. The route dips to 3,900 feet where it parallels the Green River at Potato Bottom. Over the course of the trip, expect to gain approximately 3,000 feet with about half of that occurring while chugging up either the Shafer Trail or Horsethief Trail, depending on direction of travel.

Season: Like all Canyon Country rides, spring (late March through May) and fall (September through October) offer the most moderate temperatures. The White Rim can be snowbound and impassable during the winter and unbearably hot during midsummer. Be prepared for sudden changes in weather at all times of the year. Insects can become a nuisance by late May and can make an otherwise enjoyable trip miserable.

Services: There is no drinking water or services along this route. Pack all necessities and luxuries in your support vehicle or on your bike. Vehicle and bicycle campers are restricted to designated camping sites (outhouses only). All overnight trips require a permit (see "Notes"). All visitor services and provisions are found in Moab.

Hazards: The lack of water is the single greatest limitation on the White Rim. The Park Service does not make water available for bike tour groups at the visitor center, so pack along all you will need. Plan on each person consuming one gallon per day *minimum* plus additional supplies for cooking and cleaning. Do not rely on sandstone potholes as a water source after rainstorms. Since there is very little shade, carry adequate sun protection.

During wet conditions, portions of the route may become quite muddy, especially on the Green River bottomlands. All support vehicles should be high clearance and equipped with four-wheel-drive, a full-size spare tire, and a sturdy jack.

Rescue index: Most bike groups have support vehicles, so help is usually not far away. Park rangers patrol the White Rim, but not on a regular basis. Numerous hiking trails connect the White Rim with the high rim overlooks above. Two key foot routes are Gooseberry Trail (on the east side) and Murphy Trail (on the west side). The park can arrange for helicopter rescue in the event of serious injury. (Expect to pay a premium price.) Report all injuries to the Island in the Sky Visitor Center.

Land status: Canyonlands National Park (Island in the Sky District) and Bureau of Land Management (Moab Field Office).

Maps: USGS Bowknot Bend, Horsethief Canyon, Mineral Canyon, Monument Basin, Musselman Arch, The Knoll, Turks Head, and Upheaval Dome, Utah; USGS 1:62,500 scale topographic map: Canyonlands National Park; and USGS 1:100,000 metric topographic series: Hanksville, La Sal, Moab, and San Rafael Desert, Utah.

Access: From the center of Moab, travel north on U.S. Highway 191 for 11 miles. Turn left on Utah State Highway 313 and drive 21.6 miles to the Island in the Sky Visitor Center. (An overnight parking area is less than 0.5 mile to the south.) To knock off 9 miles of pavement and nearly 13 miles of tedious dirt road, shuttle a vehicle to the top of the Horsethief Trail switchbacks, if riding clockwise.)

Notes on the trail: First some fine print. Permits are required for all overnight stays in the backcountry, including bicycle and vehicle camping. Canyonlands charges a non-refundable advance reservation fee of $25 per group for bicycle and vehicle campers. In addition, an entrance fee is required: $10 per vehicle or $5 per bicyclist. Group size in the Island in the Sky District is limited to 15 people and 3 vehicles. All group members must be present for a regulation talk prior to trip departure.

Reservation requests are accepted no earlier than the second Monday in July for the following year. (It would behoove you to plan and apply well in advance. Competition for White Rim trips is high, and weekends in April and May book quickly.) All requests must be mailed or faxed. Reservations may not be made by phone. Use the application form or supply all the necessary information in a letter of intent: trip leader name and phone number, dates and campsites with alternates, number of people in the group, and the description of vehicles with license plate numbers entering the park. Include your method of payment with your reservation request: check, money order, or credit card. Mail or fax your reservation request to Canyonlands National Park Reservation Office, 2282 South West Resource Boulevard, Moab, UT, 84532, 435-259-4285. Reservation office staff are available by phone to answer questions and assist trip planning Monday through Friday 8 A.M. to 12:30 P.M., (MST) at 435-259-4351 (and until 4 P.M. if work load permits). Additional information and a reservation application form can be found on the Canyonlands web site at http://www.nps.gov/cany

Pets are not allowed in the backcountry. Wood fires are prohibited. Use a gas stove or charcoal with a fire pan. All ashes (and trash) *must* be packed out. Bicycles are vehicles and must stay on the White Rim Trail and on designated spur roads. Cross-country travel is strictly prohibited. When hiking, stay to trails, slickrock, or sandy washes to avoid trampling cryptobiotic soils. Practice minimum impact techniques at all times. Do not disturb sites of antiquity or collect artifacts.

When vehicle-supported, it makes little difference which direction you ride, although many trips prefer clockwise. Unless you're hell-bent on riding the complete century, consider leaving a shuttle vehicle at the top of the Horsethief Trail switchbacks and embarking from the junction with UT 313. You'll warmup with 9 miles of pavement to the visitor center for your regulation talk prior to descending the Shafer Trail and avoid the tedious washboarded miles across the mesa at the end. But remember, each biker and the support vehicle must pay the park entrance fee. If you tackle the route self-supported, you may prefer to travel counterclockwise, which puts 9 miles of pavement and 13 miles of otherwise mundane dirt road first. But you'll face the dreaded Shafer Trail and no water sources at the end of your trip.

The following notes take a clockwise approach beginning at the visitor center. Head north 1 mile and fork right on the Shafer Trail. Although you've just begun your century ride, pause a long while atop the Shafer Trail to assimilate the gravity of your surroundings. In a moment's time, you'll descend 1,000 feet from the park's rim to the White Rim on the precariously placed road. Originally, the Shafer Trail was nothing but a cattle path; then in the 1950s it was upgraded—a generous word—to vehicular standards. Now, it serves as gateway, or exit, to this classic Canyon Country tour.

Below the switchbacks, fork right on the White Rim Trail (proper) where the Shafer Trail continues to the park's eastern boundary. (See Ride 84 Jughandle Loop.) Your first side trip approaches in 1.2 miles: the Gooseneck Overlook. The 0.7-mile out-and-back hike (no bikes) leads to a view of the crafty Colorado River as it makes a 180-degree bend around the photogenic mesa. Musselman Arch, 2 miles farther, is a default photo opportunity where

Spires in Monument Basin.

members regroup atop the natural span, but you must leave your bikes behind on the White Rim Road.

Easy cruising along the near level White Rim bench is interrupted by a bump separating Little Bridge and Lathrop Canyons (mile 15). Pyramid-shaped Airport Tower draws you around Lathrop Canyon and past campsites named for the butte (mile 18).

Washer Woman Arch and Monster Tower, each trying in earnest to distance themselves from the Wingate coaming, keep you in their watchful gaze as you round the first of the three incised prongs of Buck Canyon. Thereafter, a 4-mile-long horseshoe loop in the road crosses a lonely plain to Gooseberry Canyon, Trail, and Camp (mile 29). Leaving Gooseberry, the road wanders far inland from the Rim's edge for many miles. Except for the changing profile of Family Procession butte, you may find yourself engrossed with inner thoughts because startling views are wanting.

The rim draws near once more and the earth opens to a basin the color of a rich dessert (mile 33). Erosion has scooped away the White Rim and the softer, underlying Organ Rock Shale in Monument Basin leaving behind crumbs of rock that stand as frosting-capped slivers and solitary pillars. You'll salivate over the delectable views for the next several miles.

Two miles past your last view of Monument Basin, fork left on the 1.5-mile spur to White Crack (mile 37). Except for Grand View Point high above on the Island's rim, this is the one point where you can look back to where you have come from and forward to where you are headed. Southward, the park's three districts—Island in the Sky, Maze, and Needles—converge where the Colorado and Green Rivers culminate their meandering courtship at their confluence. Archaeological artifacts are widespread throughout the area. Enjoy their existence, but do not disturb them. It is morally responsible, and it is the law!

Back on route, the road passes Junction Butte, where the Green River enters stage left; then the road clips the edge of Vertigo Void (mile 40). Slither up to the edge and dangle your noggin over the rim. (Keep your bike on the road, naturally.)

For several miles the road fails to maintain a straight line as it is bullied by the shape of the land. After a descent to a wash where the Murphy Trail takes off for the rim, your heart gets a jumpstart on the warm-up approach to the insanely steep Murphy Hogback (mile 45). Painfully, but quickly, your effort is rewarded by yet another ridiculously broad view from the ridge-top camp. The drop down the other side can be exciting, especially for the designated driver.

Curl around dendritic canyons that press Soda Springs Basin back from the Green River, cap another hump in the road called Turks Pass, and pass Candlestick Camp (mile 56). It's easy to blow past Holeman Slot when you're being bombarded constantly with confounding panoramas. But if you have faith in friction, you can slip inside the confine on foot and be soothed by the beating of the desert's heart.

An hour's worth of pedaling takes you across the Green River's bottom lands and to Potato Bottom Camp (mile 67). The trail's namesake sandstone has since thinned and vanished from the rock record. Hardscrabble Hill, on the other hand, surfaces up ahead. A climb like this can make any bike trip memorable, no doubt. But after you visit the prehistoric Indian ruins and abandoned cabin from more modern days at Fort Bottom (left), you'll realize that pensiveness is an inescapable element of the White Rim. Stay right at Hardscrabble Bottom, unless you're logging in at the camp to the left.

Beyond Upheaval Canyon and Labyrinth Camp, the road passes the long spur up Taylor Canyon (mile 73), which leads to the popular rock-climbing towers of Zeus and Moses. A few miles farther you exit Canyonlands National Park and pass tamarisk-choked river bottoms to the junction with the Horsethief Trail—the coup de grâce of your White Rim tour. High fives, empathetic hugs, and photos to document your effort are in order once you conquer the climb. If you parked a vehicle here, your tour is over; otherwise, put your nose to the bar and grind out 13 tedious miles across the mesa to pavement and another 9 miles back to the visitor center.

RIDE 90 *DEADMANS TRAIL-HORSESHOE CANYON*

With a name like Deadmans Trail, one might envision terrain that is fraught with gloom and despair. You *will* pass through some of Utah's most remote and desolate backcountry on Deadmans Trail. But your destination, Horseshoe Canyon, is mystical and full of intrigue.

The canyon itself is an inspiring sight after crossing seemingly unproductive land. A spring-fed creek nourishes desert flowers, succulent grasses, and tenacious sage. Magnificent cottonwoods shade the canyon floor, and sheer sandstone walls glow with brilliant radiance. However, Horseshoe Canyon is more than a precious sanctuary amidst an arid wilderness. It hosts what many consider the most significant, and certainly most spectacular, prehistoric Indian rock art in North America. These pictographs are of the Barrier Canyon style created by an archaic Indian tribe that inhabited the area 8,000 years ago. Fremont Indians, who later inhabited central Utah between 700 A.D. and 1200 A.D., also produced rock art in this area.

Of the canyon's many murals, the Great Gallery is the most bewildering. The panel features dozens of well-preserved, life-size pictographs of armless, mummy-shaped humanoids with either blank faces or hollow, sunken eyes plus box-shaped antelopes and indecipherable shapes. Many figures are adorned with intricate shields and breastplates. Are these mysterious paintings the exaltation of deities? Are they the souls of the dead floating to the heavens,

RIDE 90 DEADMANS TRAIL-HORSESHOE CANYON

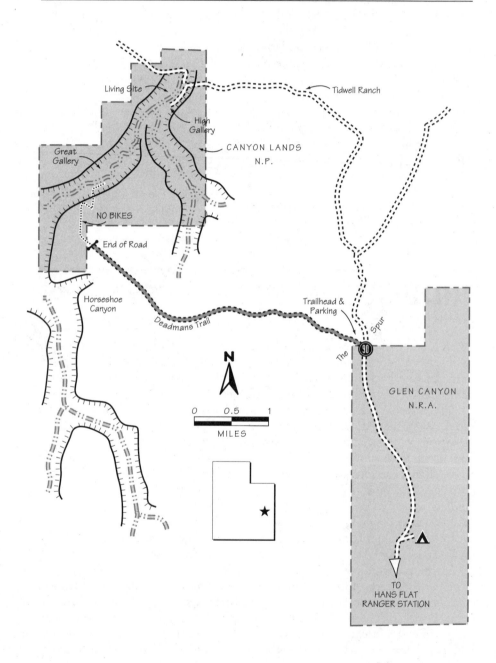

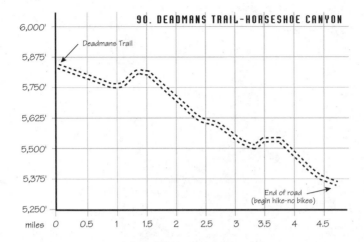

visitors from another world, demons bearing omens, or simply artistic expressions? Whatever the answer, the images will leave you spellbound.

To reach the Great Gallery you must hike 3 miles out-and-back on a primitive footpath across slickrock and sand, so wear shoes that are suitable for biking and hiking.

General location: 80 miles southwest of Green River or 65 miles northeast of Hanksville.

Distance: 9 miles out-and-back with a 3 mile out-and-back hike.

Tread: Sand and rock doubletracks.

Aerobic level: Moderate. Low hills, with sand and rock stretches on the doubletrack. The 3-mile, round-trip hike crosses slickrock and descends to a sandy wash.

Technical difficulty: Level 3. Variably sandy and rocky doubletrack with a couple of short, steep, rough sections thrown in for good measure. The hiking trail crosses slickrock and descends steeply to a sand wash.

Elevation change: Deadmans Trail begins at 5,760 feet and ends at 5,360 feet. Adding in the road's undulations, total elevation gain is about 700 feet, the majority of which is on the way out. The hike into Horseshoe Canyon descends about 600 feet over its 1.5-mile length.

Season: Spring (March into June) and fall (September through October). Temperatures can cap the century mark and bugs can be annoying by June. Always carry plenty of water both on the bike and in the car, regardless of the season.

Services: There are no services or drinking water at Hans Flat Ranger Station or throughout the Maze, and all surface waters should be purified. Camping is restricted to designated primitive sites within the National Park (no outhouses or water taps). Limited visitor services (motels, food, and gasoline) are available at Hanksville, located 65 miles west and south of Hans Flat. Green

A portion of the Great
Gallery in Horseshoe
Canyon.

River, 80 miles away, has more extensive services. The closest bike shop is in
Price.

Hazards: This is one of the most remote areas of Utah, so preparedness is
prerequisite. The light-duty dirt road to Hans Flat Ranger Station is suitable
for passenger cars when dry (rough locally), but may be impassable when wet.
The road from Hans Flat to the Deadmans Trailhead is graded but still
necessitates high-clearance. Other four-wheel-drive roads in the Maze are
extremely difficult, present considerable risk of vehicle damage, and should
not be attempted by inexperienced drivers. You should be prepared to make
basic road and vehicle repairs and should carry the following items: a full-size
spare tire, extra gasoline, high-lift jack, shovel, extra water, plus a generous
helping of common sense. Sunscreen and insect repellent are recommended.

The hike to Horseshoe Canyon crosses open slickrock. Wear shoes that are
good for desert biking and hiking.

Rescue index: Visitors are not common in Horseshoe Canyon and less so along the Deadmans Trail. Hans Flat Ranger Station has cell phone communication but no pay phone. Green River has a medical clinic, but it is 80 miles and several hours away by vehicle.

Land status: Canyonlands National Park (Maze District).

Maps: USGS Head Spur and Sugarloaf Butte, Utah.

Access: From Green River, travel 12 miles west on Interstate 70, take Exit 147 for Hanksville and Capitol Reef, and travel 25 miles south on Utah State Highway 24. Between mileposts 137 and 136, turn left for the Maze, etc. (0.5 mile south of the Goblin Valley/Temple Mountain junction, or about 20 miles north of Hanksville). Take the light-duty dirt road 25 miles and fork right for "Hans Flat Ranger Station 21." (The left fork is signed "Horseshoe Canyon Foot Trail 7.") Fork left after 7 miles for French Spring 15 and Flint Trail 25 (Ekker Ranch is the right fork) and travel 14 miles to Hans Flat Ranger Station. *Note: The graded access road is suitable for passenger cars when dry (rough locally) but can be impassable when wet.*

From Hans Flat, travel north (past the outhouses) 12.5 miles on a doubletrack signed "Horseshoe Canyon 22." (A high-clearance vehicle is required). Park at the junction signed for Deadmans Trail.

Notes on the trail: Backcountry permits are required for all overnight stays within Canyonlands National Park and adjoining Glen Canyon National Recreation Area: $25 for vehicle and bicycle campers and $10 for backpackers. Permits are issued to walk-ins, on a space-available basis, and to confirmed reservation holders. (Call Canyonlands National Park at 435-259-4351 for reservations information.) Vehicle and bicycle campers must provide their own washable, reusable toilet system.

Archaeological sites are protected by federal law. Do not touch rock art because it can cause irreversible damage. Bikes are not allowed on the foot trail into Horseshoe Canyon. Carry a cable lock if you are hesitant about leaving your bike unattended while hiking into the Maze.

Take the undulating sand and rock doubletrack west for Deadmans Trail across a high desert plateau. Knolls striped with tan, orange, and purple sediments enliven such desolation. Monumental buttes and canyons entombed by white sandstone spark curiosity and justify continued pursuit.

After 4.5 miles, the road ends at a small parking area signed "Deadmans Trail, Canyon Bottom 1.5, no vehicles or dogs allowed." (Carry a cable lock if you are hesitant about leaving your bike unattended.) Hike the primitive foot trail northwest toward a widening canyon. Posts and cairns periodically mark the way. You must scramble over steep slopes of barren slickrock before you pass through a wire fence and drop down a boulder-ridden path to the canyon. Follow the braided path north and downstream about 0.5 mile to the Great Gallery. Hike 2 miles more to view additional rock art sites.

The panel here is flooded with sunlight during the morning hours but is draped in shadow by early afternoon. Photographers might use a polarizing lens when the panel is exposed to direct sunlight and a tripod when it's in shadow.

You can make this a strenuous, 34-mile, out-and-back trip by starting at the Hans Flat Ranger Station. You will encounter easy cruising on the way out but steady climbing on the return (1,000-foot gain) and possibly deep sand. Budget all day and a gallon of water for the trip.

RIDE 91 *PANORAMA POINT*

From atop the 600-foot-tall Orange Cliffs, Panorama Point affords dizzying views of the Maze District of Canyonlands National Park. The Maze is replete with confusing and hostile terrain; its tortuous topography is an inverted and tangled wilderness of sandstone canyons that appear impossible to reconnoiter. Around nearly every bend in its web of convoluted canyons stands a wall. Direct cross-country travel is futile and becomes a matter of trial and error. Although Moab is less than 50 miles away by line of sight, Canyonlands' four districts, Island in the Sky, Needles, Rivers, and Maze, force the wayward traveler to circumnavigate by hundreds of miles.

Panorama Point extends from the North Point mesa like a thumb protruding from a hand. The North Point mesa in turn stems from an alcove-rimmed plateau like an arm from a contortionist's body. Over millions of years, the relentless process of headward erosion has gnawed away at the plateau's edge, throwing out a promontory here and there. Elaterite, Bagpipe, and Ekker buttes, along with other outlying spires and freestanding chimneys, are remnants of the once all-encompassing plateau that have since been relegated to solitary isolation.

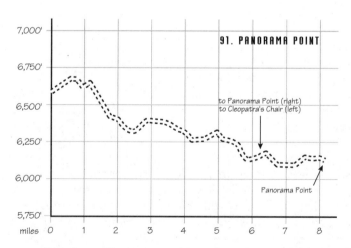

RIDE 91 PANORAMA POINT

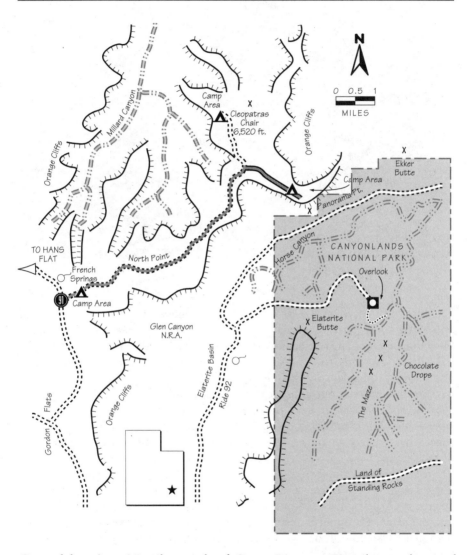

General location: 85 miles south of Green River or 70 miles northeast of Hanksville.

Distance: 16.5 miles out-and-back.

Tread: Packed and soft sand with sporadic rocks and pavement sandstone.

Aerobic level: Moderate. Most of the climbing is on the return leg, where drift sand and loose tread can sap your energy. The optional spur to Cleopatra's Chair is also moderate.

Rimrocked at Panorama Point.

Technical difficulty: Level 2 to 4. You'll have to plow through some drift sand and battle a few patches of rocks, but the route is non-threatening overall.

Elevation change: The trailhead/parking area is at 6,600 feet. The North Point road descends gently to Panorama Point at 6,160 feet. Accounting for a few undulations, total elevation gain is about 800 feet. (Tack on an extra 300-foot gain for the optional out-and-back trip to Cleopatra's Chair.)

Season: Spring (March into June) and fall (September through October). Midsummer temperatures can cap 100 degrees and bugs can be annoying by June. Always carry plenty of water both on the bike and in the car, regardless of the season.

Services: There are no services or drinking water at Hans Flat Ranger Station nor throughout the Maze, and all surface waters should be purified. French Spring, near the trailhead, flows perennially from a pipe but might be purified just the same. Camping is restricted to designated primitive sites within the National Park (no outhouses or water taps). Limited visitor services (motels, food, and gasoline) are available at Hanksville, located 65 miles west and south of Hans Flat. Green River, 80 miles from Hans Flat, has more extensive services. The closest bike shop is in Price over 140 miles away.

Hazards: The Maze District is one of the most remote areas of Utah, so preparedness is prerequisite. The light-duty dirt road to Hans Flat Ranger Station is suitable for passenger cars when dry (rough locally), but may be impassable when wet. The road from Hans Flat to the trailhead may require high-clearance because of sporadic pavement bedrock. Other four-wheel-drive roads in the Maze are extremely difficult, present considerable risk of vehicle damage, and should not be attempted by inexperienced drivers. You should be prepared to make basic road and vehicle repairs and should carry the following items: a full-size spare tire, extra gasoline, high-lift jack, shovel, extra water, plus a generous helping of common sense. Sunscreen is mandatory and insect repellent is recommended.

Rescue index: Panorama Point is seldom visited. Hans Flat Ranger Station, located 2.5 miles from the trailhead, has cell phone communication but no pay phone. Green River has a medical clinic, but it is over 100 miles and several hours away by vehicle.

Land status: Canyonlands National Park (Maze District) and Glen Canyon National Recreation Area.

Maps: USGS Cleopatra's Chair, Elaterite Butte, and Gordan Flats, Utah.

Access: From Green River, travel 12 miles west on Interstate 70, take Exit 147 for Hanksville and Capitol Reef, and travel 25 miles south on Utah State Highway 24. Between mileposts 137 and 136, turn left for the Maze, etc. (0.5 mile south of the Goblin Valley/Temple Mountain junction, or about 20 miles north of Hanksville). Take the graded dirt road 25 miles and fork right for "Hans Flat Ranger Station 21." (The left fork is signed "Horseshoe Canyon Foot Trail 7.") Fork left after 7 miles for French Spring 15 and Flint Trail 25 (Ekker Ranch is the right fork) and travel 14 miles to Hans Flat Ranger Station. *Note: The access road is suitable for passenger cars when dry (rough locally) but may be impassable when wet.*

From Hans Flat, travel southeast toward the Flint Trail. After 2 miles, pass the left fork leading to French Spring (a reliable water source). Immediately thereafter, park near the junction with the North Point Road signed for Panorama Point and Cleopatra's Chair.

Notes on the trail: Backcountry permits are required for all overnight stays within the Maze District: $25 for vehicle and bicycle campers and $10 for backpackers. Permits are issued to walk-ins, on a space-available basis, and to confirmed reservation holders. (Call Canyonlands National Park at 435-259-4351 for reservations information.) Vehicle and bicycle campers must provide their own washable, reusable toilet system. Bikes are not allowed on any foot trails.

From the parking area, pedal northward on the North Point Road across the high desert peninsula speckled with sage, juniper, and pinyon. Through the scattered foliage are distant views of the Orange Cliffs (Wingate Sandstone), which rim the plateau with vertical scarps.

After 6.5 miles, fork right following a sign for Panorama Point. You'll reach the Point after another 1.5 miles of near-level pedaling. You could spend hours out here dangling your feet from the rim and staring out across the vast emptiness. When you've had your fill of solitude and scenery, head back to the trailhead. To extend the ride an extra 4 miles, fork right to visit Cleopatra's

Chair. The tread is packed and loose sand, punctuated with loose rocks and pavement bedrock (technical level 3 to 4). The road ends on the butte's south side. Stash your bike and hike the trail to the overlook of Millard Canyon for more jaw-dropping views. Return to the junction for Panorama Point and then make the 6.5-mile gradual but tedious climb back to the parking area.

RIDE 92 *THE MAZE OVERLOOK*

The Maze District, located just west of the Colorado River, is Canyonlands National Park at its wildest. Its name conjures up striking images of convolute topography: dead-end canyons, twisted corridors, and sandstone hallways. The Maze is Nature's jigsaw puzzle cut from sandstone.

Few regions in Utah, if not the nation, are as remote and inaccessible. To some, the Maze is a stark and inhospitable land; to others, this hostile terrain sparks intrigue and offers many earthly pleasures—solitude, silence, and challenges of self-reliance—not found within the confines of civilization.

Today recreationists visit the Maze to seek temporary liberation from urban lifestyles, but this area has a history of inhabitation by outlaws, ranchers, and miners. And long before modern cultures attempted a living or sought refuge in the Maze, ancient Native Americans prospered in the canyon bottoms. Ruins, artifacts, and rock art panels dispersed throughout the region are irreplaceable vestiges of these archaic peoples.

General location: 100 miles south of Green River or 85 miles northwest of Hanksville.

Distance: 23.5 miles out-and-back.

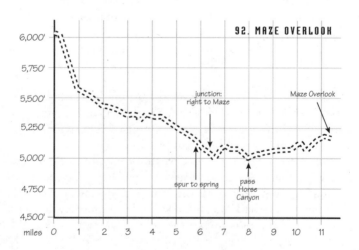

RIDE 92 THE MAZE OVERLOOK

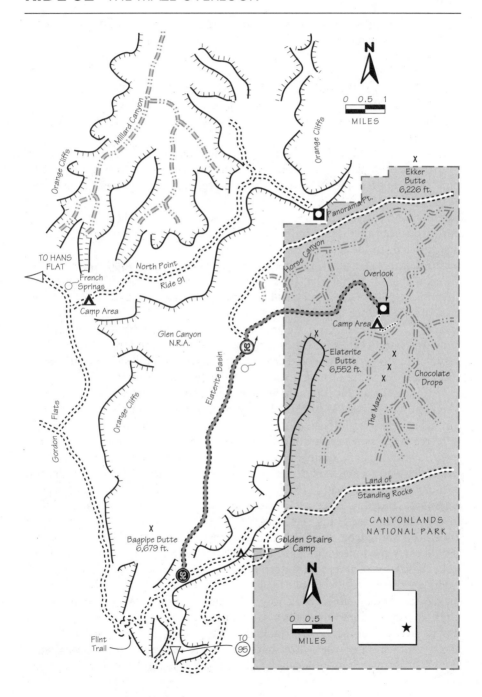

Tread: Sand and rock doubletracks.

Aerobic level: Strenuous, especially if you take the optional hike into the Maze.

Technical difficulty: Level 2 to 5. Doubletracks can have deep soft sand, rocks, and pavement outcrop (level 2 to 3). The initial descent off the mesa plummets over eroded rock ledges and is rated level 4 to 5, but it's manageable (and advised) to walk the toughest spots.

Elevation change: The trailhead is the highest elevation at 6,040 feet. The trail drops to 5,000 feet at the north end of Elaterite Basin prior to the Maze Overlook. Total elevation gain is about 1,300 feet, almost all of which is on the return leg.

Season: Spring (March into June) and fall (September through October). Midsummer temperatures can cap 100 degrees and bugs can be annoying by June. Always carry plenty of water both on the bike and in the car, regardless of the season.

Services: There are no services or drinking water at Hans Flat Ranger Station nor throughout the Maze, and all surface waters should be purified. Camping is restricted to designated primitive sites within the National Park (no outhouses or water taps). Limited visitor services (motels, food, and gasoline) are available at Hanksville, located 65 miles west and south of Hans Flat. Green River, 80 miles from Hans Flat, has more extensive services. The closest bike shop is in Price over 140 miles away.

Hazards: Do not underestimate your body's need for water. You'll need *at least* two large water bottles for the bike trip plus two more if hiking into the Maze. Have plenty of water reserved for the uphill return leg because that's when you'll need it most. Sunscreen and insect repellent are recommended.

This is one of the most remote areas of Utah, so preparedness is prerequisite. The light-duty dirt road to Hans Flat Ranger Station is suitable for passenger cars when dry (rough locally), but may be impassable when wet.

To reach the suggested trailhead, you must drive the notorious Flint Trail, a steep, switchbacking doubletrack that drops off the Orange Cliffs. Four-wheel-drive and a stalwart driver are required. The switchbacks are tight and in many places the road is one-lane wide. The Flint Trail can be impassable when wet and is subject to washout during spring thaw and after severe storms. Contact the Hans Flat Ranger Station *before* venturing onto the Flint Trail. You should be prepared to make basic road and vehicle repairs and should carry the following items: a full-size spare tire, extra gasoline, high-lift jack, shovel, extra water, plus a generous helping of common sense.

Hiking the Maze Overlook Trail to the canyons below involves crossing slickrock, wedging through narrow slots, and climbing "Moki" steps (small footholds chipped into the barren sandstone).

Rescue index: The Maze Overlook is a base camp and jump-off point for hikers venturing into the Maze, but visitors are few. Self-sufficiency is vital. Hans Flat Ranger Station, located 17 miles from the trailhead, has cell phone communication but no pay phone, and the rough Flint Trail lies in between. Green River has a medical clinic, but it is over 100 miles and one-half day away by vehicle.

Land status: Canyonlands National Park (Maze District) and Glen Canyon National Recreation Area.

Maps: USGS Clearwater Canyon, Elaterite Butte, Spanish Bottom, and Teapot Rock, Utah.

Access: From Green River, travel 12 miles west on Interstate 70, take Exit 147 for Hanksville and Capitol Reef, and travel 25 miles south on Utah State Highway 24. Between mileposts 137 and 136, turn left for the Maze, etc. (0.5 mile south of the Goblin Valley/Temple Mountain junction, or about 20 miles north of Hanksville). Take the graded dirt road 25 miles and fork right for "Hans Flat Ranger Station 21." (The left fork is signed "Horseshoe Canyon Foot Trail 7.") Fork left after 7 miles for French Spring 15 and Flint Trail 25 (Ekker Ranch is the right fork) and travel 14 miles to Hans Flat Ranger Station. *Note: The access road is suitable for passenger cars when dry (rough locally) but may be impassable when wet.*

From Hans Flat, travel 14 miles southeast following signs for the Flint Trail (high clearance is recommended). There is a pullout at the top of the Flint Trail where vehicles can turn around or lock in four-wheel-drive hubs. The Flint Trail drops 1.7 miles off the cliffs. One mile from the bottom, fork left for Golden Stairs 2, Maze Overlook 12. (The right fork leads to Utah State Highway 95, Doll House, and Standing Rocks.) The road to the Golden Stairs splits 1 mile farther; park and embark on the left fork for the Maze Overlook. (The right fork leads to the Golden Stairs Trail and campsite.)

Note: There are two roads out of the Maze: the Flint Trail/Hans Flat Road to the west and the Hite Road to the south. Although the Hite Road is only 33 miles long from this trailhead, it can take three hours or more to travel. High clearance, preferably four-wheel-drive, is required, and the rough doubletrack is painstakingly slow. Sure, the switchbacks of the Flint Trail can be daunting, but once surmounted, cross-country travel is relatively swift.

Notes on the trail: Backcountry permits are required for all overnight stays within the Maze District: $25 for vehicle and bicycle campers and $10 for backpackers. Permits are issued to walk-ins, on a space-available basis, and to confirmed reservation holders. (Call Canyonlands National Park at 435-259-4351 for reservations information.) Vehicle and bicycle campers must provide their own washable, reusable toilet system. Bikes are not allowed on the foot trail into the Maze. Carry a cable lock if you are hesitant about leaving your bike unattended while hiking into the Maze.

Take the Maze Overlook Road north and down a steep technical descent over rock ledges (technical level 4 to 5). Thereafter the doubletrack is smoother and faster, but is lined with a central berm, so pick your lane carefully. After about 5.5 miles, stay straight; the road to the right dead-ends at a spring. Drop into a wash 1 mile farther, staying right for the Maze

Overlook. (Anderson Bottom is to the left.) Cross the boundary for Canyon-lands National Park and wrap around the head of slickrock-bound Horse Canyon. Three miles ahead, around the northern point of Elaterite Butte, you come to the Maze Overlook—the route's turnaround.

To hike into the Maze, start at the trailhead to the north of the Maze Overlook. The 2-mile, out-and-back foot trail descends into the canyon bottom. En route, you'll have to cross open slickrock, wedge through cracks, and scramble down a set of "Moki" steps. Explore the canyon bottom, then return to your bike and pedal back through this romantically wild country of desert growth, redrock fortresses, and blue sky.

RIDE 93 COLORADO RIVER OVERLOOK

Saddle up the whole family and venture to an overlook of the river that has become synonymous with Canyonlands National Park—the Colorado River. The Spanish gave the river its name, which means reddish-tainted river. After a contorted run through the Island in the Sky District, the Colorado takes on a straighter course to its confluence with the Green River just out of sight downstream. But the Colorado's down-cutting temperament has not changed, for it has carved a corridor nearly 900-feet deep through varicolored sandstones. Yet again, the Colorado makes known its intention of reaching the Pacific Ocean via the shortest possible route and taking with it anything earthen that lies in its way.

Most of the route is easy pedaling on a sandy doubletrack across black-brush plains interrupted by sandstone outcrops. However, the last 2 miles cross barren rock that has eroded to a chipped surface with tiny potholes that

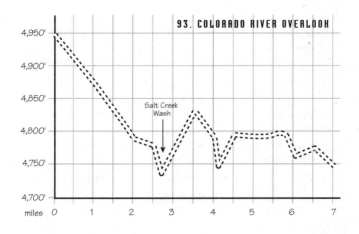

RIDE 93 COLORADO RIVER OVERLOOK

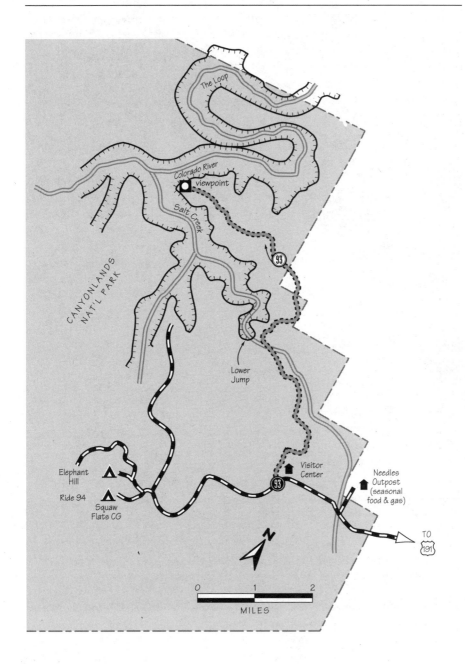

The Colorado cuts deeply into the earth's crust.

might be too rough for tag-along child trailers. Still, this is a wonderful introduction to the Needles District that ends with yet another sublime overlook of southern Utah's master sculpture.

General location: 75 miles southwest of Moab in the Needles District of Canyonlands National Park.

Distance: 14 miles out-and-back.

Tread: Sandy doubletracks with roughened slickrock.

Aerobic level: Moderate. The return leg takes a bit more effort than the ingoing leg.

Technical difficulty: Level 2 to 3. Doubletracks may have sand pockets, washboards, and ruts. The route crosses choppy slickrock near the turnaround with a few ledges thrown in for good measure (level 3).

Elevation change: The visitor center is the high point at 4,920 feet. The road undulates and descends to 4,800 feet at the turnaround. Total gain is about 650 feet.

Season: Spring (March into June) and fall (September through October). Midsummer is hot and insects may become a problem by June. Always carry plenty of water regardless of the season and use a liberal amount of sunscreen.

Services: There is no drinking water along this route. Water is available at the visitor center and at park campgrounds. Limited camping supplies, groceries, gasoline, and showers are at the Needles Outpost, located 1 mile before the visitor center. Monticello is the closest full-service town, located 50 miles from the trailhead, but it has no bike shop.

Hazards: Carry ample water and food, tools, and appropriate clothing. Use caution around cliff areas at the Colorado River Overlook.

Rescue index: The route is traveled by bikers and motorists on a regular basis, by local standards, but you may experience complete solitude at any given time. Four-wheel-drive vehicles will have a rough go over the last 2 miles. Emergency contacts can be made from the visitor center.

Land status: Canyonlands National Park (Needles District).

Maps: USGS The Loop, Utah.

Access: Drive 40 miles south of Moab or 15 miles north of Monticello on U.S. Highway 191. Between mileposts 86 and 87, take Utah State Highway 211 for 35 miles to the Needles Visitor Center, passing Newspaper Rock after 13 miles.

Notes on the trail: You must pay an entrance fee for visiting Canyonlands National Park. Within the park, mountain bikes must stay on roads that are designated open to vehicles. Bikes are prohibited on all foot trails. Carry a cable lock if you are hesitant about leaving your bike unattended while hiking to the overlook.

From the visitor center, take the doubletrack at the north side of the parking lot and follow the sign pointing left. The sandy doubletrack descends ever-so-gently across grass and black-brush prairies and past outcrops of banded sandstone. After nearly 2.5 miles, the road crosses upper Salt Creek wash and

Newspaper Rock—a sandstone tabloid.

bends north/right. You'll gaze into Salt Creek's incised meanders from the overlook later on. Or park at the wash and hike 0.2 mile to the Lower Jump where the wash pours over a 100-foot ledge. (Biking is not allowed.)

The road rises uphill and then gradually bends west to cross a broad plain of black brush. Nearly 5 miles from the visitor center, the sandy doubletrack ends on the fringe of barren rock. Vehicles with low clearance often park here. Now your route crosses slickrock that has been eroded to tiny white caps and solution holes that are too rough to pedal over while seated. To call the sandstone slickrock would be misleading because it's far from smooth; chicken-pox rock might be more appropriate. More than a mile of chattering takes you to the route's end and to the overlook of the 900-foot-deep Colorado River gorge. The "wow-factor" increases if you scramble out across the rocks, but be cautious.

Upstream, the Colorado exits a 6-mile-long gooseneck meander around The Loop; a few miles downstream, it merges with the Green River. Chesler Park to the south is a silent city of spire-capped temples, and the Abajo Mountains are one of three mountainous islands poking up from the desert floor. To the northwest, bikers on the White Rim Trail are no doubt gazing your way from White Crack Camp. Remember that trivial wash you crossed earlier. Here Salt Creek has flexed its erosional muscle and carved a huge twisting chasm that flows intermittently to the Colorado.

The return is simply a redo of your incoming tracks, but you can expect a bit more uphill component. A westerly breeze at your back will help make easy work of the miles.

RIDE 94 *CONFLUENCE OVERLOOK*

The confluence of the Colorado and Green rivers divide Canyonlands National Park into three districts: Island in the Sky to the north, the Maze to the west, and the Needles to the southeast. The Colorado and Green themselves comprise a fourth district called the Rivers. This route leads to a rimmed-side view of the districts' intersection.

The Needles District is a jumble of colorful rock formations eroded into a startling and diverse landscape of spires, arches, canyons, and valleys. The contrasting names of formations reflect the diversity of the land itself: Devils Kitchen and Angels Landing; Elephant Hill and Caterpillar Arch; Gothic Arch and Paul Bunyan's Potty. The route to the Confluence Overlook follows long, grassy valleys separated by fluted ridges. This route, like many of the hiking trails that lead to more remote reaches, rewards the adventurer with geologic wonders that border surrealism.

Newspaper Rock State Park, passed along the paved Needles access road, is an added bonus. Both ancient and modern Indian tribes etched petroglyphs on a tarnished sandstone alcove. It is perhaps the greatest concentration of Indian rock art at a single location on the Colorado Plateau. The Navajo call it Tse Hani or "rock that tells a story."

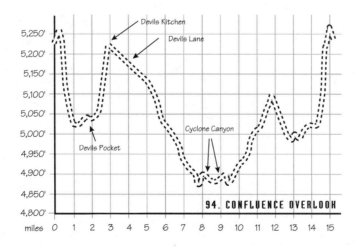

RIDE 94 CONFLUENCE OVERLOOK

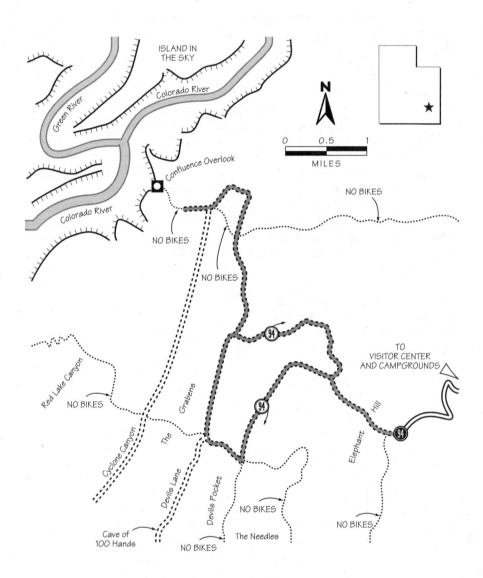

General location: 80 miles southwest of Moab in the Needles District of Canyonlands National Park.

Distance: 15 miles, combination out-and-back with loop in the middle.

Tread: Sand doubletracks with pavement bedrock. Elephant Hill is one big slickrock staircase.

Aerobic level: Strenuous because of the many sand traps and the steep, technically difficult Elephant Hill.

Technical difficulty: Level 2 to 5. Most doubletracks are harmless except for sand bogs. Elephant Hill is steep, ledgy bedrock (level 5), but it's manageable to walk the toughest parts.

Elevation change: The trailhead/parking area is at 5,200 feet. The route's lowest elevation is 4,800 feet at the Confluence Overlook. There are numerous climbs and descents along the way, so total gain is about 1,300 feet.

Season: Spring (March into June) and fall (September into November). Midsummer is hot, and insects may become a problem by June. Always carry plenty of water regardless of the season and use a liberal amount of sunscreen. Because of the excessive amount of sand on the route, the best time to ride is a day or so after it rains (but not when the route is saturated).

Services: There is no drinking water along this route. Water is available at the visitor center and at park campgrounds. The parking area/trailhead has an outhouse. Developed campgrounds (fee areas) are available 3 miles from the trailhead. Limited camping supplies, groceries, gasoline, and showers are at the Needles Outpost, located 1 mile before the visitor center. Monticello is the closest full-service town, located 55 miles from the trailhead, but it has no bike shop.

Hazards: Carry ample water and food, tools, and appropriate clothing; this is remote desert bicycling. Don't forget to use sunscreen. Elephant Hill is a highly technical, four-wheel-drive road that crosses ledgy bedrock; other sections are pocketed with drift sand. Use caution around cliff areas at the Confluence Overlook.

Rescue index: This area is not regularly patrolled. Encounters with other travelers are variable. Rescue by vehicle will be difficult because of Elephant Hill. Emergency contacts can be made at the park's visitor center, located 6 miles from the trailhead. Monticello and Moab have medical facilities.

Land status: Canyonlands National Park (Needles District).

Maps: USGS Druid Arch, Spanish Bottom, and The Loop, Utah.

Access: Drive 40 miles south of Moab or 15 miles north of Monticello on U.S. Highway 191. Between mileposts 86 and 87, take Utah State Highway 211 for 35 miles to the Needles Visitor Center, passing Newspaper Rock after 13 miles. From the visitor center, travel west 3.5 miles following signs for Elephant Hill. Before you enter campground B, turn right on a gravel road that leads 2.7 miles to the Elephant Hill Trailhead/parking area. (This road makes for a good warm-up ride if you're camping in the park.)

Notes on the trail: You must pay an entrance fee to visit Canyonlands

The Needles enclose Devils Lane.

National Park. Within the national park, mountain bikes must stay on roads that are designated open to vehicles. Bikes are prohibited on all foot trails. Carry a cable lock if you are hesitant about leaving your bike unattended while hiking to the overlook.

From the trailhead/parking area, the route begins immediately and without opportunity for warm-up with the merciless, technical climb over Elephant Hill. Attack with vigor. The descent off the sandstone fin is more confounding. (You must be an intrepid driver to negotiate this white-knuckle route by vehicle.) Remember, Elephant Hill must be tackled on the way out, too. And the backside is even longer.

At the junction for the one-way loop, stay left/west and slide unrestricted through the sandstone corridor of Devils Pocket. (You'll return on the right fork.) Judging from tire marks on the opposing walls and gouged bedrock in the road's tread, vehicles have difficulty doing the same. At the Devils Kitchen junction, turn right/west for Devils Lane and descend gradually.

At the T junction with Devils Lane, signed "Chesler Park 5" (left) and "Confluence Overlook 4" (right), fork left for an optional 2 miles out-and-back spur to the Cave of 100 Hands. You'll slog through long sand traps, but the sight of the handprint pictographs is worth the effort. Plus, you'll view the rock formations of distant Chesler Park that give the Needles District its name.

Devils Lane is one of many parallel valleys pinned between ridges known collectively as the Grabens ("graves" in German). This geologic structure is the product of parallel faulting and slumping of alternating crustal blocks. The underlying Paradox Formation (300-million-year-old evaporites) accentuated this process when the weight of overlying rocks, coupled with the uplift and tilt of the Colorado Plateau, caused this lens of subterranean salt to flow like toothpaste. This action fractured the overlying rocks and some sections sank. Further erosion by water, wind, and alternating freezing and thawing carved up a plethora of spires, towers, fins, furrows, and long valleys. The fanciful and intricately ornamented Needles District is an expression of the Cutler and Cedar Mesa formations, an interfingering of red land-derived sediment and white beach deposits, respectively.

Back at the Devils Lane junction, head north up Devils Lane to a junction signed "Confluence Overlook 3" (straight/north), "Elephant Hill 3" (right/east). The route makes a large, box-shaped U-turn to the head of Cyclone Canyon, another graben. Turn right and pedal 0.5 mile to the Confluence Trailhead, marked by a sole picnic table sheltered beneath a lowly pinyon. A 0.5 hike (marked with cairns) leads to the 800-foot-high viewpoint where the Green River joins the Colorado. The Maze District is across the river, Island in the Sky is to the north, and the Needles District is to the southeast.

Return to the junction at the north end of Devils Lane, turn left/east for Elephant Hill, and come to the junction with the one-way loop after 2 miles. Turn left again to finish the route with the cursed assault on Elephant Hill.

RIDE 95 *KOKOPELLI'S TRAIL*

Imagine mountain biking 142 miles across the remote desert backcountry, over sun-baked redrock, through deep river canyons, and past forested mountain slopes. Dream of a premier mountain-biking trail that connects two states but recognizes no border between them. Picture volunteers and private businesses banding together—without a budget, without bylaws, and without bickering. Think of federal land agencies lending feverish support, cutting through often beleaguering red tape to approve the construction of hand-built singletrack. And, envision the Hopi Indians performing a sacred dance to bless the route.

All of these "would-be" dreams came true for a dedicated group of bicycling enthusiasts under the guidance of the Colorado Plateau Mountain Bike Trail Association (COPMOBA). With the assistance of the Bureau of Land Management, Forest Service, private businesses, and dozens of volunteers, Kokopelli's Trail—a visionary trail linking Grand Junction, Colorado, with Moab, Utah—was created and built. Fueled by undying motivation and ceaseless determination, COPMOBA created a trail system that has become an inspirational model to future trail builders and a world-class adventure for those who make the pilgrimage.

RIDE 95 KOKOPELLI'S TRAIL

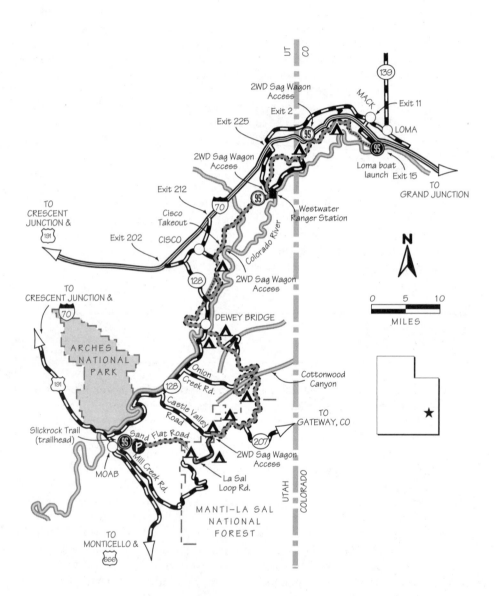

UT CO

139

2WD Sag Wagon
Access

MACK

Exit 11

Exit 2

Exit 225

95

LOMA

2WD Sag Wagon
Access

Loma boat
launch Exit 15

95

TO
GRAND JUNCTION

Exit 212

70

95

Westwater
Ranger Station

TO
CRESCENT
JUNCTION &
191

Cisco
Takeout

Exit 202

CISCO

Colorado River

128

2WD Sag Wagon
Access

TO
CRESCENT JUNCTION &
70

DEWEY BRIDGE

N

0   5   10

MILES

ARCHES
NATIONAL
PARK

191

Onion

Creek Rd.

128

Cottonwood
Canyon

Castle Valley

Road

TO
GATEWAY, CO

207

Slickrock Trail
(trailhead)

95

Sand Flat Road

P

TO
MONTICELLO &
666

MOAB

Mill Creek Rd.

2WD Sag Wagon
Access

La Sal
Loop Rd.

MANTI–LA SAL
NATIONAL
FOREST

UTAH

COLORADO

★

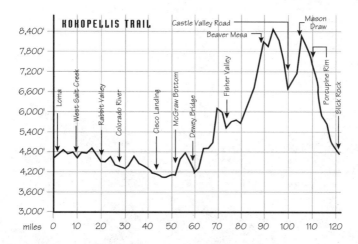

COPMOBA asserts that "mountain biking is a vehicle to promote low-impact outdoor recreation, natural history education, bike safety, and land use ethics on the Colorado Plateau. We believe mountain biking is not a fad; it's the future because it combines fun, fitness, and fantastic scenery—always with an eye on protecting the land we love."

Kokopelli's Trail, like the mystical humpbacked flute player of Hopi legend, wanders across the Colorado Plateau, crossing deserts, canyons, and mountainsides along the way. The trail is 142 miles of Canyon Country travel at its best. The route combines all aspects of mountain-bike travel from improved dirt roads, to rugged four-wheel-drive roads, to exacting singletracks. There's even some slickrock thrown in for good measure.

There are three approaches to riding Kokopelli's Trail: self-supported by packing all your gear on your bike; using one support vehicle that meets you at the end of each section (this includes being catered by a tour outfitter); or using two vehicles and configuring shuttles each day for each section.

Regardless, Kokopelli's is typically ridden as a six-day tour, based largely on convenient vehicle-access points and camping areas. You can shorten your tour a day by splitting section 5 and tacking it to the previous and following sections. This will be necessary if your support vehicle is a passenger car because via the Onion Creek Road may be too rough. All other access points are by way of paved or gravel roads suitable for passenger cars.

General location: Kokopelli's Trail begins at Loma, Colorado (15 miles west of Grand Junction), and ends in Moab, Utah (or vice versa, since it can be ridden in either direction).

Distance: 142 miles point-to-point. Section 1: Loma Boat Launch to Rabbit Valley—21 miles. Section 2: Rabbit Valley to Cisco Boat Landing—37 miles. Section 3: Cisco Boat Landing to Dewey Bridge—19 miles. Section 4: Dewey Bridge to Fisher Valley—18 miles. Section 5: Fisher Valley to Castle Valley—23 miles. Section 6: Castle Valley to Moab—24 miles.

The Colorado River—lifeblood of the Intermountain West. PHOTO COURTESY OF COPMOBA.

Tread: You name it and Kokopelli's delivers it. The route offers every type of desert riding medium from gravel to four-wheel-drive roads and from singletrack to slickrock. You'll face the whole gamut on many sections.

Aerobic level: Six days in the saddle averaging 24 miles per day is nothing to scoff at, given the often rough and sandy conditions. If you're bike-packing and hauling all your gear, this is an Olympic-caliber event and you deserve a gold medal. Mortals with vehicle support will still rate Kokopelli's as strenuous. If you share the driving duties, you can knock down the difficulty a half level.

Technical difficulty: Level 2 to 4. Most notable are the miles of sand and rock singletracks on Section 1 (level 2 to 4); the Sahara-size sand traps on section 3 (level 4 to 5); the rough descents and climbs through the Cottonwood Canyons on section 4 (level 3 to 4); and the jackhammer descents along eroded doubletracks on section 6 (level 3 to 4).

Elevation change: The elevation of the Loma Trailhead is 4,460 feet; the elevation of the Slickrock Bike Trail in Moab is 4,600. You'll reach the highest elevation of 8,500 feet between Beaver and Fisher Mesas. Total elevation gain greatly exceeds net elevation by thousands of feet, for the route crosses canyons, tops mesas, climbs the flanks of the La Sal Mountains, and drops back to the desert over its lengthy course.

Season: Early spring (March through mid-May) and fall (September through October) are the best times of the year to plan a Kokopelli's trip. Temperatures during midsummer can cap 100 degrees, and insects can be bothersome by June. Snow may close high elevation segments during early spring and late fall. Contact the BLM and Forest Service for current trail conditions.

Services: Grand Junction and Moab offer all visitor services, including bike shops. Both cities have medical facilities. Along the route, services are essentially nonexistent. Although Kokopelli's Trail passes near Cisco, this railside town site does not offer any services. So, pack in all necessities and pack out all leftovers.

Hazards: Lack of preparedness and lack of water are the two greatest hazards faced on Kokopelli's Trail. Riders should be well equipped both on bike and in support vehicles for all emergencies. Do not skimp on water consumption. The combination of strenuous activity, dry climate, and warm temperatures can cause dehydration and heat exhaustion. Carry sufficient water supplies on the bike and in the vehicle if supported, and be aware of water sources along the route. Conversely, high elevations and cool temperatures can cause hypothermia. Pack along clothes that provide good thermal insulation and that dry fast. Rainstorms may occur, especially at higher elevations, so carry rain gear.

Portions of the route are rough and technical. Honestly assess both your physical fitness and skill level before you embark on this ride. If you're riding as part of a group, remember the old adage about the weak link in the chain.

Rescue index: Much of Kokopelli's allure lies in its remoteness, which means emergency contacts and assistance are few and far between. A telephone *might* be found at the Westwater Ranger Station (seasonal) or at a residence in Cisco. The trail crosses several roadways, but motorists are not common. Remember, self-sufficiency is the key. Medical facilities are located in Moab and Grand Junction.

Land status: Bureau of Land Management (Moab Field Office and Grand Junction Field Office), Manti-La Sal National Forest (Moab-Monticello Ranger District), and private property.

Maps: USGS (east to west): Mack and Ruby Canyon, Colorado; Bitter Creek Well and Westwater, Utah/Colorado; Agate, Big Triangle, Cisco, Dewey, Blue Chief Mesa, Fisher Valley, Mount Waas, Warner Lake, Rill Creek, and Moab, Utah; USGS 1:100,000 scale topographic series: Grand Junction, Colorado; Westwater and Moab, Utah.

Access: Eastern Trailhead (Loma): From Interstate 70, take Exit 15 for Loma, cross to the south, and turn east away from the Port of Entry. The Loma Boat Launch (parking area) is a short distance down the gravel road.

Western Trailhead (Slickrock Bike Trail, Moab): From the intersection of Main and Center Streets, travel east to 400 East and turn right. Turn left after 0.4 mile on Mill Creek Drive; then 0.5 mile farther, stay straight on Sand Flats Road (near the cemetery) where Mill Creek bends right/south. The Slickrock Bike Trail parking area is 0.7 mile past the Sand Flats Recreation Area entrance station (fee required).

Rabbit Valley (Section 1 to 2): From I-70, take Exit 2 (Colorado) for Rabbit Valley and look for the parking area in just under 0.3 mile. The trail enters a bit farther down the road.

Cisco Boat Landing (Section 2 to 3): From I-70, take Exit 202 (Utah) and follow Utah State Highway 128. (Exit 212 provides access via a gravel road.) Where the highway turns right to Moab, continue straight for Cisco. Turn right on Pumphouse Road upon entering Cisco and after 2.8 miles fork left at a junction signed for Cisco Boat Landing and Fish Ford. Travel 0.9 mile, cross

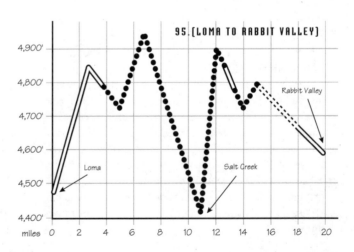

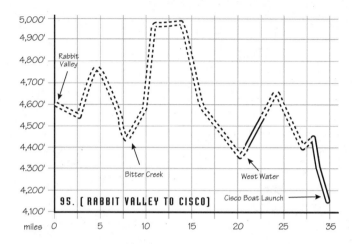

95. [RABBIT VALLEY TO CISCO]

the bridge, and fork left away from the boat launch which is to the right. Park in the area provided west of the cattle guard. From Moab, travel 43 miles on UT 128 to Cisco and proceed as above.

Dewey Bridge (Section 3 to 4): Follow the access for Cisco but continue south on UT 128 toward Moab for 12 miles to the Colorado River crossing. Dewey Bridge is about 28 miles northeast along UT 128 from the intersection with U.S. Highway 191 just north of Moab.

Fisher Valley (Section 4 to 5): Access is via the Onion Creek Road off UT 128 located 10 miles southwest of Dewey Bridge or 18 miles northeast of the intersection with US 191 just north of Moab. This 10-mile-long access road crosses Onion Creek two dozen times and may not be suitable for passenger cars. Alternate access is by way of Castle Valley.

Castle Valley (section 5 to 6) The Castle Valley Road turns south from UT 128 about 15 miles southwest of the Dewey Bridge or 13 miles from the

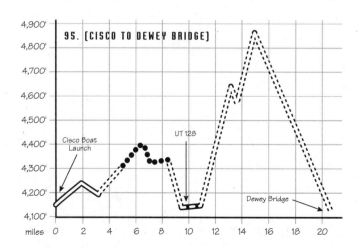

95. [CISCO TO DEWEY BRIDGE]

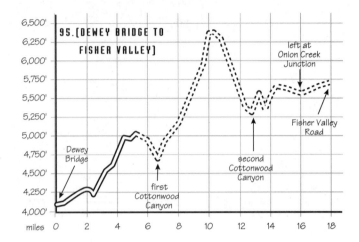

intersection with US 191 just north of Moab. Take the Castle Valley Road 11.5 miles to the junction of the paved La Sal Mountain Loop Road (right) and the Castleton Gateway Road (left). Kokopelli's Trail intersects the Castleton Gateway Road (Section 5) at the head of Fisher Valley about 8 miles to the left/east.

Sources of additional information: Colorado Plateau Mountain Bike Trail Association (COPMOBA) (See Appendix B).

Notes on the trail: Providing a turn-by-turn description of Kokopelli's Trail is exasperating. Contact the BLM or COPMOBA to obtain *Kokopelli's Trail Map*. Although the map itself is generalized, the trail log is precise. Here are some highlights.

Section 1, Loma to Rabbit Valley: Heading out from the Loma Boat Launch, the route cuts through gray and purple shales of the dinosaur-graveyard Morrison Formation as it roughly parallels I-70. The route alternates between easy four-wheel-drive roads and difficult singletrack, both of which afford

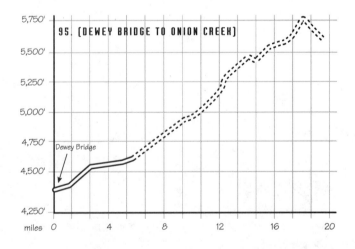

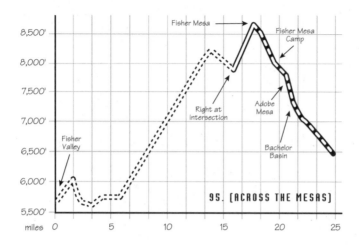

spectacular views of Horsethief Canyon, where the Colorado River flows several hundred feet below. Rim-riding and a short section of slickrock precede the difficult descent to Salt Creek.

Beyond Salt Creek, the trail follows the Colorado's bottom lands, then ascends a grueling hike-a-bike section on a rugged trail. Its summit affords splendid views of the austere Book Cliffs towering to the north while the Colorado River slips through Westwater Canyon to the southwest. Six miles of dirt and gravel roads take you to the junction providing access from I-70.

Section 2, Rabbit Valley to Cisco Boat Landing: This is the tour's longest section, but it is fast-paced because of the many miles on gravel roads and doubletracks. As you continue south toward the river, grayish-green shale gives way to pink sandstone formations, and Rabbit Valley opens up to rolling desert prairies. The route travels through the Bittercreek drainage, climbs across the rim of a mesa, and then follows the access road to the Westwater Ranger Station and parallels the railroad tracks. From a high point, an incredible view of the Priest and Nuns formation in distant Castle Valley is beautifully framed by the La Sal Mountains. Rolling hills punctuate the route as it passes near the 1950s railroad boomtown of Cisco, now reduced to a few shacks in the desert.

Section 3, Cisco Boat Landing to Dewey Bridge: Your wake up call begins with several miles of easy dirt roads that bypass Cisco. Doubletracks take over and narrow to a singletrack paralleling the river to McGraw Bottom, where Kokopelli's meets UT 128. The route then leaves the highway and heads up Yellow Jacket Canyon where gorgeous Entrada Sandstone bluffs tower above sculpted slickrock at the top of the canyon. To get there you must endure a steep, sandy, 10-mile slog through cow country. The salmon-colored formations are a godsend, but you'll wish your two-wheeler was a camel. The alternative is to stay on UT 128 for a leisurely, 10-mile stroll to the historic Dewey Suspension Bridge, sans Entrada scenery.

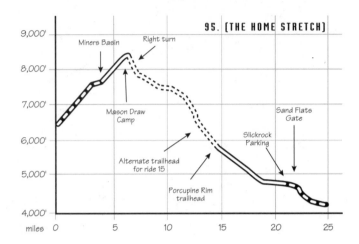

From 1916 to the mid-1980s, this span of white-washed boards and steel cables provided the only crossing of the Colorado River between Grand Junction and Moab. Presently, the historic bridge is open to foot and bike traffic; vehicles are directed to a modern bridge nearby. You are now halfway into the trail (or halfway out of, depending on your perspective).

Section 4, Dewey Bridge to Fisher Valley: This section is perhaps the most remote. From the Dewey Bridge, the route climbs on dirt roads past slickrock play areas toward Blue Chief and Sevenmile Mesas. The going gets tough where the route crosses Cottonwood Canyon with a steep and rough ascent and ensuing climb. Atop Sevenmile Mesa, you can practically retrace the entire length of Kokopelli's back toward Grand Junction. The following descent to a second canyon named Cottonwood would be welcomed if not for the increasingly technical conditions. Despite the difficult and technical conditions, the growing views of the La Sal Mountains and the opportunity to spy wildlife ease the effort. The day winds down along the edge of Fisher Valley with visions of John Wayne riding at your side through a movie scene of mountains, valleys, and redrock.

Section 5, Fisher Valley to Castle Valley: Chow down a jumbo bowl of Wheaties topped with Powerbars for breakfast because today you climb. After jumping out of Fisher Valley, the route descends briefly, then climbs for over 10 miles to Polar and North Beaver mesas flanking the lofty La Sal Mountains. Cacti and sage give way to ponderosa and aspen as you ride through the national forest. But views of Fisher and Castle Rock towers interrupting the valley below are constant reminders of the surrounding desert. A screaming descent leads down the Castleton-Gateway Road to the junction of the La Sal Mountain Loop Road.

Section 6, Castle Valley to Moab: It is a dirty trick, but one more obnoxiously steep climb (to Porcupine Draw) is between you and Moab. Fortunately, it is on pavement. The remainder of the route is generally downhill on dirt roads but hardly anticlimactic, for the views into Castle Valley from a spur on Porcupine Rim are among the best enjoyed so far. The Moab Rim on the western sky reels you down the Sand Flats Road to Moab. And if your legs have not been ground to hamburger after 140 miles, take a lap around the Slickrock Bike Trail.

RIDE 96 *THREE LAKES*

The Three Lakes loop explores the La Sal Mountains' Geyser Pass region, which is the topographic break separating the central and northern group of peaks. Although the route utilizes unavoidable dirt roads, it incorporates large sections of elusive singletracks. Be forewarned, these trails are not the buffed-out tracks of the Wasatch Range or Brian Head; these are exacting trails that test mind-set against muscle, against metal, against mountain. If you are game for a singletrack adventure, then you will score big in the La Sals.

The trip passes three small lakes: Oowah, Clark, and Warner. Each is nestled in a distinctively pristine alpine setting. Between the lakes, much of the ride threads through forests of aspen and fir that engulf a patchwork of meadows sprinkled with flowers. More impressive are the desert views that extend 100 miles from the mountain's side across Canyon Country and to distant plateaus.

General location: 30 miles east of Moab in the La Sal Mountains.

Distance: 16-mile figure-eight loop.

Tread: 8 miles of gravel and light-duty dirt roads, 8 miles of singletrack.

Aerobic level: Strenuous. Rough trails require some portaging. The ford of Mill Creek can be knee-deep in early summer. Route-finding skills are required for the sometimes-indistinct trails and less-than-obvious junctions.

Technical difficulty: Level 1 to 5. Dirt roads have variable gravel and washboards. Parts of the Trans La Sal Trail can be vicious on a bike (level 5). The trail from Oowah Lake to Warner Lake requires a short portage over blocky bedrock. You'll find the whole gamut of singletrack goodies on other sections. The ford of Mill Creek can be knee-deep, rocky, and frigid in early summer.

Elevation change: Oowah Lake sits at 8,800 feet. The first loop rises to Geyser Pass (elevation 10,600 feet) and then drops back to Oowah Lake for a gain of about 2,400 feet. The second loop rises to Warner Lake (elevation 9,360 feet), and then descends to 8,080 feet on the Oowah Lake Road for a gain of 1,280 feet. Total gain for the day is 3,680 feet.

Season: Mid-June into October, depending on seasonal snowmelt and snowfall. Daytime temperatures during midsummer are temperate and nights are crisp.

RIDE 96 THREE LAKES

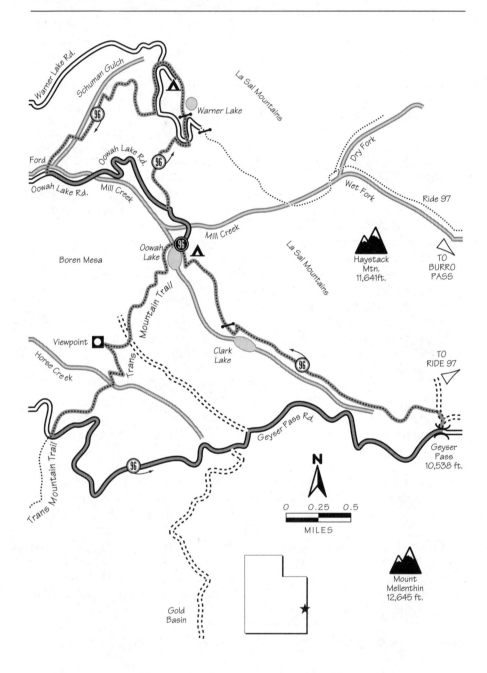

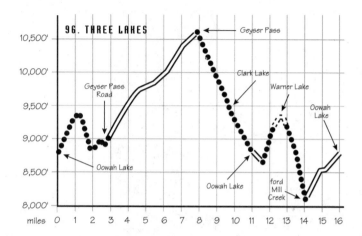

Services: Oowah Lake has a Forest Service non-fee camping area with four sites and an outhouse, but no water taps. Warner Lake is a Forest Service fee-area campground with 20 sites and water taps. No other services are available along the route and all surface waters should be purified. Moab has all visitor services, including bike shops.

Hazards: Singletracks exist in a semi-primitive condition and do not receive maintenance on a regular basis. Expect to encounter multiple obstacles, including loose and imbedded rocks, exposed roots, water bars, deadfall, narrow tread, off-camber trail, steep slopes, sharp switchbacks, and exposed bedrock, to name a few. Portions may require dismounting and portaging. Near the route's end, you must ford Mill Creek, which can be knee-deep, swift-flowing, rocky, and icy cold in early summer. Later in the summer it's calf-deep.

Rescue index: Recreationists frequent Oowah and Warner Lakes, especially on weekends and holidays. Moab has a hospital.

Land status: Manti–La Sal National Forest (Moab/Monticello Ranger District).

Maps: USGS Mount Peale, Mount Tukuhnikivatz, and Warner Lake, Utah.

Access: From the center of Moab, travel 8 miles south on U.S. Highway 191. Turn left/east at milepost 118 on County Road 126 for La Sal Mountain Road, Oowah Lake, etc. Immediately ahead at the T junction, turn right/south for La Sal Mountain Loop and pass the Red Rock Speedway. Stay left at the Pack Creek junction and rise out of Spanish Valley up a sandstone hogback. (Treat yourself to the fascinating view of mountains, stream-fed valleys, and redrock palisades from the Spanish Valley Overlook.) About 1.5 miles past the turnoff for Geyser Pass, turn right/east at Mill Creek on Forest Road 076 and travel 3 miles to Oowah Lake.

Notes on the trail: From Oowah Lake, cross the dam and start up the protracted La Sal Trans Mountain Trail. After 1 mile, the rutted trail reaches

Spindly aspens form an eerie tunnel.

the open tabletop of Boren Mesa and crosses a doubletrack. Head *due west* on the less-than-obvious singletrack toward a carsonite post tagged "trail." At the fourth marker, the trail turns left/south for a highly technical descent (technical level 5). But first, take a long quaff of Canyonlands' intoxicating view. The Moab Rim, denoted by rusty palisades topped with sandstone dollops, bounds Spanish Valley. Into the Moab Portal slips the Colorado River. The terraced land of plateaus topped with mesas, which the Colorado River carved up millions of years ago, fades to the western haze. Over 100 miles away, the horizon is shaped by lofty highlands of the Aquarius, Fish Lake, and Wasatch Plateaus, and the Henry Mountains.

As you descend the cobbles-over-cobbles trail, fork right at a signed T junction, then round a dogleg left and drop down to Horse Creek. Follow trail markers to the Geyser Pass Road. Climb steadily for 5 miles to Geyser Pass, at first on gravel and washboards, then on hard-packed dirt. At the pass, fork left/north toward "Forest Boundary" on a doubletrack marked with a bike emblem. Within 200 yards, fork left/north again on a second doubletrack. One hundred feet farther (at the interface between aspens and open slope), fork left on a game-trail-turned-singletrack. (Do *not* climb the doubletrack northward up the steep hill.)

Pass through a haunting corridor of twisted sapling aspens and cross more meadows. Drop to a marshy clearing marked by a cattle salt lick made from an old 55-gallon drum. Turn right/west (90 degrees) and head toward a young pine that has a split trunk about 3 feet from its base. Really! Avoid the temptation to cross a stream 0.6 miles ahead; instead, follow the stream down through the woods and across more meadows.

Carefully descend (or preferably walk) the switchbacks down to Clark Lake, go through the gated fence, and head west on more singletrack. After passing another cattle salt lick, the trail drops to a creek crossing filled with willows and shrubs (the crossing is actually 50 feet back uphill), and then heads north into the forest once more. The first loop culminates with a hair-raising descent full of fat-tire antics down to Oowah Lake.

If you still feel fresh, continue on the second loop to Warner Lake. Coast down the Oowah Lake Road 0.4 miles. Dump your chain into a low gear and fork right up a steep, singletrack ramp signed "Warner Lake Guard Station 1.5." At first, the serendipitous trail is ridable, but then it's clogged with bedrock and boulders that require a bike-on-shoulders portage for several hundred yards. Cross a doubletrack and continue the uphill battle to a trail registration box and carsonite post. Upon intersecting a good doubletrack (may be posted "Oowah Lake"), fork right. Up ahead you come to a junction signed "Burro Pass, Beaver Basin" (right). Follow the narrow path left/north along a wooden fence to reflective Warner Lake.

Now pedal through the campground to its entrance and turn left on a doubletrack signed "Dead End." When you break out of the aspens, there are good views of La Sals' high peaks. Here a sign tacked to an aspen (on your left) announces "Shafer Creek Trail, Mill Creek 2." Turn right/west on the faint singletrack marked with wooden directional arrows. (If you continue straight on the doubletrack, you'll loop back to the intersection for Warner Lake.)

The trail weaves northward through aspens and descends to Schuman Gulch. (Hmm, so shouldn't this be called the Schuman Gulch Trail instead of the Shafer Creek Trail?) The seldom-used path is loaded with advanced-level maneuvers plus lots of steaming guacamole that passing cattle have served up. Tortillas anyone? Ride parallel to the Schuman Gulch Creek, and then come to its confluence with Mill Creek. Shoulder your bike and trudge straight across an irrigation ditch and into the swamped-out, riparian jungle draping Mill Creek. Oowah Lake Road is atop the creek's embankment (marked with another sign for Shafer Creek Trail). Finish the adventure with 2 miles of moderate climbing to Oowah Lake.

And now for the geology lesson for the day: The La Sal Mountains, like the Abajo and Henry Mountains, were formed when chambers of magma sought the earth's surface millions of years ago. Stymied by the excessive weight and continuity of the overlying sedimentary crustal rocks, the molten mass could do no better than bow the cap rocks and spread laterally between their layers. Geologists call this a laccolithic intrusion. To the layman, the La Sals are volcano wanna-bes. Erosion, most recently by streams and glaciers, has hence exposed the massif's crystallized core and carved the range into a trio of sovereign crowns. The central cluster hosts the La Sal's monarch, Mt. Peale, which rises to 12,721 feet.

RIDE 97 *BURRO PASS*

To most fat-tire zealots who seek divinity on Moab's lithified dune field, the La Sal Mountains are little more than an idyllic backdrop to countless slickrock photographs. During spring and fall when Canyon Country is blessed with comfortable climes, and when most of us make our semi-annual pilgrimage to Utah's mountain-bike Mecca, the La Sals are largely unapproachable. Triumphant 12,000-foot-plus peaks harbor snow well into late spring, and by autumn are dusted by pre-winter flurries. A midriff of verdant forests overlain by snowy caps separates the ultramarine sky from a sun-baked mélange of sandstone fins and towers, mesas and plateaus, canyons and valleys. This is how the mountainous island is portrayed time and time again in postcards of and photo essays on Canyonlands. And this is how most bikers recall the La Sals when they are reminiscing about their Moab excursions from distant abodes.

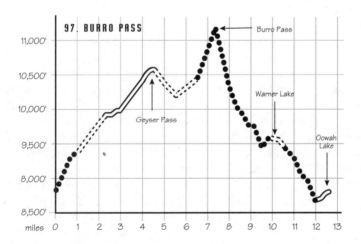

RIDE 97 BURRO PASS

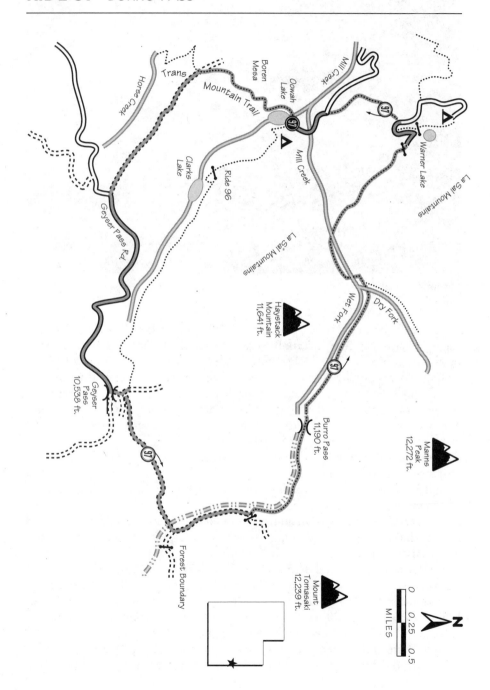

Mount Tomasaki.

Return to the Rock during midsummer and your brain will sizzle like a fried egg in an anti-drug commercial. By now, snow in the La Sals has receded to the protected confines of high-elevation cirques, and the mountains entice the bedraggled desert biker with promises of crisp alpine breezes wafting through dense timber; of peaks, ridges, and glacially-molded tarns; of uninterrupted solitude, other than the dewy-eyed gaze of deer; and of pursuable mountain-bike terrain replete with profound vistas. Along the Burro Pass loop, you'll experience the allure of the La Sal Mountains.

General location: 30 miles east of Moab in the La Sal Mountains.

Distance: 12.5-mile loop.

Tread: 8.5 miles of gravel roads and good doubletracks, 0.8 mile of not-so-good doubletrack, 3.2 miles of singletrack.

Aerobic level: Strenuous. The initial climb on the Trans Mountain Trail from Oowah Lake is rough and tough as well as the climb to Burro Pass. The technical descent off Burro is also mentally strenuous.

Technical difficulty: Level 1 to 5. The Trans Mountain Trail, the descent off Burro Pass, and the descent on the Warner Lake Trail are all level 4 to 5.

Elevation change: The elevation of Oowah Lake is 8,800 feet. It's mostly uphill to Burro Pass at 11,180 feet. Thereafter, it's mostly downhill to Warner Lake and finally to Oowah Lake. Total elevation gain is 3,100 feet.

Season: Late June/early July through September, depending on seasonal snowmelt and snowfall. Midsummer brings temperate daytime temperatures and cool nights. The descent off Burro Pass can harbor snowdrifts into July and be very wet even after they melt out. Chilling afternoon rainstorms accompanied by lightning are not uncommon.

Services: There is a Forest Service campground at Warner Lake (fee area and water taps) and a semi-developed Forest Service camping area at Oowah Lake (no fee, no water taps). There are no other services along this route and all surface waters should be purified. Moab offers all visitor services, including bike shops.

Hazards: Singletrack sections can be highly technical and warrant prudent biking. Portions may require dismounting and portaging. Deadfall and lingering snowdrifts may block the trail, especially on the descent from Burro Pass, which is a known winter avalanche zone.

Rescue index: Warner and Oowah Lakes are popular with campers and anglers, especially on weekends and holidays. Burro Pass is remote and difficult to reach by vehicle. Moab has a hospital.

Land status: Manti–La Sal National Forest (Moab/Monticello Ranger District).

Maps: USGS Mount Peale, Mount Tukuhnikivatz, Mount Waas, and Warner Lake, Utah.

Access: From the center of Moab, travel 8 miles south on U.S. Highway 191. Turn left/east at milepost 118 on County Road 126 for La Sal Mountain Road, Oowah Lake, etc. Immediately ahead at the T junction, turn right/south for La Sal Mountain Loop and pass the Red Rock Speedway. Stay left at the Pack Creek junction and rise out of Spanish Valley up a sandstone hogback. (Treat yourself to the fascinating view of mountains, stream-fed valleys, and redrock palisades from the Spanish Valley Overlook.) About 1.5 miles past the turnoff for Geyser Pass, turn right/east at Mill Creek on Forest Road 076 and travel 3 miles to Oowah Lake.

Notes on the trail: From Oowah Lake, cross over the dam and begin with a humorously steep climb on the La Sal Trans Mountain Trail. After 1 mile, the rutted path reaches the treeless tabletop of Boren Mesa and intersects a doubletrack. (The Trans Mountain Trail heads left/west, a viable but extremely technical route to the Geyser Pass Road. See Ride 96, Three Lakes.) Turn left/southeast and follow the doubletrack along the interface between aspens and meadows, then through dispersed forests to the Geyser Pass Road. Forested Geyser Pass is 2.2 miles away to the left and uphill.

At Geyser Pass, fork left/north on a rock-studded doubletrack toward Forest Boundary (note the carsonite post with a bike decal), and then fork right at the junction a couple hundred yards farther. (See Ride 96, Three Lakes.) Descend eastward through vast meadows for just over 1 mile. La Sal peaks swirl overhead. Haystack Mountain and Mount Tomasaki embrace the topographic void of Burro Pass to the north, and the sky above Burro is blocked by the bouldery crown of Manns Peak. Southward across Geyser Pass, Mount Mellenthin commands the scene with Mounts Tukuhnikivatz and Peale peering over its shoulders.

Just before the forest boundary, turn left/north up Forest Road 240. At the fence, where a sign reads, "Burro Pass Trail, Warner Lake CG," the route can be confusing. Pass through the gate and ride parallel to the fence a few feet. Just before you drop into the shallow gully, look carefully for the faint trail and hoof up to Burro Pass where a sign welcomes you. The short, but vertical, scramble toward Manns Peak offers a top-of-the-world view of the blazing desert and of fading mesas more than a vertical mile below these timbered slopes.

The singletrack descent off Burro Pass is upbeat, to say the least, and periodically redlines the crash-and-burn meter. During midsummer, a profusion of wildflowers drape the trail and effectively conceal obstacles that await your front tire; that is, except for entire trees that have been bowled down by winter's avalanches.

Upon joining Dry Fork (a misnomer, for it flows with confidence), take the trail downstream. Shortly past the gated wire fence, a pile of strategically placed rocks indicates that the trail crosses Mill Creek. Cross back over Mill Creek within 0.5 mile and then the Wilson Mesa Ditch (an earthen canal). Follow the doubletrack up through aspens and past a trail register box. Cross a small clearing and come to a junction signed for Burro Pass (reverse) and Oowah Lake (left).

Before you complete the loop, take the side trip to Warner Lake by following the path along the log fence. The lake is a small, aquatic mirror framed by luxuriant grasses that reflects aspen- and rock-shawled Manns Peak.

Return to the junction and turn downhill on the doubletrack toward Oowah Lake. Within 200 yards, fork left at a post (may be signed for Oowah Lake) that marks the Warner Lake Trail. The trail gets rockier before it gets smoother, and all but elite trail riders will have to portage down the boulder-ridden staircase. The trail exits quickly to the Oowah Lake Road, so use caution here. Oowah Lake is 0.5 mile left and uphill.

Four Corners

RIDE 98 *HOVENWEEP NATIONAL MONUMENT*

Hovenweep is a Ute Indian word meaning "deserted valley," which was applied to the area by the famous pioneer photographer William H. Jackson in 1874. The word reflects the haunting relics of stone masonry that were constructed by prehistoric Pueblo Indians who inhabited the region of the San Juan River 700 to 2,000 years ago. Initially, the nomadic natives sought shelter in caves as they foraged for food, but when they developed rudimentary farming techniques, they adopted a more sedentary lifestyle and built small villages of multi-story stone dwellings. They became expert craftsmen and artisans and developed social and religious bonds within the community. But hardships, whether brought on by drought or warfare, no one knows for sure, forced them to abandon their homes about 1300 A.D., and they drifted southward into Arizona and New Mexico, never to return. The ruins they left behind are all noted for their square, oval, circular, and D-shaped towers that are often perched on valley ledges or atop isolated boulders.

Granted, Hovenweep is not the tourist attraction of nearby Mesa Verde National Park, which houses the finest Native American adobe architecture in the nation. That means solitude is often the norm at Hovenweep and its dirt roads are ideal for mountain bikes. This tour takes you from the visitor center to outlying sites, some of which are difficult to reach by passenger car. There you can reflect in silence upon the lifestyles of these ancient people and envision the sights, sounds, and scents of the ancient Indian village.

General location: 35 miles northeast of Bluff, Utah, 40 miles southeast of Blanding, Utah, or about 40 miles west of Cortez, Colorado.

Distance: 31 miles, combination out-and-back with integrated loop.

Tread: The main thoroughfare is a graded, light-duty dirt road that is suitable for passenger cars when dry. Spur roads leading to ruin sites are on sand and rock doubletracks that may not be suitable for passenger cars.

Aerobic level: Moderate to strenuous. You can lessen the difficulty by visiting only one or two sites instead of the entire monument.

Technical difficulty: Level 1 to 3. The main road may develop sand and washboards. Side roads will have sand, rock, and ruts.

Elevation change: The visitor center is at 5,240 feet. The Pleasant View Road rises imperceptibly to 6,040 feet over 10 miles. A few hills are encountered on side routes leading to ruin sites; most are inconsequential. Total gain for the entire tour is about 1,600 feet.

RIDE 98 HOVENWEEP NATIONAL MONUMENT

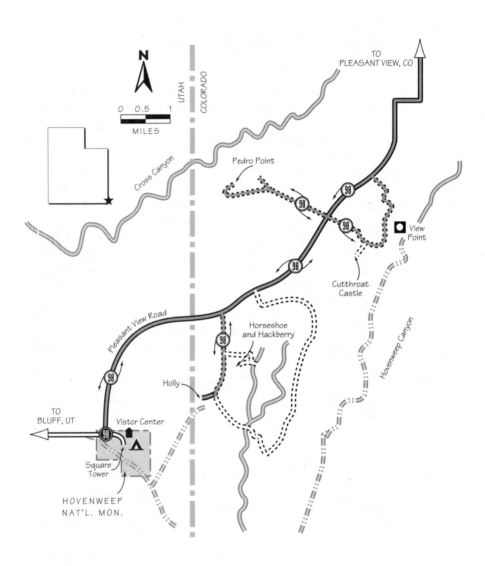

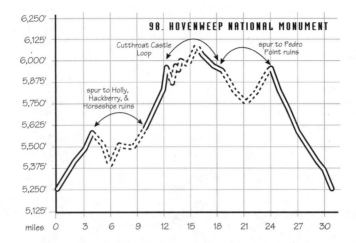

Season: Hovenweep National Monument is open year-round although spring (March through June) and fall (September through November) are the best times of year. Midsummer can be very warm. A winter visit is possible, but expect cool daytime temperatures and below freezing at night. Snowfall is intermittent and usually does not linger.

Services: Water taps are at the campground (fee area) and visitor center. The visitor center has a soda vending machine. The last outposts for supplies and overnight accommodations are in Blanding and Bluff, Utah, and Cortez, Colorado, each more than an hour away by vehicle. Limited supplies and gasoline *might* be found at Hatch and Ismay Trading Posts.

Hazards: Do not climb on any ruins; the ancient masonry is fragile and may crumble. Use caution when walking along and under cliffs and ledges. Be aware of the presence of others above or below you when near cliffs. Late spring and summer bring insects. Rattlesnakes may reside in cliff recesses and under rocks.

Dirt roads throughout the area may become impassable when wet. Call for current weather conditions and forecasts. Be alert to motorists when pedaling the Pleasant View Road.

Rescue index: Because of their remoteness and sometimes rough access roads, outlying ruin sites are seldom visited by tourists. Park patrols are infrequent. Emergency contacts can be made at the visitor center, but medical attention must be sought in Cortez, Colorado.

Land status: Hovenweep National Monument and Bureau of Land Management (San Juan Resource Area).

Maps: USGS Ruin Point, Utah/Colorado and Negro Canyon, Colorado.

Access: From Bluff, travel 11 miles north on U.S. Highway 163, or from Blanding, travel 15 miles south on U.S. Highway 191; then turn east on Utah State Highway 262 for the 24-mile approach to Hovenweep National

Boulder House (foreground) and Great House (background)—Holly Ruins.

Monument. After about 9 miles, fork left (UT 262 turns south to Montezuma Creek) following signs for Hovenweep and pass Hatch Trading Post after about 6.5 miles. Continue east on paved and dirt roads for 9 miles to Hovenweep.

From Cortez, Colorado, the most direct route (on relatively high-quality roads) is to travel south a few miles on U.S. Highways 160/666, west for 30 miles on McElmo Road, and then 12 miles on secondary paved and dirt roads to Hovenweep.

A third access route originates from Pleasant View, Colorado, located 19 miles north of Cortez on US 666. Travel west on County Road BB signed for Hovenweep National Monument. After 6 miles, turn left (at a sign for Hovenweep) and follow the graded Pleasant View Road 20 miles to the Visitor Center.

Sources of additional information: Mesa Verde Country Tourism and Convention Bureau (See Appendix B).

Notes on the trail: First some fine print. Under the Federal Antiquities Act, it is unlawful to appropriate, excavate, injure, or destroy any historic or prehistoric ruin or monument, or any object of antiquity located on federal lands. Violations are punishable by fines and/or imprisonment. Bicycles are allowed only on roads designated open to vehicles and are not allowed on any foot trails. Do not climb on ruins. Carry a lock if you are hesitant about leaving your bike unattended while walking to ruins.

Before embarking on this bike tour, spend plenty of time at the Monument's main attraction, Square Tower Ruin, to learn about the masonry and living conditions of this ancient Indian culture.

From the visitor center, pedal north on the Pleasant View Road. A cattle guard marks the Utah/Colorado border 3.5 miles out. One-half mile farther, fork right for the 5.2-mile out-and-back spur to Horseshoe/Hackberry group and Holly ruins (signed "Hovenweep"). The Horseshoe ruins consist of a half-circle-shaped structure composed of a large central room adjoined by three smaller rooms; none of the rooms are connected by windows or doors. A short trail leads past a retaining dam, handprints on a wall, and a small kiva. Holly ruins feature Tilted Tower and Boulder House, two stone structures built atop huge boulders. The main attraction is Holly Great House, a large structure where archaeologists have unearthed a plaster floor with a fire pit, grinding stones, and ceramic vessels.

Return to the Pleasant View Road and turn right to continue the tour. Pedal 3.2 miles to a junction, crossing two cattle guards along the way. Immediately past the second cattle guard, the obscure road to Cutthroat Castle branches right, next to a sign for Carbon Dioxide Pipeline. Portions of the road can be rough. (This side loop is 5.5 miles long.)

Cutthroat Castle is a large kiva situated on the edge of an overhanging cliff. It is bound on one side by a wall forming an attached room. (Kivas are used in modern Pueblo villages for ceremonies, to store dance costumes, accessories, and sacred objects, and as social centers.) From Cutthroat Castle, pedal right/south for 0.5 mile. The road then turns north and rises up a small hill. Atop this hill, look for a short spur to the right that leads to a cliff-edge viewpoint of upper Hovenweep Canyon and the La Plata Mountains. If you have a sharp eye, you will spot Painted Hand Ruin tucked below the overhanging cliff. From the viewpoint, return to the Cutthroat Castle road and pedal north to its junction with the Pleasant View Road. Turn left on the Pleasant View Road and pedal back to the original turnoff for Cutthroat Castle.

Time and endurance permitting, pedal 6 miles out-and-back to Pedro Point. The spur branches westward from the Cutthroat Castle turnoff near the carbon dioxide pipeline sign. About 2.3 miles out along the Pedro Point Road, fork left. This doubletrack will soon turn northward, hugging the rim of Cross Canyon, and lead to a small group of ruins. Thereafter, return 8 miles to the visitor center to reminisce the day's explorations under the setting sun.

RIDE 99 *VALLEY OF THE GODS*

Valley of the Gods is a prelude to Monument Valley and the Four Corners Area, where space is open and endless, and where the air is filled with a lucid sense of remoteness. Dispersed throughout these perpetually hapless desert plains are rock features of positive relief that resemble imaginary animals, troops of soldiers displaced from their platoons, or statues of exalted gods. More of these fanciful figures will be liberated in time as erosion slowly but relentlessly attacks the burnt umber ramparts of Cedar Mesa.

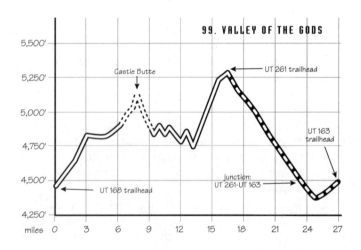

RIDE 99 VALLEY OF THE GODS

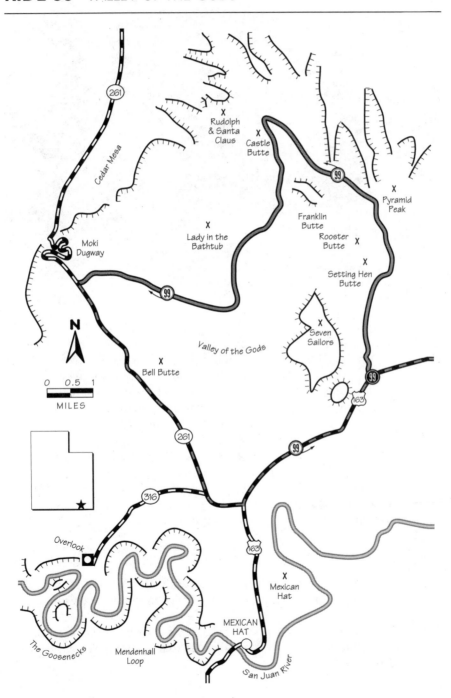

261

Rudolph
& Santa
Claus
X

Castle
Butte
X

99

Cedar Mesa

Pyramid
Peak
X

Franklin
Butte
X

Lady in the
Bathtub
X

Rooster
Butte
X

Moki
Dugway

99

Setting Hen
Butte
X

N

Valley of the Gods

Seven
Sailors
X

Bell Butte
X

0   0.5   1

MILES

99

163

261

99

316

Overlook

163

Mexican
Hat
X

MEXICAN
HAT

The Goosenecks

Mendenhall
Loop

San Juan River

The Goosenecks of the San Juan River.

As a side trip, you can pedal to the Goosenecks of the San Juan overlook. Geologists consider this one of the finest examples of entrenched meanders in the world. The San Juan River's looping pattern originated several million years ago when it flowed sluggishly over a relatively flat plain, much like the Mississippi River does today. When the Colorado Plateau was slowly uplifted, the San Juan followed its initial course, cutting downward 1,000 feet. Now the San Juan flows on a circuitous 6-mile course to cover less than a mile as the crow flies.

Got a mountain bike tandem? Break it out for this loop and you'll click away the miles with ease.

General location: 18 miles southwest of Bluff, 28 miles south of Natural Bridges National Monument, 8 miles north of Mexican Hat, 30 miles north of the Utah-Arizona border near Monument Valley, or smack-dab in the middle of nowhere.

Distance: 27-mile loop with an optional but highly recommended 7-mile out-and-back spur.

Tread: 16.5 miles of light-duty dirt road mixed with sand and rock double-track, 10.5 miles of pavement. Tack on 7 miles more of pavement for the Goosenecks Overlook.

Aerobic level: Moderate to strenuous. Lots of steady hills but no crushing climbs.

Technical difficulty: Level 1 to 3. Sand, washboards, and pavement bedrock on the off-road segment.

Elevation change: The Valley of the Gods' eastern trailhead off U.S. Highway 163 is at 4,440 feet. The dirt road rises to 5,130 feet at Castle Butte, drops to an intermediate low of 4,660 feet, and then rises back up to 5,300 feet at its western trailhead off Utah State Highway 261. The highway descends gradually (with a few gentle uphill pulses) back around to the eastern trailhead. Total elevation gain for the loop is about 1,600 feet. Add on an extra 700 feet of vertical for the spur to the Goosenecks.

Season: Spring (March into June) and fall (September into November). Midsummer is very hot, and bugs can be a nuisance, especially near water sources. Depending on snowfall and subsequent drying, winter months might be enjoyable.

Services: There are no services along this route or any reliable water sources. Carry ample water on your bike and in your vehicle. Limited visitor services are available in Bluff, located 18 miles east on US 163, or in Mexican Hat, located 10 miles south on US 163. Neither has a bike shop. Backcountry camping is allowed along the Valley of the Gods Road or at the Goosenecks Overlook, but no water is available. A primitive Bureau of Land Management campground is located at Sand Island just south of Bluff (no water tap).

Hazards: Running out of water will be your greatest concern. Carry plenty of water both on your bike and in your car. Use caution when pedaling paved highways; RV traffic is frequent and the roads' shoulders are narrow to nonexistent. Stay to the "right of the white."

Rescue index: Recreationists and motorists are few and far between along the Valley of the Gods road. Motorists are frequent on the highways. A phone *may* be found at the Valley of the Gods bed-and-breakfast near the western trailhead (Lee's Ranch on topographical maps), but *do not* seek water or refreshments there. Both food and water are trucked in and are valued highly by the owners and their guests. A medical clinic is located at Goulding (22 miles south of Mexican Hat, then a few miles west of Monument Valley).

Land status: Bureau of Land Management (San Juan Field Office). All land south of the San Juan River lies within the Navajo Indian Reservation. Camping and off-road travel is not allowed without prior and explicit permission from the Navajo Nation.

Maps: USGS Cedar Mesa-South, Cigarette Spring Cave, Mexican Hat, and The Goosenecks, Utah.

Access: The Valley of the Gods' eastern trailhead is located 18 miles southwest of Bluff along US 163 (milepost 29). Its western trailhead is 28 miles south of Natural Bridges National Monument on UT 261 (1 mile below the steep switchbacks of Moki Dugway). Both ends of Valley of the Gods Road are signed. Park at your discretion.

From the south (Arizona approach), head north on US 163 past Monument Valley to Mexican Hat. Continue north on US 163 3.5 miles to its junction with UT 261. The Valley of the Gods' eastern trailhead is 4 miles farther on US 163, and its western trailhead is about 6.5 miles along UT 261.

Notes on the trail: You can ride this loop in either direction with little change in difficulty. On the counterclockwise version described here, your highway miles are mostly downhill.

From the trailhead on US 163, pedal generally northward 7 miles toward looming orange-brown cliffs lining Cedar Mesa. It is slightly uphill and easy pedaling to where the road bends southward at Castle Butte. About 5 miles of upbeat descending are followed by a 4-mile, shallow rise on a sandy and sometimes washboarded road to UT 261. Turn left/south and catch a tail wind (hopefully) down the paved highway. Turn right for the Goosenecks after 5.5 miles. An additional 7 miles of pavement (out-and-back) lead to the overlook.

Continue southward on UT 261 about a mile to its junction with US 163. Your vehicle is 4 miles to the north along the rolling highway.

RIDE 100 *MONUMENT VALLEY NAVAJO TRIBAL PARK*

Monument Valley is a sublime landscape, one full of astonishing vastness and intangible beauty. Amidst this denuded valley stand rock monuments, buttes, and mesas of fascinating form and rich color. When you pedal past Mitten Buttes, Three Sisters, and Totem Pole; round Rain God Mesa; or stop at Artist's Point and North Window, you'll be awestruck and silenced by this ethereal desert tableau. Are these surreal features simply the byproduct of erosion or are they the divine creations of some Great Architect? It is no wonder that the Navajo Indian Nation (who call themselves "the Dinah," or "the people") look upon Monument Valley with sacred reverence.

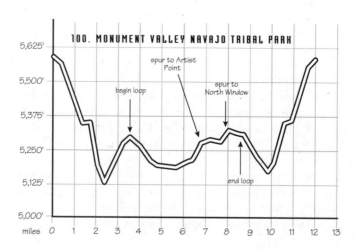

RIDE 100 MONUMENT VALLEY NAVAJO TRIBAL PARK

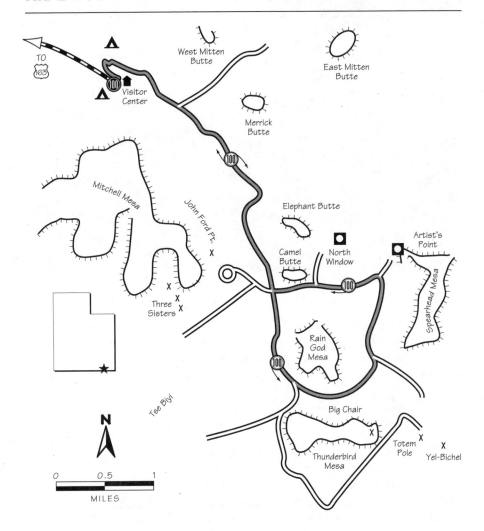

Both amateur and professional photographers find that Monument Valley seduces their camera lenses. Not only has the valley's splendor been the subject of countless postcards, calendars, and commercials, but it has also been the backdrop to a number of movies, including the 1936 John Ford classic "Stagecoach" (featuring John Wayne), "How the West Was Won," and "Back to the Future III." It is one of the nation's most celebrated landscapes and has become synonymous with the eternal dignity of Native Americans.

Technically, Monument Valley Navajo Tribal Park is located just over the border in Arizona. But since the park's mailing address has a Utah zip code, it

Mitten Buttes.

sneaks in under the wire and rounds out this guidebook. Besides, it is impossible to segregate Monument Valley to Arizona alone. The erodible Cutler Formation and tower-forming de Chelly Sandstone are sequential chapters in the sedimentary compendium that comprises the entire Colorado Plateau.

General location: 25 miles southeast of Mexican Hat, Utah, straddling the Utah-Arizona border in the Four Corners area.

Distance: 12-mile loop.

Tread: Sand and washboard light-duty dirt roads, suitable for passenger cars when dry.

Aerobic level: Moderate. Drift sand can stall your rotational progress. The moderately steep return climb to the visitor center is the toughest hill.

Technical difficulty: Level 1 to 2. The scenic drive is sand and washboard with scattered rocks on the first few miles.

Elevation change: The visitor center (parking area/trailhead) is at 5,600 feet. The scenic drive drops to 5,200 feet and then loops through the park with little elevation change. Total elevation gain is 800 feet with half of that on the 2.5-mile climb back to the visitor center.

Season: Spring (March through mid-June) and fall (September through November). Expect warm days and pleasant nights. Midsummer is hot and bugs can be annoying. Depending on snowfall and subsequent drying, winter months can be enjoyable. Sunrise and sunset are spectacular times to pedal through Monument Valley; the sun's low angle rays intensify the glowing warmth of the valley's features. The visitor center and scenic road are open during the summer (April through October) 8 A.M. to 6 P.M. and in winter (November through March) 8 A.M. to 5 P.M.

Services: A small convenience store is at the visitor center. Developed camping (fee area) is at the park's entrance. There is no drinking water along the scenic road. Goulding's Trading Post, 6 miles west of the visitor center, offers lodging, dining, private campgrounds, showers, and limited supplies. There are no bike shops within a day's drive.

Hazards: The graded scenic road is generally suitable for passenger cars. With that in mind, be alert to motorists and tour operators. The route may be very warm, so carry plenty of water. And don't forget the sunscreen.

Rescue index: Emergency assistance can be summoned from the visitor center. Motorists are frequent on the scenic drive. You might hitch a lift with a tour operator, but expect to pay a fee for services rendered. Goulding's Trading Post has medical facilities.

Land status: Navajo Indian Nation.

Maps: USGS Mitten Buttes, Arizona/Utah.

Access: The turnoff for Monument Valley is located about 22 miles south of Mexican Hat or about 0.5 mile north of the Utah/Arizona border on U.S. Highway 163. The park entrance is 3 miles to the east. Park at the visitor center.

Notes on the trail: You must pay a fee and check in at the visitor center before pedaling through the park. Vehicular and bicycle travel is restricted to the main loop road, unless you are accompanied by a tour operator. Abide all signs restricting travel. Photography for personal use is allowed. Close-up photographs of Navajo residents are by permission only, and a gratuity is expected.

From the visitor center, pedal past the steel gate and begin the quick descent into the park past Mitten Buttes. After about 3.5 miles, you come to the turnoff for John Ford Point and the beginning of the scenic loop road. Ride the loop counterclockwise with the flow of traffic. Wrap around Rain God Mesa and go past the spur for the Totem Pole and Sand Springs. Continue around the loop while taking must-do spurs to Artist's Point and North Window. Both offer distinct perspectives of this wonderfully vacant land. Merrick and Mitten Buttes guide you back to the visitor center.

APPENDICES

Appendix A

ATB	All terrain bike. An outdated term referring to a mountain bike.
ATV	All-terrain vehicle, including dirt motorcycles, three- and four-wheelers designed for off-highway use. See OHV also.
Bail	Getting off the bike, usually in a hurry, voluntarily or involuntarily.
Blaze	A mark on a tree made by chipping away a piece of the bark, usually done to designate a trail. The standard marking looks like a dotted "i".
Buffed	A very smooth trail.
Bunny hop	Leaping up, while riding, and lifting both wheels off the ground to jump over an obstacle (or for sheer joy).
Cant-and-ratchet	To rock the bike slightly side to side while backpedaling periodically to avoid hitting rocks or other obstacles with your pedals.
Catch air	To jump off the ground while on your bike, to launch, to leave Mother Earth, to sky. Evel Knievel was famous for catching *big* air.
Clean	To ride without touching a foot (or other body part) to the ground; to ride a tough section successfully; to ride without leaving evidence of your passage, i.e., "to ride cleanly."
Contour	A line on a topographic map that represents equal elevation. As a verb it means to follow a near level course across a hill or slope.
Dab	To put a foot or hand down (or hold onto or lean on a tree or other support) while riding. If you have to dab, then you haven't ridden a piece of trail clean.
Dotted i	A mark on a tree made by chipping away pieces of the bark such that it resembles a lowercase i, usually done to designate a trail.

504

Downfall	Trees or parts of trees that have fallen across the trail.
Doubletrack	An unimproved road or track consisting of two parallel treads, typically with vegetation growing in between; a jeep road. Optimists see doubletracks as parallel single-tracks, thus, twice the fun.
Dugway	A steep, unpaved, switchbacking road.
Endo	To lift the back wheel off the ground to such a degree that you are pitched over handlebars and the front wheel, a.k.a. nose dive, face plant.
Fall line	The angle and direction of a slope; the line you follow when gravity is in control and you aren't.
Feather	Using a light touch on the brake lever, depressing it lightly many times rather than very hard or locking the brake.
Ford	to carry your bike across a creek or stream that is too deep to ride.
Fork	A split in the road or trail that resembles tines of a fork. Used as a verb, it means to turn in the direction indicated when at a junction in a road or trail.
Game trail	A narrow unmaintained trail made by deer, elk or other wildlife.
Graded	When a dirt or gravel road is scraped level to smooth out the washboards, potholes, or eroded conditions, it is graded.
Gravel road:	A graded road that has a fortified road bed of dirt and gravel and is periodically maintained. Gravel roads are *generally* suitable for passenger cars when wet.
Light-duty dirt road	A graded dirt road that is periodically maintained but has a roadbed of native surface. Light-duty dirt roads are *generally* suitable for passenger cars when dry but may be impassable when wet.
Hammer	To ride hard; to "put the hammer down."
Hike-a-bike	To walk with your bike in tow when a trail is too tough or rough to ride. An extended hike-a-bike up or down a severe slope is a portage.

Line — The route (or trajectory) between or over obstacles or through turns. Tread or trail refers to the ground you're riding on; the line is the path you choose with the tread (and exists only in the eye of the beholder).

Loop — A ride configuration that begins at a designated trailhead and returns to the same location via a different route or simply the continuation of the same route. You are always forging ahead across new terrain.

Multi-use — A designation of land or a trail that is open to many uses.

Off-the-seat — Moving your butt off the back of your seat and over the rear tire; used for control on extremely steep descents. This position increases braking power, helps prevent endos, and reduces skidding.

OHV — A motorized off-highway vehicle. An unlicensed ATV, dirt motorbike, or four-wheel-drive vehicle that is intended for off-highway use.

Out-and-back — A ride configuration that begins at a designated trailhead, leads to a distant point, and then returns to the original trailhead by backtracking in the opposite direction. You will ride and see the trail from two points of view.

Point-to-point — A ride configuration that begins at a designated trailhead and ends at a distant location other than the originating point. You'll need to arrange a vehicle shuttle (or hitch a ride) to return to the original trailhead.

Portage — To carry the bike up or down a steep hill or across unridable obstacles.

Quads — The extensor muscle in the front of the thigh or a topographic map; the expression "Nice quads" refers always to the former, except in instances when the speaker is a cartographer.

Rock garden — A particularly rocky stretch of trail that requires great concentration and perhaps canting-and-ratcheting to clean without dabbing.

Singletrack — A single narrow tread followed by game, hikers, horses, or mountain bikers. Next to slickrock, arguably, singletrack is the ultimate riding medium.

Slickrock	In general, any variety of barren sandstone typical of the desert Southwest; specifically, the Moab Slickrock Bike Trail.
Snowmelt	Runoff produced by melting snow.
Snowpack	Unmelted snow accumulated over weeks or months of the winter.
Spu	A side road or trail that forks from the main route.
Surf	Riding through loose gravel or sand, when the wheels sway from side to side.
Switchback	A zigzagging road or trail designed to ease the gradient when climbing or descending steep terrain; it is *bad form* to skid around switchbacks.
Talus	The rocky debris at the base of a cliff or steep slope.
Topo	Short for topographic map, the kind that shows elevation change with contour lines. "Topo" is pronounced with both vowels long.
Track stand	Balancing on a bike in one place without rolling forward appreciably. It takes practice, but comes in handy at stoplights, on switchbacks, and when trying to free a foot before falling.
Tread	The riding surface, particularly regarding singletrack.
Washboards	A road that is surfaced with many ridges spaced closely together, like the ripple on a washboard; these make for very rough and tedious riding.
Water bar	An earthen, rock, or wooden structure placed across the trail that diverts water off the trail to prevent erosion of the tread.
Whoop-dee-doo	Earthen mounds or undulations in a road or trail that create a roller coaster ride. When taken with speed, you can catch air and possibly endo.

Appendix B

SOURCES OF ADDITIONAL INFORMATION

United States Forest Service
Antelope Island State Park
4528 West 1700 South
Syracuse, UT 84075
Entrance gate: 801-773-2941
http://www.nr.state.ut.us/parks/
  utahstpk.htm

Ashley National Forest
Supervisor's Office and Vernal
  Ranger District
353 North Vernal Avenue
Vernal, UT 84078
435-789-1181

Flaming Gorge National
  Recreation Area
c/o Manila Ranger District
P.O. Box 279
Manila, UT 84046
435-784-3445
435-789-1181

Dixie National Forest
Supervisor's Office
82 North 100 East
Cedar City, UT 84720-2686
435-865-3700

Cedar City Ranger District
P.O. Box 627
82 North 100 East
Cedar City, UT 84721-0627
435-865-3200

Escalante Ranger District
Escalante Interagency Federal
  Building
755 West Main
P.O. Box 246
Escalante, UT 84726
435-826-5400

Pine Valley Ranger District
196 East Tabernacle Street,
  Room 40
St. George, UT 84770
435-652-3100

Powell Ranger District
225 East Center
P.O. Box 80
Panguitch, UT 84759
435-676-8815

Red Canyon Visitor Center
5375 East Highway 12
Panguitch, UT 84759
435-676-2676

Fish Lake National Forest
Supervisor's Office
115 East 900 North
Richfield, UT 84701
435-896-9233

Beaver Ranger District
575 South Main
P.O. Box E
Beaver, UT 84713
435-438-2436

Fillmore Ranger District
390 South Main
P.O. Box 265
Fillmore, UT 84631
435-743-5721

Loa Ranger District
138 South Main
P.O. Box 129
Loa, UT 84747
435-836-2811

Richfield Ranger District
115 East 900 North
Richfield, UT 84701
435-896-9233

Manti-La Sal National Forest
Supervisor's Office and
Price Ranger District
599 West Price River Drive
Price, UT 84501
435-637-2817

Sanpete Ranger District
540 North Main, #32-14
Ephraim, UT 84627-1117
435-283-4151

Ferron Ranger District
115 West Canyon Road
P.O. Box 310
Ferron, UT 84523
435-384-2372

Moab-Monticello Ranger Districts
2290 South West Resource Blvd.
Moab, UT 84532
435-259-7155

Uinta National Forest
Supervisor's Office
88 West 100 North
Provo, UT 84601
801-342-5100

Heber Ranger District
2460 South Highway 40
P.O. Box 190
Heber City, UT 84032
435-654-0470

Pleasant Grove Ranger District
390 North 100 East
Pleasant Grove, UT 84062
801-785-3563

Spanish Fork Ranger District
44 West 400 North
Spanish Fork, UT 84660
801-798-3571

Wasatch-Cache National Forest
Supervisor's Office
8236 Federal Building
125 South State Street
Salt Lake City, UT 84138
801-524-5030

Kamas Ranger District
50 East Center Street
P.O. Box 68
Kamas, UT 84036
435-783-4338

Logan Ranger District
1500 East Highway 89
Logan, UT 84321-4373
435-755-3620

Ogden Ranger District
507 25th Street, Suite 103
Ogden, UT 84401
801-625-5112

Salt Lake Ranger District
6944 South 3000 East
Salt Lake City, UT 84121
801-943-1794

Bureau of Land Management
Utah State Office
324 South State Street, Suite 301
P.O. Box 45155
Salt Lake City, UT 84145-0155
801-539-4010

Salt Lake Field Office
2370 South 2300 West
Salt Lake City, UT 84119
801-977-4300

Cedar City Field Office
176 East D.L. Sargent Drive
Cedar City, UT 84720
435-586-2401

Dixie Field Office
345 East Riverside Drive
St. George, UT 84790
435-688-3200

Escalante Field Office
P.O. Box 225
Escalante, UT 84726
435-826-4291

Escalante Interagency Visitor
Center
755 West Main
Escalante, UT 84726
435-826-5499

Henry Mountain Field Office
P.O. Box 99
Hanksville, UT 84734
435-542-3461

Kanab Field Office
318 North First East
Kanab, UT 84741
435-644-2672

Moab Field Office
82 East Dogwood
Moab, UT 84532
435-259-2100

Price Field Office
125 South 600 West
Price, UT 84501
435-636-3600

San Juan Field Office
435 North Main Street
Monticello, UT 84535
435-587-1500

Vernal Field Office
170 South 500 East
Vernal, UT 84078
435-781-4400

Grand Junction Resource Area
2815 H Road
Grand Junction, Colorado 81506
970-244-3050

National Parks and Monuments
http://www.nps.gov/parks.html
Canyonlands National Park
2282 South West Resource Blvd.
Moab, UT 84532-8000
435-259-4351
435-259-7164
http://www.nps.gov/cany
   Island in the Sky District
   435-259-4712
   Needles District
   435-259-4711
   Maze District
   435-259-2652

Arches National Park
P.O. Box 907
Moab, UT 84532
435-259-8161
http://www.nps.gov/arch

Grand Staircase-Escalante
  National Monument
337 South Main, Suite 010
Cedar City, UT 84720
435-865-5100
http://www.ut.blm.gov/monument/

Hovenweep National Monument
McElmo Route
Cortez, Colorado 81321
970-749-0510 (Colorado)
435-459-4344 (Utah)

Glen Canyon National Recreation
Area
P. O. Box 1507
Page, Arizona 86040
General Information:
520) 608-6404
Headquarters: 520-608-6200

State Parks
Fremont Indian State Park
11550 West Clear Creek Canyon
Road
Sevier, UT 84766-9999
435-259-2444

County Parks
Utah County Parks
2855 South State
Provo, UT 84606
801-370-8605

Tooele County Department of
Parks and Recreation
435-843-3156

City
Ogden Trail Network
c/o Ogden City Planning
Department
2484 Washington Boulevard
Ogden, UT 84401

Provo City Parks and Recreation
P.O. Box 1849
Provo, UT 84603
801-379-6600

Utah Department of Natural Resources
1594 West North Temple
Salt Lake City, UT 84116
801-538-7200
State Parks and Recreation
801-538-7220
Utah Geological Survey (Book-
store and Map Sales)
801-537-3320
Wildlife Resources Division
801-538-4700

Mountain Bike Associations
International Mountain Bike
Association (IMBA)
PO Box 7578
Boulder, CO 80306
1121 Broadway; Suite 202, 80302
303-545-9011
E-mail: imba@aol.com
http://www.imba.com

Colorado Plateau Mountain Bike
Trail Association (COPMOBA)
P.O. Box 4602
Grand Junction, Colorado
81502-4602

Utah Mountain Bike Association
P.O. Box 573657
Murray, UT 84157-3657
801-968-1269
www.redrocks.com/local/umba
e-mail:
jmcconn@rjh.mury.k12.ut.us

Bonneville Shoreline Trail
Committee
P.O. Box 581136
Salt Lake City, UT 84158-1136

Color Country Cycling Club
P.O. Box 416
Cedar City, UT 84720
435-586-7567

The Community Sand Flats Team
435-259-2444

Mountain Trails Foundation
P.O. Box 754
Park City, UT 84060
435-649-6839

Ski and Mountain Bike Resorts
Brian Head Resort
P.O. Box 19008
369 South Highway 143
Brian Head, UT 84719
435-677-2035
http://www.brianheadutah.com/

Deer Valley Resort
P.O. Box 889
Park City, UT 84060
800-424-DEER (3337)/
  435-649-1000
http://www.deervalley.com/

Park City Mountain Resort
P.O. Box 39
1345 Lowell Avenue
Park City, UT 84060
435-649-8111
http://www.parkcitymountain.com/

Skyhaven Lodge (Ferron Reservoir)
435-835-5342

Sundance
RR 3, Box A-1
Utah State Highway 92
Sundance, UT 84604
435-225-4107
800-892-1600 (outside Utah)
http://www.sundance-utah.com/

Bicycle Trip Planning
The Utah Travel Council
Council Hall/Capitol Hill
Salt Lake City, Utah 84114-1396
801-538-1030
800-200-1160
http://www.utah.com

Castle Country Travel Council
P.O. Box 1037
Price, Utah 84501
435-835 5324

Mesa Verde Country Tourism and
  Convention Bureau
928 East Main 1
Cortez, CO 81421
800-346-6528

Internet resources
http://www.utah.com/resource/offices
.htm (A complete listing of county,
regional, and local travel bureaus and
information centers throughout Utah.)

http://www.bikeutah.com (a satellite
site of www.utah.com)

http://www.moabutah.com

Referenced bicycle shops
Bicycles Unlimited
90 South 100 East
St. George, UT 84770
435-673-4492

Red Rock Bicycle Company
190 South Main
St. George, UT 84770
435-652-8382

Altitude Cycles
510 East Mian, Suite 7
Vernal, UT 84078
435-781-2595

Appendix C

RECOMMENDED READING

TRAVEL, DESCRIPTION, AND HISTORY

Abbey, Edward. *Desert Solitaire*. New York: Ballantine Books, 1968.

————. *Slickrock*. New York: Sierra Club/Charles Scribner & Sons, 1971.

Aitchison, Stewart. *Utah Wildlands*. Salt Lake City, Utah: Utah Geographical Series, Inc., 1987.

Bickers, Jack. *Off-Road Vehicle Trails: Maze Area*. Moab, Utah: Canyon Country Publications, 1988.

Bruhn, Arthur F. *Southern Utah's Land of Color*. Bryce Canyon, Utah; Bryce Canyon Natural History Association, 1962.

Carr, Stephen L. *The Historical Guide to Utah Ghost Towns*. Salt Lake City, Utah: Western Epics, 1972.

Crampton, C. Gregory. *Standing Up Country: The Canyon Lands of Utah and Arizona*. New York: Alfred A. Knopf, 1964.

Hayward, C. Lynn. *The High Uintas: Utah's Land of Lakes and Forest*. Provo, Utah: Monte L. Bean Life Science Museum, 1983.

Hinchman, Fred. *Bryce Canyon National Park*. Bryce Canyon, Utah: Bryce Canyon Natural History Association.

Hinchman, Sandra. *Hiking the Southwest's Canyon Country*. Seattle, Washington: The Mountaineers, 1990.

Kelsey, Michael R. *Hiking Utah's San Rafael Swell*. Provo, Utah: Kelsey Publishing, 1986.

Lambrechtse, Rudy. *Hiking the Escalante*. Salt Lake City, Utah: Wasatch Publishers, Inc., 1985.

Martin, Don and Betty. *Utah Discovery Guide*. Columbia, California: Pine Cone Press, Inc., 1995.

McClenahan, Owen. *Utah's Scenic San Rafael Swell*. N.p.: n.p., 1986.

Porter, Eliot. *The Place No One Knew: Glen Canyon on the Colorado*. Salt Lake City, Utah: Peregrine Smith Books, 1988.

Powell, Allan Kent. *The Utah Guide, 2nd Edition*. Golden, Colorado: Fulcrum Publishing, 1998.

Roylance, Ward J. *Utah, A Guide to the State*. Salt Lake City, Utah: Utah Arts Council, 1982.

Reynolds, Katherine. *Park City. A 100 Year History: Silver Mining to Skiing*. Park City, Utah: The Weller Institute for the Cure of Design, Inc., 1984.

Ringholz, Raye Carleson. *Park City Trails*. Salt Lake City, Utah: Wasatch Publishers,

Inc., 1984.

Smart, William B. *Old Utah Trails*. Salt Lake City, Utah: Utah Geographical Series, Inc., 1988.

Stegner, Wallace. *Beyond the Hundredth Meridian: John Wesley Powell and the Second Opening of the West*. Lincoln, Nebraska: University of Nebraska Press, 1954.

Telford, John, and Terry Tempest Williams. *Coyote's Canyon*. Salt Lake City, Utah: Gibbs Smith, Publisher, 1989.

Thompson, George A. and Fraser Buck. *Treasure Mountain Home: Park City Revisited*. Salt Lake City, Utah: Dream Garden Press, 1981.

Van Cott, John W. *Utah Place Names*. Salt Lake City, Utah: The University of Utah Press, 1990.

Weir, Bill and W. C. McRae. *Utah Handbook 5th Edition*. Chico California: Moon Publications, 1997.

Wharton, Tom and Gayen. *Utah*. Oakland, California: Compass American Guides, Inc., 1991.

Wilson, Ted. *Utah's Wasatch Front*. Salt Lake City, Utah: Utah Geographical Series, Inc., 1987.

ARCHAEOLOGICAL AND GEOLOGICAL REFERENCES

Barnes, F. A. *Canyon Country Geology for the Layman and Rockhound*. Salt Lake City, Utah: Wasatch Publishers, 1978.

———. *Canyon Country Prehistoric Rock Art*. Salt Lake City, Utah: Wasatch Publishers, 1982.

Barnes, F. A., and Michaelene Pendleton. *Canyon Country Prehistoric Indians: Their Culture, Ruins, Artifacts, and Rock Art*. Salt Lake City, Utah: Wasatch Publishers, 1979.

Bloom, Arthur L. *Geomorphology: A Systematic Analysis of Late Cenozoic Landforms*. Englewood, New Jersey: Prentice Hall, 1978.

Castleton, Kenneth B. *Petroglyphs and Pictographs of Utah*. Vol. 1. Salt Lake City, Utah: Utah Museum of Natural History, 1978.

Chronic, Halka. *Roadside Geology of Utah*. Missoula, Montana: Mountain Press Publishing, 1990.

Dutton, Clarence. E. *Tertiary History of the Grand Cañon District*. Washington, D. C.: United States Geological Survey, 1882. Reprinted by Peregrine Smith, Inc., Santa Barbara and Salt Lake City, 1977.

———. *Report on the Geology of the High Plateaus of Utah*. Washington, D. C.: U. S. Geographical and Geological Survey of the Rocky Mountain Region, 1880.

Foster, Robert J. *General Geology*. Columbus, Ohio: Charles E. Merrill Publishing Company, 1978.

Hintze, Lehi F. *Geologic History of Utah*. Provo, Utah: Brigham Young University, Department of Geology.

Schaafsma, Polly. *Indian Rock Art of the Southwest*. Santa Fe, New Mexico: School of American Research, 1982.

Stokes, William Lee. *Geology of Utah*. Salt Lake City, Utah: Utah Museum of Natural History, Occasional Paper No. 6, 1986.

SUPPLEMENTAL MOUNTAIN BIKING GUIDEBOOKS

Barnes, F. A., and Tom Kuhne. *Canyon Country Mountain Biking*. Moab, Utah: Canyon Country Publications, 1988.

Bromka, Gregg. *Mountain Biking Utah's Wasatch & Uinta Mountains*. Salt Lake City, Utah: Off-Road Publications, 1996.

———. *Mountain Biking Utah's Brian Head-Bryce Country*. Salt Lake City, Utah: Off-Road Publications, 1998.

Campbell, Todd. *Above and Beyond Slickrock*. Salt Lake City, Utah: Wasatch Publishers, 1995.

Crowell, David. *Mountain Biking Moab*. Helena, Montana: Falcon Publishing, Inc., 1997.

Kirksey, Matt. *Wasatch & Beyond Mountain Bike Trail Guide (The Wasatch, Sun Valley, Jackson Hole, Brian Head)*. Salt Lake City, Utah: High Desert Publishing, 1996.

McCoy, Michael. *Mountain Bike Adventures in the Four Corners Region*. Seattle, Washington: The Mountaineers, 1990.

Utesch, Peggy. *The Utah-Colorado Mountain Bike Trail System: Route 1, Moab to Loma—Kokopelli's Trail*. Moab, Utah: Canyon Country Publications, 1990.

Ward, Bob. *Moab, Utah: A Travelguide to the Slickrock Bike Trail and Mountain Biking Adventures*. La Crescenta, California: Mountain Ní Air Books, 1995.

SUPPLEMENTAL MOUNTAIN BIKING AND RECREATIONAL MAPS

Arches National Park, Utah. Evergreen, Colorado: Trails Illustrated, 1996.

Canyons of the Escalante: Grand Staircase-Escalante National Mon., Dixie National. Forest, Glen Canyon N.R.A., Utah. Evergreen, Colorado: Trails Illustrated, 1998.

Canyonlands National Park: Maze & N.E. Glen Canyon N.R.A., Utah. Evergreen, Colorado: Trails Illustrated, 1997.

Canyonlands National Park: Needles & Island in the Sky, Utah. Evergreen, Colorado: Trails Illustrated, 1996.

Fish Lake North, Capitol Reef, Utah. Evergreen, Colorado: Trails Illustrated, 1996.

Flaming Gorge, East Uinta Mountains, Utah. Evergreen, Colorado: Trails Illustrated, 1995.

Moab East Mountain Biking & Recreation. Boulder, Colorado: Latitude 40-, 1993.

Moab Map—Mountain Biking, Hiking, & 4WD. Evergreen, Colorado: Trails Illustrated, 1997.

Moab West Mountain Biking & Recreation. Boulder, Colorado: Latitude 40-, 1997.

Slickrock Bike Trail—Map Moab, Utah. Boulder, Colorado: Latitude 40-, n/d.

Uinta National Forest: Lone Peak, Mt. Timpanogos, Mt. Nebo, Utah. Evergreen, Colorado: Trails Illustrated, 1998.

Wasatch Front, Strawberry Valley, Utah. Evergreen, Colorado: Trails Illustrated, 1994.

Note: All mountain biking guidebooks and maps are available from Off-Road Publications, Salt Lake City, Utah 801-486-0698, 888-477-3374, http://www.offroadpub.com

Appendix D

INDEX OF RIDES

	NORTHERN	CENTRAL	SOUTHERN
Beginner's Luck and Family Fun Rides	1 Green Canyon 8 Logan River Trail 19 Albion Basin 23 Provo River Parkway 31 Beaver Creek Trail 35 Dowd Mountain	41 Nine Mile Canyon 46 Lakeshore National Recreation Trail 50 Powell Point	59 Buckhorn Wash-The Wedge Overlook 60 Black Dragon Canyon 72 Warner Valley 82 Hurrah Pass 93 Colorado River Overlook
Sweet Singletracks (may also include portions of gravel roads and doubletracks)	2 Jardine Juniper 6 Ricks Canyon-Steel Hollow 9 Herd Hollow-Richards Hollow 11 Skyline Trail 12 Wheeler Creek Trail 13 Bonneville Shoreline Trail (Ogden Section) 14 Mueller Park Trail 15 Bonneville Shoreline Trail (Salt Lake City Section) 16 Mill Creek Pipeline Trail 17 Big Water Trail 18 Wasatch Crest Trail 21 Ridge Trail 157 22 Sundance 25 Diamond Fork-Strawberry Ridge 27 Blackhawk Trail 28 Park City Mountain Resort 29 Tour de Suds 30 Deer Valley 33 Little South Fork of Provo River	43 Petes Hole 45 Mytoge Mountain 48 Skyline National Recreation Trail 51 Casto Canyon 54 Virgin River Rim Trail 55 Right Fork of Bunker Creek 56 Dark Hollow-Second Left Hand Canyon 57 Scout Camp Loop	62 Iron Divide Trail System 69 Gooseberry Mesa 73 Red Rock Rampage 74 Green Valley 75 Stucki Spring 87 Porcupine Rim 96 Three Lakes 97 Burro Pass

	NORTHERN	CENTRAL	SOUTHERN
Sweet Singletracks (continued)	34 Elk Park 36 Canyon Rim Trail-Swett Ranch 37 Little Hole National Recreation Trail		
Road Rides (gravel roads and/or doubletracks)	1 Green Canyon 4 Beaver Creek-Sink Hollow 5 Old Ephraim's Grave 10 Antelope Island State Park 19 Albion Basin 20 Copper Pit Overlook 24 Squaw Peak Road 26 Monks Hollow 32 Soapstone Basin 38 Red Cloud Loop 40 Horseshoe Bend	41 Nine Mile Canyon 44 U M Pass 47 Velvet Ridge 49 Kimberly Road 50 Powell Point 52 Sunset Cliffs 53 Pink Cliff 58 Twisted Forest	59 Buckhorn Wash-The Wedge Overlook 60 Black Dragon Canyon 61 Reds Canyon 63 Temple Mountain 64 Tantalus Flats 65 Mount Ellen 66 Wolverine Road 67 Fiftymile Bench 68 Hole-in-the-Rock 70 Silver Reef 72 Warner Valley 78 Courthouse Wash 79 Gemini Bridges 82 Hurrah Pass 84 Jughandle Loop 88 Pritchett Canyon 90 Deadmans Trail-Horseshoe Canyon 91 Panorama Point 92 The Maze Overlook 93 Colorado River Overlook 94 Confluence Overlook 98 Hovenweep National Monument 99 Valley of the Gods 100 Monument Valley Navajo Tribal Park
Killer Climbs	5 Old Ephraim's Grave 7 Logan Peak 11 Skyline Trail 18 Wasatch Crest Trail 21 Ridge Trail 157	49 Kimberly Road 54 Virgin River Rim Trail	65 Mount Ellen 67 Fiftymile Bench 83 Jackson Hole 84 Jughandle Loop 85 Moab Rim

	NORTHERN	CENTRAL	SOUTHERN
Killer Climbs (continued)	24 Squaw Peak Road 25 Diamond Fork-Strawberry Ridge		86 Slickrock Bike Trail 97 Burro Pass
Dynamite Downhills	3 Bear Hollow Trail-Twin Creek 7 Logan Peak 22 Sundance 30 Deer Valley Resort	49 Kimberly Road 55 Right Fork of Bunker Creek 56 Dark Hollow-Second Left Hand Canyon	64 Tantalus Flats 84 Jughandle Loop
Technical Tests	11 Skyline Trail 39 Red Mountain	48 Skyline National Recreation Trail	62 Iron Divide Trail System 69 Gooseberry Mesa 71 Church Rocks 74 Green Valley 80 Poison Spider Mesa 81 Amasa Back 83 Jackson Hole 85 Moab Rim 86 Slickrock Bike Trail 87 Porcupine Rim 94 Confluence Overlook 96 Three Lakes 97 Burro Pass
Multi-day Treks		42 Skyline Drive	89 White Rim Trail 95 Kokopelli's Trail
Epic Rides	7 Logan Peak 11 Skyline Trail 18 Wasatch Crest Trail 21 Ridge Trail 157 25 Diamond Fork-Strawberry Ridge	48 Skyline National Recreation Trail 49 Kimberly Road 54 Virgin River Rim Trail	62 Iron Divide Trail System 84 Jughandle Loop 89 White Rim Trail
Scintillating Slickrock			69 Gooseberry Mesa 71 Church Rocks 76 Bartlett Wash 77 Klondike Bluffs 80 Poison Spider Mesa 81 Amasa Back 85 Moab Rim 86 Slickrock Bike Trail

About the Author

A native of upstate New York, Gregg Bromka ventured west in the early 1980s to pursue graduate studies in geology at the University of Utah in Salt Lake City. Instead of receiving a master's degree, he became captivated by Utah's diverse scenery and discovered mountain biking as the preeminent means of backcountry travel. Searching for enticing mountain bike trails became Greg's obsession, and writing about his pursuits was a natural progression.

In addition to *Mountain Biking Utah,* Gregg has written *Mountain Biking Utah's Wasatch & Uinta Mountains, Mountain Biking Utah's Brian Head-Bryce Country,* and co-authored *Mountain Biking Colorado.* Mountain biking has become an integral part of Greg's lifestyle, whether exploring Utah's mountains and deserts, capturing his experiences in print or on film, or racing in the expert veteran's class.

For information on these publications and related photographs, contact Off-Road Publications, 1590 South 1400 East, Salt Lake City, Utah 84105, http://www.offroadpub.com

Gregg and Tricia toast to the good life.

FALCONGUIDES ® Leading the Way™

FALCONGUIDES ® are available for where-to-go hiking, mountain biking, rock climbing, walking, scenic driving, fishing, rockhounding, paddling, birding, wildlife viewing, and camping. We also have FalconGuides on essential outdoor skills and subjects and field identification. The following titles are currently available, but this list grows every year. For a free catalog with a complete list of titles, call FALCON toll-free at 1-800-582-2665.

MOUNTAIN BIKING GUIDES

Mountain Biking Arizona
Mountain Biking Colorado
Mountain Biking Georgia
Mountain Biking New Mexico
Mountain Biking New York
Mountain Biking Northern New England
Mountain Biking Oregon
Mountain Biking South Carolina
Mountain Biking Southern California
Mountain Biking Southern New England
Mountain Biking Utah
Mountain Biking Wisconsin
Mountain Biking Wyoming

LOCAL CYCLING SERIES

Fat Trax Bozeman
Mountain Biking Bend
Mountain Biking Boise
Mountain Biking Chequamegon
Mountain Biking Chico
Mountain Biking Colorado Springs
Mountain Biking Denver/Boulder
Mountain Biking Durango
Mountain Biking Flagstaff and Sedona
Mountain Biking Helena
Mountain Biking Moab
Mountain Biking Utah's St. George/Cedar City Area
Mountain Biking the White Mountains (West)

■ *To order any of these books, check with your local bookseller or call FALCON ® at **1-800-582-2665**.*
Visit us on the world wide web at:
www.FalconOutdoors.com

FALCON®

FALCONGUIDES ® Leading the Way

FIELD GUIDES

Bitterroot: Montana State Flower
Canyon Country Wildflowers
Central Rocky Mountains
  Wildflowers
Great Lakes Berry Book
New England Berry Book
Ozark Wildflowers
Pacific Northwest Berry Book
Plants of Arizona
Rare Plants of Colorado
Rocky Mountain Berry Book
Scats & Tracks of the Pacific
  Coast States
Scats & Tracks of the
  Rocky Mountains
Southern Rocky Mountain
  Wildflowers
Tallgrass Prairie Wildflowers
Western Trees
Wildflowers of Southwestern
  Utah
Willow Bark and Rosehips

FISHING GUIDES

Fishing Alaska
Fishing the Beartooths
Fishing Florida
Fishing Glacier National Park
Fishing Maine
Fishing Montana
Fishing Wyoming
Fishing Yellowstone
  National Park

ROCKHOUNDING GUIDES

Rockhounding Arizona
Rockhounding California
Rockhounding Colorado
Rockhounding Montana
Rockhounding Nevada
Rockhound's Guide to New
  Mexico
Rockhounding Texas
Rockhounding Utah
Rockhounding Wyoming

MORE GUIDEBOOKS

Backcountry Horseman's
  Guide to Washington
Camping California's
  National Forests
Exploring Canyonlands &
  Arches National Parks
Exploring Hawaii's Parklands
Exploring Mount Helena
Exploring Southern California
  Beaches
Recreation Guide to WA
  National Forests
Touring California & Nevada
  Hot Springs
Touring Colorado Hot Springs
Touring Montana & Wyoming
  Hot Springs
Trail Riding Western
  Montana
Wild Country Companion
Wilderness Directory
Wild Montana
Wild Utah

BIRDING GUIDES

Birding Minnesota
Birding Montana
Birding Northern California
Birding Texas
Birding Utah

PADDLING GUIDES

Floater's Guide to Colorado
Paddling Minnesota
Paddling Montana
Paddling Okefenokee
Paddling Oregon
Paddling Yellowstone & Grand
  Teton National Parks

HOW-TO GUIDES

Avalanche Aware
Backpacking Tips
Bear Aware
Desert Hiking Tips
Hiking with Dogs
Leave No Trace
Mountain Lion Alert
Reading Weather
Route Finding
Using GPS
Wilderness First Aid
Wilderness Survival

WALKING

Walking Colorado Springs
Walking Denver
Walking Portland
Walking St. Louis
Walking Virginia Beach

■To order any of these books, check with your local bookseller
or call FALCON ® at **1-800-582-2665**.
Visit us on the world wide web at:
www.FalconOutdoors.com

FALCON®